W9-APF-102

# Accounting
## for Managers
### Text and Cases

### SECOND EDITION

## William J. Bruns, Jr.

Harvard Business School

SOUTH-WESTERN College Publishing

*An International Thomson Publishing Company*

Copyright © 1999
by South-Western College Publishing
*An International Thomson Publishing Company*

Portions of this work have been reprinted by permission of the President and Fellows of
Harvard College.

All Rights Reserved. No part of this book may be reproduced, stored in a retrieval system, or trans-
mitted, in any form or by any means, electronic, mechanical, photocopying, recording, or otherwise, without the prior written permission of the copyright holder. The copyright on each case in
this book unless otherwise noted is held by the President and Fellows of Harvard College and they
are published herein by express permission. Permission requests to use individual Harvard copy-
righted cases should be directed to the Permission Manager, Harvard Business School Publishing
Division, Boston, MA 02163.

Case material of the Harvard Graduate School of Business Administration is made possible by the
cooperation of business firms and other organizations which may wish to remain anonymous by
having names, quantities, and other identifying details disguised while maintaining basic relationships. Cases are prepared as the basis for class discussion rather than to illustrate either effective or ineffective handling of an administrative situation.

Library of Congress Cataloging-in-Publication Data

Bruns, William J.
    Accounting for managers : text and cases / William J. Bruns, Jr. -
- 2nd ed.
      p.    cm.
    Includes bibliographical references and index.
    ISBN 0-538-88777-X (alk. paper)
    1. Managerial accounting. 2. Managerial accounting--Case studies.
  I. Title.
  HF5657.4.B78  1999
  658.15'11--dc21
                                              98-2670
                                                  CIP

2 3 4 5 6 7 8 9 D1 7 6 5 4 3 2 1 0 9

Printed in the United States of America

I(T)P®
International Thomson Publishing
South-Western College Publishing is an ITP Company.
The ITP trademark is used under license.

Team Director: Richard K. Lindgren
Senior Acquisitions Editor: David L. Shaut
Senior Developmental Editor: Ken Martin
Production Editor: Kara ZumBahlen
Marketing Manager: Maureen Riopelle
Manufacturing Coordinator: Gordon Woodside
Cover Design: Sandy Kent, Kent and Co. Design
Cover Photograph: Copyright Superstock
Production House: Cover to Cover Publishing
Composition: Janet Sprowls

# Table of Contents

## PART 3   MANAGING FINANCIAL REPORTING

## REVIEW CASES

# Preface

Accounting systems, information, and reports have the potential to provide managers with critical data and information about their organizations and those of customers and competitors. Unfortunately, however, many managers never learn how to use and exploit that potential. The complexity of modern accounting systems and standards can be daunting in spite of the apparent simplicity of basic accounting frameworks. Untrained in the complexities, many managers retreat from accounting, content to leave it to the accountants, and never to admit their uneasiness with accounting information and reports.

*Accounting for Managers* was written with the belief that managers must learn to work with accounting and accountants, but they do not need to learn how to be accountants themselves. Managers need to know what accountants do and what they do not do. They need to know the vocabulary, perspectives, and bias that underlie accounting processes and reports. Managers need to know how to ask accountants for data and information they want, and they need to know how to use accounting as a strategic tool. But managers do not need to become accountants themselves.

In 1989, the faculty of the Harvard Business School established a new required course titled *Financial Reporting and Management Accounting* (now *Financial Reporting and Control*). Although the charter and objectives for the course were vague, the mandate was to create an accounting course that would focus on what accountants do and why they do it, rather than how they do it. The course was to focus on how managers could manage better because of what accountants do, and how managers could use accounting reports, systems, and information as effectively as possible.

Case studies are an ideal way to achieve these objectives because they illustrate and describe what accountants do and provide a basis for discussions about alternatives and implications of accounting standards, procedures, and reports. Cases allow the reader to understand that accountants make choices that determine what information managers, as well as outsiders, will see, and the form it will take.  If the manager needs other information or wants to present another accounting picture, the manager needs to intervene and provide direction through questions or requests.  By doing so, the manager uses accounting as a tool to accomplish his or her objectives.

Some of the case studies in *Accounting for Managers* look deceptively easy, while others look impossibly difficult.  The former are usually more complex than they look because of the nuances that underlie any accounting.  The latter can usually be broken into easy-to-understand parts because of the power of the basic accounting models that underlie financial reporting, product costing, and measurements for control.  The majority of cases are based on information gathered from actual organizations and present real problems managers have to solve.

Most case studies contain ambiguities and complexities that preclude any single correct answer.  Individual study of cases is best followed by small group and class discussions.  In these exchanges, learning is enhanced.  The role of the instructor or discussion leader is to ensure that alternative analyses and conclusions are carefully considered along with their implications.  The goal for everyone in a case discussion should be to improve his or her ability to approach, analyze, and reach conclusions about the next newspaper or magazine story about accounting or the next accounting problem or case study that he or she will encounter.

Accounting is too important to managers, organizations, and societies to be left to accountants alone.  Accounting information is often a basis for decisions.  Accounting reports are often the basis on which the effectiveness of stewardship, decisions, and actions are evaluated.  Effective managers are always aware of the potentials and problems that accountants and accounting processes can create.  Your study of this text and the case situations should help you to become a more effective manager, and better management helps everyone.

# Acknowledgments

**M**any people have helped to create and improve *Accounting for Managers*. More than 8,000 students in the Harvard Business School MBA Classes of 1990 through 1999 have commented, made suggestions, and corrected errors in many of the cases and chapters that comprise this book. Students since 1994 have made many suggestions that have improved this Second Edition.

The colleagues with whom I have been privileged to teach this material in a group-teaching, file-sharing environment have contributed much and have helped to improve it. These include Mary Barth, Sharon Bruns, Brian Bushee, James Chang, Chuck Christenson, Srikant Datar, Bala Dharan, Marc Epstein, Dave Hawkins, Paul Healy, Julie Hertenstein, Regi Herzlinger, Gerald Holtz, Ken Merchant, V.G. Narayanan, Chris Noe, Dick Nolan, Tom Piper, Donella Rapier, Ratna Sarkar, Bob Simons, Amy Sweeney, Guy Weyns, Pete Wilson, and Karen Wruck. Many of these wrote material included in *Accounting for Managers*, and all others will find their influences in several places. Gerald Holtz and my Harvard classmate, Alfred King, encouraged me to prepare a second edition and made valuable suggestions for it.

Other faculty contributors to this book include Bob Anthony, Robin Cooper, Bob Kaplan, Krishna Palepu, Peter Turney, and Dave Wilson. I appreciate their allowing me to include some of their cases and notes.

Six research associates contributed greatly to this project, and I acknowledge the great contributions of Jeremy Cott, Dave Ellison, Susan Harmeling, Terry Nichols, Eric Petro, and Marc Zablatsky.

The Harvard Business School and Deans John H. McArthur and Kim B. Clark provided encouragement and a supporting environment for what has been one of the most satisfying teaching assignments of my career. *Business Horizons*, *Forbes*, and the *Harvard Business Review* each agreed to allow me to reprint articles.

Finally, special thanks are due to the group who helped to put this material together. The staff of the Word Processing Center at the Harvard Business School provided invaluable help in making the cases and notes readable, and their service went beyond that which I had any right to expect. My assistant, Patty Powers, again kept the project on schedule. Her cheerful acceptance of unreasonable demands for countless drafts revised on tight deadlines will not be forgotten. At South-Western College Publishing, the contributions of Ken Martin and Kara ZumBahlen also deserve special mention. Sandy Thomson of Cover to Cover Publishing provided invaluable editorial assistance and suggestions for improvement.

Finally, my wife, Shay, supported this project with affection, help, and needed criticism. She read drafts, improved presentations, contributed ideas, and taught several cases to her students before making suggestions about improvements. Her ideas are to be found throughout this book.

William J. Bruns, Jr.
Boston, Massachusetts

# Reviewers

The following faculty and instructors have used *Accounting for Managers* or cases and notes from it in their courses and have provided valuable feedback and suggestions:

Robert D. Austin (Harvard)
Mary E. Barth (Stanford)
Sharon M. Bruns (Northeastern)
Brian J. Bushee (Harvard)
James Chang (Harvard)
Srikant M. Datar (Harvard)
Bala G. Dharan (Rice)
Marc J. Epstein (INSEAD)
David F. Hawkins (Harvard)
Paul M. Healy (Harvard)
Julie H. Hertenstein (Northeastern)
Regina E. Herzlinger (Harvard)
Gerald Holtz (Boston College)
Alfred M. King
Kenneth A. Merchant (University of Southern California)
V.G. Narayanan (Harvard)
Christopher F. Noe (Harvard)
Richard L. Nolan (Harvard)
Thomas R. Piper (Harvard)
Donella Rapier (Harvard)
Ratna G. Sarkar (Harvard)
Robert L. Simons (Harvard)
Amy P. Sweeney (Harvard)
Kiran Verma (University of Massachusetts—Boston)
Guy Weyns (Harvard)
G. Peter Wilson (Boston College)
Karen Wruck (Harvard)

To Shay . . . my wife and friend

# Introduction

*Accounting for Managers* is a text for managers who want to make the most of accounting information in the business environment. It is not a comprehensive accounting text. Instead, readers are broadly exposed to the way in which accountants contribute to organizations and some of the things accountants do that every manager should know.

## WHY MANAGERS NEED TO KNOW WHAT ACCOUNTANTS DO

Accountants are the scorekeepers who observe, measure, and report on the economic aspects of organizations. Using the rules and procedures that have been developed over many years, they measure the effects of economic activities. Managers have played important roles in the development of these rules and procedures, and they will continue to do so as those principles and practices evolve in the future. Managers who know something about the status and use of accounting standards will be more effective in telling their story and in getting the information they really need.

Accounting is a language system that facilitates efficient communication between managers about economic aspects of organizations. Standardized terminology developed and used by accountants facilitates discussion of complex aspects of economic conditions and the performance of organizations. If managers do not understand the vocabulary and accounting methodology, communication in the organization becomes awkward and inefficient. In turn, the possibility of confusion or mistakes increases.

Accountants maintain records that become the basis for financial reports. Such reports summarize the financial status of the organization at one or more points in time, and they may describe how the financial structure and strength of the organization has changed over a period of time.

Financial reports are important to managers for two reasons. First, they allow managers to evaluate how their strategies and decisions are affecting the economic status and viability of their organization. By comparing the expected results to those that have been reported by accountants, managers can judge their own success and decide whether changes in strategy or decisions are needed. Second, since external parties often have interests in the financial status and success of organizations, financial statements are commonly used to report on those interests. Managers need a basic understanding of the way in which accountants summarize economic activities and prepare financial reports, so they can assess how their actions will appear to others both inside and outside of the organization.

The structure of financial reports is part of the language that accounting brings into an organization. As managers try to anticipate how their decisions might affect the organization, the framework provided by financial reports is often a useful way of summarizing the possible effects and consequences of actions.

Accounting records are often the most comprehensive records that any organization maintains. As a result, those records often provide useful information to managers trying to solve problems or decide between alternative decisions or courses of action. By knowing what kind of information is kept in accounting records and by knowing where it is maintained, managers can more efficiently request needed information and understand the proper use of that information for decisions at hand.

## AN OVERVIEW OF THE TEXT

*Accounting for Managers* has seven parts:

Part I provides an overview of accounting and financial reporting. The accounting framework and some accounting concepts are introduced so that managers can immediately begin working with financial statements.

Part II is concerned with how accountants measure and report on the assets, liabilities, and equities different parties have in an organization. In this part, classifications and elements of financial statements are examined separately to give managers an understanding of some of the difficulties that both managers and accountants have in measuring and describing the economic substance of an organization.

Part III introduces the idea that managers can choose a reporting strategy in presenting their organization to those who may request and use financial statements. A combination of accounting policies that underlie a set of financial statements can be described as conservative or aggressive. By taking an active role in the financial reporting process, managers can minimize the risk that their strategic directions will be misunderstood by outsiders who seek to understand and appraise an organization based on financial statements alone.

Part IV introduces some of the concepts of cost used by managers in decision making, planning, and controlling operations.

Part V is concerned with procedures accountants use in estimating product costs and provides an introduction to cost management. Accounting for costs is primarily an activity that takes place for the benefit of managers. Product costs are useful for pricing and product line decisions. In addition, measurements of product costs can be compared against expectations in determining whether or not planned efficiencies have been attained.

Part VI introduces capital investment analyses. Capital investment analyses are a special kind of cost management problem because they affect the future of the organization for longer periods of time.

Part VII presents some of the ways in which accounting measurements are used by managers in planning and controlling organizational activities. Because of their expertise, accountants are often called upon by managers to make measurements, to communicate, to motivate, and to provide a basis of evaluating part of an organization and the products or services that it provides. The case studies in Part VII illustrate how some organizations have sought to improve their internal measurement and management systems to benefit from their knowledge that what gets measured matters.

## A BRIEF SUMMARY OF TEXT OBJECTIVES

Six objectives have guided the development and selection of the text and case studies that comprise *Accounting for Managers*. When you have finished this text, you should:

- Be familiar with the accounting framework and how it is used in evaluating economic conditions and success and in decision making in organizations.
- Have a sense for the conceptual basis of accounting as it is carried out in organizations today.
- Be familiar with financial statements, accounting reports, and the vocabulary found within them.
- Have a sense for how managers use a reporting strategy in communicating with each other and with parties external to their organization.
- Understand the complexity of determining and using information on the cost of products and services produced by an organization.
- Understand the power of measurements in coordinating, motivating, and evaluating the activities of employees and managers in modern organizations.

Some of the case studies are based on situations where managers are trying to solve one or more complex problems that may not have a solution that will satisfy the objectives and needs of all the affected parties. In other cases, complex problems have been greatly simplified using hypothetical situations and descriptions to allow students to discover why problems in accounting often demand extensive examination and discussion.

# Part One

## An Overview of Accounting and Financial Reporting

The Accounting Framework, Financial Statements, and Some Accounting Concepts

*Chemalite, Inc.*

Introduction to Accounting Records

*Hanson Ski Products*

*Thumbs-Up Video, Inc.*

*Monterrey Manufacturing Company*

Introduction to Financial Ratios and Financial Statement Analysis

*Identify the Industries—1996*

*Colgate–Palmolive Company: Analyzing an Annual Report*

# The Accounting Framework, Financial Statements, and Some Accounting Concepts

Providing information for decisions about the deployment and use of resources in an organization and in the economy is one of the top objectives of accounting and accountants. Over many years, certain formats and procedures for presenting accounting information have come into wide use. Financial statements are based on a framework appropriately called *The Accounting Framework*.

## THE BASIC ACCOUNTING FRAMEWORK

The accounting framework rests on two premises. The first is the idea that it is possible to distinguish an *accounting entity*—the person or organization for which a set of accounts is kept—from other persons or organizations that are associated with it. The second premise is that for any accounting entity, the resources available will be exactly equal to the resources provided by creditors and owners. This second assumption is usually called *the accounting equation*, and is written as follows:

### Assets = Equities

The accounting processes of observing, measuring, and reporting are always carried out with an eye to maintaining this fundamental equality of assets and equities.

Copyright © 1992 by the President and Fellows of Harvard College. Harvard Business School case 193-028.

## Assets

In general, assets may be thought of as all things of value that the organization has a right to use. They consist of financial resources, equipment and other physical resources, and other resources having value to the entity. Most business organizations have a wide variety of assets, which they may classify according to common characteristics. Some prevalent financial assets include cash and cash balances in banks, amounts owed to the organization by customers, and marketable securities held by the firm. Operating assets often include land, buildings, equipment used in carrying out the activities of the organization, and inventories of unsold products. Other assets might include such intellectual property as copyrights or patents, conveying exclusive rights to profit from the use of property or process.

## Equities

Equities in an organization represent claims on its resources or assets. In a crude way, equities reveal the suppliers of an organization's resources. Some parties provide resources and expect to be repaid; these are creditors. Others contribute resources and thereby become participants; these are owners. Equities of nonowners include amounts owed to employees or suppliers, amounts owed on short-term loans, and loans represented by other debts of one kind or another. Owners share in both the risks and whatever profits accrue. Equities of owners include the amount of resources that they originally contributed as well as some portion of the earnings that they have not withdrawn.

## Assets = Equities

The accounting equation demands that, in accounting for an organization, the equality of assets and equities must be preserved. Thought of in another way, if the resources owned by an entity increase, the new resources had to have come from somewhere, and that source has a claim against them. If the things of value owned by an organization increase, the corresponding increase either in the amount of obligations or in the equities of owners must be recognized. Likewise, if the things of value owned by an entity decrease, obligations to nonowners may have been satisfied, or the equity of owners may have been reduced.

## Classifications of Assets and Equities

Although there are decision situations in which information about total assets or total equities can be useful, in most cases greater detail is desired. Both assets and equities come in very different forms with very different characteristics, as we have already noted.  For this reason, it is customary in accounting to adopt a scheme for classifying assets and equities of various types.  The classifications can be as large or as small as necessary to achieve the objectives for measuring and reporting.  As the number of classifications increases, the cost of measuring, record keeping, and reporting increases, so there is usually an economic constraint that limits the number of classifications actually employed.

The basic accounting equation is commonly expanded to highlight the two major equity classifications:

### Assets = Liabilities + Owners' Equity

This expansion recognizes that there is a fundamental difference between the obligations the organization has to outsiders, or those who are not members or owners, and the obligation it has to owners, or shareholders—those who have invested capital in the organization.  In the event the organization is dissolved, obligations to creditors must be met before assets are distributed to owners.  This legal distinction provides the basis for this additional classification.

One reason why this expanded form of the accounting equation is used relates to the fundamental distinction between an organization or entity and its owners.  The owners contribute capital, but they are not the entity.  If the excess of assets over liabilities increases, owners' equity is increased.  As long as owners do not make additional capital contributions or withdrawals from the assets of the firm, increases in owners' equity are usually associated with income-generating activities of an organization, whereas decreases usually result from losses.

## BASIC FINANCIAL STATEMENTS

The nature and format of financial statements are derived directly from the basic accounting framework and the accounting equation.  A *balance sheet* (or *statement of financial position*) lists the assets, liabilities, and owners' equity at a specified point in time.  An asset-flow statement (the *statement of cash flows* is the most common) summarizes the reasons why a class of assets has increased or decreased over a period of time.  A *statement of income* (or *earnings*) explains why the retained earnings classification within owners' equity has changed over a period of time, assuming owners have not taken assets from the firm in the form of dividends.

Although financial statements are prepared in many different formats and may use account classifications that differ substantially, a reader of financial reports who understands the basic accounting equation can usually figure out how to read the financial reports of an organization regardless of the particular reporting scheme that the organization has chosen.  The consolidated financial statements of the Coca-Cola Company and Subsidiaries for 1996 provide an illustration of the relationship between the accounting equation and a set of financial reports for a corporation. The consolidated balance sheet (see **Exhibit 1**) illustrates the basic equality between assets and equities. The consolidated statement of income (see **Exhibit 2**) measures how retained earnings were affected by operations before the payment of cash dividends, and the consolidated statement of cash flows (see **Exhibit 3**) shows why the amount of cash and cash equivalents changed because of operating, investing, and financing activities.

These financial reports provide an outline for reviewing some of the elements that will be found in every set of financial reports of a corporation.

## The Balance Sheet

The *balance sheet* (or *statement of financial position*) presents a company's financial position as of a specific date, based on measurements made in accordance with *generally accepted accounting principles (GAAP)* or some other reporting basis. By definition, the measured amount of total assets is always equal to the measured amount of liabilities and owners' equity. Except for monetary amounts such as cash, accounts receivable, and accounts payable, the measurements of each classification will rarely be equal to the actual current value or cash value shown. This is due to the fact that most measurements in accounting are made at the time a transaction took place in the past, and these historical measurements are retained in the accounts, even though the values of assets and some obligations may increase or decrease with the occurrence of events or passage of time. It is essential to remember that no statement of financial position will ever present the true financial value of an organization or the financial significance of the classifications used in the reports.

The classifications used by the Coca-Cola Company in its consolidated balance sheet (**Exhibit 1**) are typical of those that will be found in the balance sheets of other companies. *Current Assets* include cash and other assets used in operations during the normal operating cycle of the business, or within one year if the operating cycle is shorter than one year. The *normal operating cycle* of a company is that period of time required to acquire services and materials to create a product or service, which is sold to a customer, who then pays for the product or service, thus supplying the cash to begin the cycle again. *Cash and cash equivalents* are measured at their face amounts, whether they are in the possession of the company or deposited in banks. *Marketable securities* represent temporary investments, which can be easily converted to cash if more cash is needed. *Trade accounts receivable* are amounts that are due from customers who have purchased goods or services on credit. *Inventories* typically include materials that will be converted into product, work-in-process inventory, and finished goods that are ready for sale or have not yet been delivered to customers. *Prepaid expenses* include expenditures that have been made to acquire future benefits or services (an insurance policy would be an example), but for which the benefits have not been obtained at the date of the financial reports.

Following the current assets are a number of other assets that are *not* current; that is, they are not expected to be used up within a year or within the normal operating cycle of the business.

Many companies, particularly large companies, have assets that are not used directly in their operations or for which they do not have majority ownership. These are considered "nonoperating" assets and are usually called *Investments*. Coca-Cola has a number of such "investments." *Marketable securities* are securities of other companies similar to the marketable securities in the "Current Assets" section, except that *these* securities are expected to be held for a long-term period. *Equity method investments* are also investments in the securities of other companies, but these have to be accounted for somewhat differently (under the *equity method*) because the investor (here, Coca-Cola) owns enough of the companies to have "significant influence" over them (usually presumed to be 20% or more of their outstanding stock but less than 50%). The equity method of accounting essentially records the investor's pro rata share of all of the earnings of the investee and represents a more elaborate way of accounting for the investment than occurs with ordinary "marketable securities." Other kinds of "investments" (not represented here) might be the cash surrender value of life insurance or special-purpose funds that accumulate cash in a systematic way to meet some specific future needs.

*Property, Plant and Equipment* represents the cost of long-lived, tangible assets that are used in the company's operations. Land is almost always included at its original cost, while other assets are stated at their original cost less the proportion of original cost that has been included in the expenses of prior periods' operations as depreciation.

If a company has purchased another company for a price in excess of the fair market value of its identifiable assets, *goodwill* is assumed to have been acquired and will be recorded as an additional asset. Goodwill represents intangible things like the acquired company's excellent reputation or highly marketable brand names.

On the other side of the accounting equation are liabilities and the owners' equity. *Liabilities* are obligations that an organization must satisfy by transferring assets to or performing services for a person or organization at some time in the future. *Current liabilities* are those that an organization expects to satisfy either with assets that have been classified as current or in the course of normal operations or during the following year. Liabilities not falling within these categories are usually shown as *long-term debts* or *other liabilities*.

*Shareowners' Equity* (or *Stockholders' Equity*) represents the interest of the owners in the organization. Mathematically, its total is always equal to the amount that remains after deducting the total liabilities of the organization from its total assets. Only by coincidence would this amount be equal to the true value of the organization to its owners. Instead, the total is very much an artifact of the measurements and accounting procedures that have been used to record and account for assets and liabilities.

The amount of assets that owners originally committed to the organization (usually cash paid for stock) is usually shown separately in the owners' equity section of the Balance Sheet.   In the case of the Coca-Cola Company, that amount consists of *Common stock* with a certain "par value" (which is a nominal, base value) plus *Capital surplus* (often called *Additional paid-in capital*), which represents the money that owners paid for stock in excess of the par value.   Once these original assets are turned over to an organization, no further measurements are made, and the market value of the shares representing ownership may differ substantially from the original amount paid by the original owners.

*Reinvested earnings* (often referred to as *Retained earnings*) shows the accumulated net income of an organization from its origin to the present, after deducting dividends to shareholders.

Following this, Coca-Cola shows four additional, special components of Shareowners' Equity.  *Unearned compensation* refers to the value of stock that has been awarded to certain officers of the company but not yet earned.  *Foreign currency translation adjustment* and *Unrealized gain* on securities *available for sale* represent temporary changes that have occurred in the value of certain assets.  Because they are temporary in nature, they aren't immediately recorded as part of the income statement.  Instead, they are recorded as temporary additions to or subtractions from the value of Shareowners' Equity and are adjusted from period to period until they become permanent or fully realized.  Lastly, *Treasury stock* measures amounts that Coca-Cola has paid to reacquire its own stock.  Although these shares have not been canceled, they are no longer outstanding and therefore do not represent any owners' interest at the date of the Balance Sheet.

## The Statement of Income

The results of operations of business over a period of time are shown in the *statement of income*, or the *income statement*.  Just as the balance sheet can be represented by the accounting equation, the income statement can be represented by the following equation:

**Revenues – Expenses  =  Net Income (or Net Loss)**

In actual reports, this equation is expanded considerably and usually includes details about the nature of important categories, particularly in footnotes to the statement.

*Revenues* result from selling products or services to customers.  In its consolidated statement of income (see **Exhibit 2**), Coca-Cola shows a single figure for its "Net operating revenues" during the designated periods of time (that is, the years ending December 31, 1996 and 1995).  Some companies might give figures for different kinds of revenue.

This is immediately followed by *Cost of goods sold*, which represents, for Coca-Cola, the direct, factory-related cost of producing the products it sold. (If Coca-Cola were a retailer rather than a manufacturer, cost of goods sold would represent the amount of money it paid to outside suppliers for the merchandise that it then resold to the public.) Coca-Cola's *Gross profit* represents simply the difference between revenues and cost of goods sold.

Following this is what Coca-Cola labels *Selling, administrative, and general expenses*. Other companies sometimes call it *Operating expenses* or will sometimes break it down into a few different categories. This represents general overhead expenses that the company incurred during the designated periods of time. Deducting these general overhead expenses from the gross profit figure yields the company's *Operating income*, which is thus a measure of the income derived from the principal operations of the company.

The consolidated statement of income of Coca-Cola is typical in that, in addition to operating income, other income and expense items must be added and subtracted before the *net income* total is measured. In many organizations, these nonoperating amounts are significant, but they are shown separately to enable a reader of the financial report to make alternative assumptions about the efficiency and success of operations in the current or future periods.

## The Statement of Cash Flows

The *statement of cash flows* details the reasons why the amount of cash (and cash equivalents) changed during an accounting period. Just as the statement of income describes how retained earnings have changed during an accounting period, the statement of cash flows describes how the amount of cash and cash equivalents has changed during the accounting period. The statement's format reflects the three categories of activities that affect cash. Cash can be increased or decreased (1) because of *operations*, (2) because of the acquisition or sale of assets or *investments*, or (3) from changes in debt or stock or other *financial activities*.

Although it may not be self-evident from the consolidated statement of cash flows from the Coca-Cola Company (see **Exhibit 3**), the statement of cash flows can be thought of as containing much of the same kind of information as a checkbook register or bankbook. Sales or purchases of assets increase or decrease the amount of cash that can be deposited. Borrowing cash or payment of debt affect the balance similarly. Operations have similar effects on the balance of cash available. The reason this analogy to a bank balance is not obvious may be due to the most common form in which the statement of cash flows is presented. This common format reconciles the net income reported in the income statement to the net cash provided by operations. Upon further study, it will become apparent why statements of cash flows are often presented in this format rather than by showing directly the demands for cash made by operations and the receipts of cash provided by operations.

## ACCOUNTING CONCEPTS

Four basic accounting concepts underlie the presentation in any statement of income. They are the *accounting period concept*, the *accrual concept*, the *realization* or *recognition concept*, and the *matching concept*.

A statement of income is always presented for a period of time. In fact, part of the heading of the statement of income must include a description of the time period for which the income has been measured. The *accounting period concept* covers the period over which a statement of income has been prepared. The accounting period can be of any length, but customarily it is related to a calendar period such as one year, one-half year, or perhaps one month. It is often useful to think of the accounting period as the time between the preparation and presentation of two successive statements of financial position by an organization. The statement of income presents the changes in owners' equity due to operations and other events between one balance sheet and the next.

The *accrual concept* supports the idea that income should be measured at the time major efforts or accomplishments occur rather than simply when cash is received or paid. Revenue and expenses can be recognized before or after cash flows. If revenue is recognized, but cash has not been received, then it will be recorded among current assets as accounts receivable. Correspondingly, if an expense has been incurred, but cash has not been paid, it will be recorded as a current liability.

What accountants call the *realization concept* is really a family of rules that might be more clearly labeled *recognition concepts*. These rules aid the accountant in determining that a revenue or expense has occurred, so that it can be measured, recorded, and reported in financial reports. There is actually a large number of these rules, many of which are conditional on circumstances affecting a particular organization at a particular point in time. For example, revenue is often realized (recognized) when a product is shipped to a customer. However, in other circumstances where a customer has contracted for a special product, some portion of revenue might be recognized at the end of an accounting period, even though the product is not complete and has not been delivered. In general, revenue is recognized along with associated expenses when an exchange has taken place, the earnings process is complete, the amount of income is determinable, and collection of amounts due is reasonably assured.

The amount of expenses to be deducted in each accounting period is determined by the *matching concept* through which the expenses associated with revenue are identified and measured. The accountant attempts to match the cost and expenses of producing a product or service with revenues obtained from its delivery to customers, so that net income can be measured. This matching of revenues and expenses allows readers to understand better the possible expenses of future revenues the organization will try to earn.

Our introduction to the accounting framework and financial reports illustrates four additional accounting concepts. These concepts include the *money measurement concept*, the *business entity concept*, the *going concern concept*, and the *cost concept*.

Accountants measure things in terms of money. The *money measurement concept* has the advantage of expressing all measurements in a common monetary unit that can be added, subtracted, multiplied, and divided to produce reports which themselves can become the subject of further analysis. Nevertheless, there are many things that affect an organization but are difficult or impossible to measure in terms of money. The knowledge and skills of members or employees of an organization have great value, but they are virtually impossible to measure in terms of money. Customer loyalty may ensure future profitability, but only past revenues will be shown in past reports. Because accountants employ the money measurement concept, readers of accounting reports should not expect to find a complete picture or all the facts about an organization.

The *business entity concept* delineates the boundaries of the organization for which accounts are kept and reports are made. The reports of the Coca-Cola Company that we have examined contain no information about who the owners or the managers of the Coca-Cola Company are. At the same time, because the accounts of many parts of the Coca-Cola Company have been consolidated, we cannot see the financial condition or financial success of a particular sales office or product line. Common sense tells us that within the Coca-Cola Company, accounts are probably maintained and reports prepared for each of those entities. The entity concept means that anyone who uses financial reports has to be sure that those reports are for the exact entity in which he or she is interested, whether it be the organization as a whole or a particular subset of it.

Financial reports assume that the entity is a *going concern*. Reports are not prepared on a basis that would show the liquidation value of an organization or what would happen if the organization was liquidated. Instead, the accountant works on the assumption that an entity will continue to operate much as it has been operating for an indefinitely long period in the future.

A fourth concept seen in the financial reports you have examined is the *cost concept*. Transactions provide the information necessary for measuring and recording assets in the accounts and subsequently reporting about them. Although a reader of a financial report may be interested in the value of assets or the value of an organization, the accountant is not. Assets are initially recorded by measuring the amount paid for them. When that cost is matched with revenues, it is matched at its historical amount rather than at the current value of the asset used to create a product or service. The cost concept means that as time passes asset measurements are not changed even if the current value of those assets is changing. Likewise, when coupled with the money measurement concept, no allowance is made for changes in the purchasing power of the currency that may have been used to acquire an asset. There can be no doubt that the cost concept greatly simplifies the accountant's job in maintaining a record that can become the basis for financial reports. But it does so by sacrificing the relevance of those reports to many kinds of economic decision making.

Three other concepts are important to financial reporting, even though they are somewhat less obvious. These are the concepts of *conservatism, consistency,* and *materiality.*

The *conservatism concept* operates as a safeguard to overstatement of asset values and owners' equity. It requires that accountants be slower to recognize revenues and gains and quicker to recognize expenses and losses. This potentially negative bias in the accountant's behavior is the basis for many jokes about the differences in the way accountants and other managers see things occurring in organizations.

The *consistency concept* requires that once an entity has selected an accounting method for a kind of event or a particular asset, that same method should be used for all future events of the same type and for that asset. The consistency concept enhances the comparability of accounting reports from one period to that of another. In that way, it enhances the usefulness of financial reports. Nevertheless, certain caution must be attached to any discussion of the consistency concept because accountants use the term consistency in a narrower sense than found in other uses. Consistency is required all the time, but there is no requirement for logical consistency at a moment in time. For example, assets that may appear identical may be accounted for using different accounting methods. All that is required is that the same method be used for the same asset over time, not that all like assets be accounted for using the same method. This means that financial statement users must be constantly alert for the specific accounting methods used in different parts of financial reports. Just because a reader of financial reports understands the way in which factory machinery has been measured and reported does not necessarily mean that the same reader will have any idea how trucks or delivery equipment have been measured and reported.

Finally, arching over the entire process of accounting and financial reporting is the *materiality concept.* This concept allows that the accountant does not need to attempt to measure and record events that are insignificant or to highlight events that differ from the usual or the norm. Events or assets judged to be insignificant can be ignored or disregarded. On the surface, this concept seems to make good sense, as it focuses both the accountant and the financial report reader's attention on important things. Unfortunately, the exact line between what is significant and what is insignificant is very difficult to define. Furthermore, something may seem insignificant to the accountant but might be regarded as very significant to a managing director. The materiality concept is both a strength and a weakness in financial reporting, and a wise reader of reports must be constantly on guard for its occasionally pernicious effects.

## SUMMARY

The accounting equation

**Assets  =  Equities**

or in its expanded form

**Assets  =  Liabilities + Owners' Equity**

provides the basis for the accounting framework.  The format for the statement of financial position derives directly from the accounting equation, and the assumed equality of assets and equities provides a basis for accounting record systems as well as the balance sheet.

Two additional financial reports stem directly from the accounting equation.  The statement of income explains the change in the owners' equity that occurs during an accounting period by giving details of both revenues that increase owners' equity and expenses that decrease owners' equity.  It provides a basis for analyzing the effectiveness of operations.  The statement of cash flows explains why the amount of cash and equivalents has increased or decreased during a period of time.  It details whether or not operations have provided additional cash or have themselves consumed cash.  It also reveals cash that is provided by new loans or that has been used to pay off debts, and how cash has been invested or obtained by selling assets.

This brief overview of the accounting framework and financial reporting has served as an introduction to eleven important accounting concepts, financial reports, and the work of accountants.  Only practice and further study can give real meaning to these accounting concepts, but understanding their existence is critical to studying the work of accountants, and some of the reasons why they operate as they do.  The eleven concepts introduced here are accounting period, accrual, realization, matching, money measurement, business entity, going concern, cost, consistency, conservatism, and materiality.  We will see in detail how these concepts are applied as we continue in our study of accounting principles.

**EXHIBIT 1**
**The Coca-Cola Company and Subsidiaries—Consolidated Balance Sheet (in millions except share data)**

| December 31 | 1996 | 1995 |
|---|---|---|
| **ASSETS** | | |
| **Current** | | |
| Cash and cash equivalents | $ 1,433 | $ 1,167 |
| Marketable securities | 225 | 148 |
| | 1,658 | 1,315 |
| Trade accounts receivable, less allowance of $30 in 1996 and $34 in 1995 | 1,641 | 1,695 |
| Inventories | 952 | 1,117 |
| Prepaid expenses and other assets | 1,659 | 1,323 |
| **Total Current Assets** | 5,910 | 5,450 |
| **Investments and Other Assets** | | |
| Equity method investments: | | |
| Coca-Cola Enterprises, Inc. | 547 | 556 |
| Coca-Cola Amatil Limited | 881 | 682 |
| Other, principally bottling companies | 2,004 | 1,157 |
| Cost method investments, principally bottling companies | 737 | 319 |
| Marketable securities and other assets | 1,779 | 1,597 |
| | 5,948 | 4,311 |
| **Property, Plant and Equipment** | | |
| Land | 204 | 233 |
| Buildings and improvements | 1,528 | 1,944 |
| Machinery and equipment | 3,649 | 4,135 |
| Containers | 200 | 345 |
| | 5,581 | 6,657 |
| Less allowances for depreciation | 2,031 | 2,321 |
| | 3,550 | 4,336 |
| **Goodwill and Other Intangible Assets** | 753 | 944 |
| | $16,161 | $15,041 |

**EXHIBIT 1 (continued)**
**The Coca-Cola Company and Subsidiaries—Consolidated Balance Sheet (in millions except share data)**

| December 31 | 1996 | 1995 |
|---|---|---|
| **LIABILITIES AND SHAREOWNERS' EQUITY** | | |
| **Current** | | |
| Accounts payable and accrued expenses | $ 2,972 | $ 3,103 |
| Loans and notes payable | 3,388 | 2,371 |
| Current maturities of long-term debt | 9 | 552 |
| Accrued income taxes | 1,037 | 1,322 |
| **Total Current Liabilities** | 7,406 | 7,348 |
| **Long-term Debt** | 1,116 | 1,141 |
| **Other Liabilities** | 1,182 | 966 |
| **Deferred Income Taxes** | 301 | 194 |
| **Shareowners' Equity** | | |
| Common stock, $.25 par value | | |
| Authorized: 5,600,000,000 shares | | |
| Issued: 3,432,956,518 shares in 1996; 3,423,678,994 in 1995 | 858 | 856 |
| Capital surplus | 1,058 | 863 |
| Reinvested earnings | 15,127 | 12,882 |
| Unearned compensation related to outstanding restricted stock | (61) | (68) |
| Foreign currency translation adjustment | (662) | (424) |
| Unrealized gain on securities available for sale | 156 | 82 |
| | 16,476 | 14,191 |
| Less treasury stock, at cost (951,963,574 shares in 1996; 919,081,326 shares in 1995) | 10,320 | 8,799 |
| | 6,156 | 5,392 |
| | $16,161 | $15,041 |

**EXHIBIT 2**
**The Coca-Cola Company and Subsidiaries—**
**Consolidated Statement of Income (in millions, except per share data)**

| Year Ended December 31 | 1996 | 1995 | 1994 |
|---|---|---|---|
| **Net Operating Revenues** | $18,546 | $18,018 | $16,181 |
| Cost of goods sold | 6,738 | 6,940 | 6,168 |
| **Gross Profit** | 11,808 | 11,078 | 10,013 |
| Selling, administrative, and general expenses | 7,893 | 7,052 | 6,376 |
| **Operating Income** | 3,915 | 4,026 | 3,637 |
| Interest income | 238 | 245 | 181 |
| Interest expense | 286 | 272 | 199 |
| Equity income | 211 | 169 | 134 |
| Other income (deductions)—net | 87 | 86 | (25) |
| Gains on issuances of stock by equity investees | 431 | 74 | — |
| **Income before Income Taxes** | 4,596 | 4,328 | 3,728 |
| Income taxes | 1,104 | 1,342 | 1,174 |
| **Net Income** | $ 3,492 | $ 2,986 | $ 2,554 |
| **Net Income per Share** | $ 1.40 | $ 1.18 | $ .99 |
| **Average Shares Outstanding** | 2,494 | 2,525 | 2,580 |

**EXHIBIT 3**
**The Coca-Cola Company and Subsidiaries—Consolidated Statement of Cash Flows (in millions)**

| Year Ended December 31 | 1996 | 1995 | 1994 |
|---|---|---|---|
| **Operating Activities** | | | |
| Net income | $ 3,492 | $ 2,986 | $ 2,554 |
| Depreciation and amortization | 479 | 454 | 411 |
| Deferred income taxes | (145) | 157 | 58 |
| Equity income, net of dividends | (89) | (25) | (4) |
| Foreign currency adjustments | (60) | (23) | (6) |
| Gains on issuances of stock by equity investees | (431) | (74) | — |
| Other noncash items | 181 | 45 | 41 |
| Net change in operating assets and liabilities | 36 | (192) | 307 |
| Net cash provided by operating activities | 3,463 | 3,328 | 3,361 |
| **Investing Activities** | | | |
| Acquisitions and investments, principally bottling companies | (645) | (338) | (311) |
| Purchases of investments and other assets | (623) | (403) | (379) |
| Proceeds from disposals of investments and other assets | 1,302 | 580 | 299 |
| Purchases of property, plant, and equipment | (990) | (937) | (878) |
| Proceeds from disposals of property, plant, and equipment | 81 | 44 | 109 |
| Other investing activities | (175) | (172) | (55) |
| Net cash used in investing activities | (1,050) | (1,226) | (1,215) |
| Net cash provided by operations after reinvestment | 2,413 | 2,102 | 2,146 |
| **Financing Activities** | | | |
| Issuances of debt | 1,122 | 754 | 491 |
| Payments of debt | (580) | (212) | (154) |
| Issuances of stock | 124 | 86 | 69 |
| Purchases of stock for treasury | (1,521) | (1,796) | (1,192) |
| Dividends | (1,247) | (1,110) | (1,006) |
| Net cash used in financing activities | (2,102) | (2,278) | (1,792) |
| Effect of Exchange Rate Changes on Cash and Cash Equivalents | (45) | (43) | 34 |
| **Cash and Cash Equivalents** | | | |
| Net increase (decrease) during the year | 266 | (219) | 388 |
| Balance at beginning of year | 1,167 | 1,386 | 998 |
| Balance at end of year | $ 1,433 | $ 1,167 | $ 1,386 |

# Chemalite, Inc.

In late 1990, Bennett Alexander, a consulting chemical engineer, applied for and received a patent for one of his inventions, a Chemalite. A small, fragile glass vial of one chemical was inserted into a plastic, translucent cylinder that was then filled with a second chemical and sealed. Bending the cylinder caused the glass vial inside to break, allowing the two chemicals to mix. When combined, the two chemicals gave off a bright yellow-green glow.

Alexander anticipated a substantial market for the Chemalite. It had the appeal of being readily available in case of emergencies, but yet it did not require any form of ignition. He anticipated a considerable demand from the armed forces and manufacturers of flares and similar safety equipment.

On January 2, 1991, Alexander, together with a number of relatives and friends, established Chemalite, Inc.; 500,000 shares were issued, of which Alexander received 125,000 in exchange for his patent, and the remainder were sold to the other investors at $1 per share. During the period January 2, 1991, through June 30, 1991, Chemalite, Inc., made the following expenditures:

- January 15—Paid $7,500 in legal fees, charter costs, and printing expenses associated with the incorporation of the company.
- June 15—Spent $62,500 building the machinery that would be used to produce the first commercial models of the Chemalite.
- June 24—Purchased $75,000 worth of plastics and chemicals for use in the production of commercial Chemalites.

*Visiting Professor David A. Wilson prepared this case and it was revised by Professor Charles Christenson.*

Copyright © 1976 by the President and Fellows of Harvard College. Harvard Business School case 177-078.

Toward the end of June, Alexander, who had assumed a very active role in the management of Chemalite, Inc., met with the rest of the stockholders to present a state of the corporation report and to discuss strategies for the future marketing of the Chemalites. He was hopeful that the company would be producing Chemalites by the end of August. Susan Peterson, a friend of Alexander who had invested a substantial sum in the company, indicated at the meeting that she had received inquiries from an auto parts distributor about the availability of Chemalites and their expected price. The distributor wished to purchase a substantial number of the lights as part of a highway safety promotion and was interested in pursuing the possibility of private branding.

At this point in the meeting, Mr. Larson, one of the stockholders, but a man with very little business experience and even less understanding of financial statements, interjected: "All this discussion of what we are going to do is well and good, but all I can see is that six months ago we had $375,000 and now we have $230,000. By my reckoning, we've managed to lose $145,000 in six months and haven't much to show for it."

Some of the stockholders agreed with Larson. Indeed, between January 2 and June 30, the company's bank balance had fallen from $375,000 to $230,000. Ms. D'Cruz, a stockholder, suggested that since Chemalite's operations were not in full swing, these preoperating outlays should probably be considered more as investments in the business by the business rather than as losses. After considerable discussion by all the stockholders, it was agreed that they would meet again in early January 1992 to study the state of the corporation. It was generally felt that the company should be in full operation by then and that the problems created by the preoperating period spoken of would be overcome by year-end.

During the last half of 1991, Chemalite, Inc., did indeed go into full operation. To prepare for the stockholder's meeting in early January 1992, Bill Murray, the firm's recently hired bookkeeper, produced the following data:

1.  In early July 1991, a consulting engineer delivered the prototypes of the Chemalite that he had been developing, and he was paid a total of $23,750.
2.  During the six months from July to December 1991, Chemalite sold $754,500 of its product. The largest single purchaser, the auto parts distributor with whom Peterson had negotiated, still owed Chemalite, Inc., $69,500. All other customers' accounts were paid in full by year-end.
3.  Additional chemicals and plastics were purchased for a total of $175,000. All of these purchases were paid for in cash.
4.  Chemalite, Inc., spent $22,500 on television and trade journal advertising to introduce the product.
5.  During the six months ended December 31, 1991, the company expended $350,000 on direct manufacturing labor and on manufacturing-related overhead (rent, utilities, supervisory labor). An additional $80,000 was spent on corporate salaries and other corporate expenses.

6.  In early July, a further $150,000 was spent on machinery to be used in the production of Chemalites.
7.  During the period, the company had borrowed $50,000 for a short time and repaid the loan by year-end. The interest paid on the loan amounted to $750.

In preparing his state of the corporation report, Alexander noted with some anxiety that the company's bank balance had fallen a further $117,000 from the $230,000 reported in June to only $113,000. It bothered him because he believed that the company was really doing quite well, and he failed to understand why the bank account did not appear to reflect this condition. In surveying the cash outflows incurred by Chemalite, Inc., over the entire year, he noted the following:

1.  There was still a stock at December 31 of $55,000 worth of plastics and chemicals in the warehouse; however, there were no finished or partially finished Chemalites at year-end.
2.  Although the patent that the company had acquired from Alexander had a legal life of 17 years, he expected competitors to develop equivalent products that did not use the patented technique in about five years.
3.  The machinery used in the production of the Chemalites was general purpose machinery, not restricted to Chemalite production, that might reasonably be expected to last for 10 years, six months of which had already passed.
4.  Alexander was quite confused by the worth of the prototypes. They had directly resulted in the development of the product the company was presently selling, so perhaps their value had actually increased over the last six months of 1991.
5.  The committee organizing Barcelona '92, The Games of the XXV Olympiad, had placed a firm order with the company for 60,000 Chemalites at a price of $1.50 each. It was their intention to give a Chemalite to each person at the opening ceremony of the 1992 Olympic Games and to have athletes and fans light their Chemalites, symbolic of the Olympic flame.

Alexander was an inventor, not a businessperson, and he was perplexed about how to report the events of the year to the stockholders. He had a feeling that things were going well, but he did not know how to convey this message to his fellow stockholders.

## QUESTIONS

1.  Prepare a summary of the cash transactions for the six months ended June 30, 1991.
2.  Prepare an income statement for the six months ended June 30, 1991.  Did the company incur a loss as Mr. Larson suggested?
3.  Prepare a statement of financial position at June 30, 1991, and a statement of cash flows for the six-month period.
4.  Prepare a set of financial statements for the stockholders for the year 1991: a statement of financial position at December 31, 1991; an income statement; and a statement of cash flows for the year ended December 31, 1991.
5.  How would you have reported to stockholders on the financial performance of Chemalite, Inc., for its first year, January 1, 1991 to December 31, 1991?

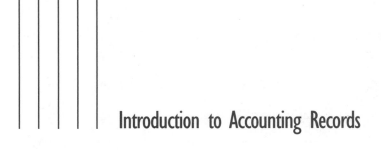

# Introduction to Accounting Records

**A**lmost all accounting systems have two major components. One of these, called the *journal*, is a sequential listing of events that have had a measurable effect on an organization's economic condition. The journal is, in effect, a diary of the economic events that have taken place on a day-to-day basis. The second component, called *accounts*, consists of summaries by categories of all events that have occurred during a period or since the formation of the entity. A complete set of accounts is called a *ledger*. A set of accounts for assets, liabilities, and owners' equity is called a *general ledger*. The purpose of this introduction is to illustrate briefly the nature of a journal and a ledger and to describe some of the conventions used in maintaining them.

The development of electronic media, such as computers, has drastically changed the way records are kept in most organizations. The introduction of new technologies, however, has not displaced the terminology and basic record-keeping functions of the double-entry bookkeeping system originally developed before the end of the fifteenth century.

## THE JOURNAL

The journal is a sequential record of events and their effects on the entity. The double-entry bookkeeping system is a means of ensuring that the accounting equation of *assets* = *equities* remains in balance. Entries are made in the journal using this system. It is labeled *double entry* because there will always be at least two parts to the entry. For example, if an asset increases, something else must

Copyright © 1992 by the President and Fellows of Harvard College. Harvard Business School case 192-153.

occur to keep the equation in balance (such as an equity increase or another asset decrease).

A typical journal entry might look like this:

| | | | |
|---|---|---|---|
| January 2 | Cash | 100 | |
| | Capital Stock | | 100 |

The significance of the location of the parts of the entry will become clear shortly. At this point, simply note that one line has a different margin than the other. This left-versus-right format is a conventional way of describing whether these accounts have increased or decreased. Convention dictates that all lines with left margins are presented first, with all indented lines following in each individual journal entry. **Exhibit 1** summarizes the nine classes of changes that can affect assets, liabilities, and owners' equity. Note that the above example is in the third category mentioned in **Exhibit 1** (Increase in assets, Increase in owners' equity). Cash, an asset, increases by $100 because an owners' equity account increases due to an owner's purchase of capital stock for $100.

Inspection of **Exhibit 1** reveals some important characteristics of almost all journals. Each event is dated. Where a date is not shown, it is presumed to be the same as that of the preceding entry. A description is included giving details about classifications that are increased or decreased. Finally, the amount of increase or decrease is listed in two columns labeled *debit* (dr.) or *credit* (cr.). The words debit and credit in accounting have no meaning other than left and right, and no attempt should be made to relate the meaning of these two words in other contexts to the way in which they are used in accounting records. An inspection of **Exhibit 1** will reveal that increases in assets and decreases in liabilities and owners' equity are always entered in the left-hand or debit column, and decreases in assets and increases in liabilities and owners' equity are always listed in the right-hand or credit column.

A journal may contain other information as well, as illustrated in the explanations in parentheses under several journal entries in **Exhibit 3**. This descriptive detail allows a reader to more quickly understand the journal entry.

## ACCOUNTS

The entries for events or transactions listed in the journal are then transferred to accounts in a ledger and accumulated. An account is maintained for each classification of assets, liabilities, or owners' equity that has been established by a journal entry. No entry is made in an account until a record has been made in the journal, and every entry in the journal results in a change in the status of two or more accounts.

Many different forms of accounts are used. Typically, the form of account provides space for keeping a record of the date of a change and whether it represents an increase or decrease. In addition, space may be provided for maintaining a running balance and/or for entering a description of the type of event or transaction that resulted in the change. Entries in the accounts are almost always cross-referenced to the journal; that is, a page number or journal entry number is included so that the accountant can move from the account back to the record of original journal entry without difficulty.

In the study of accounting and in discussions of accounting problems by managers, a skeleton form of account—called a "T" account—is frequently used. The left-hand side is called the debit side, and the right-hand side is called the credit side. **Exhibit 2** illustrates T accounts and summarizes the general rules for entry of amounts of change in the accounts. These correspond exactly to the placement of amounts listed in the journal.

It is unusual to find accounts that are headed solely by the classification assets or liabilities and owners' equities. Subclassifications are used, that is, separate asset accounts for cash, amounts receivable from customers, amounts owed to creditors, amounts contributed by owners, and so forth. The number of accounts corresponds to the number of classifications that have been established by the accountant.

An important characteristic of conventional accounting records can now be pointed out. Because the amount of increase and decrease entered in each half of a journal entry is identical, the total amount of debits will always be equal to the total amounts of credits. When these amounts are transferred to accounts, the amount of debits and the amount of credits remain the same. Therefore, if a listing of all accounts in a general ledger is made showing their debit or credit balances, and these are summed, the amounts should be equal. A listing such as this is called a *trial balance*, and it provides a check on the clerical accuracy of the record. As indicated earlier, a group of accounts is called a ledger. The clerical accuracy of entries made in the general ledger is often "proven" by checking to see that the equality of debits and credits has been maintained.

## SPECIALIZED RECORDS

The forms that are illustrated in **Exhibits 1** and **2** are general in character; many accounting systems use forms that are quite different. When a large number of entries of the same type is to be made in the journal, often a *special journal* will be established to simplify the clerical task involved in making that group of entries. In some cases, a variety of journals may be used to take advantage of special characteristics of the accounting task in a particular firm or situation.

For the same reasons that special journals are sometimes used, special ledgers are sometimes established. In particular, rather than maintain a separate account in the general ledger for each customer or creditor, subsidiary ledgers are established that relate in total to an account maintained in the general ledger of the accounting system. When a *subsidiary ledger* is used, the total of all debits and credits in the subsidiary ledger will be equal to the total amounts listed in the *control account* in the general ledger.

It is not within the scope of this introduction to illustrate all possible forms of journals or ledgers and the ways in which they are used. The design of an effective accounting record system depends upon the comprehension and ingenuity of the accountant and the needs of the business and its managers, who must develop and adopt an effective system from the generic forms illustrated herein.

## AN ILLUSTRATION

To demonstrate the way in which the general journal form and T accounts can be used to record information about an entity, consider the following example:

> On September 1, 1999, Robert Greene opened a store, the Greene Paint Company. On preceding days he had taken $3,500 of his own cash and had placed it in a separate bank account, which he intended to use only for the store. In addition, he borrowed $2,000 from the local bank. He used some cash to acquire equipment, but he was able to purchase on credit the rest of his equipment and some merchandise inventory. By the time he opened his doors for business on September 1, the business, the Greene Paint Company, could be represented by the following statement of financial position:

**Greene Paint Company—Statement of Financial Position, September 1, 1999**

| Assets | | Liabilities and Owners' Equity | |
|---|---|---|---|
| Cash | $3,300 | Amounts owed to suppliers | $1,500 |
| Merchandise inventories | 700 | Loans owed | 2,000 |
| Equipment | 3,000 | Owners' equity | 3,500 |
| | $7,000 | | $7,000 |

During the month of September, business was much slower than Mr. Greene had hoped it would be. Nevertheless, four kinds of events took place. They were:

1. Additional merchandise was purchased at a cost of $1,000, and Mr. Greene promised to pay the suppliers as soon as he could.
2. $900 cash was paid on accounts already owed to suppliers.
3. The merchandise that he had purchased at the beginning of the month for $1,000 was sold for $1,500, with the customer promising to pay within 30 days.

4.    Mr. Greene estimated that his equipment had depreciated $100 during the month.

Exhibit 3 shows the journal of the Greene Paint Company for August and September, and **Exhibit 4** shows the accounts. Note that the accountant established some temporary accounts in September to keep track of details affecting Greene's equity, then closed those accounts to a new account called *retained earnings*. **Exhibit 5** shows the statement of financial position for the Greene Paint Company at the end of September.

## THE BOOKKEEPING CYCLE

As economic events are observed and measured by the accountant, their effects are measured and recorded sequentially in a journal. The journal tells the accountant which accounts have been affected and which need to be updated. Temporary accounts are usually established to keep track of details of events which affect owners' equity. At the end of each accounting period, the length of which is determined by the needs or interests of managers or owners, the accountant may adjust the balances in some accounts before summarizing the effects of entries in temporary accounts on retained earnings. Permanent accounts comprise the statement of financial position. Information in the temporary accounts is used to prepare the statement of income. This exercise, repeated each accounting period, is known as *the bookkeeping cycle*.

**EXHIBIT 1**
## A Journal Showing Nine Classes of Events

| Date | Description | Dr. | Cr. |
|---|---|---|---|
| (Each event or transaction is dated.) | (Details about classifications increased or decreased are included in the description.) | (The left-hand column, the *debit* column, records amounts of increases of assets and decreases in equities.) | (The right-hand column, the *credit* column, records amounts of decreases of assets and increases in equities.) |
| **1999** | | | |
| January 1 | Increase in assets | XX | |
| | Decrease in assets | | XX |
| January 2 | Increase in assets | XX | |
| | Increase in liabilities | | XX |
| | Increase in assets | XX | |
| | Increase in owners' equity | | XX |
| January 3 | Decrease in liabilities | XX | |
| | Decrease in assets | | XX |
| | Decrease in owners' equity | XX | |
| | Decrease in assets | | XX |
| January 4 | Decrease in liabilities | XX | |
| | Increase in liabilities | | XX |
| | Decrease in liabilities | XX | |
| | Increase in owners' equity | | XX |
| | Decrease in owners' equity | XX | |
| | Increase in liabilities | | XX |
| | Decrease in owners' equity | XX | |
| | Increase in owners' equity | | XX |

**EXHIBIT 2**
## T Accounts

| Assets | | Liabilities and Owners' Equities | |
|---|---|---|---|
| Increases in asset accounts are entered on the left-hand side of the account | Decreases in asset accounts are entered on the right-hand side of the account | Decreases in liability and owners' equity accounts are entered on the left-hand side of the account | Increases in liability and owners' equity accounts are entered on the right-hand side of the account |

**EXHIBIT 3**
**Journal of Greene Paint Company**

| Date | | Description | Dr. | Cr. |
|---|---|---|---|---|
| **1999** | | | | |
| August | | Entries to record creation of entity | | |
| | (A1) | Cash | $3,500 | |
| | | Owners' equity, B. Greene | | $3,500 |
| | | (investment of cash) | | |
| | (A2) | Cash | 2,000 | |
| | | Loans owed | | 2,000 |
| | (A3) | Merchandise inventory | 700 | |
| | | Amount owed to suppliers | | 700 |
| | | (purchase of inventory) | | |
| | (A4) | Equipment | 3,000 | |
| | | Amount owed to suppliers | | 800 |
| | | Cash | | 2,200 |
| | | (purchase of equipment) | | |
| September | | | | |
| | (S1) | Merchandise inventory | 1,000 | |
| | | Amounts owed to suppliers | | 1,000 |
| | | (purchase of more paint) | | |
| | (S2) | Amount owed to suppliers | 900 | |
| | | Cash | | 900 |
| | | (payment to suppliers) | | |
| | (S3) | Amounts owed by customers | 1,500 | |
| | | Sales | | 1,500 |
| | | (sales of merchandise) | | |
| | (S4) | Cost of goods sold | 1,000 | |
| | | Merchandise inventory | | 1,000 |
| | | (cost of merchandise sold) | | |
| | | An adjusting entry: | | |
| | (S5) | Depreciation | 100 | |
| | | Equipment | | 100 |
| | | A closing entry: | | |
| | (S6) | Sales | 1,500 | |
| | | Cost of goods sold | | 1,000 |
| | | Depreciation | | 100 |
| | | Retained earnings | | 400 |
| | | (to close three temporary accounts) | | |

**EXHIBIT 4**
**General Ledger of Greene Paint Company**

### Assets

**Cash**

| | | | |
|---|---|---|---|
| (A1) | $3500 | (A4) | $2200 |
| (A2) | 2000 | | |
| Bal., Sept. 1 | $3300 | (S2) | $ 900 |
| Bal., Sept. 30 | $2400 | | |

**Amounts Owed by Customers**

| | | | |
|---|---|---|---|
| (S3) | $1500 | | |
| Bal., Sept. 30 | $1500 | | |

**Merchandise Inventory**

| | | | |
|---|---|---|---|
| (A3) | $ 700 | | |
| Bal., Sept. 1 | $ 700 | (S4) | $1000 |
| (S1) | 1000 | | |
| Bal., Sept. 30 | $ 700 | | |

**Equipment**

| | | | |
|---|---|---|---|
| (A4) | $3000 | | |
| Bal., Sept. 1 | $3000 | (S5) | $ 100 |
| Bal., Sept. 30 | $2900 | | |

### Liabilities and Owners' Equity

**Amounts Owed to Suppliers**

| | | | |
|---|---|---|---|
| | | (A3) | $ 700 |
| | | (A4) | $ 800 |
| (S2) | $ 900 | Bal., Sept. 1 | $1500 |
| | | (S1) | 1000 |
| | | Bal., Sept. 30 | $1600 |

**Loans Owed**

| | | | |
|---|---|---|---|
| | | (A2) | $2000 |
| | | Bal., Sept. 1 | $2000 |
| | | Bal., Sept. 30 | $2000 |

**Owners' Equity, B. Greene**

| | | | |
|---|---|---|---|
| | | (A1) | $3500 |
| | | Bal., Sept. 1 | $3500 |
| | | Bal., Sept. 30 | $3500 |

**Retained Earnings**

| | | | |
|---|---|---|---|
| | | (S6) | $ 400 |

### Temporary Accounts

**Sales**

| | | | |
|---|---|---|---|
| (S6) | $1500 | (S3) | $1500 |

**Cost of Goods Sold**

| | | | |
|---|---|---|---|
| (S4) | $1000 | (S6) | $1000 |

**Depreciation**

| | | | |
|---|---|---|---|
| (S5) | $ 100 | (S6) | $ 100 |

**EXHIBIT 5**
**Greene Paint Company—Statement of Financial Position, September 30, 1999**

| Assets | | Liabilities and Owners' Equity | |
|---|---|---|---|
| Cash | $2,400 | Amounts owed to suppliers | $1,600 |
| Amounts owed by customers | 1,500 | Loans owed | 2,000 |
| Merchandise inventories | 700 | Owners' equity | 3,500 |
| Equipment | 2,900 | Retained earnings | 400 |
| | $7,500 | | $7,500 |

# Hanson Ski Products

In early July 1986, Alden (Denny) Hanson, president and chief executive officer of Hanson Ski Products, was preparing for a meeting with his executive committee on the company's current and longer-term financing needs. For one thing, Mr. Hanson wanted to review the plans for fiscal year (FY) 1987.[1] Although the company's bankers had provided a $4.2 million line of credit to meet the year's seasonal cash needs, Denny wanted to recheck his figures to be sure that this credit would be sufficient, particularly since Hanson Ski Products was scheduled to repay stockholder loans of $841,000 in November.

## COMPANY BACKGROUND

Hanson Ski Products was a leading manufacturer of high-quality ski boots located in Boulder, Colorado. Although it was a relatively new entrant to the market, its revenues ranked among the top 10 ski boot manufacturers worldwide by 1984. Hanson commanded a 20% share of the U.S. market for high-quality ski boots, which was growing at an estimated 10% per year. While the focus of operations was U.S. skiers, the international portion of the company's business was growing faster than the domestic portion. The company expected

---

*Professor Julie H. Hertenstein and Professor William J. Bruns, Jr. adapted this case from "Hanson Industries, (B)," No. 179-077 and "Hanson Industries," No. 297-066. Dates of events and selected financial information have been changed and disguised.*

Copyright © 1986 by the President and Fellows of Harvard College. Harvard Business School case 187-038.

---

[1] Fiscal year 1987 at Hanson Ski Products began on April 1, 1986, and ended on March 31, 1987.

that in FY 1987, its international revenues would represent about 30% of total sales.

One of the keys to Hanson's successful penetration of this tough market was the unique design of its ski boots. The revolutionary patented rear-entry concept, designed by Chris Hanson, balanced the objectives of comfort and skiing performance sought by the experienced skier. In May 1977, *Fortune* named the specially engineered boot in a worldwide competition "one of the 25 best-designed products available in America." By 1986, Hanson was marketing four models of adult boots, and newer models were continually being added as older models were dropped.

## PAST OPERATING PERFORMANCE

Hanson Ski Products was founded in 1973. The first year of operations, FY 1974, was devoted to development of boot design and preparation for production. In FY 1975, Hanson shipped 2,300 pairs of boots to retailers. By FY 1986, this figure had grown to 85,000 pairs, and revenues had reached $9.8 million (see **Exhibits 1** and **2**).

Hanson management expected net revenues to continue to grow at an impressive rate during FY 1987. Sales projections made early in the planning process had later been revised upward so that it was now expected that net sales would reach $12 million for the year. By FY 1991, Hanson predicted revenues from ski boots would approximate $26 million; beyond that point it was expected that unit volume of sales would only increase proportionately to the overall growth in the market.

## THE ORDER CYCLE

Hanson's boot business was extremely seasonal and could be broken down into the ordering, shipment, and collection phases. The ordering phase was composed of two parts: the stocking order period and the reorder period. During the stocking order period from March through June, sales representatives conducted an intensive marketing campaign, commencing with the equipment dealers' annual Ski Show held in Las Vegas in March. The timing of this show was important in that it was held just after the end of the previous ski season when both manufacturers and equipment dealers were aware of past equipment sales performance and retail inventory levels. Hanson usually received 25% to 30% of its total orders at this ski show and another 55% to 60% of the orders between April and June, when its sales representatives contacted all dealers who had not attended the show. Discounts ranging from 4% to 12% were offered to customers, and accounts were typically payable on the tenth day of the second or third month following shipment, depending upon the date of their requested shipment. These terms were similar to and slightly tighter than the terms offered by Hanson's competitors.

The reorder period accounted for the remaining 10% to 20% of Hanson's sales and started in July, when dealers reordered to replenish their supplies. A 2% discount was available to these customers for payment by the tenth of the month following shipment.

Sparse snow years affected the order phase in two fiscal years. The first effect was felt almost immediately in the year there was no snow and manifested itself as a reduction in the reorders received. The second and more pronounced effect was felt during the stocking order period in the following spring. At that time, dealers' inventories were higher than their normal levels, and dealers were wary of placing large initial stocking orders for fear of experiencing two consecutive poor snow years and the consequent falloff in demand.

Shipments began in July, peaked in August, and remained at a high level until December, when they trailed off. The largest part of Hanson's collections of accounts receivable began in December following the shipment phase. In a normal business year, the collection period was about 75 days. However, a poor snow year had the effect of significantly stretching the collection period.

## THE PRODUCTION AND FINANCING CYCLE

Manufacturing of the following season's products commenced in January, and production schedules were subsequently modified and adjusted as the shape and size of the order pattern became clearer. A level production policy was adopted for three reasons. Hanson did not want to lay off skilled workers (50% of their 123-person production force) who were key to the manufacture of the ski boots. In addition, the company did not have sufficient physical capacity to turn out an entire year's production after March, when the first orders were received. Finally, management had sufficient confidence in its sales forecasts to manufacture up to 60% of such forecasts in advance of firm orders.

Hanson's seasonal marketing efforts and level manufacturing operations created a substantial financial management challenge. Although by June the company had produced approximately 60% of the year's expected volume of finished boots, it was not until November that most of the year's finished goods inventory was converted to accounts receivable; it was December before the bulk of receivables collections began flowing in.

David Snyder, Hanson's treasurer, typically developed a preliminary cash budget in January, before the start of the fiscal year. On the basis of that projection, he made appropriate arrangements for funding the coming season's cash needs. Based on the results of sales efforts and orders received during the spring, the budget was reviewed in June, and revisions were made as necessary. The proposed final budgets for fiscal year 1987 are shown in **Exhibits 3** and **4**, which also include Snyder's estimates of the balance in each current asset and current liability category at the end of each quarter.

Hanson's management also practiced very tight internal cash management. In fact, Mr. Snyder believed that the optimum target for the firm's cash balances was zero, since Hanson was highly leveraged financially and would have had to pay interest to support any cash balances maintained at the bank. In practice, the cash balances averaged about $100,000.

Despite these efforts to conserve or stretch cash within the firm, Hanson had still found it necessary to arrange substantial short-term loans from banks, finance companies, and from principal stockholders. Although current seasonal financing was being handled exclusively with a group of commercial banks, Hanson had made use of some commercial financing in the past. Commercial financing companies made more frequent audits of the borrower's operations and finances than was typical for the banks and usually levied a higher interest charge. Because of frequent monitoring and higher interest rates, the commercial finance companies felt comfortable in extending a larger amount of funds against inventory and accounts receivable collateral than would normally be true for a commercial bank.

It was the company's goal, however, to move toward exclusive reliance on commercial bank funding, primarily because of the potentially lower cost of such borrowings to Hanson and secondarily because of the higher-quality corporate image it portrayed. In February 1986, Hanson had obtained approval of a $4.2 million revolving line of credit for fiscal 1987 at 3.75% over prime[2] with a group of three banks led by the United Bank of Denver, which was in a good geographical position to maintain day-to-day contact with Hanson. Hanson could draw against this line of credit to the extent of 70% of the cost of inventories and 80% of current accounts receivable.

The banks' reduction of the interest rate charge in FY 1987 was seen by Denny Hanson as an indication of the company's improved credit standing in the eyes of these lenders. That conviction was further strengthened when the banks informed Hanson that the personal guarantees of the major stockholders would not be required as a condition of the 1987 credit line.

As of June 15, 1986, Hanson Ski Products had no plans to issue more stock, and, because of growth, no liquidations of plant or equipment were contemplated. The company had never paid a cash dividend, and it did not plan to initiate dividend payments in fiscal year 1987.

The final element of financial plans for fiscal year 1987 about which Denny Hanson was concerned was the set of loans from shareholders. A total of $841,000 in loans would become due in November 1986. An estrangement had developed between a key shareholder of the group and Mr. Hanson, and only if the loans were paid could Mr. Hanson be sure of maintaining personal control of operations. He hoped the bank line of credit was sufficient to enable the company to pay the loans in full and on time.

---

[2] In July 1986 the prime rate was 8%. The credit line for fiscal 1986 had also been $4.2 million but had carried an interest rate of 4% over prime.

## QUESTIONS

1.  Using the information in the balance sheet for March 31, 1986 (**Exhibit 2**), and the fiscal year 1987 budgets (**Exhibits 3** and **4**), prepare a projected balance sheet for Hanson Ski Products for March 31, 1987. (To do this, you will need to estimate the size of the commercial bank loan—"Notes–bank"—on that date.) Does your balance sheet tell you whether or not the plans on which the budgets are based are feasible?

2.  Project the size of the commercial bank loan at the end of each quarter of FY 1987. Can Hanson stay within the commercial banks' line of credit of $4.2 million? Will the company have sufficient collateral?

3.  Prepare quarterly balance sheets for Hanson Ski Products for June 30, 1986; September 30, 1986; and December 31, 1986. What do the four balance sheets you have prepared tell you about the financial structure and strength of Hanson Ski Products?

4.  Denny Hanson was particularly concerned that the stockholder loans be paid off in November 1986 when they were due, and he asked Dave Snyder, treasurer, to prepare a cash budget by months for the third quarter of FY 1987 (**Exhibit 5**). Do you see any problems in paying off the loans on time? What could Hanson do to be sure the loans can be paid?

**EXHIBIT 1**
**Hanson Ski Products, Income Statements ($000)**

|  | FY 1984 | FY 1985 | FY 1986 |
|---|---|---|---|
| Net sales | $5,753 | $7,671 | $9,776 |
| Cost of goods sold[a] | 3,040 | 4,140 | 5,177 |
| Gross margin | $2,713 | $3,531 | $4,599 |
| Selling, general, and administration | 1,585 | 2,109 | 2,519 |
| Product development | 152 | 189 | 260 |
| Operating earnings | $ 976 | $1,233 | $1,820 |
| Interest expense | 436 | 428 | 507 |
| Income before tax and extraordinary item | $ 540 | $ 805 | $1,313 |
| Tax provision | 314 | 468 | 400 |
| Earnings before extraordinary item | $ 226 | $ 337 | $ 913 |
| Extraordinary item tax benefit from utilization of operating loss carryforwards | 314 | 468 | 251 |
| Net earnings | $ 540 | $ 805 | $1,164 |
| Earnings per common share: |  |  |  |
|    Earnings before extraordinary item | 0.39 | 0.57 | 1.50 |
|    Extraordinary item | 0.53 | 0.79 | 0.41 |
|    Net earnings | 0.92 | 1.36 | 1.91 |
| Weighted average number of common shares outstanding | 585,889 | 590,566 | 607,761 |

[a] Depreciation and amortization for 1984, 1985, and 1986 was $341, $396, and $561, respectively.

**EXHIBIT 2**
**Hanson Ski Products, Consolidated Balance Sheets ($000)**

|  | 3/31/84 | 3/31/85 | 3/31/86 |
|---|---|---|---|
| **Current Assets** | | | |
| Cash | $  163 | $  81 | $  156 |
| Receivables, net | 692 | 1,378 | 1,556 |
| Inventories | 1,352 | 2,104 | 1,729 |
| Prepaid expenses | 99 | 124 | 262 |
| Total current assets | $ 2,306 | $ 3,687 | $ 3,703 |
| **Fixed Assets** | | | |
| Plant, property, and equipment | 1,430 | 1,958 | 3,393 |
| Less accumulated depreciation and amortization | 569 | 836 | 1,255 |
| Total net fixed assets | $  861 | $ 1,122 | $ 2,138 |
| Other assets | 171 | 191 | 207 |
| Total Assets | $ 3,338 | $ 5,000 | $ 6,048 |
| **Liabilities** | | | |
| Accounts payable | $  536 | $  967 | $ 1,586 |
| Notes payable—banks | 1,100 | 2,082 | 1,547[a] |
| Income taxes payable | — | — | 149 |
| Current installments—long-term debt | 109 | 35 | 1,010[b] |
| Total current liabilities | $ 1,745 | $ 3,084 | $ 4,292 |
| Long-term debt | | | |
| Term loan | 1,423 | 1,407 | — |
| Notes payable to banks | 506 | — | — |
| Total | $ 1,929 | $ 1,407 | $   — |
| **Stockholders' Equity:** | | | |
| Common stock | 1,126 | 1,166 | 1,249 |
| Additional paid-in capital | 105 | 105 | 105 |
| Retained earnings (deficit) | (1,567) | (762) | 402 |
| Total stockholders' equity | $  (336) | $  509 | $ 1,756 |
| Total Equities | $ 3,338 | $ 5,000 | $ 6,048 |

---

[a] Borrowings under the revolving line of credit were personally guaranteed by the major stockholders and were secured by all of the accounts receivable, inventories, machinery and equipment, furniture, trademarks, and patent rights.

[b] Current installments on long-term debt (3/31/86):

| | |
|---|---|
| Officers and stockholders | $  841,000 |
| Installment purchases | 169,000 |
| Capital leases | — |
| | $1,010,000 |

**EXHIBIT 3**
**FY 1987 Final Budget (June 15, 1986—$000)**

| | 1st Quarter | 2nd Quarter | 3rd Quarter | 4th Quarter | |
| | April–June 1986 | July–September 1986 | October–December 1986 | January–March 1987 | TOTAL |
|---|---|---|---|---|---|
| Net revenues | $ 391 | $ 5,893 | $ 4,769 | $ 832 | $ 11,885 |
| Cost of goods sold | 344 | 2,630 | 2,176 | 491 | 5,641 |
| Gross margin | $ 47 | $ 3,263 | $ 2,593 | $ 341 | $ 6,244 |
| Operating expenses | 779 | 1,204 | 1,256 | 926 | 4,165 |
| Operating income | ($ 732) | $ 2,059 | $ 1,337 | ($ 585) | $ 2,079 |
| Tax allowance | — | 432 | 261 | — | 693 |
| Net income (loss) | ($ 732) | $ 1,627 | $ 1,076 | ($ 585) | $ 1,386 |

**EXHIBIT 4**
**FY 1987 Cash Budget and Selected Expense and Balance Sheet Items (June 15, 1986—$000)**

| | 1st Quarter | 2nd Quarter | 3rd Quarter | 4th Quarter |
|---|---|---|---|---|
| | April–June 1986 | July–September 1986 | October–December 1986 | January–March 1987 |
| Cash receipts | $1,487 | $1,764 | $4,572 | $3,800 |
| **Cash outflows** | | | | |
| For materials, labor, and operating expenses (except for interest but including income taxes)[a] | 1,928 | 2,967 | 2,698 | 2,022 |
| Interest | 67 | 110 | 168 | 86 |
| Capital expenditures for fixed assets | 177 | 238 | 179 | 301 |
| Pay back stockholder loans | — | — | 841 | — |
| Depreciation | 143 | 166 | 179 | 195 |
| **Assets at end of quarter** | | | | |
| Planned cash balance | 100 | 100 | 100 | 100 |
| Receivables, net | 507 | 4,580 | 4,739 | 1,741 |
| Inventories | 2,808 | 1,690 | 1,166 | 1,869 |
| Prepaid expenses | 241 | 294 | 198 | 283 |
| Other assets | 201 | 247 | 283 | 302 |
| **Liabilities at end of quarter** | | | | |
| Accounts payable | 1,849 | 1,717 | 1,755 | 1,664 |
| Income taxes payable | — | — | — | — |
| Current installments long-term debt | 980 | 1,060 | 207 | 189 |

Notes payable—banks (to be determined)

[a] In general, corporations must pay current year income taxes on a quarterly basis. However, the precise payment requirements are based on a complex set of rules that are different for large or small corporations.

**EXHIBIT 5**
**Third Quarter FY 1987 Cash Budget by Months ($000)**

|  | October | November | December |
|---|---|---|---|
| Cash receipts | $1,000 | $1,054 | $2,518 |
| Cash outflow | | | |
| For materials, labor, and operating expenses | | | |
| (except for interest) | 830 | 1,065 | 803 |
| Interest | 54 | 56 | 58 |
| Capital expenditures | 69 | 62 | 48 |
| Pay back stockholder loans | — | 841 | — |
| Collateral for bank loans at end of month | | | |
| Receivables | 5,420 | 5,517 | 4,739 |
| Inventory | 1,331 | 1,363 | 1,166 |

# Thumbs-Up Video, Inc.

In October 1988, Linda Williams was determined to open a video cassette rental store that would have a wider selection of tapes and could operate more efficiently than the few small video rental stores located in and around her hometown of Mystic, Connecticut. Williams knew that more than one-half of the homes in Mystic were equipped with video cassette recorders, but based on informal discussions with her friends and neighbors, she learned that these recorders were infrequently used. She felt that with this installed base of recorders, a new, upscale, well-stocked video cassette rental store would surely succeed.

After preparing a business plan, Williams approached a long-time friend who she felt would invest in this new venture. After considerable thought, this friend was willing to invest $66,000 with Williams putting up the remaining $99,000 to purchase shares in the new corporation, which was to be called Thumbs-Up Video, Inc.

In November 1988, Williams left her job as a real estate broker and began to establish her new enterprise. She first consulted with a lawyer to have the business incorporated. Because this was a fairly simple organization, the legal fees incurred were only $2,700. Her next task was to find some land and a building in which to operate. Her connections in real estate allowed her to negotiate a favorable price of $48,000 for a building near the center of town. The building was old and needed renovation work. The purchase documents allocated $43,000 to the land and only $5,000 to the building, due to its age and

*Eric J. Petro prepared this case under the supervision of Professor William J. Bruns, Jr.*

Copyright © 1989 by the President and Fellows of Harvard College. Harvard Business School case 189-193.

run-down appearance. A mortgage of $33,600 was secured for the purchase, with the remaining $14,400 paid in cash. Williams felt that the current building was structurally sound, and with renovation work the life of the building could be extended to 25 years. She ordered the renovation work, costing $20,000, to begin immediately. The work lasted through December 1988. Williams paid $5,000 in advance for the renovations, with the remainder paid in full at completion of the work on December 31, 1988.

In anticipation of the store's opening on January 2, 1989, Williams began negotiations with the major film distribution companies for purchase of a rental tape inventory. By the end of December 1988, Williams had purchased 2,000 tapes (1,000 different titles) at an average cost of $50 per tape. Since Thumbs-Up Video was a new entity with no credit history, every vendor required a personal guarantee from Williams before they shipped the tapes "on account." All tapes were paid for by December 31, 1988. Although this represented a very large investment, Williams was certain that a wide selection of tapes would ensure the success of her new store.

In December 1988, equipment worth $6,700, including a computer priced at $3,000, was purchased for cash. Williams paid an additional $1,000 for a computer software package to be used by the company. The software, which was specifically designed for Thumbs-Up Video, would efficiently track those tapes out on rental and those on the shelves. All of the equipment had estimated useful lives of five years. Also at the end of December 1988, $500 of miscellaneous office supplies were ordered for delivery January 2, 1989, to be paid cash on delivery.

Williams then contracted with a local advertising agency to provide various forms of advertising for a period of one year. On January 2, 1989, $6,000 was paid for advertising through December 1989.

The new store opened as scheduled on January 2, 1989. During the subsequent months, Williams was pleased with the way the business was developing. Confident of the success of the store, Williams purchased another 250 tapes for $75 each on June 1, 1989. The entire amount remained unpaid at June 30. These tapes were considered new releases of feature films and multiple copies (10 copies each of 25 different titles) were purchased to satisfy expected initial demand.

For the six months ended June 30, 1989, sales amounted to $96,000. Due to the nature of the business, most of the sales were cash sales. A limited number of customers were allowed to charge their rentals, and at June 30, 1989, only $2,200 had not been collected from charge sales of the previous six months. Employees earned wages of $32,000 during this six-month period. Williams drew a salary of $30,000.

When Williams met with her accountant at the end of June 1989, she was pleased that the bank account showed a balance of $45,500, considering that significant expenditures were made just to get the business started. She wondered if she should declare a dividend as a signal to her investor friend that the business was doing well.  The accountant reminded Williams that certain accruals, including interest on the mortgage of $2,900, still needed to be made before dividends could be declared.

While discussing the results of the business through June 30, 1989, Williams and her accountant puzzled over how to account for a certain item. They knew that the tapes held for rental had a physical life of three years, and the cost of the tapes should be amortized over that period.  However, they were unsure how to account for the new release tapes.  They had the same physical life, but the initial demand (which warranted 10 copies of each title to be purchased versus the usual 2) was sure to wane significantly after only one year on the shelves.  Williams felt that most of the revenues from these new releases would occur in the first year, and thereafter the store would derive little or no benefit from 8 extra copies of the same title.

This matter of the amortization of new releases and several other concerns needed to be resolved before financial statements of Thumbs-Up Video, Inc., could be issued.

## QUESTIONS

1.  Construct a set of T accounts to record the transactions that occurred at Thumbs-Up Video, Inc., from November 1988 through June 1989.
2.  Prepare a statement of financial position as of June 30, 1989, for Thumbs-Up Video, Inc.
3.  Prepare an income statement for Thumbs-Up Video, Inc., from incorporation through June 30, 1989.  Disregard any income taxes that might be due.

# Monterrey Manufacturing Company

T he management of the Monterrey Manufacturing Company prepared annually a budget of expected financial operations for the ensuing calendar year. The completed budget provided information on many aspects of the coming year's operations. It included summaries of the projected estimated transactions for the budget year, the resulting assets and liabilities as of the end of that year, the sales, expense, and profit forecast for the year.

The final preparation of statements was accomplished only after careful integration of detailed computations submitted by each department to ensure that the operation of all departments were balanced with one another. For example, the finance department needed to base its schedules of loan operations and collections disbursements on figures that were dependent upon manufacturing, purchasing, and selling expectations. The scale of manufacture would, of course, be geared to the forecasts of the sales department, and purchasing would be geared to the proposed manufacturing schedule. In short, it was necessary to integrate the estimates of each department and to revise them in terms of the overall effect on operations to arrive at a well-formulated and profitable plan of operations for the coming year. The budget statements ultimately derived from the adjusted estimated transactions would then serve the company as a reliable guide and measure of the coming year's operations.

At the time the 1996 budget was being prepared in November of 1995, estimated 1995 financial statements were compiled for use as a comparison with the budgeted figures. These 1995 statements were based on nine months' actual and three months' estimated transactions. See **Exhibits 1** and **2**.

Copyright © 1996 by the President and Fellows of Harvard College. Harvard Business School case 197-023.

Below is the summary of expected operations for the budget year 1996 as it was finally accepted.

## SUMMARY OF EXPECTED OPERATIONS FOR BUDGET YEAR 1996

1.  **Sales** (on credit) $2,442,000; sales returns and allowances, $18,000; sales discounts taken by customers, $48,000. (The sales figure is net of expected bad debts.)
2.  **Purchases of goods and services:**
    a.  New Assets:
        Purchased for cash: manufacturing plant and equipment, $120,000; prepaid manufacturing taxes and insurance, $36,000.
        Purchased on accounts payable: raw materials, $822,000; supplies, $78,000.
    b.  Services used to convert raw materials into goods in process which will increase the "value" of goods in process inventory:[1] Purchased for cash: direct manufacturing labor, $420,000; indirect manufacturing labor, $174,000; social security taxes on labor, $61,200; power, heat, and light, $92,400. (Accrued payroll was ignored in these estimates.)
    c.  Sales and administrative services: Purchased for cash, $402,000.
3.  **Conversion of assets into goods in process:** This appears as an increase in the "value" of goods in process and a decrease in the appropriate asset accounts.
    Depreciation of plant and equipment, $80,400; expiration of prepaid taxes and insurance, $30,000; supplies used in manufacturing, $90,000; raw materials put into process, $786,000.
4.  **Transfer of work in process into finished goods:** This appears as an increase in finished goods and a decrease in goods in process.
    Total cost accumulated on goods that are expected to be completed and transferred to finished goods inventory, $1,650,000.
5.  **Cost of finished goods sold to customers:** $1,638,000.

---

[1] In a merchandising company, the cost of goods sold is roughly equal to the purchase price of these goods. In a manufacturing company, however, the cost of goods sold is the sum of the raw material in these goods plus the "value added by manufacture." Thus, inventory is assumed to increase in value by the amounts spent to convert raw materials into salable products. These amounts include the items listed in 2(b) plus the items listed in (3) below. Three inventory items are used to collect information about this process: (1) raw materials; (2) goods in process, which shows the value built up on goods that are in the factory; and (3) finished goods, showing the value of goods that have been completed and are awaiting sale. Values are transferred from one to another in the manner suggested by items 3 and 4.

6. **Financial transactions:**
   a.   Borrowed, $462,000 on notes payable to bank.
   b.   Retired bank loans, $528,000.
   c.   Cash payment to bank of $7,200 for interest on loans.
7. **Cash receipts** from customers on accounts receivable, $2,425,800.
8. **Cash payments of liabilities:**
   a.   Payment of accounts payable, $958,800.
   b.   Payment of accrued 1995 Federal Income Tax, $21,000.
9. **Estimated Federal Income Tax** on 1996 income, accrued but unpaid as of December 31, 1996, $94,200.
10. **Dividends** declared for year and paid in cash, $126,000.

This summary presents the complete cycle of the Monterrey Manufacturing Company's budgeted yearly operations from the purchases of goods and services through their various stages of conversion to completion of the finished product to the sale of this product. All costs and cash receipts and disbursements involved in this cycle are presented, including the necessary provision for federal income tax and the payment of dividends.

In preparing the budget the management was interested in an analysis of the effect of each of these transactions upon the balance sheet items as of January 1, 1996. T accounts to facilitate this analysis are shown in **Exhibit 3**. The T accounts are categorized into asset accounts, liability accounts, and owners' equity accounts. Temporary accounts for income and expenses are also included.

## QUESTIONS

1.   Enter the year's projections on the T accounts. Entries should be coded as illustrated by the sample entry for sales of $2,442,000 (coded 1).
2.   Prepare pro forma 1996 financial statements similar to **Exhibits 1** and **2**.
3.   Prepare a pro forma statement of cash flows for the Monterrey Manufacturing Company for 1996.

**EXHIBIT 1**
**Monterrey Manufacturing Company—Estimated Statement of Financial Position, December 31, 1995**

**Assets**
*Current Assets*

| | | | |
|---|---|---|---|
| Cash | | $ 153,000 | |
| Accounts receivable (net of allowance for doubtful accounts) | | 363,000 | |
| Inventories: | | | |
| Raw materials | $ 330,000 | | |
| Work in process | 145,200 | | |
| Finished goods | 85,800 | | |
| Supplies | 99,000 | 660,000 | |
| Prepaid taxes and insurance | | 34,200 | |
| Total current assets | | | $ 1,210,200 |

*Fixed Assets*

| | | | |
|---|---|---|---|
| Manufacturing plant and equipment (original cost) | $ 1,920,000 | | |
| Less accumulated depreciation | 600,000 | | 1,320,000 |
| | | | $ 2,530,200 |

**Liabilities and Capital**
*Current Liabilities*

| | | | |
|---|---|---|---|
| Notes payable | | $ 198,000 | |
| Accounts payable | | 120,000 | |
| Unpaid estimated federal income taxes | | 21,000 | |
| Total current liabilities | | | $ 339,000 |

*Owners' Equity*

| | | | |
|---|---|---|---|
| Capital stock | | $ 1,980,000 | |
| Retained earnings | | 211,200 | 2,191,200 |
| | | | $ 2,530,200 |

**EXHIBIT 2**

**Monterrey Manufacturing Company—Estimated Statement of Income for Year Ended December 31, 1995**

| | | | |
|---|---:|---:|---:|
| Sales | | | $2,184,000 |
| Less: Sales returns and allowances | $ 16,800 | | |
| Sales discounts | 42,600 | | 59,400 |
| | | | $2,124,600 |
| Net Sales | | | |
| Cost of Goods Sold: | | | |
| Finished goods inventory, 1/1/95 | | $ 504,000 | |
| Work in process inventory, 1/1/95 | | $ 156,000 | |
| Raw materials inventory, 1/1/95 | $270,000 | | |
| Raw materials purchased | 600,000 | | |
| | $870,000 | | |
| Raw materials inventory, 12/31/95 | 330,000 | | |
| Raw materials used | | 540,000 | |
| Direct manufacturing labor | | 294,000 | |
| Factory overhead: | | | |
| Indirect manufacturing labor | $114,000 | | |
| Power, heat, and light | 54,000 | | |
| Depreciation of plant and equipment | 76,800 | | |
| Social security taxes | 45,000 | | |
| Factory, insurance and taxes | 30,000 | | |
| Supplies | 47,400 | 367,200 | |
| | | $1,357,200 | |
| Less: Work in process, inventory, 12/31/95 | | 145,200 | |
| Cost of goods manufactured (i.e., completed) | | 1,212,000 | |
| | | $1,716,000 | |
| Less: Finished goods inventory, 12/31/95 | | 85,800 | |
| Cost of goods sold | | | 1,630,200 |
| Gross margin | | | $ 494,400 |
| Sales and administrative expenses | | $ 360,000 | |
| Interest expense | | 7,200 | 367,200 |
| New profit before federal income tax | | | $ 127,200 |
| Estimated income tax | | | 21,000 |
| Net profit after federal income tax | | | $ 106,200 |

**EXHIBIT 3**
**Asset T Accounts**

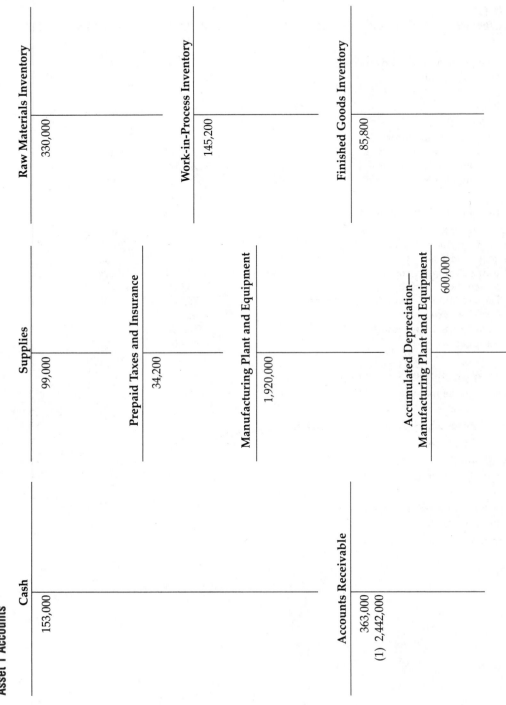

Cash

153,000

Accounts Receivable

363,000
(1) 2,442,000

Supplies

99,000

Prepaid Taxes and Insurance

34,200

Manufacturing Plant and Equipment

1,920,000

Accumulated Depreciation—
Manufacturing Plant and Equipment

600,000

Raw Materials Inventory

330,000

Work-in-Process Inventory

145,200

Finished Goods Inventory

85,800

**EXHIBIT 3 (continued)**
**T Accounts**

*Liability T Accounts*

**Notes Payable**

| | 198,000 |
|---|---|

**Accounts Payable**

| | 120,000 |
|---|---|

**Accrued Federal Income Taxes**

| | 21,000 |
|---|---|

*Owner's Equity T Accounts*

**Capital Stock**

| | 1,980,000 |
|---|---|

**Retained Earnings**

| | 211,200 |
|---|---|

**EXHIBIT 3 (continued)**
**Temporary T Accounts**

Sales

(1) 2,442,000

Sales Returns and Allowances

Sales Discount

Selling and Administrative Expenses

Interest Expense

Federal Income Taxes

Cost of Goods Sold

Profit and Loss Summary

# Introduction to Financial Ratios and Financial Statement Analysis

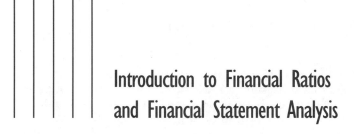

There is almost always a reason why someone picks up an organization's financial statements and begins to analyze them. Lenders or creditors may be interested in determining whether they will be repaid money they have lent or may lend to the organization. Investors may be interested in comparing a potential investment in one organization with that of another. Employees may want to compare the current performance or financial status of their employer with earlier periods. Regulatory agencies often need to assess organizational or industry financial health and performance. Financial analysis is always based on a set of questions, and the specific questions requiring answers depend on who the financial statement user is and the reasons for his or her analysis.

Financial analyses based on accounting information consistently involve comparisons. Amounts or ratios may be compared with industry norms, the same measurement in a prior period, the same measurement in a competitor's organization, or with planned and budgeted amounts previously established. Figuring out which comparisons will best answer the questions motivating the analysis is one of the necessary steps in making the best use of accounting information.

Financial ratios can help describe the financial condition of an organization, the efficiency of its activities, its comparable profitability, and the perception of investors as expressed by their behavior in financial markets. Ratios often permit an analyst or decision maker to piece together a story about where an organization has come from, its current condition, and its possible future. In most cases, the story is incomplete, and important questions may remain unanswered.

Copyright © 1992 by the President and Fellows of Harvard College. Harvard Business School case 193-029.

Even though the analyst or decision maker is better informed as a result of doing the ratio analysis, the indiscriminate use of financial ratios can be extremely dangerous. Decision rules that rely on a specific or minimum value of a ratio can easily lead to missed opportunities or losses. Even the best ratio is not always indicative of the health, status, or performance of an organization. Ratios between apparently similar measurements in financial statements may be affected by differences in accounting classifications or by deliberate manipulation.

The ease with which ratios can be manipulated and the danger in using them as criteria lead many analysts to concentrate on trends in ratio measurements rather than on the absolute value or proportion expressed by the ratio itself. When a trend in the value of a ratio between financial attributes is observed, questions can be raised about why the trend is occurring. The answers to such questions provide new information, not necessarily contained in financial reports, but perhaps highly relevant and useful to the decision maker and the problem at hand.

Similarly, comparisons of firms only on the basis of ratios can lead to erroneous conclusions. The diversity inherent in available accounting practices and principles can lead to differences in ratios between organizations being compared. Comparisons between companies can be made, but they must be made with care and with full attention to the underlying differences in basic accounting methods used in the reports as well as in the companies themselves. With these cautions in mind, we can proceed to examine briefly some commonly used financial ratios.

# PROFITABILITY RATIOS

Profitability ratios seek to associate the amount of income earned with either the amount of resources used or the amount of activity that has taken place. These correspond to efficiency measures often used in economic and engineering theory. Ideally, the firm should produce as much income as possible with a given amount of resources or a satisfactory amount of income using as few resources as possible.

## Return on Investment (ROI)

Dividing net income by the amount of investment expresses the idea of economic efficiency. Return on assets (ROA), return on investment capital (ROIC), and return on owners' equity (ROE) are all used in financial analysis as measures of the effectiveness with which assets have been employed.

*Return on assets (ROA)* relates net income to the investment in all of the financial resources at the command of management. It is most useful as a measure of the effectiveness of resource utilization without regard to how those resources have been obtained and financed. The formula for this ratio is:

**Return on Assets (ROA) =** $\dfrac{\overset{\frown{\text{Net}}}{\text{Income}}}{\text{Assets} - \text{All}}$

The consolidated statement of earnings, consolidated balanced sheets, and consolidated statements of cash flows for the Gillette Company and Subsidiary Companies (hereafter the Gillette Company) are shown in **Exhibit 1**. These financial statements will be used as a basis for illustrating the calculation of each financial ratio in this introduction. For 1995, return on assets for the Gillette Company was:

**Return on Assets (ROA) =** $\dfrac{\$823.5}{\$6,340.3} = 13.0\%$

*Return on invested capital (ROIC)* relates all net income to all resources committed to the firm for ~~long periods of time~~. It is calculated by dividing net income by the total amount of noncurrent liabilities and stockholders' equity. The formula for this ratio is:

**Return on Invested Capital (ROIC) =** $\dfrac{\overset{\frown{\text{Net}}}{\text{Net Income}}}{\substack{\text{Total Liabilities and} \\ \text{Stockholders' Equity} \\ - \text{Current Liabilities}}}$

Return on invested capital in 1995 for the Gillette Company was:

**Return on Invested Capital (ROIC) =** $\dfrac{\$823.5}{\$6,340.3 - \$2,124.0} = 19.5\%$

① Two variations in these two ratios are often observed. Because their purpose is to compare how efficiently a pool of capital has been used—a pool that includes long-term debt as well as stockholders' equity—the aftertax interest expense is often ~~added back to income in the numerator~~. This can be easily calculated by the formula:

**Interest expense × (1 – tax rate) = Aftertax interest expense**

The amount of the adjustment is the *net* interest cost. Interest expense is tax deductible, and the formula calculates the aftertax interest expense by multiplying the total interest expense by the complement of the tax rate. The rationale for this adjustment is that it is a better measure of the income flow generated by management, considering all of the sources of long-term financing it has chosen to use. ~~Without the adjustment, the income understates the earnings generated by the total pool of capital.~~

① = N.I. w/o Interest Expense

② A second variation is appropriate when the amount of assets or invested capital is changing. Since income is earned over a period of time, the appropriate denominator in the two ratios above is probably *average* assets or *average*

Ex 1
Income = Rev − I
Taxes = t(R−I)
NI = (R−I) − t(R−I)

$NI_2 = NI + I*(1-t) = (R-I) - t(R-I) + I*(1-t)$
$= R-I-t*R+t*I+I-t*I$
$= R(1-t) \leftarrow$ w/o Int. Exp.

invested capital. This is easily approximated by adding the beginning and ending measurements together and dividing by two. The analyst has to decide if these refinements to the ratios will improve his or her ability to answer the questions at hand.

*Return on equity (ROE)* relates net income to the amount invested by stockholders. It is a measure of the efficiency with which the stockholders' investment through their original capital contributions and earnings retained in the business have been used. The formula for this ratio is:

$$\text{Return on Equity (ROE)} = \frac{\text{Net Income}}{\text{Stockholders' Equity}}$$

Return on equity in 1995 for the Gillette Company was:

$$\text{Return on Equity (ROE)} = \frac{\$823.5}{\$2,513.3} = 32.8\%$$

Note that for this ratio stockholders' equity is the correct denominator because the ratio is an attempt to understand what the investment by the owners alone has earned.

## Earnings per Share (EPS)

Because corporations have many owners, not all of whom own an equal number of shares, it is quite common to express earnings of a company on a per-share basis for those who wish to calculate their proportional share of earnings. The calculation of earnings per share can be complicated if there is more than one class of ownership, each with differing claims against the income of the firm. Preferred stock or other securities that are convertible into common shares are often treated as common stock equivalents in making this calculation. In published financial reports, this ratio is required to be presented, often in several variations such as "basic" or "diluted" (a very conservative form) EPS. Although the actual formulas for EPS are usually very complex, a simplified formula showing the basic common elements is:

$$\text{Earnings per Share (EPS)} = \frac{\text{Net Income} - \text{Preferred Stock Dividends}}{\substack{\text{Number of Shares of} \\ \text{Common Stock} + \text{Equivalents}}}$$

Net earnings per share for the Gillette Company for 1995 were $1.85.

## Profit Margin

This ratio, which gives a rate of return on sales, relates two statement of income measurements to each other. For this reason, it is not a measure of efficiency, but instead, gives some indication of the sensitivity of income to price changes or changes in cost structure.  The formula for this ratio is:

**Profit Margin** = $\dfrac{\text{Net Income}}{\text{Net Sales}}$

*Must also look at amount of investment required*

It is important to note that neither a high nor low profit margin necessarily means good performance.  A company with a high profit margin but high investment may not be returning a great amount to investors.  A firm with a very low profit margin may have required only a very small investment so that it proves highly profitable to those who invest in it.

The profit margin in 1995 for Gillette was:

**Profit Margin** = $\dfrac{\$823.5}{\$6,794.7}$ = 12.1%

# ACTIVITY RATIOS

Activity ratios provide an indication of how well assets are utilized by the organization.  Efficiency in using assets minimizes the need for investment by lenders or owners.  Activity ratios provide measurements of how well assets or capital are being utilized.

## Asset Turnover

This ratio measures the company's effectiveness in utilizing all of its assets. The formula for this ratio is:

**Asset Turnover** = $\dfrac{\text{Net Sales}}{\text{Total Assets}}$

For the Gillette Company in 1995, the asset turnover was:

**Asset Turnover** = $\dfrac{\$6,794.7}{\$6,340.3}$ = 1.1x

Since different industries require very different asset structures, comparing asset turnover ratios from one industry to those in another is potentially meaningless and must be done with caution.  Likewise, when an organization participates in many industries, the exact meaning of an asset turnover ratio can be obscured, and the most valid comparisons of an asset turnover ratio at one date may be to that of the same firm at another recent date.

Asset turnover ratios can be calculated for any group of assets.  Accounts receivable, inventory, and total working capital are all asset classifications for which comparison of turnover is potentially interesting and important.

## Days' Receivables

Evidence about the amount of time that lapses between sales and receipt of payment from customers can be important information about the financial structure of a company. An approximation of the number of days that elapse can be obtained by dividing the amount of accounts receivable (and notes receivable if these are related to customer accounts) by the average day's sales. In cases where cash sales are a significant portion of the total, the amount of charge sales must be estimated for use in judging the length of collection.

The collection period for accounts receivable can be calculated by first dividing net sales by 365 days to determine average sales per day.

$$\text{Average Day's Sales} = \frac{\text{Net Sales}}{365}$$

Then calculate the collection period using the following formula:

$$\text{Days' Receivables} = \frac{\text{Accounts Receivable}}{\text{Average Day's Sales}}$$

Days' receivables in 1995 for the Gillette Company was:

$$\text{Average Day's Sales} = \frac{\$6,794.7}{365} = \$18.6 \text{ million}$$

$$\text{Days' Receivables} = \frac{\$1,659.5}{\$18.6} = 89 \text{ days}$$

## Inventory Turnover

Determining the number of times that inventory is sold during the year provides some measure of its liquidity and the ability of the company to convert inventories to cash quickly if that were to become necessary. When turnover is slow, it may indicate that inventories are not a liquid asset and suggest they should be excluded from that category for analytical purposes. On the other hand, when turnover is quite rapid, that is when inventory is sold several times each year, the liquid character of inventory can provide funds if needed in the short term and may protect the firm against inventory obsolescence.

Inventory turnover is calculated by dividing the cost of goods sold by the inventory cost. The average inventory for the year should be calculated or approximated if there has been a significant change in inventory cost from the beginning to the end of the period. Usually it is sufficient simply to add the beginning and ending inventory amounts and to use one-half of that total as the average inventory for the year. Once the inventory turnover is determined, it can be converted to days' inventory by dividing inventory turnover into 365 days.

$$\text{Inventory Turnover} = \frac{\text{Cost of Goods Sold}}{\text{Average Inventory}}$$

$$\text{Inventory Turnover Period in Days} = \frac{365}{\text{Inventory Turnover}}$$

In some financial reports issued for stockholders, the cost of goods sold is not revealed. In these cases, it is necessary to use sales as the numerator of the ratio, which gives the appearance of providing faster inventory turnover. If the relationship between price and cost does not change, the trend in turnover period would be approximately the same between two periods. Nevertheless, it is wise to use the ratio of sales to inventory with somewhat greater care.

Inventory turnover in 1995 for the Gillette Company was:

$$\text{Inventory Turnover} = \frac{\$2,540.2}{(\$1,035.1 + \$941.2) \div 2} = 2.6x$$

$$\text{Days' Inventory} = \frac{365}{2.6x} = 140 \text{ days}$$

### Working Capital Turnover

Working capital turnover is a measure of the speed with which funds are provided by current assets to satisfy current liabilities. The formula for this ratio is:

$$\text{Working Capital Turnover} = \frac{\text{Net Sales}}{\text{Average Current Assets} - \text{Average Current Liabilities}}$$

Working capital turnover in 1995 for the Gillette Company was:

$$\text{Working Capital Turnover} = \frac{\$6,794.7}{(\$2,902.5 - \$1,930.1)} = 7.0x$$

## SOLVENCY AND LEVERAGE RATIOS

When an organization is unable to meet its financial obligations, it is said to be insolvent. Because insolvency leads to organizational distress, or even to bankruptcy or organization extinction, ratios to test solvency are often used by investors and creditors. By measuring a company's ability to meet its financial obligations as they become current, solvency ratios give an indication of the liquidity of the company.

## Current Ratio

This ratio is commonly used for testing liquidity or solvency.  The formula for this ratio is:

$$\text{Current Ratio} = \frac{\text{Current Assets}}{\text{Current Liabilities}}$$

The size of the current ratio that a healthy company needs to maintain is dependent upon the relationship between inflows of cash and the demands for cash payments.  A company that has a continuous inflow of cash or other liquid assets, such as a public utility or taxi company, may be able to meet currently maturing obligations easily despite the fact that its current ratio may be small.  On the other hand, the manufacturing firm with a long product development and manufacturing cycle may need to maintain a larger current ratio.

The current ratio at the end of 1995 for the Gillette Company was:

$$\text{Current Ratio} = \frac{\$3,104.5}{\$2,124.0} = 1.46$$

## Acid Test Ratio

In cases where there is a desire or a need to confirm the absolute liquidity of an organization, the current ratio is modified by eliminating from current assets all that cannot be liquidated on very short notice.  Typically, then, this ratio consists of the ratio of so-called "quick" assets (cash, marketable security, and some forms of accounts receivable) to current liabilities.

$$\text{Acid Test Ratio} = \frac{\text{Quick Assets}}{\text{Current Liabilities}}$$

For 1995, add the cash, short-term investments, and receivables to calculate the acid test ratio for the Gillette Company.

$$\text{Acid Test Ratio} = \frac{\$1,709.0}{\$2,124.0} = .80$$

## Debt Ratio

The degree to which the activities of a company are supported by liabilities and long-term debt as opposed to owner contributions is referred to as *leverage.*  A firm that has a high proportion of debt to stockholder contributions would be referred to as being highly leveraged.  The advantage to the owners of the firm of having high debt is that profits earned after payment of interest accrue to a smaller group of owners. On the other hand, when a firm is highly leveraged, risk rises when profits and cash flows fall. A company can be forced to the point of insolvency by the cost of interest on the debt.

The debt ratio is widely used in financial analysis because it reveals the effect of financial leverage. The debt ratio is calculated in different ways, and we will illustrate two here. First,

$$\text{Debt Ratio} = \frac{\text{Total Debt}}{\text{Total Assets}}$$

Alternatively, the debt to equity ratio is sometimes calculated by dividing total liabilities by the amount of stockholders' equity. The formula for this ratio would be:

$$\text{Debt-to-Equity Ratio} = \frac{\text{Total Liabilities}}{\text{Owners' Equity}}$$

Care must be taken in interpreting either of these ratios because there is no absolute level that can be referred to as being better than another. In general, as the ratio increases in size, returns to owners are higher but so also is risk higher. The trend in this ratio may reveal important management decisions about the financing of activities comparing two organizations. Differences in the size of the ratio may reveal management attitude toward risks and alternative strategies toward financing the activities of the respective entities.

Using the second of the two formulas above, the 1995 debt-to-equity ratio for the Gillette Company was:

$$\text{Debt-to-Equity Ratio} = \frac{\$6,340.3 - \$2,513.3}{\$2,513.3} = 1.52$$

## Times Interest Earned

Almost every firm has continuing commitments that must be met by future flows if the company is to remain solvent. Interest payments are an example of such commitments. The common ratio that measures the ability of a company to meet its interest payments is times interest earned. The formula for this ratio is:

$$\text{Times Interest Earned} = \frac{\text{Pretax Operating Income + Interest Expense}}{\text{Interest Exp.}}$$

The number of times interest payments are covered by current earnings offers some measure of the degree to which income could fall without causing insolvency in this account. In many cases, this is not so much a test of solvency as a test of staying power under adversity. Times interest earned for 1995 for the Gillette Company was:

$$\text{Times Interest Earned} = \frac{\$1,296.9 + \$59.0}{\$59.0} = 23x$$

## MARKET-RELATED AND DIVIDEND RATIOS

Two ratios are affected by the market price for shares of ownership in corporations. These are the price earnings ratio and the dividend yield ratio. In addition, analysts sometimes calculate a dividend payout ratio as a measure of the degree to which the firm is likely to be able to continue its dividend payments provided there is fluctuation in future income.

### Price Earnings Ratio (PE)

The relationship of the market price of shares of stock to the earnings of the company is of great interest to investors. Companies that are growing rapidly and are thought to have good potential for future growth often find that their shares are traded at a multiple of earnings per share much higher than companies thought to have less promise. The price earnings ratio is often included in stock market tables in investment information prepared by analysts. The formula for this ratio is:

$$\text{Price Earnings Ratio (PE)} = \frac{\text{Market Price per Share of Stock}}{\text{Earnings per Share}}$$

Since the market price of shares frequently fluctuates, this ratio is sometimes calculated using an average market price for a period of time.

During 1995, the market price per share of stock in the Gillette Company was as low as $35.38 and as high as $55.38. Calculating a price earnings ratio using each of these figures shows that during the year, Gillette's price earnings ratio fluctuated between 19.1 and 29.9.

$$\text{1995 Low Price Earnings Ratio} = \frac{\$35.38}{\$1.85} = 19.1$$

$$\text{1995 High Price Earnings Ratio} = \frac{\$55.38}{\$1.85} = 29.9$$

## Dividend Yield Ratio

The dividend yield to common shareholders is dependent upon the market price originally paid for the share and is calculated by dividing dividends received by the market price originally paid for the shares. For a prospective investor, dividend yield is the dividend per share divided by the current market price of the stock.

$$\text{Dividend Yield} = \frac{\text{Dividends per Share}}{\text{Market Price per Share}}$$

If the market price of shares in the Gillette Company was $55, the dividend yield in 1995 when dividends per share of $.60 were paid to shareholders would have been:

$$\text{Dividend Yield} = \frac{\$.60}{\$55} = 1.1\%$$

## Dividend Payout

The dividend payout ratio shows the proportion of net income that was paid in dividends. Both the dividend yield and dividend payout ratio are useful for forecasting future dividend streams to investors in the company's common stock. The formula for this ratio is:

$$\text{Dividend Payout} = \frac{\text{Dividends}}{\text{Net Income (available to common stockholders)}}$$

For the Gillette Company in 1995, dividends paid to common stockholders totaled $266.3 million; therefore the dividend payout was:

$$\text{Dividend Payout} = \frac{\$266.3}{\$818.8} = 33\%$$

# USING RATIOS TO THINK ABOUT MANAGEMENT STRATEGIES

Sometimes it is useful when conducting a financial analysis to think about the interrelationships between ratios and to use them to think about the strategies that management has adopted or might adopt. One well-known algebraic construction using ratios is known as the *du Pont model* because financial analysts at the E. I. du Pont de Nemours & Co. are credited with its development and use during the 1920s. The du Pont model multiplies profit margin times asset turnover times a ratio of assets over equity to calculate return on stockholders' equity. If we look at this algebraic construction, we can see why it is so useful.

Profit   x  Asset
Margin      Turnover

$$\frac{\text{Income}}{\text{Sales}} \times \frac{\text{Sales}}{\text{Assets}} \times \frac{\text{Assets}}{\text{Owners' Equity}} = \text{Return on Owners' Equity}$$

The first ratio, profit margin, can be used to focus management's attention on the relationship between the price and cost of products or services sold. The second ratio, asset turnover, emphasizes the efficient use of resources in producing products and services. The third ratio, assets over equity, focuses on the ability of management to leverage the firm properly to provide maximum return to stockholders. Each of these major classes of decisions that managers must make can be examined in light of its ability to provide the overall objective of increasing return to stockholders.

## COMMON SIZE FINANCIAL STATEMENTS

In order to examine the changing financial structure of a firm through time and the changing nature of operations, many analysts like to create common size financial statements in which the balance sheet and the statement of income are prepared in the percentage format. In a common size balance sheet, each asset, liability, and owners' equity amount is expressed as a percentage of total assets. In a common size statement of income, sales is set at 100%, and each item is expressed as a percentage of sales.

Common size financial statements facilitate the comparison of firms of a different size as well. Although firms may be in the same industry, they may be of significantly different sizes, and common size statements allow an analyst to focus on the efficiency with which managements of different firms have created a capital structure and have achieved efficient operations.

Common size balance sheets and statements of income for the Gillette Company are presented in **Exhibit 2**.

**EXHIBIT 1**
**The Gillette Company and Subsidiary Companies—Consolidated Statement of Income and Earnings Reinvested in the Business for Years Ended December 31, 1995, 1994, and 1993 ($ million, except per share amounts)**

|  | 1995 | 1994 | 1993 |
|---|---|---|---|
| **Net sales** | $6,794.7 | $6,070.2 | $5,410.8 |
| Cost of sales | 2,540.2 | 2,221.9 | 2,044.3 |
| **Gross profit** | 4,254.5 | 3,848.3 | 3,366.5 |
| Selling, general, and administrative expenses | 2,883.2 | 2,621.6 | 2,279.2 |
| Realignment expense | — | — | 262.6 |
| **Profit from operations** | 1,371.3 | 1,226.7 | 824.7 |
| Nonoperating charges (income) |  |  |  |
| Interest income | (9.9) | (19.0) | (27.3) |
| Interest expense | 59.0 | 61.1 | 59.8 |
| Other charges—net | 25.3 | 80.5 | 109.5 |
|  | 74.4 | 122.6 | 142.0 |
| **Income before income taxes and cumulative effect of accounting changes** | 1,296.9 | 1,104.1 | 682.7 |
| Income taxes | 473.4 | 405.8 | 255.8 |
| **Income before cumulative effect of accounting changes** | 823.5 | 698.3 | 426.9 |
| Cumulative effect of accounting changes | — | — | (138.6) |
| **Net income** | 823.5 | 698.3 | 288.3 |
| Preferred stock dividends, net of tax benefit | 4.7 | 4.7 | 4.7 |
| **Net income available to common stockholders** | 818.8 | 693.6 | 283.6 |
| Earnings reinvested in the business at beginning of year | 2,830.2 | 2,357.9 | 2,259.6 |
|  | 3,649.0 | 3,051.5 | 2,543.2 |
| Common stock dividends declared | 266.3 | 221.3 | 185.3 |
| Earnings reinvested in the business at end of year | $3,382.7 | $2,830.2 | $2,357.9 |
| **Income per common share before cumulative effect of accounting changes** | $1.85 | $1.57 | $ .96 |
| Cumulative effect of accounting changes | — | — | (.32) |
| **Net income per common share** | $1.85 | $1.57 | $ .64 |
| Dividends declared per common share | $ .60 | $ .50 | $ .42 |
| Weighted average number of common shares outstanding (millions) | 443.5 | 442.3 | 440.9 |

**EXHIBIT 1 (continued)**
**The Gillette Company and Subsidiary Companies—**
**Consolidated Balance Sheets, December 31, 1995 and 1994 ($ millions)**

|  | 1995 | 1994 |
|---|---|---|
| **Assets** | | |
| **Current assets** | | |
| Cash and cash equivalents | $ 47.9 | $ 43.8 |
| Short-term investments, at cost, which approximate market value | 1.6 | 2.3 |
| Receivables, less allowances: 1995—$59.2; 1994—$52.1 | 1,659.5 | 1,379.5 |
| Inventories | 1,035.1 | 941.2 |
| Deferred income taxes | 220.2 | 220.6 |
| Prepaid expenses | 140.2 | 113.0 |
| **Total current assets** | 3,104.5 | 2,700.4 |
| **Property, plant and equipment**, at cost less accumulated depreciation | 1,636.9 | 1,411.0 |
| **Intangible assets**, less accumulated amortization | 1,221.4 | 887.4 |
| **Other assets** | 377.5 | 314.6 |
|  | $6,340.3 | $5,313.4 |
| **Liabilities and stockholders' equity** | | |
| **Current liabilities** | | |
| Loans payable | $ 576.2 | $ 344.4 |
| Current portion of long-term debt | 26.5 | 28.1 |
| Accounts payable and accrued liabilities | 1,273.3 | 1,178.2 |
| Income taxes | 248.0 | 185.5 |
| **Total current liabilities** | 2,124.0 | 1,736.2 |
| **Long-term debt** | 691.1 | 715.1 |
| **Deferred income taxes** | 72.7 | 53.1 |
| **Other long-term liabilities** | 919.2 | 774.3 |
| **Minority interest** | 20.0 | 17.4 |
| **Stockholders' equity** | | |
| 8.0% Cumulative Series C ESOP Convertible Preferred, without par value, issued: | | |
|     1995—160,701 shares; 1994—162,928 shares | 96.9 | 98.2 |
| Unearned ESOP compensation | (34.3) | (44.2) |
| Common stock, par value $1 per share | | |
| Authorized 1,160,000,000 shares; Issued: 1995—559,718,438 shares; | | |
|     1994—558,242,404 shares | 559.7 | 558.2 |
| Additional paid-in capital | 31.1 | (1.4) |
| Earnings reinvested in the business | 3,382.7 | 2,830.2 |
| Cumulative foreign currency translation adjustments | (477.0) | (377.1) |
| Treasury stock, at cost: 1995—115,254,353 shares; 1994—115,343,404 shares | (1,045.8) | (1,046.6) |
| **Total stockholders' equity** | 2,513.3 | 2,017.3 |
|  | $6,340.3 | $5,313.4 |

**EXHIBIT 1 (continued)**
**The Gillette Company and Subsidiary Companies—Consolidated Statements**
**of Cash Flows for Years Ended December 31, 1995, 1994, and 1993 ($ millions)**

|  | 1995 | 1994 | 1993 |
|---|---|---|---|
| **Operating activities** | | | |
| Net income | $823.5 | $698.3 | $288.3 |
| Adjustments to reconcile net income to net cash provided by operating activities: | | | |
| Cumulative effect of accounting changes | — | — | 138.6 |
| Provision for realignment expense | — | — | 164.1 |
| Depreciation and amortization | 248.4 | 215.4 | 218.5 |
| Other | (3.1) | 15.1 | 51.8 |
| Changes in assets and liabilities, net of effects from acquisition of businesses: | | | |
| Accounts receivable | (286.1) | (147.4) | (101.8) |
| Inventories | (94.1) | (66.7) | (56.0) |
| Accounts payable and accrued liabilities | 67.0 | 93.7 | 10.8 |
| Other working capital items | 60.7 | 37.4 | (30.7) |
| Other noncurrent assets and liabilities | 4.2 | (40.3) | 48.1 |
| Net cash provided by operating activities | 820.5 | 805.5 | 731.7 |
| **Investing activities** | | | |
| Additions to property, plant and equipment | (471.1) | (399.8) | (352.0) |
| Disposals of property, plant and equipment | 30.0 | 24.9 | 10.2 |
| Acquisition of businesses, less cash acquired | (276.7) | (25.6) | (452.9) |
| Other | 12.1 | 16.9 | (35.6) |
| Net cash used in investing activities | (705.7) | (383.6) | (830.3) |
| **Financing activities** | | | |
| Proceeds from exercise of stock option and purchase plans | 31.6 | 18.4 | 24.5 |
| Proceeds from long-term debt | — | — | 500.0 |
| Reduction of long-term debt | (19.6) | (200.7) | (414.8) |
| Increase (decrease) in loans payable | 133.6 | (12.9) | 177.5 |
| Dividends paid | (259.7) | (217.1) | (183.3) |
| Net cash provided by (used in) financing activities | (114.1) | (412.3) | 103.9 |
| **Effect of exchange rate changes on cash** | 3.4 | (2.9) | (3.5) |
| **Increase in cash and cash equivalents** | 4.1 | 6.7 | 1.8 |
| **Cash and cash equivalents at beginning of year** | 43.8 | 37.1 | 35.3 |
| **Cash and cash equivalents at end of year** | $ 47.9 | $ 43.8 | $ 37.1 |
| Supplemental disclosure of cash paid for: | | | |
| Interest | $ 62.4 | $ 61.6 | $ 72.5 |
| Income taxes | $289.1 | $240.6 | $180.9 |
| Noncash investing and financing activities: | | | |
| Acquisition of businesses | | | |
| Fair value of assets acquired | $394.9 | $ 19.0 | $705.8 |
| Cash paid | 278.3 | 25.6 | 481.1 |
| Liabilities assumed | $116.6 | $ (6.6) | $224.7 |

**EXHIBIT 2**
**The Gillette Company and Subsidiary Companies—Common Size**
**Statement of Income for the Years Ended December 31, 1995, 1994, and 1993 (%)**

|  | 1995 | 1994 | 1993 |
|---|---|---|---|
| **Net sales** | 100.0% | 100.0% | 100.0% |
| Cost of sales | 37.4 | 36.6 | 37.8 |
| **Gross profit** | 62.6% | 63.4% | 62.2% |
| Selling, general, and administrative expenses | 42.4 | 43.2 | 42.1 |
| Realignment expense | — | — | 4.9 |
| **Profit from operations** | 20.2% | 20.2% | 15.2% |
| Nonoperating charges (income) |  |  |  |
|    Interest income | (.1) | (.3) | (.5) |
|    Interest expense | .8 | 1.0 | 1.1 |
|    Other charges—net | .4 | 1.3 | 2.0 |
|  | 1.1% | 2.0% | 2.6% |
| **Income before income taxes and cumulative effect of accounting changes** | 19.1 | 18.2 | 12.6 |
| Income taxes | 7.0 | 6.7 | 4.7 |
| **Income before cumulative effect of accounting changes** | 12.1% | 11.5% | 7.9% |
| Cumulative effect of accounting changes | — | — | (2.6) |
| **Net income** | 12.1% | 11.5% | 5.3% |

**EXHIBIT 2 (continued)**
**The Gillette Company and Subsidiary Companies—**
**Common Size Balance Sheets December 31, 1995 and 1994 (%)**

|  | 1995 | 1994 |
|---|---|---|
| **Assets** | | |
| **Current assets** | | |
| Cash and cash equivalents | .8% | .8% |
| Short-term investments, at cost, which approximates market value | — | — |
| Receivables, less allowances | 26.2 | 26.0 |
| Inventories | 16.3 | 17.7 |
| Deferred income taxes | 3.5 | 4.2 |
| Prepaid expenses | 2.2 | 2.1 |
| Total current assets | 49.0% | 50.8% |
| **Property, plant and equipment**, at cost less accumulated depreciation | 25.8 | 26.6 |
| **Intangible assets**, less accumulated amortization | 19.3 | 16.7 |
| **Other assets** | 5.9 | 5.9 |
|  | 100.0% | 100.0% |
| **Liabilities and stockholders' equity** | | |
| **Current liabilities** | | |
| Loans payable | 9.1% | 6.5% |
| Current portion of long-term debt | .4 | .5 |
| Accounts payable and accrued liabilities | 20.1 | 22.2 |
| Income taxes | 3.9 | 3.5 |
| Total current liabilities | 33.5% | 32.7% |
| **Long-term debt** | 10.9 | 13.5 |
| **Deferred income taxes** | 1.1 | 1.0 |
| **Other long-term liabilities** | 14.5 | 14.6 |
| **Minority interest** | .3 | .3 |
| **Stockholders' equity** | | |
| 8.0% Cumulative Series C ESOP Convertible Preferred, without par value, Issued: 1995—160,701 shares; 1994—162,928 shares | 1.5 | 1.8 |
| Unearned ESOP compensation | (.5) | (.8) |
| Common stock, par value $1 per share Authorized 1,160,000,000 shares; Issued: 1995—559,718,438 shares; 1994—558,242,410 shares | 8.8 | 10.5 |
| Additional paid-in capital | .5 | — |
| Earnings reinvested in the business | 53.4 | 53.3 |
| Cumulative foreign currency translation adjustments | (7.5) | (7.1) |
| Treasury stock, at cost: 1995—115,254,353 shares; 1994—115,343,404 shares | (16.5) | (19.7) |
| Total stockholders' equity | 39.7% | 38.0% |
|  | 100.0% | 100.0% |

# Identify the Industries—1996

**C**ommon size balance sheets of twelve firms are presented on the following page, along with some useful ratios. These companies were chosen because they consist of primarily one major business segment, and the relationships between balance sheet items, profit, and operations are fairly typical of these industries. The following companies are involved:

- Regional bank
- Temporary office personnel agency
- For-profit hospital chain
- Warehouse club
- Major passenger airline
- Major regional utility company
- Manufacturer of oral, personal, and household care products
- Hotel chain
- Upscale department store chain
- Discount department store chain
- International oil company
- Defense contractor

The financial statement dates are noted at the top of each column. Use the ratios, common size statements, and your knowledge of business operations and conditions at the time these data were generated to identify the companies.

---

*Research Associate Jeremy Cott prepared this case under the supervision of Professors Sharon M. McKinnon of Northeastern University and William J. Bruns, Jr.*

Copyright © 1997 by the President and Fellows of Harvard College. Harvard Business School case 198-017.

## EXHIBIT 1

| | Jun-96 A | Dec-95 B | Dec-95 C | Jan-96 D | Dec-95 E | Jan-96 F | Dec-95 G | Dec-95 H | Dec-95 I | Dec-95 J | Dec-95 K | Sep-96 L |
|---|---|---|---|---|---|---|---|---|---|---|---|---|
| Cash and Marketable Securities | 13.5 | 2.1 | 2.0 | 0.9 | 32.6 | 0.2 | 13.4 | 3.3 | 0.2 | 1.2 | 17.7 | 2.1 |
| Receivables | 7.9 | 9.4 | 7.7 | 32.7 | 63.2 | 2.3 | 7.2 | 14.7 | 6.0 | 13.4 | 55.4 | 2.8 |
| Inventories | — | 37.8 | 6.2 | 22.9 | — | 42.6 | 0.5 | 10.1 | 1.6 | 2.0 | — | 30.6 |
| Other Current Assets | 5.4 | 4.3 | 3.1 | 2.5 | — | 1.1 | 2.4 | 2.8 | 1.6 | 4.5 | 4.6 | 1.8 |
| Total Current Assets | 26.8 | 53.6 | 19.0 | 59.0 | 95.8 | 46.2 | 23.5 | 30.9 | 9.4 | 21.1 | 77.7 | 37.3 |
| Plant & Equipment | 55.6 | 16.1 | 71.7 | 40.4 | 1.8 | 50.3 | 55.4 | 28.2 | 81.1 | 49.0 | 11.7 | 58.8 |
| Investments | 6.0 | 1.9 | 6.2 | — | — | — | 19.4 | — | 0.7 | 10.5 | — | — |
| Goodwill | 2.2 | 25.7 | — | — | 0.3 | — | — | 35.9 | — | 17.6 | 7.7 | 1.0 |
| Other Noncurrent Assets | 9.4 | 2.7 | 3.1 | 0.6 | 2.1 | 3.5 | 1.7 | 5.0 | 8.8 | 1.8 | 2.9 | 2.9 |
| Total Noncurrent Assets | 73.2 | 46.4 | 81.0 | 41.0 | 4.2 | 53.8 | 76.5 | 69.1 | 90.6 | 78.9 | 22.3 | 62.7 |
| **Total Assets** | 100.0 | 100.0 | 100.0 | 100.0 | 100.0 | 100.0 | 100.0 | 100.0 | 100.0 | 100.0 | 100.0 | 100.0 |
| Accounts Payable | 12.6 | 10.6 | 9.3 | 10.1 | 84.7 | 17.2 | 10.0 | 9.7 | 3.7 | 4.2 | 7.4 | 25.3 |
| Notes Payble | — | 12.2 | 1.9 | 8.5 | 6.0 | 6.5 | — | 2.7 | 3.5 | — | — | 1.2 |
| Current Portion of L/T Debt | 0.8 | 0.1 | 0.5 | 2.7 | — | 0.9 | 7.1 | 0.5 | 2.8 | 1.2 | — | 0.2 |
| Unearned Revenues | 11.6 | 3.5 | — | — | — | — | — | — | — | — | — | — |
| Other Current Liabilities | 4.8 | 11.1 | 8.8 | 9.1 | 0.9 | 5.9 | 0.4 | 10.1 | 5.2 | 8.4 | 26.3 | 9.4 |
| Total Current Liabilities | 29.8 | 37.5 | 20.5 | 30.4 | 91.6 | 30.6 | 7.5 | 23.0 | 15.2 | 13.8 | 33.7 | 36.1 |
| L/T Debt | 17.8 | 15.1 | 8.5 | 13.4 | 0.5 | 28.2 | 34.9 | 39.2 | 31.8 | 35.9 | — | 25.0 |
| Other Noncurrent Liabilities | 30.5 | 3.8 | 26.7 | 4.1 | — | 1.9 | 6.6 | 15.9 | 20.0 | 14.5 | — | 2.7 |
| *Total Liabilities* | 78.1 | 56.4 | 55.7 | 47.9 | 92.1 | 60.7 | 59.0 | 78.1 | 67.0 | 64.2 | 33.7 | 63.8 |
| Preferred Stock | 1.1 | — | (0.1) | — | — | — | — | 5.3 | 5.9 | — | — | — |
| Common Stock | 1.8 | 2.4 | 3.1 | 6.1 | 0.3 | 0.6 | 4.2 | 2.4 | 1.3 | 0.0 | 5.6 | 0.0 |
| Additional Paid-in Capital | 21.5 | 2.6 | — | — | 3.0 | 1.5 | — | 13.5 | 18.7 | 22.6 | 1.0 | 6.5 |
| Retained Earnings | (1.0) | 38.5 | 58.7 | 47.8 | 4.5 | 38.3 | 41.7 | 31.3 | 7.1 | 12.9 | 60.5 | 31.2 |
| Adjustments to Retained Earnings | 1.0 | 0.1 | 1.5 | — | 0.1 | (1.1) | (0.2) | (11.7) | — | 0.3 | — | (1.5) |
| Treasury Stock | (2.5) | — | (18.9) | (1.8) | — | — | (4.7) | (18.9) | — | — | (0.8) | — |
| *Total Stockholders' Equity* | 21.9 | 43.6 | 44.3 | 52.1 | 7.9 | 39.3 | 41.0 | 21.9 | 33.0 | 35.8 | 66.3 | 36.2 |
| **Total Liabilities & Stockholders' Equity** | 100.0 | 100.0 | 100.0 | 100.0 | 100.0 | 100.0 | 100.0 | 100.0 | 100.0 | 100.0 | 100.0 | 100.0 |
| **Selected Ratios** | | | | | | | | | | | | |
| Current Ratio | 0.90 | 1.43 | 0.92 | 1.94 | 1.05 | 1.51 | 1.34 | 1.35 | 0.63 | 1.53 | 2.31 | 1.03 |
| Inventory Turns (X) | N.M. | 2.5 | 8.9 | 4.5 | N.M. | 5.0 | N.M. | 5.8 | 2.6 | N.M. | N.M. | 11.9 |
| Receivables Collection Period | 28 | 29 | 27 | 79 | N.M. | 3 | 51 | 49 | 49 | 55 | 54 | 3 |
| Net Sales/Total Assets | 1.019 | 1.191 | 1.357 | 1.505 | 0.066 | 2.524 | 0.539 | 1.094 | 0.447 | 0.890 | 3.741 | 3.983 |
| Net Profits/Net Sales | 0.053 | 0.068 | 0.052 | 0.040 | 0.171 | 0.029 | 0.105 | 0.021 | 0.069 | 0.060 | 0.026 | 0.013 |
| Net Profits/Total Assets | 0.054 | 0.080 | 0.071 | 0.060 | 0.011 | 0.073 | 0.057 | 0.023 | 0.031 | 0.053 | 0.096 | 0.051 |
| Net Profits/Net Worth | 0.217 | 0.185 | 0.160 | 0.116 | 0.144 | 0.186 | 0.138 | 0.102 | 0.113 | 0.147 | 0.145 | 0.140 |

*Notes:*

* "Adjustments to Retained Earnings" consists primarily of foreign translation adjustments.
* "N.M." means that the ratio is not meaningful, even if calculable, for this company.

# Colgate-Palmolive Company

## ANALYZING AN ANNUAL REPORT

The Colgate-Palmolive annual report presents an opportunity to analyze a company as you might initially evaluate any public company (see pp. 1-83 to 1-105). Annual reports are published by companies to provide important financial information to shareholders, financial analysts, and other outside parties. The focus of an annual report is the income statement, balance sheet, and statement of cash flows. Companies are also required to provide other types of information including an auditor's report, notes to the financial statements, management's discussion and analysis, business segment information, and certain historical data. In addition, an annual report may contain information about the company's products, facilities, strategies, or other topics at management's discretion.

This exercise is a guided analysis through the fundamental financial statements of a company. You will want to calculate a number of financial ratios to analyze the basic financial statements and to highlight significant points underlying trends. In order to understand many of these points you will have to study management's discussion of financial condition and results of operations as well as the notes to the financial statements.

A complete financial analysis could take several hours to complete, which may be more than you will be able to spend while preparing for class.

Included in this exercise are comparable financial data from several companies in consumer nondurable, personal products, and health care products businesses. Such data normally are not available pre-prepared to an analyst; the analyst has to select comparable companies and work through the basic

Copyright © 1996 by the President and Fellows of Harvard College. Harvard Business School case 196-116.

financial analysis for each company. For your convenience we have provided financial ratio analysis and comparable income statements and balance sheets from recent fiscal years for six companies, which may or may not be comparable to Colgate-Palmolive.

## Overview of Colgate-Palmolive Company Annual Report

The Colgate-Palmolive annual report is made up of several sections. The various components include:

**Highlights**
Financial highlights from the last three fiscal years, including per-share information.

**Management Interview**
A basic discussion of the results of the past year, including financial results, operating highlights, financial objectives, management changes, and future outlook.

**Global Brands, Global Investment, Global Growth**
Description of the company's consumer products brands sold in markets around the world, global investments to improve manufacturing and supply of the company's products, and the company's strategies for global growth in product sales and profits.

**Global Business Review**
A review of operating performance in four geographical segments of the world and in the company's pet food business.

**Financial Review**
A description of the scope of business:

- Results of Operations by Business and Geographical Segments.
- Company Liquidity and Capital Resources
- Outlook for 1995
- Report of Management

    Management's responsibility for the financial statements and for the internal control systems designed to safeguard assets and ensure accuracy of the financial records and reports.

- Report of Independent Public Accountants

    Independent auditors' audit opinion after their review of the financial statements in the annual report.

- Consolidated Financial Statements

Consolidated financial statements for the latest year and two previous years.  Includes:

- Consolidated Statements of Income
- Consolidated Balance Sheets
- Consolidated Statements of Retained Earnings
- Consolidated Statements of Changes in Capital Accounts
- Consolidated Statements of Cash Flows

**Notes to Consolidated Financial Statements**

Notes to financial statements providing detail for understanding and interpretating statements.  Notes are considered to be an integral part of the financial statements.  Includes notes on:

| | |
|---|---|
| Note One: | Summary of Significant Accounting Policies |
| Note Two: | Acquisitions |
| Note Three: | Long-Term Debt and Credit Facilities |
| Note Four: | Leases |
| Note Five: | Capital Stock and Stock Option Plans |
| Note Six: | Employee Stock Ownership Plan |
| Note Seven: | Retirement Plans and Other Postretirement Benefits |
| Note Eight: | Income Taxes |
| Note Nine: | Foreign Currency Translation |
| Note Ten: | Earnings per Share |
| Note Eleven: | Other Income Statement Information |
| Note Twelve: | Balance Sheet Information |
| Note Thirteen: | Commitments and Contingent Liabilities |
| Note Fourteen: | Quarterly Financial Data |
| Note Fifteen: | Market and Dividend Information |
| Note Sixteen: | Subsequent Event—Purchase of Kolynos Oral Care Business |

**Board of Directors and Management**

A directory of the board of directors, corporate officers, other planning and staff executives, and other principal operating executives.

**Historical Financial Summary**

History of reported financial reports for the past 11 years.  Includes operations, financial position, and share and other information.

**Shareholder Information**

Information for shareholders including information about corporate responsibility and environmental policy.

## I. Ratio Analysis

Calculate the following ratios for Colgate-Palmolive for the last two fiscal years and compare with industry averages from **Exhibit 1**.

|  | Latest Year | Previous Year | Industry |
|---|---|---|---|

### A.   Profitability Ratios

Profit margin

Return on assets (ROA)

Return on equity (ROE)

### B.   Activity Ratios

Asset turnover

Days' receivables

Inventory turnover

## I.   Ratio Analysis (continued)

| | Latest Year | Previous Year | Industry |
|---|---|---|---|
| **C.   Leverage Ratios** | | | |
| Debt ratio | | | |
| Times interest earned | | | |
| Days' payable | | | |
| **D.   Liquidity Ratios** | | | |
| Current ratio | | | |
| Quick ratio | | | |
| **E.   Market Ratios** | | | |
| Price earnings ratio | | | |
| Dividend yield | | | |

## II. Common Size Balance Sheet Analysis

A. Calculate a common size balance sheet for the last two fiscal years. Use the total assets line for each year as the denominator in each calculation.

|  | Latest Year | Previous Year |
|---|---|---|
| Total current assets |  |  |
| Land, buildings and equipment |  |  |
| Other assets | ____ | ____ |
| Total assets | 100.0% | 100.0% |
| Total current liabilities |  |  |
| Long-term debt |  |  |
| Deferred income taxes |  |  |
| Other liabilities |  |  |
| Total liabilities | ____ | ____ |
| Common stock |  |  |
| Retained earnings |  |  |
| Common stock in treasury |  |  |
| Cumulative foreign exchange earnings adjustments | ____ | ____ |
| Total equity | ____ | ____ |
| Total liabilities and stockholders' equity | 100.0% | 100.0% |

B. How does Colgate-Palmolive's balance sheet compare with those of other consumer products companies highlighted in **Exhibit 2**?

## III. Common Size Income Statement Analysis

A.   Calculate a common size income statement for the last two fiscal years.  Use total sales in each year as the denominator in each calculation.

|  | Latest Year | Previous Year |
|---|---|---|
| Sales | 100.0% | 100.0% |
| Cost & expenses | | |
| Cost of sales | | |
| SG&A | | |
| Depreciation & amortization | ___ | ___ |
| Interest expense | | |
| Total costs and expenses | | |
| Earnings from continuing operations before tax | | |
| Income taxes | | |
| Earnings from continuing operations | | |
| Discontinued operations after tax | ___ | ___ |
| Net earnings | | |

B.   How does Colgate-Palmolive's income statement compare with those of other consumer products companies in **Exhibit 3**?

## IV.  Cash Flow Analysis

What were the primary sources and uses of cash for Colgate-Palmolive in the latest fiscal year?

## V.  Other Questions

A.  How would you go about choosing comparable companies to Colgate-Palmolive?  How would you calculate an industry average?

B.  How well positioned is Colgate-Palmolive to meet the financial goals stated in the Management Interview?

C.  What are Colgate-Palmolive's prospects for future growth?  Can the company continue at its present growth rate?

**EXHIBIT 1**
**Financial Ratios for Selected Consumer Products Companies**

| | Gillette (12/31/94) | Bristol-Myers Squibb (12/31/94) | American Home Products (12/31/94) | Kimberly-Clark (12/31/94) | Johnson & Johnson (1/1/95) | Procter & Gamble (6/30/95) | Average of Six Companies |
|---|---|---|---|---|---|---|---|
| **1. Profitability Ratios** | | | | | | | |
| Profit margin | 11.50% | 15.37% | 17.04% | 7.27% | 12.75% | 7.91% | 11.97% |
| Return on assets | 13.65% | 15.06% | 10.88% | 9.35% | 14.99% | 10.95% | 12.48% |
| Return on equity | 39.93% | 31.64% | 37.59% | 21.18% | 31.62% | 27.24% | 31.53% |
| **2. Activity Ratios** | | | | | | | |
| Asset turnover | 114.57% | 95.83% | 61.07% | 112.45% | 112.75% | 124.61% | 103.55% |
| Days' receivables | 78 | 59 | 77 | 39 | 55 | 36 | 57 |
| Inventory turnover | 2.45 | 2.30 | 1.74 | 6.23 | 2.73 | 6.20 | 3.61 |
| **3. Leverage Ratios** | | | | | | | |
| Debt to equity | 1.72 | 1.26 | 4.09 | 1.59 | 1.20 | 1.66 | 1.92 |
| Times interest earned | 27.29 | 38.57 | 18.65 | 7.29 | 19.88 | 9.20 | 20.15 |
| Days' payables | 183 | 77 | 64 | 25 | 67 | 50 | 78 |
| **4. Liquidity Ratios** | | | | | | | |
| Current ratio | 1.54 | 1.57 | 1.69 | 0.88 | 1.57 | 1.25 | 1.42 |
| Quick ratio | 0.80 | 1.04 | 0.94 | 0.42 | 0.77 | 0.66 | 0.77 |
| **5. Market Ratios** | | | | | | | |
| Price earnings ratio | 26 | 19 | 15 | 16 | 20 | 20 | 19 |
| Dividend yield | 1.39% | 5.03% | 4.52% | 3.26% | 2.26% | 2.30% | 3.13% |

**EXHIBIT 2**
**Common Size Balance Sheets for Selected Consumer Products Companies**

| | Gillette (12/31/94) | Bristol-Myers Squibb (12/31/94) | American Home Products (12/31/94) | Kimberly-Clark (12/31/94) | Johnson & Johnson (1/1/95) | Procter & Gamble (6/30/95) | Average of Six Companies |
|---|---|---|---|---|---|---|---|
| Total current assets | 50.00% | 51.97% | 36.08% | 26.95% | 42.63% | 38.55% | 41.03% |
| Land, buildings and equipment | 25.68 | 28.40 | 17.59 | 62.52 | 31.34 | 39.20 | 34.12 |
| Other assets | 24.32 | 19.63 | 46.33 | 10.53 | 26.03 | 22.25 | 24.85 |
| Total assets | 100.0% | 100.0% | 100.0% | 100.0% | 100.0% | 100.0% | 100.0% |
| Total current liabilities | 32.46% | 33.11% | 21.31% | 30.66% | 27.23% | 30.75% | 29.25% |
| Long-term debt | 13.01 | 4.99 | 46.01 | 13.85 | 14.03 | 18.35 | 18.37 |
| Deferred income taxes | 3.40 | | 4.50 | 9.13 | 0.83 | 1.89 | 3.29 |
| Other liabilities | 14.42 | 17.72 | 8.55 | 7.73 | 12.45 | 11.36 | 12.04 |
| Total liabilities | 63.29 | 55.82 | 80.37 | 61.37 | 54.54 | 62.35 | 62.95 |
| Common stock | 11.12 | 3.49 | 5.18 | 3.41 | 4.43 | 11.71 | 6.56 |
| Retained earnings | 51.51 | 58.87 | 14.89 | 40.99 | 57.23 | 25.71 | 41.53 |
| Common stock in treasury | -19.06 | -15.85 | 0.00 | -1.15 | -15.98 | 0.00 | -8.67 |
| Cumulative foreign exchange earnings adjustments | -6.86 | -2.33 | -0.44 | -4.62 | -0.22 | 0.23 | -2.37 |
| Total equity | 36.71 | 44.18 | 19.63 | 38.63 | 45.46 | 37.65 | 37.05 |
| Total liabilities and stockholders' equity | 100.0% | 100.0% | 100.0% | 100.0% | 100.0% | 100.0% | 100.0% |
| Total assets ($ millions) | $5,494.0 | $12,910.0 | $21,674.0 | $6,716.0 | $15,668.0 | $28,125.0 | |

**EXHIBIT 3**
**Common Size Income Statements for Selected Consumer Products Companies**

| | Gillette (12/31/94) | Bristol-Myers Squibb (12/31/94) | American Home Products (12/31/94) | Kimberly-Clark (12/31/94) | Johnson & Johnson (1/1/95) | Procter & Gamble (6/30/95) | Average of Six Companies |
|---|---|---|---|---|---|---|---|
| Sales | 100.0% | 100.0% | 100.0% | 100.0% | 100.0% | 100.0% | 100.0% |
| Costs and expenses | | | | | | | |
| Cost of sales | 36.61 | 26.05 | 31.18 | 66.88 | 33.68 | 58.69 | 42.18 |
| SG&A | 43.19 | 53.33 | 44.54 | 22.00 | 48.76 | 28.81 | 40.11 |
| Interest expense | 0.69 | 0.57 | 1.28 | 1.75 | 0.90 | 1.46 | 1.11 |
| Total costs and expenses | 80.49 | 79.95 | 77.00 | 90.63 | 83.34 | 88.96 | 83.40 |
| Operating income | 19.51 | 20.05 | 23.00 | 9.37 | 16.66 | 11.04 | 16.61 |
| Other income | −1.32 | 1.27 | −0.36 | 0.69 | 0.38 | 0.92 | 0.26 |
| Income before taxes | 18.19 | 21.32 | 22.64 | 10.06 | 17.04 | 11.96 | 16.87 |
| Income taxes | 6.69 | 5.95 | 5.60 | 3.76 | 4.29 | 4.05 | 5.06 |
| Income from continuing operations | 11.50 | 15.37 | 17.04 | 6.30 | 12.75 | 7.91 | 11.81 |
| Discontinued operations | 0.00 | 0.00 | 0.00 | −0.96 | 0.00 | 0.00 | −0.16 |
| Net earnings | 11.50 | 15.37 | 17.04 | 7.27 | 12.75 | 7.91 | 11.97 |
| % of revenue by marketing segment | Blades/razors (39%)<br>Personal care (26%)<br>Stationery products (12%)<br>Household appliances (23%) | Pharmaceutical (58%)<br>Medical devices (14%)<br>Nonprescription health (17%)<br>Beauty aids (11%) | Health care (88%)<br>Food products (11%)<br>Agricultural (1%) | Disposable diapers (23%)<br>Household tissue (24%)<br>Feminine care (10%)<br>Other (43%) | Consumer (33%)<br>Pharmaceutical (33%)<br>Professional (34%) | Laundry and cleaning (32%)<br>Paper (28%)<br>Beauty care (19%)<br>Food and beverage (12%)<br>Health care (9%) | |

**EXHIBIT 4**
**Income Statements for Selected Consumer Products Companies ($ in millions)**

| | Gillette (12/31/94) | Bristol-Myers Squibb (12/31/94) | American Home Products (12/31/94) | Kimberly-Clark (12/31/94) | Johnson & Johnson (1/1/95) | Procter & Gamble (6/30/95) |
|---|---|---|---|---|---|---|
| Sales | $6,070 | $11,984 | $8,966 | $7,364 | $15,734 | $33,434 |
| Costs and expenses | | | | | | |
| Cost of sales | 2,222 | 3,122 | 2,796 | 4,925 | 5,299 | 19,623 |
| SG&A | 2,622 | 6,391 | 3,993 | 1,620 | 7,672 | 9,632 |
| Interest expense | 42 | 68 | 115 | 129 | 142 | 488 |
| Total costs and expenses | 4,886 | 9,581 | 6,904 | 6,674 | 13,113 | 29,743 |
| Operating income | 1,184 | 2,403 | 2,062 | 690 | 2,621 | 3,691 |
| Other income | –80 | 152 | –32 | 51 | 60 | 309 |
| Income before taxes | 1,104 | 2,555 | 2,030 | 741 | 2,681 | 4,000 |
| Income taxes | 406 | 713 | 502 | 277 | 675 | 1,355 |
| Income from continuing operations | 698 | 1,842 | 1,528 | 464 | 2,006 | 2,645 |
| Discontinued operations | | | | –71 | | |
| Net earnings | $ 698 | $ 1,842 | $1,528 | $ 535 | $ 2,006 | $ 2,645 |

Part One  An Overview of Accounting and Financial Reporting

**EXHIBIT 5**
**Balance Sheets for Selected Consumer Products Companies ($ in millions)**

| | Gillette (12/31/94) | Bristol-Myers Squibb (12/31/94) | American Home Products (12/31/94) | Kimberly-Clark (12/31/94) | Johnson & Johnson (1/1/95) | Procter & Gamble (6/30/95) |
|---|---|---|---|---|---|---|
| Total current assets | $2,747 | $ 6,710 | $ 7,821 | $1,810 | $ 6,680 | $10,842 |
| Land, buildings and equipment | 1,411 | 3,666 | 3,812 | 4,199 | 4,910 | 11,026 |
| Other assets | 1,336 | 2,534 | 10,041 | 707 | 4,078 | 6,257 |
| Total assets | $5,494 | $12,910 | $21,674 | $6,716 | $15,668 | $28,125 |
| | | | | | | |
| Total current liabilities | $1,783 | $ 4,274 | $ 4,618 | $2,059 | $ 4,266 | $ 8,648 |
| Long-term debt | 715 | 644 | 9,973 | 930 | 2,199 | 5,161 |
| Deferred income taxes | 187 | | 975 | 613 | 130 | 531 |
| Other liabilities | 792 | 2,288 | 1,854 | 519 | 1,951 | 3,196 |
| Total liabilities | $3,477 | $ 7,206 | $17,420 | $4,121 | $ 8,546 | $17,536 |
| | | | | | | |
| Common stock | 611 | 451 | 1,123 | 229 | 694 | 3,293 |
| Retained earnings | 2,830 | 7,600 | 3,226 | 2,753 | 8,966 | 7,231 |
| Common stock in treasury | -1,047 | -2,046 | | -77 | -2,503 | |
| Cumulative foreign exchange earnings adjustments | -377 | -301 | -95 | -310 | -35 | 65 |
| Total equity | 2,017 | 5,704 | 4,254 | 2,595 | 7,122 | 10,589 |
| | | | | | | |
| Total liabilities and stockholders' equity | $5,494 | $12,910 | $21,674 | $6,716 | $15,668 | $28,125 |

**Colgate-Palmolive Company 1996 Annual Report**

# Highlights

| Dollars in Millions Except Per Share Amounts | 1996 | 1995* | Change |
|---|---|---|---|
| Worldwide Sales | **$8,749.0** | $8,358.2 | + 5% |
| Unit Volume | | | +5.5% |
| Gross Profit Margin | **49.1%** | 47.9% | |
| Earnings Before Interest & Taxes | **$1,152.0** | $1,029.4 | + 12% |
| Percent of Sales | **13.2%** | 12.3% | |
| Net Income | **$ 635.0** | $ 541.2 | + 17% |
| Earnings Per Share | **$ 4.19** | $ 3.58 | + 17% |
| Dividends Paid Per Share | **$ 1.88** | $ 1.76 | + 7% |
| Operating Cash Flow | **$ 917.4** | $ 810.2 | + 13% |
| Capital Expenditures | **$ 459.0** | $ 431.8 | + 6% |
| Number of Common Shareholders | **45,500** | 46,600 | |
| Number of Common Shares Outstanding | **147.1** | 145.8 | |

\* Excludes a 1995 restructuring provision of $369.2 or $2.54 per share aftertax.

Financial information, throughout this report, has not been adjusted to reflect the two-for-one common stock split to be effective April 25, 1997.

- **Colgate achieved record-breaking 1996 results.**
- **Every operating division worldwide contributed to excellent, profitable growth in 1996.**
- **Growth was fastest in the high growth markets of the developing world, unit volume increasing 7 percent in both Latin America and Asia/Africa.**
- **Total sales rose 7 percent, excluding the effect of the strengthening of the U.S. dollar.**
- **Profitability improved sharply, with gross profit margin up 1.2 percentage points to a record 49.1 percent.**
- **Colgate's strong unit volume growth is the result of aggressive global new product activity and market share gains. Colgate introduced 602 new products worldwide in 1996, a new record.**
- **Operating cash flow also set a new record at $917 million, up 13 percent, providing funds for reinvesting in growth and dividends to shareholders.**
- **On March 6, 1997, the Board of Directors declared a 17 percent dividend increase and a two-for-one stock split, effective April 25, 1997.**

1

Reprinted with permission of Colgate-Palmolive Company.

# Financial Review

(Dollars in Millions Except Per Share Amounts)

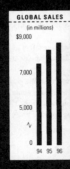

GLOBAL SALES
(in millions)

18

## Results of Operations

| Worldwide Net Sales by Business Segment and Geographic Region | 1996 | 1995 | 1994 |
|---|---|---|---|
| Oral, Personal and Household Care | | | |
| North America | **$1,869.0** | $1,784.7 | $1,623.1 |
| Europe | **2,148.5** | 2,159.7 | 1,968.2 |
| Latin America | **2,124.8** | 1,977.2 | 1,736.5 |
| Asia/Africa | **1,738.0** | 1,644.1 | 1,408.0 |
| Total Oral, Personal and Household Care | **7,880.3** | 7,565.7 | 6,735.8 |
| Total Pet Nutrition and Other* | **868.7** | 792.5 | 852.1 |
| **Total Net Sales** | **$8,749.0** | $8,358.2 | $7,587.9 |

*Sales outside North America represented approximately 29%, 29% and 25% of total sales of Pet Nutrition and Other products in 1996, 1995 and 1994, respectively.

### NET SALES

Worldwide net sales increased 5% to $8,749.0 in 1996 on volume growth of 5%, reflecting increases in every geographic region. Sales in the Oral, Personal and Household Care segment were up 4% on 5% volume growth.

In 1996, sales in North America rose 5% on the same percentage of volume growth. Market share climbed for three of the region's key product categories: toothpaste, dishwashing liquid and deodorants. Products contributing to the sales growth included Colgate Baking Soda & Peroxide toothpaste, Palmolive antibacterial dishwashing liquid, Speed Stick gel and Irish Spring Sport soap.

Overall sales in Europe decreased slightly in 1996 on 3% higher volume, due primarily to the negative effects of weaker European currencies. Volume was up sharply in Russia. New product launches including Colgate Triple Stripe toothpaste, Fabuloso fabric softener and Ajax Expel cleaner, as well as the relaunching of Palmolive shower gel, enabled the region to achieve higher volume and increase market share for a majority of its core categories.

Sales in Latin America were up 8% on 7% volume growth. Leading the way in this region were Argentina, Brazil, Chile, Dominican Republic and Ecuador, which were partially offset by the negative impact of Venezuela caused by the country's economic downturn. Mexican operations are beginning to recover from the economic downturn of 1995. New product introductions contributed to the rapid expansion of sales in this region, which is evidenced by the success of Colgate Total Fresh Stripe toothpaste and Colgate Baking Soda & Peroxide toothpaste, Protex Fresh soap, Fab Total detergent and Suavitel fabric softener refills.

The Asia/Africa region posted an overall sales increase of 6% on 7% volume growth for the year, largely due to a combination of new product introductions and geographic expansion, especially in China. The successful introductions of new products elsewhere in the region including Fabuloso fragranced cleaner, Protex Fresh soap, Dynamo antibacterial detergent, Palmolive Optims shampoo and Palmolive Shower Cream also contributed to the volume growth.

Sales for the Pet Nutrition and Other segment increased 10% on 6% volume growth. Hill's Pet Nutrition completed its transition to a company-owned distribution and sales network. During 1996, Hill's also relaunched the entire Science Diet line and added three new products. Due to Hill's rapid expansion in international markets, a European manufacturing facility was added in 1996 in order to support this growth.

Worldwide net sales in 1995 increased 10% to $8,358.2, reflecting growth among all divisions. Asia/Africa with sales growth of 17% on 13% higher volume and Latin America with 14% sales growth on 21% higher volume led the way on the strength of oral and personal care product sales. North America posted overall sales increases of 10% on 9% volume growth, largely due to the introduction of new products. Sales in Europe were up 10% on flat volumes, primarily reflecting the positive effects of stronger European currencies. Sales for the Pet Nutrition and Other segment declined, reflecting the sale of non-core businesses in 1994, partially offset by a modest sales increase of 2% at Hill's.

### GROSS PROFIT

Gross profit margin was 49.1%, above both the 1995 level of 47.9% and the 1994 level of 48.4%. The 1996 increase reflects cost-reduction programs, focus on high margin products, the initial benefits of the 1995 restructuring program and economic recovery in Mexico.

### SELLING, GENERAL AND ADMINISTRATIVE EXPENSES

Selling, general and administrative expenses as a percentage of sales were 35% in 1996, 34% in 1995 and 35% in 1994. The modest increase in 1996 represents increased advertising spending, increased investment in China, India and Russia as well as slightly higher distribution costs. The Company continues to focus on expense-containment strategies including the 1995 restructuring program. It is anticipated that these initiatives will provide incremental funds to further increase investments in research and development as well as media advertising to support growth.

### PROVISION FOR RESTRUCTURED OPERATIONS

In September 1995, the Company announced a major worldwide restructuring of its manufacturing and administrative operations designed to further enhance profitable growth over the next several years by generating significant efficiencies and improving competitiveness. The charge included employee termination costs and expenses associated with the realignment of the Company's global manufacturing operations, as well as settlement of contractual obligations. The worldwide restructuring program resulted in a 1995 third quarter pretax charge of $460.5 ($369.2 net of tax) or $2.54 per share for the year. To date, 14 factories have been closed or reconfigured, and the realignments in facilities around the world are expected to be substantially completed during 1997.

### OTHER EXPENSE, NET

Other expense, net of other income, consists principally of amortization of goodwill and other intangible assets, minority interest in earnings of less-than-100% owned consolidated subsidiaries, earnings from equity investments and asset sales. Amortization expense increased in each of the three years presented due to higher levels of intangible assets stemming from the Company's recent acquisitions, most notably Kolynos in 1995 and Cibaca in India in 1994.

| Worldwide Earnings by Business Segment and Geographic Region | 1996 | 1995 As Reported | 1995 Excluding Restructuring | 1994 |
|---|---|---|---|---|
| Oral, Personal and Household Care | | | | |
| North America | $ **214.1** | $ 24.5 | $ 178.3 | $148.3 |
| Europe | **234.3** | 59.9 | 207.8 | 198.4 |
| Latin America | **397.1** | 313.7 | 342.9 | 298.4 |
| Asia/Africa | **187.8** | 153.5 | 187.5 | 164.5 |
| Total Oral, Personal and Household Care | **1,033.3** | 551.6 | 916.5 | 809.6 |
| Total Pet Nutrition and Other | **125.7** | 53.0 | 117.7 | 162.0 |
| Total Segment Earnings | **1,159.0** | 604.6 | 1,034.2 | 971.6 |
| Unallocated Expense, Net | **(7.0)** | (35.7) | (4.8) | (5.0) |
| **Earnings Before Interest and Taxes** | **1,152.0** | 568.9 | 1,029.4 | 966.6 |
| Interest Expense, Net | **(197.4)** | (205.4) | (205.4) | (86.7) |
| **Income Before Income Taxes** | $ **954.6** | $ 363.5 | $ 824.0 | $879.9 |

### EARNINGS BEFORE INTEREST AND TAXES

Earnings before interest and taxes (EBIT) increased 12% in 1996 to $1,152.0 compared with $1,029.4 (excluding restructuring) in the prior year. EBIT for the Oral, Personal and Household Care segment was up 13%, with North America, Europe and Latin America posting gains of 20%, 13% and 16%, respectively. Results in Asia/Africa were flat, reflecting a significant increase in advertising spending in the region. The Pet Nutrition and Other segment rebounded from 1995 with an increase of 7%.

In 1995, EBIT was impacted by the provision for restructured operations of $460.5. Excluding this charge, EBIT for the Oral, Personal and Household Care segment was up 13%, with North America, Asia/Africa and Latin America posting gains of 20%, 14% and 15%, respectively. Results in Europe showed modest improvement in 1995. Overall EBIT was tempered by the 27% decline in the Pet Nutrition and Other segment, principally due to the sale of non-core businesses in 1994 as well as a realignment of the sales force and distribution at Hill's.

### INTEREST EXPENSE, NET

Interest expense, net of interest income, was $197.4 in 1996 compared with $205.4 in 1995 and $86.7 in 1994. The decrease in 1996 is primarily a result of lower debt levels for the year. The increase in net interest expense in 1995 versus the prior year is a result of higher debt for the full year, incurred primarily to finance Kolynos and other acquisitions, and slightly higher effective interest rates in 1995.

### INCOME TAXES

The effective tax rate on income was 33.5% in 1996 versus 52.7% in 1995 and 34.1% in 1994. The overall effective rate in 1995 was impacted by the charge for restructuring, the tax benefit of which was 20% due to the effect of tax benefits in certain jurisdictions not expected to be realized. Excluding the charge, the effective income tax rate was 34.3% in 1995. Global tax planning strategies benefited the effective tax rate in all three years presented.

### NET INCOME

Net income was $635.0 in 1996 or $4.19 per share compared with $172.0 in 1995 or $1.04 per share including the provision for restructured operations of $369.2 or $2.54 per share. Excluding the special charge in 1995, earnings were $541.2 or $3.58 per share compared with $580.2 or $3.82 per share in 1994.

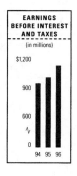

**EARNINGS BEFORE INTEREST AND TAXES**
(in millions)

| Identifiable Assets | **1996** | 1995 | 1994 |
|---|---|---|---|
| Oral, Personal and Household Care | | | |
| North America | **$2,531.4** | $2,497.7 | $2,416.0 |
| Europe | **1,192.1** | 1,271.0 | 1,293.8 |
| Latin America | **2,365.1** | 2,158.3 | 845.2 |
| Asia/Africa | **1,045.7** | 967.2 | 889.0 |
| Total Oral, Personal and Household Care | **7,134.3** | 6,894.2 | 5,444.0 |
| Total Pet Nutrition and Other | **578.6** | 545.5 | 509.6 |
| Total Corporate | **188.6** | 202.6 | 188.8 |
| **Total Identifiable Assets** | **$7,901.5** | $7,642.3 | $6,142.4 |

## Liquidity and Capital Resources

Net cash provided by operations increased 13% to $917.4 in 1996 compared with $810.2 in 1995 and $829.4 in 1994. The increase in cash generated by operating activities in 1996 reflects the Company's improved profitability and working capital management. Cash generated from operations was used to fund capital spending, reduce debt levels and increase dividends.

During 1996, long-term debt decreased from $3,029.0 to $2,897.2. The Company continued to focus on enhancing its debt portfolio, resulting in the refinancing of a substantial portion of commercial paper and other short-term borrowings to longer term instruments. In 1996, the Company entered into a $496.3 loan agreement and obtained a $406.0 term loan with foreign commercial banks. In addition, the Company issued $100.0 of notes in a private placement and issued $75.0 of medium-term notes under previously filed shelf registrations.

As of December 31, 1996, $341.9 of domestic and foreign commercial paper was outstanding. These borrowings carry a Standard & Poor's rating of A1 and a Moody's rating of P1. The commercial paper as well as other short-term borrowings are classified as long-term debt at December 31, 1996, as it is the Company's intent and ability to refinance such obligations on a long-term basis. The Company has additional sources of liquidity available in the form of lines of credit maintained with various banks. At December 31, 1996, such unused lines of credit amounted to $1,785.7. In addition, at December 31, 1996, the Company had $697.8 available under previously filed shelf registrations.

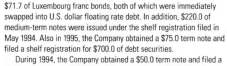

NET CASH PROVIDED BY OPERATIONS
(in millions)
$1,000
750
500
0
94 95 96

During 1995, the Company issued $89.2 of Swiss franc bonds and $71.7 of Luxembourg franc bonds, both of which were immediately swapped into U.S. dollar floating rate debt. In addition, $220.0 of medium-term notes were issued under the shelf registration filed in May 1994. Also in 1995, the Company obtained a $75.0 term note and filed a shelf registration for $700.0 of debt securities.

During 1994, the Company obtained a $50.0 term note and filed a shelf registration for $500.0 of debt securities, of which $208.0 medium-term notes were issued in that year.

The Company utilizes interest rate agreements and foreign exchange contracts to manage interest rate and foreign currency exposures. The principal objective of such financial derivative contracts is to moderate the effect of fluctuations in interest rates and foreign exchange rates. The Company, as a matter of policy, does not speculate in financial markets and therefore does not hold these contracts for trading purposes. The Company utilizes what are considered straightforward instruments, such as forward foreign exchange contracts and non-leveraged interest rate swaps, to accomplish its objectives. As of December 31, 1996, the Company had $925.9 notional amount of interest rate swaps outstanding converting floating rate debt to fixed rate debt and $285.0 of swaps outstanding converting fixed rate debt to floating.

The ratio of net debt to total capitalization (defined as the ratio of the book values of debt less cash and marketable securities ["net debt"] to net debt plus equity) decreased to 58% during 1996 from 64% in 1995. The decrease is primarily the result of higher Company earnings in 1996 as well as effective working capital management and lower acquisitions than in prior years. The ratio of market debt to market capitalization (defined as above using fair market values) decreased to 17% during 1996 from 23% in 1995. The Company primarily uses market value analyses to evaluate its optimal capitalization.

| | **1996** | 1995 | 1994 |
|---|---|---|---|
| **Capital Expenditures** | | | |
| Oral, Personal and Household Care | **$413.6** | $354.9 | $343.1 |
| Pet Nutrition and Other | **45.4** | 76.9 | 57.7 |
| **Total Capital Expenditures** | **$459.0** | $431.8 | $400.8 |
| **Depreciation and Amortization** | | | |
| Oral, Personal and Household Care | **$286.2** | $273.8 | $213.0 |
| Pet Nutrition and Other | **30.1** | 26.5 | 22.1 |
| **Total Depreciation and Amortization** | **$316.3** | $300.3 | $235.1 |

Capital expenditures were 5.2% of net sales in both 1996 and 1995 and were 5.3% of net sales in 1994. Capital spending continues to be focused primarily on projects that yield high aftertax returns, thereby reducing the Company's cost structure. Capital expenditures for 1997 are expected to continue at the current rate of approximately 5% of net sales.

Other investing activities in 1996, 1995 and 1994 included strategic acquisitions and equity investments worldwide. During 1996, the Company acquired the Profiden oral care business in Spain, the Seprod fabric care business in Jamaica and other regional brands in the Oral, Personal and Household Care segment. During 1995, the Company acquired Kolynos in Latin America and Odol oral care products in Argentina and made other regional investments. During 1994, the Company acquired the Cibaca toothbrush and toothpaste business in India and several other regional brands across the Oral, Personal and Household Care segment. The aggregate purchase price of all 1996, 1995 and 1994 acquisitions was $38.5, $1,321.9 and $149.8, respectively.

During 1994, the Company repurchased a significant amount of common shares in the open market and private transactions to provide for employee benefit plans and to maintain its targeted capital structure. Aggregate repurchases for the year approximated 6.9 million shares with a total purchase price of $411.1.

Dividend payments were $296.2 in 1996, up from $276.5 in 1995 and $246.9 in 1994. Common stock dividend payments increased to $1.88 per share in 1996 from $1.76 per share in 1995 and $1.54 in 1994. The Series B Preference Stock dividends were declared and paid at the stated rate of $4.88 per share in all three years.

Internally generated cash flows appear to be adequate to support currently planned business operations, acquisitions and capital expenditures. Significant acquisitions, such as the acquisition of Kolynos discussed previously, would require external financing.

The Company is a party to various superfund and other environmental matters and is contingently liable with respect to lawsuits, taxes and other matters arising out of the normal course of business. Management proactively reviews and manages its exposure to, and the impact of, environmental matters. While it is possible that the Company's cash flows and results of operations in particular quarterly or annual periods could be affected by the one-time impacts of the resolution of such contingencies, it is the opinion of management that the ultimate disposition of these matters, to the extent not previously provided for, will not have a material impact on the Company's financial condition or ongoing cash flows and results of operations.

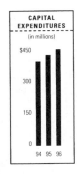

**CAPITAL EXPENDITURES**
(in millions)

94  95  96

## Outlook

Looking forward into 1997, the Company is well positioned for strong growth in developing markets, particularly Asia and Latin America. However, economic uncertainty in Venezuela and the pace of recovery in Mexico may continue to impact overall results from Latin America, and its projected growth may be tempered until these economies become more stable. In addition, in 1996, the antitrust regulatory authorities in Brazil approved the acquisition of Kolynos subject to certain conditions. The Company is currently negotiating undertakings related to those conditions with the Brazilian authorities. The undertakings, which the Company hopes to execute soon, are expected to include a commitment by the Company to suspend the Kolynos trademark on toothpaste sold in Brazil for four years. During this time, the Company will market an alternate brand of toothpaste. The Company will continue to use the Kolynos name in Brazil for other oral care products, such as toothbrushes, mouthwash and dental floss. The undertakings are also expected to require the Company to contract manufacture toothpaste on commercial terms for third parties in Brazil. Although management is confident Kolynos can successfully operate in Brazil within these conditions, there cannot, of course, be absolute assurance that the conditions will not have an adverse impact on the Company's performance in Brazil. The acquisition is discussed further in Notes 3 and 16 to the Consolidated Financial Statements. Competitive pressures in Western European markets are expected to persist as business in this region will continue to be affected by slow economic growth, high unemployment and retail trade consolidation. Movements in foreign currency exchange rates can also impact future operating results as measured in U.S. dollars. Effective January 1997, the Company changed the functional currency of its Mexican operations from the Mexican peso to the U.S. dollar. The effect of this change on future results of operations is not determinable. Savings from the 1995 worldwide restructuring began in the latter half of 1996 and are expected to reach $100.0 annually by 1998.

The Company expects the continued success of Colgate Total, using patented proprietary technology, to bolster worldwide oral care leadership and expects new products in all other categories to add potential for further growth. Overall, the global economic situation for 1997 is not expected to be materially different from that experienced in 1996 and the Company expects its positive momentum to continue. Historically, the consumer products industry has been less susceptible to changes in economic growth than many other industries, and therefore the Company constantly evaluates projects that will focus operations on opportunities for enhanced growth potential. Over the long term, Colgate's continued focus on its consumer products business and the strength of its global brand names, its broad international presence in both developed and developing markets, and its strong capital base all position the Company to take advantage of growth opportunities and to continue to increase profitability and shareholder value.

# Report of Management

The management of Colgate-Palmolive Company has prepared the accompanying consolidated financial statements and is responsible for their content as well as other information contained in this annual report. These financial statements have been prepared in accordance with generally accepted accounting principles and necessarily include amounts which are based on management's best estimates and judgments.

The Company maintains a system of internal accounting control designed to be cost-effective while providing reasonable assurance that assets are safeguarded and that transactions are executed in accordance with management's authorization and are properly recorded in the financial records. Internal control effectiveness is supported through written communication of policies and procedures, careful selection and training of personnel, and audits by a professional staff of internal auditors. The Company's control environment is further enhanced through a formal Code of Conduct which sets standards of professionalism and integrity for employees worldwide.

The Company has retained Arthur Andersen LLP, independent public accountants, to examine the financial statements. Their accompanying report is based on an examination conducted in accordance with generally accepted auditing standards, which includes a review of the Company's systems of internal control as well as tests of accounting records and procedures sufficient to enable them to render an opinion on the Company's financial statements.

The Audit Committee of the Board of Directors is composed entirely of non-employee directors. The Committee meets periodically and independently throughout the year with management, internal auditors and the independent accountants to discuss the Company's internal accounting controls, auditing and financial reporting matters. The internal auditors and independent accountants have unrestricted access to the Audit Committee.

Reuben Mark
Chairman and Chief Executive Officer

Stephen C. Patrick
Chief Financial Officer

# Report of Independent Public Accountants

To the Board of Directors and Shareholders of
Colgate-Palmolive Company:

We have audited the accompanying consolidated balance sheets of Colgate-Palmolive Company (a Delaware corporation) and subsidiaries as of December 31, 1996 and 1995, and the related consolidated statements of income, retained earnings, changes in capital accounts and cash flows for each of the three years in the period ended December 31, 1996. These financial statements are the responsibility of the Company's management. Our responsibility is to express an opinion on these financial statements based on our audits.

We conducted our audits in accordance with generally accepted auditing standards. Those standards require that we plan and perform the audit to obtain reasonable assurance about whether the financial statements are free of material misstatement. An audit includes examining, on a test basis, evidence supporting the amounts and disclosures in the financial statements. An audit also includes assessing the accounting principles used and significant estimates made by management, as well as evaluating the overall financial statement presentation. We believe that our audits provide a reasonable basis for our opinion.

In our opinion, the financial statements referred to above present fairly, in all material respects, the financial position of Colgate-Palmolive Company and subsidiaries as of December 31, 1996 and 1995, and the results of their operations and their cash flows for each of the three years in the period ended December 31, 1996, in conformity with generally accepted accounting principles.

Arthur Andersen LLP

New York, New York
March 6, 1997

23

# Consolidated Statements of Income

| Dollars in Millions Except Per Share Amounts | 1996 | 1995 | 1994 |
|---|---|---|---|
| Net sales | $8,749.0 | $8,358.2 | $7,587.9 |
| Cost of sales | 4,451.1 | 4,353.1 | 3,913.3 |
| Gross profit | 4,297.9 | 4,005.1 | 3,674.6 |
| Selling, general and administrative expenses | 3,052.1 | 2,879.6 | 2,625.2 |
| Provision for restructured operations | – | 460.5 | – |
| Other expense, net | 93.8 | 96.1 | 82.8 |
| Interest expense, net of interest income of $34.3, $30.6 and $34.2, respectively | 197.4 | 205.4 | 86.7 |
| Income before income taxes | 954.6 | 363.5 | 879.9 |
| Provision for income taxes | 319.6 | 191.5 | 299.7 |
| Net income | $ 635.0 | $ 172.0 | $ 580.2 |
| Earnings per common share, primary | $ 4.19 | $ 1.04 | $ 3.82 |
| Earnings per common share, assuming full dilution | $ 3.90 | $ 1.02 | $ 3.56 |

See Notes to Consolidated Financial Statements.

# Consolidated Balance Sheets

| Dollars in Millions Except Per Share Amounts | 1996 | 1995 |
|---|---|---|
| **Assets** | | |
| Current Assets | | |
| Cash and cash equivalents | $ 248.2 | $ 208.8 |
| Marketable securities | 59.6 | 47.8 |
| Receivables (less allowances of $33.8 and $31.9, respectively) | 1,064.4 | 1,116.9 |
| Inventories | 770.7 | 774.8 |
| Other current assets | 229.4 | 211.9 |
| Total current assets | 2,372.3 | 2,360.2 |
| Property, plant and equipment, net | 2,428.9 | 2,155.2 |
| Goodwill and other intangibles, net | 2,720.4 | 2,741.7 |
| Other assets | 379.9 | 385.2 |
| | $ 7,901.5 | $ 7,642.3 |
| **Liabilities and Shareholders' Equity** | | |
| Current Liabilities | | |
| Notes and loans payable | $ 172.3 | $ 204.4 |
| Current portion of long-term debt | 110.4 | 37.0 |
| Accounts payable | 751.7 | 738.7 |
| Accrued income taxes | 93.1 | 76.7 |
| Other accruals | 776.8 | 696.3 |
| Total current liabilities | 1,904.3 | 1,753.1 |
| Long-term debt | 2,786.8 | 2,992.0 |
| Deferred income taxes | 234.3 | 237.3 |
| Other liabilities | 942.0 | 980.1 |
| Shareholders' Equity | | |
| Preferred stock | 392.7 | 403.5 |
| Common stock, $1 par value (500,000,000 shares | | |
| authorized, 183,213,295 shares issued) | 183.2 | 183.2 |
| Additional paid-in capital | 1,101.6 | 1,033.7 |
| Retained earnings | 2,731.0 | 2,392.2 |
| Cumulative translation adjustments | (534.7) | (513.0) |
| | 3,873.8 | 3,499.6 |
| Unearned compensation | (370.9) | (378.0) |
| Treasury stock, at cost | (1,468.8) | (1,441.8) |
| Total shareholders' equity | 2,034.1 | 1,679.8 |
| | $ 7,901.5 | $ 7,642.3 |

See Notes to Consolidated Financial Statements.

# Consolidated Statements of Retained Earnings

| Dollars in Millions | 1996 | 1995 | 1994 |
|---|---|---|---|
| Balance, January 1 | $2,392.2 | $2,496.7 | $2,163.4 |
| Add: | | | |
| Net income | 635.0 | 172.0 | 580.2 |
| | 3,027.2 | 2,668.7 | 2,743.6 |
| Deduct: | | | |
| Dividends declared: | | | |
| Series B Convertible Preference Stock, net of income taxes | 20.9 | 21.1 | 21.1 |
| Preferred stock | .5 | .5 | .5 |
| Common stock | 274.8 | 254.9 | 225.3 |
| | 296.2 | 276.5 | 246.9 |
| Balance, December 31 | $2,731.0 | $2,392.2 | $2,496.7 |

# Consolidated Statements of Changes in Capital Accounts

| Dollars in Millions | Common Stock | | Additional Paid-In Capital | Treasury Stock | |
|---|---|---|---|---|---|
| | Shares | Amount | | Shares | Amount |
| Balance, January 1, 1994 | 149,256,603 | $183.2 | $1,000.9 | 33,956,692 | $1,124.0 |
| Shares issued for stock options | 1,803,574 | – | 1.6 | (1,803,574) | (63.4) |
| Treasury stock acquired | (6,923,325) | – | – | 6,923,325 | 411.1 |
| Other | 267,385 | – | 17.9 | (267,385) | (9.3) |
| Balance, December 31, 1994 | 144,404,237 | 183.2 | 1,020.4 | 38,809,058 | 1,462.4 |
| Shares issued for stock options | 2,252,955 | – | 13.7 | (2,252,955) | (85.5) |
| Treasury stock acquired | (1,117,099) | – | – | 1,117,099 | 77.7 |
| Other | 313,779 | – | (.4) | (313,779) | (12.8) |
| Balance, December 31, 1995 | 145,853,872 | 183.2 | 1,033.7 | 37,359,423 | 1,441.8 |
| Shares issued for stock options | 2,557,282 | – | 44.4 | (2,557,282) | (100.5) |
| Treasury stock acquired | (1,798,574) | – | – | 1,798,574 | 149.9 |
| Other | 521,238 | – | 23.5 | (521,238) | (22.4) |
| **Balance, December 31, 1996** | **147,133,818** | **$183.2** | **$1,101.6** | **36,079,477** | **$1,468.8** |

See Notes to Consolidated Financial Statements.

# Consolidated Statements of Cash Flows

| Dollars in Millions | 1996 | 1995 | 1994 |
|---|---|---|---|
| **Operating Activities** | | | |
| Net income | $ **635.0** | $ 172.0 | $ 580.2 |
| Adjustments to reconcile net income to net cash provided by operations: | | | |
| Restructured operations, net | **(105.6)** | 424.9 | (39.1) |
| Depreciation and amortization | **316.3** | 300.3 | 235.1 |
| Deferred income taxes and other, net | **(23.0)** | (62.9) | 64.7 |
| Cash effects of changes in: | | | |
| Receivables | **(15.4)** | (44.1) | (50.1) |
| Inventories | **(1.2)** | (26.1) | (44.5) |
| Other current assets | **–** | (42.4) | (7.8) |
| Payables and accruals | **111.3** | 88.5 | 90.9 |
| Net cash provided by operations | **917.4** | 810.2 | 829.4 |
| **Investing Activities** | | | |
| Capital expenditures | **(459.0)** | (431.8) | (400.8) |
| Payment for acquisitions, net of cash acquired | **(59.3)** | (1,300.4) | (146.4) |
| Sale of marketable securities and other investments | **26.3** | 6.2 | 58.4 |
| Other, net | **(12.0)** | (17.2) | 31.1 |
| Net cash used for investing activities | **(504.0)** | (1,743.2) | (457.7) |
| **Financing Activities** | | | |
| Principal payments on debt | **(1,164.6)** | (17.1) | (88.3) |
| Proceeds from issuance of debt, net | **1,077.4** | 1,220.0 | 316.4 |
| Proceeds from outside investors | **8.5** | 30.5 | 15.2 |
| Dividends paid | **(296.2)** | (276.5) | (246.9) |
| Purchase of common stock | **(27.4)** | (9.0) | (357.9) |
| Proceeds from exercise of stock options and other, net | **30.7** | 28.3 | 18.5 |
| Net cash (used for) provided by financing activities | **(371.6)** | 976.2 | (343.0) |
| Effect of exchange rate changes on cash and cash equivalents | **(2.4)** | (4.3) | (2.9) |
| Net increase in cash and cash equivalents | **39.4** | 38.9 | 25.8 |
| Cash and cash equivalents at beginning of year | **208.8** | 169.9 | 144.1 |
| Cash and cash equivalents at end of year | $ **248.2** | $ 208.8 | $ 169.9 |
| **Supplemental Cash Flow Information** | | | |
| Income taxes paid | $ **253.7** | $ 292.5 | $ 261.1 |
| Interest paid | **229.1** | 228.6 | 96.9 |
| Non-cash consideration in payment for acquisitions | **–** | 48.9 | 8.0 |
| Principal payments on ESOP debt, guaranteed by the Company | **(5.0)** | (4.4) | (4.0) |

See Notes to Consolidated Financial Statements.

# Notes to Consolidated Financial Statements

*Dollars in Millions Except Per Share Amounts*

## 1. NATURE OF OPERATIONS

The Company manufactures and markets a wide variety of products in the U.S. and around the world in two distinct business segments: Oral, Personal and Household Care, and Pet Nutrition. Oral, Personal and Household Care products include toothpastes, oral rinses and toothbrushes, bar and liquid soaps, shampoos, conditioners, deodorants and antiperspirants, baby and shave products, laundry and dishwashing detergents, fabric softeners, cleansers and cleaners, bleaches and other similar items. These products are sold primarily to wholesale and retail distributors worldwide. Pet Nutrition products include pet food products manufactured and marketed by Hill's Pet Nutrition. The principal customers for Pet Nutrition products are veterinarians and specialty pet retailers. Principal global trademarks include Colgate, Palmolive, Mennen, Kolynos, Protex, Ajax, Soupline/Suavitel, Fab, Science Diet and Prescription Diet in addition to various regional trademarks.

The Company's principal classes of products accounted for the following percentages of worldwide sales for the past three years:

|  | 1996 | 1995 | 1994 |
| --- | --- | --- | --- |
| Oral Care | **30%** | 30% | 26% |
| Personal Care | **22** | 22 | 24 |
| Household Surface Care | **16** | 16 | 17 |
| Fabric Care | **18** | 18 | 18 |
| Pet Nutrition | **10** | 9 | 11 |

Company products are marketed under highly competitive conditions. Products similar to those produced and sold by the Company are available from competitors in the U.S. and overseas. Product quality, brand recognition and acceptance, and marketing capability largely determine success in the Company's business segments. The financial and descriptive information on the Company's geographic area and industry segment data, appearing in the tables contained in management's discussion, is an integral part of these financial statements. More than half of the Company's net sales, operating profit and identifiable assets are attributable to overseas operations. Transfers between geographic areas are not significant.

The Company's products are generally marketed by a sales force employed by each individual subsidiary or business unit. In some instances, distributors and brokers are used. Most raw materials used worldwide are purchased from others, are available from several sources and are generally available in adequate supply. Products and commodities such as tallow and essential oils are subject to wide price variations. No one of the Company's raw materials represents a significant portion of total material requirements.

Trademarks are considered to be of material importance to the Company's business; consequently, the practice is followed of seeking trademark protection by all available means. Although the Company owns a number of patents, no one patent is considered significant to the business taken as a whole.

## 2. SUMMARY OF SIGNIFICANT ACCOUNTING POLICIES

*Principles of Consolidation*
The Consolidated Financial Statements include the accounts of Colgate-Palmolive Company and its majority-owned subsidiaries. Intercompany transactions and balances have been eliminated. Investments in companies in which the Company's interest is between 20% and 50% are accounted for using the equity method. The Company's share of the net income from such investments is recorded as equity earnings and is classified as other expense, net in the Consolidated Statements of Income.

*Revenue Recognition*
Sales are recorded at the time products are shipped to trade customers. Net sales reflect units shipped at selling list prices reduced by promotion allowances.

*Accounting Estimates*
The preparation of financial statements in conformity with generally accepted accounting principles requires management to make estimates and assumptions that affect the reported amounts of assets and liabilities and disclosure of contingent gains and losses at the date of the financial statements and the reported amounts of revenues and expenses during the reporting period. Actual results could differ from those estimates.

*Cash and Cash Equivalents*
The Company considers all highly liquid investments with maturities of three months or less when purchased to be cash equivalents. Investments in short-term securities that do not meet the definition of cash equivalents are classified as marketable securities. Marketable securities are reported at cost, which equals market.

*Inventories*
Inventories are valued at the lower of cost or market. The last-in, first-out (LIFO) method is used to value substantially all inventories in the U.S. as well as in certain overseas locations. The remaining inventories are valued using the first-in, first-out (FIFO) method.

28

### Property, Plant and Equipment

Land, buildings, and machinery and equipment are stated at cost. Depreciation is provided, primarily using the straight-line method, over estimated useful lives ranging from 3 to 40 years.

### Goodwill and Other Intangibles

Goodwill represents the excess of purchase price over the fair value of identifiable tangible and intangible net assets of businesses acquired. Goodwill and other intangibles are amortized on a straight-line basis over periods not exceeding 40 years. The recoverability of carrying values of intangible assets is evaluated on a recurring basis. The primary indicators of recoverability are current and forecasted profitability of a related acquired business. For the three-year period ended December 31, 1996, there were no material adjustments to the carrying values of intangible assets resulting from these evaluations.

### Income Taxes

Deferred taxes are recognized for the expected future tax consequences of temporary differences between the amounts carried for financial reporting and tax purposes. Provision is made currently for taxes payable on remittances of overseas earnings; no provision is made for taxes on overseas retained earnings that are deemed to be permanently reinvested.

### Postretirement and Postemployment Benefits

The cost of postretirement health care and other benefits is actuarially determined and accrued over the service period of covered employees.

### Translation of Overseas Currencies

The assets and liabilities of subsidiaries, other than those operating in highly inflationary environments, are translated into U.S. dollars at year-end exchange rates, with resulting translation gains and losses accumulated in a separate component of shareholders' equity. Income and expense items are converted into U.S. dollars at average rates of exchange prevailing during the year.

For subsidiaries operating in highly inflationary environments, inventories, goodwill, and property, plant and equipment are translated at the rate of exchange on the date the assets were acquired, while other assets and liabilities are translated at year-end exchange rates. Translation adjustments for these operations are included in net income.

### Geographic Areas and Industry Segments

The financial and descriptive information on the Company's geographic area and industry segment data, appearing in the tables contained in management's discussion of this report, is an integral part of these financial statements.

### 3. ACQUISITIONS

During 1996, the Company acquired the Profiden oral care business in Spain, the Seprod fabric care business in Jamaica as well as other regional brands in the Oral, Personal and Household Care segment. The Company also expanded its investment in the Pet Nutrition segment in the Netherlands. The aggregate purchase price of all 1996 acquisitions was $38.5.

On January 10, 1995, the Company acquired the worldwide Kolynos oral care business ("Kolynos") for $1,040.0. Kolynos is an oral care business operating primarily in South America. The transaction was structured as a multinational acquisition of assets and stock and was accounted for under the purchase method of accounting. The net book value of Kolynos assets was approximately $50.0. As further described in Note 16, during 1996, the antitrust regulatory authorities in Brazil approved the acquisition subject to certain conditions.

The following unaudited pro forma summary combines the results of the operations of the Company and Kolynos as if the acquisition had occurred as of the beginning of 1994 after giving effect to certain adjustments, including amortization of goodwill, increased interest expense on the acquisition debt incurred and the related income tax effects.

Summarized Pro Forma Combined Results of Operations
For the Year Ended December 31, 1994

| | |
|---|---|
| Net sales | $7,864.0 |
| Income before income taxes | 835.4 |
| Net income | 550.9 |
| Primary earnings per common share | 3.62 |
| Fully diluted earnings per common share | 3.38 |

The pro forma financial information is not necessarily indicative of either the results of operations that would have occurred had the Company and Kolynos actually been combined during the year ended December 31, 1994, or the future results of operations of the combined companies. There are certain other benefits that are anticipated to be realized from the implementation of the Company's integration plans which are not included in the pro forma information.

In addition, during 1995, the Company acquired the Odol oral care business in Argentina, the Barbados Cosmetic Products business in the Caribbean as well as other regional brands in the Oral, Personal and Household Care segment. The aggregate purchase price of all 1995 acquisitions was $1,321.9.

During 1994, the Company acquired the Cibaca toothpaste and toothbrush business in India, the NSOA laundry soap business in Senegal as well as several other regional brands in the Oral, Personal and Household Care segment. The aggregate purchase price of all 1994 acquisitions was $149.8.

All of these acquisitions have been accounted for as purchases, and, accordingly, the purchase prices were allocated to the net tangible and intangible assets acquired based on estimated fair values at the dates of the respective acquisitions. The results of operations have been included in the Consolidated Financial Statements since the respective acquisition dates. The inclusion of pro forma financial data for all acquisitions except Kolynos prior to the dates of acquisition would not have materially affected reported results.

### 4. LONG-TERM DEBT AND CREDIT FACILITIES

Long-term debt consists of the following at December 31:

| | Weighted Average Interest Rate | Maturities | 1996 | 1995 |
|---|---|---|---|---|
| Notes | 7.3% | 1997-2025 | **$1,292.9** | $1,149.2 |
| ESOP notes, guaranteed by the Company | 8.6 | 2001-2009 | **385.2** | 390.2 |
| Payable to banks | 5.5 | 2000-2003 | **836.0** | 101.8 |
| Commercial paper and other short-term borrowings, reclassified | 5.1 | 1997 | **375.1** | 1,378.2 |
| Capitalized leases | | | **8.0** | 9.6 |
| | | | **2,897.2** | 3,029.0 |
| Less: current portion of long-term debt | | | **110.4** | 37.0 |
| | | | **$2,786.8** | $2,992.0 |

Commercial paper and certain other short-term borrowings are classified as long-term debt as it is the Company's intent and ability to refinance such obligations on a long-term basis. Scheduled maturities of debt outstanding at December 31, 1996, excluding short-term borrowings reclassified, are as follows: 1997–$110.4; 1998–$184.9; 1999–$167.1; 2000–$339.6; 2001–$97.6, and $1,622.5 thereafter. The Company has entered into interest rate swap agreements and foreign exchange contracts related to certain of these debt instruments (see Note 12).

At December 31, 1996, the Company had unused credit facilities amounting to $1,785.7. Commitment fees related to credit facilities are not material. The weighted average interest rate on short-term borrowings, excluding amounts reclassified, as of December 31, 1996 and 1995 was 7.5% and 8.3%, respectively.

The Company's long-term debt agreements include various restrictive covenants and require the maintenance of certain defined financial ratios with which the Company is in compliance.

### 5. CAPITAL STOCK AND STOCK COMPENSATION PLANS

*Preferred Stock*

Preferred Stock consists of 250,000 authorized shares without par value. It is issuable in series, of which one series of 125,000 shares, designated $4.25 Preferred Stock, with a stated and redeemable value of $100 per share, has been issued and is outstanding. The $4.25 Preferred Stock is redeemable only at the option of the Company.

*Preference Stock*

In 1988, the Company authorized the issuance of 50,000,000 shares of Preference Stock, without par value. The Series B Convertible Preference Stock, which is convertible into two shares of common stock, ranks junior to all series of the Preferred Stock. At December 31, 1996 and 1995, 5,849,039 and 6,014,615 shares of Series B Convertible Preference Stock, respectively, were outstanding and issued to the Company's ESOP.

*Shareholder Rights Plan*

Under the Company's Shareholder Rights Plan, each share of the Company's common stock carries with it one Preference Share Purchase Right ("Rights"). The Rights themselves will at no time have voting power or pay dividends. The Rights become exercisable only if a person or group acquires 20% or more of the Company's common stock or announces a tender offer, the consummation of which would result in ownership by a person or group of 20% or more of the common stock. When exercisable, each Right entitles a holder to buy one two-hundredth of a share of a new series of preference stock at an exercise price of $87.50.

If the Company is acquired in a merger or other business combination, each Right will entitle a holder to buy, at the Right's then current exercise price, a number of the acquiring company's common shares having a market value of twice such price. In addition, if a person or group acquires 30% or more of the Company's common stock, other than pursuant to a cash tender offer for all shares in which such person or group increases its stake from below 20% to 80% or more of the outstanding shares, each Right will entitle its holder (other than such person or members of such group) to purchase, at the Right's then current exercise price, a number of shares of the Company's common stock having a market value of twice the Right's exercise price.

Further, at any time after a person or group acquires 30% or more (but less than 50%) of the Company's common stock, the Board of Directors may, at its option, exchange part or all of the Rights (other than Rights held by the acquiring person or group) for shares of the Company's common stock on a one-for-one basis.

The Company, at the option of its Board of Directors, may redeem the Rights for $.005 at any time before the acquisition by a person or group of beneficial ownership of 20% or more of its common stock. The Board of Directors is also authorized to reduce the 20% and 30% thresholds to not less than 15%. Unless redeemed earlier, the Rights will expire on October 24, 1998.

*Incentive Stock Plan*

The Company has a plan which provides for grants of restricted stock awards for officers and other executives of the Company and its major subsidiaries. A committee of non-employee members of the Board of Directors administers the plan. During 1996 and 1995, 126,229 and 237,019 shares, respectively, were awarded to employees in accordance with the provisions of the plan.

*Stock Option Plans*

The Company's 1987 and 1996 Stock Option Plans ("Plans") provide for the issuance of non-qualified stock options to officers and key employees. Options are granted at prices not less than the fair market value on the date of grant. At December 31, 1996, 811,843 shares of common stock were available for future grants.

The Plans contain an accelerated ownership feature which provides for the grant of new options when previously owned shares of Company stock are used to exercise existing options. The number of new options granted under this feature is equal to the number of shares of previously owned Company stock used to exercise the original options and to pay the related required U.S. income tax. The new options are granted at a price equal to the fair market value on the date of the new grant and have the same expiration date as the original options exercised.

Stock option plan activity is summarized below:

| | 1996 Shares | Weighted Average Exercise Price | 1995 Shares | Weighted Average Exercise Price |
|---|---|---|---|---|
| Options outstanding, January 1 | 10,495,895 | $57 | 10,261,408 | $51 |
| Granted | 2,854,611 | 82 | 2,581,173 | 69 |
| Exercised | (2,557,282) | 57 | (2,252,955) | 44 |
| Canceled or expired | (85,625) | 61 | (93,731) | 53 |
| Options outstanding, December 31 | 10,707,599 | 64 | 10,495,895 | 57 |
| Options exercisable, December 31 | 6,991,922 | 58 | 6,770,039 | 53 |

The following table summarizes information relating to currently outstanding and exercisable options as of December 31, 1996:

| Range of Exercise Prices | Weighted Average Remaining Contractual Life In Years | Options Outstanding | Weighted Average Exercise Price | Options Exercisable | Weighted Average Exercise Price |
|---|---|---|---|---|---|
| $19.53-$52.13 | 4 | 2,385,707 | $39 | 2,385,707 | $39 |
| $52.38-$60.98 | 6 | 2,408,409 | 57 | 1,934,196 | 57 |
| $61.00-$72.07 | 7 | 2,450,844 | 68 | 1,434,389 | 67 |
| $72.31-$87.06 | 8 | 2,431,654 | 80 | 737,630 | 78 |
| $87.25-$99.79 | 5 | 1,030,985 | 94 | 500,000 | 98 |
| | 6 | 10,707,599 | 64 | 6,991,922 | 58 |

The Company applies Accounting Principles Board Opinion No. 25, "Accounting for Stock Issued to Employees," and related interpretations in accounting for options granted under the Plan. Accordingly, no compensation expense has been recognized. Had compensation expense been determined based on the Black-Scholes option pricing model value at the grant date for awards in 1996 and 1995 consistent with the provisions of Statement of Financial Accounting Standards No. 123, "Accounting for Stock-Based Compensation" (SFAS 123), the Company's net income, primary earnings per common share and fully diluted earnings per common share would have been $621.7, $4.09 per share and $3.82 per share, respectively, in 1996 and $166.1, $1.00 per share and $.98 per share, respectively, in 1995. The SFAS 123 method of accounting has not been applied to options granted prior to January 1, 1995, and the resulting pro forma compensation expense may not be indicative of pro forma expense in future years.

The weighted average Black-Scholes value of grants issued in 1996 and 1995 was $10.81 and $9.45, respectively. The Black-Scholes value of each option granted is estimated using the Black-Scholes option pricing model with the following assumptions: option term until exercise ranging from 2 to 4 years, volatility ranging from 17% to 18%, risk-free interest rate ranging from 5.8% to 6.4% and an expected dividend yield of 2.5%. The Black-Scholes model used by the Company to calculate option values was developed to estimate the fair value of short-term freely tradable, fully transferable options without vesting restrictions and was not designed to value reloads, all of which significantly differ from the Company's stock option awards. The value of this model is also limited by the inclusion of highly subjective assumptions which greatly affect calculated values.

### 6. EMPLOYEE STOCK OWNERSHIP PLAN

In 1989, the Company expanded its employee stock ownership plan (ESOP) through the introduction of a leveraged ESOP covering certain employees who have met certain eligibility requirements. The ESOP issued $410.0 of long-term notes due through 2009 bearing an average interest rate of 8.6%. The long-term notes, which are guaranteed by the Company, are reflected in the accompanying Consolidated Balance Sheets. The ESOP used the proceeds of the notes to purchase 6.3 million shares of Series B Convertible Preference Stock from the Company. The Stock has a minimum redemption price of $65 per share and pays semiannual dividends equal to the higher of $2.44 or the current dividend paid on two common shares for the comparable six-month period. Each share may be converted by the Trustee into two shares of common stock.

Dividends on these preferred shares, as well as common shares also held by the ESOP, are paid to the ESOP trust and, together with contributions, are used by the ESOP to repay principal and interest on the outstanding notes. Preferred shares are released for allocation to participants based upon the ratio of the current year's debt service to the sum of total principal and interest payments over the life of the loan. At December 31, 1996, 1,275,380 shares were allocated to participant accounts.

Dividends on these preferred shares are deductible for income tax purposes and, accordingly, are reflected net of their tax benefit in the Consolidated Statements of Retained Earnings.

Annual expense related to the leveraged ESOP, determined as interest incurred on the notes, less employee contributions and dividends received on the shares held by the ESOP, plus the higher of either principal repayments on the notes or the cost of shares allocated, was $3.9 in 1996, $8.3 in 1995 and $8.0 in 1994. Similarly, unearned compensation, shown as a reduction in shareholders' equity, is reduced by the higher of principal payments or the cost of shares allocated.

Interest incurred on the ESOP's notes amounted to $33.5 in 1996, $33.9 in 1995 and $34.2 in 1994. The Company paid dividends on the stock held by the ESOP of $31.1 in 1996, $31.7 in 1995 and $32.3 in 1994. Company contributions to the ESOP were $4.1 in 1996, $6.4 in 1995 and $5.7 in 1994. Employee contributions to the ESOP were $5.9 in 1996 and $0 in 1995 and 1994.

### 7. RETIREMENT PLANS AND OTHER POSTRETIREMENT BENEFITS

*Retirement Plans*

The Company, its U.S. subsidiaries and a majority of its overseas subsidiaries maintain pension plans covering substantially all of their employees. Most plans provide pension benefits that are based primarily on years of service and employees' career earnings. In the Company's principal U.S. plans, funds are contributed to trustees in accordance with regulatory limits to provide for current service and for any unfunded projected benefit obligation over a reasonable period. To the extent these requirements are exceeded by plan assets, a contribution may not be made in a particular year. Plan assets consist principally of common stocks, guaranteed investment contracts with insurance companies, investments in real estate funds and U.S. Government obligations.

Net periodic pension expense of the plans includes the following components:

| | 1996 U.S. | 1996 Overseas | 1995 U.S. | 1995 Overseas | 1994 U.S. | 1994 Overseas |
|---|---|---|---|---|---|---|
| Service cost—benefits earned during the period | $ 24.5 | $ 15.1 | $ 19.1 | $ 15.4 | $ 23.1 | $ 17.9 |
| Interest cost on projected benefit obligation | 64.4 | 17.5 | 64.5 | 16.8 | 63.1 | 15.3 |
| Actual return on plan assets | (96.9) | (13.6) | (134.7) | (13.0) | (3.1) | (2.2) |
| Net amortization and deferral | 26.1 | 4.0 | 61.5 | 4.7 | (69.1) | (7.0) |
| Net pension expense | $ 18.1 | $ 23.0 | $ 10.4 | $ 23.9 | $ 14.0 | $ 24.0 |

The following table sets forth the funded status of the plans at December 31:

| | 1996 U.S. | 1996 Overseas | 1995 U.S. | 1995 Overseas |
|---|---|---|---|---|
| Plan assets at fair value | $842.8 | $ 171.2 | $ 817.5 | $ 157.2 |
| Actuarial present value of benefit obligations: | | | | |
| Vested obligation | 836.2 | 219.2 | 806.5 | 223.5 |
| Nonvested obligation | 41.1 | 16.5 | 57.7 | 23.5 |
| Accumulated benefit obligation | 877.3 | 235.7 | 864.2 | 247.0 |
| Additional benefits related to assumed future compensation levels | 48.4 | 36.2 | 58.1 | 37.2 |
| Projected benefit obligation | 925.7 | 271.9 | 922.3 | 284.2 |
| Plan assets less than projected benefit obligation | (82.9) | (100.7) | (104.8) | (127.0) |
| Deferral of net actuarial changes and other, net | 75.9 | 4.9 | 161.4 | 6.7 |
| Unrecognized prior service cost | 50.9 | 4.2 | 21.1 | 2.1 |
| Unrecognized transition asset | (21.6) | (4.2) | (28.3) | (3.6) |
| Additional liability | – | (1.2) | – | (.2) |
| Prepaid (accrued) pension cost recognized in the Consolidated Balance Sheets | $ 22.3 | $ (97.0) | $ 49.4 | $(122.0) |

The actuarial assumptions used to determine the projected benefit obligation of the plans were as follows:

| | U.S. 1996 | U.S. 1995 | U.S. 1994 | Overseas (weighted average) 1996 | Overseas (weighted average) 1995 | Overseas (weighted average) 1994 |
|---|---|---|---|---|---|---|
| Settlement rates | 7.50% | 7.00% | 8.75% | 8.23% | 8.46% | 8.38% |
| Long-term rates of compensation increase | 5.50 | 5.50 | 5.75 | 5.38 | 5.47 | 5.53 |
| Long-term rates of return on plan assets | 9.25 | 9.25 | 9.25 | 10.91 | 10.50 | 10.88 |

When remeasuring the pension obligation, the Company reassesses each actuarial assumption. The settlement rate assumption is pegged to long-term bond rates to reflect the cost to satisfy the pension obligation currently, while the other assumptions reflect the long-term outlook of rates of compensation increases and return on assets.

*Other Postretirement Benefits*

The Company and certain of its subsidiaries provide health care and life insurance benefits for retired employees to the extent not provided by government-sponsored plans. The Company utilizes a portion of its leveraged ESOP, in the form of future retiree contributions, to reduce its obligation to provide these postretirement benefits. Postretirement benefits currently are not funded.

Postretirement benefits expense includes the following components:

| | 1996 | 1995 | 1994 |
|---|---|---|---|
| Service cost–benefits earned during the period | $ 1.7 | $ 1.9 | $ 2.2 |
| Annual ESOP allocation | (5.0) | (4.2) | (5.7) |
| Interest cost on accumulated postretirement benefit obligation | 12.6 | 13.7 | 14.2 |
| Amortization of unrecognized net gain | (2.2) | (3.4) | (.1) |
| Net postretirement expense | $ 7.1 | $ 8.0 | $10.6 |

The actuarial present value of postretirement benefit obligations included in Other liabilities in the Consolidated Balance Sheets is comprised of the following components, at December 31:

| | 1996 | 1995 |
|---|---|---|
| Retirees | $144.8 | $145.2 |
| Active participants eligible for retirement | 1.0 | 2.0 |
| Other active participants | 6.9 | 9.2 |
| Accumulated postretirement benefit obligation | 152.7 | 156.4 |
| Unrecognized net gain | 43.8 | 44.4 |
| Accrued postretirement benefit liability | $196.5 | $200.8 |

The principal actuarial assumptions used in the measurement of the accumulated benefit obligation were as follows:

| | 1996 | 1995 | 1994 |
|---|---|---|---|
| Discount rate | 7.50% | 7.00% | 8.75% |
| Current medical cost trend rate | 6.50 | 8.00 | 10.00 |
| Ultimate medical cost trend rate | 5.00 | 5.00 | 6.25 |
| Medical cost trend rate decreases ratably to ultimate in year | 1999 | 1999 | 2001 |
| ESOP growth rate | 10.00% | 10.00% | 10.00% |

When remeasuring the accumulated benefit obligation, the Company reassesses each actuarial assumption.

The cost of these postretirement medical benefits is dependent upon a number of factors, the most significant of which is the rate at which medical costs increase in the future. The effect of a 1% increase in the assumed medical cost trend rate would increase the accumulated postretirement benefit obligation by approximately $14.8; annual expense would not be materially affected.

## 8. INCOME TAXES

The provision for income taxes consists of the following for the years ended December 31:

| | 1996 | 1995 | 1994 |
|---|---|---|---|
| United States | $ 67.2 | $ 18.0 | $ 43.3 |
| Overseas | 252.4 | 173.5 | 256.4 |
| | $319.6 | $191.5 | $299.7 |

Differences between accounting for financial statement purposes and accounting for tax purposes result in taxes currently payable being (lower) higher than the total provision for income taxes as follows:

| | 1996 | 1995 | 1994 |
|---|---|---|---|
| Excess of tax over book depreciation | $(15.9) | $(18.9) | $(32.8) |
| Net restructuring (spending) accrual | (26.3) | 70.5 | (19.0) |
| Other, net | 21.5 | (5.3) | 5.6 |
| | $(20.7) | $ 46.3 | $(46.2) |

The components of income before income taxes are as follows for the three years ended December 31:

| | 1996 | 1995 | 1994 |
|---|---|---|---|
| United States | $171.3 | $(121.1) | $181.8 |
| Overseas | 783.3 | 484.6 | 698.1 |
| | $954.6 | $ 363.5 | $879.9 |

The difference between the statutory United States federal income tax rate and the Company's global effective tax rate as reflected in the Consolidated Statements of Income is as follows:

| Percentage of Income Before Tax | 1996 | 1995 | 1994 |
|---|---|---|---|
| Tax at U.S. statutory rate | 35.0% | 35.0% | 35.0% |
| State income taxes, net of federal benefit | .3 | .6 | .6 |
| Earnings taxed at other than U.S. statutory rate | (1.4) | (.4) | (.3) |
| Restructured operations | – | 18.4 | – |
| Other, net | (.4) | (.9) | (1.2) |
| Effective tax rate | 33.5% | 52.7% | 34.1% |

In addition, net tax benefits of $28.9 in 1996 and $6.8 in 1995 were recorded directly through equity.

The components of deferred tax assets (liabilities) are as follows at December 31:

| | 1996 | 1995 |
|---|---|---|
| Deferred Taxes–Current: | | |
| Accrued liabilities | $ 63.7 | $ 64.1 |
| Restructuring | 24.5 | 20.0 |
| Other, net | 28.2 | 13.9 |
| Total deferred taxes current | 116.4 | 98.0 |
| Deferred Taxes–Long-term: | | |
| Intangible assets | (212.9) | (212.2) |
| Property, plant and equipment | (175.7) | (215.9) |
| Postretirement benefits | 73.1 | 73.1 |
| Restructuring | 50.7 | 141.1 |
| Tax loss and tax credit carryforwards | 116.3 | 124.8 |
| Other, net | 29.1 | (30.0) |
| Valuation allowance | (114.9) | (118.2) |
| Total deferred taxes long-term | (234.3) | (237.3) |
| Net deferred taxes | $(117.9) | $(139.3) |

The major component of the 1996 and 1995 valuation allowance relates to tax benefits in certain jurisdictions not expected to be realized.

## 9. FOREIGN CURRENCY TRANSLATION

Cumulative translation adjustments, which represent the effect of translating assets and liabilities of the Company's non-U.S. entities, except those in highly inflationary economies, were as follows:

| | 1996 | 1995 | 1994 |
|---|---|---|---|
| Balance, January 1 | $(513.0) | $(439.3) | $(372.9) |
| Effect of balance sheet translations | (21.7) | (73.7) | (66.4) |
| Balance, December 31 | $(534.7) | $(513.0) | $(439.3) |

Foreign currency charges, resulting from the translation of balance sheets of subsidiaries operating in highly inflationary environments and from foreign currency transactions, are included in the Consolidated Statements of Income.

## 10. EARNINGS PER SHARE

Primary earnings per share are determined by dividing net income, after deducting preferred stock dividends net of related tax benefits ($21.4 in 1996, $21.6 in 1995 and 1994), by the weighted average number of common shares outstanding (146.6 million in 1996, 145.2 million in 1995 and 146.2 million in 1994).

Earnings per common share assuming full dilution are calculated assuming the conversion of all potentially dilutive securities, including convertible preferred stock and outstanding options, unless the effect of such conversion is antidilutive. This calculation also assumes reduction of available income by pro forma ESOP replacement funding, net of income taxes.

## 11. INCOME STATEMENT INFORMATION

Other expense, net consists of the following for the years ended December 31:

| | 1996 | 1995 | 1994 |
|---|---|---|---|
| Amortization of intangibles | $ 91.7 | $ 87.7 | $ 56.3 |
| Earnings from equity investments | (7.8) | (7.3) | (1.3) |
| Minority interest | 33.4 | 37.1 | 37.8 |
| Other | (23.5) | (21.4) | (10.0) |
| | $ 93.8 | $ 96.1 | $ 82.8 |

The following is a comparative summary of certain expense information for the years ended December 31:

| | 1996 | 1995 | 1994 |
|---|---|---|---|
| Interest incurred | $244.4 | $250.7 | $130.6 |
| Interest capitalized | 12.7 | 14.7 | 9.7 |
| Interest expense | $231.7 | $236.0 | $120.9 |
| Research and development | $162.7 | $156.7 | $147.1 |
| Maintenance and repairs | 107.1 | 108.2 | 110.1 |
| Media advertising | 565.9 | 561.3 | 543.2 |

## 12. BALANCE SHEET INFORMATION

Supplemental balance sheet information is as follows:

| Inventories | 1996 | 1995 |
|---|---|---|
| Raw materials and supplies | $311.5 | $313.8 |
| Work-in-process | 34.3 | 38.3 |
| Finished goods | 424.9 | 422.7 |
| | $770.7 | $774.8 |

Inventories valued under LIFO amounted to $203.7 at December 31, 1996 and $207.2 at December 31, 1995. The excess of current cost over LIFO cost at the end of each year was $52.6 and $42.9, respectively.

| Property, Plant and Equipment, Net | 1996 | 1995 |
|---|---|---|
| Land | $ 126.4 | $ 126.0 |
| Buildings | 655.9 | 623.1 |
| Machinery and equipment | 3,048.5 | 2,850.3 |
| | 3,830.8 | 3,599.4 |
| Accumulated depreciation | (1,401.9) | (1,444.2) |
| | $2,428.9 | $2,155.2 |

| Goodwill and Other Intangible Assets, Net | 1996 | 1995 |
|---|---|---|
| Goodwill and other intangibles | $3,107.4 | $3,037.0 |
| Accumulated amortization | (387.0) | (295.3) |
| | $2,720.4 | $2,741.7 |

| Other Accruals | 1996 | 1995 |
|---|---|---|
| Accrued payroll and employee benefits | $293.0 | $271.0 |
| Accrued advertising | 135.7 | 117.6 |
| Accrued interest | 48.6 | 46.0 |
| Accrued taxes other than income taxes | 47.9 | 51.1 |
| Restructuring accrual | 115.2 | 100.0 |
| Other | 136.4 | 110.6 |
| | $776.8 | $696.3 |

| Other Liabilities | 1996 | 1995 |
|---|---|---|
| Minority interest | $232.2 | $214.1 |
| Pension and other benefits | 393.9 | 411.7 |
| Restructuring accrual | 38.0 | 175.9 |
| Other | 277.9 | 178.4 |
| | $942.0 | $980.1 |

*Fair Value of Financial Instruments*

In assessing the fair value of financial instruments at December 31, 1996 and 1995, the Company has used available market information and other valuation methodologies. Some judgment is necessarily required in interpreting market data to develop the estimates of fair value, and, accordingly, the estimates are not necessarily indicative of the amounts that the Company could realize in a current market exchange.

The estimated fair value of the Company's financial instruments at December 31 are summarized as follows:

| | 1996 | | 1995 | |
|---|---|---|---|---|
| | Carrying Amount | Fair Value | Carrying Amount | Fair Value |
| Assets: | | | | |
| Cash and cash equivalents | $ 248.2 | $ 248.2 | $ 208.8 | $ 208.8 |
| Marketable securities | 59.6 | 59.6 | 47.8 | 47.8 |
| Long-term investments | 8.1 | 7.9 | 13.3 | 14.2 |
| Liabilities: | | | | |
| Notes and loans payable | (172.3) | (172.3) | (204.4) | (204.4) |
| Long-term debt, including current portion | (2,897.2) | (2,980.6) | (3,029.0) | (3,161.1) |
| Other liabilities: | | | | |
| Foreign exchange contracts | 4.0 | 4.8 | .4 | 1.3 |
| Interest rate instruments | (10.3) | (.4) | (11.0) | (68.1) |
| Equity: | | | | |
| Foreign exchange contracts to hedge investment in subsidiaries | (1.7) | (1.4) | (2.3) | (2.1) |

*Financial Instruments and Rate Risk Management*

The Company utilizes interest rate agreements and foreign exchange contracts to manage interest rate and foreign currency exposures. The principal objective of such contracts is to moderate the effect of fluctuations in interest rates and foreign exchange rates. The Company, as a matter of policy, does not speculate in financial markets and therefore does not hold these contracts for trading purposes. The Company utilizes what it considers straightforward instruments, such as forward foreign exchange contracts and non-leveraged interest rate swaps, to accomplish its objectives.

The Company primarily uses interest rate swap agreements to effectively convert a portion of its floating rate debt to fixed rate debt in order to manage interest rate exposures in a manner consistent with achieving a targeted fixed to variable interest rate ratio. The net effective cash payment of these financial derivative instruments combined with the related interest payments on the debt that they hedge are accounted for as interest expense. Those interest rate instruments that do not qualify as hedge instruments for accounting purposes are marked to market and carried on the balance sheets at fair value. As of December 31, 1996 and 1995, the Company had agreements outstanding with an aggregate notional amount of $1,210.9 and $1,142.2, respectively, with maturities through 2025.

The Company uses forward exchange contracts principally to hedge foreign currency exposures associated with its net investment in foreign operations and overseas debt. This hedging minimizes the impact of foreign exchange rate movements on the Company's financial position. The terms of these contracts are generally less than five years.

As of December 31, 1996 and 1995, the Company had approximately $676.9 and $972.0, respectively, of outstanding foreign exchange contracts. At December 31, 1996, approximately 15% of outstanding foreign exchange contracts served to hedge net investments in foreign subsidiaries, 40% hedged intercompany loans, 40% hedged third-party firm commitments and the remaining 5% hedged certain transactions that are anticipated to settle in accordance with their identified terms. The Company makes net settlements for foreign exchange contracts at maturity, based on rates agreed to at inception of the contracts.

Gains and losses from contracts that hedge the Company's investments in its foreign subsidiaries are shown in the cumulative translation adjustments account included in shareholders' equity. Gains and losses from contracts that hedge firm commitments are recorded in the balance sheets as a component of the related receivable or payable until realized, at which time they are recognized in the statements of income.

The contracts that hedge anticipated sales and purchases do not qualify as hedges for accounting purposes. Accordingly, the related gains and losses are calculated using the current forward foreign exchange rates and are recorded in the statements of income as other expense, net. These contracts mature within 15 months.

The Company is exposed to credit loss in the event of nonperformance by counterparties on interest rate agreements and foreign exchange contracts; however, nonperformance by these counterparties is considered remote as it is the Company's policy to contract only with counterparties that have a long-term debt rating of A or higher. The amount of any such exposure is generally the unrealized gain on such contracts, which at December 31, 1996 was not significant.

## 13. MARKET AND DIVIDEND INFORMATION

The Company's common stock and $4.25 Preferred Stock are listed on the New York Stock Exchange. The trading symbol for the common stock is CL. Dividends on the common stock have been paid every year since 1895, and the amount of dividends paid per share has increased for 34 consecutive years.

**Market Price**

| Quarter Ended | Common Stock | | | | $4.25 Preferred Stock | | | |
| | 1996 | | 1995 | | 1996 | | 1995 | |
| | High | Low | High | Low | High | Low | High | Low |
|---|---|---|---|---|---|---|---|---|
| March 31 | $83.00 | $68.88 | $67.88 | $58.63 | $73.00 | $69.00 | $67.00 | $62.00 |
| June 30 | 85.63 | 75.38 | 77.00 | 66.25 | 71.50 | 67.50 | 71.00 | 64.50 |
| September 30 | 88.75 | 78.13 | 73.13 | 65.75 | 69.00 | 64.50 | 71.00 | 67.50 |
| December 31 | 95.50 | 86.00 | 76.38 | 66.13 | 72.00 | 65.50 | 72.00 | 69.00 |
| Closing Price | $92.25 | | $70.25 | | $70.00 | | $72.00 | |

**Dividends Paid Per Share**

| Quarter Ended | 1996 | 1995 | 1996 | 1995 |
|---|---|---|---|---|
| March 31 | $ .47 | $ .41 | $1.0625 | $1.0625 |
| June 30 | .47 | .41 | 1.0625 | 1.0625 |
| September 30 | .47 | .47 | 1.0625 | 1.0625 |
| December 31 | .47 | .47 | 1.0625 | 1.0625 |
| Total | $1.88 | $1.76 | $4.25 | $4.25 |

## 14. QUARTERLY FINANCIAL DATA (Unaudited)

| | First Quarter | Second Quarter | Third Quarter | Fourth Quarter |
|---|---|---|---|---|
| **1996** | | | | |
| Net sales | $2,053.7 | $2,167.3 | $2,230.6 | $2,297.4 |
| Gross profit | 1,003.3 | 1,061.0 | 1,094.8 | 1,138.8 |
| Net income | 143.5 | 148.9 | 160.9 | 181.7 |
| Earnings per common share: | | | | |
| Primary | .95 | .98 | 1.06 | 1.20 |
| Assuming full dilution [1] | .89 | .92 | .99 | 1.12 |
| 1995 | | | | |
| Net sales | $1,980.3 | $2,090.7 | $2,134.4 | $2,152.8 |
| Gross profit | 969.8 | 980.1 | 1,024.7 | 1,030.5 |
| Net income (loss) | 156.5 | 143.2 | (250.2)[2] | 122.5 |
| Earnings (loss) per common share: | | | | |
| Primary | 1.05 | .95 | (1.76)[2] | .80 |
| Assuming full dilution [1] | .97 | .88 | (1.76)[2] | .76 |

[1] The sum of the quarterly fully diluted earnings (loss) per share amounts is not equal to the full year because the computations of the weighted average number of shares outstanding and the potential impact of dilutive securities for each quarter and for the full year are required to be made independently.

[2] The third quarter of 1995 includes a provision for restructured operations of $460.5 ($369.2 aftertax) or $2.54 per share on a primary basis and $2.50 per share on a fully diluted basis.

### 15. RESTRUCTURED OPERATIONS

In September 1995, the Company announced a major worldwide restructuring of its manufacturing and administrative operations designed to further enhance profitable growth over the next several years by generating significant efficiencies and improving competitiveness. As a result of this rationalization, 24 of the 112 factories worldwide will be closed or significantly reconfigured, of which 14 had been closed or reconfigured at the end of 1996.

The changes are expected to be substantially completed during 1997 in facilities around the world, but primarily in North America and Europe. The charge includes employee termination costs, expenses associated with the realignment of the Company's global manufacturing operations as well as settlement of contractual obligations.

The worldwide restructuring program resulted in a 1995 pretax charge of $460.5 ($369.2 net of tax) or $2.54 per share for the year.

A summary of the restructuring reserve established is as follows:

| | Original Reserve | Utilized in 1995 | Balance at Dec. 31, 1995 | Utilized in 1996 | Balance at Dec. 31, 1996 |
|---|---|---|---|---|---|
| Workforce | $210.0 | $ (4.2) | $205.8 | $ (93.4) | **$112.4** |
| Manufacturing plants | 204.1 | (7.2) | 196.9 | (118.6) | **78.3** |
| Settlement of contractual obligations | 46.4 | (13.5) | 32.9 | (20.4) | **12.5** |
| | $460.5 | $(24.9) | $435.6 | $(232.4) | **$203.2** |

Of the restructuring reserve remaining as of December 31, 1996 and 1995, $115.2 and $100.0, respectively, is classified as a current liability, $38.0 and $175.9, respectively, as a noncurrent liability, and $50.0 and $159.7, respectively, as a reduction of fixed assets.

### 16. COMMITMENTS AND CONTINGENCIES

Minimum rental commitments under noncancellable operating leases, primarily for office and warehouse facilities, are $70.0 in 1997, $58.4 in 1998, $51.7 in 1999, $47.5 in 2000, $44.7 in 2001 and $193.1 for years thereafter. Rental expense amounted to $93.3 in 1996, $91.8 in 1995 and $83.4 in 1994. Contingent rentals, sublease income and capital leases, which are included in fixed assets, are not significant.

The Company has various contractual commitments to purchase raw materials, products and services totaling $123.4 that expire through 1998.

The Company is a party to various superfund and other environmental matters and is contingently liable with respect to lawsuits, taxes and other matters arising out of the normal course of business. Management proactively reviews and manages its exposure to, and the impact of, environmental matters. While it is possible that the Company's cash flows and results of operations in particular quarterly or annual periods could be affected by the one-time impacts of the resolution of such contingencies, it is the opinion of management that the ultimate disposition of these matters, to the extent not previously provided for, will not have a material impact on the Company's financial condition or ongoing cash flows and results of operations.

As discussed in Note 3, the acquisition of Kolynos was reviewed by antitrust regulatory authorities in Brazil. The antitrust regulatory authorities in Brazil approved the acquisition subject to certain conditions. The Company is currently negotiating undertakings related to those conditions with the Brazilian authorities. Among other things, those undertakings would result in the substitution by the Company of a new toothpaste brand for Kolynos in Brazil for four years and the Company contract manufacturing toothpaste in Brazil for third parties during this period.

### 17. SUBSEQUENT EVENT

On March 6, 1997, the Company's Board of Directors approved a two-for-one common stock split effected in the form of a 100% stock dividend. As a result of the split, shareholders will receive one additional share of Colgate common stock for each share they hold as of April 25, 1997. Par value will remain at $1 per share. Giving retroactive effect for the stock split, common shares issued as of December 31, 1996 would have been 366,426,590. Earnings per share, after giving retroactive effect to the two-for-one split, are presented below for each of the three years ended December 31:

| | 1996 | 1995 | 1994 |
|---|---|---|---|
| Primary | **$2.09** | $.52 | $1.91 |
| Fully diluted | **1.95** | .51 | 1.78 |

Financial information contained elsewhere in this annual report has not been adjusted to reflect the impact of the common stock split.

# Shareholder Information

**CORPORATE OFFICES**

Colgate-Palmolive Company
300 Park Avenue
New York, New York 10022-7499
(212) 310-2000

**ANNUAL MEETING**

The annual meeting of Colgate shareholders will
be Thursday, May 8, 1997 at 10:00 a.m. in the
Broadway Ballroom of the Marriott Marquis Hotel,
Sixth Floor, Broadway at 45th Street, New York, NY.
Please sign and return your proxy promptly even if
you plan to attend the meeting.

**STOCK EXCHANGES**

The common stock of Colgate-Palmolive Company is
listed and traded on the New York Stock Exchange
under the symbol CL and on other world
exchanges including those in Amsterdam,
Frankfurt, London, Paris and Zurich.

**CL**
**Listed**
**NYSE**

**FINANCIAL INFORMATION ON-LINE
AND BY 800 NUMBER**

Financial results, dividend news and other information
are available on Colgate's World Wide Web site on the
Internet. The address is http://www.colgate.com/
Information can also be requested by e-mail from the
Company at Investor_Relations@colpal.com

Colgate also offers earnings information, dividend news and other corporate announcements
on a toll-free telephone line: 1-800-850-2654.
The information can be read to the caller and can
also be received by mail or fax.

**SHAREOWNER ACCOUNT ASSISTANCE**

To transfer stock, report address changes or pose
questions about dividend checks or Colgate's
Dividend Reinvestment Plan, contact the Company's
transfer agent and registrar:

Attn: Colgate-Palmolive Company
First Chicago Trust Company of New York
P. O. Box 2500
Jersey City, NJ 07303-2500
TOLL-FREE: 1-800-756-8700
FAX: (201) 222-4842
e-mail: fctc@em.fcnbd.com
Internet address: http://www.fctc.com

**DIVIDEND REINVESTMENT PLAN**

Colgate offers an automatic Dividend Reinvestment
Plan for common and $4.25 preferred stockholders
and a voluntary cash feature. Any brokers' commissions or service charges for stock purchases under
the Plan are paid by Colgate-Palmolive.

**OTHER SHAREHOLDER CONTACTS**

Copies of annual or interim reports, product
brochures, Form 10-K and other publications are
available from the Investor Relations Department.
Those can be requested by mail directed to the
corporate address, by e-mail, by calling
1-800-850-2654 or by calling Investor Relations
at (212) 310-3207.

Individual investors with other requests: please
write Investor Relations at the corporate address or
call (212) 310-2575.

Institutional investors should call Bina
Thompson at (212) 310-3072.

**INDEPENDENT PUBLIC ACCOUNTANTS**

Arthur Andersen LLP

**CORPORATE RESPONSIBILITY**

Colgate-Palmolive does business in over 200 countries
and territories worldwide, affecting the lives of a
highly diverse population of employees, consumers,
shareholders, business associates and friends. We are
committed to the highest standard of ethics, fairness
and humanity in all our activities and operations.
All employees are guided by a worldwide Code of
Conduct, which sets forth Colgate policies on
important issues such as nondiscriminatory employment, involvement in community and educational
programs, care for the environment, employee safety,
and our relationship with consumers, shareholders
and government.

**ENVIRONMENTAL POLICY**

Colgate-Palmolive is committed to the protection of
the environment everywhere. Our commitment is
an integral part of Colgate's mission to become the
best truly global consumer products company.

We continue to work on developing innovative
environmental solutions in all areas of our business
around the world. The health and safety of our customers, our employees and the communities in
which we operate is paramount in all that we do.

Dollars In Millions Except Per Share Amounts

**Operations**
Net sales
Results of operations:
  Net income
  Per share, primary
  Per share, assuming full dilution
Depreciation and amortization expense

**Financial Position**
Working capital
Current ratio
Property, plant and equipment, net
Capital expenditures
Total assets
Long-term debt
Shareholders' equity

**Share and Other**
Book value per common share
Cash dividends declared and paid per common share
Closing price
Number of common shares outstanding (in millions)
Number of shareholders of record:
  $4.25 Preferred
  Common
Average number of employees

Colgate-Palmolive's concern has been translated
into many varied programs dealing with our products, packaging, factories and business decisions.
Projects such as concentrated cleaners and detergents, refill packages, recycled and recyclable bot-
tles, and packaging materials are all part of working
toward long-term solutions.

To obtain a copy of Colgate's Environmental
Policy Statement, Code of Conduct, Advertising
Placement Policy Statement, the Product Safety
Research Policy or our 1996 Report of Laboratory
Research with Animals, please write to Consumer
Affairs at Colgate-Palmolive.

**RUSSIA:**

**Colgate is becoming a household name in this vast
market; strong brands including Colgate, Protex,
Palmolive and Axion contributed to sales that
more than doubled in 1996.**

# Eleven-Year Financial Summary [*][(1)]

| Ten-Year Compound Annual Growth Rate | 1996 | 1995 | 1994 | 1993 | 1992 | 1991 | 1990 | 1989 | 1988 | 1987 | 1986 |
|---|---|---|---|---|---|---|---|---|---|---|---|
| 8.8% | **$8,749.0** | $8,358.2 | $7,587.9 | $7,141.3 | $7,007.2 | $6,060.3 | $5,691.3 | $5,038.8 | $4,734.3 | $4,365.7 | $3,768.7 |
| 18.7 | **635.0** | 172.0[(2)] | 580.2[(3)] | 189.9[(4)] | 477.0 | 124.9[(5)] | 321.0 | 280.0 | 152.7[(6)] | .9[(8)] | 114.8 |
| 17.9 | **4.19** | 1.04[(2)] | 3.82[(3)] | 1.08[(4)] | 2.92 | .77[(5)] | 2.28 | 1.98 | 1.11[(6)] | .01[(8)] | .81 |
| 17.0 | **3.90** | 1.02[(2)] | 3.56[(3)] | 1.05[(4)] | 2.74 | .75[(5)] | 2.12 | 1.90 | 1.10[(6)] | .01[(8)] | .81 |
| 18.0 | **316.3** | 300.3 | 235.1 | 209.6 | 192.5 | 146.2 | 126.2 | 97.0 | 82.0 | 70.1 | 60.3 |
| | **468.0** | 607.1 | 648.5 | 676.4 | 635.6 | 596.0 | 516.0 | 907.5 | 710.9 | 439.5 | 428.7 |
| | **1.2** | 1.3 | 1.4 | 1.5 | 1.5 | 1.5 | 1.4 | 1.9 | 1.7 | 1.3 | 1.4 |
| | **2,428.9** | 2,155.2 | 1,988.1 | 1,766.3 | 1,596.8 | 1,394.9 | 1,362.4 | 1,105.4 | 1,021.6 | 1,201.8 | 1,113.7 |
| | **459.0** | 431.8 | 400.8 | 364.3 | 318.5 | 260.7 | 296.8 | 210.0 | 238.7 | 285.8 | 220.9 |
| | **7,901.5** | 7,642.3 | 6,142.4 | 5,761.2 | 5,434.1 | 4,510.6 | 4,157.9 | 3,536.5 | 3,217.6 | 3,227.7 | 2,845.9 |
| | **2,786.8** | 2,992.0 | 1,751.5 | 1,532.4 | 946.5 | 850.8 | 1,068.4 | 1,059.5 | 674.3 | 694.1 | 522.0 |
| | **2,034.1** | 1,679.8 | 1,822.9 | 1,875.0 | 2,619.8 | 1,866.3 | 1,363.6 | 1,123.2 | 1,150.6 | 941.1 | 979.9 |
| | **13.68** | 11.34 | 12.45 | 12.40 | 16.21 | 12.54 | 10.12 | 8.39 | 8.24 | 6.77 | 6.91 |
| | **1.88** | 1.76 | 1.54 | 1.34 | 1.15 | 1.02 | .90 | .78 | .74[(7)] | .695 | .68 |
| | **92.25** | 70.25 | 63.38 | 62.38 | 55.75 | 48.88 | 36.88 | 31.75 | 23.50 | 19.63 | 20.44 |
| | **147.1** | 145.8 | 144.4 | 149.3 | 160.2 | 147.3 | 133.2 | 132.2 | 138.1 | 137.2 | 140.1 |
| | **350** | 380 | 400 | 450 | 470 | 460 | 500 | 500 | 550 | 600 | 600 |
| | **45,500** | 46,600 | 44,100 | 40,300 | 36,800 | 34,100 | 32,000 | 32,400 | 33,200 | 33,900 | 35,900 |
| | **37,900** | 38,400 | 32,800 | 28,000 | 28,800 | 24,900 | 24,800 | 24,100 | 24,700 | 37,400 | 37,900 |

[*] On March 6, 1997, the Board of Directors approved a two-for-one common stock split. Financial information has not been adjusted to reflect the impact of the split.

[(1)] All share and per share amounts have been restated to reflect the 1991 two-for-one stock split.

[(2)] Income in 1995 includes a net provision for restructured operations of $369.2 ($2.54 per share on a primary basis or $2.50 per share on a fully diluted basis).

[(3)] Income in 1994 includes a one-time charge of $5.2 for the sale of a non-core business, Princess House.

[(4)] Income in 1993 includes a one-time impact of adopting new mandated accounting standards, effective in the first quarter of 1993, of $358.2 ($2.30 per share on a primary basis or $2.10 per share on a fully diluted basis).

[(5)] Income in 1991 includes a net provision for restructured operations of $243.0 ($1.80 per share on a primary basis or $1.75 per share on a fully diluted basis).

[(6)] Income in 1988 includes Hill's service agreement renegotiation net charge of $42.0 ($.30 per share on both a primary and fully diluted basis).

[(7)] Due to timing differences, 1988 includes three dividend declarations totaling $.55 per share and four payments totaling $.74 per share while all other years include four dividend declarations.

[(8)] Income in 1987 includes a net provision for restructured operations of $144.8 ($1.06 per share on a primary basis or $1.05 per share on a fully diluted basis).

♻ Printed entirely on recycled paper.
© 1997 Colgate-Palmolive Company

Design by Robert Webster Inc.
Major photography by Richard Alcorn
Other photos by Tom Ferraro
Printing by Acme Printing Company
Typography by Boro Graphic Technologies, Inc.

# Part Two

## How Accountants Measure and Report

Accounting for Current Assets

*LIFO or FIFO? That Is the Question*

Recognizing Revenues and Expenses: When Is Income Earned?

*R. J. Reynolds Tobacco Company*

*Circuit City Stores, Inc. (A)*

*The Intel Pentium Chip Controversy (A)*

Accounting for Property, Plant, and Equipment and Other Assets

*Depreciation at Delta Air Lines and Singapore Airlines (A)*

*Depreciation at Delta Air Lines and Singapore Airlines (B)*

*Kansas City Zephyrs Baseball Club, Inc.*

*Buying Time*

Liabilities and Time

*Laurinburg Precision Engineering*

*Belgrave Corporation*

*Accounting for Frequent Fliers*

Introduction to Owners' Equity

*FMC Corporation*

Solving the Puzzle of the Cash Flow Statement

*Statements of Cash Flows: Three Examples*

*Crystal Meadows of Tahoe, Inc.*

# Accounting for Current Assets

**C**urrent assets are those resources that are expected to benefit the organization within the next operating cycle. Current assets reported by the Gillette Company and Subsidiary Companies in its 1995 Annual Report are typical (see **Exhibit 1**). *Cash and cash equivalents and short-term investments* always head the list of current assets, and they are the means by which current operating expenses can be met. Other current assets are usually listed in an order that approximates their nearness to cash; *inventories* are available for sale to customers, whose accounts then become *accounts receivable*, which when paid become cash to replenish the inventory pool to start the cycle again. These flows are ongoing, and the balance sheet merely provides a view at one moment in time.

## CASH, CASH EQUIVALENTS, AND OTHER TEMPORARY INVESTMENTS

The term *cash and cash equivalents* has become very prevalent as more and more organizations engage in cash management techniques. Since idle cash provides no return, financial managers try to invest any temporary excess amounts of cash in highly liquid, short-term investments. Money market funds, government securities, certificates of deposit, or high-grade commercial paper are some of the investments that may be used for this purpose. Because they can be readily resold and converted into cash, accounting treats them as if they are cash.

Copyright © 1992 by the President and Fellows of Harvard College. Harvard Business School case 193-048.

Forecasting cash receipts and disbursements is an important part of the treasury function in most corporations. Since the yield (interest earned) on investments tends to be higher on marketable securities that are less liquid, many organizations invest a part of their excess cash in other marketable securities, which are listed separately as temporary investments. For most purposes, the distinction between cash equivalents and other temporary investments in marketable securities is unimportant, except as an indication of the investment horizon in a cash management program.

## ACCOUNTS RECEIVABLE

When a sale to a customer is made on terms other than cash, an account receivable is created. Accounts receivable from customers are reported at the amount that is expected to be received from customers in settlement of their obligations. This may differ from the total of stated selling prices for two reasons. First, as an inducement for prompt payment, customers may be offered a *cash discount* if they pay within a short period of time. Second, although there is an assumption at the time of every sale that customers will pay, in practice not all do. For this reason, a valuation adjustment, or *allowance for doubtful accounts*, is normally recorded to recognize that some accounts will become *bad debts* and to bring the accounts receivable balance to a more realistic level.

Cash discounts are normally anticipated at the time of sale and deducted from sales, creating an allowance for cash discounts that is deducted from the total amount owed by customers to arrive at the amount of accounts receivable included in the balance sheet. The amount of the allowance is almost always based on the company's past experience with cash discounts taken by customers.

The problem in estimating the amounts that customers will not pay (bad debts) is somewhat more complex. Most organizations know from experience that some customers will be unable or unwilling to pay the amounts they owe. The problem is that at the time a sale is made and a receivable is recorded, managers do not know which customers will pay and which will not. The solution to this problem lies in making an estimate that is based on past experience of the portion of accounts receivable that will not be paid in full either at the time it is due or within some reasonable time thereafter.

A number of methods are used to estimate the *allowance for doubtful accounts*, also called the *allowance for bad debts*. Sometimes a percentage of the total amount of sales is charged to expense during the period in which sales are made, and that amount is established as an allowance against which bad accounts are offset when they are finally identified. The percentage of sales taken is customarily based on the experience of the firm with its particular group of customers, and it may vary with the type of customer to which sales are made.

Alternatively, an examination could be made of the distribution of accounts according to how long they have been outstanding. The percentage used to estimate default on accounts already overdue can be different from that applied to accounts that have not reached the point where payment is expected. Estimating the amount of accounts that will not be collected is an important aspect of reporting realistic figures for accounts receivable. If no allowance for doubtful accounts is made, the amount of accounts receivable may be overstated.

# INVENTORIES

Inventories are considered a significant current asset in many firms. By holding an inventory of finished product, an organization can fill orders more quickly and provide better customer service. Even when products or services have to be created after a customer order is received, inventories of raw materials speed the process of satisfying customer demands.

Accounting for inventories has two important aspects. First, the cost of inventory that is purchased or manufactured has to be determined. That cost is then held in the inventory accounts of the firm until the product is sold. Once the product has been shipped or delivered to a customer, the cost becomes an expense to be reported in the income statement as the cost of goods sold.

To understand the process of inventory accounting, you have to imagine costs flowing into the inventory account and then being removed from that account and charged to cost of goods sold in the income statement. Just as products are physically moved onto shelves or into a warehouse and then physically removed as they are delivered to customers, so too is the cost of inventory moved into an account and later removed from it. It is important to recognize, however, that the flows need not be parallel; that is, the flow of costs into and out of the inventory account need not be in the same order as the flow of goods into and out of the warehouse.

## Inventory Cost Flows

At first glance, it seems there is no need to make an assumption about how costs flow through the inventory account. The cost of each item placed in physical inventory can be entered into the account, and then, as the item is physically taken from inventory, the cost can be removed from the account. In this way, the costs accumulated in the account match perfectly with the items physically held, and the costs of goods sold equal the sum of the cost of each item actually delivered to a customer. Such an inventory cost system is known as a *specific identification* system.

Specifically identifying each item in inventory is relatively easy if each item is unique, such as an art object, expensive jewelry, or custom-made furniture, or if each item has an identification number, such as an automobile. However, specific identification is not practical for a company having a large number of inventory items that are not easily identifiable individually. In these cases, it is common for accountants to assume a flow of cost through the inventory account that is unrelated in any way to the actual physical flow of goods.

Three common assumptions used in accounting for inventory cost are (1) average cost, (2) first-in, first-out (FIFO), and (3) last-in, first-out (LIFO). A company can choose any of these assumptions and use them consistently for each classification of inventory regardless of the way in which goods physically move into and out of inventory.

Using the *average-cost method* requires calculating the average cost of items in the beginning inventory plus purchases made during the accounting period to determine the cost of goods sold and the cost of inventory on hand at the end of the period. The average cost is assumed to be a representative cost of all the items available for sale during the accounting period. Rather than wait until the end of an accounting period to calculate the average cost, some companies use a predetermined unit cost of all transactions that take place during the accounting period. This is a *standard-cost system* and is a variation of the average-cost method. Any difference between the actual average unit cost and the predetermined standard cost during a period is usually added to or subtracted from the cost of goods sold for that period.

If the *first-in first-out*, or *FIFO*, assumption is used, the oldest costs in the inventory account are the first to be transferred to cost of goods sold when merchandise is sold. Using this assumption means that the costs retained in the inventory account will always be those most recently incurred for the purchase or manufacture of inventory. For this reason, the FIFO assumption produces an inventory account balance that usually comes the closest of the three methods to approximating the replacement cost of the inventory.

The *last-in first-out*, or *LIFO*, assumption is the opposite of FIFO. Cost of goods sold is measured using the cost of the most recent additions to inventory, and the inventory account always retains the oldest cost of items purchased or manufactured. *This assumed cost flow may be quite different from the actual physical flow of goods, and it usually is when the LIFO method is used.* If older costs are retained in the inventory account for some time because the inventory is never depleted, and if prices change substantially in the accounting periods during which these old costs are retained, the LIFO inventory balance will likely bear little relation to the current value of the same amount of inventory recently purchased.

Use of the LIFO assumption is not permitted in some countries. It is, however, permitted in the United States and is quite popular. The reasons for this popularity are rooted in the fact that the United States has experienced fairly continuous inflation and cost increases for many commodities and goods. Since the LIFO assumption can be used in reporting income for income taxation purposes, firms choose to use it to reduce income taxes that are due in the current period. For most accounting methods, there is no requirement under U.S. tax law that the same method be employed in financial reports issued to shareholders and in financial reports on which taxes are based. However, LIFO is an exception. A company that chooses to save taxes by using the LIFO assumption must also use the LIFO method in its reports to shareholders. For this reason, the cost associated with paying lower taxes comes from the fact that management must then report to shareholders lower earnings than might be the case if an alternative inventory assumption were used.

These three common assumptions—average cost, LIFO, and FIFO—are illustrated in **Exhibit 2**. The differences caused by the differing flow assumptions are a function of the rate at which prices have changed during the period as well as the length of time old costs have been retained in the account because of the LIFO assumption. The important thing to remember is that the inventory cost flow assumption has an impact on cost of goods sold, reported net income, and the inventory value that will be shown among the current assets in the balance sheet. The amount of difference between cost of goods sold reported under one assumption and cost of goods sold reported under another will depend on the speed with which costs of inventory are changing.

A reader of financial reports also has to be alert for situations in which the LIFO assumption has been used and inventory costs acquired many periods before have been allowed to flow into cost of goods sold. Assuming the costs of inventory have risen, dipping into these old inventory costs by reducing the size of inventory on hand (called a LIFO liquidation) will give a burst of net income, which may not be sustainable in future periods.

We can sum up our discussion of inventory accounting to this point quite simply. Inventory accounting consists of measuring the cost of items that are added to inventory and then choosing the flow assumption to determine which of those costs are moved first to cost of goods sold when inventory is sold and delivered to customers. In organizations that only purchase items for their own use or for resale to others, the only other issue that arises is whether a perpetual record of inventory purchases and deliveries is kept or whether the firm relies on a periodic inventory count to determine the quantity of inventory on hand at the end of an accounting period that will be carried forward as the beginning inventory in the subsequent period. However, many organizations buy materials, expend labor on changing their character, and manufacture products or create services, which all add cost to the products eventually delivered to customers. These firms require additional records and account classifications in order to properly record and report their inventories.

## ACCOUNTING FOR MANUFACTURED INVENTORIES

The record keeping required to maintain control of inventory items as their form and character change is often complex and voluminous. A branch of accounting known as *cost accounting* is devoted to analysis and study of the type of problems encountered in measuring and recording information necessary to determine the cost of inventories and the effects of expenditures and expenses incurred during the manufacturing process.

In the case of manufactured inventory, it is necessary to choose a flow assumption just as we would in a case where inventory was only purchased and sold. Since inventories are typically in several different forms in the manufacturing firm—raw materials, work in process, and finished goods—the record-keeping task is necessarily more complex. Labor and supplies may be used to alter raw materials, increasing the amount and cost of work in process. Raw materials and labor may be necessary to create finished goods. Costs now flow not only within classifications of the inventory according to assumptions (FIFO, LIFO, and so on), but the amount used becomes the input for another class of inventory. In a typical manufacturing firm, the flow is like that depicted in **Exhibit 3**. **Exhibit 4** is a numerical illustration of the way in which costs might be assumed to flow through the inventory accounts in a simple manufacturing company. **Exhibit 5** shows how the cost of goods sold can be detailed in a comprehensive statement of income for the same firm.

Although the application of particular flow assumptions used in the manufacturing firm demands care (and occasionally ingenuity) on the part of the accountant, the problems of inventory accounting are essentially the same in all organizations. As inventories become a relatively larger portion of the total working capital or total assets of a firm, issues of inventory costing and measurement become more important and demand more attention of management.

## OTHER CURRENT ASSETS

The major category of other current assets that you are likely to encounter in financial reports is *prepaid expenses*. In most cases, these are expenditures that have not yet become expenses because they have future value to the firm. They will be matched with revenue in subsequent accounting periods as their usefulness has been realized. Typical examples might be rents paid in advance for machinery or facilities that will be used in future months, amounts paid as insurance premiums at the beginning of insurance coverage, and travel expense advances to employees for trips to be taken. These deferred expenses are typically used up over a short period of time, and for this reason they are classified as current assets.

## SUMMARY

Because the items classified as current assets are so important to current operations, they tend to turn over fairly quickly.  The amounts shown on the balance sheet are usually fairly close to the amount that would be paid for a replacement asset of the same classification.  The major exception to this is the inventory account during periods of rapid price changes, or if the LIFO inventory flow assumption is used.

In most organizations, there is a logical flow through those assets reported as current assets.  Cash is used to purchase or create inventory.  Inventory is delivered to customers, and their accounts become receivables.  Receivables are collected, making cash available for operations.  This flow is what operations are about.  These operating assets are what demand management's day-to-day attention as inventories are turned into more liquid assets to finance the creation of more inventories ready to satisfy customer orders.

**EXHIBIT 1**
**Current Assets, The Gillette Company and Subsidiary Companies**
**(Excerpt from Consolidated Balance Sheets) ($ millions)**

| Current Assets | December 31, 1995 | December 31, 1994 |
|---|---|---|
| Cash and cash equivalents | $    47.9 | $    43.8 |
| Short-term investments, at cost which approximates market | 1.6 | 2.3 |
| Receivables  less allowances:  1995—$59.2; 1994—$52.1 | 1,659.5 | 1,379.5 |
| Inventories | 1,035.1 | 941.2 |
| Deferred income taxes | 220.2 | 220.6 |
| Prepaid expenses | 140.2 | 113.0 |
| **Total Current Assets** | $3,104.5 | $2,700.4 |

**Notes to Consolidated Financial Statements**

**Cash and Cash Equivalents**
Cash and cash equivalents include cash, time deposits, and all highly liquid debt instruments with an original maturity of three months or less.

**Inventories**

| (Millions of dollars) | December 31, 1995 | December 31, 1994 |
|---|---|---|
| Raw materials and supplies | $   231.8 | $207.3 |
| Work in process | 127.3 | 95.0 |
| Finished goods | 676.0 | 638.9 |
| | $1,035.1 | $941.2 |

Inventories are stated at the lower of cost or market.  In general, cost is currently adjusted standard cost, which approximates actual cost on a first-in, first-out basis.

**Income Taxes**
Beginning in 1993, deferred taxes are provided for using the asset and liability method for temporary differences between financial and tax reporting.

**EXHIBIT 2**
**Inventory Cost Flow Assumptions Illustrated**

The Xitan Plumbing Supply Company maintained an inventory of standard brass faucets for sale to plumbers.  In 1999, because of increasing copper prices, the price paid to suppliers increased significantly.  A record of purchases in 1999 showed the following:

| | | | |
|---|---|---|---|
| February 1 | 50 @ | $ 6.00 | $   300 |
| April 1 | 50 @ | 7.50 | 375 |
| May 1 | 50 @ | 8.50 | 425 |
| July 1 | 50 @ | 9.00 | 450 |
| October 1 | 50 @ | 10.50 | 525 |
| | | | $2,075 |

Prices had been stable prior to 1999.  On January 1, 1999, there were 29 faucets on hand, each of which had cost $5.00.  At the end of the year on December 31, there were 54 faucets on hand.

If inventories are valued periodically, the value of inventory in terms of historical prices and the cost of faucets sold depends on the inventory flow assumption adopted, as shown below.

**Xitan Plumbing Supply Company—Expense Standard Brass Faucets—1999**

| | Assumed Flow of Costs | | |
|---|---|---|---|
| | First-In, First-Out | Average Cost | Last-In, First-Out |
| Brass faucets, January 1, 1999 | | | |
| 29 @ $5.00 | $  145 | $  145 | $  145 |
| Purchases, 1999 | 2,075 | 2,075 | 2,075 |
| Available for sale, 1999 | $2,220 | $2,220 | $2,220 |
| Brass faucets, December 31, 1999 | | | |
| FIFO:  50 @ $10.50 = $525 | | | |
| 4 @    9.00 =   36 | 561 | | |
| Average cost:  54 @ $7.96[a] | | 430 | |
| LIFO:  29 @ $5.00 = $145 | | | |
| 25 @   6.00 =  150 | | | 295 |
| Cost of faucets sold, 1999 | $1,659 | $1,790 | $1,925 |

[a]  Average cost is measured here by taking the total cost of brass faucets purchased and dividing it by the total number of faucets purchased ($2,220 ÷ 2.79).

**EXHIBIT 3**
## Inventory Flows in Manufacturing

1. Materials and parts are purchased for use in manufacturing

   Raw Materials at Beginning of Period
   + Purchases
   − To work in process

2. Cost flow of raw materials into manufacturing processes is assumed as labor and other costs are assumed to add to value

   Work in Process at Beginning of Period
   + Raw materials used
   + Cost of labor
   + Other manufacturing costs (cost of management; heat, power, and light; supplies used; depreciation)
   − To finished goods

3. Cost flow of goods finished is assumed as products are completed and ready for sale

   Finished Goods at Beginning of Period
   + Goods completed
   + Goods purchased ready for sale
   − Cost of products sold

### EXHIBIT 4
### Manufactured Inventory Accounting Illustrated

The Astroweld Company produces and distributes an advanced technology home welding unit.  From two suppliers, the company purchases two parts assemblies—one electrical and one mechanical—for each finished welding unit.  These are assembled by company employees using company-owned equipment in a rented factory building. The firm uses LIFO flow assumptions for all inventories except work in process.

   During May of last year these inventory accounts showed the following conditions and events:

**Raw Materials—Electrical Parts Assemblies**

| | | |
|---|---|---:|
| On hand, May 1 | 15 @ $33 | $  495 |
| May purchases | 10 @ $39 | 390 |
| | | $  885 |
| On hand, May 31 | 13 @ $33 | 429 |
| May usage (10 @ $39, 2 @ $33) | 12 | $  456 |

**Raw Materials—Mechanical Parts Assemblies**

| | | |
|---|---|---:|
| On hand, May 1 | 19 @ $10 | $  190 |
| May purchases | 10 @ $11 | 110 |
| | | $  300 |
| On hand, May 31 | 14 @ $10 | 140 |
| May usage (10 @ $11, 5 @ $10) | 15 | $  160 |

**Manufacturing Costs for May**

| | |
|---|---:|
| Assembly labor | $  650 |
| Supervisory salaries | 220 |
| Heat, light, and power | 56 |
| Depreciation of equipment | 120 |
| Supplies used | 32 |
| Total | $ 1,078 |

**EXHIBIT 4 (continued)**
**Manufactured Inventory Accounting Illustrated**

**Work in Process**

| | | |
|---|---:|---:|
| In process, May 1 | | None |
| | | |
| *Processing in May* | | |
| 12 electrical parts | $ 456 | |
| 15 mechanical parts | 160 | |
| Manufacturing costs | 1,078 | |
| | | $1,694 |
| | | |
| *In process, May 31* | | |
| 3 mechanical parts (3 @ $10) | $ 30 | |
| Labor cost | 40 | |
| Cost of supervision | 10 | |
| | | 80 |
| Transferred to finished goods in May | | $1,614 |

**Finished Welders**

| | |
|---|---:|
| On hand, May 1 (5 @ $127.50) | $ 637.50 |
| May production from work in process | 1,614.00 |
| On hand, May 31 (2 @ $127.50) | (255.00) |
| Cost of welders sold in May | $1,996.50 |

Since 12 welders were completed in May and transferred to finished goods at a total cost of $1,614, the average cost of each welder manufactured was $134.50.

An income statement for May for Astroweld might show expense of goods sold as shown in **Exhibit 5**.

**EXHIBIT 5**
**Astroweld Company—Cost of Welders Sold—May**

**Raw Materials Cost**

| | | | |
|---|---|---|---|
| Raw materials—electrical, May 1 | $495.00 | | |
| Purchases | 390.00 | | |
| Total available | $885.00 | | |
| Raw materials—electrical, May 31 | 429.00 | | |
| To work in process | | $  456.00 | |
| Raw materials—mechanical, May 1 | $190.00 | | |
| Purchases | 110.00 | | |
| Total available | $300.00 | | |
| Raw materials—mechanical, May 31 | 140.00 | | |
| To work in process | | 160.00 | |
| Work in process, May 1 | | 0 | |
| Add:  Manufacturing costs for May | | 1,078.00 | |
| | | $1,694.00 | |
| Work in process, May 31 | | 80.00 | |
| To finished welders | | | $1,614.00 |
| Finished welders, May 1 | | | 637.50 |
| Welders available for sale | | | $2,251.50 |
| Finished welders, May 31 | | | 255.00 |
| Cost of welders sold, May | | | $1,996.50 |

# LIFO or FIFO? *That* Is the Question

**A**ccounting for inventories is a tricky business. This is particularly true because a company's level of inventories cannot be judged precisely short of an actual count, verification, and appraisal of value. Because it is expensive to do this, companies maintain careful records of purchases and goods manufactured and sold. Record keeping requires choices about what to include in the cost of inventory purchased or manufactured and the flow of those costs through the inventory accounts as inventory is used or sold to customers.

It is rarely possible to associate the actual cost of a particular item with that item as it enters, resides in, and is removed from an inventory account. Only if items are very expensive (such as precious gemstones) or have specific identifying numbers (such as automobiles) is the effort to keep track of particular items considered worth the effort by accountants. Instead, like items are classified in an account, and an assumption is made about the cost of items used or sold. If prices or costs are changing, the assumption about the cost of items removed from inventory will affect reported expenses or cost of goods sold.

Three common assumptions about the flow of costs through inventory accounts define the most widely used inventory accounting methods. If it is assumed that the oldest costs are matched with revenues first, the method is called the first-in, first-out, or FIFO, inventory valuation method. If it is assumed that the most recent costs are matched with revenues first, the method

---

*Susan S. Harmeling prepared this note under the supervision of Professor William J. Bruns, Jr.*

Copyright © 1991 by the President and Fellows of Harvard College. Harvard Business School case 192-046.

is called the last-in, first-out method, or LIFO.[1]  The average-cost method is based on the assumption that an "average cost" is matched with revenues.  It is important to note that the actual physical flow of items does not need to correspond to the assumed flow of costs, and it rarely does.  In accounting for milk or bread in a retail grocery store, an accountant could use a LIFO assumption, even though the grocer would probably want to maintain a FIFO physical flow.

It is useful to visualize layers of cost built up over time in the inventory account.  FIFO always takes the cost from the oldest layer.  LIFO always takes the cost from the most recent layer, with the result that the bottom layers may be costs measured well in the past.

In the United States, the Internal Revenue Code permits companies to use the LIFO assumption in calculating income subject to taxation.  If costs and prices are rising, more recent high costs increase expenses and cost of goods sold, reduce income, and reduce tax payments if the LIFO assumption is used.  A company that elects to use the LIFO assumption in accounting for all or part of its inventories for tax purposes must also use that assumption in its published financial reports.  This LIFO conformity requirement is the only rule which dictates that financial reports prepared for shareholders must be based on the same accounting assumptions as those used in preparing tax returns.

If prices and costs are rising, the opportunity to save cash by reducing tax payments will look attractive to many managers and they will be attracted to using the LIFO assumption.  However, by choosing LIFO they will also be forced to report lower income than they would have reported if they used the FIFO or average-cost method.  Often the choice managers make is determined in part by their belief about whether shareholders, investors, or lenders will understand that even though reported income is lower when LIFO is used in a time of rising costs, cash flow has been improved because lower taxes were paid.

Companies rarely change inventory flow assumptions.  But when they do, management and independent auditors are required to note and highlight the change.  The general requirement for any change in accounting method is that the new method be preferable to the old one.  A different inventory valuation method from that previously used can be preferable for many reasons, so there is little to keep a management that wants to change from doing so.  Of course, if their present inventory valuation method were adopted very recently, another change would cause readers to be suspicious about the new accounting and about what management was trying to show or conceal.

A change in accounting method for inventories frequently signals a change in management assumptions about the future of their company, their industry, or the economy.  In other cases, managers may change accounting methods to use the same methods used by other companies to which they hope to be

---

[1] Use of the LIFO method is not permitted in many countries.

compared. For these reasons, when a change is made, it frequently pays a reader of financial statements to think carefully about the reasons why management chose to change accounting methods.

In 1987 and 1988, three large corporations made changes in the methods each used to account for inventories. Blount, Inc., an international company with operations in machinery and equipment manufacturing, specialty steel products, and construction, adopted FIFO on September 1, 1987. The company had previously used LIFO. **Exhibit 1** shows their consolidated statements of operations, consolidated balance sheets, excerpts from the notes to the financial statements, and the independent accountants' report.

The Penn Central Corporation, a diversified company whose principal operating businesses were the manufacture of products and the supply of services in the areas of industrial manufacturing, defense services, insurance, and energy, decided to change its method of valuing a significant component of its electrical wire inventories from the FIFO to the LIFO method effective January 1, 1988. **Exhibit 2** shows their statement of income, balance sheet, and excerpts from the notes to financial statements and the independent auditor's report.

Quaker Oats, a large multinational consumer products company with sales of more than $5.3 billion in 1988, decided in that year to adopt the LIFO cost flow assumption for valuing the majority of its remaining U.S. grocery products inventories. **Exhibit 3** shows their consolidated statements of income, consolidated balance sheets, and excerpts from the notes to consolidated financial statements and the auditor's report.

## QUESTIONS

1. Why do you think each company decided to change its inventory accounting method in 1987 and 1988? Did the change impact the balance sheet or income statement in a material way? Did the reasons given for the change make sense? Why, or why not?
2. What can explain why a move from LIFO was preferable for Blount, Inc. at the same time a move to LIFO was preferable to Penn Central and Quaker Oats?

## EXHIBIT 1
### Blount, Inc. and Subsidiaries, Consolidated Statements of Operations

For the Years Ended the Last Day of February

| (in thousands, except share data) | 1988 | 1987[a] | 1986[a] |
|---|---|---|---|
| Revenues | $ 666,812 | $ 729,081 | $ 659,793 |
| Sales | 563,880 | 504,859 | 501,714 |
| Total sales and revenues | $1,230,692 | $1,233,940 | $1,161,507 |
| Cost of revenues | $ 657,925 | $ 713,066 | $ 629,083 |
| Cost of sales | 410,276 | 365,097 | 382,688 |
| Selling, general, and administrative expenses | 122,963 | 114,391 | 120,005 |
| Total costs and operating expenses | $1,191,164 | $1,192,554 | $1,131,776 |
| Income from operations | $ 39,528 | $ 41,386 | $ 29,731 |
| Interest expense, net | (22,682) | (24,738) | (29,282) |
| Other income (expense), net | (2,563) | (3,192) | 1,399 |
| Income before provision for income taxes and extraordinary gain | $ 14,283 | $ 13,456 | $ 1,848 |
| Provision for income taxes | 6,356 | 6,044 | (215) |
| Income before extraordinary gain | $ 7,927 | $ 7,412 | $ 2,063 |
| Extraordinary gain on termination of pension plans (less applicable income taxes of $7,558) | | | 8,873 |
| Net income | $ 7,927 | $ 7,412 | $ 10,936 |
| Per share of common stock | | | |
| Income before extraordinary gain | $    .66 | $    .62 | $    .16 |
| Extraordinary gain | | | .74 |
| Net income | $    .66 | $    .62 | $    .90 |
| Weighted average number of common shares outstanding | 11,974,882 | 11,934,132 | 12,023,793 |

[a] Restated

**EXHIBIT 1 (continued)**
**Blount, Inc. and Subsidiaries, Consolidated Balance Sheets**

| As of the Last Day of February (in thousands, except share data) | 1988 | 1987[a] |
|---|---|---|
| **Assets** | | |
| Current assets: | | |
| Cash, including short-term investments of $2,098 and $5,006 | $ 4,858 | $ 7,920 |
| Accounts receivable, net | 198,997 | 284,331 |
| Inventories | 78,333 | 71,983 |
| Costs and recognized profits in excess of billings on uncompleted contracts | 19,074 | 46,378 |
| Other current assets | 11,040 | 9,945 |
| Total current assets | $312,302 | $420,557 |
| Property, plant, and equipment, net | 199,204 | 211,305 |
| Excess of cost investment in subsidiaries over net assets acquired, net | 61,894 | 68,312 |
| Other assets | 26,714 | 26,282 |
| Total assets | $600,114 | $726,456 |
| **Liabilities and Shareholders' Equity** | | |
| Current liabilities: | | |
| Notes payable and current maturities of long-term debt | $ 21,683 | $ 32,971 |
| Accounts payable | 152,458 | 239,432 |
| Accrued expenses | 57,956 | 55,479 |
| Billings in excess of costs and recognized profits on uncompleted contracts | 21,132 | 22,115 |
| Deferred income taxes | 17,303 | 34,568 |
| Total current liabilities | $270,532 | $384,565 |
| Long-term debt, exclusive of current maturities | 154,208 | 173,165 |
| Deferred income taxes, exclusive of current portion | 17,652 | 10,037 |
| Other liabilities | 14,802 | 21,169 |
| Total liabilities | $457,194 | $588,936 |
| **Commitments and Contingent Liabilities** | | |
| **Shareholders' Equity** | | |
| Preference stock:  par value $.10 per share; 5,086 and 10,174 shares issued and outstanding | 1 | 1 |
| Common stock:  par value $1.00 per share; | | |
| Class A:  7,312,363 and 7,170,154 shares issued and outstanding | 7,312 | 7,170 |
| Class B:  4,626,165 and 4,725,092 shares issued and outstanding | 4,626 | 4,725 |
| Capital in excess of par value of stock | 4,715 | 4,837 |
| Retained earnings | 119,062 | 116,307 |
| Accumulated translation adjustment | 7,204 | 4,480 |
| Total shareholders' equity | $142,920 | $137,520 |
| Total liabilities and shareholders' equity | $600,114 | $726,456 |

The accompanying notes are an integral part of these statements.

[a]  Restated (see Note 1)

**EXHIBIT 1 (continued)**
**Notes to Financial Statements**

**Excerpt from Note 1: Summary of Significant Accounting Policies**

*Inventories*

The company adopted the lower of first-in, first-out ("FIFO") cost or market in valuing all its inventories effective September 1, 1987. Previously, a significant amount of the company's inventories had been valued by the lower of last-in, first-out ("LIFO") cost or market method. The change resulted in an increase in net income of $3.7 million ($.31 per share) for the year ended February 29, 1988. The adoption of this policy was applied retroactively and, as a result, retained earnings at March 1, 1985 were decreased by $2.5 million and net income was increased by $197,000 ($.02 per share) in 1987 and decreased by $1.3 million ($.11 per share) in 1986. The company believes that the FIFO method of inventory valuation is a better measure of the financial position of the company as it reflects more recent costs in the balance sheet. The change to FIFO will conform all the company's inventories to the same valuation method. The company continues to emphasize Japanese manufacturing techniques and just-in-time methods and, as a result of this focus, the company expects inventory reductions and lower production costs in certain manufacturing operations in future years. Under the current economic environment of low inflation and an expected reduction in inventory and lower production costs, the company believes that the FIFO method results in a better matching of costs and revenues as compared to the LIFO method.

**Independent Accountants' Report**

To the Board of Directors and Shareholders
Blount, Inc.

We have examined the consolidated balance sheets of Blount, Inc. and subsidiaries as of the last day of February 1988 and 1987, and the related consolidated statements of operations, retained earnings, changes in capital stock accounts and changes in financial position for each of the three years in the period ended February 29, 1988. Our examinations were made in accordance with generally accepted auditing standards and, accordingly, included such tests of the accounting records and such other auditing procedures as we considered necessary in the circumstances.

In our opinion, the aforementioned financial statements present fairly the consolidated financial position of Blount, Inc. and subsidiaries as of the last day of February 1988 and 1987, and the results of their operations and the changes in their financial position for each of the three years in the period ended February 29, 1988, in conformity with generally accepted accounting principles applied on a consistent basis after restatement for the change, with which we concur, in the method of determining cost for certain inventories as described in Note 1 to the financial statements and except for the change, with which we concur, in the method of accounting for pensions as described in Note 7 to the financial statements.

Coopers & Lybrand
Atlanta, Georgia
April 8, 1988

**EXHIBIT 2**
**The Penn Central Corporation and Consolidated Subsidiaries, Statement of Income**

| (in millions, except per share amounts) | For the Years Ended December 31, | | |
| --- | --- | --- | --- |
| | 1989 | 1988 | 1987 |
| Revenues | | | |
| Net sales | $1,454.0 | $1,546.5 | $1,261.1 |
| Net insurance premiums earned | 231.1 | — | — |
| Net investment income from insurance operations | 39.9 | — | — |
| | $1,725.0 | $1,546.5 | $1,261.1 |
| Costs and expenses | | | |
| Cost of sales | $ 889.6 | $ 952.4 | $ 700.7 |
| Operating expenses | 433.7 | 419.9 | 397.4 |
| Insurance losses and expenses | 233.6 | — | — |
| General and administrative expenses | 69.0 | 68.8 | 63.8 |
| | $1,625.9 | $1,441.1 | $1,161.9 |
| Operating income | $ 99.1 | $ 105.4 | $ 99.2 |
| Interest and dividend income | $ 108.3 | $ 93.7 | $ 81.1 |
| Net gain on the disposal of businesses | 74.7 | — | — |
| Interest and debt expense | (27.9) | (27.0) | (12.8) |
| Corporate and administrative expenses | (21.2) | (21.1) | (23.1) |
| State, foreign and other income taxes | (8.3) | (16.2) | (14.7) |
| Other income (expense)—net | 7.7 | (6.3) | (81.5) |
| | $ 133.3 | $ 23.1 | $ (51.0) |
| Income from continuing operations before Federal income tax | $ 232.4 | $ 128.5 | $ 48.2 |
| Deduction in lieu of current Federal income tax, which is not accruable or payable | (58.3) | (34.4) | (17.8) |
| Income from continuing operations | $ 174.1 | $ 94.1 | $ 30.4 |
| Discontinued operations | | | |
| Income from operations | — | 3.9 | 5.8 |
| Gain on disposal | — | 5.4 | — |
| Net income | $ 174.1 | $ 103.4 | $ 36.2 |
| Net income per share of common stock | | | |
| Continuing operations | $ 2.48 | $ 1.33 | $ .39 |
| Discontinued operations | — | .13 | .07 |
| | $ 2.48 | $ 1.46 | $ .46 |
| Weighted average number of common shares | 70.3 | 71.0 | 78.0 |

**EXHIBIT 2 (continued)**
**The Penn Central Corporation and Consolidated Subsidiaries, Balance Sheet**

|  | December 31, | |
| --- | --- | --- |
| (in millions, except per share data) | 1989 | 1988 |

**Assets**

| | | |
| --- | --- | --- |
| Cash | $ 16.1 | $ 53.6 |
| Receivables | 372.8 | 241.2 |
| Inventories | 280.6 | 246.0 |
| Investments | 1,209.1 | 1,256.8 |
| Investments of insurance operations | 488.3 | — |
| Property, plant, and equipment | 335.6 | 301.5 |
| Cost in excess of net assets acquired ~ goodwill ~ above market of Net Assets. (vs. Book " " " ) | 333.1 | 80.8 |
| Other assets | 142.6 | 220.4 |
| Total assets | $3,178.2 | $2,400.3 |

**Liabilities and Common Shareholders' Equity**

| | | |
| --- | --- | --- |
| Accounts payable and accrued liabilities | $ 350.2 | $ 290.5 |
| Insurance claims and reserves | 457.5 | — |
| Debt | 378.8 | 168.4 |
| Minority interests in subsidiaries | 17.5 | 13.3 |
| Deferred income taxes | 29.7 | 29.7 |
| Other liabilities | 117.7 | 128.5 |
| Total liabilities | $1,351.4 | $ 630.4 |

| | | |
| --- | --- | --- |
| Common stock, $1.00 par value—issued and issuable 89,831,241 and 88,659,646 shares | $ 89.8 | $ 88.7 |
| Capital surplus | 1,942.7 | 1,861.2 |
| Retained earnings | 669.3 | 524.4 |
| Treasury stock | (875.0) | (704.4) |
| Total common shareholders' equity | $1,826.8 | $1,769.9 |
| Total liabilities and common shareholders' equity | $3,178.2 | $2,400.3 |

See accompanying notes to financial statements

**EXHIBIT 2 (continued)**
## Excerpts from Notes to Financial Statements

1. **Summary of Significant Accounting Policies**

*Inventories*

Inventories are stated at the lower of cost or market value. Due to the diversified nature of the company's operations, several methods of determining cost are used, including last-in/first-out ("LIFO") for electrical wire and first-in/first-out ("FIFO") for substantially all of the company's other inventories. See Note 6 for a discussion of the change in the method of valuing electrical wire inventories effective January 1, 1988.

6. **Inventories**

Inventories consist of the following:

|  | (In Millions) | |
|---|---|---|
| December 31, | 1989 | 1988 |
| Raw materials | $ 64.8 | $ 48.2 |
| Work-in-progress | 88.0 | 87.6 |
| Finished goods | 127.2 | 102.3 |
| Other | .6 | 7.9 |
| Total | $ 280.6 | $ 246.0 |

Effective January 1, 1988, the company changed its method of valuing a significant component of its electrical wire inventories from the FIFO to the LIFO method. Management believes the LIFO method will result in a better matching of current costs with current revenues.

At December 31, 1989 and 1988, $54.9 million and $53.8 million, respectively, of inventories were valued using the LIFO method. Approximate replacement cost of inventories valued using the LIFO method totaled $69.6 million at December 31, 1989 and $73.9 million at December 31, 1988.

The effect of the change in 1988 was to decrease both income from continuing operations and net income by $7.4 million, or $.10 per share. The cumulative effect of this accounting change and the pro forma effects on prior years' earnings have not been included because such effects are not reasonably determinable.

## Excerpt from Independent Auditor's Report

We have audited the accompanying balance sheet of The Penn Central Corporation and Consolidated Subsidiaries as of December 31, 1989 and 1988 and the related statements of income and cash flows for each of the three years in the period ended December 31, 1989. . . .

In our opinion, such consolidated financial statements present fairly, in all material respects, the financial position of the company at December 31, 1989 and 1988 and the results of its operations and its cash flow for each of the three years in the period ended December 31, 1989 in conformity with generally accepted accounting principles.

As discussed in Note 6 of Notes to Financial Statements, in 1988 the company changed its method of accounting for electrical wire inventories.

Deloitte & Touche
Cincinnati, Ohio
February 9, 1990

**EXHIBIT 3**
**The Quaker Oats Company and Subsidiaries, Consolidated**
**Statements of Income (dollars in millions, except per share data)**

| Year Ended June 30 | 1989 | 1988 | 1987 |
|---|---|---|---|
| Net sales | $5,724.2 | $5,329.8 | $4,420.6 |
| Cost of goods sold | 3,188.7 | 2,906.7 | 2,436.6 |
| | | | |
| Gross profit | $2,535.5 | $2,423.1 | $1,984.0 |
| Selling, general, and administrative expenses | 1,996.2 | 1,905.4 | 1,534.2 |
| Interest expense—net of $12.4, $15.1, and $20.6 interest income | 63.5 | 47.8 | 41.1 |
| Other expense—net | 147.1 | 56.3 | 50.3 |
| | | | |
| Income from continuing operations before income taxes | $ 328.7 | $ 413.6 | $ 358.4 |
| Provision for income taxes | 125.7 | 157.9 | 172.7 |
| | | | |
| Income from continuing operations | $ 203.0 | $ 255.7 | $ 185.7 |
| | | | |
| Income from discontinued operations—net of tax | — | — | 2.4 |
| Income from the disposal of discontinued operations—net of tax | — | — | 55.8 |
| | | | |
| Income from discontinued operations (net of income tax of $27.0) | — | — | 58.2 |
| | | | |
| Net income | $ 203.0 | $ 255.7 | $ 243.9 |
| Per Common Share: | | | |
|    Income from continuing operations | $ 2.56 | $ 3.20 | $ 2.36 |
|    Income from discontinued operations | — | — | .74 |
| | | | |
|    Net income | $ 2.56 | $ 3.20 | $ 3.10 |
|    Dividends declared | $ 1.20 | $ 1.00 | $ .80 |
| | | | |
| Average number of common shares outstanding (in 000s) | 79,307 | 79,835 | 78,812 |

**EXHIBIT 3 (continued)**
**The Quaker Oats Company and Subsidiaries, Consolidated Balance Sheets**

| June 30 | Dollars in Millions | | |
| --- | --- | --- | --- |
| | 1989 | 1988 | 1987 |
| **Assets** | | | |
| Current assets: | | | |
| Cash and cash equivalents | $ 21.0 | $ 55.6 | $ 311.5 |
| Short-term investments, at cost which approximates market | 2.7 | 35.6 | 48.4 |
| Receivables—net of allowances | 872.1 | 826.0 | 752.9 |
| Inventories: | | | |
| Finished goods | 396.4 | 359.4 | 334.6 |
| Grain and raw materials | 154.0 | 143.4 | 114.1 |
| Packaging materials and supplies | 39.0 | 37.0 | 37.7 |
| Total inventories | $ 589.4 | $ 539.8 | $ 486.4 |
| Other current assets | 113.0 | 33.3 | 197.4 |
| Total current assets | $ 1,598.2 | $ 1,490.3 | $ 1,796.6 |
| Other Receivables and Investments | 26.4 | 20.7 | 14.8 |
| Property, plant, and equipment | 1,725.2 | 1,628.6 | 1,515.9 |
| Less accumulated depreciation | 633.3 | 600.2 | 533.9 |
| Properties—net | $ 1,091.9 | $ 1,028.4 | $ 982.0 |
| Intangible Assets, Net of Amortization | 505.4 | 435.2 | 456.7 |
| Total assets | $ 3,221.9 | $ 2,974.6 | $ 3,250.1 |
| Current Liabilities | $ 902.4 | $ 1,072.8 | $ 1,288.7 |
| Long-Term Debt | 766.8 | 299.1 | 527.7 |
| Other Liabilities | 89.5 | 101.0 | 79.1 |
| Deferred Income Taxes | 326.1 | 250.6 | 267.1 |
| Preferred Stock, no par value, authorized 1,750,000 shares; issued 1,282,051 of $5.46 cumulative convertible shares in 1989 (liquidating preference $78 per share) | 100.0 | — | — |
| Deferred Compensation | (100.0) | — | — |
| Common Shareholders' Equity: | | | |
| Common stock, $5 par value, authorized 200,000,000 shares; issued 83,989,396 shares | 420.0 | 420.0 | 420.0 |
| Additional paid-in capital | 18.1 | 19.5 | 13.1 |
| Reinvested earnings | 1,106.2 | 998.4 | 822.6 |
| Cumulative exchange adjustment | (56.6) | (36.5) | (43.0) |
| Deferred compensation | (165.8) | (17.4) | (18.9) |
| Treasury common stock, at cost, 5,221,981 shares; 4,593,664 shares; and 4,505,250 shares, respectively | (184.8) | (132.9) | (106.3) |
| Total common shareholders' equity | 1,137.1 | 1,251.1 | 1,087.5 |
| Total Liabilities and Common Shareholders' Equity | $ 3,221.9 | $ 2,974.6 | $ 3,250.1 |

See accompanying notes to consolidated financial statements

**EXHIBIT 3 (continued)**
**Excerpts from Notes to Financial Statements**

### Note 1  Summary of Significant Accounting Policies

*Inventories*

Inventories are valued at the lower of cost or market, using various cost methods, and include the cost of raw materials, labor and overhead.  The percentage of year-end inventories valued using each of the methods is as follows:

| June 30 | 1989 | 1988 | 1987 |
|---|---|---|---|
| Average quarterly cost | 21% | 54% | 52% |
| Last-in, first-out (LIFO) | 65 | 29 | 31 |
| First-in, first-out (FIFO) | 14 | 17 | 17 |

Effective July 1, 1988, the company adopted the LIFO cost flow assumption for valuing the majority of remaining U.S. Grocery Products inventories.  The company believes that the use of the LIFO method better matches current costs with current revenues.  The cumulative effect of this change on retained earnings at the beginning of the year is not determinable, nor are the pro forma effects of retroactive application of LIFO to prior years.  The effect of this change on fiscal 1989 was to decrease net income by $16.0 million, or $.20 per share.

If the LIFO method of valuing certain inventories were not used, total inventories would have been $60.1 million, $24.0 million and $14.6 million higher than reported at June 30, 1989, 1988, and 1987, respectively.

*Reserve*

The company takes positions in the commodity futures market as part of its overall raw materials purchasing strategy in order to reduce the risk associated with price fluctuations of commodities used in manufacturing.  The gains and losses on futures contracts are included as a part of product cost.

### Excerpt from Auditor's Report

We have audited the accompanying consolidated balance sheets of The Quaker Oats Company (a New Jersey corporation) and Subsidiaries as of June 30, 1989, 1988, and 1987, and the related consolidated statements of income, common shareholders' equity and cash flows for the years then ended. . . .

In our opinion, the financial statements referred to above present fairly, in all material respects, the financial position of The Quaker Oats Company and Subsidiaries as of June 30, 1989, 1988, and 1987, and the results of their operations and their cash flows for the years then ended in conformity with generally accepted accounting principles.

As discussed in Note 1 to the financial statements, effective July 1, 1988, the company adopted the Last-In, First-Out method of determining cost for the majority of its U.S. Grocery Products inventories.

Arthur Andersen & Co.
Chicago, Illinois
August 7, 1989

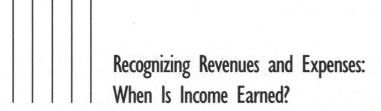

# Recognizing Revenues and Expenses: When Is Income Earned?

The *accrual concept* forces accountants and managers to focus on changes in owners' equity rather than merely reporting changes to the cash or other asset accounts. The *matching concept* relates revenues and expenses so that owners' equity is neither overstated nor understated at any point in the stream of events that constitutes operations. The *realization concept* underlies the decision rules that accountants use in determining when revenues should be recognized and expenses matched to them.

Questions about the time at which revenue should be measured and recognized in reports are not always easy to answer, particularly if the accountant seeks to provide reliable and verifiable information. At first glance, the easy answer would be to recognize revenue only when cash is received. Recognizing and measuring revenues when cash is received constitute the *cash basis for accounting*. Using the cash basis, expenses are recognized when cash is expended. In contrast, when revenues are recognized and measured on the *accrual basis*, delivery of product or service is one cue accountants use to know to measure and report revenues even if cash has not yet been received; expenses are measured and recognized in the same accounting period as the revenues to which they relate. When revenues or expenses have been earned so that they are recognizable and measurable, they are often said to have been *realized*.

The only reason for considering use of the cash basis for accounting for revenues and expenses is simplicity. By counting cash received, revenues are easily measured. By counting cash spent, expenses are easily measured. But cash is only one of the resources that most organizations employ in carrying out operations and seeking to enhance the wealth of owners. The accrual basis is

Copyright © 1992 by the President and Fellows of Harvard College. Harvard Business School case 193-047.

usually assumed to provide better information to owners on the results of operations and better information to those who use information from financial reports in making decisions.

The advantages of cash accounting need not be completely lost when the accrual basis is used. A summary of the monetary transactions of an organization or a statement of cash flows can easily be prepared to supplement balance sheets and income statements prepared on an accrual basis. Because no information is lost, and because there appear to be important reasons to favor the accrual basis for income determination, the accrual basis has become the standard for the measurement and recognition of revenues, expenses, and income within companies and other organizations and in public reports about them.

## WHEN SHOULD REVENUE BE RECOGNIZED?

Revenues arise in events and from transactions, and if revenues exceed expenses, income is earned and the organization grows in value. For most business entities, the largest and most important source of revenues is sales of goods and services to customers.

There are many points when revenue may be recognized as a result of sale of goods or services to customers. Five of the most common are:

1. The point at which an order is obtained from a customer.
2. The point at which an order is accepted and the terms of the sale are finalized.
3. The point at which goods are delivered to a customer.
4. The point at which the customer is billed.
5. The point at which payment is received from the customer.

Managers, especially those in marketing and sales, will probably favor revenue recognition practices that use either point 1 or point 2 as cues to begin the matching process. On the other hand, the *concept of conservatism* draws accountants toward point 3 or point 4, or perhaps even some later point in time such as point 5. At those points, there has been an observable market exchange that satisfies the criteria of feasibility, reliability, freedom from bias, verifiability, and high probability of cash collection.

The accrual concept provides the counterbalance to the concept of conservation to support the revenue recognition rules most often used. In most cases, generally accepted accounting principles call for revenues to be recognized at the time goods or services are delivered to the customer. Depending upon the legal form of the sales contract, delivery can take place when goods or services are shipped by the seller or when they are received by the buyer. This is the earliest point at which an outsider can independently determine that a sale has been completed in the terminology of accounting practice. Revenues are "realized" and are measured and reported when a sale is completed by delivery of goods to a customer. At that point in time, most critical earnings events have taken place, and the pragmatic issues of probable collection of receivables can be addressed.

## Applying the Revenue Recognition Rule

One advantage of using the rule that revenue should be recognized when goods or services are delivered is that recognizing revenue at that time is fairly simple. When a customer buys goods in a retail store and carries the goods out the door, it is clear that something has happened and easy to see that a sale has been completed. In other cases where goods or services are delivered to customers, these events can be observed, and revenue can be recognized and measured. The ease of applying the rule for recognizing revenue at the time of delivery does not mean, however, that there are not important judgments to be made by managers and accountants about revenue recognition. Some of these judgments involve deciding how much revenue should be recognized, and others stem from other events that might take place. What, for example, should be done if merchandise is returned? What if additional services are required to satisfy the customer?

Since it is inevitable that some merchandise will be returned for credit, the amount actually reported as revenue frequently is reduced by estimated or actual returns for credit or refund, or for discounts that have been offered for prompt payment. Thus, it is not uncommon for the first line of an income statement to be labeled *net sales*. If there are important timing differences between the delivery of merchandise and the time it is returned or cash discounts taken, allowances for returns and discounts may be established as accounts and may appear in the balance sheet as liabilities.

## Measuring Revenue Prior to Delivery

Sometimes recognizing revenue on delivery does not provide the best information concerning actual events. One example is when an item is created or manufactured over a long period of time under contract to a customer. Large buildings, ships, and special production facilities designed and constructed as a special order for a customer are examples of items that may take several accounting periods to complete. The entire effort of an organization may be spent working several periods completing one item. In these cases, deferring recognition of income until the contract work is completely satisfied and the customer accepts the finished outcome does not give readers of financial reports an adequate sense of what is really happening.

In cases where the production cycle is long and involves large items, and where the income pattern of the firm will be distorted by deferring all recognition of revenue and hence all income to the period of delivery, accountants use procedures by which some of the anticipated income from a project can be recognized as parts of it are completed.  Using these *percentage-of-completion methods*, a portion of the total revenue on a project is recognized in each period over the life of the project, and an appropriate amount of expenses is matched to it.  Although this method is a deviation from the general rule that revenues should be recognized at the time of delivery of goods or services, for some industries it provides a better picture of the pattern of earnings activities.

A second situation where recognition of revenue is sometimes not deferred until time of delivery occurs when there is a price fixed by law or a well-established market price for the product.  Precious metals, grains and other agricultural products, and marketable securities have readily determinable prices and can sometimes be sold without significant effort.  When this is true, revenues are sometimes recognized at the point the production process is complete and the product ready for delivery, or when prices of the assets change.

## APPLYING THE MATCHING CONCEPT

Once revenues have been recognized, the cost of creating the goods and services that were sold and the expenses of supporting the organization during the accounting period are matched to the revenues.  Many times there is a fairly obvious and straightforward relationship between expenditures that have been made to create the revenue-producing process and the revenues themselves.  In other situations, such as expenditures for advertising or research and development, the relationship between expenditures and revenues is less clear, and expenditures for these efforts will be matched to revenues in the period in which the expenditure takes place.

Finally, there is a kind of expense which can be difficult to observe, measure, and recognize.  These are commitments that arise because promises of future expenditures have been made during the period in which revenues have been earned.  Promises to employees for pensions or other post-retirement benefits are examples of this kind of promise.  In these cases, transactions do not provide information about the amount of expense.  Instead, estimates of the amount of future liability must be made so that the current expense can be matched against the revenue that created the commitment and hence a future obligation.

## A FINAL COMMENT

Within many organizations, there is continual conflict between managers and accountants on the proper ways in which revenues should be recognized.  Although everyone in an organization is biased toward recognizing organizational success quickly, accounting conventions for recognizing revenue and the underlying accounting concept of conservatism operate as checks on early revenue recognition. Everyone in an organization may be thrilled when a large contract is signed and sure that the value of the organization has been enhanced, but until the products and services promised under the contract have been delivered to customers, or criteria of the percentage of completion process have been met, no revenue will be reported.

# R. J. Reynolds Tobacco Company

O n September 13, 1989, Louis V. Gerstner, chief executive officer (CEO) of RJR Nabisco Holding Corp. for five months, received a call from James W. Johnston, the executive he had recruited in June to head the R. J. Reynolds Tobacco Company (RJRT), RJR Nabisco's U.S. tobacco division. Since his return to the company that he had left in 1984, Johnston had been investigating the buildup of excess cigarette inventories in the warehouses of RJRT's independent distributors. Johnston's opposition to this practice of "trade loading" had been a factor in his departure five years earlier, when he was a marketing executive, and now he was in a position to put an end to it. In 1988 the company had instituted and then abandoned a three-year plan to eliminate trade loading gradually, but Johnston now proposed to do it immediately. It would be, he said, "a real statement of change in emphasis and direction," and "there's probably no single thing . . . that would [energize] the place as much" as this action.[1] He asked for Gerstner's approval.

## COMPANY BACKGROUND

### History

RJRT was founded in 1875 in Winston-Salem, North Carolina, by Richard Joshua Reynolds, a 25-year-old businessman from Virginia. Its first product

*Research Associate Charles A. Nichols, III prepared this case under the supervision of Professor William J. Bruns, Jr.*

Copyright © 1990 by the President and Fellows of Harvard College. Harvard Business School case 191-038.

---

[1] Carol J. Loomis, "The $600 Million Cigarette Scam," *Fortune*, 4 Dec. 1989, 100.

was chewing tobacco, a business Reynolds had learned from the chewing-tobacco factory owned by his father. The company rose to prominence among its many local competitors, and in 1899, Reynolds sold a two-thirds interest in it to James B. Duke's American Tobacco Company for $3 million and a guarantee that Reynolds would retain operating control. The company grew rapidly in the next 10 years by purchasing many competing local firms, becoming the largest employer in North Carolina. In 1911, Teddy Roosevelt's trust-busting policies forced the liquidation of Duke's tobacco trust, and RJRT regained its independence. To preserve it, Reynolds arranged for the purchase of much of the company's stock by its own employees and created a special "Class A" stock to consolidate all voting power into the hands of the workers. As a result, from the early 1920s until the 1950s, employees controlled a majority of the company's stock.

RJRT has had a history of innovation. The company was the first to blend saccharin with chewing tobacco to make it sweeter. Then in the early years of the twentieth century, Reynolds introduced a national brand of pipe tobacco named Prince Albert, after the Prince of Wales, who had become King Edward VII. The product's success was ensured by a national advertising campaign and by discounted prices to retailers and distributors to encourage large purchases. In 1913, RJRT was the first to market a national brand of ready-to-smoke cigarettes. Previous cigarette brands had been only regional and had a poor reputation for taste; at the time, most smokers preferred to roll their own. But with a clever advertising campaign and prices at half those of the rival brands, Camel cigarettes swamped the competitors and became the first cigarette to be sold by the carton. RJRT obtained an exclusive contract to supply cigarettes to U.S. servicemen fighting in Europe during World War I.

Following Reynolds' death in 1918, the company drifted under local management. Its success bred complacency and a lack of attention to marketplace trends, such as the growth of smoking among women. It lost its first position in the market to American Tobacco Company's Lucky Strikes in 1929, but regained it in the next decade through aggressive advertising. In the 1940s, management's attention was devoted to breaking a union that the workers had formed. Although management succeeded, in the process RJRT again lost its lead position in sales to American Tobacco.

Early reports about the dangers of cigarette smoking led in 1954 to RJRT's introduction of Winston, the first major filtered cigarette. Shortly thereafter it came out with Salem, the first mass-marketed menthol cigarette. With these two new products, RJRT's sales again passed those of American Tobacco in 1959. RJRT confined its activities to the tobacco industry until the 1960s, when it diversified into transportation, energy, and food. Beginning in the late 1970s it focused its efforts on consumer products, acquiring Del Monte in 1979; Heublein, Inc. in 1982; and Nabisco (including Planters LifeSavers) in 1985. During the 1980s, RJR divested itself of its transportation, energy, restaurant, and spirits and wines businesses, retaining only its tobacco and food products operations. However, in 1983, a new rival, Philip Morris, overtook RJRT's leading position in the industry with its popular Marlboro brand. In November 1988, RJR Nabisco agreed to be purchased by the investment firm of Kohlberg Kravis Roberts & Company (KKR) in a leveraged buyout agreement worth approximately $25 billion.

## The Buyout

The idea for a buyout of the company originated with F. Ross Johnson, RJR Nabisco's flamboyant chairman. Johnson had risen to his position through a series of victories in corporate power struggles and company mergers and acquisitions. In 1976 he became CEO of Standard Brands, a middle-sized food company with products such as Chase and Sanborn coffee and Fleischmann's margarine. In 1981 he negotiated a merger with Nabisco through a $1.9 billion stock swap, at that time one of the largest in consumer-product companies. Johnson became CEO of the new Nabisco Brands in 1984, and in 1985, he helped to engineer the merger with RJRT. The tobacco company, in its search for ways to diversify its operations, felt that its skill in marketing established brands would find a perfect match in a consumer products company such as Nabisco Brands. Through careful cultivation of board members, Johnson developed the support he needed to be made chairman of RJR Nabisco in 1986.

As chairman of RJR Nabisco, Johnson felt dissatisfied with the value the market placed on the company's stock. The stock traded consistently in the $50 to $60 per-share range, and Johnson was sure that the company was worth much more. In the fall of 1988, his concern resulted in a proposal he laid in front of a surprised board: He would lead a management buyout of the giant corporation at $75 per share, a transaction valued at the unprecedented amount of $17 billion. The board's response was to form a special committee of its members to put RJR Nabisco up for auction. This action led to a bidding war of several rounds, which involved practically all of the major takeover specialists on Wall Street. Ultimately Johnson and his backers at the Shearson Lehman Hutton brokerage unit of American Express lost to KKR, whose winning bid of $109 per share, $25 billion in total, was financed by high-yielding, unsecured junk bonds. On February 9, 1989, the day KKR officially acquired ownership of RJR Nabisco, Johnson resigned his position at the company, taking with him a "golden parachute" valued at $53 million. KKR quickly hired Gerstner, formerly a top executive at American Express, to take over as CEO in April.

Gerstner assumed control of a company with a very different financial profile from the one run by Johnson. In the second quarter of 1989, RJR Holdings Corporation, the corporate entity set up by KKR that ultimately owned RJR Nabisco, was liable for over $1 billion of interest and debt expense and showed a long-term debt of $22.3 billion. In comparison, the publicly held RJR Nabisco paid only $145 million in interest and debt expense in the second quarter of 1988, and its total long-term debt at the end of 1988 was $4.9 billion.

## Current Position

In 1988, RJRT was the second-largest cigarette manufacturer in the United States with an overall share of 31.8% of cigarette sales and 5 of the top 11 largest-selling cigarette brands in the United States (see **Exhibit 1**). Together with RJR Nabisco's international tobacco operations, sales of $7.1 billion generated operating income of $1.9 billion, compared to $6.3 billion and $1.8 billion, respectively, in 1987 (see **Exhibit 2**). Substantially all of the company's manufacturing facilities were located in or near Winston-Salem, North Carolina. RJRT sold its cigarettes primarily to chain stores, other large retail outlets, and through distributors to retail and wholesale outlets. No customer accounted for more than 5% of sales in 1988. But although the company's customers were retailers and distributors, it aimed its advertising and marketing efforts at its ultimate consumer—the general public. Image-oriented advertising techniques included the use of newspapers and magazines, billboards, coupons, point-of-sale displays, and sponsorship of recreational events.

## SMOKING AND SOCIETY

With cigarette sales having peaked in the early 1980s and having declined since then, the U.S. tobacco industry was in decline. Earlier in this century, tobacco companies marketed their products as actually promoting health, with endorsements by doctors as well as by celebrities in their advertisements. However, early in the 1950s, researchers published studies linking cigarette smoking and lung cancer. The industry vigorously disputed these results, arguing that the research showed at best a correlation between smoking and disease and did not establish a causal connection. However, the mounting evidence against smoking led to the 1964 report by the Surgeon General of the United States that condemned smoking as carcinogenic. Laws were passed requiring that warnings about the health effects of smoking be printed prominently on all packages of cigarettes and on advertising for them. In 1971, tobacco advertisements were banned from radio and television.

The 1980s saw the growth of movements to ban smoking in public places, and many localities passed laws to put such prohibitions into effect. In the later part of the decade, the Surgeon General called for the creation of a "smoke-free society" by the year 2000, and California passed a 35¢-per-pack cigarette tax used to fund an advertising campaign against smoking. Cigarette smoke inhaled by nonsmokers had been recommended for the EPA list of "Group A" carcinogens, which included the most dangerous compounds such as asbestos. However, the cigarette industry continued to fight a rearguard action against the antismoking movement. With little or no support from the scientific community, it questioned the link between smoking and disease. It spent massive amounts of money in lobbying efforts and on election campaign contributions for politicians. A spokesperson for Philip Morris offered this diagnosis of the situation:

*It's part of the whole anti-business movement, the Green Movement . . . . People have more time to think these days, and so they're more and more critical of everything. Look how critical they are of governments. And there's this health-consciousness movement running through the world.[2]*

Yet it was clear that the tide had turned against the tobacco industry. According to a 1987 survey in a report by the Surgeon General, the incidence of smoking varied inversely with level of education, ranging from 36% of those who never finished high school to 16% of college graduates. Smoking, in 1960 the socially accepted habit of 58% of men and 34% of women, was rapidly becoming the socially unacceptable "vice" of a minority.

## THE RESPONSE OF THE TOBACCO INDUSTRY

In more recent years, the population of cigarette smokers in the United States had been shrinking at an annual rate of 2½% to 3%. However, manufacturers had offset this decline by increasing the price of their product by about 10% per year. Company executives had long held that the demand for cigarettes by brand-loyal smokers was inelastic and therefore little affected by price increases, but the rise of the "savings segment" in the cigarette market had cast doubt on this view. In this segment, which included generic cigarettes and discount brands (such as RJRT's Doral), prices were 30¢ to 55¢ below those of the regular branded products. By 1989, the savings segment share of the cigarette market had reached 15%, double its level in 1985.

To maintain profitability, cigarette manufacturers had two options: expansion in the world market or diversification into other businesses. Both options, however, faced the same basic problem: There was no other business that generated the extraordinary operating margins of the domestic cigarette trade. In 1989 RJRT's operating margin on its U.S. cigarette business was over 42%, whereas the Nabisco operations returned only 12%. Profits on foreign sales of cigarettes were much lower than domestic sales largely because of the difference in taxes. Whereas the average of combined federal and state taxes accounted for 28% of the cost of a package of cigarettes in the United States, the corresponding worldwide average figure was 66%.

Finally, U.S. cigarette makers were confronted with a dilemma in the structure of the world market for cigarettes, a market that was growing at an annual rate of 1%. In the less-developed countries, where the growth was greatest (over 2% per year), smokers could not afford the more expensive imported brands; but the richer countries were experiencing slower growth or actual declines in consumption. Advertising restrictions and public health education campaigns similar to those in the United States were certainly major factors in

---

[2]  Maggie Mahar, "Going Up in Smoke?" *Barrons*, 9 July, 1990, 21.

the lessened popularity of smoking in the more-developed countries. The marketing of cigarettes in less-developed countries often went unregulated and unopposed due to lack of governmental resources.

All the large tobacco companies had taken steps to diversify their operations, to the point where most of their sales revenue came from nontobacco sources. However, because of the profitability of the cigarette industry, more than one-half of the operating income for each company flowed from cigarette sales. In particular, RJR Nabisco depended upon cigarettes for 73% of its income, a situation the company expected would continue for the foreseeable future.

## THE MECHANICS OF TRADE LOADING

Trade loading was fueled by "push," inducements by the manufacturer to wholesalers to buy more of a product than they needed, and by "pull," manufacturer-financed promotions at the retail level. In both push and pull, price discounts were a major tactic.

Trade loading produced problems in the tobacco industry for three reasons. First, the pull was more difficult because unit sales of cigarettes in the United States were falling as smoking became less popular. Second, the manufacturer had to pay a 16¢-per-pack federal excise tax on all cigarettes shipped to wholesalers, which increased the up-front costs of trade loading. Third, the tobacco industry had a full-return policy for cigarettes more than six months old, which were regarded as too stale to sell (the **Appendix** shows current FASB standards for revenue recognition when a right of return exists). Although the manufacturer received an excise tax credit for returned cigarettes, the costs of producing the excess cigarettes had been wasted.

By its nature, trade loading tended to perpetuate itself. If a manufacturer wanted to report steady or increasing results, it would find it difficult to do so without continuing the practice of trade loading. Gerald H. Long, a retired senior executive of RJRT, remembered the corporate philosophy under F. Ross Johnson in this way: "My friend Ross said, 'Jerry, you have one great big major objective, and that's producing over $300 million a quarter in operating profits.'"[3]

RJRT also found itself increasing its reliance on trade loading because it was losing ground to Philip Morris, its competitor for market share. Company executives estimated that in 1984 the size of RJRT wholesaler inventory was 5 billion cigarettes, rising to 14 billion at the beginning of 1988. In customer warehouses at the beginning of 1989, there was an excess of 18.5 billion RJRT cigarettes, a surplus supply of 42 days over the ideal wholesale stock of 4½ days of supply or 2 billion cigarettes. Inventory runoff, reduction in shipments, and

---

[3]  Loomis, 96.

unusually large numbers of returned cigarettes reduced the excess to 1 billion cigarettes by September 1989. However, a continuation of the existing practice of trade loading would have resulted in another inflated inventory by early 1990, perhaps even larger than before.

Although RJRT was the company with the largest trade load, its competitors in the tobacco industry also participated in the process. The business magazine *Fortune* estimated that the wholesaler excess inventory of 18.5 billion RJRT cigarettes was matched by an additional 30 billion excess inventory of other brands.[4]

## THE WHOLESALER PERSPECTIVE

One incentive for wholesalers to participate in trade loading was price discounts for large volume purchases. Equivalently, the prospect of a price increase could encourage wholesalers to purchase more product than usual for inventory. Thus, the practice was given a boost in late 1982 when cigarette vendors were faced with a doubling of the federal excise tax on cigarettes in January 1983. In addition, starting in 1983, cigarette manufacturers adopted a policy of regular price increases in June and December, whereas previously price increases had followed no fixed schedule. Thus, wholesalers responded by making large semiannual annual purchases of cigarettes, boosting reported earnings for manufacturers in the June and December quarters. Smaller peaks in purchasing also occurred in April and September, motivated by manufacturer price discounts and favorable payment terms.

In fact, the profits of wholesalers in some cases had become dependent upon the artificial end-of-quarter increases resulting from trade loading. Eliminating the practice would transform them into break-even or money-losing operations.

Because of the large volume of small retail outlets such as newspaper stands and convenience stores that lacked scanner technology to count sales, good figures on retail sales of cigarettes were not available. Thus, manufacturers have had to rely on sales to wholesalers as a proxy to calculate shares of the consumer market.

## THE COMPANY RESPONSE

In 1988, RJRT adopted a three-year plan to gradually eliminate the trade loading problem in such a way that projected semiannual increases in cigarette prices would offset reductions in reported unit sales from bringing down trade inventories. By limiting shipments to wholesalers at the end of the second

---

[4]   Ibid., 94.

quarter, excess inventories were brought down to 10 billion cigarettes. However, the plan was neglected in the latter part of 1988 as management focused all of its attention on the negotiations leading up to the buyout of RJR Nabisco in November. Shipments to wholesalers were not limited in December, resulting in the 18.5 billion inventory load in early 1989.

Trade loading also contributed to the return of 2.5 billion cigarettes to RJRT in 1988, 1.4% of the 177 billion sold in that year. Indications were that the company's problem with returns was worse than its competitors: in Texas, RJRT, with approximately one-third of the market, accounted for 43% of returns in a recent period. As head of RJRT, one of Johnston's greatest concerns was the fear that the return figures were only the tip of an iceberg. They suggested that because of the difficulty of keeping track of massive cigarette inventories, stale cigarettes were actually ending up in stores. Resulting consumer dissatisfaction would lead to further erosion of RJRT's market share.

Johnston realized he needed more information about the scope of the problem. In the past, estimates of the trade load had been educated guesses at best. Soon after he became CEO, Johnston commissioned a wholesaler inventory count, a task that was complicated by the fact that wholesalers, having run out of space in their own warehouses, were renting additional ones to store excess inventories.

Johnston's analysis showed that while trade loading was propping up reported income, its effects on cash flow were negative. The excessive demand at ends of quarters disrupted production schedules and added to production costs, and the manufacturer's need to "push" trade loading through price discounts also drained cash from the company. By eliminating trade loading, the company would increase its net cash flow by a small amount, probably less than $20 million.

## CONCLUSION

The end of the quarter was fast approaching. Wholesalers would add yet another layer to their cigarette inventories unless the company took action to restrain them. Gerstner had to make a decision about trade loading soon.

**EXHIBIT 1**
**1988 RJRT Market Share and Position**

| Brand | Market Share[a] | Market Position[a] |
|-------|-----------------|--------------------|
| Winston | 10.7% | # 2 |
| Salem | 7.3 | 3 |
| Camel | 4.3 | 6 |
| Doral | 3.4 | 9 |
| Vantage | 2.9 | 11 |
| RJRT overall | 31.8% | 2 |

Source:  RJR Nabisco, Form 10-K (1988): 6.

[a] Based on independent estimated 1988 shipments to wholesalers.

**EXHIBIT 2**
**Excerpts from 1988 RJR Nabisco, Inc., Financial Statements**

REPORT OF ERNST & WHINNEY, INDEPENDENT AUDITORS

RJR Nabisco, Inc.
Its Directors and Stockholders

We have audited the consolidated financial statements and related schedules of RJR Nabisco, Inc. and subsidiaries listed in Item 14(a)(1) and (2) of the annual report on Form 10-K of RJR Nabisco, Inc. for the year ended December 31, 1988. These financial statements and related schedules are the responsibility of the Company's management. Our responsibility is to express an opinion on these financial statements and related schedules based on our audits.

We conducted our audits in accordance with generally accepted auditing standards. Those standards require that we plan and perform the audit to obtain reasonable assurance about whether the financial statements and related schedules are free of material misstatement. An audit includes examining, on a test basis, evidence supporting the amounts and disclosures in the financial statements and related schedules. An audit also includes assessing the accounting principles used and significant estimates made by management, as well as evaluating the overall financial statement presentation. We believe that our audits provide a reasonable basis for our opinion.

In our opinion, the financial statements referred to above present fairly, in all material respects, the consolidated financial position of RJR Nabisco, Inc. and subsidiaries at December 31, 1988 and 1987, and the consolidated results of their operations and their cash flows for each of the three years in the period ended December 31, 1988 in conformity with generally accepted accounting principles. Further, it is our opinion that the schedules referred to above present fairly, in all material respects, the information set forth therein in compliance with the applicable accounting regulation of the Securities and Exchange Commission.

ERNST & WHINNEY

Atlanta, Georgia
January 30, 1989

Source: RJR Nabisco, Form 10-K (1988): F-1.

**EXHIBIT 2 (continued)**

### RJR NABISCO, INC.
### CONSOLIDATED FINANCIAL STATEMENTS

The Summary of Significant Accounting Policies and the Notes to Consolidated Financial Statements on pages F-6 through F-20 are integral parts of the accompanying financial statements.

### SUMMARY OF SIGNIFICANT ACCOUNTING POLICIES

This summary of significant accounting policies is presented to assist in understanding the Company's financial statements included in this report. These policies conform to generally accepted accounting principles and have been consistently followed by the Company in all material respects.

**Consolidation**
The Company includes in its consolidated financial statements the accounts of the parent and all subsidiaries.

**Cash Equivalents**
The Company classifies as cash equivalents all short-term, highly liquid investments that are readily convertible to known amounts of cash and so near maturity that they present insignificant risk of changes in value because of changes in interest rates.

**Inventories**
In all of the Company's businesses, inventories are stated at the lower of cost or market. Various methods are used for determining cost. The cost of domestic inventories is determined principally under the LIFO method. The cost of remaining inventories is determined under the FIFO, specific lot and weighted average methods. In accordance with recognized trade practice, stocks of tobacco, which must be cured for more than one year, are classified as current assets.

**Depreciation**
Property, plant and equipment are depreciated principally by the straight-line method.

**Goodwill and Trademarks**
Goodwill and trademarks are generally amortized on a straight-line basis over a 40-year period.

**Other Income and Expense**
The Company includes interest income, gains and losses on foreign currency transactions and other financial items in "Other income (expense), net." The 1988 amount also includes $50 million in connection with advisory fees incurred in anticipation of the Merger described in Note 1 to the Consolidated Financial Statements.

**Income Taxes**
The Company uses the flow-through method in accounting for investment tax credits, whereby the provision for income taxes is reduced in the year the tax credits first become available. Deferred income taxes are accounted for under the deferred method since the Company has not yet adopted the liability method of Statement of Financial Accounting Standards ("SFAS") No. 96.

**Excise Taxes**
Excise taxes are excluded from "Net sales" and "Cost of products sold."

**Restricted Stock**
On the date of grant to certain officers and other employees, restricted shares are recorded as issued and outstanding and the cost, based on market value at grant date, is deducted from stockholders' equity as "Unamortized value of restricted stock." The unvested amount is amortized to compensation expense over the vesting period, generally three years.

---

Source:   RJR Nabisco, Form 10-K (1988): F-2.

**EXHIBIT 2 (continued)**

### RJR NABISCO, INC.
### CONSOLIDATED STATEMENTS OF INCOME AND RETAINED EARNINGS
**For the Years Ended December 31**

| | 1988 | 1987 | 1986 |
|---|---|---|---|
| | (Dollars in Millions Except Per Share Amounts) | | |
| Net sales* | $16,956 | $15,766 | $15,102 |
| Costs and expenses: | | | |
| Cost of products sold* | 8,786 | 8,221 | 7,920 |
| Selling, advertising, administrative and general expenses | 5,322 | 4,991 | 4,842 |
| Restructuring expense, net (Note 16) | — | 250 | — |
| Operating income | 2,848 | 2,304 | 2,340 |
| Interest and debt expense (net of capitalized amounts of $34, $19 and $71, respectively) | (579) | (489) | (565) |
| Other income (expense), net | 17 | 1 | 7 |
| Income from continuing operations before provision for income taxes | 2,286 | 1,816 | 1,782 |
| Provision for income taxes (Note 2) | 893 | 735 | 757 |
| Income from continuing operations | 1,393 | 1,081 | 1,025 |
| Income (loss) from discontinued operations, net of taxes (Note 3) | — | (7) | 78 |
| Gain (loss) on sale of discontinued operations, net of taxes (Note 3) | — | 215 | (39) |
| Income before extraordinary item | 1,393 | 1,289 | 1,064 |
| Extraordinary item—loss from early extinguishment of debt, net of taxes (Note 4) | — | 80 | — |
| Net income | 1,393 | 1,209 | 1,064 |
| Less preferred dividends | 15 | 30 | 102 |
| Net income applicable to Common Stock | 1,378 | 1,179 | 962 |
| Retained earnings at beginning of year | 5,548 | 4,832 | 4,357 |
| Less: | | | |
| Cash dividends on Common Stock | 475 | 440 | 378 |
| Retirement of Company's stocks (Notes 12 and 13) | 1,102 | 23 | 109 |
| Retained earnings at end of year | $ 5,349 | $ 5,548 | $ 4,832 |
| Income per common share: | | | |
| Continuing operations | $5.92 | $4.19 | $3.68 |
| Discontinued operations | — | 0.83 | 0.15 |
| Extraordinary item | — | (0.32) | — |
| Net income | $5.92 | $4.70 | $3.83 |
| Average number of common shares outstanding (in thousands) | 232,587 | 250,612 | 251,073 |

*Excludes excise taxes of $3,448, $3,314 and $3,057 for 1988, 1987 and 1986, respectively.

Source: RJR Nabisco, Form 10-K, (1988): F-3.

**EXHIBIT 2 (continued)**

**RJR NABISCO, INC.**
**CONSOLIDATED STATEMENTS OF CASH FLOWS**
**For the Years Ended December 31**

|  | 1988 | 1987 | 1986 |
|---|---|---|---|
|  | (Dollars in Millions) | | |
| Cash flows from operating activities (Note 5) | $ 1,840 | $ 1,769 | $ 1,718 |
| Cash flows from investing activities: | | | |
| Capital expenditures | (1,142) | (936) | (1,022) |
| Deposits on fresh fruit vessels | (126) | — | — |
| Proceeds from sale of capital assets | 52 | 48 | 59 |
| Proceeds from dispositions of businesses | 489 | 1,597 | 1,321 |
| Acquisitions of businesses and minority interests | (189) | (72) | — |
| Collections of notes receivable | 19 | 92 | 128 |
| Net cash flows (used in) from investing activities | (897) | 729 | 486 |
| Cash flows from financing activities: | | | |
| Dividends paid | (494) | (474) | (514) |
| Proceeds from the issuance of long-term debt | 1,435 | 1,288 | 1,125 |
| Payments to retire long-term debt | (236) | (2,680) | (960) |
| Increase (decrease) in notes payable | 9 | (89) | (121) |
| Proceeds from issuance of Company's stocks | 22 | 11 | 12 |
| Repurchase of Company's stocks | (1,380) | (317) | (1,467) |
| Net cash flows (used in) financing activities | (644) | (2,261) | (1,925) |
| Effect of exchange rate changes on cash and cash equivalents | 38 | 24 | 1 |
| Net change in cash and cash equivalents | 337 | 261 | 280 |
| Cash and cash equivalents at beginning of year | 1,088 | 827 | 547 |
| Cash and cash equivalents at end of year | $ 1,425 | $ 1,088 | $   827 |

See Note 5 for Supplemental Cash Flows Information.

Source:  RJR Nabisco, Form 10-K (1988): F-4.

**EXHIBIT 2 (continued)**

## RJR NABISCO, INC.
## CONSOLIDATED BALANCE SHEETS
### December 31

|  | 1988 | 1987 |
|---|---|---|
|  | (Dollars in Millions) | |
| **ASSETS** | | |
| **Current assets:** | | |
| Cash and cash equivalents | $ 1,425 | $ 1,088 |
| Accounts and notes receivable (less allowances of $84 and $61, respectively) | 1,920 | 1,745 |
| Inventories (Note 6) | 2,571 | 2,678 |
| Prepaid expenses and excise taxes | 265 | 329 |
| Total current assets | 6,181 | 5,840 |
| Property, plant and equipment—at cost (Note 7) | 8,363 | 7,563 |
| Less accumulated depreciation | 2,214 | 1,716 |
| Net property, plant and equipment | 6,149 | 5,847 |
| Goodwill and trademarks (net of amortization of $442 and $326, respectively) | 4,555 | 4,525 |
| Other assets and deferred charges | 866 | 649 |
|  | $17,751 | $16,861 |
| **LIABILITIES AND STOCKHOLDERS' EQUITY** | | |
| **Current liabilities:** | | |
| Notes payable (Note 8) | $   423 | $   442 |
| Accounts payable and accrued accounts (Note 9) | 3,220 | 3,187 |
| Current maturities of long-term debt (Note 10) | 337 | 162 |
| Income taxes accrued | 300 | 332 |
| Total current liabilities | 4,280 | 4,123 |
| Long-term debt (Note 10) | 4,975 | 3,884 |
| Other noncurrent liabilities | 1,617 | 1,797 |
| Deferred income taxes | 1,060 | 846 |
| Commitments and contingencies (Note 11) | | |
| Redeemable preferred stock (Note 12) | 125 | 173 |
| Common stockholders' equity (Notes 13 and 14): | | |
| Common stock | 229 | 251 |
| Paid-in capital | 290 | 312 |
| Cumulative translation adjustments | 101 | 86 |
| Retained earnings | 5,349 | 5,548 |
| Treasury stock, at cost | (190) | (159) |
| Unamortized value of restricted stock | (85) | — |
| Total common stockholders' equity | 5,694 | 6,038 |
|  | $17,751 | $16,861 |

Source:   RJR Nabisco, Form 10-K (1988): F-5.

**EXHIBIT 2 (continued)**

**RJR NABISCO, INC.**
**NOTES TO CONSOLIDATED FINANCIAL STATEMENTS—(Continued)**

**Note 17—Segment Information**
*Lines of Business Data*
The company classifies its continuing operations into two principal lines of business which are described in Management's Discussion and Analysis, appearing elsewhere herein.  Summarized financial information for these operations for each of the past three years is shown in the following tables.

| | 1988 | 1987 | 1986 |
|---|---|---|---|
| Net sales: | | | |
| Tobacco | $ 7,068 | $ 6,346 | $ 5,866 |
| Food | 9,888 | 9,420 | 9,236 |
| Consolidated net sales | $16,956 | $15,766 | $15,102 |
| Operating income: | | | |
| Tobacco | $ 1,924 | $ 1,822 | $ 1,660 |
| Food | 1,215 | 1,035 | 944 |
| Restructuring expense, net (1) | — | (250) | — |
| Corporate (includes amortization of intangibles) (2) | (291) | (303) | (264) |
| Consolidated operating income | $ 2,848 | $ 2,304 | $ 2,340 |
| Assets at December 31: | | | |
| Tobacco | $ 5,393 | $ 5,208 | $ 4,882 |
| Food | 10,382 | 10,117 | 9,822 |
| Corporate (3) | 1,976 | 1,536 | 1,281 |
| | 17,751 | 16,861 | 15,985 |
| Net assets of discontinued operations | — | — | 716 |
| Consolidated assets | $17,751 | $16,861 | $16,701 |
| Capital expenditures: | | | |
| Tobacco | $    459 | $    433 | $    613 |
| Food | 621 | 445 | 344 |
| Corporate | 62 | 58 | 65 |
| Consolidated capital expenditures | $ 1,142 | $    936 | $ 1,022 |
| Depreciation expense: | | | |
| Tobacco | $    203 | $    178 | $    145 |
| Food | 279 | 260 | 246 |
| Corporate | 14 | 12 | 11 |
| Consolidated depreciation expense | $    496 | $    450 | $    402 |

(1) Restructuring expense, net for 1987 includes $(261) million, $18 million and $(7) million for Tobacco, Food and Corporate, respectively (see Note 16 to the Consolidated Financial Statements).
(2) Includes amortization of intangibles for Tobacco and Food, respectively for 1988, $1 million and $124 million; for 1987, $1 million and $120 million; and for 1986, $1 million and $124 million.
(3) All cash and cash equivalents are included in Corporate assets.

Source:   RJR Nabisco, Form 10-K (1988): F-19.

## EXHIBIT 2 (continued)

### RJR NABISCO, INC.
### NOTES TO CONSOLIDATED FINANCIAL STATEMENTS—(Continued)

**Note 17—Segment Information—(Continued)**
*Geographic Data*
The following table shows certain financial information relating to the Company's continuing operations in various geographic areas.

|  | 1988 | 1987 | 1986 |
|---|---|---|---|
| **Net sales:** | | | |
| United States | $12,525 | $11,721 | $11,338 |
| Canada | 853 | 850 | 1,060 |
| Europe | 2,698 | 2,361 | 2,055 |
| Other geographic areas | 1,786 | 1,387 | 1,217 |
| Less transfers between geographic areas (1) | (906) | (553) | (568) |
| Consolidated net sales | $16,956 | $15,766 | $15,102 |
| **Operating income:** | | | |
| United States | $ 2,375 | $ 2,261 | $ 2,128 |
| Canada | 76 | 119 | 92 |
| Europe | 393 | 247 | 186 |
| Other geographic areas | 295 | 230 | 198 |
| Restructuring expense, net (2) | — | (250) | — |
| Corporate (includes amortization of intangibles) | (291) | (303) | (264) |
| Consolidated operating income | $ 2,848 | $ 2,304 | $ 2,340 |
| **Assets at December 31:** | | | |
| United States | $11,217 | $10,881 | $10,982 |
| Canada | 862 | 700 | 896 |
| Europe | 2,307 | 2,293 | 1,660 |
| Other geographic areas | 1,389 | 1,451 | 1,166 |
| Corporate | 1,976 | 1,536 | 1,281 |
|  | 17,751 | 16,861 | 15,985 |
| Net assets of discontinued operations | — | — | 716 |
| Consolidated assets | $17,751 | $16,861 | $16,701 |
| Liabilities of the Company's continuing operations located in foreign countries at December 31 | $ 1,940 | $ 1,831 | $ 1,578 |

(1) Transfers between geographic areas (which consist principally of fresh and canned fruit from Latin America, Africa and the Philippines transferred to the United States and Europe and tobacco principally from the United States to Europe) are generally made at fair market value.
(2) Restructuring expense, net for 1987 includes $(428) million and $178 million for the United States and Canada, respectively (see Note 16 to the Consolidated Financial Statements).

Source:   RJR Nabisco, Form 10-K (1988): F-20.

**EXHIBIT 2 (continued)**

RJR NABISCO, INC.
NOTES TO CONSOLIDATED FINANCIAL STATEMENTS—(Continued)

**Note 18—Quarterly Results of Operations (Unaudited)**
The following is a summary of the quarterly results of operations for the years ended December 31:

| | First | Second | Third | Fourth |
|---|---|---|---|---|
| | | (Dollars in Millions Except Per Share Amounts) | | |
| **1988** | | | | |
| Net sales | $3,792 | $4,286 | $4,160 | $4,718 |
| Operating income (1) | 527 | 708 | 706 | 907 |
| Income from continuing operations | 273 | 354 | 355 | 411 |
| Net income (2) | 273 | 354 | 355 | 411 |
| Income from continuing operations per common share | 1.09 | 1.50 | 1.55 | 1.78 |
| Net income per common share | 1.09 | 1.50 | 1.55 | 1.78 |
| **1987** | | | | |
| Net sales | $3,489 | $4,023 | $3,835 | $4,419 |
| Operating income (3) | 277 | 632 | 650 | 745 |
| Income from continuing operations | 92 | 299 | 320 | 370 |
| Net income (4) | 220 | 299 | 320 | 370 |
| Income from continuing operations per common share | 0.33 | 1.16 | 1.24 | 1.46 |
| Net income per common share (4) | 0.84 | 1.16 | 1.24 | 1.46 |

(1) Effective January 1, 1988, the deferral method of accounting for crop expenditures was changed to a method of currently expensing such costs in the year incurred. In the first, third and fourth quarters of 1988, the Company recorded gains on the sale of certain operations. The first quarter gains were more than offset by charges resulting from the accounting change mentioned above. Third quarter gains were partially offset by writedowns for the permanent impairment of the investment in certain foreign operations. Fourth quarter results include a pre-tax gain of $130 million from the sale of the Company's cereal and confectionery businesses in the United Kingdom.

(2) The effective tax rate increased to 46.5% for the fourth quarter of 1988 compared to 35.3% for the first three quarters of 1988 due to tax provisions on the repatriation of certain foreign earnings in anticipation of the Tender Offer and Merger.

(3) Operating income for the first, second and third quarters of 1987 included $219 million, $12 million and $19 million, respectively for net restructuring expense (see Note 16 to the Consolidated Financial Statements).

(4) Net income in the first quarter of 1987 included the net gain on the sale of the Company's discontinued operations of $215 million or 86 cents per share and the extraordinary loss from the early extinguishment of debt of $80 million or 32 cents per share (see Notes 3 and 4 to the Consolidated Financial Statements).

Source: RJR Nabisco, Form 10-K (1988): F-21.

## APPENDIX
## FASB Standards for Revenue Recognition

### Profit and Revenue Recognition

.101   Profit is realized when a sale in the ordinary course of business is effected, unless the circumstances are such that the collection of the sale price is not reasonably assured. [Accordingly,] revenues shall ordinarily be [recognized] at the time a transaction is completed, with appropriate provision for uncollectible accounts.

### Criteria for Recognizing Revenue When Right of Return Exists

.107   If an enterprise sells its product but gives the buyer the right to return the product, revenue from the sales transaction shall be recognized at time of sale only if *all* of the following conditions are met:

a.   The seller's price to the buyer is substantially fixed or determinable at the date of sale.

b.   The buyer has paid the seller, or the buyer is obligated to pay the seller and the obligation is not contingent on resale of the product. [Footnote: This condition is met if the buyer pays the seller at time of sale or if the buyer does not pay at time of sale but is obligated to pay at a specified date or dates. . . .]

c.   The buyer's obligation to the seller would not be changed in the event of theft or physical destruction or damage of the product.

d.   The buyer acquiring the product for resale has economic substance apart from that provided by the seller. [Footnote: This condition relates primarily to buyers that exist "on paper," that is, buyers that have little or no physical facilities or employees. It prevents enterprises from recognizing sales revenue on transactions with parties that the sellers have established primarily for the purpose of recognizing such sales revenue.]

e.   The seller does not have significant obligations for future performance to directly bring about resale of the product by the buyer.

f.   The amount of future returns can be reasonably estimated (. . .).

Sales revenue and cost of sales that are not recognized at time of sale because the foregoing conditions are not met shall be recognized either when the return privilege has substantially expired or if those conditions subsequently are met, whichever occurs first.

.108   If sales revenue is recognized because the conditions of paragraph .107 are met, any costs or losses that may be expected in connection with any returns shall be accrued . . . . Sales revenue and cost of sales reported in the income statement shall be reduced to reflect estimated returns.

---

Source:  FASB Accounting Standards Current Text, Sec. R75, 39747-49.

# Circuit City Stores, Inc. (A)

Michael Chalifoux, the senior vice president and chief financial officer of Circuit City Stores, a discount specialty retailer, was disturbed about a problem that had been brewing for some time. The issue involved Circuit City's accounting practices, specifically regarding the recognition of revenue from the sale of extended warranty and product maintenance contracts.

Chalifoux had just learned that the Financial Accounting Standards Board (FASB) had released a proposed FASB technical bulletin that would require Circuit City Stores to change its accounting for extended warranty and product maintenance contracts. The proposed accounting change would delay full recognition of revenue and income until the warranty period had expired. As a result, reported income would be lower than currently reported under Circuit City's present accounting policies.

Circuit City believed that revenue from sales of extended warranty contracts most closely matched costs under the partial revenue recognition method. The FASB was proposing that the deferral of revenue method was more appropriate, whereas Circuit City argued that this would result in a mismatch of revenues and expenses.

## BACKGROUND

Circuit City Stores was one of the first consumer electronics and major appliance retailers to adopt the concept of low pricing, selection, and service. By 1990 the company operated 149 retail outlets, 125 of which were designated Circuit City superstores. These 32,000-square-foot stores were designed to

*Susan S. Harmeling prepared this case under the supervision of Professor William J. Bruns, Jr.*

Copyright © 1990 by the President and Fellows of Harvard College. Harvard Business School case 191-086.

display a broad product selection from 2,800 brand-name items sold by Circuit City. In a typical superstore, customers could choose from almost 150 color televisions, more than 50 video cassette recorders, 30 camcorders, 30 compact disc players, 45 refrigerators, and 25 washer-and-dryer pairs. In addition, the selections could include car stereos, microwaves, cellular phones, telephones, telephone answering machines, and facsimile machines. Large in-store warehouses provided instant product availability, and mechanized distribution centers allowed overnight inventory replenishment. Complete delivery, installation, and service were offered for almost every item sold.

Circuit City had experienced rapid growth in sales and profitability. Net revenues had increased from $705 million in 1986 to $2.1 billion in 1990. During the same period, net earnings had increased from $22 million to $78 million. Financial statements included in the 1990 annual report of Circuit City Stores are shown in **Exhibit 1**.

Circuit City Stores and other discount retailers like it made substantial profit margins on extended warranty contracts. An example of a typical transaction would be the following scenario. A retailer would sell a stereo system with a cost of $900 for $1,000. At the same time, the retailer offered the customer the option to purchase a two-year service contract for $100. Under the terms of the service contract, the retailer would clean and inspect the stereo every six months and would cover the cost of parts and labor should it need repair. Future costs to perform under the contract were estimated at $20. The retailer generally sold service contracts only to customers who also purchased a stereo from that retailer. The transaction could be summarized as follows:

|          | Stereo  | Contract | Total   |
| -------- | ------- | -------- | ------- |
| Revenue  | $1,000  | $100     | $1,100  |
| Cost     | 900     | 20       | 920     |
| Profit   | 100     | 80       | 180     |

The joint sale of equipment and service contracts was part of Circuit City's corporate strategy. By successfully selling extended warranty and service contracts to a substantial portion of equipment customers, Circuit City could price its merchandise more competitively and draw customers to its stores through advertising. Circuit City had had much experience with the combined sale of equipment and extended warranty contracts. They looked on the combined sale as one transaction because they could predict with great certainty the percentage of customers, between 40% and 70% depending on the product, who would purchase both the item for sale and the warranty contract.

## ACCOUNTING FOR EXTENDED WARRANTY CONTRACTS

There were several approaches to accounting for extended warranty contracts:

**Approach 1: Full revenue recognition**  Proponents of this approach would recognize total revenue of $1,100 and total cost of $920 at the date of the sale (that is, profit of $180). If actual costs under the service contract either fell short of or exceeded the $20 estimate, an adjustment would be made later during the contract period.

Proponents of Approach 1 used the FASB's Statement of Financial Accounting Concepts No. 5, "Recognition and Measurement in Financial Statements of Business Enterprises," to support their position. A summary of this reasoning is shown in **Exhibit 2**.

**Approach 2: Deferral of revenue**  Proponents of this approach would view the sale of the stereo and the sale of the extended warranty contract as two distinctly separate transactions that should be accounted for separately. They would recognize only the revenue and cost associated with the stereo at the point of the sale. Therefore, profit of $100 on the sale of the stereo would be recognized at that time. The $100 contract revenue would be deferred and recognized as revenue over the two-year contract period using some systematic allocation method. Costs under the contract would be recognized as incurred.

Proponents of deferring the revenue from the service contract believed it was inappropriate to recognize revenue at the point of sale because none of the services associated with the contract had yet been rendered, and therefore the revenue had not been earned.

Proponents of Approach 2 looked to a proposed Statement of Position of the American Institute of Certified Public Accountants (AICPA), "Accounting for Certain Service Transactions," for support. A summary of this reasoning is shown in **Exhibit 3**.

**Approach 3: Partial revenue recognition**  Companies such as Circuit City Stores used and supported an approach whereby a portion of the total revenue on the combined transaction would be recognized at the time of sale, with the remainder deferred and recognized over the contract period. Costs under the extended warranty contract would be recognized as incurred. This treatment would be allowable for financial reporting in only very limited circumstances.

**Sample calculation of Approach 3**  On a sale of $1,100 for a stereo and warranty with a combined expected cost of $900 + $20, this approach would result in $1,076 of revenue recognized at the time of sale, with the remaining $24 deferred and recognized over the contract period, as calculated below.

$$\frac{\$900}{\$920} \times \$1,100 = \$1,076 \quad \text{Recognized at time of sale}$$

$$\frac{\$20}{\$920} \times \$1,100 = \underline{\$\quad 24} \quad \text{Deferred revenue}$$

$$\$1,100 \quad \text{Total revenue}$$

Profit of $176 ($1,076 revenue less $900 cost) would be recognized at the time of sale. Costs under the contract would be recognized as incurred throughout the contract period.

Those who supported Approach 3 believed it was appropriate to consider the sale of the product and service contract as a package when the conditions outlined in **Exhibit 4** were met.

## CIRCUIT CITY'S DILEMMA

The issue of how to account for the retail sale of an extended warranty contract had initially been addressed and was thought to have been resolved in discussions between the Securities and Exchange Commission (SEC) and Highland Superstores, Inc. in March 1989. At that time, the SEC's staff required Highland to adopt the partial recognition method for extended warranty contract revenues.

However, FASB's proposed technical bulletin had now reopened discussions on the proper accounting method for extended warranty contracts, and Mike Chalifoux was concerned. He felt that if Circuit City were required to adopt the full deferral method, the negative impact on shareholder's equity of the largest companies in the merchandising industry would be significant.

Given the issue's importance to Circuit City Stores and its shareholders, Mr. Chalifoux wanted to be sure his reasoning on the proper accounting policies for extended warranties was correct and that he had properly explored all sides of the issue. If so, he had to decide how to make his argument clear and persuasive in a letter to FASB on the proposed bulletin. Finally, he had to consider how corporate strategy and policy might have to change if the proposed bulletin were issued as it stood at that time.

One possible way to avoid the adverse effects of the proposed accounting change would be to continue to sell extended warranty contracts but then to resell them to another party. The resale would "lock in" the profitability of the sale, but total margins would have to be reduced somewhat to allow the buyer of the contracts to earn a profit as well. Although this method might allow Circuit City to avoid the adverse effects of the proposed accounting change, it seemed at first glance to be choosing "form over substance" by letting the accounting method drive the selection of the firm's competitive strategy.

## QUESTIONS

1. Which of the three approaches to accounting for extended warranty and service contracts is most consistent with the actual substance of a sales transaction involving equipment and an extended warranty contract? Explain your selection and your reasoning fully.
2. What should Mike Chalifoux do?

**EXHIBIT 1**
**Independent Auditors' Report**

The Board of Directors and Stockholders of Circuit City Stores, Inc.:

We have audited the accompanying consolidated balance sheets of Circuit City Stores, Inc. and subsidiaries as of February 28, 1990 and 1989, and the related consolidated statements of earnings, stockholders' equity, and cash flows for each of the years in the three-year period ended February 28, 1990. These consolidated financial statements are the responsibility of the Company's management. Our responsibility is to express an opinion on these consolidated financial statements based on our audits.

We conducted our audits in accordance with generally accepted auditing standards. Those standards require that we plan and perform the audits to obtain reasonable assurance about whether the financial statements are free of material misstatement. An audit includes examining, on a test basis, evidence supporting the amounts and disclosures in the financial statements. An audit also includes assessing the accounting principles used and significant estimates made by management, as well as evaluating the overall financial statement presentation. We believe that our audits provide a reasonable basis for our opinion.

In our opinion, the consolidated financial statements referred to above present fairly, in all material respects, the financial position of Circuit City Stores, Inc. and subsidiaries at February 28, 1990 and 1989, and the results of their operations and their cash flows for each of the years in the three-year period ended February 28, 1990, in conformity with generally accepted accounting principles.

KPMG Peat Marwick
Richmond, Virginia
April 5, 1990

**EXHIBIT 1 (continued)**
**Circuit City Stores, Inc. Consolidated Statements of Earnings ($ in thousands, except per-share data)**

| Years Ended February 28 or 29 | 1990 | 1989 | 1988 |
|---|---|---|---|
| **Net sales and operating revenues (note 9)** | **$ 2,096,588** | $ 1,721,497 | $ 1,350,425 |
| Cost of sales, buying and warehousing | **1,477,502** | 1,219,570 | 961,345 |
| **Gross profit** | **619,086** | 501,927 | 389,080 |
| Selling, general and administrative expenses (note 9) | **482,229** | 379,045 | 291,489 |
| Interest expense | **8,757** | 8,382 | 8,391 |
| **Total expenses** | **490,986** | 387,427 | 299,880 |
| Earnings before income taxes | **128,100** | 114,500 | 89,200 |
| Provision for income taxes | **50,000** | 45,025 | 38,800 |
| **Net earnings** | **$ 78,100** | $ 69,475 | $ 50,400 |
| Average common shares outstanding—primary | **46,068** | 45,542 | 44,850 |
| **Net earnings per common share:** | | | |
| Primary and fully diluted | **$ 1.70** | $ 1.53 | $ 1.12 |

**EXHIBIT 1 (continued)**
**Circuit City Stores, Inc. Consolidated Balance Sheets ($ in thousands)**

| At February 28 | 1990 | 1989 |
|---|---:|---:|
| **Assets** | | |
| **Current assets:** | | |
| Cash and cash equivalents | $ 91,712 | $ 46,124 |
| Accounts and notes receivable | 9,721 | 11,558 |
| Merchandise inventory | 331,244 | 302,596 |
| Other current assets | 9,531 | 6,615 |
| **Total current assets** | 442,208 | 366,893 |
| | | |
| Property and equipment, net | 250,006 | 206,052 |
| Deferred income taxes | 6,460 | 3,023 |
| Other assets | 14,981 | 11,513 |
| **Total assets** | $ 713,655 | $ 587,481 |
| | | |
| **Liabilities and stockholders' equity:** | | |
| Current liabilities: | | |
| Current installments of long-term debt | $ 2,038 | $ 2,002 |
| Accounts payable | 165,545 | 143,426 |
| Accrued expenses and other liabilities | 31,837 | 26,957 |
| Accrued income taxes | 22,823 | 19,765 |
| **Total current liabilities** | 222,243 | 192,150 |
| | | |
| Long-term debt | 93,882 | 94,674 |
| Other liabilities | 66 | 79 |
| Deferred revenue | 38,178 | 26,961 |
| **Total liabilities** | 354,369 | 313,864 |
| | | |
| **Stockholders' equity:** | | |
| Common stock of $1 par value | 45,860 | 22,617 |
| Capital in excess of par value | 17,454 | 29,710 |
| Retained earnings | 295,972 | 221,290 |
| **Total stockholders' equity** | 359,286 | 273,617 |
| | | |
| **Total liabilities and stockholders' equity** | $ 713,655 | $ 587,481 |

**EXHIBIT 1 (continued)**
**Circuit City Stores, Inc. Consolidated Statements of Cash Flows ($ in thousands)**

| Years Ended February 28 or 29 | 1990 | 1989 | 1988 |
|---|---|---|---|
| **Operating activities:** | | | |
| Net earnings | $ 78,100 | $ 69,475 | $ 50,400 |
| Adjustments to reconcile net earnings to net cash provided by operating activities: | | | |
| Depreciation and amortization | 21,890 | 16,981 | 13,592 |
| Deferred revenue | 11,217 | 8,086 | 7,266 |
| Loss on sale of property and equipment | 262 | 70 | 157 |
| Decrease (increase) in accounts and notes receivable | 1,837 | (4,423) | 5,184 |
| Increase in merchandise inventory, deferred income taxes, and other assets | (36,873) | (96,754) | (58,636) |
| Increase in accounts payable, accrued expenses, and other liabilities | 30,044 | 75,309 | 16,448 |
| **Net cash provided by operating activities** | 106,477 | 68,744 | 34,411 |
| **Investing activities:** | | | |
| Purchases of property and equipment | (110,879) | (81,948) | (74,186) |
| Proceeds from sale of property and equipment | 43,177 | 14,091 | 52,404 |
| **Net cash used in investing activities** | (67,702) | (67,857) | (21,782) |
| **Financing activities:** | | | |
| Additions to long-term debt | 1,227 | — | 146 |
| Principal payments on long-term debt | (1,983) | (1,359) | (4,378) |
| Proceeds from issuance of common stock | 10,987 | 5,206 | 3,410 |
| Dividends paid | (3,418) | (2,477) | (1,668) |
| **Net cash provided (used) by financing activities** | 6,813 | 1,370 | (2,490) |
| Increase in cash and cash equivalents | 45,588 | 2,257 | 10,139 |
| Cash and cash equivalents at beginning of year | 46,124 | 43,867 | 33,728 |
| **Cash and cash equivalents at end of year** | $ 91,712 | $ 46,124 | $ 43,867 |
| **Supplemental disclosures of cash flow information:** | | | |
| Cash paid during the year for: | | | |
| Interest | $ 11,928 | $ 10,043 | $ 11,129 |

**EXHIBIT 1 (continued)**
**Selected Notes to Consolidated Financial Statements**

1.  **Summary of Significant Accounting Policies**

    **(G) Deferred Revenue:**   The Company sells extended warranty contracts beyond the normal manufacturers' warranty period, usually with terms of coverage (including the manufacturers' warranty period) between 12 and 60 months.  A portion of the extended warranty contract revenue is recognized immediately, and the remainder is deferred and recognized in income in a systematic manner over the contract period.  The portion deferred represents an estimate of future costs under the contract plus a profit margin based on the combined profit of the sale of the product and contract.  Direct costs under the contract are charged to expenses as incurred.

9.  **Supplementary Income Statement Information**

    Net extended warranty contract revenue, which is included in net sales and operating revenues in the accompanying consolidated statements of earnings, amounted to $112,933,000, $92,808,000, and $70,800,000 (5.4%, 5.4%, and 5.2%, respectively, of net sales and operating revenues) in fiscal years 1990, 1989, and 1988, respectively.

    Advertising expense, which is included in selling, general and administrative expenses in the accompanying consolidated statements of earnings, amounted to $129,177,000, $102,626,000, and $77,702,000 (6.2%, 6.0%, and 5.8%, respectively, of net sales and operating revenues) in fiscal years 1990, 1989, and 1988, respectively.

## EXHIBIT 2
### Support for Full Revenue Recognition in the Sale of an Extended Warranty Contract

Guidance for revenue recognition is provided in the Statement of Financial Accounting Concepts No. 5, "Recognition and Measurement in Financial Statements of Business Enterprises." Revenue must be both realized and earned prior to the recognition. In the case of the sale of an extended warranty, all the cash is received at the time the extended warranty is sold. Thus, the first criterion is met at the time of sale.

Further, revenue is considered to have been earned when the entity has substantially accomplished what it must do to be entitled to the benefits represented by the revenues. At the time of sale, an entity will be considered to have substantially completed the earning process if:

- It incurs the selling costs (the single largest cost).
- It has an established service network, which is there for the most part to provide the customer with the service associated with the manufacturer's warranty.
- Relatively few customers call for service during the extended period.
- There is a deductible (i.e., the customer must make a cash payment to obtain service), which in large part offsets the cost of the service to be provided.
- Estimates can be made with relative certainty as to future costs to be incurred under the extended warranty.

Thus the earning process is complete at the time of sale.

Appropriate revenue recognition principles require that all relevant tests as to certainty of revenue collection, relative risks associated with future anticipated costs, and the significance of such costs be considered.

Mike Chalifoux, for example, felt that deferral of revenue was not required because of uncertainties. In Circuit City's case, the revenues from extended warranties were collected at the time of the sale; the extended warranty was not subject to cancellation and prorated return of fee like an insurance policy. Thus no uncertainties existed as to realization. A long historical experience had shown that costs incurred to "perform under the contracts" after the year of sale could be estimated with great certainty and were small in relation to the extended warranty revenue amount. Costs were even smaller when considering the combined revenue from the sale of merchandise and the contract, thus representing an inconsequential future cost and low relative risk. These low uncertainties and low future costs were such that the deferral of revenue method would not be justifiable for Circuit City, and an argument might be made for using full revenue recognition.

## EXHIBIT 3
### Support for Deferral of Revenue on the Sale of an Extended Warranty Contract

The AICPA proposed Statement of Position (SOP), "Accounting for Certain Service Transactions," attempts to define criteria for determining when a service or product is incidental to a transaction.

The draft SOP acknowledges that determining when a service or product is incidental to a transaction can be difficult. According to the draft SOP, the following may indicate an incidental nature:

1.  The inclusion of the product or service does not result in a variance in the total transaction price from what would be charged excluding that product or service.
2.  The product is not sold or the service is not rendered separately in the seller's normal business.

(According to the draft SOP, "if a service is incidental to the sale of a product, the service transaction would be accounted for separately.")

Proponents of Approach 2 believed that the draft SOP would support accounting for the sale of an appliance or electronic item, for example, a stereo, and an extended warranty contract was incidental and would be accounted for separately. Customers clearly had the option to purchase the stereo without the service contract. Both the stereo and service contract had distinctly separate prices. Therefore, two transactions had taken place that required different accounting treatments.

The draft SOP further stated that if separate service transaction accounting was warranted, revenue on the service contract would be recognized on the basis of the seller's performance of the transaction. The draft SOP stated that performance was "the execution of a defined act or acts or occurs with the passage of time." The draft SOP would support recognition of the revenue over the contract period. Direct costs of providing the service would be recognized as incurred.

Proponents of Approach 2 also looked to the FASB's Statement of Financial Accounting Standards No. 60, "Accounting and Reporting by Insurance Enterprises," which discussed accounting for short-duration insurance contracts. Short-duration insurance contracts provided insurance protection for a short fixed period and enabled the insurer to cancel the contract or adjust the provisions of the contract at the end of any contract period. Statement No. 60 said that premiums from such contracts ordinarily were earned and recognized as revenue over the period of the contract. Costs under the insurance contract were recognized as insured events occurred. Proponents of Approach 2 believed that service contracts were similar to insurance contracts. The seller insured that certain services would be provided and repair claims would be covered. Therefore, in their view the accounting for service contracts should follow Statement No. 60.

At least one automobile manufacturer that sold extended warranty contracts followed Approach 2, but it also attempted to spread costs out evenly over the contract period similar to the manner in which revenue was recognized.

**EXHIBIT 4**
**Support for Partial Revenue Recognition on**
**the Sale of an Extended Warranty Contract**

It is appropriate to consider the sale of the product and its extended warranty contract as a package when the following conditions are met:

1.  The pricing of the sale of an extended warranty contract is an integral part of pricing the related product (that is, a substantial portion of customers purchasing the product also purchase extended warranty contracts and, therefore, the retailer prices the product and contract assuming both will be sold).
2.  The extended warranty contract relates to a product sold by the company (sales of contracts unaccompanied by product sales should be rare and only incidental to the company's business).
3.  The profit margin on the extended warranty contract is unusually high in comparison to the profit margin on the product.
4.  The estimated costs to be incurred to render services under the contract can be estimated with a high degree of reliability and are nominal in relation to the service contract sales price.

When the above conditions were met, supporters of partial revenue recognition would recognize a portion of the combined revenue based on the relative costs of the product and extended warranty and service.

# The Intel Pentium Chip Controversy (A)

*H-E-L-L-Ooooooooo! Who is the paying customer here? Now if Intel were giving away buggy chips, maybe, just maybe I could understand their "profit margin" mentality. Intel . . . after monopolizing the PC industry for so long, you disappoint me as a PREVIOUS customer! You made millions and you still don't understand who got you to where you are/were today . . . THE CUSTOMER!*

—Internet message posted on comp.sys.intel

**"IBM halts shipments of Pentium-based personal computers based on company research**. SOMERS, N.Y., Dec. 12, 1994 . . . IBM today announced that it has stopped shipment of all IBM personal computers based on the Intel Pentium microprocessor. The action is based on tests conducted by the IBM Research Division. . . . 'indicat[ing] that common spreadsheet programs, recalculating for 15 minutes a day, could produce Pentium-related errors as often as once every 24 days. For a customer with 500 Pentium-based PCs, this could result in as many as 20 mistakes a day. . . .'" [1]

Andrew Grove, Intel's president and CEO, quickly retorted with an Intel press release about the computational flaw in Intel's most advanced microprocessor, the Pentium: "Based on the work of our scientists analyzing real world applications, and the experience of millions of users of Pentium processor-based systems, we have no evidence of increased probability of encountering the flaw. . . . You can always contrive situations that force this error. In other words, if you know where a meteor will land, you can go there and get hit." [2]

---

*James Evans prepared this case with Professor V. G. Narayanan.*

Copyright © 1995 by the President and Fellows of Harvard College. Harvard Business School case 196-091.

---

[1] Bart Ziegler, "IBM, Intel Continue Their Wrangling Over Liability for Pentium Repair Bill," *The Wall Street Journal*, December 14, 1994, p. B6.

[2] [[Intel]] webmaster@www.intel.com, "Tell us what you think!," Copyright © 1994, Intel Corporation. All rights reserved.

"Grove . . . was caught off guard by IBM's decision to halt shipments."[3] IBM's "research" was not good science to the Berkeley-educated chemical engineering Ph.D. and his staff of engineers. Further, "Intel's engineers simply couldn't grasp consumers' demands that the Pentiums be replaced"[4]— dismissing the Pentium chip flaw as a small problem" in response to customers' fear and anger.[5] More and more computer users were calling for replacements even though Intel's research had shown that the one-in-nine billion chance of error would never affect most of them; their computers would disintegrate before the 27,000 years passed that it would take for the error to appear at Intel's estimates.

Grove offered replacements only to those heavy-duty users who could prove their vulnerability to the error.[6] Calls poured in on Intel's new hotline, which Grove had staffed with over a thousand engineers and office support personnel, expressing concerns about the error.[7] Grove had built an egalitarian engineering culture at Intel which encouraged anyone to stop by Grove's own, standard cubicle and challenge his decisions.[8] This elicited a few suggestions to make a no-questions-asked returns policy soon after the newspapers published high profile stories on the flaw in late November, but Grove kept his course.

The decision facing Intel was how to respond to these demands—whether or not to replace the defective Intel chips of all concerned users with no questions asked. The week following IBM's announcement, an Intel crisis team assembled by Grove and made up of several dozen Intel employees drawn from all parts of the company continued to meet before and after work each day to analyze and resolve the consumer crisis on their hands.[9] At an all-day meeting instigated by Grove on Monday, December 17, 1994, which was "marked . . . by passionate discussion, the decision to change the policy on the Pentium replacements was adopted and rescinded several times."[10] Both decisions had their risks and liabilities and now it was time to choose.

---

[3] Brian Gillooly, "The Chips Are Down," *Information Week*, 26 December 1994, p. 40.

[4] Robert D. Hof, "The Education of Andy Grove," *Business Week*, 16 January 1995, pp. 29-33.

[5] Bart Ziegler and Don Clark, "Chip Shot: Computer Giants' War Over Flaw in Pentium Jolts the PC Industry," *The Wall Street Journal*, 13 December 1995, p. A1.

[6] Ibid., p. A1.

[7] Hof, "The Education of Andy Grove," p. 31.

[8] Ibid., p. 29.

[9] John Markoff, "Intel's Crash Course on Consumers," *The New York Times*, 21 December 1994, p. D1.

[10] Ibid., p. D1.

## HISTORY

Microprocessing chips are the "brains" of computers sold for both home and business use. Intel was the first, the biggest, and regarded by many as the best microprocessor-maker in the computer industry. This success was won at the price of constant innovation; huge spending in marketing, production, and cycle-time improvement; and "pummeling rivals in court"[11]—the hunt for copycat competitors. Their first microprocessors for computers, the 8086 and 8088 (sold in the first IBM computer) were followed by their 80186, 80286, 80386, and 80486 editions, each with markedly more memory and processing speed than the previous generation. By 1993, when the first Pentium was introduced, a number of competitors, including AMD, Cyrix, and NexGen, were already producing clones of Intel's 486. These clones appeared on the market more quickly after Intel's 486 than the clones that followed Intel's 386 and 286 chips. Profit margins were gradually diminishing and analysts cautioned that this could affect the resources plowed back into research and development.[12] Regardless, as the competition rose, Intel's efforts to maintain its dominant position in the microprocessor market intensified.

Intel had prepared its next generation microprocessor, the Pentium, with more testing than any manufactured product ever, according to Andrew Grove, Intel's CEO.[13] "They ran the hell out of all the software they could find," said Joseph Costello, CEO of a chip-design software maker.[14] A full year of testing involving trillions of random mathematical processes was performed to detect any problems with the chip before and soon after it went on the market; a quadrillion more were performed in the year after that. Still, however, chip-testing technology was a generation behind chip-making technology; the roll-out of any new microprocessor was unavoidably risky.

Intel had strategically prepared this new chip for market with the increased patent protection available to the name, "Pentium," rather than calling it what the market had slated as the 80586. Intel began to steer the market towards this newer, faster chip while they had the market to themselves by trying to convince personal and corporate computer users that the 486 was outmoded. With an advertising blitz of unprecedented size, estimated at $150 million, the microprocessor giant advertised the logo Intel Inside® with the new trademarked name Pentium in every type of media possible. As the third

---

[11]  Don Clark, "Intel Balks at Replacing Pentium Chip Without Asking Owners Any Questions," *The Wall Street Journal*, 14 December 1994, p. A3.

[12]  J. J. Lazlo, "Intel Corp.—Company Report," PaineWebber Inc., p. 4; Gillooly, "Chips Are Down," *Information Week*, p. 12.

[13]  Jim Carlton and Stephen Kreider Yoder, "Computers: Humble Pie: Intel to Replace Its Pentium Chips," *The Wall Street Journal*, 21 December 1994, p. B1.

[14]  Robert D. Hof, "The 'Lurking Time Bomb' of Silicon Valley," *Business Week*, 19 December 1994, p. 118.

quarter of 1994 ended, Intel had shipped nearly two million of the chips to computer producers (**Exhibit 1**).

To match market dominance with internal performance, Intel designed an extensive incentive plan linking employee compensation to both profits and stock price. The plan included a cash bonus for all employees based on pretax profits and stock options for key Intel employees and executives.

## THE FLAW DISCOVERED

Dr. Thomas Nicely, a mathematics professor at Lynchburg College in Virginia, discovered inconsistencies beyond the ninth decimal of his Pentium-driven mathematical results early in the summer of 1994. Nicely was trying to prove that PCs could do mathematical work heretofore only performed on larger systems, and his continuous number crunching included processes in which the number one was divided by large reciprocal numbers. He discovered a division flaw not in his software, but in the processor of his Pentium that affected only rare combinations of numbers. The problem was in the floating point unit of the chip, the part that calculates numbers expressed in scientific notation. At the end of October, Nicely published a note on the Internet querying other users about the Pentium flaw, and a discussion emerged at the Internet news group "comp.sys.intel." The tone of discussion rapidly heightened from a calm discussion of arcane technical tests to flaming accusations and threats aimed at the massive microprocessor company.

On November 7, 1994, an *Electrical Engineering Times* article by Alexander Wolfe, pooled from the Internet discussion, prompted Intel's response that it had uncovered the flaw during tests the previous June. Although Intel had repaired the next planned version of the Pentium, it had not informed customers of the problem. Furthermore, Intel ran a series of tests from which it assessed and stated that the problem would occur only once every nine billion random calculations, or every 27,000 years for most users. The microprocessor maker reservedly offered to replace the chips of only those users who could prove that the technical nature of their work demanded a precision at risk with the rare divisional flaw. The Internet discussion group continued to "flame" the company on-line. This discussion group soon attracted the attention of reporters, and on November 22, 1994, Cable News Network (CNN) broadcast a story that revealed the chip flaw for the first time to the general public, Intel's computer-making customers, and the rest of the media.

On November 24, 1994, the beginning of a long Thanksgiving holiday weekend, the front page of *The New York Times* business section read "Flaw undermines the accuracy of Intel's Pentium."[15] That day *The Boston Globe* carried the same story on its front page, and the news began to unfold in a

---

[15] John Markhoff, "Circuit Flaw Causes Pentium Chip to Miscalculate, Intel Admits," *The New York Times*, 24 December 1994, p. B1.

month-long media blitz.  On November 25 Intel's stock was down two percentage points from its steady rise since late September.

The mounting consumer pressure to fix the Pentium flaw was hitting PC manufacturers as it had hit Intel.  Who would take responsibility for fixing the flaw?  Dell, a computer manufacturer, began advertising their Pentium with a built-in computer fix to remedy the latent flaw.  On November 28, Sequent, a mainframe manufacturer, stopped shipping Pentium machines until it could get a software solution installed.[16]  On November 30, 1994,  IBM—a major Intel customer—announced that it would replace the Pentium processor in any of its machines at the customer's request.  IBM, however, did not have Intel's support to fulfill such a promise and would potentially have had to purchase replacements on its own account.

As the second week of December passed, the media began to quiet down and Pentium flaw stories lost their sensational front-page status.  December Pentium sales continued to increase as planned, but several thousand Pentium owners were calling Intel daily.  In response Intel had rallied over a thousand of its own employees to respond and carefully assess whether or not the users were performing functions that would engage the damaged floating point unit.[17]

Intel claimed that it could replace any defective chips while continuing to meet demand for new orders.  In fact, Intel's new high production Fab 10 facility in Leixlip, Ireland, could alone produce an estimated 12.5 million Pentium chips[18] per year.  This quantity was more than twice the 5.5 million defective processors Intel sold in 1993 and 1994[19]—two-thirds of which ended up in personal computers bought by individuals, while the other third were used in computers purchased by businesses.[20]  Unfortunately, the reality of Intel's manufacturing and upgrading processes required some Intel plants to continue producing defective chips through the first quarter of 1995.[21] This implied that they could not change all production to the new chip without producing under the estimated demand. The "company's use of more robots, employment of statistical process control methodologies and implementation of Japanese manufacturing philosophies" like just-in-time in the late 1980s revealed Intel's concern for efficiency in their operations as well as innovation in their product

---

[16]  Don Clark, "Technology and Health: Intel Finds Pumped-Up Image Offers A Juicy Target in Pentium Brouhaha," *The Wall Street Journal*, 5 December 1994, p. B5.

[17]  Hof, "The Education of Andy Grove," p. 31.

[18]  Fahnestock & Co. Inc., "Intel Corporation," *The Wall Street Journal Transcript*, pp. 113, 676.

[19]  J. J. Lazlo, "Intel Corporation—Company Report," PaineWebber Inc., 26 January 1995, pp. 7-9.

[20]  Don Clark, "Intel Balks at Replacing Pentium Chip Without Asking Owners Any Questions," *The Wall Street Journal*, 14 December 1995, p. A3.

[21]  Carlton, "Humble Pie," p. B1.

line.[22]  These process improvements were matched in the early 1990s with increasingly automatic chip-testing methods.  Intel financial statements for 1993 revealed this commitment to production with record spending of $970 million on R&D and $1.93 billion on additions to property, plant, and equipment (**Exhibit 2**).  Intel had opened or expanded five new semiconductor facilities internationally in 1994, which had prepared it for everything but a run on the chip bank.

Then, on December 12, 1994, IBM dropped the bomb by publicly halting shipments of their Pentium PCs without any prior notice to Intel.  News coverage and consumer fears reignited.  IBM claimed that further testing had revealed the bug to be more common than Intel had reported.  On certain spreadsheet programs, IBM researchers claimed, the problematic number combinations were not random but much more common.  Calculations for a continuous fifteen minutes per day could produce an error once every 24 days.  Intel's stock plummeted $2.50 within an hour of IBM's announcement.[23]

Intel was faced with the decision of whether or not to replace the flawed Pentium chips of all concerned users.  If they did decide to replace the Pentium chips, would they also pay for the actual labor and other incidental costs of physically replacing the defective chips with new ones?  These labor and incidental costs were estimated to range from $31 to $750, averaging over $400 per chip replaced.[24]

## ACCOUNTING ISSUE

A company faced with an unanticipated product recall could account for it in one of three broad ways.  First, revenue can be recognized on the defective product already sold.  To match expenses correctly against this revenue, a provision can be made for estimated contingency losses (e.g., cost of replacing the product already sold).  The company may also decide to write off unsold defective inventory.  Second, companies can defer recognition of revenue until the defective products are actually replaced on the basis that revenue has not yet been earned. This option could be applied prospectively to future sales of defective products or retrospectively by reversing revenue that has already been recognized. If Intel followed this method, it could choose to defer, in part or in full, revenue on the 5.5 million defective Pentium chips already sold and recognized as revenue.  Third, companies can avoid reflecting the event in the books of the company at all on the basis that it is not material.  Each choice would have different implications for the financial statements.

---

[22] Alden M. Hayashi, "The New Intel: Moore Mature, Moore Competitive," *Electronic Business*, 15 November 1987, pp. 54-62.

[23] Peter Lewis, "IBM Deals Blow to a Rival As It Suspends Pentium Sales," *The New York Times*, p. A1.

[24] Brian Gillooly, "The Real Cost—Intel's 'free' Pentium Replacement Plan May End up Costing Large Users a Bundle," *Information Week*, 9 January 1995, p. 34.

**EXHIBIT 1**
**Based on PaineWebber "Intel Corporation Company Report."[a]**

Intel Corporation Company Report

| 1993 | Total Pentium | | |
|---|---|---|---|
| | Units[b] | ASP[c] | Sales[d] |
| 1Q | 0.00 | 0 | 0 |
| 2Q | 0.00 | 0 | 0 |
| 3Q | 0.05 | 660 | 33 |
| 4Q | 0.20 | 665 | 133 |
| Year | 0.25 | $ 664 | 166 |

| 1994 | Total Pentium | | | Total 486 | | |
|---|---|---|---|---|---|---|
| | Units | ASP | Sales | Units | ASP | Sales |
| 1Q | 0.40 | 625 | 250 | 7.50 | 169 | 1268 |
| 2Q | 0.80 | 528 | 422 | 8.56 | 165 | 1410 |
| 3Q | 1.50 | 483 | 725 | 8.00 | 138 | 1105 |
| 4Q | 3.00 | 375 | 1125 | 8.50 | 138 | 1175 |
| Year | 5.71 | $ 442 | 2522 | 32.67 | 151 | 4958 |

| 1994 | Total | | |
|---|---|---|---|
| | Units | ASP | Sales |
| 1Q | 7.91 | 192 | 1518 |
| 2Q | 9.34 | 196 | 1831 |
| 3Q | 9.48 | 193 | 1830 |
| 4Q | 11.50 | 200 | 2300 |
| Year | 38.12 | 196 | 7479 |

| Estimated 1995 | Total Pentium | | |
|---|---|---|---|
| | Units | ASP | Sales |
| 1Q | 4.00 | 341 | 1365 |
| 2Q | 5.00 | 326 | 1630 |
| 3Q | 6.00 | 283 | 1700 |
| 4Q | 7.01 | 268 | 1879 |
| Year | 21.99 | 299 | 6574 |

[a] J. J. Lazlo, "Intel Corporation—Company Report," PaineWebber Inc., 26 January 1995, pp. 7-9.

[b] Units in millions

[c] Average Selling Price

[d] Total sales in millions of dollars

**EXHIBIT 2**
**Selected Intel Financial Statements[a]**

### CONSOLIDATED STATEMENTS OF INCOME

Three Years Ended December 25, 1993
*(In millions—except per share amounts)*

| | 1993 | 1992 | 1991 |
|---|---|---|---|
| **Net revenues** | $8,782 | $5,844 | $4,779 |
| Cost of sales | 3,252 | 2,557 | 2,316 |
| Research and development | 970 | 780 | 618 |
| Marketing, general and administrative | 1,168 | 1,017 | 765 |
| Operating costs and expenses | 5,390 | 4,354 | 3,699 |
| **Operating Income** | **3,392** | **1,490** | **1,080** |
| Interest expense | (50) | (54) | (82) |
| Interest income and other, net | 188 | 133 | 197 |
| Income before taxes | 3,530 | 1,569 | 1,195 |
| Provision for taxes | 1,235 | 502 | 376 |
| **Net Income** | **$2,295** | **$1,067** | **$ 819** |
| Earnings per common and common equivalent share | $ 5.20 | $ 2.49 | $ 1.96 |
| Weighted average common and common equivalent shares outstanding | 441 | 429 | 418 |

*See accompanying notes.*

[a]  Intel Corporation Annual Report, 1994, p. 14.

**EXHIBIT 2 (continued)**
**The Intel Pentium Chip Controversy (A)**

## CONSOLIDATED[b] BALANCE SHEETS

December 25, 1993 and December 26, 1992
*(In millions—except per share amounts)*

| | 1993 | 1992 |
|---|---|---|
| **Assets** | | |
| Current assets: | | |
| Cash and cash equivalents | $ 1,659 | $ 1,843 |
| Short-term investments | 1,477 | 993 |
| Accounts receivable, net of allowance for doubtful accounts of $22 | | |
| ($26 in 1992) | 1,448 | 1,069 |
| Inventories | 838 | 535 |
| Deferred tax assets | 310 | 205 |
| Other current assets | 70 | 46 |
| **Total current assets** | **5,802** | **4,691** |
| Property, plant and equipment: | | |
| Land and buildings | 1,848 | 1,463 |
| Machinery and equipment | 4,148 | 2,874 |
| Construction in progress | 317 | 311 |
| | 6,313 | 4,648 |
| Less accumulated depreciation | 2,317 | 1,832 |
| **Property, plant and equipment, net** | **3,996** | **2,816** |
| **Long-term investments** | **1,416** | **496** |
| **Other assets** | **130** | **86** |
| **Total assets** | **$11,344** | **$ 8,089** |
| **Liabilities and Stockholders' Equity** | | |
| Current liabilities: | | |
| Short-term debt | $    399 | $    202 |
| Long-term debt redeemable within one year | 98 | 110 |
| Accounts payable | 427 | 281 |
| Deferred income on shipments to distributors | 200 | 149 |
| Accrued compensation and benefits | 544 | 435 |
| Other accrued liabilities | 374 | 306 |
| Income taxes payable | 391 | 359 |
| **Total current liabilities** | **2,433** | **1,842** |
| **Long-term debt** | **426** | **249** |
| **Deferred tax liabilities** | **297** | **180** |
| **Put warrants** | **688** | **373** |
| **Commitments and contingencies** | | |
| Stockholders' equity: | | |
| Preferred stock, $.001 par value, 50 shares authorized; none issued | — | — |
| Common stock, $.001 par value, 1,400 shares authorized; 418 issued | | |
| and outstanding in 1993 (419 in 1992) and Capital in excess of par value | 2,194 | 1,776 |
| Retained earnings | 5,306 | 3,669 |
| **Total stockholders' equity** | **7,500** | **5,445** |
| **Total liabilities and stockholders' equity** | **$11,344** | **$ 8,089** |

[b]  Intel Corporation Annual Report, 1994, p. 15.

**EXHIBIT 2 (continued)**
**The Intel Pentium Chip Controversy (A)**

### CONSOLIDATED STATEMENTSᶜ OF CASH FLOWS

Three Years Ended December 25, 1993
*(In millions)*

| | 1993 | 1992 | 1991 |
|---|---|---|---|
| **Cash and cash equivalents, beginning of year** | **$1,843** | **$1,519** | **$1,620** |
| Cash flows provided by (used for) operating activities: | | | |
| Net income | 2,295 | 1,067 | 819 |
| Adjustments to reconcile net income to net cash provided by operating activities: | | | |
|   Depreciation | 717 | 518 | 418 |
|   Net loss on retirements of property, plant and equipment | 36 | 57 | 25 |
|   Amortization of debt discount | 17 | 16 | 16 |
|   Change in deferred tax assets and liabilities | 12 | 13 | (19) |
| Changes in assets and liabilities: | | | |
|   (Increase) decrease in accounts receivable | (379) | (371) | 11 |
|   (Increase) in inventories | (303) | (113) | (7) |
|   (Increase) decrease in other assets | (68) | (61) | 31 |
|   Increase (decrease) in accounts payable | 146 | 112 | (41) |
|   Tax benefit from employee stock plans | 68 | 55 | 35 |
|   Increase (decrease) in income taxes payable | 32 | 207 | (89) |
|   Increase in other liabilities | 228 | 136 | 149 |
|     Total adjustments | 506 | 569 | 529 |
| **Net cash provided by operating activities** | **2,801** | **1,636** | **1,348** |
| Cash flows provided by (used for) investing activities: | | | |
|   Additions to property, plant and equipment | (1,933) | (1,228) | (948) |
|   (Increase) decrease in short-term investments, net | (244) | 28 | (420) |
|   Additions to long-term investments | (1,165) | (293) | (127) |
|   Sales and maturities of long-term investments | 5 | 13 | 37 |
| **Net cash (used for) investing activities** | **(3,337)** | **(1,480)** | **(1,458)** |
| Cash flows provided by (used for) financing activities: | | | |
|   Increase (decrease) in short-term debt, net | 197 | 29 | (30) |
|   Additions to long-term debt | 148 | — | 2 |
|   Retirement of long-term debt | — | (20) | (75) |
|   Proceeds from sales of shares through employee stock plans and other | 133 | 138 | 98 |
|   Proceeds from sale of Step-Up Warrants, net | 287 | — | — |
|   Proceeds from sales of put warrants, net of repurchases | 62 | 42 | 14 |
|   Repurchase and retirement of common stock | (391) | — | — |
|   Payment of dividends to stockholders | (84) | (21) | — |
| **Net cash provided by financing activities** | **352** | **168** | **9** |
| **Net (decrease) increase in cash and cash equivalents** | **(184)** | **324** | **(101)** |
| **Cash and cash equivalents, end of year** | **$1,659** | **$1,843** | **$1,519** |
| Supplemental disclosures of cash flow information: | | | |
| Cash paid during the year for: | | | |
|   Interest | $ 39 | $ 32 | $ 59 |
|   Income taxes | $1,123 | $ 227 | $ 448 |

ᶜ Intel Corporation Annual Report, 1994, p. 16.

# Accounting for Property, Plant, and Equipment and Other Assets

**E**xpenditures for property and capital equipment represent a commitment of some of an organization's resources to investments that are likely to be utilized over several periods. The *matching concept* requires that the cost of such investments be matched with the revenues in the periods in which benefits are obtained by using the capital equipment. For buildings and equipment, the amount of expense matched with revenues is called *depreciation*. If the asset is a natural resource, such as forest land or mineral deposits, similar expenses might be called *depletion*. If the assets are intangible, the original cost is said to be *amortized* over the periods when benefits are obtained, or in some cases, over an arbitrary period.

In practice, accounting for the cost of assets that provide benefits over several periods (also called *fixed assets*) consists of three distinct phases: determining the cost of a fixed asset, amortizing the cost over the useful life of the asset, and removing it from the accounts at the end of the asset's life.

## THE COST OF FIXED ASSETS

The cost of the fixed asset and the amount at which it will be initially measured in reports consist of the total amount of expenditures necessary to ready the asset for its intended use. To the price of acquiring legal title to ownership of an asset are added costs of delivery, installation, training of employees, and modification of facilities that are necessary in order to use the asset as planned. (**Exhibit 1** is an illustration of how the cost of a new asset might be measured.)

Copyright © 1992 by the President and Fellows of Harvard College. Harvard Business School case 193-046.

# ESTIMATING DEPRECIATION

At the beginning of the life of an asset, an estimate of the asset's *salvage value* is made. The salvage value is the expected selling price of the asset less any removal costs at the end of its useful life to the organization. The difference between the cost and the salvage value is called the *depreciable cost,* and it is this cost that is to be matched in some way to revenues earned in the accounting periods over which the asset will be used.

Determining depreciation expense using generally accepted accounting principles is not particularly difficult. Having determined depreciable cost, all that remains is to select a method for allocating that cost to periods when the asset will be used to generate revenues. The market prices provided by an asset purchase and an eventual sale provide information about an asset's value at those times. However, in between these points of time, when commonly used depreciation methods are employed, there is no assurance that the asset values are accurately estimated by the unamortized cost reported in the statement of financial position.

In allocating the depreciable cost, any one of several methods is acceptable. Although the methods may appear to be arbitrary, they meet two criteria. The most important criterion requires that the amount of depreciation charged is not subject to manipulation by management in such a way that income for any period can be capriciously distorted. The second criterion is that the amounts charged bear some resemblance to the decline in value of the asset measured on an historical cost basis. There are two methods of depreciation in common use with occasional variations in each: straight-line depreciation and declining balance depreciation. A third method that is sometimes used is sum-of-the-years' digits depreciation.

## Straight-Line Depreciation

Under the straight-line method of depreciation, an equal portion of the depreciable cost is charged according to some measure of the length of an asset's life. The measure may be periods of time or units of product. Under this method, as under any of the methods of depreciation commonly used, the amount charged to expense is usually accumulated and shown in balance sheets as a deduction from the historical cost of the asset. This *accumulated depreciation* is called a *contra asset.* It is always associated with the asset to which it is related, and its balance offsets part of the original cost that has already been matched against revenues. **Exhibit 2** shows how depreciation can be estimated using the straight-line method.

## Declining Balance Depreciation

In an attempt to reflect the fact that an asset is often most productive in the early years of its use in an organization, accountants often employ methods that charge a larger proportion of the total depreciation expense in the early years of life than in later periods. One common method for accomplishing this is to charge to each period a fixed percentage of the *original cost of the asset less any previously accumulated depreciation* (note the difference from straight-line depreciation in which the depreciation rate is applied to the entire depreciable cost of the asset each period). Commonly, this percentage will be 150% or 200% of the depreciation rate used under the straight-line method. Because the declining balance method will never completely amortize the original cost of an asset, it is customary not to deduct salvage value of the asset from the original cost prior to applying the depreciation percentage. **Exhibit 3** shows how depreciation can be estimated using the declining balance method.

## Sum-of-the-Years' Digits Method

A third depreciation method that may be used in financial reporting in the United States is the sum-of-the-years' digits method. Under this method, depreciation is related to time in annual periods. The numbers used to identify each year of life, from 1 to *n*, are summed. The depreciation expense for each year is estimated by taking in inverse order the number of the period as the numerator of a fraction having as its denominator the sum of the years of the asset's life. This fraction is multiplied by the depreciable cost, based on cost less salvage value, to estimate the year's depreciation expense. One should not waste any time searching for the logic of this method, for there is none. However, it does satisfy the criteria for an acceptable depreciation amount. **Exhibit 4** shows how depreciation can be estimated using the sum-of-the-years' digits method.

# GAIN OR LOSS ON DISPOSAL OF ASSET

A decision to sell or otherwise dispose of a fixed asset may come any time after it is acquired. In some cases, assets thought to be useful to the firm will prove not to be so useful. It may be that they are more valuable to the organization when sold for cash. For this reason, assets are sometimes sold before the end of their original expected useful life, so that the resources committed to them can be redeployed more effectively.

In other situations, assets may be held over a longer period of time than expected and employed in their intended uses very profitably. At some point, however, the cost of maintenance and repair necessary to maintain a favorable stream of income for the organization becomes prohibitive, and the asset must be sold or scrapped. In other cases, technological developments will cause an asset to become obsolete. Assets can also be sold or exchanged for another asset. Occasionally, however, an organization may have to pay to have a useless asset destroyed or hauled away.

When an asset is sold or otherwise disposed of, it is usually necessary to account for the fact that earlier estimates about the salvage value or life of the asset were not correct. Differences between the *book value* and the amount actually obtained upon disposal are shown either as a gain or loss in the period in which the asset disposal takes place. Although gains and losses resulting from the disposal of assets represent miscalculations made in other periods, it is usually not considered necessary to adjust estimates of income in those earlier periods except in the most extreme cases.

Typically, the used asset is sold, and the items relating to the asset disappear from the accounts of the firm. We use the difference between the book value of the assets and the amount of cash or other resources received to determine whether or not the gain or loss on disposal of the asset should be recognized. In either case, the cash received from the sale is not included in revenue, and the amount of gain or loss is usually reported separately in the income statement as gain or loss on sale of assets.

## SOME FINAL COMMENTS ABOUT DEPRECIATION

This section has introduced in a cursory way three methods of allocating as expense all or part of the original cost of an asset over the life of that asset. Other methods have been proposed, and some are employed by business organizations. The importance of the depreciation estimate lies in its relationship to the proper determination of income. While the criterion of accurate estimation of periodic income should dictate the choice of depreciation method, in practice other criteria often dominate: simplicity of application, tax and other legal requirements, or the desire on the part of management to show earnings more favorable or less favorable than those that would be shown if another method were used. Estimates of depreciation expense, therefore, must be used and interpreted with great care.

One other aspect of depreciation accounting deserves mention. We have dealt with the depreciation of individual assets because this was the easiest way to illustrate different methods of depreciation. In practice, however, a large firm may have many assets of a certain type—for example, personal computers. The problems of accounting for acquisition, depreciation, and disposal of these types of assets may not be too different from those encountered when accounting for inventory. Sometimes, when there are large numbers of similar items, rather than keep track of each asset, accountants find it more feasible to depreciate them as a group. A full discussion of methods of *group depreciation* or *composite depreciation* is unnecessary, but you should be aware of the fact that such groupings are frequently used to simplify the recording and reporting tasks.

## ACCOUNTING FOR LAND

Like other fixed assets, land is recorded in the accounting records at the cost needed to upgrade it to the condition necessary for its intended use. Purchase price, fees or taxes incurred in the purchase, the cost of clearing or grading land, or the cost of developing drainage would all be included in the amount of cost for purchase of a tract of land.  In contrast to other fixed assets, land is not depreciated and is held at original cost until such time as it is sold, traded, or abandoned.

## ACCOUNTING FOR LONG-TERM INVESTMENTS IN OTHER ORGANIZATIONS

Organizations often find it in their interest to acquire an investment in companies that they regard as subsidiaries.  These investments in subsidiaries are considered long term.  If the investment in a subsidiary is 20% or less of the total ownership of the subsidiary, the investment is usually accounted for using a *cost method*.  The investment is carried at its original cost in the owning company's accounts, and any dividends are reported as current income.

If the investment in the affiliated company is greater than 20% but less than 50%, the parent company will usually account for the investment using a method known as the *equity method*.  In this method, a share of the subsidiary's earnings proportional to the share of company ownership is added to the investment in the company accounts, whether the earnings have been distributed as dividends or not.  If dividends are paid by the subsidiary, they reduce the equity investment shown in the parent company's account.

When ownership in a subsidiary exceeds 50% of the total ownership, consolidation of the accounts of both parent and subsidiary on a line-by-line basis is normally required.  In these cases, other owners' interest may appear as a liability under the title *minority interest in subsidiaries*.

## ACCOUNTING FOR INTANGIBLE ASSETS AND GOODWILL

In spite of their desire to produce the most useful information and reports, accountants frequently ignore many intangibles in balance sheets.  Unless intangibles have been purchased, it is difficult to estimate their value with any precision.  Instead, expenditures for the purposes of developing trademarks or advertising programs which create customer loyalty or expenditures for research and development are expensed in the periods they are incurred.  Current income is reduced during the period in which the expenditures are made, and no recognition is given to future benefits that may accrue from these expenditures.

One common intangible asset frequently found in financial reports is *goodwill*.  When one company purchases another, paying more than fair value of the net assets of the acquired company, the difference is called goodwill and may be shown as an asset on the balance sheet of the purchasing firm.  The amount of goodwill should be expensed against revenue in future periods just as we match the cost of capital assets against the periods when benefits accrue.  In the

United States, goodwill must be amortized over a period not to exceed 40 years. When goodwill is deemed not to be of any further consequence, it can be written off against the owners' equity of the acquiring organization. In some countries, it is common to make this write-off at the date goodwill is acquired rather than to confuse the reported income in future periods with an expense that represents nothing more than an arbitrary allocation.

Plant assets, intangible assets, and other assets reported by the Gillette Company and Subsidiary Companies in its consolidated balance sheets for 1995 and 1994 are shown in **Exhibit 5**, along with the associated footnotes. In particular, the notes to financial statements illustrate several of the ideas and financial reporting concepts that have been discussed in this section.

## EXHIBIT 1
## Measuring the Cost of a New Asset

Western Metallurgical purchased a new laboratory furnace on January 1, 1999. The price of the new furnace was $13,000, but the manufacturer agreed to allow a trade-in of $3,000 for an old furnace and a $500 discount because Western agreed to pay $9,500 cash for the balance. To the $12,500 given in exchange for the new furnace, the following items were added to the cost of the new asset: $500 for freight charges for delivery, $2,000 paid to an electrician and engineer for installation, and $1,000 paid to reimburse two key employees for expenses incurred while visiting the manufacturer's plant in another city to receive instructions on operating the new equipment. The cost of the asset, and hence a measure of its value on the first day it was ready for operation, was estimated to be $16,000, as shown below.

| Cost of New Laboratory Furnace—January 1, 1999 | | |
|---|---|---|
| Cash paid for new furnace: | | |
| Purchase price | $13,000 | |
| Less: Trade-in allowance | 3,000 | |
| Less: Discount for cash | 500 | |
| | $ 9,500 | |
| Value of old furnace | | 3,000 |
| Total assets paid | | $12,500 |
| Freight charges for delivery | | 500 |
| Installation costs | | 2,000 |
| Training costs for employees | | 1,000 |
| Total cost | | $16,000 |

**EXHIBIT 2**
## Estimating Straight-Line Depreciation

Following the purchase of the new furnace, the management of Western Metallurgical turned to the problem of selecting a method of depreciation. It estimated that the furnace would have a salvage value of $6,000 at the end of its useful life of five years. Thus, the depreciable cost was estimated to be $10,000.

    The accountant suggested that the $10,000 depreciable cost could be allocated on a straight-line basis at a rate of $2,000 per year over the five years the furnace would be used. As an alternative, he suggested that the firm might estimate the total number of pounds of metal that would be melted in the furnace over the five-year period and then charge depreciation expense in relation to the amount of metal melted as a proportion of the expected total. Management expected that it would melt about 250,000 pounds of metal in the next five years; therefore in each year, depreciation expense would be calculated by taking the number of pounds of metal melted and multiplying it by $.04. The depreciation expense that might be shown if the straight-line method were adopted is shown below.

Straight-Line Depreciation Schedule for Laboratory Furnace

| Depreciable cost: | |
|---|---:|
| Price of furnace | $13,000 |
| Less: Discount | 500 |
| | $12,500 |
| Freight charge | 500 |
| Installation | 2,000 |
| Training expenses | 1,000 |
| Total cost | $16,000 |
| Less: Salvage value | 6,000 |
| Depreciable cost | $10,000 |

Estimated life: 5 years
Expected metal melt: 250,000 pounds
Schedule of depreciation expense:

| Year | Expected Melt (in pounds) | Time Base | Use Base |
|---|---:|---:|---:|
| 1 | 40,000 | $ 2,000 | $ 1,600 |
| 2 | 45,000 | 2,000 | 1,800 |
| 3 | 50,000 | 2,000 | 2,000 |
| 4 | 55,000 | 2,000 | 2,200 |
| 5 | 60,000 | 2,000 | 2,400 |
| Total | 250,000 | $10,000 | $10,000 |

## EXHIBIT 3
## Estimating Declining Balance Depreciation

<u>Declining Balance Depreciation Schedule for Laboratory Furnace</u>

Depreciable cost: $16,000
Estimated life: 5 years
Schedule of depreciation expense:

| Year | Book Value at Beginning of Year | Depreciation Expense (40% of book value) | Book Value at End of Year |
|---|---|---|---|
| 1 | $16,000 | $ 6,400 | $9,600 |
| 2 | 9,600 | 3,840 | 5,760 |
| 3 | 5,760 | 2,304 | 3,456 |
| 4 | 3,456 | 1,382 | 2,074 |
| 5 | 2,074 | 830 | 1,245 |
| Total | | $14,756 | |

Management was disturbed by the fact that the use of this method would depreciate the asset by such an amount that the reported value after the second year would be less than the expected salvage value and that it would apparently show a large gain when the asset was sold at the end of its useful life. The accountant explained that it would be possible to find a percentage rate that would exactly amortize the $10,000 depreciable cost over the five-year period if management preferred to do that rather than use an arbitrary 200% of the straight-line depreciation rate.

**EXHIBIT 4**
**Estimating Sum-of-the-Years' Digits Depreciation**

Sum-of-the-Years' Digits Depreciation Schedule for Laboratory Furnace

Depreciable cost:  $10,000
Estimated life:  5 years
Sum of digits:  $1 + 2 + 3 + 4 + 5 = 15$[a]
Schedule of depreciation expense:

| Year | Depreciation Factor | Depreciation Expense |
|------|---------------------|----------------------|
| 1 | 5/15 | $ 3,333 |
| 2 | 4/15 | 2,667 |
| 3 | 3/15 | 2,000 |
| 4 | 2/15 | 1,333 |
| 5 | 1/15 | 667 |
| | | $10,000 |

[a]  The sum-of-the-years' digits can be calculated using

$$SYD = \frac{n(n + 1)}{2}$$

where $SYD$ = sum of years, and $n$ = number of years of life.

**EXHIBIT 5**
**Noncurrent Assets, The Gillette Company and Subsidiary Companies**
**(Excerpt from Consolidated Balance Sheets) ($ million)**

|  | December 31, 1995 | December 31, 1994 |
| --- | --- | --- |
| Property, plant and equipment, at cost less accumulated depreciation | $1,636.9 | $1,411.0 |
| Intangible assets, less accumulated amortization | 1,221.4 | 887.4 |
| Other assets | 377.5 | 314.6 |

**Notes to Consolidated Financial Statements**
*Property, Plant and Equipment*

|  | | |
| --- | --- | --- |
| Land | $ 37.4 | $ 36.9 |
| Buildings | 509.9 | 465.8 |
| Machinery and equipment | 2,714.2 | 2,399.5 |
|  | 3,261.5 | 2,902.2 |
| Less accumulated depreciation | 1,624.6 | 1,491.2 |
|  | $1,636.9 | $1,411.0 |

*Intangible Assets*

|  | | |
| --- | --- | --- |
| Goodwill ($43.8 million not subject to amortization) | $1,229.4 | $ 905.0 |
| Other intangible assets | 187.4 | 148.1 |
|  | 1,416.8 | 1,053.1 |
| Less accumulated amortization | 195.4 | 165.7 |
|  | $1,221.4 | $ 887.4 |

*Depreciation*
Depreciation is computed primarily on a straight-line basis over the estimated useful lives of assets.

*Intangible Assets*
Intangible assets principally consist of goodwill, which is amortized on the straight-line method, generally over a period of 40 years. Other intangible assets are amortized on the straight-line method over a period of from 13 to 40 years. The carrying amounts of intangible assets are assessed for impairment when operating profit from the applicable related business indicates that the carrying amount of the assets may not be recoverable.

# Depreciation at Delta Air Lines and Singapore Airlines (A)

**P**roperty, plant, and equipment (PP&E) is a significant asset category of most airline companies. PP&E usually constitutes more than 50% of the total assets of an airline, and depreciation of these assets is a major operating expense.

However, unlike many expenses—for example, salaries, the cost of aircraft fuel, the cost of meals and beverages, all of which are significant operating expenses for airlines—depreciation of PP&E is different in that the methods and estimates used to determine the amount of this expense can vary widely among companies. Moreover, the methods and estimates used can have a significant impact on companies' reported earnings. Thus, unless the user of financial statements sifts through the footnotes to sort out the details, comparability among companies within an industry can be problematic.

Consider, for example, the depreciation practices of two major airlines—Delta Air Lines and Singapore Airlines—in 1993.

## DELTA AIR LINES

Delta Air Lines was one of the major passenger airlines in the United States, with almost $12 billion in annual revenues. It served 161 cities in 44 states in the United States, and it also operated flights to 33 foreign countries. In terms

*Research Associate Jeremy Cott prepared this case under the supervision of Professor William J. Bruns, Jr.*

Copyright © 1997 by the President and Fellows of Harvard College. Harvard Business School case 198-001.

of operating revenues and revenue passenger miles flown,[1] it was, in 1993, the third largest U.S. airline. (American Airlines and United Airlines were the largest.)

Delta had been expanding its international operations. In fiscal year 1990 it entered into a partnership with Singapore Airlines that was meant to coordinate some of their scheduling and marketing efforts. In November 1991, Delta purchased most of the transatlantic route authorities of Pan Am, which had gone bankrupt. Thus in fiscal year 1993 revenues from international flights represented 21% of total operating revenues. This represented a large increase from earlier years, but it was still a smaller proportion of total revenues than what was the case for some other major carriers. (For example, in 1993, 38% of United's revenues and 26% of American's revenues came from international flights.) Although Delta was the third largest U.S. airline in terms of operating revenues and revenue passenger miles flown, it was the largest in terms of the number of airline departures and the number of passengers carried.

**Exhibit 1** shows key financial and operational data for Delta for the years 1989 through 1993.

Delta was in the throes of difficulties affecting most American airlines. Deregulation of the industry in 1978 had led to increasing price competition; in the 1980s and early 1990s, airline fares didn't even remotely keep pace with inflation. Major carriers like Delta—with high cost structures left over from an earlier, regulated environment—were hit hard by competition from low-cost, no-frills airlines like Southwest and People's Express. In the late 1980s and early 1990s, the difficulties mounted: Iraq's invasion of Kuwait discouraged passenger travel and caused fuel prices to skyrocket; the American economy went into a recession; and fare wars intensified. In four years, 1990–1993, the American industry as a whole lost $12.8 billion. Delta went about reassessing its marketing programs and cutting back on staff in an effort to control costs. "The work we are doing to cut costs and raise revenues," the 1993 Annual Report stated, "fits within a comprehensive effort to transform our Company into a high performing organization."

Delta's property and equipment totaled $7.1 billion on its 1993 balance sheet. The largest part of this ($5.5 billion) consisted of aircraft and other flight equipment. (See **Exhibits 2** and **3**, which show the dollar values of Delta's fixed assets and the composition of its aircraft fleet.) The average age of Delta's aircraft was 8.8 years, which was relatively young by industry standards. Among other major airlines, the average age of aircraft varied a good deal. At American and United, the two largest passenger airlines in the United States, the average age of aircraft was 8.9 and 10.8 years, respectively. At Continental, the fifth largest airline, it was 15.3. At TWA, the seventh largest, it was 18.7.

---

[1] "Revenue passenger miles" is a widely used measurement of traffic volume in the airline industry. It represents the number of miles flown by all revenue-paying passengers.

(There was no necessary connection, however, between the average age of an airline's fleet and the assumption it made regarding the fleet's depreciable life.)

In April 1993, Delta announced a change in its depreciation assumptions regarding flight equipment. The last time Delta had made such a change had been in July 1986. (See the excerpts from the footnotes to Delta's financial statements regarding this change in **Exhibit 4**.)[2]

## SINGAPORE AIRLINES

Singapore Airlines was the largest private-sector employer in Singapore's booming economy. At the end of fiscal year 1993, its route network covered 70 cities in 40 countries. Singapore was a transit point for a good deal of travel in Asia, but the airline also handled a lot of traffic to other continents: for example, it flew regularly to the United States across both the Atlantic and Pacific Oceans, and flew nonstop to and from London nine times a week. Of its total operating revenues, about 44% came from flights to Asia, 23% from flights to Europe, 22% from flights to North and South America, and 11% from flights to the Southwest Pacific. In fiscal year 1993 its total operating revenues ($5.1 billion in Singapore dollars, $3.1 billion in U.S. dollars) would have made it the seventh largest airline in the United States—larger, for example, than Trans World Airlines and Southwest.[3]

**Exhibit 5** shows key financial and operational data for Singapore for the years 1989 through 1993.

The airline was renowned for its high level of customer service, geared largely to business travelers. It continuously won awards from various trade associations and travel magazines for the quality of its service. The average age of its aircraft was 5.1 years, which was the youngest of any major airline in the world. (See **Exhibits 6** and **7**, which show the dollar values of Singapore's fixed assets and the composition of its aircraft fleet.) According to an industry publication, Singapore's exclusive MEGATOP 747-400, which it bought from

---

[2] During fiscal year 1993 Delta also changed one of its assumptions regarding pension accounting. "Effective April 1, 1993, Delta increased from 9% to 10% its assumption regarding the expected return on plan assets associated with defined benefit pension plans. This change in accounting estimate resulted in a decrease in pension expense of $12.7 million in fiscal 1993, and is expected to reduce pension expense by an estimated $56 million in fiscal 1994" (1993 Annual Report).

[3] Singapore Airlines was actually a wholly owned subsidiary of a holding company named SIA, 90% of whose revenues came from the airline operation. All of the financial and operating data cited in this case regarding Singapore Airlines, however, pertains solely to Singapore Airlines, not the holding company. (The holding company's other investments were in engineering and airport terminal services, a regional airline, and various hotel properties.)

Boeing, was "the largest, fastest, long-haul aircraft in the world, offering state-of-the-art technology and comfort."[4]

Much of the Asian airline market was regulated. Moreover, slightly more than half of Singapore Airlines' common stock was owned by the Singapore government. However, the company received no government subsidy and operated under most of the usual pressures from international competition and the investment community. Its stock was followed by more than 20 investment analysts.

Asian airlines at this time were generally more profitable than American airlines, but they definitely did not feel immune to the problems in the industry. In 1993, Singapore Airlines' net profit dropped (in Singapore dollars) from $922 million to $741 million—or (in American dollars) from $555 million to $452 million. In its Annual Report for the year, the company said that the year had been "a difficult one for most airlines. The industry continued to be saddled with huge financial losses. . . . Singapore Airlines was not spared." As a result, the company's briefing for reporters was held at a much more modest hotel than usual, and staff bonuses were reduced from the 3.4 months of the previous year to a half-month. The company said that it was continuing with its expansion plans, expecting an eventual recovery in the business cycle. Its capital expenditures, however, were running about $2 billion a year (Singapore dollars) and, as a result, the company's Annual Report said, "it is possible that, in a few years' time, we shall have to incur debt."[5]

During fiscal year 1993, the company's assumptions regarding its depreciation of flight equipment remained unchanged. The last time Singapore had changed its depreciation policy regarding flight equipment had been in April 1989. (See the excerpts from the footnotes to Singapore's financial statements regarding this change in **Exhibit 8**.)

---

[4] *Business Wire,* November 29, 1996.

[5] *Business Times* in Singapore reported on May 20, 1993, that "even with the lower earnings" in fiscal year 1993, Singapore Airlines "retained its position as the world's most profitable airline." The company's director of corporate affairs reported a conversation he had with an industry analyst in which "the analyst said that if an American airline had reported such figures, the market would have rejoiced at the news." In response, the company's director of corporate affairs said to the analyst, "You must forgive the local press because it is influenced by the performance of other Singapore companies."

## QUESTIONS

1. Calculate the annual depreciation expense that Delta and Singapore would record for each $100 gross value of aircraft.
   (a) For Delta, what was its annual depreciation expense (per $100 of gross aircraft value) prior to July 1, 1986; from July 1, 1986 through March 31, 1993; and from April 1, 1993 on?
   (b) For Singapore, what was its annual depreciation expense (per $100 of gross aircraft value) prior to April 1, 1989; and from April 1, 1989 on?
2. Are the differences in the ways that the two airlines account for depreciation expense significant? Why would companies depreciate aircraft using different depreciable lives and salvage values? What reasons could be given to support these differences? Is different treatment proper?
3. Assuming the average value of flight equipment that Delta had in 1993, how much of a difference do the depreciation assumptions it adopted on April 1, 1993 make? How much more or less will its annual depreciation expense be compared to what it would be if it were using Singapore's depreciation assumptions?
4. Singapore Airlines maintains depreciation assumptions that are very different from Delta's. What does it gain or lose by doing so? How does this relate to the company's overall strategy?
5. Does the difference in the average age of Delta's and Singapore's aircraft fleets have any impact on the amount of depreciation expense that they record? If so, how much?

**EXHIBIT 1**
**Delta Air Lines: Key Financial and Operational Data ($ millions)**

| | For the fiscal years ending June 30 | | | | |
| --- | --- | --- | --- | --- | --- |
| | 1993 | 1992 | 1991 | 1990 | 1989 |
| Total assets | 11,871 | 10,162 | 8,411 | 7,227 | 6,484 |
| Fixed assets | 7,141 | 7,093 | 5,641 | 5,399 | 4,478 |
| Fixed assets/Total assets | 60.2% | 69.8% | 67.1% | 74.7% | 69.1% |
| Long-term debt (including capital leases) | 3,717 | 2,833 | 2,058 | 1,315 | 703 |
| Total debt/Total assets | 31.3% | 27.9% | 24.5% | 18.2% | 10.8% |
| Total operating revenues | 11,997 | 10,837 | 9,170 | 8,582 | 8,089 |
| Total operating expenses | 12,572 | 11,512 | 9,621 | 8,163 | 7,411 |
| Depreciation expense for fixed assets | 679 | 585 | 512 | 453 | 378 |
| Depreciation expense/Total operating expense | 5.4% | 5.1% | 5.3% | 5.5% | 5.1% |
| Operating profit | (575) | (674) | (450) | 420 | 678 |
| Operating profit/Revenues | −4.8% | −6.2% | −4.9% | 4.9% | 8.4% |
| Gain on sale of flight equipment (pretax) | 65 | 35 | 17 | 18 | 17 |
| Net profit (excluding cumulative effect of accounting change) | (415) | (506) | (324) | 303 | 461 |
| Net profit/Revenues | −3.5% | −4.7% | −3.5% | 3.5% | 5.7% |
| Revenue passenger miles (millions) | 82,406 | 72,693 | 62,086 | 58,987 | 55,904 |
| Number of revenue passengers carried (millions) | 85 | 77 | 69 | 67 | 64 |
| Average passenger trip length (miles) | 969 | 944 | 900 | 880 | 874 |
| Available passenger miles (millions) | 132,282 | 123,102 | 104,328 | 96,463 | 90,742 |
| Capacity utilization | 62.3% | 59.1% | 59.5% | 61.1% | 61.6% |

Source:   Company Annual Reports and 10-Ks; shaded numbers calculated by casewriter.

**EXHIBIT 2**
**Delta Air Lines: Property and Equipment ($ millions)**

|  | June 30 | |
| --- | --- | --- |
|  | 1993 | 1992 |
| Flight equipment owned | 9,043 | 8,354 |
| Less: Accumulated depreciation | (3,559) | (3,213) |
|  | 5,484 | 5,141 |
| Flight equipment under capital leases | 173 | 173 |
| Less: Accumulated depreciation | (128) | (112) |
|  | 45 | 61 |
| Ground property and equipment | 2,373 | 2,211 |
| Less: Accumulated depreciation | (1,143) | (983) |
|  | 1,230 | 1,228 |
| Advance payments for equipment | 383 | 663 |
| Total | 7,142 | 7,093 |

Source:  Company Annual Reports.

**EXHIBIT 3**
**Delta Air Lines:  Aircraft Fleet as of June 30, 1993**

| Type of Aircraft | Average Seats per Aircraft | Owned | Leased | Total |
|---|---|---|---|---|
| A310-200 | 177 | 3 | 4 | 7 |
| A310-300 | 178 | — | 15 | 15 |
| B727-200 | 148 | 106 | 43 | 149 |
| B737-200 | 107 | 1 | 57 | 58 |
| B737-300 | 127 | 3 | 13 | 16 |
| B757-200 | 182 | 43 | 41 | 84 |
| B767-200 | 204 | 15 | — | 15 |
| B767-300 | 254 | 2 | 23 | 25 |
| B767-300ER | 218 | 7 | 7 | 14 |
| L1011-1 | 302 | 32 | — | 32 |
| L1011-200 | 300 | 1 | — | 1 |
| L-1011-250 | 266 | 6 | — | 6 |
| L1011-500 | 223 | 17 | — | 17 |
| MD-11 | 253 | 1 | 8 | 9 |
| MD-88 | 142 | 59 | 57 | 116 |
| MD-90 | 150 | — | — | 0 |
| Total | | 296 | 268 | 564 |

Note:  All of the aircraft shown above as "leased" were being operated under "operating" leases.

Source:  Company Annual Reports.

**EXHIBIT 4**
## Delta Air Lines' Depreciation Policy

**Excerpt from Delta Air Lines' "Notes to Consolidated Financial Statements" (for fiscal year 1993)**

Depreciation and Amortization—Prior to April 1, 1993, substantially all of the Company's flight equipment was being depreciated on a straight-line basis to residual values (10% of cost) over a 15-year period from the dates placed in service. As a result of a review of its fleet plan, effective April 1, 1993, the Company increased the estimated useful lives of substantially all of its flight equipment. Flight equipment that was not already fully depreciated is being depreciated on a straight-line basis to residual values (5% of cost) over a 20-year period from the dates placed in service.

**Excerpt from Delta Air Lines' "Notes to Consolidated Financial Statements" (for fiscal year 1987)**

Depreciation and Amortization—Prior to July 1, 1986, substantially all of the Company's flight equipment was being depreciated on a straight-line basis to residual values (10% of cost) over a 10-year period from dates placed in service. As a result of a comprehensive review of its fleet plan, effective July 1, 1986, the Company increased the estimated useful lives of substantially all of its flight equipment. Flight equipment that was not already fully depreciated is now being depreciated on a straight-line basis to residual values (10% of cost) over a 15-year period from dates placed in service. The effect of this change was a $130 million decrease in depreciation . . . for the year ended June 30, 1987.

---

Note: Delta's assumptions regarding the depreciable life and salvage value of fixed assets other than flight equipment were quite different and were, in any case, unchanged in 1993.

**EXHIBIT 5**
**Singapore Airlines: Key Financial and Operational Data ($ millions, Singapore dollars)**

| | For the fiscal years ending March 31 | | | | |
| --- | --- | --- | --- | --- | --- |
| | 1993 | 1992 | 1991 | 1990 | 1989 |
| Total assets | 9,417 | 9,366 | 8,516 | 7,708 | 6,365 |
| Fixed assets | 6,729 | 5,876 | 4,960 | 4,515 | 3,926 |
| Fixed assets/Total assets | 71.5% | 62.7% | 58.2% | 58.6% | 61.7% |
| Long-term debt (including capital leases) | 0 | 421 | 450 | 518 | 624 |
| Total debt/Total assets | 0.0% | 4.5% | 5.3% | 6.7% | 9.8% |
| Total operating revenues | 5,135 | 5,013 | 4,602 | 4,730 | 4,272 |
| Total operating expenses | 4,480 | 4,149 | 3,760 | 3,601 | 3,407 |
| Depreciation expense for fixed assets | 708 | 614 | 513 | 439 | 550 |
| Depreciation expense/Total operating expense | 15.8% | 14.8% | 13.6% | 12.2% | 16.1% |
| Operating profit | 655 | 863 | 842 | 1,129 | 865 |
| Operating profit/Revenues | 12.8% | 17.2% | 18.3% | 23.9% | 20.2% |
| Gain on sale of flight equipment (pretax) | 42 | 129 | 208 | 195 | 96 |
| Net profit (excluding cumulative effect of accounting change) | 741 | 922 | 887 | 1,177 | 928 |
| Net profit/Revenues | 14.4% | 18.4% | 19.3% | 24.9% | 21.7% |
| Revenue passenger miles (millions) | 23,663 | 21,808 | 19,582 | 19,210 | 17,991 |
| Number of revenue passengers carried (millions) | 8.7 | 8.1 | 7.1 | 6.8 | 6.2 |
| Average passenger trip length (miles) | 2,720 | 2,692 | 2,758 | 2,825 | 2,902 |
| Available passenger miles (millions) | 33,174 | 29,659 | 26,063 | 24,523 | 22,789 |
| Capacity utilization | 71.3% | 73.5% | 75.1% | 78.3% | 78.9% |
| Note: March 31 exchange rate for conversion of Singapore dollars to U.S. dollars | $1.64 | $1.66 | $1.80 | $1.89 | $1.96 |

Source: Company Annual Reports and 10-Ks; shaded numbers calculated by casewriter.

**EXHIBIT 6**
**Singapore Airlines:  Fixed Assets  ($ millions, Singapore dollars)**

|  | March 31 | |
|---|---|---|
|  | 1993 | 1992 |
| Flight equipment | 9,224 | 7,814 |
| Less: Accumulated depreciation | (3,914) | (3,330) |
|  | 5,310 | 4,484 |
| Ground property and equipment | 1,020 | 1,018 |
| Less: Accumulated depreciation | (549) | (589) |
|  | 471 | 429 |
| Advance and progress payments | 947 | 962 |
| Total | 6,728 | 5,875 |

Source:  Company Annual Reports.

**EXHIBIT 7**
**Singapore Airlines:  Aircraft Fleet as of March 31, 1993**

| Type of aircraft | In operation |
|---|---|
| B747-400 (MEGATOP) | 18 |
| B747-300 (BIG TOP) | 11 |
| B747-300 (COMBI) | 3 |
| B747-200 | 3 |
| B747-200 Freighter | 1 |
| B737-200 Freighter | 2 |
| B737-300 Freighter | 1 |
| A310-300 | 12 |
| A310-200 | 6 |
| Total | 57 |

Note:  Singapore Airlines owned all of its aircraft; it did not operate any under "operating" leases.  (Confirmed by company in June 6, 1997 phone conversation.)

Source:  Company Annual Reports.

**EXHIBIT 8**
**Singapore Airlines' Depreciation Policy**

**Excerpt from Singapore Airlines' "Notes to the Accounts" (for fiscal year 1993)**
Depreciation of Fixed Assets—The Company depreciates its new aircraft, spares and spare engines over 10 years to 20% residual values. . . . For used aircraft less than 5 years old, the Company depreciates them over the remaining life (10 years less age of aircraft) to 20% residual value. In the case of used aircraft more than 5 years old, they are depreciated over 5 years to 20% residual value.

**Excerpt from Singapore Airlines' "Notes to the Accounts" (for fiscal year 1990)**
Depreciation of Fixed Assets—[Prior to April 1, 1989], the operational lives of the aircraft fleet were estimated to be 8 years with 10% residual values. . . . [Effective] April 1, 1989, the Company depreciated its aircraft, spares and spare engines over 10 years to 20% residual values. . . . This arises from a review of the operational lives and residual values of the aircraft fleet.

---

Note: Singapore's assumptions regarding the depreciable life and salvage value of fixed assets other than flight equipment were quite different and were, in any case, unchanged in 1993.

# Depreciation at Delta Air Lines and Singapore Airlines (B)

**D**elta Air Lines and Singapore Airlines used different assumptions regarding the depreciable life and salvage life of their aircraft in 1993. Furthermore, the financial structures of their aircraft fleets were also different. As indicated in **Exhibits 3** and **7** of the "(A)" case, close to half of Delta's planes operated under "operating" leases, whereas Singapore owned all of its aircraft; it did not operate any under "operating" leases.

Delta Air Lines disclosed, in its 1992 and 1993 Annual Reports, information regarding its minimum rental commitments under capital leases and noncancelable operating leases. This information is shown in **Exhibit 1**.

Singapore Airlines indicated that, at the end of fiscal year 1993, it had no liabilities for capital leases. Legally, it did have capital lease obligations amounting to $2.8 million (Singapore dollars), but this was matched by $2.8 million in cash that it had deposited with a financial institution "under defeasance"—meaning that the deposited money was to be used solely for the purpose of satisfying the company's capital lease obligations—and therefore this amount was not considered debt for financial reporting purposes. Singapore's 1993 Annual Report did indicate that it leased a good deal of space for offices, air terminals, and maintenance and training facilities—presumably under operating leases—but it did not disclose information, comparable to Delta's, regarding its future rental commitments for these things.

The "(A)" case indicated that the overall capital structures of Delta Air Lines and Singapore Airlines in 1993 were also very different. Delta had a fair

*Research Associate Jeremy Cott prepared this case under the supervision of Professor William J. Bruns, Jr.*

Copyright © 1997 by the President and Fellows of Harvard College. Harvard Business School case 198-002.

amount of long-term debt (31.3% of total assets) whereas Singapore had none. Footnotes to Delta's financial statements for 1993 indicated that Delta had outstanding, in 1993, various issues of long-term debt. All of it was unsecured and (with a couple of exceptions) carried interest rates in the range of 7% to 10.5%, with an average around 8.5%.

## QUESTIONS

1. What possible reasons might there be to explain why Delta operates almost half of its aircraft fleet under operating leases, while Singapore operates no aircraft under operating leases?
2. Comparing the balance sheets and income statements of Delta and Singapore has serious shortcomings given the extreme difference between the financial structures of the two companies' aircraft fleets. From the information provided in the case, calculate adjusted figures for Delta's aircraft fleet so as to make Delta's total depreciation expense, total assets, and total long-term debt more comparable with Singapore's.

## EXHIBIT 1
## Delta Air Lines:  Lease Obligations

**Excerpt from Delta Air Lines' "Notes to Consolidated Financial Statements" (for fiscal year 1992)**

The Company leases certain aircraft, airport terminal and maintenance facilities, ticket offices, and other property and equipment under agreements with terms of more than one year. . . .

At June 30, 1992, the Company's minimum rental commitments under capital leases and noncancelable operating leases with initial or remaining terms of more than one year were as follows (in millions of dollars):

| Years Ending June 30 | Capital Leases | Operating Leases |
|---|---|---|
| 1993 | 20 | 907 |
| 1994 | 21 | 897 |
| 1995 | 18 | 881 |
| 1996 | 18 | 895 |
| 1997 | 17 | 901 |
| After 1997 | 73 | 12,852 |
| Total minimum lease payments | 167 | 17,333 |
| Less: Amounts representing interest | (47) | |
| Present value of future minimum capital lease payments | 120 | |
| Less: Current obligations under capital leases | (10) | |
| Long-term capital lease obligations | 110 | |

**Excerpt from Delta Air Lines' "Notes to Consolidated Financial Statements" (for fiscal year 1993)**

At June 30, 1993, the Company's minimum rental commitments under capital leases and noncancelable operating leases with initial or remaining terms of more than one year were as follows (in millions of dollars):

| Years Ending June 30 | Capital Leases | Operating Leases |
|---|---|---|
| 1994 | 21 | 905 |
| 1995 | 18 | 916 |
| 1996 | 18 | 941 |
| 1997 | 18 | 940 |
| 1998 | 15 | 924 |
| After 1998 | 58 | 13,202 |
| Total minimum lease payments | 148 | 17,828 |
| Less: Amounts representing interest | (38) | |
| Present value of future minimum capital lease payments | 110 | |
| Less: Current obligations under capital leases | (12) | |
| Long-term capital lease obligations | 98 | |

Delta's Income Statements and Notes also indicated that the amounts charged to rental expense for operating leases (in millions of dollars) were (in 1993) $1,085, consisting of $729 for "Aircraft rent" and $356 for "Facilities and other rent";  and (in 1992) $997, consisting of $642 for "Aircraft rent" and $355 for "Facilities and other rent."

# Kansas City Zephyrs Baseball Club, Inc.

On April 17, 1985, Bill Ahern sat in his office and contemplated a difficult judgment he had to make in the next two days. Two weeks before, Bill had been asked to be an arbitrator in a dispute between the Owner-Player Committee (OPC, the representatives of the owners of the 26 major league baseball teams in collective bargaining negotiations) and the Professional Baseball Players Association (PBPA, the players' union).

## A BASEBALL ACCOUNTING DISPUTE

The issue Ahern had to resolve was the profitability of the major league baseball teams. The players felt they should share in the teams' profits; the owners maintained, however, that most of the teams were actually losing money each year, and they produced financial statements to support that position. The players, who had examined the owners' statements, countered that the owners were hiding profits through a number of accounting tricks and that the statements did not accurately reflect the economic reality. Ahern's decision on the profitability issue was important because it would affect the ongoing contract negotiations, particularly in the areas of minimum salaries and team contributions to the players' pension fund.

On April 9, Ahern met with the OPC and the representatives of the PBPA. They explained they wanted him to focus on the finances of the Kansas City Zephyrs Baseball Club, Inc. This club was selected for review because both

---

*Research Assistant Joseph P. Mulloy prepared this case under the supervision of Professors Kenneth A. Merchant and Krishna G. Palepu.*

Copyright © 1987 by the President and Fellows of Harvard College. Harvard Business School case 187-008.

sides agreed its operations were representative, yet it was a relatively clean and simple example to study:  the baseball club entity was not owned by another corporation and it did not own the stadium the team played in.  Furthermore, no private financial data would have to be revealed because the corporation was publicly owned.  Ahern's task was to review the Zephyrs' financial statements, hear the owners' and players' arguments, and then reach a decision as to the profitability of the team by Friday, April 19.

## MAJOR LEAGUE BASEBALL

Major league baseball in the United States was comprised of a number of components bound together by sets of agreements and contractual relationships. At the heart of major league baseball were the 26 major league teams.  Each team operated as an independent economic unit in such matters as contracting for players, promoting games and selling tickets, arranging for the use of a stadium and other needed facilities and services, and negotiating local broadcasting of games.  The teams joined together to establish common rules and playing schedules and to stage championship games.

The business of most teams was limited exclusively to their major league activities. Very few integrated vertically by owning their own stadium or minor league teams.  Most teams were organized as partnerships or privately held corporations, although a few were subunits of larger corporations.  While baseball was often thought of as a big business, the individual teams were relatively small.  For most of them, annual revenues were between $20 and $30 million.

Each team maintained an active roster of 24 players during the playing season, plus 16 minor league players "on option," who might see major league action during the season.  This made a total of 40 players on major league contracts for each team at any one time.  Each team played a schedule of 162 games during the season, 81 at home and 81 away.

Collectively, the team owners established most of the regulations that governed the industry. The covenant that bound them was the Major League Agreement (MLA), to which was attached the Major League Rules.  The rules detailed all the procedures the clubs agreed on, including the rules for signing, trading, and dealing with players.

Under the MLA, the owners elected a commissioner of baseball for a seven-year term.  The commissioner acted as a spokesperson for the industry, resolved disputes among the clubs and the other baseball entities, policed the industry, and enforced the rules.  The commissioner had broad powers to protect the best interests of the game.  The commissioner also administered the Major Leagues Central Fund, under which he negotiated and received the revenues from national broadcast contracts for major league games. About one-half of the fund's revenues were passed on directly to the teams in approximately equal shares.

Within the overall structure of major league baseball, the 26 teams were organized into two leagues, each with its own president and administration.  The

American League had 14 teams and the National League had 12 teams, of which one was the Kansas City Zephyrs. Each league controlled the allocation and movement of its respective franchises. In addition to authorizing franchises, the leagues developed the schedule of games, contracted for umpires, and performed other administrative tasks. The leagues were financed through a small percentage share of club ticket revenues and receipts from the World Series and pennant championship games.

In addition to the major league teams, U.S. baseball included about 150 minor league teams located throughout the United States, Canada, and Mexico. Minor league teams served a dual function: they were entertainment entities in their own right and they were training grounds for major league players. Through Player Development Contracts, the major league teams agreed to pay a certain portion of their affiliated minor league teams' operating expenses and player salaries.

## MEETING WITH THE ZEPHYRS' OWNERS

Bill Ahern spent Tuesday reviewing the history of major league baseball and the relationships among the various entities that make up the major leagues. Then he met with the Zephyrs owners' representatives on Wednesday.

The owners' representatives gave Ahern a short history of the team and presented him with the team's financial statements for the years 1983 and 1984 (**Exhibits 1** and **2**). The current owner was a corporation with five major shareholders, which bought the team on November 1, 1982, for $24 million. The Zephyrs did not own any of their minor league teams or their stadium, but two of the Zephyrs' owners were part owners of the private corporation that owned the baseball stadium.

Ahern studied the financial statements for a short time and then met with Keith Strong, the owners' lawyer. The conversation can be summarized by the following exchange:

**Bill:** I would like to know more about the controversial items in your financial statements. First, could you please explain your players' salaries expense entries?

**Keith:** Sure. Here is a list of our roster players and what we paid them last year (see **Exhibit 3**). The number we show on our 1984 income statement is the total expense of $10,097,000. Most of the expense represents cash outflows in 1984. The only exception is shown in the last column of this exhibit. For our highest paid players, we have agreed to defer a portion of their salary for 10 years. That helps save them taxes and provides them with some income after their playing days are over.

**Bill:** What is the nonroster guaranteed contract expense?

**Keith:** That is also player salary expense, but we break it out separately because the salaries are paid to players who are no longer on our active roster.

The salaries are amounts we owe to players whom we released who had long-term guaranteed contracts.  The amount of $750,000 represents the amount we still owe at the end of 1984 to two players (shown in **Figure A**).  Joe Portocararo, one of our veteran pitchers, signed a four-year guaranteed contract last year, but before the season started he suffered a serious injury, and Joe and the team jointly decided it was best he retire.  We released U. R. Wilson in spring training, hoping that another team would pick him up and pay his salary, but none did.

**FIGURE A**
**Calculation of Nonroster Guaranteed Contract Expense ($000)**

| Player | Amount Owed | | | |
| | 1984 | 1985 | 1986 | Total |
| --- | --- | --- | --- | --- |
| Joe Portocararo | $300.0 | $350.0 | $400.0 | $1,050.0 |
| U. R. Wilson | 200.0 | | | 200.0 |
| | | | | $1,250.0 |

We still owe these players the amounts in their contracts.  We decided to expense the whole amount in 1984 because they are not active players; they are not serving to bring in our current revenues.  We felt it was more meaningful and conservative to recognize these losses now, as they result from the effects of past decisions that did not turn out well.

**Bill:**   Okay.  Let's move on to roster depreciation expense.

**Keith:**   When the team was bought in 1982, 50 percent of the purchase price ($12 million) was designated as the value of the player roster at that time.  This amount was capitalized and is being amortized over six years.

**Bill:**   Why 50 percent?

**Keith:**   That is the maximum percentage that the Internal Revenue Code will allow when purchasing a sports team.

**Bill:**   I see.  Is there anything else in the statements that the players dispute?

**Keith:**   No, I don't think so.  The rest of our accounting is very straightforward.  Most of our revenues and expenses result directly from a cash inflow or outflow.

**Bill:**   Well, that answers all my questions.  Thank you.

**Keith:**   I have just one more thing to say concerning baseball finances in general.  People seem to think that we generate huge profits since we have a relative monopoly, but it should be obvious that the professional baseball leagues do not exist in order to carry out traditional cartel functions. The rules and regulations governing the clubs comprising the league are essential to the creation of the league as an entity and have virtually nothing to do with pricing policies of the individual clubs. The objective of the cooperative agreements is not to constrain the economic competition among them, but rather to create the league as a joint venture that produces baseball during a season of play. Without such rules of conduct, leagues would not exist.

When this meeting was completed, Bill Ahern felt he understood the owners' accounting methods well enough.

## MEETING WITH THE PLAYERS

The following Monday, Ahern met with the PBPA representatives and their lawyer, Paul Hanrahan. They presented Ahern with income statements for the years 1983 and 1984 as they thought they should be drawn up (**Exhibit 4**). As Ahern studied them, he found the players' version of the financial statements showed profits before tax of $2.9 million for 1983 and $3.0 million for 1984 as compared to the losses of $2.4 million and $2.6 million on the owners' statements.

Ahern's conversation with Paul Hanrahan went approximately as follows:

**Bill:** The income statements you have given me are very similar to those of the owners except for a few items.

**Paul:** That's true; most of the expenses are straightforward. There are only a few areas we dispute, but these areas can have a significant impact on the overall profitability of the team. We feel that the owners have used three techniques to "hide" profits: (1) roster depreciation, (2) overstated player salary expense, and (3) related-party transactions.

**Bill:** Let's start with roster depreciation. Why have you deleted it?

**Paul:** We feel it gives numbers that aren't meaningful. The depreciation expense arises only when a team is sold, so you can have two identical teams that will show dramatically different results if one had been sold and the other had not. We also don't think the depreciation is real because most of the players actually improve their skills with experience, so if anything, there should be an increase in roster value over time, not a reduction as the depreciation would lead you to believe.

**Bill:** Okay. I understand your reasoning. I'll have to think about that. Let's move on to the next issue.

**Paul:** That's player salary expense. We think the owners overstate player expense in several ways. One is that they expense the signing bonuses in the year they're paid. We feel the bonuses are just a part of the compensation package, and that for accounting purposes the bonuses should be spread over the term of the player's contract.

We gathered information on the bonuses paid in the last four years and the contract terms (**Exhibit 5**).  Then we adjusted the owners' income statements by removing the bonuses from the current roster salary expense and by adding an "amortization of bonuses" line.  The net effect of this one adjustment on 1984, for example, was an increase in income of $373,000.[1]

**Bill:**  But the owners have really paid out all the bonuses in cash, and there is no guarantee that the players will complete their contracts.

**Paul:**  That's partly true.  Some players get hurt and are unable to compete effectively.  But the number of players who do not complete their contracts is very small, and we think it is more meaningful to assume that they will continue to play over the term of their contract.

**Bill:**  Okay.  What's next?

**Paul:**  A second adjustment we made to the players' salary line was to back out the deferred portion of the total compensation.  Many of the players, particularly those who are higher paid, receive only about 80% of their salaries in any given year.  They receive the rest 10 years later (**Exhibit 3**).  We feel that since the team is paying this money over a long period of time, it is misleading to include the whole amount as a current expense.  This adjustment increased 1984 income for the Zephyrs by $1,521,000.  No salary expense deferred from prior years was added back in because that form of contract is a relatively recent phenomenon.

**Bill:**  I've looked at some of the contracts, and it says very clearly that the player is to receive, say, $500,000, of which $100,000 is deferred to the year 1994.  Doesn't that indicate that the salary expense is $500,000?

**Paul:**  No.  The team has paid only $400,000 in cash.

**Bill:**  Doesn't the team actually set money aside to cover the future obligation?

**Paul:**  Some teams do, and in such cases, I think we would agree that it is appropriate to recognize that amount as a current expense.  But the Zephyrs don't set any money aside.

**Bill:**  Okay.  You made a third adjustment to the players' salaries.

**Paul:**  Yes, we think the salaries due to players who are no longer on the roster should be recognized when the cash is paid out, not when the players leave the roster.  Unless that is done, the income numbers will vary wildly depending on when these players are released and how large their contracts are.  Furthermore, it is quite possible that these players' contracts will be picked up

---

[1]  $1,320,000 less $947,000.

by another team, and the Zephyrs would then have to turn around and recognize a large gain because the liability it has set up would no longer be payable.

**Bill:**  Okay.  Let's go to the last area: related-party transactions.  You have listed Stadium Operations at about 80% of what the owners charged.  Why is that?

**Paul:**  You probably know that two of the Zephyrs' owners are also involved with the stadium corporation.  But what you probably don't know is that they are the sole owners of that stadium company.  We think that the stadium rent is set to overcharge the team and help show a loss for the baseball operations.

**Bill:**  How did you get your numbers?

**Paul:**  This wasn't easy, but we looked at what other teams pay for their stadiums.  Every contract is slightly different, but we are sure that two of the five shareholders in the team are earning a nice gain on the stadium-pricing agreement.

Just for your own edification, this is not the only type of related-party transaction where the owners can move profits around.  A few of the teams are owned by broadcasting organizations, and as a result they report no local broadcasting revenues.  Their individual losses are consolidated into the overall major league position, thus the overall loss is overstated.  I know it's hard to do, but an objective look must be taken at all these related-party transactions if baseball's true position is to be fairly stated.

The overall effect of all these adjustments we have made to the Zephyrs' income statements changes losses to profits.  In 1984, the change is from a loss of $1.7 million to a profit of $1.4 million.  In the labor negotiations, the owners keep claiming that they're losing money and can't afford the contract terms we feel are fair.  We just don't think that's true.  They are "losing money" only because they have selected accounting methods to hide their profits.

**Bill:**  Well, you've given me a lot to think about.  There are a lot of good arguments on both sides. Thank you for your time.  I'll have my answer for you soon.

## BILL'S DECISION

By Wednesday, April 17, Bill was quite confused.  To clarify the areas of disagreement, he prepared the summaries shown in **Exhibit 6**, but whereas the sets of numbers were clear, the answers to the conflicts were not.  Bill had expected this arbitration to be rather straightforward, but instead he was mired in difficult issues involving the accounting unit, depreciation, amortization of intangibles, and related-party transactions.  Now he was faced with a tight deadline, and it was not at all obvious to him how to define "good accounting methods" for the Zephyrs Baseball Club.

**EXHIBIT 1**
**Income Statements—Owners' Figures (000s omitted)**

|  | Year Ending October 31 | |
| --- | --- | --- |
|  | 1983 | 1984 |
| **Operating Revenues:** |  |  |
| Game Receipts | $ 16,526.0 | $ 18,620.0 |
| National Television | 2,360.8 | 2,730.8 |
| Local Broadcasting | 3,147.9 | 3,575.1 |
| Concessions | 2,886.3 | 3,294.3 |
| Parking | 525.1 | 562.0 |
| Other | 786.9 | 843.9 |
| Total Revenues | $ 26,233.0 | $ 29,626.1 |
| **Operating Expenses:** |  |  |
| Spring Training | $      545.0 | $      594.0 |
| Team Operating Expenses |  |  |
| Players' Salaries |  |  |
| Current Roster | 9,111.0 | 10,097.0 |
| Nonroster Guaranteed |  |  |
| Contract Expense | 0.0 | 1,250.0 |
| Coaches' Salaries | 756.9 | 825.7 |
| Other Salaries | 239.0 | 260.8 |
| Miscellaneous | 2,655.9 | 2,897.3 |
| Player Development | 2,996.0 | 3,269.0 |
| Team Replacement: |  |  |
| Roster Depreciation | 2,000.0 | 2,000.0 |
| Scouting | 672.8 | 734.0 |
| Stadium Operations | 4,086.0 | 4,457.0 |
| Ticketing and Marketing | 1,907.0 | 2,080.0 |
| General and Administrative | 3,541.0 | 3,663.0 |
| Total Operating Expense | $ 28,510.6 | $ 32,127.8 |
| Income from Operations | (2,277.6) | (2,501.7) |
| Other Income (Expense) | (96.0) | (101.0) |
| Income Before Taxes | (2,373.6) | (2,602.7) |
| Federal Income Tax Benefit | 855.9 | 944.2 |
| Net Income (Loss) | $ (1,517.7) | $ (1,658.5) |

**EXHIBIT 2**
**Balance Sheets—The Owners' Figures (000s omitted)**

|  | Year Ending October 31 | |
|  | 1983 | 1984 |
|---|---|---|
| **Assets** | | |
| Current Assets | | |
| Cash | $ 488.0 | $ 561.0 |
| Marketable Securities | 6,738.0 | 7,786.1 |
| Accounts Receivable | 598.0 | 681.2 |
| Notes Receivable | 256.0 | 234.0 |
| Total Current Assets | 8,080.0 | 9,262.3 |
| Property, Plant & Equipment | 1,601.0 | 1,892.0 |
| Less Accumulated Depreciation | (359.0) | (511.0) |
| Net PP&E | 1,242.0 | 1,381.0 |
| Initial Roster | 12,000.0 | 12,000.0 |
| Less Accumulated Depreciation | (4,000.0) | (6,000.0) |
| Net Initial Roster | 8,000.0 | 6,000.0 |
| Other Assets | 2,143.0 | 4,123.2 |
| Franchise | 6,500.0 | 6,500.0 |
| Total Assets | $ 25,965.0 | $ 27,266.5 |
| **Liabilities and Shareholders' Equity** | | |
| Current Liabilities | | |
| Accounts Payable | $ 909.2 | $ 1,020.2 |
| Accrued Expenses | 1,207.5 | 1,461.8 |
| Total Current Liabilities | 2,116.7 | 2,482.0 |
| Long-Term Debt | 7,000.0 | 8,073.7 |
| Other Long-Term Liabilities | 2,443.3 | 3,964.3 |
| Shareholders' Equity | | |
| Common Stock, par value $1 per share, | | |
| 500,000 shares issued | 500.0 | 500.0 |
| Additional Paid-In Capital | 10,000.0 | 10,000.0 |
| Retained Earnings | 3,905.0 | 2,246.5 |
| Total Liabilities and Shareholders' Equity | $ 25,965.0 | $ 27,266.5 |

**EXHIBIT 3**
**Detailed Players' Salary Summary—1984 (000s omitted)**

| Roster Player | Signings Bonus | Base Salary | Performance and Attendance Bonuses | Total Compensation | Portion of 1984 Salary Deferred Until 1994 |
|---|---|---|---|---|---|
| Bill Hogan | $   500.0 | $   850.0 | $   250.0 | $  1,600.0 | $   250.0 |
| Corby Megorden | 300.0 | 600.0 | 225.0 | 1,125.0 | 200.0 |
| Manuel Vasquez | 200.0 | 500.0 | 100.0 | 800.0 | 150.0 |
| Jim Showalter | | 600.0 | 100.0 | 700.0 | 200.0 |
| Scott Van Buskirk | 150.0 | 400.0 | 100.0 | 650.0 | 150.0 |
| Jerry Hyde | 150.0 | 400.0 | 50.0 | 600.0 | 150.0 |
| Dave Schafer | | 355.0 | 50.0 | 405.0 | 130.0 |
| Leslie Yamshita | | 300.0 | 37.5 | 337.5 | 100.0 |
| Earl McLain | | 220.0 | 37.5 | 257.5 | 50.0 |
| Shannon Saunders | | 210.0 | 37.5 | 247.5 | 50.0 |
| Gary Blazin | | 190.0 | 37.5 | 227.5 | 40.0 |
| Rich Hayes | | 160.0 | 25.0 | 185.0 | 30.0 |
| Sam Willett | | 140.0 | 17.5 | 157.5 | 21.0 |
| Chuck Wright | 20.0 | 115.0 | 12.5 | 147.5 | |
| Jim Urquart | | 115.0 | 12.5 | 127.5 | |
| Bill Schutt | | 115.0 | 12.5 | 127.5 | |
| Mike Hegarty | | 115.0 | 12.5 | 127.5 | |
| Bruce Selby | | 110.0 | 12.5 | 122.5 | |
| Dave Kolk | | 110.0 | 12.5 | 122.5 | |
| Bill Kelly | | 110.0 | 12.5 | 122.5 | |
| Dave Carr | | 110.0 | 12.0 | 122.0 | |
| Tom O'Conner | | 110.0 | 5.0 | 115.0 | |
| Jake Luhan | | 110.0 | | 110.0 | |
| Ray Woolrich | | 100.0 | | 100.0 | |
| John Porter | | 100.0 | | 100.0 | |
| Dusty Rhodes | | 100.0 | | 100.0 | |
| Lynn Novinger | | 100.0 | | 100.0 | |
| Bill Williams | | 95.0 | | 95.0 | |
| Jim Sedor | | 95.0 | | 95.0 | |
| Ralph Young | | 95.0 | | 95.0 | |
| Ed Marino | | 95.0 | | 95.0 | |
| Ray Spicer | | 90.0 | | 90.0 | |
| Eric Womble | | 90.0 | | 90.0 | |
| Ron Gorena | | 90.0 | | 90.0 | |
| Gene Johnston | | 90.0 | | 90.0 | |
| Jack Zollinger | | 90.0 | | 90.0 | |
| Ken Karr | | 90.0 | | 90.0 | |
| Tom Crowley | | 80.0 | | 80.0 | |
| Joe Matt | | 80.0 | | 80.0 | |
| Bill Brunelle | | 80.0 | | 80.0 | |
| Roster Player Salary | $1,320.0 | $7,605.0 | $1,172.0 | $10,097.0 | $1,521.0 |

**EXHIBIT 4**
**Income Statements—Players' Figures (000s omitted)**

| | Year Ending October 31 | |
| --- | --- | --- |
| | 1983 | 1984 |
| Operating Revenues: | | |
| Game Receipts | $16,526.0 | $18,620.0 |
| National Television | 2,360.8 | 2,730.8 |
| Local Broadcasting | 3,147.9 | 3,575.1 |
| Concessions | 2,886.3 | 3,294.3 |
| Parking | 525.1 | 562.0 |
| Other | 786.9 | 843.9 |
| Total Revenues | $26,233.0 | $29,626.1 |
| | | |
| Operating Expenses: | | |
| Spring Training | $ 545.0 | $ 594.0 |
| Team Operating Expenses | | |
| Players' Salaries | | |
| Current Roster | 5,897.4 | 7,256.5 |
| Nonroster Guaranteed | | |
| Contract Expense | 0.0 | 500.0 |
| Amortization of Bonuses | 716.0 | 947.0 |
| Coaches' Salaries | 756.9 | 825.7 |
| Other Salaries | 239.0 | 260.8 |
| Miscellaneous | 2,655.9 | 2,897.3 |
| Player Development | 2,996.0 | 3,269.0 |
| Team Replacement: | | |
| Scouting | 672.8 | 734.0 |
| Stadium Operations | 3,300.0 | 3,500.0 |
| Ticketing and Marketing | 1,907.0 | 2,080.0 |
| General and Administrative | 3,541.0 | 3,663.0 |
| Total Operating Expenses | $23,227.0 | $26,527.3 |
| Income from Operations | 3,006.0 | 3,098.8 |
| Other Income (Expense) | (96.0) | (101.0) |
| | | |
| Income Before Taxes | 2,910.0 | 2,997.8 |
| Provision for Federal Income Taxes[a] | 1,338.6 | 1,379.0 |
| City and State Taxes | 236.0 | 253.0 |
| Net Income | $ 1,335.4 | $ 1,365.8 |

[a] Tax rate assumed to be 46%.

## EXHIBIT 5
### Summary of Signing Bonuses ($000)

| | Bonuses for Contracts Starting in | | | |
|---|---|---|---|---|
| Contract Length (Years) | 1981 | 1982 | 1983 | 1984 |
| 4 | 240 | 550 | 350 | 800 |
| 3 | 210 | 200 | 250 | 200 |
| 2 | 360 | 250 | 170 | 320 |

## EXHIBIT 6
### Summary of Items of Disagreement Between Owners and Players (000s)

| | 1983 | | | 1984 | | |
|---|---|---|---|---|---|---|
| Items of Dispute | Owners | Players | Difference | Owners | Players | Difference |
| Roster depreciation | $2,000.0 | $   0.0 | $2,000.0 | $ 2,000.0 | $   0.0 | $2,000.0 |
| Current roster salary | 9,111.0 | 5,897.4 | 3,213.6 | 10,097.0 | 7,256.5 | 2,840.5 |
| Amortization of signing bonuses | 0.0 | 716.0 | (716.0) | 0.0 | 947.0 | (947.0) |
| Nonroster guaranteed contract expense | 0.0 | 0.0 | — | 1,250.0 | 500.0 | 750.0 |
| Stadium operations | 4,086.0 | 3,300.0 | 786.0 | 4,457.0 | 3,500.0 | 957.0 |
| Total effect on net income | | | $5,283.6 | | | $5,600.5 |

| Effect on Net Income (Before Tax): | 1983 | 1984 |
|---|---|---|
| Income before tax per owners' financial statements (Exhibit 1) | ($2,373.6) | ($2,602.7) |
| Total items of disagreement | 5,283.6 | 5,600.5 |
| Income before tax per players' financial statements (Exhibit 4) | $2,910.0 | $2,997.8 |

# Buying Time

The concept of compound interest allows managers to connect money with time. Managers whose organizations lack the cash to pay for desirable projects can offer to pay interest to others for the use of their cash for a period of time. People with cash they do not currently need find the prospect of earning interest attractive because it means their claim to cash will be larger at a future date. Higher interest rates will make more money available to those who can use it most effectively over time periods of any length.

Suppose you need about $1,000 to purchase new computer software that you are sure will double your productivity. That increase in productivity leaves no doubt that you will have plenty of cash a year from now, even though you are a little short of cash today. The dealer who hopes to sell you the software proposes to lend you the cash you need for the purchase, provided you agree to pay interest at a rate of 10% per year. You agree to the deal, get the software, and repay the loan at the end of one year. You have used the dealer's cash, and you buy the use of that cash for one year's time. In money terms, the deal looks like this:

|  |  | To be Repaid at the End of Year |
| --- | --- | --- |
| Original Loan | $1,000 | $1,000 |
| Interest Rate | x   10%  per year | 100 |
|  |  | $1,100 |

---

*Professor William J. Bruns, Jr. and Susan S. Harmeling prepared this case.*

Copyright © 1991 by the President and Fellows of Harvard College. Harvard Business School case 192-045.

You paid $100 to use the cash you needed to improve your productivity. That was the interest on the dealer's cash.

Another dealer offers a new printer for about $1,000. With such a printer you would reproduce your productive results with greater clarity and effectiveness. This dealer will also lend you the money to buy this equipment, but the 10% interest is deducted from the loan when it is made. Again, you are using the dealer's cash, and you must buy the use of that cash for one year's time. In money terms, the deal looks like this:

|  |  | To be Repaid at the End of Year |
|---|---|---|
| Original Loan | $909 | $ 909 |
| Interest Rate | x  10%  per year | 91 |
|  |  | $1,000 |

Note that in this case you get less cash, but you still pay interest at 10%. The interest cost is less because you actually borrowed less.

We can view each of these loans using terms that managers use to describe the costs of buying time to use the cash that will be paid to others. The **present value** of the loan is the amount received or credited to the sale on the day we buy the software or equipment. The **future value** of the loan is the amount to which the loan has grown at the time payment is due. In our examples, these terms could be used as follows:

|  | Present Value |  | Future Value |
|---|---|---|---|
| Loan from dealer #1 | $1,000 | at 10% interest  = | $1,100 |
| Loan from dealer #2 | $ 909 | at 10% interest  = | $1,000 |

The interest rate ties the present value of cash to its future value, and our example shows how we can look either forward or backward at a loan of "about $1,000." It is as if the present value and the future value represent the same amount of cash at two points in time, connected by an interest rate that determines what the borrower will pay for "buying time."

Two algebraic formulas provide bases for solving most business problems involving money and time. The future value of an amount earning **compound interest** can be calculated using the formula

$$PV (1 + i)^n = FV$$

where   PV = present value of principal amount

$i$ = interest rate

$n$ = number of periods interest will compound

FV = future value

Actually, most managers have no need to remember this or any other compound interest formula because compound interest tables have been constructed to ease the burden of computation of future or present values. Also, many calculators and computer software products are programmed to assist in such calculations.

Many business decisions involve a comparison of a present value of an amount of cash to be received in the future to the current price of the right to obtain the future payment. The present value of an amount to be received in $n$ periods in the future can be calculated by rearranging the formula above:

$$PV = \frac{FV}{(1 + i)^n}$$

To facilitate the calculation of present values, tables are constructed based on this formula. An example is shown in **Table 1**.

**TABLE 1**
**Present Value of $1**

| Periods | 8% | 10% | 12% |
|---------|-------|-------|-------|
| 1 | .9259 | .9091 | .8929 |
| 2 | .8573 | .8264 | .7972 |
| 3 | .7938 | .7513 | .7118 |
| 4 | .7350 | .6830 | .6355 |
| 5 | .6806 | .6209 | .5674 |
| 6 | .6302 | .5645 | .5066 |

To use the table to find the present value of any future cash payment, you need only multiply the amount shown for the number of periods and chosen interest rate by the amount of the payment. For example, the present value of $1,000 to be paid or received in three years at 10% interest would be $751.30:

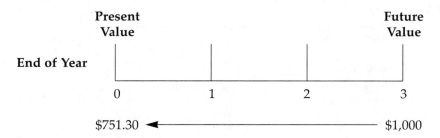

The process of calculating the present value of a future cash amount is called **discounting**.

Many investments generate a stream of cash receipts over a number of future periods. If the amount of cash to be received in each period is the same, it is sometimes called an **annuity**. The formula for calculating the present value of an annuity to be received for $n$ periods is

$$PV = PMT \left[ \frac{1 - \frac{1}{(1 + i)^n}}{i} \right]$$

A table constructed to facilitate the calculation of the present value of an ordinary annuity, based on this formula, is shown in **Table 2**.

**TABLE 2**
**Present Value of an Ordinary Annuity of $1**

| Periods | 8% | 10% | 12% |
|---------|--------|--------|--------|
| 1 | .9259 | .9091 | .8929 |
| 2 | 1.7833 | 1.7355 | 1.6901 |
| 3 | 2.5771 | 2.4869 | 2.4018 |
| 4 | 3.3121 | 3.1699 | 3.0373 |
| 5 | 3.9927 | 3.7908 | 3.6048 |
| 6 | 4.6229 | 4.3553 | 4.1114 |

**Table 2** can be used to find the present value of a stream of equal future cash payments to be paid or received for a number of periods at a chosen interest rate. For example, the present value of $1,000 to be paid or received for three years at 10% interest would be $2,486.90. This is actually the sum of the present values of each of the three payments to be received over the waiting period for each. Using **Table 1** we could have calculated:

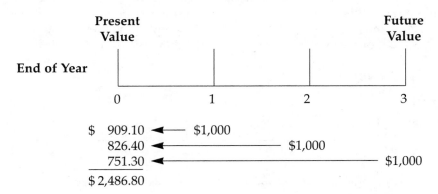

The small discrepancy in the two answers is the result of rounding within the **present value tables**. This often occurs, but it is rarely a problem in actual situations. If you want to be precise, use of a calculator or software program instead of present value tables is recommended.

# THE USE OF COMPOUND INTEREST AND PRESENT VALUE IN ACCOUNTING

Companies make many contracts that call for the future receipt or payment of cash. Some examples of payments could include a loan to be repaid over several time periods, a financial contract calling for interest payments and re-payment of borrowed principal after a time (a bond), payments due under a contract for leased equipment (a lease), or payments promised to employees after their retirement from active employment (a pension). When receipts or payments are due within a short period of time—trade accounts receivable or payable, for example—they are rarely discounted to their present value. How-ever, almost all amounts due after a year or more would be discounted to their present value. Interest expense (or revenue) then accumulates at the rate of interest used in the original discounting.

# PRACTICE EXAMPLE #1: RENT-A-LEMON, INC.

Hank Ford, founder of Rent-a-Lemon, Inc., needed to borrow some money, and he needed it fast. He was a pioneer in the business of buying older cars and renting them to college students visiting southern Florida on spring break. Rapid expansion of his rental locations was necessary to discourage competi-tors from entering the business. In 1991, he hoped to open two new offices in Daytona Beach. To do this, Rent-a-Lemon would need about $2.5 million for location development and purchase of a fleet of well-used automobiles.

Ford's personal assistant, Ms. I. Countem, told him that he could get the money Rent-a-Lemon needed from Money-for-Nothing, Inc. (MFNI), a local loan broker. She suggested Rent-a-Lemon offer MFNI three annual payments of $1 million each, the first to be due one year from the date of the loan, and the second and third at subsequent one-year intervals. Ms. Countem said that Rent-a-Lemon would receive a loan of about $2,486,900 if MFNI would be sat-isfied with an interest rate of 10%. She also explained that during the first year, interest expense on the loan would total $248,690, and when the first $1 million payment was made, the principal owed to MFNI would be reduced by the dif-ference between the $1 million paid and the interest expense.

## Questions

1. How did Ms. Countem know that Rent-a-Lemon would get nearly $2.5 million if MFNI would lend at a 10% interest rate?
2. Assume Ms. Countem is right, and MFNI is willing to lend on Mr. Ford's promises to pay $1 million each year for three years. How much will Rent-a-Lemon owe on the day the loan is taken? How much will it owe one year later just before the first payment of $1 million is made to MFNI?

What will be the liability of Rent-a-Lemon just **after** the first $1 million payment is made to MFNI?

3.  Calculate the interest expense for Rent-a-Lemon for the second year of the loan and the liability at the end of that year after the annual $1 million payment is made. Repeat the exercise for the third year. What does MFNI mean when they say they want to earn a 10% interest rate?

4.  Ms. Countem told Mr. Ford that she could be wrong about the interest rate MFNI might accept. It could be as low as 8% or as high as 12%. At these extremes, if Rent-a-Lemon offers the three annual payments of $1 million, how much will MFNI lend to Rent-a-Lemon, and what will be the interest expense in each year of the loan?

## PRACTICE EXAMPLE #2:  I. COUNTEM'S ALTERNATIVE

Ms. Countem had suggested to Hank Ford that there was an alternative to dealing with the local Florida [loan] sharks. She thought Rent-a-Lemon could float a bond issue. She suggested selling 2,500 bonds with a face value of $1,000 each and a coupon interest rate of 10% to be paid annually. The principal amount of the bonds, $2.5 million, would be due and paid at the end of the third year.

### Questions

5.  If Rent-a-Lemon decides to issue the bonds suggested by I. Countem, and investors wish to earn exactly 10% interest on their investment, how much will Rent-a-Lemon get from selling the bonds? On the day the bonds are issued, is that the total amount of Rent-a-Lemon's liability? Why or why not?

6.  What will Rent-a-Lemon's total liability be at the end of the first year just before the interest payment is made? Just after? At the end of the second year? The third year?

7.  What will be the proceeds of the 10% bond issue if investors are content to earn an 8% interest rate? How will this affect interest expense each year? What if investors demand 12% interest?

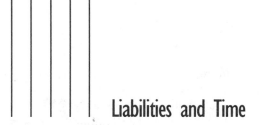

# Liabilities and Time

**W**hen an organization makes a commitment to an outside party to pay resources at some time in the future, the commitment is a *liability*. If the payment is due within one "operating cycle" (often assumed to be one year) of the organization's activities, the commitment will usually be classified as a *current liability*. *Noncurrent liabilities* are those that will be paid in a subsequent operating cycle or at a time beyond one year. The distinction between short-term liabilities and long-term liabilities is rarely precise. Likewise, the exact time period is rarely critical. Nevertheless, the distinction often determines how an accountant will measure the future burden of the liability and how it will be reported in financial reports.

## CURRENT LIABILITIES

Short-term or current liabilities of an individual or organization are created by exchanges or events that may involve a variety of sources. For example, accounts payable may be due to many different creditors. Current liabilities are usually labeled according to the party or class of creditor to which payments will be made. Classifications may be broad or narrow, depending upon the amount of detail that managers and their accountants wish to show in financial reports.

**Exhibit 1** shows the liabilities reported for the Gillette Company and Subsidiary Companies at the end of 1995 and 1994. Additional detail on the amount of liabilities and debt is contained in the notes to financial statements,

Copyright © 1992 by the President and Fellows of Harvard College. Harvard Business School case 193-051.

which are also shown in **Exhibit 1**. Gillette reports four classifications of current liabilities but groups all other liabilities into three classifications.

Many current liabilities arise from transactions involving employees and suppliers. These *accounts payable* report amounts owed to suppliers who have provided materials or services, but who have not yet been paid. This use of credit not only provides resources to the organization incurring a liability but also facilitates activity in that it is not necessary to pause and make payments continuously as transactions take place or services are rendered. Most organizations normally have a significant number of accounts payable. Gillette labels this item *accounts payable* and *accrued liabilities*. These include amounts payable to suppliers for purchased goods and services, to employees for wages and salaries that were unpaid at the balance sheet date, to government agencies as a result of payroll or property taxes, and so forth. If Gillette had wanted to show greater detail, it could have shown other categories in separate classifications.

Current liabilities are usually measured using the amount of cash or other assets that would currently satisfy the obligation if it were paid. If interest is associated with a liability, the amount of interest expense already incurred will be added to the original liability incurred. Measuring current liabilities is usually fairly straightforward, and understanding the future burden that they will place on the organization is usually simple, provided sufficient detail has been included in the balance sheet.

Two kinds of liabilities, *unearned revenue* and *deferred credits,* are often found among current liabilities and deserve special mention. Each shows the obligation of the organization to customers or clients. In many types of businesses customers pay in advance for services, and in return the organization promises to provide future services or products. Magazine subscriptions are typically sold on this basis, as are tickets for artistic or athletic events and airline transportation. The amount of resources received in advance for services that have not as yet been provided is clearly a liability. The organization promises to provide a good or service in the future to the same degree of certainty as if it had promised to provide payment in the future. The fact that the obligation will not be settled by payment of cash or assets does not mean a liability does not exist.

These situations result in *unearned revenue,* which is included in current liabilities if the product or service is to be delivered within the next operating cycle. Then, when the product or service is delivered, the revenue previously unearned becomes revenue of that operating period. The expenses to provide the product or service are matched with the revenue recognized in measuring and reporting the income at the time the product or service is delivered.

Deposits received from customers can also create liabilities. Deposits are frequently called *deferred credits*. If the deposit is an advance payment for a product or service, the deposit will be added to other revenues obtained when the product or service is delivered and will be removed from the liability account at that time. Other types of deferred credits might include deposits on shipping containers or other items of value provided by the seller to a customer. The deposit serves as security, and when the container or other items are returned, the refund of the deposit reduces cash and eliminates the liability.

Finally, as time passes, liabilities once classified as long-term come within the reach of the next operating period when they will be satisfied. That portion to be paid in the subsequent operating period is transferred from long-term liability categories to current liabilities, where it may be identified as the *current portion of long-term debt*. Amounts that will not be paid in the next period will continue to be shown as long-term debts.

## LONG-TERM DEBT

Agreements to pay at some future point of time or at intervals of time in the future represent an important source of resources to many organizations. Such agreements frequently take the form of loan contracts between the organization as a borrower and another individual or entity. They may take the form of debt security, such as debenture bonds, which lenders are free to trade among themselves and which are frequently traded in the securities markets. Loans can take other forms as well and may be known as mortgages, trust notes, or any of a number of other possible types of debt instruments. The characteristics that set these apart from other liabilities are their contractual nature and the extended period over which interest is to be accrued or payments are to be made.

Perhaps the simplest type of long-term debt is a contractual agreement to pay some specified amount at some time in the future. Consider the firm that has agreed to pay $1,000 in cash five years from today to another party.

At first glance, the $1,000 commitment might seem to have a value equal to cash or other resources the organization will have to give up when the debt falls due. Thus, we might simply say the liability has a value of $1,000. On the other hand, if we consider the investment decision of the person with whom we have made this agreement, the creditor, we would surely recognize that the value is less than the $1,000 amount stated in the liability agreement.

Suppose we were to go to the creditor and ask how much we would have to pay today to be released from our future obligation. Alternatively, we might go to a third party and ask it how much we would have to pay it to assume our promise to pay in the future.

Providing the creditor has alternative uses for the resources that we would offer today to cancel our future obligation, we should be able to settle for less than $1,000. If the market rate of interest is 10%, then we might expect that the creditor would accept the present value of $1,000 five years from now, or $620.92 today, and release us from our future commitment.[1] That is the amount

---

[1] The present value of $1,000 five years from now can be calculated by the formula:
Present Value = $1,000 ÷ $(1 + .10)^5$.

that a person would have to invest today to have $1,000 five years hence if the available interest rate is 10%. Actually, we might have to pay slightly more than $620.92 to compensate the creditor for the inconvenience of locating another investment. The nature of the liability compels us to measure its value in terms of what we would have to pay to satisfy the creditor.   Pv

When an organization incurs a liability such as a promise of $1,000 to be paid at the end of five years, the proper measurement of the claim is never the amount promised in the future. Instead, it would be the present value considering alternative uses (for five years) of the resources that can be made by any other parties to the contract. Even if the creditor should reject the offer to settle a future commitment at a level reflecting the market rate of interest, there is no reason for concern. The entity committed to a future payment can invest resources at the market rate of interest and thus accumulate the amount necessary to satisfy its obligation when it finally falls due. **Exhibit 2** illustrates how the present burden of a liability can be estimated and related to the amount that will have to be paid when the settlement date of the obligation finally occurs.

Discounting future expenditures to their present value rather than observing only their contractual amount is important for valuing long-term liabilities. Although the same arguments could be applied to current liabilities, the fact that these liabilities will be settled soon usually leads accountants to treat current liabilities as if the difference between the present value of the amount to be paid and the contractual amount is immaterial.

## Bonds

The amounts that business firms and other organizations wish to borrow are sometimes quite large—larger than any single lender may be willing or able to provide. For this reason, securities are created. One general category of borrowing instruments is that of bond indentures. The terms of a loan are specified in a master contract between the entity, which is the borrower, and the bondholders, who are the lenders. Each bondholder receives a certificate showing the total indebtedness represented by the certificate and the terms of his or her contract with the firm.

All bond agreements have three basic features:

1.  The *term* of the loan is specified.
2.  A *face amount* of the loan is specified.
3.  The *repayment schedule* is shown either in detailed amounts or as a percentage rate of interest to be paid at intervals based upon the face amount of the bond.

Other terms such as the privilege of conversion to other forms of securities may also be included in some bonds, but for simplicity we will ignore those complications here.

Bonds are typically issued in multiples of $1,000, so let us assume that an organization is offering to sell a bond with a term of 10 years, a face amount of $1,000, and annual payments based on an interest rate of 8%.  Now what do these contractual terms mean?

The face amount of the bond determines the amount that the issuers will pay the holder at the end of the life of the bond.  In this example, at the end of 10 years, the issuer of the bond will pay $1,000 to whomever presents it. The "nominal" interest rate, 8%, determines the amount of annual payments that will be made in addition to the terminal payment at the end of the bond term. Since that rate in our example is 8%, the annual payments on the $1,000 bond will be $80.  For this reason, when the borrower firm offers this bond for sale, it is asking, "How much will you lend me for promises to pay $80 at the end of each year for 10 years and, in addition, for the promise that I will pay $1,000 at the end of 10 years?"[2]

The amount that a lender will be willing to offer for a bond is dependent upon the desired rate of interest, or *yield*, that the lender wishes to earn on the amount about to be invested.  **Exhibit 3** illustrates the procedure that three investors might use to decide what to bid on a bond offering, assuming that each is willing to earn a different rate of interest on the investment.  The lender willing to bid the highest amount determines the *prevailing market interest rate* for the bonds offered.

The difference between the face amount of the bond and the amount received by the borrower when the bond is initially issued is referred to as discount or premium.  If the amount received is *larger* than the face amount, the difference is called *premium*.  If it is *smaller*, the difference is called *discount*. Premium or discount results whenever the nominal interest rate, that stated on the face of a bond, is different from the current market rate of interest demanded by lenders.  Only after a bond is issued can the borrower determine the *effective interest rate* on the debt.  The effective interest rate is the prevailing interest rate determined by the successful bid for the bonds.

The amount of the liability created by issuing a bond includes the premium (or excludes the discount), which will be amortized by the difference between the *interest expense* each period and the *interest payment* actually made. At any given time, the liability will be the face amount of the bond plus or minus the unamortized premium or discount created when the bond was first sold.  From **Exhibit 4**, we can surmise that Investor A, who is willing to invest to earn 6% interest, would at any time be willing to allow Eastern Coast Company to buy back the bond for the amount of liability at the beginning of the year, plus current interest not yet paid, plus perhaps a small premium for

---

[2]  By convention, bond interest rates are quoted in annual terms, but one-half of the quoted interest rate is used to determine the amount of *semiannual* interest payments. However, for this illustration annual payments are assumed in order to simplify **Exhibits 3** and 4.

inconvenience.  Near the end of the tenth year, the amount would be about $1,000 plus current interest earned but not paid.

A similar analysis could be applied to bond discounts, except that the positions would be somewhat different.  We can see by referring to **Exhibit 3** that if on the day after Eastern Coast had issued the bond to Investor C for $877, the company wished to cancel the agreement, Investor C probably would have been quite willing to accept $1,000 for it.  On the other hand, if we assume that other investments offering a 10% interest rate are available and that Investor C would be able to reinvest at the same rate, it would not be surprising to find that Investor C would be willing to cancel the future obligations in return for a payment for something near $877.07 plus any current interest already earned but not yet paid.

In accounting for bonds, the reduction in liability due to the fact that the periodic payments on bonds issued at a premium exceed the effective interest is referred to as the *amortization of bond premium*.  If bonds are issued at discount, the periodic payments will be less than the effective interest, and the liability will grow because of *amortization of bond discount*.  When bonds are issued for exactly the face amount, there is no premium or discount to amortize, and since the effective rate of interest is equal to the stated rate, interest each period will be equal to the periodic payments.  You should note that as the liability differs in each succeeding year due to amortization of premium or discount, so will the amount of interest expense change, even though the annual payment set by the contract will remain the same.

**Exhibit 5** provides another illustration, somewhat more extensive than **Exhibits 3** and **4**, of a proposed bond issue.

If all bonds were as simple as those we have used here to illustrate the problems of accounting for long-term debt, observing, measuring, and reporting on liabilities of this type would be much easier than they frequently are in practice.  As the number of conditions attached to a bond increases or the options open to either the bondholder (for example, the right to turn in the bond in return for ownership shares) or the borrower (for example, the right to pay off the bond at a specified sum at any point of time during its life) multiply, the more difficult become the problems of accounting for bonds.

## Long-Term Leases

Many organizations secure the future benefits of land, buildings, and equipment through lease agreements rather than through purchase.  A lease agreement conveys to the organization the right to use a resource in return for a promise to pay a specified amount at some future time or at many times in the future.  The owner of property or equipment who enters into such an agreement is called a *lessor*; the entity that secures the rights to use the resources in return for a promise to pay is called the *lessee*.

The terms of lease agreements vary widely.  Some are for long periods, others are for short.  Some demand that the lessee pay all expenses in maintaining and using the property, while others confer on the lessee the rights of use but leave the burdens of maintenance and replacement on the lessor.

Organizations that lease assets rather than purchase them may do so for a number of reasons. In many cases, leasing provides a type of financing. The products and benefits of using resources can be obtained through leasing without paying for them until receipts can be obtained from customers. This frees the firm from the necessity of other forms of borrowing and preserves liquid assets. In some instances, lease agreements are only veiled purchase agreements. This is particularly true when payments are to be made over a period of time, after which legal title to the leased property is transferred to the lessee.

Since a lease agreement requires the outflow of cash or other resources in the future, it has the essential characteristics of a liability. In many cases, this liability resembles long-term bonds, and the problem of accounting for the liability is quite similar to that for bonds. Because of their kinship to long-term liabilities, we might expect to find lease agreements included with long-term debts when reports on liabilities or the value of the firm are prepared. However, in practice, at least in public reports, long-term leases and their related obligations are often reported only in footnotes. Only when lease agreements are essentially agreements to purchase and simply provide a means for the buyer to delay payment for the assets do generally accepted accounting principles call for full disclosure of the liability inherent in the lease agreement.

## CONDITIONAL LIABILITIES

An important class of liabilities to many business organizations is one in which the promises to pay are contingent upon the occurrence of other events. Product guarantees and pension payments are two important types of conditional liabilities. When an entity promises to expend resources if certain events occur, a *conditional liability* has been created.

The observation and measurement problems associated with conditional liabilities are somewhat more difficult than those for contractual liabilities, but not impossibly so. The accountant must consider what the probable payments may be and then calculate the present value of the expected future payments.

### Product Guarantees

Often a business firm, in order to promote a product, will promise to refund the purchase price if the product fails to satisfy the customer. Alternatively, a replacement unit or cash refund based on use may be offered. Products returned under the guarantee rarely have any resale value. They have been used, and therefore they are often either given away or destroyed. The amount of liability created by such an agreement depends upon the frequency with which customers return the product and on the terms of the guarantee. The frequency will, in turn, be dependent upon factors, many of which are not easily measurable even when they are observed by the accountant. Product quality, product price, consumer expectations, and other factors all enter into the individual consumer's decision process in considering whether to return a product for refund. Despite the difficulty of projecting possible costs under product guarantees, it can be important in some circumstances. Thus, the accountant must employ as much ingenuity as possible in attempting to observe, measure, and report them.

## Postretirement Benefits

Frequently, in order to increase the attractiveness of employment or to reward faithful service, an entity enters into an agreement with its employees to provide them with a pension or other benefits on their retirement. A pension is a promise to pay a specified amount periodically for a specified period of time. Typically, a pension agreement guarantees that a certain amount will be paid each month to an employee after he or she retires. The conditional nature of such a liability makes the measurement difficult, for many factors can change during the years that intervene before an employee's retirement date arrives and the payments begin. Furthermore, the period of time over which the payments must be made depends upon whether employees die before retirement, soon after, or live for many years.

A postretirement agreement consists in most cases of a fairly long list of promises with stipulations. Typically, it provides that a specified amount will be paid periodically or as a lump sum, provided that the employee has met certain conditions: that he or she has continued in the employment of the entity until his or her retirement; that he or she has served some minimum of time prior to retirement; and that he or she has contributed some proportion of the amount necessary to make payments. The amounts of payments may vary depending upon the salary earned for all employees.

In practice, liabilities for pensions are sometimes eliminated by paying premiums to insurance or other fiduciary or trust agencies which then assume the liability. Since the liability is transferred to another organization, the liability is no longer a liability of the organization that created it.

As in the case of any other long-term liability, the amount of pension liability can be affected by a change in the agreement, by a change in the work force resulting in older or younger employees, or by a change in the rate at which future payments are discounted. Environmental events can have an important impact on the amount of the liability and should be reflected in accounting for pension liabilities.

## Deferred Taxes

When the amount of income taxes paid differs from the tax expense that should be reported in financial reports, the difference is recorded and reported as *deferred taxes.* Measuring and reporting deferred taxes create some of the most complicated reporting problems accountants face because of the complexity of income tax regulations and the conditional nature of income taxes not yet due.

## SUMMARY

Liabilities are commitments to transfer resources to another person or organization at some time in the future. Current liabilities are usually measured and reported at the amount that will be paid to satisfy the claims of creditors. Long-term liabilities are usually reported at the present value of the amounts of claim or estimates of what will eventually be paid.

On a balance sheet, liabilities show the sources other than owners' contributions and retained earnings of the resources (assets) of the organization. Just as assets must be managed, liabilities need attention to make the best use of this important source of resources while preserving the credit worthiness of the organization.

**EXHIBIT 1**
**The Gillette Company and Subsidiary Companies—Liabilities**
**(Excerpt from Consolidated Balance Sheets) ($ millions)**

| | December 31, | |
| --- | --- | --- |
| | 1995 | 1994 |
| **Liabilities and Stockholders' Equity** | | |
| **Current Liabilities** | | |
| Loans payable | $ 576.2 | $ 344.4 |
| Current portion of long-term debt | 26.5 | 28.1 |
| Accounts payable and accrued liabilities | 1,273.3 | 1,178.2 |
| Income taxes | 248.0 | 185.5 |
| Total current liabilities | $2,124.0 | $1,736.2 |
| **Long-Term Debt** | $ 691.1 | $ 715.1 |
| **Deferred Income Taxes** | 72.7 | 53.1 |
| **Other Long-Term Liabilities** | 919.2 | 774.3 |
| **Minority Interest** | 20.0 | 17.4 |

**EXHIBIT 1 (continued)**
## Notes to Consolidated Financial Statements

ACCOUNTS PAYABLE AND ACCRUED LIABILITIES

| (Millions of dollars) | December 31, 1995 | 1994 |
|---|---|---|
| Accounts payable | $ 400.3 | $ 334.6 |
| Advertising and sales promotion | 227.5 | 218.0 |
| Payroll and payroll taxes | 221.3 | 197.8 |
| Other taxes | 71.1 | 45.5 |
| Interest payable | 8.8 | 12.2 |
| Dividends payable on common stock | 66.7 | 55.4 |
| Realignment expense | 30.2 | 107.3 |
| Miscellaneous | 247.4 | 207.4 |
| | $1,273.3 | $1,178.2 |

## Income Taxes

Beginning in 1993, deferred taxes are provided for using the asset and liability method for temporary differences between financial and tax reporting.

## Debt

Loans payable at December 31, 1995 and 1994, included $223 million and $142 million, respectively, of commercial paper. The company's commercial paper program is supported by its revolving credit facilities.

Long-term debt is summarized as follows:

| (Millions of dollars) | December 31, 1995 | 1994 |
|---|---|---|
| Commercial paper | $150.0 | $150.0 |
| 5.75% Notes due 2005 | 200.0 | 200.0 |
| 6.25% Notes due 2003 | 150.0 | 150.0 |
| 4.75% Notes due 1996 | 150.0 | 150.0 |
| 8.03% Guaranteed ESOP notes due through 2000 | 41.2 | 51.5 |
| Other, primarily foreign currency borrowings | 26.4 | 41.7 |
| Total long-term debt | $717.6 | $743.2 |
| Less current portion | 26.5 | 28.1 |
| Long-term portion | $691.1 | $715.1 |

## Other Long-Term Liabilities

| | | |
|---|---|---|
| Pensions | $449.6 | $368.4 |
| Postretirement medical | 209.1 | 193.1 |
| Incentive plans | 131.6 | 116.6 |
| Realignment expense | (11.0) | 15.0 |
| Miscellaneous | 139.9 | 81.2 |
| | $919.2 | $774.3 |

## EXHIBIT 1 (continued)

At December 31, 1995 and 1994, the company had swap agreements that converted $500 million in U.S. dollar-denominated long-term fixed rate debt securities into multicurrency principal and floating interest rate obligations over the term of the respective issues. As of December 31, 1995, the $150 million notes due 1996 were swapped into floating interest rate U.S. dollar obligations, and the $150 million notes due 2003 and the $200 million notes due 2005 were swapped to Deutschmark principal and floating interest rate obligations, resulting in an agreement principal amount of $533 million at a weighted average interest rate of 4.7%. At December 31, 1994, the aggregate principal amounted to $500 million, with a weighted average interest rate of 5.6%

In addition, at December 31, 1995, the company had a forward exchange contract, maturing in 1996, that established a $42 million Yen principal, .5% interest obligation with respect to $43 million of U.S. dollar commercial paper debt included in long-term debt. At December 31, 1994, the Company had forward exchange contracts that established Deutschmark and Yen principal and interest obligations with respect to $119 million of U.S. dollar commercial paper debt included in long-term debt, with a weighted average interest rate of 3.7%.

Exchange rate movements give rise to changes in the values of these agreements that offset changes in the values of the underlying exposure. Amounts associated with these agreements were liabilities of $32.6 million at December 31, 1995, and were nil at December 31, 1994.

The weighted average interest rate on loans payable was 5.8% at December 31, 1995, and 6.5% at December 31, 1994. The weighted average interest rate on total long-term debt, including associated swaps and excluding the guaranteed ESOP notes, was 4.7% at December 31, 1995, compared with 5.3% at December 31, 1994.

The company has a $100 million revolving bank credit agreement that expires in June 1996 and a $300 million revolving bank credit agreement expiring in June 2000, both of which may be used for general corporate purposes. Under the agreements, the company has the option to borrow at various interest rates, including the prime rate, and is required to pay a weighted average facility fee of 0.65% per annum. At year-end 1995 and 1994, there were no borrowings under these agreements.

Based on the company's intention and ability to maintain its $300 million revolving credit agreement beyond 1996, $150 million of commercial paper borrowings and the $150 million notes due 1996 were classified as long-term debt at December 31, 1995. As of December 31, 1994, $150 million of commercial paper borrowings was so classified.

Aggregate maturities of total long-term debt for the five years subsequent to December 31, 1995, are $176.5 million, $15.1 million, $10.7 million, $8.8 million, and $5.1 million, respectively.

Unused lines of credit, including the revolving credit facilities, amounted to $1.02 billion at December 31, 1995.

**EXHIBIT 2**
**The Value of a Promise to Pay $1,000**
**at the End of Five Years (rate of interest = 10%)**

| End of Year | Total Liability, Which Is Equal to the Amount of Creditor's Investment | Interest Accumulated During Year |
|---|---|---|
| 5 | $1,000.00 | $90.91 |
| 4 | 909.09 | 82.64 |
| 3 | 826.45 | 75.13 |
| 2 | 751.32 | 68.30 |
| 1 | 683.02 | 62.10 |
| Now | 620.92 | |

**EXHIBIT 3**
**Analysis of a Bond by Three Investors**

Eastern Coast Company—Analysis of Value of 10-Year, 8%, $1,000 Bonds to Three Investors Who Seek 6%, 8%, and 10% Return, Respectively

Investor A demands 6%.
Investor B demands 8%.
Investor C demands 10%.

Bond contract ("indenture") promises:
a) Ten payments of $80 at end of each of 10 years.
b) One payment of $1,000 at end of 10 years.

| Present Value of $1.00 | At 6% Interest | At 8% Interest | At 10% Interest |
|---|---|---|---|
| Received annually for 10 years | 7.3601 | 6.7101 | 6.1446 |
| Received at end of 10 years | .5584 | .4632 | .3855 |

Value to Investors at Issue Date

| A | | | B | | | C | | |
|---|---|---|---|---|---|---|---|---|
| 7.3601 × $ 80 = | $ 588.81 | | 6.7101 × $ 80 = | $ 536.80 | | 6.1446 × $ 80 = | $491.57 | |
| .5584 × 1,000 = | 558.40 | | .4632 × 1,000 = | 463.20 | | .3855 × 1,000 = | 385.50 | |
| Total | $1,147.21[a] | | Total | $1,000.00 | | Total | $877.07 | |

| A will pay a premium of $147.21 over the face amount of the bond. | B will pay the face amount of $1,000. | C demands a discount of $122.93 off the face amount of the bond. |
|---|---|---|

[a] The value of the liability and hence the amount that the business firm issuing this bond will receive are dependent on the rate of return that the investors wish to earn on their investment. Because Investor A demands only 6% on his or her investment, he or she is willing to lend more, given the fixed terms of the contract. The entity issuing these bonds would be foolish not to accept his or her high bid of $1,147.21 for the bond.

## EXHIBIT 4
## A Investment in a Bond from the Investor's Point of View

Assume that the Eastern Coast Company issued the bond described in **Exhibit 3** to Investor A and received $1,147.21 from him or her. Investor A has accepted a yield rate of interest of 6%, which is the rate of interest Eastern Coast now will pay on the *actual* amount borrowed. Its original promises remain constant, however, it will make 10 payments of $80 at the end of each year for 10 years and 1 payment of $1,000 at the end of 10 years.

If the original liability of Eastern Coast is assumed to be equal to the amount received, the table below shows how that liability increases during each year because of the interest owed to Investor A, then falls as each $80 payment is made until at the end of 10 years it is exactly equal to the $1,000 terminal payment originally promised.

| Year | Liability at Beginning of Year | Interest at 6% = Yield Rate | Liability at End of Year Before Payment | Payment | Liability at End of Year |
|---|---|---|---|---|---|
| 1 | $1,147.21 | $ 68.83[a] | $1,216.04 | $   80.00 | $1,136.04 |
| 2 | 1,136.04 | 68.16 | 1,204.20 | 80.00 | 1,124.20 |
| 3 | 1,124.20 | 67.45 | 1,191.65 | 80.00 | 1,111.65 |
| 4 | 1,111.65 | 66.70 | 1,178.35 | 80.00 | 1,098.35 |
| 5 | 1,098.35 | 65.90 | 1,164.25 | 80.00 | 1,084.25 |
| 6 | 1,084.25 | 65.06 | 1,149.31 | 80.00 | 1,069.31 |
| 7 | 1,069.31 | 64.16 | 1,133.47 | 80.00 | 1,053.47 |
| 8 | 1,053.47 | 63.21 | 1,116.68 | 80.00 | 1,036.68 |
| 9 | 1,036.68 | 62.20 | 1,098.88 | 80.00 | 1,018.88 |
| 10 | 1,018.88 | 61.13 | 1,080.01 | 80.00 | 1,000.01 |
| 10 | — | — | 1,000.00 | 1,000.00 | 0.00 |
| Totals | | $652.79 | | $1,800.00 | |

| | |
|---|---|
| Total borrowed | $1,147.21 |
| Add interest | 652.79 |
| Total paid | $1,800.00 |

---

[a] We can calculate the interest Investor A expects during the first year by multiplying the amount received by the interest rate used by Investor A (6.0%) originally to value the promised cash payments.

# EXHIBIT 5
## Proposed Bond Issue of Indet Corporation

The Indet Corporation is planning to issue bonds with a face value of $1,000,000, bearing a nominal interest rate of 5%, and payable at the end of 20 years. Interest is to be paid semiannually. The treasurer of the corporation has prepared three schedules to show the way in which the liability of the corporation will change over the life of the bonds under varying conditions with respect to yield rates. That is, if the prevailing market interest rate at the date the bonds are issued will be either 4%, 5%, or 6%, the measurement of the liability will be affected as shown in these schedules (**Exhibits 5a, 5b,** and **5c**).

The schedules of liability prepared by the treasurer show some important features of long-term liabilities with contractual payments that have the same form as bonds. Until the last period, all payments remain the same. When payments are made semiannually, the annual rate of interest must be adjusted to reflect the time period stated for interest. In this case, since payments are to be made semiannually, the interest expense for each period is calculated using half the annual rate. The interest expense is based on the total outstanding liability at the beginning of the period. In cases where premium or discount has been created because the bonds sold at a yield rate different from the stated rate, the difference between the semiannual payment and the interest expense amortizes premium or discount as the case may demand. By the end of the last period of the life of the bonds, the liability is the amount equal to the terminal payment, which includes repayment of principle as well as payment of interest for the last period.

# EXHIBIT 5a
## Indet Corporation—Projected Liability at Selected Intervals Due to Sale of $1,000,000, 5%, 20-Year Bonds with Interest Due Semiannually, Sold to Yield 4% to Investors

| Interest Period (6 months) | Total Liability at Beginning of Period | Unamortized Premiums | Interest Expense for Period at 4% (2% for 6 months) | Liability at End of Period before Payment | Payment at End of Period | Liability at End of Period after Payment |
|---|---|---|---|---|---|---|
| 1 | $1,136,787 | $136,787 | $22,735 | $1,159,522 | $ 25,000 | $1,134,522 |
| 2 | 1,134,522 | 134,552 | 22,690 | 1,157,212 | 25,000 | 1,132,212 |
| 20 | 1,085,080 | 85,080 | 21,702 | 1,106,782 | 25,000 | 1,081,872 |
| 40 | 1,004,902 | 4,902 | 20,098 | 1,025,000 | 1,025,000 | 0 |

**EXHIBIT 5b**
**Indet Corporation—Projected Liability at Selected Intervals Due to Sale of $1,000,000, 5%, 20-Year Bonds with Interest Due Semiannually, Sold to Yield 5% to Investors**

| Interest Period (6 months) | Total Liability at Beginning of Period | Unamortized Premiums | Interest Expense for Period at 5% (2½% for 6 months) | Liability at End of Period before Payment | Payment at End of Period | Liability at End of Period after Payment |
|---|---|---|---|---|---|---|
| 1 | $1,000,000 | $0 | $25,000 | $1,025,000 | $ 25,000 | $1,000,000 |
| 2 | 1,000,000 | 0 | 25,000 | 1,025,000 | 25,000 | 1,000,000 |
| • • • | • • • | • • • | • • • | • • • | • • • | |
| 20 | 1,000,000 | 0 | 25,000 | 1,025,000 | 25,000 | 1,000,000 |
| • • • | • • • | • • • | • • • | • • • | • • • | |
| 40 | 1,000,000 | 0 | 25,000 | 1,025,000 | 1,025,000 | 0 |

**EXHIBIT 5c**
**Indet Corporation—Projected Liability at Selected Intervals Due to Sale of $1,000,000, 5%, 20-Year Bonds with Interest Due Semiannually, Sold to Yield 6% to Investors**

| Interest Period (6 months) | Total Liability at Beginning of Period | Unamortized Premiums | Interest Expense for Period at 6% (3% for 6 months) | Liability at End of Period before Payment | Payment at End of Period | Liability at End of Period after Payment |
|---|---|---|---|---|---|---|
| 1 | $884,470 | $115,530 | $26,534 | $ 911,004 | $ 25,000 | $886,004 |
| 2 | 886,004 | 113,996 | 26,580 | 912,584 | 25,000 | 887,584 |
| • • • | • • • | • • • | • • • | • • • | • • • | |
| 20 | 922,875 | 77,125 | 27,686 | 950,561 | 25,000 | 925,561 |
| • • • | • • • | • • • | • • • | • • • | • • • | |
| 40 | 995,146 | 4,854 | 29,854 | 1,025,000 | 1,025,000 | 0 |

# Laurinburg Precision Engineering

**O**liver MacKinnon and Beacham McDougald founded Laurinburg Precision Engineering in 1992 to manufacture precision injection-molded parts for use in medical devices. After an uncertain start-up period, the company won contracts from several different manufacturers. Using special machinery and expertise in injection molding of specialty plastics, the company prospered.

In early 1997, the company was experiencing a cash crisis caused by rapid growth and the desire to extend capabilities through the acquisition of new molding machines. The partners had no additional capital to finance the expansions, and they were reluctant to sell equity to anyone else. A bank loan was considered, but financial projections indicated the loan could not be paid down for almost five years. Because of prevailing interest rates, local banks were unwilling to make a loan commitment of that duration.

Their local bank had introduced MacKinnon and McDougald to a small investment banking firm in Charlotte, North Carolina. After a consultation with MacKinnon and McDougald, Sheila Cox, a partner in the investment banking firm, suggested a $1 million bond issue with a term of five years. The bond issue would be secured by the new machinery and placed with private investors. Cox told MacKinnon and McDougald that she expected the bonds would have to be sold to yield almost 10% interest. She proposed setting the interest rate on the bonds at 10%, with semiannual interest payments and the principal due at the end of the fifth year, and she prepared a schedule of the interest and principal repayments that would be due if the bonds were sold to yield 10% interest exactly (see **Exhibit 1**).

Although the proposal seemed to be a reasonable solution to the problem facing MacKinnon and McDougald, both were worried about the semiannual

Copyright © 1993 by the President and Fellows of Harvard College. Harvard Business School case 193-098.

interest payments in the early years. They expected operating cash flows would remain tight as Laurinburg Precision Engineering continued to grow. When they expressed this concern to Cox by telephone, she suggested a second alternative. Laurinburg Precision Engineering could issue zero-coupon bonds at the same interest rate and terms. On these bonds no interest payments would be made during the five years the bonds would be outstanding, and all interest and principal would be due on January 15, 2002, when the bonds matured. The principal amount of the zero-coupon bonds would be greater than that of the 10% bonds, but Laurinburg would have five years to prepare to pay interest and principal from either operations or additional financing.

## QUESTIONS

1.  Using the present value tables in **Exhibits 2** and **3**, estimate the number of zero-coupon bonds (each with a face value of $1,000) that will have to be offered to provide the $1 million Laurinburg Precision Engineering needs for expansion, if investors seek a yield of 10%. Assume interest will compound on a semiannual basis over the life of the five-year bond issue. Prepare a schedule similar to **Exhibit 1** that shows the interest expense and end-of-period bond liability for each semiannual compounding period. Why is the interest expense for the zero-coupon bonds different from the interest expense on the five-year bonds summarized in **Exhibit 1**?

2.  Assume that MacKinnon and McDougald decide to issue bonds to finance the expansion of Laurinburg Precision Engineering. The terms of the $1,000 bonds to be due January 15, 2002, specify an interest rate of 10% with semiannual compounding or interest payments. However, Sheila Cox is able to find a group of investors who will accept a yield of 8% interest. How much will the investors be willing to pay for the 10% bonds? Prepare a schedule like **Exhibit 1** showing principal, interest payments, interest expense, and amortization of bond premium for these bonds. Why does the bond premium amortize to zero?

3.  If zero-coupon bonds with semiannual compounding to be due January 15, 2002, are issued, what will be the amount due on that date if enough bonds are issued to provide $1 million on January 15, 1997, if the investors seek a yield of 8%? Prepare a schedule of interest expense and bond liabilities for each semiannual compounding period.

4.  How should Oliver MacKinnon and Beacham McDougald decide which bonds to issue? What factors should they consider? Why?

**EXHIBIT 1**
**Schedule of Interest Payments, Interest Expense, and Bond Liability for a 10%, Five-Year Bond with Semiannual Interest Payments Issued to Yield 10% Interest**

| Date | Interest Payment | Interest After Expense | Interest Payment | Principal to be Paid |
|---|---|---|---|---|
| 1/15/97 | — | — | $1,000,000 | — |
| 7/15/97 | $50,000 | $50,000 | 1,000,000 | — |
| 1/15/98 | 50,000 | 50,000 | 1,000,000 | — |
| 7/15/98 | 50,000 | 50,000 | 1,000,000 | — |
| 1/15/99 | 50,000 | 50,000 | 1,000,000 | — |
| 7/15/99 | 50,000 | 50,000 | 1,000,000 | — |
| 1/15/00 | 50,000 | 50,000 | 1,000,000 | — |
| 7/15/00 | 50,000 | 50,000 | 1,000,000 | — |
| 1/15/01 | 50,000 | 50,000 | 1,000,000 | — |
| 7/15/01 | 50,000 | 50,000 | 1,000,000 | — |
| 1/15/02 | 50,000 | 50,000 | 1,000,000 | $1,000,000 |

**EXHIBIT 2**
**Present Value of $1**

$$PV= \frac{1}{(1 + i)^n}$$

| Period | 3% | 4% | 5% | 6% | 7% | 8% | 10% |
|---|---|---|---|---|---|---|---|
| 1 | .9709 | .9615 | .9524 | .9434 | .9346 | .9259 | .9091 |
| 2 | .9426 | .9246 | .9070 | .8900 | .8734 | .8573 | .8264 |
| 3 | .9151 | .8890 | .8638 | .8396 | .8163 | .7938 | .7513 |
| 4 | .8885 | .8548 | .8227 | .7921 | .7629 | .7350 | .6830 |
| 5 | .8626 | .8219 | .7835 | .7473 | .7130 | .6806 | .6209 |
| 6 | .8375 | .7903 | .7462 | .7050 | .6663 | .6302 | .5645 |
| 7 | .8131 | .7599 | .7107 | .6651 | .6227 | .5835 | .5132 |
| 8 | .7894 | .7307 | .6768 | .6274 | .5820 | .5403 | .4665 |
| 9 | .7664 | .7026 | .6446 | .5919 | .5439 | .5002 | .4241 |
| 10 | .7441 | .6756 | .6139 | .5584 | .5083 | .4632 | .3855 |

**EXHIBIT 3**
**Present Value of Ordinary Annuity of $1**   @ End of Period

$$PV_A = \frac{1}{i}\left[\,1 - \frac{1}{(1+i)^n}\,\right]$$

| Period | 3% | 4% | 5% | 6% | 7% | 8% | 10% |
|--------|--------|--------|--------|--------|--------|--------|--------|
| 1 | .9709 | .9615 | .9524 | .9434 | .9346 | .9259 | .9091 |
| 2 | 1.9135 | 1.8861 | 1.8594 | 1.8334 | 1.8080 | 1.7833 | 1.7355 |
| 3 | 2.8286 | 2.7751 | 2.7232 | 2.6730 | 2.6243 | 2.5771 | 2.4869 |
| 4 | 3.7171 | 3.6299 | 3.5460 | 3.4651 | 3.3872 | 3.3121 | 3.1699 |
| 5 | 4.5797 | 4.4518 | 4.3295 | 4.2124 | 4.1002 | 3.9927 | 3.7908 |
| 6 | 5.4172 | 5.2421 | 5.0757 | 4.9173 | 4.7665 | 4.6229 | 4.3553 |
| 7 | 6.2303 | 6.0021 | 5.7864 | 5.5824 | 5.3893 | 5.2064 | 4.8684 |
| 8 | 7.0197 | 6.7327 | 6.4632 | 6.2098 | 5.9713 | 5.7466 | 5.3349 |
| 9 | 7.7861 | 7.4353 | 7.1078 | 6.8017 | 6.5152 | 6.2489 | 5.7590 |
| 10 | 8.5302 | 8.1109 | 7.7217 | 7.3601 | 7.0236 | 6.7101 | 6.1446 |

# Belgrave Corporation

Late one evening in January 1989, Alex Banks sat in his office struggling with his new assignment. Alex had just met with Charles Belgrave, president of Belgrave Corporation, who was concerned about the current interest rate environment and its effect on the corporation's outstanding bond issue. Mr. Belgrave instructed Alex to analyze what the effects would be if the bonds issued back in 1981 were repurchased on the open market and new bonds issued in their place at a much lower interest rate. Mr. Belgrave indicated that Alex's analysis should include the effects of the potential transaction on cash flows, reported earnings, and financial position. The company had reported impressive earnings growth in the past eight or so years, and Mr. Belgrave hoped that the transaction would not mar this trend.

## THE COMPANY

Belgrave Corporation manufactured high-quality brass lamps and other brass lighting fixtures for sale in the United States and many countries abroad. Although Belgrave's stock and debt were publicly traded, the corporation was principally family owned. As a closely held corporation, Belgrave operated very conservatively. Its conservative financial policies were evidenced by the absence of long-term debt up until 1981 when its first debt issue was sold to the public.

The late 1970s were difficult for Belgrave because of rising raw material and labor costs, and because an internal family dispute diverted management's

*Eric J. Petro prepared this case under the supervision of Professor William J. Bruns, Jr.*

Copyright © 1989 by the President and Fellows of Harvard College. Harvard Business School case 190-056.

attention away from the company at a critical time. Unexpectedly, the company was forced to issue $10 million in debt with a coupon rate of 15% in 1981 to fund needed capital expenditures and growth in working capital. Management felt that issuing debt was more prudent than issuing additional equity. At the time Belgrave issued the debt the market interest rate for debt of the type and risk class issued by Belgrave was a hefty 16.5%.

## CURRENT SITUATION

Charles Belgrave had told Alex that he felt the time might be ripe to refund the 1981 bond issue and replace it with bonds bearing lower interest rates. Mr. Belgrave had met with the company's investment bankers, who told him that $10 million in new 10% bonds could be issued to yield the company exactly $10 million, not considering underwriting costs and legal fees that were expected to be nominal. The bonds would pay $500,000 interest every January 2 and July 1, with a payment of $10 million in principal at the end of 10 years. If 11% bonds were issued, the proceeds would be $10.6 million.

Beginning his research, Alex obtained a copy of Belgrave Corporation's 1988 Annual Report. Alex was confused as to why the liability for the $10 million bonds issued in 1981 was only $9.2 million at the end of 1988. (See **Exhibit 1** for the Liabilities and Shareholders' Equity section of Belgrave's 1988 balance sheet.) To clarify his confusion, Alex called upon the company's controller and learned that the 1981 bonds had been issued at a discount. Only approximately $9.1 million was received when the bonds were issued. For further information, the controller referred Alex to footnote 10 of the company's 1988 financial statements (**Exhibit 2**).

Next, Alex looked in *The Wall Street Journal* to determine the market price of the company's bonds. The current price was 134½. This meant that each $1,000 bond would have to be bought back at $1,345. The company would have to spend $13.45 million to retire bonds that were valued on the balance sheet at $9.2 million. The $4.25 million loss would probably shrink 1989's projected earnings to lower than what was reported in 1988. Alex knew that this would not make Mr. Belgrave happy. However, the lower interest expense associated with a new issue would help earnings in future years.

Since it was getting late and the office was deserted, Alex cleared his desk and left the office for the week. For the entire train ride home and throughout the weekend, Alex wondered about his assignment. The recommendation he would make needed to be supported with a clear, straightforward analysis of the situation that carefully weighed each of the variables that concerned Mr. Belgrave.

# QUESTIONS

1. Belgrave Corporation's controller told Alex that the bonds were issued in 1981 at a discount and that only approximately $9.1 million was received in cash. Explain what is meant by the terms "premium" or "discount" as they relate to bonds. Compute exactly how much the company received from its 15% bonds if the rate prevailing at the time of the original issue was 16.5% as indicated in **Exhibit 2**. Also, recompute the amounts shown in the balance sheet at December 31, 1987, and December 31, 1988, for long-term debt.

2. If you were Alex Banks, would you recommend issuing $10 million, 10% bonds and using the proceeds and other cash to refund the existing $10 million, 15% bonds? Will it cost more, in terms of principal and interest payments, to keep the existing bonds or to issue new ones at a lower rate? Be prepared to discuss the impact of a bond refunding on the following areas:

   - cash flows
   - current year earnings
   - future years' earnings
   - balance sheet presentation

   Note: For purposes of your computations assume that refunding, if selected, occurs effective January 2, 1989, at a price of 134½. Also, ignore the effects of income taxes.

3. Assume that $13.45 million in 10% bonds could be issued and the proceeds used to refund the existing bonds. Compare the effects of these transactions to those calculated in Question 2. If you were Alex Banks, what amount of new bonds would you recommend and why?

4. Assuming the company does refund the 1981 bonds, how should it decide between issuing, in their place, 10% bonds or 11% bonds?

**EXHIBIT 1**
**Liabilities and Shareholders' Equity as of December 31 ($ thousands)**

|  | 1988 | 1987 |
|---|---|---|
| Current Liabilities | | |
| Notes payable | $ 14,043 | $ 11,863 |
| Accounts payable and accrued expenses | 22,788 | 18,674 |
| Income taxes payable | 4,743 | 3,491 |
| Total current liabilities | 41,574 | 34,028 |
| Long-term debt (Note 10) | $ 9,227 | $ 9,207 |
| Shareholders' Equity | | |
| Common shares, $1 par value (5,000,000 shares authorized; 2,837,593 issued) | 2,838 | 2,838 |
| Additional paid-in capital | 69,482 | 69,482 |
| Retained earnings | 157,811 | 140,279 |
| Total shareholders' equity | 230,131 | 212,599 |
| Total liabilities and shareholders' equity | $280,932 | $ 255,834 |

**EXHIBIT 2**
**Long-Term Debt Footnote**

**Note 10:  Long-Term Debt**
On January 2, 1981, the company issued $10 million, 15% bonds payable on January 2, 2001.  Interest is payable semiannually on January 2 and July 1.  The prevailing interest rate at the time was 16.5%.  For financial reporting purposes, the discount on bonds payable is being amortized using the effective interest method over the life of the bonds. These bonds are presented in the financial statements net of such discounts as follows (in thousands of dollars):

|  | 1988 | 1987 |
|---|---|---|
| Bonds payable | $10,000 | $10,000 |
| Less:  unamortized discount | 773 | 793 |
| Bonds payable—net | $ 9,227 | $ 9,207 |

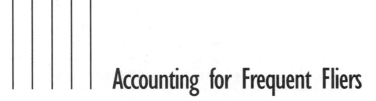

# Accounting for Frequent Fliers

**B**y 1991, almost all U.S. airline companies offered frequent flier programs to their passengers. Under these programs, passengers could become members of a program where the miles they flew would be recorded and accumulated to earn free future flights. The proliferation and growth of frequent flier programs created concerns about the proper way to account for and report them in financial reports. The airlines, the Securities and Exchange Commission (SEC), the American Institute of Certified Public Accountants (AICPA), and the Financial Accounting Standards Board (FASB) had each voiced concerns about measuring the expenses and reporting airlines' obligations under frequent flier programs.

The percentage of revenue passenger miles (the number of miles flown by revenue passengers, including free flight award passengers, computed by multiplying the number of revenue passengers by the miles they have flown) flown under free travel awards was less than 5% for all U.S. airlines combined. However, on some routes for some airlines (U.S. mainland to Hawaii, for example) the percentage of revenue passenger miles represented by free flights exceeded 12%. And there was some evidence that the problem was growing.

## BACKGROUND OF FREQUENT FLIER PROGRAMS

American Airlines first introduced frequent flier programs in 1981. Initially the program was meant to be a promotional gimmick designed to attract more customers. The program's immediate success in generating repeat business

*Susan S. Harmeling prepared this case under the supervision of Professor William J. Bruns, Jr.*

Copyright © 1991 by the President and Fellows of Harvard College. Harvard Business School case 192-040.

shocked the industry.  This success forced other carriers to introduce their own free mileage programs, each promising better and better rewards to customers who would sign up.  Through agreements with hotels, auto rental companies, and financial institutions, airlines made it possible for program participants to earn free miles by choosing where to stay, what auto to rent, or what credit card to use.  By 1988, frequent flier programs were so popular that airlines owed more than 3 million round-trip domestic tickets to their free mileage program members.  These tickets amounted to a minimum of 5.4 billion free miles according to one published report.

The question was how, when, and whether participants would use their free miles.  The worst scenario for the airline industry would have all their free fliers cashing in over a short period of time, taking up revenue-producing seats on many flights.  In 1984, for example, Pan Am forced frequent fliers to use their awards or lose them, and the result was chaos at the check-in counter and a $50 million revenue loss.  By 1991, all airlines limited the number of free travel award seats on some flights and used "blackout" dates during peak holiday travel periods when very limited or no free travel awards could be used.  However, controls such as these had to be used cautiously to avoid diluting the promotional value of the programs.  Members of a program who had earned a free flight but who then found it hard to schedule could easily switch their allegiance to another airline.

## THE ACCOUNTING ISSUE

By 1990, all major airlines offered similar frequent flier programs.  Members of a program would receive miles credited to their accounts based on the actual miles flown on the particular airline.  In some cases, additional bonus miles were credited to members flying First or Business Class and, in certain circumstances, for flying certain routes or during periods when special promotions were offered.

The use of free mileage from frequent flier programs represented between 2% and 6% of total revenue passenger miles for each airline offering such awards in 1990.  Based on the issuance of free travel awards to qualified members, coupled with program characteristics and the use of "blackout" dates during peak holiday periods, airlines generally did not consider the liability of free travel awards to be material.

In contrast, the airlines' auditors were concerned that growth of the programs might eventually force airlines to change the way in which they accounted for free miles.  As more and more tickets were given away, and as paying passengers were replaced on flights by free fliers, a "new reality" might soon have to be reflected on the balance sheet and income statement.

The AICPA considered new rules that would likely force the airlines to change their accounting practices in 1988.  When they did not take action, many observers thought the FASB might take up the problem, but the FASB did not add the issue to its agenda. Ultimately, the SEC issued a rule that required the airlines to disclose in their filings with the SEC, beginning in 1991, the number of free trips taken by frequent flier participants.

## UNITED AIR LINES, INC.

One of the largest frequent flier programs was that of United Air Lines (United). Travel awards redeemed in 1990 by members of United's program totaled 1.2 million free trips, an increase of 200,000 over the prior year. By early 1991, United had enrolled more than 13.3 million members in its frequent flier program and was adding 130,000 new members each month. **Exhibits 1** and **2** contain some disclosures of financial and flight data taken from the 1990 Annual Report and Form 10K filed with the SEC by United in early 1991.

## QUESTIONS

1.  The cost of United's frequent flier program:
    a.  What are the various methods United might use to measure the costs of its frequent flier program? What are the potential differences in dollars of the cost measured by each method?
    b.  What method should United use to measure the cost of its frequent flier program? Estimate the cost of the program using this method. Show all calculations and indicate the assumptions you make.
    c.  If you were the chief financial officer (CFO) of United, how would you determine if continuing the frequent flier program would be beneficial to United?
2.  Financial disclosure for United's frequent flier program:
    a.  Do you believe that United should account in its published financial statements for the frequent flier program or is "disclosure" in public filings with the SEC sufficient? Why?
    b.  In either case, what is it that should be accounted for or disclosed? Why?
    c.  What possible ways might United choose to account for the program in its published financial statements if it chooses to do so?
    d.  How do you believe United should account for the program in its published financial statements? Explain and support your chosen method and why you rejected other approaches. Show by some means (such as journal entries, T accounts, or pro forma statements) how your chosen method would be applied and all of the accounts that would be affected by the accounting you believe to be best.
    e.  If you were CFO of United, what would you do?

**EXHIBIT 1**
**United Air Lines, Inc. Statement of Consolidated**
**Financial Position (in thousands, except share data)**

| | December 31, | |
| --- | --- | --- |
| | 1990 | 1989 |
| **Assets** | | |
| **Current assets:** | | |
| Cash and cash equivalents | $  221,401 | $  465,181 |
| Short-term investments | 973,695 | 957,312 |
| Receivables, less allowance for doubtful accounts (1990—$13,129; 1989—$11,719) | 912,663 | 888,015 |
| Aircraft fuel, spare parts and supplies, less obsolescence allowance (1990—$57,406; 1989—$55,493) | 322,866 | 248,581 |
| Prepaid expenses | 209,435 | 178,711 |
| | 2,640,060 | 2,737,800 |
| **Operating property and equipment:** | | |
| Owned— | | |
| Flight equipment | 5,677,428 | 5,217,535 |
| Advances on flight equipment purchase contracts | 641,281 | 427,616 |
| Other property and equipment | 1,747,415 | 1,537,401 |
| | 8,066,124 | 7,182,552 |
| Accumulated depreciation and amortization | (3,565,590) | (3,557,440) |
| | 4,500,534 | 3,625,112 |
| Capital leases— | | |
| Flight equipment | 420,452 | 420,452 |
| Other property and equipment | 100,337 | 101,015 |
| | 520,789 | 521,467 |
| Accumulated amortization | (272,394) | (248,117) |
| | 248,395 | 273,350 |
| | 4,748,929 | 3,898,462 |
| **Other assets:** | | |
| Intangibles, less accumulated amortization (1990—$55,023; 1989—$42,074) | 128,884 | 175,780 |
| Deferred income taxes | 49,193 | 71,022 |
| Other | 426,755 | 323,628 |
| | 604,832 | 570,430 |
| | $7,993,821 | $7,206,692 |

Notes are omitted.

**EXHIBIT 1 (continued)**
**(In thousands, except share data)**

|  | December 31, | |
|---|---|---|
|  | 1990 | 1989 |
| **Liabilities and Shareholders' Equity** | | |
| **Current liabilities:** | | |
| Short-term borrowings | $ 447,260 | $ 446,276 |
| Long-term debt maturing within one year | 61,607 | 60,928 |
| Current obligations under capital leases | 27,174 | 22,863 |
| Advance ticket sales | 842,665 | 660,639 |
| Accounts payable | 552,780 | 596,435 |
| Accrued salaries, wages and benefits | 675,547 | 585,983 |
| Accrued aircraft rent | 380,775 | 181,997 |
| Accrued income taxes | 86,945 | 62,656 |
| Other accrued liabilities | 682,514 | 606,046 |
|  | **3,757,267** | 3,223,823 |
| Long-term debt | **887,749** | 945,667 |
| Long-term obligations under capital leases | **361,246** | 388,419 |
| Other liabilities and deferred credits: | | |
| Deferred pension liability | 367,958 | 363,781 |
| Deferred gains on sale and | | |
| leaseback transactions | 922,862 | 655,657 |
| Other | 24,493 | 62,945 |
|  | **1,315,313** | 1,082,383 |
| **Redeemable preferred stock:** | | |
| 5½% cumulative prior preferred stock, | | |
| $100 par value | **1,590** | 2,067 |
| **Common shareholders' equity:** | | |
| Common stock, $5 par value; authorized, | | |
| 125,000,000 shares; issued, 23,467,880 | | |
| shares in 1990 and 23,419,953 shares | | |
| in 1989 | 117,339 | 117,100 |
| Additional capital invested | 52,391 | 47,320 |
| Retained earnings | 1,620,885 | 1,526,534 |
| Unearned compensation | (8,053) | (14,538) |
| Common stock held in treasury— | | |
| 1,582,900 shares in 1990 and | | |
| 1,585,400 shares in 1989 | (111,906) | (112,083) |
|  | **1,670,656** | 1,564,333 |
| Commitments and contingent liabilities | | |
|  | **$7,993,821** | $7,206,692 |

Notes are omitted.

**EXHIBIT 1 (continued)**
**United Air Lines, Inc. Statement of Consolidated Operations (in thousands, except per share)**

| | Year Ended December 31, | | |
| --- | --- | --- | --- |
| | 1990 | 1989 | 1988 |
| **Operating Revenues:** | | | |
| Passenger | $ 9,633,627 | $8,536,000 | $7,723,139 |
| Cargo | 592,872 | 521,274 | 509,639 |
| Contract services and other | 810,978 | 736,361 | 748,965 |
| | **11,037,477** | 9,793,635 | 8,981,743 |
| **Operating Expenses:** | | | |
| Salaries and related costs | 3,549,981 | 3,158,414 | 2,837,599 |
| Aircraft fuel | 1,811,417 | 1,352,511 | 1,179,571 |
| Commissions | 1,718,902 | 1,335,537 | 1,101,755 |
| Depreciation and amortization | 559,585 | 516,989 | 518,387 |
| Purchased services | 658,781 | 614,834 | 572,933 |
| Rentals and landing fees | 829,311 | 574,425 | 408,228 |
| Aircraft maintenance materials and repairs | 388,139 | 348,602 | 293,522 |
| Food and beverages | 241,583 | 213,693 | 193,367 |
| Advertising and promotion | 203,215 | 200,711 | 206,493 |
| Personnel expenses | 202,176 | 185,000 | 158,351 |
| Other | 910,663 | 828,379 | 846,609 |
| | **11,073,754** | 9,329,096 | 8,316,815 |
| Earnings (loss) from operations | **(36,277)** | 464,539 | 664,928 |
| **Other deductions (income):** | | | |
| Interest expense | 192,228 | 221,186 | 245,306 |
| Interest capitalized | (71,323) | (51,884) | (30,983) |
| Interest income | (122,615) | (120,913) | (100,873) |
| Equity in earnings of Covia Partnership | (16,220) | (45,441) | (87,460) |
| Gain on sale of Covia Partnership interests | — | — | (393,006) |
| Net gains on disposition of property | (285,846) | (106,422) | (13,989) |
| Other, net | 103,131 | 29,502 | 57,145 |
| | **(200,645)** | (73,972) | (323,860) |
| Earnings from continuing operations before income taxes | 164,368 | 538,511 | 988,788 |
| Provision for income taxes | 69,903 | 214,330 | 388,874 |
| Earnings from continuing operations | 94,465 | 324,181 | 599,914 |
| Discontinued operations: | | | |
| Earnings from discontinued operations, less income taxes | — | — | 457 |
| Gain on sales of discontinued operations, less income taxes | — | — | 523,929 |
| Net earnings | $     94,465 | $   324,181 | $1,124,300 |
| Net earnings per share: | | | |
| Continuing operations | $       4.33 | $     14.96 | $     20.20 |
| Discontinued operations | — | — | 17.67 |
| Net earnings | $       4.33 | $     14.96 | $     37.87 |

Notes are omitted.

**EXHIBIT 2**
**Selected Operating Statistics for United Air Lines, Inc.**

| | Year Ended December 31, | | | | |
|---|---|---|---|---|---|
| | 1990 | 1989 | 1988 | 1987 | 1986 |
| Revenue aircraft miles (millions)[a] | 597 | 552 | 543 | 553 | 507 |
| Revenue aircraft departures | 654,555 | 621,111 | 626,809 | 670,790 | 627,943 |
| Available seat miles (millions)[b] | 114,995 | 104,547 | 101,721 | 101,454 | 91,409 |
| Revenue passenger miles (millions)[c] | 76,137 | 69,639 | 69,101 | 66,348 | 59,312 |
| Revenue passengers (thousands) | 57,598 | 54,859 | 56,175 | 55,089 | 50,419 |
| Average passenger journey (miles) | 1,322 | 1,269 | 1,230 | 1,204 | 1,176 |
| Average flight length (miles) | 912 | 888 | 866 | 824 | 807 |
| Passenger load factor[d] | 66.2% | 66.6% | 67.9% | 65.4% | 64.9% |
| Breakeven load factor[e] | 66.5% | 63.0% | 62.2% | 63.0% | 64.1% |
| Average yield per revenue passenger mile[f] | 12.6¢ | 12.2¢ | 11.1¢ | 10.3¢ | 10.0¢ |
| Cost per available seat mile[g] | 9.6¢ | 8.9¢ | 8.2¢ | 7.9¢ | 7.7¢ |
| Average price per gallon of jet fuel | 80.4¢ | 63.6¢ | 56.0¢ | 57.8¢ | 56.2¢ |
| Average fare per revenue passenger | $167.26 | $155.60 | $137.48 | $124.45 | $118.17 |
| Average daily utilization of each aircraft (hours: minutes)[h] | 8:14 | 8:09 | 8:29 | 9:04 | 8:46 |

[a] "Revenue aircraft miles" means the number of miles flown in revenue-producing service.

[b] "Available seat miles" represents the number of seats available for passengers multiplied by the number of miles those seats are flown.

[c] "Revenue passenger miles" represents the number of miles flown by revenue passengers including frequent flier awards.

[d] "Passenger load factor" represents revenue passenger miles divided by available seat miles.

[e] "Breakeven load factor" represents the number of revenue passenger miles at which operating earnings would have been zero (based on the actual average yield) divided by available seat miles.

[f] "Average yield per revenue passenger mile" represents the average revenue received for each mile a revenue passenger is carried.

[g] "Cost per available seat mile" represents operating expenses divided by available seat miles.

[h] "Average daily utilization of each aircraft" means the average air hours flown in service per day per aircraft for the total fleet of aircraft.

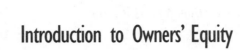

# Introduction to Owners' Equity

Almost all business organizations take one of three forms. The simplest form of organization is the *proprietorship*, or the business owned by a single individual. Typically, this individual has committed personal resources to the organization and has created the business entity. Whatever success the entity enjoys accrues to the owner as an individual. A *partnership* is a somewhat more sophisticated organization form, but it maintains several attributes of a single proprietorship. In this form, two or more persons agree to pool their resources and create a business entity, the success of which they will share equally or according to some agreement between them. The third widely used form of business organization is the *corporation*. In legal form, a corporation is more complex than either a proprietorship or partnership, but it is extremely popular for several reasons. One of the most important reasons is that it allows many investors to contribute their resources to one endeavor without the complication of agreements among them individually. Under the law, a corporation is a legal entity and as such assumes its own obligations. This frees the investor from having to use personal resources above the amount originally invested to satisfy claims against the entity, limiting liability. It also allows the use of ownership shares that can be exchanged for money or other securities should the shareholder wish to divest of ownership rights.

In terms of the aggregate amount of resources controlled by business organizations, the corporation is by far the most important form. It is for this reason that the remainder of this note will be concerned with corporation owners' equity.

---

Copyright © 1992 by the President and Fellows of Harvard College. Harvard Business School case 193-049.

# ACCOUNTING FOR OWNERSHIP IN CORPORATIONS

Several technical complexities of accounting for ownership in corporations are the result of the laws that allow the creation of the corporation. The corporation must account to owners in the form required by the laws of the state or country in which the entity was formed; if securities issued by the corporation are traded publicly, regulations of applicable Company's Acts, the Securities & Exchange Commission, stock exchanges, and other regulatory agencies must also be heeded. Legal distinctions among classes of ownership, types of capital contributions, and the retention of the accumulated retained earnings are extremely important to the accountant maintaining records of corporate activity for management or public reporting. But from our point of view, they are important only insofar as some understanding is necessary if we are to read and use intelligently the accounting information in published financial reports.

## Classification of Owners of Corporations

The owners of the common stock are the owners of the corporation. This group ultimately bears the risk of the operation of the business organization. It is also usually the last to receive distributions of income. In return for this assumption of risk not taken by others, it may receive higher returns than others if the entity is successful. It also usually has voting rights. In many respects, the common shareholder is analogous to the owner in a proprietorship.

Another important class of owners in some corporations is the preferred shareholders. The importance of the *preferred* designation usually revolves about the promise that dividends will be paid to this class of shareholders in a specified amount each period before any dividends are paid to common shareholders. Legal distinctions about payments in excess of this specified amount, or the effect of skipping a dividend payment on future dividend payments, can create a host of different legal subclassifications under the general category of preferred shareholders.

A third class of owners, who may have some rights in particular situations within corporate operations, are those who hold certain classes of debt, such as mortgage bonds or debentures, which either give them a voice in the activities of the corporation or allow them to obtain a voice if certain contractual obligations are not satisfied. Some bond agreements allow holders to convert to an ownership interest at some time in the future or under specified conditions.

## Rights and Responsibilities of Shareholders

The common shareholders are responsible for the management of the corporation. But due to the large number of shareholders typically represented, taking an active part in day-to-day management is usually impossible. This right is normally exercised through their election of a board of directors, which selects and directs the management of the corporation. While it is possible for share-holders to step forward and play a more active role in management by replacing those managers who have been selected by the board of directors with others, or even by replacing the board of directors itself, such action rarely occurs. Dissident shareholders are more apt to sell their interest in the corporation, thereby transferring their rights to others. They are then free to invest in situations in which they feel more comfortable, from which they feel they can receive a more satisfactory return, or through which they can accomplish other personal objectives.

It is important to note that the relationship between a corporation and common shareholders is not a direct one, but rather an indirect one through their acquisition of shares. The corporation sells shares originally in exchange for assets or services, usually cash, to shareholders. If original shareholders subsequently exchange their shares, transferring their rights to others, the corporation receives no added benefits. Records of current owners of shares are maintained by the company or its agents to ensure payment of dividends to current holders of shares. But the amount received by the corporation for a given share is determined only once—at the time the share is issued.

For many large corporations, shares are traded on a day-to-day basis on stock exchanges or through other electronic auction mechanisms. The prices for which shares are traded depend upon the evaluations and assessments of future corporate prospects by current shareholders and prospective investors. Except for those situations in which the corporation itself may acquire shares once held by shareholders (*treasury stock*), the owners' equity section in financial reports is unaffected by the day-to-day trading of ownership shares.

## Accounting for Dividends

Cash or other assets are paid to shareholders as a dividend only when a dividend is declared by the board of directors. The decision to pay cash dividends normally rests on the availability of resources not essential to the continued operation of the corporation and the desire of the board of directors to provide some immediate and tangible return to those who have invested in the common shares of the corporation. A cash dividend is typically declared on a per-share basis; that is, the declaration may read "the Board of Directors of the X Corporation will pay a dividend of $.125 per share to each shareholder of record as of February 28, 1999." The effect of this declaration, which might be made at any time prior to the payment date, will be to cause a dividend check to be prepared and mailed to each owner whose name is registered as the owner of shares by the secretary or agent of the corporation. The check to each shareholder will represent the dividend payment appropriate to the number of shares owned.

At the time a dividend declaration is made, the effect on owners' equity should be apparent. A new obligation is created, since the dividend declaration has a legal standing amongst the other obligations and liabilities of the corporation. Retained earnings, a part of owners' equity, is reduced, and the declared dividend becomes a liability to the corporation.

## The Sale of Stock and Stock Distributions

When you examine the owners' equity section of a balance sheet for a corporation, you are likely to find a minimum of three classifications. One of these is likely to be titled common stock; the second, paid-in-capital in excess of par or some equivalent phrase; and finally, a third, retained earnings.

When shares are issued by a corporation, they are typically issued in exchange for resources, usually cash, that are given by the investor to the organization in exchange for those rights obtained by owning shares. Usually the entire amount that an owner pays for shares is transferred to the corporation, except perhaps an amount for commissions to some selling agent for carrying out certain promotional activities related to the sales of shares. In the simplest form, a sale of stock involves recognition that the resources of the organization have been increased without a related legal obligation to pay in the future. The effect of such an exchange is to increase owners' equity in the classification of common stock. However, legal distinctions required in accounting for owners' equity frequently complicate this simple procedure.

Common stock may be legally identified as par value stock or no par stock. Par value stock typically has a money figure quoted with it; that is, the corporation may be authorized to issue up to 1,000 shares of common stock with a par value of $5.00 per share. The mechanism of stated par value at one time was designed to protect investors and creditors, but today it has lost much of its significance. For this reason, many shares are now simply identified as no par common shares. However, to complicate the task of accounting for corporate equities when no par shares are used, the laws of some countries and states require that a *stated value* per share be established, and that this be used in lieu of par value in recording the sale of shares. The use of par value or stated value means that not all the proceeds from the issuance of shares are credited to the common stock account. Those in excess of par or stated value are credited to a separate account called *paid-in-capital in excess of par* or sometimes *capital surplus*.

**Exhibit 1** shows the stockholders' equity of the Gillette Company and Subsidiary Companies at the end of 1995 and 1994. Gillette has issued a cumulative convertible preferred stock to its employee stock ownership plan; some details about this issue and its use are shown in the Notes to Consolidated Financial Statements included in **Exhibit 1**. Retained earnings are identified as *earnings reinvested in the business*. The two items shown as shareowners' equity, *treasury stock* and *cumulative foreign currency translation adjustments*, will be discussed briefly below.

Amounts of paid-in-capital and common stock are usually subjected to some restrictions under the laws of the country or state in which the corporation is incorporated. These restrictions usually prevent dividend payments to common shareholders in all cases where the net worth of the corporation is less than the sum of par or stated values.

Sometimes shares are distributed in exchange for services or for resources other than cash. The basic principles for recording ownership rights remain the same. The valuation of shares issued rests in these cases on the market value of services or resources acquired, often measured by the market value of shares given in exchange. Thus, the owners' equity, as recorded in the common stock and related paid-in-capital accounts, should give the reader of a financial statement some impression of the amount contributed by shareholders to the corporation in the form of resources or services.

In addition to the distribution of shares through sale, other means have been established for increasing the number of shares outstanding. Stock distributions can take the form of *stock splits* or *stock dividends*. While a distinction is normally made between these two types of transactions, they are essentially the same. Both can be referred to as stock distributions. (See **Exhibit 1** Notes to Consolidated Financial Statements for a description of a "100% common stock dividend" issued by the Gillette Company in 1995.)

Stock distribution takes place whenever the board of directors elects to send additional shares to each shareholder on a pro rata basis. In the case of a stock split, no entry in the records or change to the monetary amounts is shown in the reports of the organization, except that the par value changes. A memorandum stating that the number of shares outstanding has been changed is appropriate. Accounting for stock dividends is somewhat different. Provided the stock dividend increases the number of shares outstanding by 20% or less, an amount equal to the market value of the shares distributed is transferred from retained earnings to the common stock and paid-in-capital account. Because the dividend results in the permanent transfer of retained earnings to paid-in capital, the effect of a stock dividend transaction is sometimes referred to as *capitalizing retained earnings*.

## Treasury Stock

Because shares are traded on open financial markets, the corporation can purchase its own shares. Alternatively, some shareholders may express dissatisfaction with management action, and management may negotiate a purchase of the dissident shareholders' stock.

Sometimes shares are reacquired to reduce permanently the number of shares outstanding. If so, the shares are retired, and the records of their initial sale are updated to show that the shares are no longer in the shareholders' hands. Any apparent gain or loss in their cancellation affects the net worth of the remaining shares, but it has no income statement effect.

At other times, shares are reacquired and not canceled. Instead, they are held for future resale, distribution to officers or employees, use as gifts, or even as a means for satisfying obligations to other persons or organizations. Shares so held are called *treasury shares* and reduce the amount of owners' equity shown in the accounts. Treasury shares are not an asset because the corporation cannot own itself or any part of itself. Even though the shares may have value because people may buy them at the market price, that value is not an asset, nor does it belong to the corporation and the holders of shares still outstanding. Shares held in treasury receive no dividends nor may they be voted in shareholders' meetings. Their purchase price appears as a reduction of stockholders' equity until they are resold.

### Cumulative Foreign Currency Translation Adjustments

Many corporations own subsidiaries that operate in countries other than the domicile of the parent country. When the financial statements of these foreign subsidiaries are consolidated with those of the parent company, the foreign currency must be converted to the home country currency. The conversion process is referred to as foreign currency translation. Because exchange rates fluctuate over time, and because of the mechanics of translation, differences between the translated value of the subsidiaries' assets and liabilities and the translated value of the subsidiaries' owners' equity can arise. In order to maintain the equality of assets and total equities, these translation differences require recognition somewhere in the financial statements. In many circumstances, it seems inappropriate to include this difference as a gain or loss in the computation of net income, since it results only from the mechanics of the translation process. For this reason, cumulative foreign currency translation gains and losses are usually excluded from the computation of net income, but a record is maintained in the shareholders' equity section of the balance sheet to allow the integrity of that statement to be maintained, with assets equaling liabilities and owners' equity.

## MERGERS, ACQUISITIONS, AND LEVERAGED BUYOUTS (LBOs)

Because a corporation is a separate entity, it is free to purchase another corporation. Sometimes such mergers occur with the approval of the acquired firm, and sometimes they do not. An unfriendly acquisition may occur when one firm acquires another by purchasing the stock of the company being acquired by paying cash or other securities to the shareholders of the targeted firm. Unfriendly acquisitions of this type are frequently called takeovers. In a friendly merger, managers usually agree, and terms are negotiated that allow one firm to acquire another by issuing stock of the surviving company to shareholders of the firm being acquired. In most cases, whether an acquisition or merger is friendly or unfriendly, it is undertaken in the belief that operating efficiencies in management and facilities utilization will result in performance superior to that which would have been obtained if the two firms had contin-ued as separate entities.

A *leveraged buyout* takes place when the management of a firm elects to add debt in order to get the cash needed to buy the shares of public stockholders. Without shareholders (or at least nonmanagement shareholders), it is less likely that a corporation will be a target of an unfriendly acquisition. The burden of servicing the added debt and paying interest as it falls due affects both the cash flow and profitability of the corporation.

In some cases, leveraged buyouts have taken place because a group of managers hope to leverage the performance of the corporation to their own benefit by eliminating other shareholders and by using financial leverage to the advantage of the shares they own. They hope the payoffs to themselves through share ownership and control of discretionary salaries and bonuses will justify the added risk of a heavily indebted corporation.

## SUMMARY

Owners' equity is both the measure of the residual equity of the owners and a record of the sources of that entity. Corporations may have different classes of shareholders. When they do, separate records are needed to report the differ-ential rights and capitalization of the classes. Shares can usually be transferred from one owner to another without the consent of the corporation and without additional payment to the company. Usually shares are sold by the corporation only once, which keeps records to maintain the distinction between the capital directly contributed and earnings subsequently retained.

Dividends can be paid only if assets are available for distribution to share-holders and legal restrictions for protection of creditors are met. When divi-dends are declared, they become a liability of the firm. Stock dividends are not dividends at all; they merely represent an increase in the number of shares of ownership having a claim on an unchanged equity. They do, however, reduce the amount of retained earnings by transferring a measured amount of retained earnings to the common stock and paid-in capital accounts. Stock distributions or splits, which may be used to increase or decrease the number of shares out-standing, do not affect the value of owners' equity.

In recent years, the phenomenon of leveraged buyouts has led to a shift in the capital structure of many firms. Managers borrow money, thus leveraging the firm, and use the cash to acquire outstanding shares. As they do so, the amount of stockholders' equity outstanding is reduced at the same time debt is increased. The result is an increase in the size of the debt-to-equity ratio. Returns to the remaining shareholders can be leveraged dramatically if the company is able to meet the interest payments on debt assumed to retired stock.

**EXHIBIT 1**
**Stockholders' Equity—The Gillette Company and Subsidiary Companies**
**(Excerpt from Consolidated Balance Sheets) ($ millions)**

|  | December 31, 1995 | December 31, 1994 |
|---|---|---|
| **Stockholders' Equity** | | |
| 8.0% Cumulative Series C ESOP Convertible Preferred, without | | |
|     par value, Issued: 1995—160,701 shares; 1994—162,928 shares | $ 96.9 | $ 98.2 |
| Unearned ESOP compensation | (34.3) | (44.2) |
| Common stock, par value $1 per share | | |
| Authorized 1,160,000,000 shares | | |
| Issued: 1995—559,718,438 shares; 1994—558,242,410 shares | 559.7 | 558.2 |
| Additional paid-in capital | 31.1 | (1.4) |
| Earnings reinvested in the business | 3,382.7 | 2,830.2 |
| Cumulative foreign currency translation adjustments | (477.0) | (377.1) |
| Treasury stock, at cost: | | |
|     1995—115,254,353 shares; 1994—115,343,404 shares | (1,045.8) | (1,046.6) |
| **Total stockholders' equity** | $ 2,513.3 | $ 2,017.3 |

**EXHIBIT 1 (continued)**
## Notes to Consolidated Financial Statements

### Common Stock and Additional Paid-in Capital

In April 1995, stockholders voted to increase the authorized $1 par value common stock from 580 million shares to 1.16 billion shares. Accordingly, as previously authorized by the Board of Directors, the 100% common stock dividend to stockholders of record June 1, 1995, having the effect of a two-for-one split, became effective. All share information has been adjusted for this stock split.

| | (Thousands of shares) | | | (Millions of Dollars) | | |
| | Common Stock | | | | Additional | |
| | Issued | In Treasury | Outstanding | Common Stock | Paid-in Capital | Treasury Stock |
|---|---|---|---|---|---|---|
| Balance at December 31, 1992 | 555,748 | (115,410) | 440,338 | $555.8 | $(41.0) | $(1,047.2) |
| Conversion of Series C ESOP Preferred stock | — | 14 | 14 | — | .1 | .1 |
| Stock option and purchase plans | 1,427 | — | 1,427 | 1.4 | 21.7 | — |
| Balance at December 31, 1993 | 557,175 | (115,396) | 441,779 | 557.2 | (19.2) | (1,047.1) |
| Conversion of Series C ESOP Preferred stock | — | 53 | 53 | — | .3 | .5 |
| Stock option and purchase plans | 1,067 | — | 1,067 | 1.0 | 17.5 | — |
| Balance at December 31, 1994 | 558,242 | (115,343) | 442,899 | 558.2 | (1.4) | (1,046.6) |
| Conversion of Series C ESOP Preferred stock | — | 89 | 89 | — | .5 | .8 |
| Stock option and purchase plans | 1,476 | — | 1,476 | 1.5 | 32.0 | — |
| Balance at December 31, 1995 | 559,718 | (115,254) | 444,464 | $559.7 | $ 31.1 | $(1,045.8) |

## EXHIBIT 1 (continued)

### Foreign Currency Translation

Net exchange gains or losses resulting from the translation of assets and liabilities of foreign subsidiaries, except those in highly inflationary economies, are accumulated in a separate section of stockholders' equity titled, "Cumulative foreign currency translation adjustments." Also included are the effects of exchange rate changes on intercompany transactions of a long-term investment nature and transactions designated as hedges of net foreign investments.

| (Millions of dollars) | 1995 | 1994 | 1993 |
|---|---|---|---|
| Balance at beginning of year | $(377.1) | $(415.0) | $(265.2) |
| Translation adjustments, including the effect of hedging | (120.4) | 43.0 | (154.2) |
| Related income tax effect | 20.5 | (5.1) | 4.4 |
| Balance at end of year | $(477.0) | $(377.1) | $(415.0) |

Included in Other Charges are net exchange losses of $17.0 million, $77.4 million and $105.4 million for 1995, 1994 and 1993, respectively, primarily relating to subsidiaries in highly inflationary countries, principally Brazil.

### Employee Stock Ownership Plan

In 1990, the Company sold to the ESOP 165,872 shares of a new issue of 8% cumulative Series C convertible preferred stock for $100 million, or $602.875 per share.

Each share of Series C stock is entitled to vote as if it were converted to common stock and is convertible into 40 common shares at $15.07188 per share. At December 31, 1995, 160,701 Series C shares were outstanding, of which 103,860 shares were allocated to employees and the remaining 56,841 shares were held in the ESOP trust for future allocations. The 160,701 Series C shares are equivalent to 6,428,054 shares of common stock, about 1.4% of the Company's outstanding voting stock.

The Series C stock is redeemable upon the occurrence of certain changes in control or other events, at the option of the Company or the holder, depending on the event, at varying prices not less than the purchase price plus accrued dividends.

The ESOP purchased the Series C shares with borrowed funds guaranteed by the Company. The ESOP loan principal and interest is being repaid on a semiannual basis over a 10-year period by Company contributions to the ESOP and by the dividends paid on the Series C shares.

As the ESOP loan is repaid, a corresponding amount of Series C stock held in the trust is released to participant accounts. Allocations are made quarterly to the accounts of eligible employees, generally on the basis of an equal amount per participant. In general, regular U.S. employees participate in the ESOP after completing one year of service with the Company.

Unpaid balance of this loan is reported as a liability of the Company. An unearned ESOP compensation amount is reported as an offset to the Series C share amount in the equity section.

Plan costs and activity for this plan follow.

| (Millions of dollars) | 1995 | 1994 | 1993 |
|---|---|---|---|
| Compensation expense | $ 6.0 | $ 6.4 | $ 8.5 |
| Cash contributions and dividends paid | 14.2 | 13.9 | 15.8 |
| Principal payments | 10.3 | 9.2 | 10.3 |
| Interest payments | 3.9 | 4.7 | 5.5 |

# FMC Corporation

## A RECAPITALIZATION

### Background

FMC Corporation, a diversified industrial company based in Chicago, Illinois, was considering the reorganization of its financial structure through a major recapitalization. Through selective divesting, cost-cutting measures, and productivity enhancements, FMC had realized a return on equity exceeding 18% and a return on capital employed exceeding 15% for the years 1984 and 1985. (See **Exhibit 1** for consolidated financial statements.)

Robert Malott, FMC's chief executive officer (CEO), had seen his company eliminate debt and increase earnings substantially during 1984 and 1985. When Malott became CEO in 1973, the company was far-flung both geographically and operationally, and it was spending resources to "test" different operating areas for long-run potential. When the conservative Malott came in, he reduced FMC's portfolio, and the company began to throw off more and more cash from operations. In fact, cash provided from continuing operations had risen from $200 million in 1977 to $403 million in 1986. The company was by any standard a "cash machine" and was considered by many analysts to be in an enviable position.

However, in early 1986, FMC's strong cash position forced Malott to make a decision regarding the financial structure of the corporation. With so much

*Susan S. Harmeling prepared this case from a draft written by Mary Addonizio and with the assistance and supervision of Professors Julie H. Hertenstein and William J. Bruns, Jr.*

Copyright © 1990 by the President and Fellows of Harvard College. Harvard Business School case 191-084.

cash and with a stock price that was only at nine times earnings, FMC was becoming too attractive, and management feared a takeover bid by potential raiders.[1]  One option Malott considered was taking the company private in a leveraged buyout.  However, initiating a leveraged buyout would mean potentially competing with corporate raiders who might top any bid he would make.  Instead, Malott decided to recapitalize the company.

On February 23, 1986, FMC's board of directors announced that it had approved a recapitalization plan subject to the arranging of suitable financing and stockholder approval. The plan would cost about $1.9 billion to finance.  Malott explained:

> *In many cases, leveraged buyouts tend to take advantage of the public shareholders.  Management is benefitted out of proportion to the contribution they are making, [but] the public shareholders are not allowed to participate in the results of the leveraging procedure.[2]*

The recapitalization plan had three main goals: to eliminate a takeover attempt, to give FMC employees a greater stake in the company and its future by expanding employee ownership, and to invest aggressively in existing businesses and concentrate on current and related businesses.  Malott realized that the plan involved considerable risk and that earnings would be more sensitive to short-term operating fluctuations, but he expressed confidence that the company's history showed that its debt could be repaid with the cash generated from its operations.

The initial plan included the following provisions:

**Public Shareholders:**   All public shareholders would receive $70 in cash and one new share of the recapitalized company in exchange for each share held.

**Management and Employee Benefit Plans:**   All management-owned shares and shares in certain employee benefit plans would receive 5.67 new shares for each share held.

**Employee Thrift Plan Shareholders:**   These shareholders would receive $25 in cash plus four new shares in exchange for each share held.

Further, as part of the recapitalization, the company planned to redeem its outstanding convertible debt and preferred stock.  Approximately $250 million of FMC's existing debt, consisting of industrial revenue bonds and publicly traded debentures, would remain outstanding after the refinancing.  New debt, consisting of $1.3 billion in bank debt from a group of banks and $400 million in subordinated debentures, would be incurred to finance the plan.

---

[1]  G. Slutsker, *Forbes*, April 7, 1986.

[2]  Ibid.

After the recapitalization, the newly issued shares together with an outstanding deferred-share awards plan and stock options were expected to total approximately 36 million shares on a diluted basis.[3]

## The Revision

The news of FMC's recapitalization plan met with criticism by some shareholders, most notably, Ivan Boesky. Boesky, along with a group of companies he controlled, bought a 7.5% stake in the corporation.[4] In his filing with the Securities and Exchange Commission (SEC), Boesky stated that the recapitalization plan unfairly rewarded management at the expense of public shareholders, and he hinted that he would vote against the proposal at FMC's annual meeting. Said Boesky, "It is always gratifying when a management awakens to the realization that outside shareholders ought to be treated with relative fairness compared to insiders."[5]

FMC responded by "sweetening the plan in response to 'current economic and market conditions.'" The new plan announced on April 28, 1986, offered public shareholders an additional $10 per share, bringing the total to $80 per share. This new deal was approved on May 22, 1986, at FMC's annual meeting. The provisions of the revised plan were as follows:

*Public Shareholders:*   All public shareholders would receive $80 in cash and one share of the recapitalized company for each common share held.

*Management and Employee Benefit Plans:*   Management and holders of stock in employee benefit plans would receive 5.67 shares for each share held, which was equal to this provision in the original plan.

*Employee Thrift Plan Shareholders:*   These shareholders would receive 4.209 new shares and $25 per share for each share held.

In addition, 11.3 million shares held by the company's pension plan would be retired in early 1986 to ensure that they could not be seized by anyone seeking control of the company. As a result, employee ownership of FMC would rise from 19% to 41% and the proportion of stock held by the public would decline from 81% to 59%. **Exhibit 2** shows how the income statement might have appeared if the restructuring had taken place on January 1, 1985, and how the balance sheet would have appeared if the restructuring had taken place on December 31, 1985.

This recapitalization program, dubbed a "leveraged cash-out," resembled a stock split in which only the insiders' shares were split. The public share-

---

[3]  FMC Annual Report, 1985.

[4]  *The Wall Street Journal*, April 29, 1986.

[5]  Ibid.

holders' equity was diluted by the increase in insiders' shares, but the former were compensated for this dilution with a substantial cash payment and highly favorable tax treatment. (The $80 per share cash-out received capital gains tax treatment for public shareholders.)  In order to finance the sweetened plan, FMC secured a total of $1.4 billion in bank debt and a total of $625 million in subordinated debt from Goldman Sachs.  This debt increased FMC's total debt burden to $2.2 billion from $370 million.

Though initial word of the recapitalization raised FMC's stock price from $70 to $85 within days, the move met with criticism.  One analyst with a Chicago securities firm said,

> *Logically it doesn't make sense.  With a 154% debt/equity ratio up from 25% and a negative equity of 54%, FMC has made itself most unattractive to any hostile takeovers.  The company has essentially paid out all of its equity.*[6]

FMC's interest payment on debt would be about $250 million in the first year.  The company had earned $270 million in pretax income in 1985.  Others expressed concern FMC could not find better use for its money.  These critics felt that the burden of so much debt would diminish the company's ability to make acquisitions and develop internally.

## Later Developments

In 1986, the SEC charged that Ivan Boesky and others had engaged in various acts of insider trading of securities.  Among the incidents cited in SEC documents was Boesky's purchase of about 95,300 shares of FMC stock between February 18, 1986 and February 21, 1986, during which the price of shares rose from $73.75 to $85.625 per share.  Ultimately, Mr. Boesky sold these shares for a profit of approximately $975,000.

On December 18, 1986, FMC filed a lawsuit against Boesky and others alleging that their illegal insider trading added to the cost of the company's recapitalization plan.  The lawsuits charged that the insider trading meant that FMC had to sweeten the plan by $10 per share, adding approximately $225 million to the cost of the plan for FMC.

The suit also named Drexel, Burnham Lambert, Goldman Sachs, Shearson Lehman Brothers, David Brown, Dennis Levine, and Ira Sokolow.  FMC sought total damages of $260 million, including $225 million to cover its additional recapitalization costs, recovery of the $975,000 profit made by Boesky, and a $17.5 million fee paid by FMC to Goldman Sachs, its financial advisor.  In announcing the lawsuit, Mr. Malott stated, "The freedoms and obligations of the free market system have been jeopardized by Wall Street players caught in the grip of takeover fever and get-rich-quick schemes."[7]

---

[6]  Brian Moskal, *Industry Week*, June 23, 1986, p. 28.

[7]  *Boston Globe*, April 14, 1987.

## QUESTIONS

1. Using the historical and pro forma information in Exhibits 1 and 2, explain as specifically as you can how the proposed restructuring was to be accomplished and how the financial condition and performance of FMC would be affected.  Try to reconstruct the journal entries that the restructuring required.

2. Assume that cash flows from operations and investing are similar in future years to those of recent years except for the additional interest expenses associated with the restructuring.  Will FMC be able to pay down the new debt?  What actions must managers take, and what must happen in the future for this restructuring to be a financial success?  For how many years will owners' equity remain negative?  What is the meaning of negative owners' equity?

3. Would this same deal be done today?  Why or why not?

**EXHIBIT 1**
**FMC Corporation—Consolidated Statements of Changes in Financial Position ($ thousands)**

| | Year Ended December 31 | | |
| --- | --- | --- | --- |
| | 1985 | 1984 | 1983 |
| Cash provided (required) by continuing operations: | | | |
| Income from continuing operations | $ 196,553 | $ 225,863 | $ 188,400 |
| Provision for depreciation | 161,197 | 140,193 | 143,356 |
| Provision for deferred income taxes | 35,237 | (6,830) | 30,191 |
| Dividends received from unconsolidated affiliates, net of equity in earnings | (435) | 17,718 | (1,290) |
| Other | (1,464) | (8,736) | (7,351) |
| Cash provided by continuing operations before working capital changes | $ 391,088 | $ 368,208 | $ 353,306 |
| Decrease (increase) in working capital from selected items (detail below) | (13,909) | 46,391 | 107,653 |
| Cash provided by continuing operations ⟶ *Avg ≈ 400M* | $ 377,179 | $ 414,599 | $ 460,959 |
| Cash provided (required) by discontinued operations | $ 29,463 | $ (10,760) | $ 13,464 |
| Cash provided (required) by investing activities: | | | |
| Acquisition of Lithco and BS&B Engineering | $ (153,433) | — | — |
| Capital expenditures | (319,031) | (182,645) | (169,245) |
| Disposal of property, plant, and equipment | 26,472 | 18,497 | 19,771 |
| Decrease (increase) in investments | 20,827 | (239) | (49,163) |
| Cash required by investing activities | $ (425,165) | $ (164,387) | $ (198,637) |
| Cash provided (required) by financing activities: | | | |
| Increase in short-term debt | $ 8,591 | $ 10,973 | $ 5,753 |
| Increase (decrease) in long-term debt | 26,496 | (66,003) | (43,351) |
| Issue (repurchase) of capital stock | 8,947 | (466,407) | 31,799 |
| Cash provided (required) by financing activities | $ 44,034 | $ (521,437) | $ (5,799) |
| Cash required for dividends to stockholders | $ (57,571) | $ (56,907) | $ (61,980) |
| Increase (decrease) in cash and marketable securities | $ (32,060) | $ (338,892) | $ 208,007 |
| Cash and marketable securities, beginning of year | $ 193,978 | $ 532,870 | $ 324,863 |
| Cash and marketable securities, end of year | $ 161,918 | $ 193,978 | $ 532,870 |

*Foreign currency translation effects have been eliminated from the above items*

Decrease (increase) in working capital from selected items:

| | | | |
| --- | --- | --- | --- |
| Trade receivables | $ (59,497) | $ (15,515) | $ 16,160 |
| Inventories | 37,484 | (19,463) | 152,283 |
| Other current assets | (34,069) | (2,240) | 2,540 |
| Accounts payable and accruals | 75,826 | 64,824 | (51,950) |
| Income taxes payable | (31,740) | 31,817 | 7,429 |
| Net translation adjustment on working capital | (1,913) | (13,032) | (18,809) |
| Decrease (increase) in working capital from selected items | $ (13,909) | $ 46,391 | $107,653 |

**EXHIBIT 1 (continued)**
**FMC Corporation—Consolidated Balance Sheets ($ thousands)**

|  | Year Ended December 31 | |
|---|---|---|
|  | 1985 | 1984 |
| **ASSETS** | | |
| **Current Assets** | | |
| Cash | $ 6,794 | $ 7,220 |
| Marketable securities | 155,124 | 186,758 |
| Trade receivables, net | 454,373 | 384,776 |
| Inventories | 232,444 | 244,528 |
| Other current assets | 96,818 | 60,649 |
| Deferred income taxes | 158,949 | 191,351 |
| Total current assets | $ 1,104,502 | $ 1,075,282 |
| Investments | 179,054 | 188,073 |
| Property, plant, and equipment, net | 1,327,625 | 1,108,409 |
| Patents and deferred charges | 59,802 | 18,434 |
| Intangibles of acquired companies | 19,739 | 9,788 |
| Total assets | $ 2,690,722 | $ 2,399,986 |
| **LIABILITIES AND STOCKHOLDERS' EQUITY** | | |
| **Current Liabilities** | | |
| Short-term debt | $ 37,475 | $ 31,116 |
| Accounts payable, trade and other | 465,740 | 404,743 |
| Accrued payroll | 92,536 | 88,045 |
| Accrued and other liabilities | 225,452 | 199,214 |
| Reserve for discontinued operations | 117,291 | 117,244 |
| Current portion of long-term debt | 30,209 | 14,107 |
| Income taxes payable | 45,284 | 77,024 |
| Total current liabilities | $ 1,013,987 | $ 931,493 |
| Long-term debt, less current portion | 303,210 | 292,173 |
| Deferred income taxes | 243,146 | 210,895 |
| Minority interests in consolidated companies | 7,279 | 5,665 |
| **Stockholders' Equity** | | |
| Preferred stock, no par value, authorized 5,000,000 shares; $2.25 cumulative convertible; preference value $24,553 | $ 3,069 | $ 3,843 |
| Common stock, $5 par value, authorized 60,000,000 shares | 178,948 | 177,710 |
| Capital in excess of par value of capital stock | 105,354 | 101,152 |
| Retained earnings | 1,440,204 | 1,301,222 |
| Foreign currency translation adjustment | (90,684) | (106,095) |
| Treasury stock, common, at cost | (513,791) | (518,072) |
| Total stockholders' equity | $ 1,123,100 | $ 959,760 |
| Total liabilities and stockholders' equity | $ 2,690,722 | $ 2,399,986 |

**EXHIBIT 1 (continued)**
**FMC Corporation—Consolidated Statements of Income ($ thousands, except per share data)**

| | Year Ended December 31 | | |
| | 1985 | 1984 | 1983 |
|---|---|---|---|
| **Revenue** | | | |
| Sales | $3,260,847 | $3,337,839 | $3,246,758 |
| Equity in net earnings of affiliates | 15,445 | 16,573 | 17,027 |
| Interest income | 32,108 | 69,352 | 48,082 |
| Other income | 20,049 | 6,025 | 8,906 |
| Total revenue | $3,328,449 | $3,429,789 | $3,320,773 |
| **Costs and Expenses** | | | |
| Cost of sales | $2,448,544 | $2,521,576 | $2,520,056 |
| Selling, general and administrative expenses | 424,209 | 395,452 | 387,777 |
| Research and development | 149,361 | 120,578 | 102,366 |
| Interest expense | 35,490 | 42,020 | 48,991 |
| Minority interests | 1,768 | 1,518 | 1,421 |
| Total costs and expenses | $3,059,372 | $3,081,144 | $3,060,611 |
| Income before income taxes | $ 269,077 | $ 348,645 | $ 260,162 |
| Provision for income taxes | 72,524 | 122,782 | 71,762 |
| Income from continuing operations | $ 196,553 | $ 225,863 | $ 188,400 |
| Loss from discontinued operations | — | (187,895) | (19,616) |
| Net income | $ 196,553 | $ 37,968 | $ 168,784 |
| **Earnings per Common Share** | | | |
| **Primary:** | | | |
| Income from continuing operations | $7.54 | $ 7.52 | $ 5.62 |
| Loss from discontinued operations | — | (6.31) | (0.60) |
| Net income | $7.54 | $ 1.21 | $ 5.02 |
| Assuming full dilution: | | | |
| Income from continuing operations | $7.34 | $ 7.17 | $ 5.27 |
| Loss from discontinued operations | — | (5.95) | (0.55) |
| Net income | $7.34 | $ 1.22 | $ 4.72 |

## EXHIBIT 2
### Pro Forma Financial Information

The Pro Forma Consolidated Income Statement for the year ended December 31, 1985 and the Pro Forma Consolidated Balance Sheet as of December 31, 1985 have been prepared to reflect the Recapitalization, the conversion of the company's outstanding Convertible Securities, the incurrence of obligations under the Bank Agreements, the issuance of the Senior Subordinated Debentures and the Subordinated Debentures, the repayment of certain existing indebtedness, and the payment of costs related to the Recapitalization. The Recapitalization has been accounted for as a redemption of Shares not subject to purchase accounting.

The Pro Forma Consolidated Income Statement was prepared as if the Recapitalization had occurred on January 1, 1985. The Pro Forma Consolidated Balance Sheet was prepared as if the Recapitalization had occurred on December 31, 1985.

No changes in revenues and expenses have been made to reflect the results of any modification to operations that might have been made had the Recapitalization been consummated on the assumed effective dates of the Recapitalization for presenting pro forma results. The pro forma expenses include the recurring costs that are directly attributed to the Recapitalization, such as interest expense arising from the Financing and the related tax effects thereof. The pro forma financial information does not purport to be indicative of the results that would actually have been obtained had such transactions been completed as of the date and for the periods presented or that may be obtained in the future.

### Pro Forma Consolidated Income Statement (in thousands, except per share data)

| | Year Ended December 31, 1985 Actual | Pro Forma |
|---|---|---|
| | | *(unaudited)* |
| Revenue | | |
| Sales | $3,260,847 | $3,260,847 |
| Equity in net earnings of affiliates | 15,445 | 15,445 |
| Interest income | 32,108 | 17,328 |
| Other income | 20,049 | 20,049 |
| Total revenue | $3,328,449 | $3,313,669 |
| Costs and expenses | | |
| Cost of sales | 2,448,544 | 2,452,777 |
| Selling, general and administrative expenses | 424,209 | 424,209 |
| Research and development | 149,361 | 149,361 |
| Interest expense | 35,490 | 255,342 |
| Minority interests | 1,768 | 1,768 |
| Total costs and expenses | $3,059,372 | $3,283,457 |
| Income before income taxes | $ 269,077 | $ 30,212 |
| Provision for income taxes (benefit) | 72,524 | (33,387) |
| Net income | $ 196,553 | $ 63,599 |
| Earnings per common share | | |
| Primary | $7.54 | $1.73 |
| Fully diluted | $7.34 | $1.73 |
| Ratio of earnings to fixed charges | 5.3 | 1.1 |

Sources: Proxy Statement/Prospectus, May 2, 1986.

**EXHIBIT 2 (continued)**
**Pro Forma Consolidated Balance Sheet ($ thousands)**

| | Year Ended December 31, 1985 | |
| | Actual | Pro Forma |
| --- | ---: | ---: |
| | | *(unaudited)* |
| **ASSETS:** | | |
| **Current Assets:** | | |
| Cash | $ 6,794 | $ 6,794 |
| Marketable securities | 155,124 | 75,724 |
| Trade receivables, net | 454,373 | 154,373 |
| Inventories | 232,444 | 232,444 |
| Other current assets | 96,818 | 96,818 |
| Deferred income taxes | 158,949 | 158,949 |
| Total current assets | $1,104,502 | $ 725,102 |
| Investments | 179,054 | 179,054 |
| Property, plant, and equipment, net | 1,327,625 | 1,327,625 |
| Patents and deferred charges | 59,802 | 119,802 |
| Intangibles of acquired companies | 19,739 | 19,739 |
| Total assets | $2,690,722 | $2,371,322 |
| **LIABILITIES AND STOCKHOLDERS' EQUITY (DEFICIT):** | | |
| **Current Liabilities:** | | |
| Short-term debt | $ 37,475 | — |
| Accounts payable, trade and other | 465,740 | $ 465,740 |
| Accrued payroll | 92,536 | 92,536 |
| Accrued and other liabilities | 225,452 | 225,452 |
| Reserve for discontinued operations | 117,291 | 57,291 |
| Current portion of long-term debt | 30,209 | — |
| Income taxes payable | 45,284 | 45,284 |
| Total current liabilities | $1,013,987 | $ 886,303 |
| Long-term debt, less current portion | 303,210 | 1,900,310 |
| Deferred income taxes | 243,146 | 243,146 |
| Minority interests in consolidated companies | 7,279 | 7,279 |
| **Stockholders' Equity (deficit):** | | |
| Preferred stock, no par value, authorized 5,000,000 shares; | | |
|   $2.25 cumulative convertible; preference value $24,553 | $ 3,069 | — |
| Common stock, $5 par value, authorized 60,000,000 shares | 178,948 | — |
| Common stock, $.10 par value | | $ 4,531 |
| Capital in excess of par value of capital stock | 105,354 | — |
| Retained earnings | 1,440,204 | (579,563) |
| Foreign currency translation adjustment | (90,684) | (90,684) |
| Treasury stock, common, at cost | (513,791) | — |
| Total stockholders' equity (deficit) | $1,123,100 | $ (665,716) |
| Total liabilities and stockholders' equity | $2,690,722 | $2,371,322 |
| Book value per common share | $42.75 | $(19.60) |

**EXHIBIT 2 (continued)**
**Pro Forma Change in Cash Due to the Recapitalization ($ millions)**

| | |
|---|---:|
| Accounts receivable facility | $   300.0[a] |
| Revolving credit facility | 1,000.0 |
| Senior subordinated debentures | 225.0 |
| Subordinated debentures | 400.0 |
| Cash payment of $80.00 per share to public stockholders (assumes conversion of all outstanding convertible securities) | (1,735.6) |
| Cash payment of $25.00 per share for shares held by the stock fund of thrift plan | (59.6) |
| Retirement of debt outstanding at December 31, 1985 | (89.2) |
| Construction equipment receivables reacquired from FMC Finance and deducted from reserve for discontinued operations | (60.0) |
| Estimated fees and expenses | (60.0) |
| | $   (79.4) |

---

[a]  The $300.0 million reduction in trade receivables reflects the sale of accounts receivable pursuant to the accounts receivable facility.

# Solving the Puzzle of the Cash Flow Statement

The cash flow statement is one of the most useful financial statements companies prepare. When analyzed in a rational, logical manner, it can illuminate a treasure trove of clues as to how a company is balancing its receivables and payables, paying for its growth, and otherwise managing its flow of funds. But many readers seem to bypass the cash flow statement and head only for the old, familiar, comfortable income statement and balance sheet—despite the fact that the cash flow statement may provide considerable information about what is really happening in a business beyond that contained in either of the other two statements.

There are several reasons why the cash flow statement may not get the attention it deserves. First, although it has been around in its present format since mid-1988, it is still considered the "new statement": many managers were not exposed to it during their business schooling in financial analysis. If they were, they may have been taught how to prepare one but not how to interpret the story it tells.

Second, the format of the Cash Flow from Operating Activities section of the statement can be challenging to follow if presented in what is known as the "indirect" method. But perhaps most daunting to many is the mistaken idea that it takes a very sophisticated analysis of complicated ratios and relationships to use a cash flow statement effectively.

Contributing to this notion are numerous business journal articles that have appeared in the past decade. They promote the value of this statement when appropriate cash flow ratios are used in statistical packages, such as those used to predict bankruptcy. Present-day textbooks, when not merely teaching students to prepare the statement, also concentrate on describing how

Julie H. Hertenstein and Sharon M. McKinnon authored this article. Reprinted from *Business Horizons*, January-February 1997. Copyright 1997 by the Foundation for the School of Business at Indiana University. Used with permission.

ratios such as "free cash flow to net income" can be derived, but say little about what truly useful information these ratios or other information from the cash flow statement may provide.

Analyzing this statement should not present a formidable task when reviewed in the manner we are advocating here. Instead, it will quickly become obvious that the benefits of understanding the sources and uses of a company's cash far outweigh the costs of undertaking some very straightforward analyses. Executives want to know if the cash generated by the company will be sufficient to fund their expansion strategy; stockholders want to know if the firm is generating enough cash to pay dividends; suppliers want to know if their customers will be able to pay if offered credit, investors want to evaluate future growth potential; and employees are interested in the overall viability of their employer as indicated by its ability to fund its operations. These are just a few of the valuable insights to be gained from the cash flow statement.

The method we suggest for studying this valuable statement contains several steps, with the preliminary step consisting of gaining a basic understanding of the format of the cash flow statement. Once a certain "comfort level" with the structure of the statement has been attained, individual companies' statements should be examined to gain practice in using the stepwise approach described shortly. These steps consist of:

1. scanning the big picture,
2. checking the power of the cash flow engine,
3. pinpointing the good news and the bad news, and
4. putting the puzzle together.

## FORMAT OF THE CASH FLOW STATEMENT

The cash flow statement is divided into three sections: operating activities, investing activities, and financing activities. **Exhibit 1** presents an example of a simple cash flow statement with the three sections delineated in bold letters. Each section shows the cash inflows and outflows associated with that type of activity.

*Cash flow from operating activities* shows the results of cash inflows and outflows related to the fundamental operations of the basic line or lines of business in which the company engages. For example, it includes cash receipts from the sale of goods or services and cash outflows for purchasing inventory and paying rent and taxes. You will notice it does not show these items directly. It assumes that most of these cash inflows and outflows are already summarized in the "Net Income" figure, so it starts at that figure and makes an adjustment for everything that is not a true representation of "cash in and out" in net income. This approach is the "indirect format" of presenting cash flows from operating activities and is the one chosen by most companies. The indirect format can be confusing, and a longer explanation of "direct versus indirect" formats is provided in **Exhibit 2** for readers who desire more information.

Regardless of how the cash flow from operating activities section is formatted, it is important to remember that this is the most important of the three sections because it describes how cash is being generated or used by the primary activities of the company. To picture activities that affect cash flow from operations, think of the cash receipts and payments that make most working capital accounts on the balance sheet increase or decrease. For example, accounts receivable decreases when cash is collected from customers, inventory increases when goods are purchased, and accounts payable decreases when suppliers are paid for their goods.

The next section is called *cash flow from investing activities*. Here you see the cash flows associated with purchases and sales of noncurrent assets, such as building and equipment purchases, or sales of investments or subsidiaries. An easy way to picture what activities would be here is to think again of a balance sheet. If you assume current assets are associated with operations, then the activities associated with all the rest of the assets are in this section.

The third section is called *cash flow from financing activities*. Again, the balance sheet provides a handy way of discerning what would be in this section. If you eliminate the current liabilities associated with operations, then the activities of all the rest of the liabilities and the stockholders' equity accounts are summarized here. These are all the flows associated with financing the firm, everything from selling and paying off bonds to issuing stock and paying dividends.

Warning! There are exceptions to everything, and the cash flow statement format has a few to watch out for. Two working capital accounts, one asset and one liability, are dealt with outside the cash flow from operating activities section. Short-term marketable securities are treated as long-term investments and appear in cash flow from investing activities; similarly, short-term debt is treated as long-term debt and appears in cash flow from financing activities.

Another anomaly is the treatment of interest and dividends. Although dividends are handled as a cash outflow in the cash flow from financing activities section, interest payments are considered an operating outflow, despite the fact that both are payments to outsiders for using their money! In some countries, such as the United Kingdom, interest payments are included in the financing activities section. But in the United States, the Financial Accounting Standards Board (FASB) voted that interest payments should be in the operating activities section instead. In such a situation, one might have to adjust somewhat if one were trying to compare a UK company like British Petroleum to a U.S. company like Exxon.

## STEP 1: SCANNING THE BIG PICTURE

Now, sit back with your favorite company's annual report and follow these steps to understanding its cash flow picture. You can think of this as a big puzzle exercise. All the pieces are there in the statement; your task is to put them in the proper context to form a mosaic from which a picture of the firm's cash flow health emerges.  If you don't have an annual report handy, you can use **Exhibit 3**, which shows the cash flow statements for the Colgate-Palmolive Company for the years ending 1992, 1993, and 1994.  We chose Colgate-Palmolive because it represents one of the best annual reports in the country and the positive trends are clear for illustrative purposes.  Other reports may not contain such "rosy scenarios," as you will discover shortly.

Scanning the big picture involves several substeps.  The first is to place your company in context in terms of its age, industry, and size.  We expect mature companies to have different cash flows from start-up companies, and service industries to look different from heavy manufacturing industries.  Big corporations may experience declining cash flows in certain years, but the sheer immensity of their cash flows may ameliorate concerns, whereas the declining trend might be much more worrisome if they were small firms without such vast resources.

Colgate-Palmolive certainly qualifies as a mature company.  It is huge (figures are rounded to millions), and it operates primarily in consumer product markets throughout the world.  A firm like this should be involved in complex activities on a global scale.  Colgate-Palmolive certainly is, but its cash flow statement is not much more complex than what one might expect from a much smaller, perhaps simpler, company.

Continue your big picture scan by flipping through the annual report to determine how management believes the year has progressed.  Was it a good year?  Perhaps a record-breaking year in terms of revenues or net income?  Or is management explaining how the company has weathered some rough times?

A key part of the big picture scan is to look at a key summary figure of financial health—net income.  If the cash flow statement has been prepared using the indirect method for operating cash flows, as Colgate-Palmolive's has, you can find this at the top of the cash flow statement.  Otherwise you'll have to use the reconciliation of net income and operating cash flows that accompanies the cash flow statement, or take a peek at the income statement itself.  What is the bottom line?  Does it show income or losses over the past few years?  Is income (or loss) growing or shrinking?  Keep these points in mind as you examine the cash flows.  In addition, scan the comparative numbers for the past three years for unusual items you'd like to have explained eventually.

Colgate-Palmolive shows positive net income for all three years—a promising start.  The three-year trend appears to be positive, but a big drop in 1993 raises a few questions.  The statement also reveals a few items that need to be checked out.  In the operating activities section, what is that "cumulative effect on prior years of accounting changes" in 1993?  And what are those "restructured operations"?  File those away to examine later.  Note any line items that are vastly different from year to year.  Colgate-Palmolive has a few of those, including changes in its working capital accounts, the proceeds from issuance of debt, and its purchases of treasury stock.

## STEP 2:　CHECKING THE POWER OF THE CASH FLOW ENGINE

The cash flow from operating activities section is the cash flow engine of the company. When this engine is working effectively, it provides the cash flows to cover the cash needs of operations. It also provides cash necessary for routine needs, such as the replacement of worn-out equipment and the payment of dividends. There are exceptions, of course. Start-up companies, for example, usually have negative cash flows from operating activities because their cash flow engines are not yet up to speed. Companies in cyclical industries might have negative operating cash flows in a "down" year; a company that has experienced an extensive strike could also be expected to have negative cash flow from operating activities. Although occasional years of negative cash flow from operating activities do not spell disaster, on the average we should expect it to be positive.

To check the cash flow engine, first observe whether cash flow from operating activities is greater than zero. Also check whether it is growing or shrinking. Assuming it is positive, the next question is whether or not it is adequate for important, routine expenditures. Just as we do not expect a start-up company to have positive cash flow from operating activities, we also do not expect a company still in a very rapid growth phase to generate enough cash flow from operating activities to cover the investments required to rapidly expand the firm. However, we do expect the operations of a mature company to generate enough cash to "keep the company whole." This would include the amount of investment required to replace those fixed assets that are used up, worn out, or technologically obsolete, as well as cash required to pay the annual dividend shareholders have come to expect.

It is difficult to know precisely how much cash is required to keep the company's fixed assets "whole," because the cash flow statement does not separate capital expenditures for replacement and renewal from those for expansion and growth. However, the annual depreciation amount provides a very rough surrogate for the amount of fixed assets that need to be replaced each year. In periods when prices are rising, the cost to replace assets should be somewhat greater than the cost of older assets that are being depreciated. So to ensure that the firm is kept whole and is not shrinking, we should expect the portion of investing activities related to the purchase of fixed assets to exceed depreciation.

Important information about the cash flow engine is also revealed by examining the operating working capital accounts. In the Colgate-Palmolive operating activities section, these are shown under "cash effects of these changes." In a healthy, growing company, we would expect growth in operating working capital accounts such as inventory and accounts receivable as well as in accounts payable and other operating payables. Obviously there can be quite a bit of variability in working capital accounts from period to period. Streamlining a collections policy or implementing a just-in-time inventory system could shrink accounts receivable or inventory in a growing company. But on the average, inventories, receivables, and accounts payable usually grow in expanding companies. Beware of situations in which all working capital accounts increase net cash from operating activities. This likely would not happen randomly in a healthy, growing company. It normally results from deliberate management action and could indicate a company in such a cash flow crisis that managers have been forced to raid the working capital accounts to survive.

With these ground rules, let's check Colgate-Palmolive's cash flow engine. In all three years, cash flow from operating activities is greater than zero, reaching over $800 million in 1994. It increases steadily every year, unlike net income. Annual depreciation is in the vicinity of $200 million each year, and the yearly dividend is also around $200 million. Colgate-Palmolive's cash flow engine is not only generating enough cash to cover "keeping the company whole," it is also able to throw off around $400 million annually for growth and investment, and the amount of excess cash has been increasing each year.

This is a powerful cash flow engine. A glance at the working capital account differences indicates that receivables, other assets, and payables have grown (net) over the three years, while inventories have shrunk slightly. This picture is consistent with a global company increasing its scope through acquisitions and new product development.

## STEP 3:  PINPOINTING THE GOOD NEWS AND THE BAD NEWS

This step involves looking at the total cash flow statement to find where the rest of the "good news" and "bad news" lie. What you are looking for is the story the statement is trying to tell you. It will not come simply by divine revelation, but by systematic observation of the items on the statement and their trends over the years presented for your comparison.

Begin with cash flow from investing activities. What is this section trying to tell you? One systematic observation is to check whether the company is generating or using cash in its investing activities. Whereas we expect positive cash flow from operating activities, we also expect a healthy company to invest continually in more plant, equipment, land, and other fixed assets to replace the assets that have been used up or have become technologically obsolete, as well as to expand and grow. Although companies often sell assets that are no longer of use to them, they would normally purchase more capital assets than they sell. As a result, we generally expect negative cash flows from investing activities. As with operating activities, exceptions do occur, especially if the firm divests a business or subsidiary. However, watch for companies that are beginning to shrink substantially because they are generating much of their cash by selling off chunks of the business!

Colgate-Palmolive exhibits the signs of a "good news from investing activities" company. Capital expenditures are nearly 1.5 times the amount of depreciation, so they are clearly at a level well beyond that required to keep the company whole. In addition, Colgate-Palmolive makes significant expenditures for acquisitions in each year—another growth indicator. These numbers remain consistent or increase from year to year and paint a picture of a steadily growing company, with enough cash flow from operating activities to cover these expenditures and more.

Cash flows from financing activities could as easily be positive as negative in a healthy company. Moreover, they are likely to change back and forth, so finding the "good" and "bad" is more challenging. It requires viewing the cash flows from financing activities in conjunction with other information on the cash flow statement and basing your conclusions on the weight of the evidence and your own judgment. Assume a company has borrowed cash or issued stock. A "good news" scenario might be that the firm has carefully analyzed its leverage and cost of capital and chosen to finance itself through debt or equity rather than from cash from operations. Another "good news" scenario might be that a new start-up is doing well enough to issue an Initial Public Offering. On the other hand, a "bad news" scenario might be that the company has low (or negative) cash flows from operations and is being forced to generate funds from other sources. You must look at the entire package to evaluate whether your cash flows from financing are in the "good news" or "bad news" categories.

One systematic way to begin is to compare borrowing and payments on debt with each other across the years and note the trends. Colgate-Palmolive has been consistently borrowing more than it has paid back, and to a very substantial degree in 1993. Good news or bad? We have already seen the incredible amount of cash being thrown off from operations, so this increase in debt financing is probably the result of a conscious management decision and not the actions of a company desperately borrowing to survive. Nevertheless, it might be worth another more detailed look if we wanted to consider whether continued borrowing provides a likely source of funds for future growth, or whether the firm is nearing its debt capacity.[1]

---

[1] This might be the time to go looking for clues in the rest of the annual report. Where to look? A footnote on long-term debt might seem logical, but it is often almost impossible to truly understand unless you are a Chief Financial Officer. Easier and sometimes more illuminating is to do some simple ratios on the balance sheet and income statement. How has debt changed as a percentage of total liabilities and stockholders' equity? For Colgate-Palmolive, the percentage of debt to total liabilities and stockholders' equity is quite high and has gotten higher, from 67% in 1993 to 70% in 1994. The company's income statement reveals that interest expense has almost doubled in the last year, and a quick ratio analysis of "number of times interest can be paid from income" shows a sharp decline from 7 times to about 4½ times in one year. Further examination of the cash flow statement reveals that the company purchased large amounts of treasury stock. This helps explain why stockholders' equity is low in comparison to total equities, which may make that 70% debt-to-total equity ratio more understandable.

A second systematic step in uncovering the news in this section is to check the activities in the stock accounts. Colgate-Palmolive is not issuing much stock; instead, it seems to be buying back substantial amounts of treasury stock. In fact, that is the single largest use of cash outside of capital expenditures.[2] This is probably a "good news" scenario, because the company may be cashing in on what it considers a low price for its stock, or perhaps protecting itself from takeover attempts. In either event, Colgate-Palmolive appears to have sufficient cash available to make this large, non-routine investment. A little digging in the rest of the financial statements might present the whole story.

## STEP 4:  PUTTING THE PUZZLE TOGETHER

In evaluating the cash flow statement, you are evaluating many pieces of evidence to produce an overall picture. However, it would be rare to find a company in which all of the evidence is positive, or in which all of the evidence is negative. To make a balanced evaluation, you must use both the good news and the bad news identified in each section of the statement. To reach an overall conclusion, you need to judge the relative importance of each piece of evidence and assess its relationship to the overall picture. As in a legal case, your conclusion needs to be based on the "weight of the evidence."

Before proceeding with the overall evaluation, one loose end to tie up at this point might be any unusual line items you spotted in your scan of the big picture. Sometimes these demand that you ask an expert, but frequently you can think them through or search for illumination elsewhere in the annual report. Earlier we identified two unusual line items for Colgate-Palmolive. One was the "cumulative effect on prior years of an accounting change" in 1993. Without the deduction of this $358 million item from income in 1993, Colgate-Palmolive had a healthy income figure of $548 million; but after subtracting it, income fell to $190 million. The explanation is that when Colgate-Palmolive made this accounting change, all of its effects prior to 1993 were charged to income in 1993. In reality, there was no actual expenditure of cash in 1993, which is why we added this back on the cash flow statement.[3] This is good to know, because if we ignore the accounting change and the associated charge, net income has steadily increased.

The other unusual line item was called "restructured operations," which Colgate-Palmolive subtracted from net income. This means that the cash flows associated with restructuring operations occurred in a different year from when

---

2  This contrasts with minor stock repurchases that companies typically undertake to offer stock to employees in stock option plans; in such instances, modest treasury stock repurchases are offset by modest but comparable issuances of treasury stock.

3  An accounting change is just a "paper decision"; it affects the way net income is presented, but it does not change the fundamental economic activity of the firm, so it does not affect cash receipts or cash expenditures.

these costs were expensed on the income statement. In all three years presented by Colgate-Palmolive, it had more cash outflows for restructuring than it expensed in the income statement.

Good news or bad news? When a company restructures some of its operations, there is both. The bad news is that there was some kind of problem that required the restructuring. The good news is that the company recognized the problem and took action it hopes will be effective. Whether the restructuring cash costs are more or less than the restructuring expense is simply a timing issue. Because expenses are recognized as soon as reasonably possible, it typically requires several years after the expense has been recorded for all of the cash costs to be incurred. Colgate-Palmolive probably recognized these restructuring expenses in prior years and this is just the anticipated cash outflows catching up with them. Moreover, the amount on the cash flow statement is declining each year.

Whether or not to chase down explanations for unusual or unknown items is a subjective call. For example, if Colgate-Palmolive's restructuring charge differences were bigger or growing, it might be worthwhile to search for more information. However, the "weight of the evidence" so far indicates that this issue is not particularly relevant in getting at the big picture. If you encounter something you do not understand, consider its materiality. If it has a major effect on cash flow from operating activities, or if it ranks as one of the major sources or uses of cash, you should probably search for an explanation. Otherwise it may be more efficient to ignore it and concentrate on the many items you know.

Now let's summarize what we've learned by examining Colgate-Palmolive's cash flow statement. First, the good news. Net income has been positive for all three years and, if we eliminate the effects of the accounting change, has been steadily increasing. Operating cash flows have also been positive for three years; they, too, have been steadily increasing. Operating cash flows have significantly exceeded the sum of depreciation and dividends, so Colgate-Palmolive is generating enough cash from operations to expand the business. The working capital accounts are growing, consistent with the expectations for a growing business. By making capital expenditures that significantly exceed depreciation, and also by making fairly large acquisitions, Colgate-Palmolive shows that it is grooming the business for the future. There are no large-scale sales of fixed assets or divestitures that indicate any downsizing or shrinking of the business. The company has increased its dividend payments annually, an expression of management's confidence in the firm's future cash-generating capability. It also has sufficient excess cash to repurchase large amounts of its stock.

Now the bad news. The presence of charges for "restructured operations" indicates that Colgate-Palmolive has experienced problems in some portions of the business. It has borrowed significantly, in excess of repayment, which could increase leverage. The repurchase of stock could indicate management concerns with possible takeovers. And acquisitions sometimes create problems for firms; it is difficult to integrate them successfully into the company's business to ensure adequate returns.

The good news in the Colgate-Palmolive cash flow story is quite compelling. The bad news is more at the level of "concerns" rather than major cash flow problems. So considering the weight of the evidence, Colgate-Palmolive appears to have a strong positive cash flow story.

Now it's your turn. The best way to learn about cash flow statements is to study some carefully using the four steps described above. You may not become an expert but you will be able to spot the big trends and important issues involved with the management of cash in most companies.

**Exhibit 4** provides you with the opportunity to test your newfound skills. It is similar to the puzzles you encountered as a child in which you spot the things that are wrong with the picture. Poor Jones Company is having some rough times, as illuminated by their cash flow statements for 1993, 1994, and 1995. See how many of these troubling developments you can identify by putting together the Puzzle of the Cash Flow Statement!

Some possible answers are: (1) there have been losses in all three years, (2) depreciation charges have decreased, (3) capital expenditures are less than depreciation, (4) capital expenditures are less than disposals, (5) a big accounts receivable increase needs to be instigated, (6) inventories are decreasing, (7) segments of the business are being sold off, (8) the company has stopped paying dividends, (9) debt needs to be paid off with cash flow from operations, (10) there is much borrowing, and (11) there is less borrowing this year. Are creditors trusting the company less?

Opportunities for applying your new expertise are many. As an employee curious about your company's ability to cover your paycheck, you can check out the health of cash flow from operating activities. Or suppose you are a supplier whose customer has just announced a loss for the year and you are wondering whether to continue to extend credit. An analysis of the customer's cash flow from operating activities can provide you with evidence that the firm does or does not have strong enough cash flows from operating activities to pay its bills despite losses on the income statement.

If you are a stockholder, you may be interested in whether cash flow from operating activities is large enough to invest in the capital expenditures required to keep the company whole and make it grow while still paying the dividend you have come to expect. As an executive, you might examine the cash flow statement to determine whether it is likely that all of the major sources of cash—operating activities, issuing stock, and borrowing—will be sufficient to fund a major expansion program you plan to undertake. As your expertise increases, many other useful applications may appear to you.

The information contained in a cash flow statement cannot replace the information from the traditional income statement and balance sheet. But it does provide valuable input for understanding the relationships between income and its short- and long-term ability to generate cash.

# REFERENCES

Mohamed A. Rujoub, Doris M. Cook, and Leon E. Hay, "Using Cash Flow Ratios To Predict Business Failures," *Journal of Managerial Issues*, Spring 1995, pp. 75–90.

"The Top 8 Reports," *Institutional Investor*, September 1995, pp. 123–129.

**EXHIBIT 1**
**Statement of Cash Flows**    Indirect

| | |
|---|---:|
| **Cash Flow from Operating Activities** | |
| Net Income | xxx,xxx |
| Adjustments to reconcile net income to net cash provided by operating activities: | |
| Depreciation and amortization | xx,xxx |
| Changes in other accounts affecting operations: | |
| (Increase)/decrease in accounts receivable | x,xxx |
| (Increase)/decrease in inventories | x,xxx |
| (Increase)/decrease in prepaid expenses | x,xxx |
| Increase/(decrease) in accounts payable | x,xxx |
| Increase/(decrease) in taxes payable | x,xxx |
| Net cash provided by operating activities | xxx,xxx |
| | |
| **Cash Flow from Investing Activities** | |
| Capital expenditures | (xxx,xxx) |
| Proceeds from sales of equipment | xx,xxx |
| Proceeds from sales of investments | xx,xxx |
| Investment in subsidiary | (xxx,xxx) |
| Net cash provided by (used in) investing activities | (xxx,xxx) |
| | |
| **Cash Flow from Financing Activities** | |
| Payments of long-term debt | (xx,xxx) |
| Proceeds from issuance of long-term debt | xx,xxx |
| Proceeds from issuance of common stock | xxx,xxx |
| Dividends paid | (xx,xxx) |
| Purchase of treasury stock | (xx,xxx) |
| Net cash provided by (used in) financing activities | (xx,xxx) |
| | |
| **Increase (Decrease) in Cash** | xx,xxx |

EXHIBIT 2
## Cash Flow from Operating Activities:  Direct and Indirect Formats

The cash flow from operating activities section of a cash flow statement can be presented using the direct format or the indirect format.  The bottom line is the same, but the two begin at different points.  Companies are free to choose either format.

*A* is an income statement, followed by *B*, the cash flow from operating activities section for the same company presented in the two different formats.

The direct method is just like a cash tax return:  how much cash came in the door for sales and how much cash went out the door for the inventory and other operating expenditures.  Many believe the direct format is better, because it is easier to understand at first glimpse.  However, if companies choose the direct format, they must also present a reconciliation between cash flows from operating activities and net income—which is precisely what the indirect format shows!  Consequently, most firms simply choose to present the indirect format.

The indirect method starts with net income as a figure that summarizes most of the cash transactions for operating activities in a firm.  However, net income also includes transactions that were not cash, so we must eliminate the noncash transactions from the net income figure to arrive at an accurate presentation of cash flows from operating activities.

A common, typically major expense that does not involve the expenditure of any cash at all is depreciation.  Depreciation is always added back to net income under the indirect method.  Do not be confused by this presentation into thinking depreciation somehow provides cash.  It is only added back because it was subtracted to get to net income in the first place, and it must now be added back to get to cash.  If there are other expenses that did not involve cash, these too will be added back to net income.

### *A.*  Income Statement

| | |
|---|---:|
| Sales | $ 412,000 |
| Cost of goods sold | (265,000) |
| Other expenses | (117,000)* |
| Net income | $  30,000 |

*Other expenses includes $25,000 depreciation expense.

### *B.*  Cash Flow from Operating Activities (two formats)

| Direct | | Indirect | |
|---|---:|---|---:|
| Cash received from customers | $ 400,000 | Net Income | $ 30,000 |
| Cash paid to suppliers | (260,000) | Adjustments to reconcile net | |
| Cash paid to employees | (70,000) | income to net cash provided | |
| Other cash operating expenditures | (30,000) | by operating activities: | |
| | | Depreciation | 25,000 |
| Net cash provided by operating activities | $  40,000 | Changes in other accounts affecting operations: | |
| | | (Increase) in receivables | (12,000) |
| | | Decrease in inventory | 5,000 |
| | | (Decrease) in payables | (8,000) |
| | | Net cash provided by operating activities | $ 40,000 |

## EXHIBIT 2 (continued)

For most income statement items, the cash paid (or received) could be a little more, or a little less, than the income statement item. For example, cash received from customers could be a little more than revenues, especially if we collected large amounts owed to us from prior years, or it could be a little less if we made significant credit sales this year. Changes in operating working capital accounts reveal whether or not the amounts included in net income for sales, inventory costs, and other expenses really reflect the actual cash inflows and outflows. Changes in these accounts are added back to or subtracted from net income to reveal the true cash inflows and outflows.

Say the total sales number on our income statement was $412,000. But if we examined accounts receivable, we would find that receivables increased by $12,000, which customers essentially "put on their bill," and only $400,000 was actually collected in cash. So the deduction of $12,000 for "increase in receivables" in the indirect format adjusts the sales number of $412,000 down to $400,000, the actual cash received.

The inventory decrease reveals that we used some inventory purchased in prior years for sales this year. Our cost of goods sold figure in net income is therefore too high as an indicator of cash paid this year for inventory.

Similarly, it looks as if we paid some of last year's bills this year, because our payables went down by $8,000. So we must subtract an additional $8,000 to adjust the net income figure for the additional, actual cash expenditures.

There is a simple rule by which accounts should be added to or subtracted from net income: *Increases in current assets are subtracted, and increases in current liabilities are added.* The simplest approach to remember this is to pick a single account that is easy to figure out when it changes in one direction. For example, you might remember that increases in accounts receivable represent goods sold on account, but not for cash; so increases in accounts receivable must be subtracted from net income to reflect cash flows from operating activities. Once you know this, you know that a decrease in accounts receivable must be treated the opposite way: it will be added. Now you can deduce the remaining working capital accounts. The asset accounts will be treated just like accounts receivable. And the liability accounts will be exactly the opposite. Once you know one working capital account, you know them all.

Although initially it takes practice to become familiar with the indirect format, you will discover that it actually shows quite a bit of useful information you might need to search for otherwise. The quickest way to find the company's total depreciation, for example, is on the cash flow statement. In addition, it directly displays the changes in the working capital accounts. If you were to use the balance sheet for this information, you would have to perform the subtraction yourself.

**EXHIBIT 3**
**Consolidated Statements of Cash Flows:  Colgate-Palmolive**

| (In millions) | 1994 | 1993 | 1992 |
|---|---|---|---|
| **Operating Activities** | | | |
| Net Income | $ 580.2 | $ 189.9 | $ 477.0 |
| Adjustments to reconcile net income to cash provided by operations: | | | |
| Cumulative effect on prior years of accounting changes | — | 358.2 | — |
| Restructured operations, net | (39.1) | (77.0) | (92.0) |
| Depreciation and amortization | 235.1 | 209.6 | 192.5 |
| Deferred income taxes and other, net | 64.7 | 53.6 | (25.8) |
| Cash effects of these changes: | | | |
| (Increase) in receivables | (50.1) | (103.6) | (38.0) |
| (Increase)/decrease in inventories | (44.5) | 31.7 | 28.4 |
| (Increase)/decrease in other current assets | (7.8) | (4.6) | 10.6 |
| Increase/(decrease) in payables | 90.9 | 52.6 | (10.0) |
| Net cash provided by operations | 829.4 | 710.4 | 542.7 |
| **Investing Activities** | | | |
| Capital expenditures | (400.8) | (364.3) | (318.5) |
| Payment for acquisitions | (146.4) | (171.2) | (170.1) |
| Sale of securities and investments | 58.4 | 33.8 | 79.9 |
| Investments | (1.9) | (12.5) | (6.6) |
| Other, net | 33.0 | 61.7 | 17.4 |
| Net cash used for investing activities | (457.7) | (452.5) | (397.9) |
| **Financing Activities** | | | |
| Principal payments on debt | (88.3) | (200.8) | (250.1) |
| Proceeds from issuance of debt | 316.4 | 782.1 | 262.6 |
| Proceeds from outside investors | 15.2 | 60.0 | — |
| Dividends paid | (246.9) | (231.4) | (200.7) |
| Purchase of treasury stock | (357.9) | (657.2) | (20.5) |
| Proceeds from exercise of stock options | 18.5 | 21.8 | 22.6 |
| Net cash used for financing activities | (343.0) | (225.5) | (186.1) |
| Effect of exchange rate changes on cash | (2.9) | (6.2) | (9.3) |
| Net increase (decrease) in cash | $ 25.8 | $ 26.2 | $ (50.6) |

**EXHIBIT 4**
**Jones Company:  Statements of Cash Flows for Year Ending December 31**

| *Millions of Dollars* | 1995 | 1994 | 1993 |
|---|---|---|---|
| **Cash Flow from Operating Activities** | | | |
| Net income (loss) | $ (43) | $(189) | $(134) |
| Depreciation | 230 | 271 | 350 |
| (Increase) in receivables | (121) | (25) | (4) |
| Decrease in inventories | 50 | 42 | 30 |
| Changes in other current accounts | 16 | (8) | (12) |
| Net cash provided by operating activities | 132 | 91 | 230 |
| **Cash Flow from Investing Activities** | | | |
| Capital expenditures | (200) | (260) | (300) |
| Disposal of plant assets | 204 | 200 | 180 |
| Disposal of business segment | 134 | 51 | — |
| Net cash (used in)/provided by investing activities | 138 | (9) | (120) |
| **Cash Flow from Financing Activities** | | | |
| Proceeds of long-term debt | 200 | 450 | 215 |
| Reductions of long-term debt | (460) | (480) | (322) |
| Dividends paid | — | — | (30) |
| Net cash used for financing activities | (260) | (30) | (137) |
| Increase (decrease) in cash | $  10 | $  52 | $ (27) |

# Statements of Cash Flows:  Three Examples

**J**ohn Stacey, a sales engineer for Aldhus Corporation, was worried.  A flight delay had caused him to miss last week's accounting class in the evening MBA program in which he had enrolled at the suggestion of the personnel director at Aldhus, a growing manufacturer of computer peripherals.  The class he had missed had been devoted to a lecture and discussion of the statement of cash flows, and he was sure the material he had missed would be covered in the weekly quiz that was part of each class session.  A classmate had faxed Stacey some notes distributed by their instructor, but they were too cryptic to be understood by anyone who had missed the class.

In desperation, John called Lucille Barnes, the assistant controller at Aldhus, to ask if she could take a few minutes to point him in the right direction toward understanding the statement of cash flows.  She seemed delighted by the request, and they agreed to meet that afternoon.

## THE MEETING

At 2:00 P.M. John Stacey went to the office of Lucille Barnes with his notes and questions.  After they had exchanged greetings, Lucille handed John three cash flow statements from the annual reports of other high-technology companies (**Exhibits 1**, **2**, and **3**).  John was worried that Lucille would ask him to explain them, and that she would see how confused he still was about some aspects of accounting; instead, Lucille began explaining.

---

*Professors Julie H. Hertenstein and William J. Bruns, Jr. prepared this case.*

Copyright © 1993 by the President and Fellows of Harvard College.  Harvard Business School case 193-103.

**Lucille Barnes (Assistant Controller):**   The statement of cash flows is really a very useful part of the set of three statements companies are required to prepare.  In some cases, it tells more about what is actually happening in a business than either the balance sheet or income statement. The statements of cash flows that I have given you are very revealing.  Let me give you a brief overview of the structure and content of cash flow statements, and then you take some time to study these statements.  I have prepared some questions to guide your study.  Then, we can meet again tomorrow to discuss what you have learned and to answer any questions that remain.  I do not think you have to worry about your next quiz because if you understand how balance sheets and income statements are prepared, much about the statement of cash flows will seem pretty obvious.

**John Stacey:**   I hope you are right.  I really like the accounting course, and I want to do well in it and to really learn the material.  That's why I panicked when I could not understand the notes our instructor passed out last week.

**Lucille Barnes:**   Forget those notes for a while and just concentrate on studying the statements I have given you.  Notice that the statement of cash flows is divided into three sections: operating activities, investing activities, and financing activities.  Each section shows the cash inflows and the cash outflows associated with that type of activity.
   Operating activities shows the inflows and outflows related to the fundamental operations of the basic line or lines of business that the company is in. For example, it would include cash receipts from the sale of goods or services, and the cash outflows for purchasing inventory and paying wages, taxes, and rent.
   Investing activities shows cash flows for the purchase and sale of assets not generally held for resale and for the making and collecting of loans. (Maybe it should more appropriately be called the investing and disinvesting activities section.)  Here is where you would see if the company sold a building, purchased equipment, made a loan to a subsidiary, or purchased a piece of equity in its supplier.
   Finally, financing activities shows the cash flows associated with increasing or decreasing the firm's financing, for example, issuing or repurchasing stock and borrowing or repaying loans.  It also includes dividends, which are cash flows associated with equity.  However, ironically, it does not include interest payments; these are included in operating activities.

**John Stacey:**   That seems strange to me.  Since loans are the reason interest payments are made, why are they not included in the financing activities section? You know, interest is to loans as dividends are to equity?

**Lucille Barnes:**   Actually in some other countries such as the United Kingdom interest is included in the financing activities section!  But in the United States the Financial Accounting Standards Board voted that interest payments should be in the operating activities section instead.  This is one of these situations where you might have to do some adjusting if you were trying to compare a U.K. company like British Petroleum to a U.S. company like Exxon.

**John Stacey**:    That is interesting!  How can I use each section of the statement?

**Lucille Barnes:**    The operating activity section is the cash flow engine of the company.  When this engine is working effectively, it provides the cash flows to cover the cash needs of operations.  In a healthy, growing company, we would expect growth in operating working capital accounts such as inventory and accounts receivable (uses of cash) as well as in accounts payable and other operating payables (sources of cash).  Obviously there can be quite a bit of variability in working capital accounts from period to period, but on average inventories, receivables, and accounts payable usually grow in growing companies.  In addition, this operating cash flow engine provides cash for needed investments, to repay debt, and to pay dividends.  There are exceptions, of course.  Start-up companies, for example, usually have negative cash flows from operations because they have not gotten their cash flow engines up to speed.  Companies in cyclical industries may have negative operating cash flow in a "down" year; a company that has experienced an extensive strike could also be expected to have negative cash flow from operations.  Although an occasional year of negative operating cash flow does not spell disaster, nonetheless, we should expect operating cash flow, on average, to be positive.

Investing activities are a different story.  Whereas we expect positive operating cash flow, we also expect a healthy company to continually invest in more plant, equipment, land, and other fixed assets to replace the assets that have been used up or have become technologically obsolete, as well as to expand and grow.  Although companies often sell assets that are no longer of use to them, we would normally expect them to purchase more capital assets than they sell.  As a result, in general, we expect negative cash flows from investing activities.  Like operating activities, exceptions occur, especially if the firm divests a business or subsidiary.

Cash flows from financing activities could as easily be positive as negative in a healthy company, and they are likely to change back and forth.  If the company's need for cash to invest exceeds the cash flow generated by operating activities, this will require extra financing by debt or equity, therefore a positive financing cash flow.  On the other hand, if cash flow from operating activities exceeds the investing needs, the firm will have excess cash to repay debt or pay more dividends, producing negative cash flows from financing.

**John Stacey:**    I am beginning to see why you said that the statement of cash flows is so useful.  Where do you start your review and analysis?

**Lucille Barnes:**    A way to approach the cash flow statement is to begin with cash flows from operating activities.  If this is the cash flow engine, then the first question is, "Is cash flow from operating activities greater, or less, than zero?" Also of interest is the trend: is it increasing or decreasing?

**John Stacey:**   As you were talking, I glanced at the cash flows from operations sections of the first two statements (**Exhibits 1** and **2**) you gave me. They look very different. On the first, depreciation seems to provide cash flows, but there is no mention of depreciation on the second.

**Lucille Barnes:**   Oops! I forget to mention that there are two ways operating cash flows can be presented. Sometimes they are presented using the indirect method as in the first statement I gave you (**Exhibit 1**). Using that method, net income is adjusted for all noncash revenues and expenses, one of which is depreciation. Depreciation is *never* a source of cash, but it *is* deducted to compute net income, so it must be added back. Likewise, operating cash flows not included in net income, such as purchases of inventory not sold, have to be added or subtracted.

When the direct method is used to present cash flows from operations, that section of the report looks much more like a summary from the operating cash account as it does in the second report I gave you (**Exhibit 2**).

**John Stacey:**   Which of the methods is better?

**Lucille Barnes:**   I think the direct statement of cash flows from operations is easier to understand, but few companies present their operating cash flows that way. Most of the statements you will see will use the indirect method. The reason for this is that if the direct method is used, a reconciliation of income to cash flows from operations is also required (see **Exhibit 2**), so most companies simply use the reconciliation as their summary of cash flows from operations.

But let's get back to how I approach the statement of cash flows.

Assuming operating cash flows are greater than zero, the next challenge is to decide whether they are adequate for important, routine expenditures. Again, our expectations are tempered by our understanding of the company and its situation. Just as we do not expect a start-up company to have positive operating cash flows, we also do not expect a company still in a very rapid growth phase to have enough cash flow from operations to cover its investments. However, for a mature company, we expect operations to generate enough cash to "keep the company whole." This would include the amount of investment required to replace those fixed assets that are used up, worn out, or technologically obsolete as well as cash required to pay the annual dividend which the shareholders have come to expect. It is hard to know precisely how much cash is required to keep the company's fixed assets "whole," and the cash flow statement does not separate investing cash flows for replacement and renewal from those investing cash flows for expansion and growth. However, the annual depreciation amount is a very rough surrogate for the amount of fixed assets that need to be replaced each year. In periods when prices are rising, we should expect that the cost to replace assets would be somewhat greater than the cost of older assets that are being depreciated. Thus, it is common to expect the portion of investing activities related to the purchase of fixed assets to exceed the annual depreciation.

After considering whether operating cash flows cover capital expenditures and dividends, I look to see whether there are other major cash needs such as acquisitions, stock repurchase, or debt repayment. If so, how do these cash needs fit with the availability of cash? Are these needs discretionary, like acquisitions?

If there are cash shortfalls, I investigate how they are being funded. Is it by issuing stock? By borrowing? By selling businesses or assets? In each case, I consider whether the company is likely to be able to continue such funding, and for how long. Will the funding source continue to be available, or are we likely nearing the limit? Will continuing to use this source hurt the company in any way?

**John Stacey:**   Do you always have to look at all of those things in every case?

**Lucille Barnes:**   No. But if you stop short of a full review, you may miss an important part of the story.

In evaluating the cash flow statement, you are evaluating many pieces of evidence to produce an overall picture. However, it would be rare to find a company where all of the evidence is positive, or where all of the evidence is negative. To do a balanced evaluation, you must search out both the good news and the bad news in each cash flow statement. To reach an overall conclusion you need to judge the relative importance of each piece of evidence and assess its relationship to the overall picture. Like in a legal case, your conclusion needs to be based on the "weight of the evidence."

I think the best way to learn about statements of cash flow is to study some carefully. The statements I have given you are a place to start. I wrote out some questions to guide your study (the assignment). Try to develop answers, and we can meet tomorrow to discuss them. By the time we finish, I think you will be well prepared for the quiz in your next class.

# THE ASSIGNMENT

**Exhibits 1, 2,** and **3** contain cash flow statements from three companies. Each cash flow statement has three years of data. Examine the contents of these cash flow statements carefully. Answer the following questions about each of the three cash flow statements.

I.   For *each* of the years on the statement of cash flows:
  1. What were the firm's major sources of cash? Its major uses of cash?
  2. Was cash flow from operations[1] greater than or less than net income?[2] Explain in detail the major reasons for the difference between these two figures.
  3. Was the firm able to generate enough cash from operations to pay for all of its capital expenditures?[3]
  4. Did the cash flow from operations cover both the capital expenditures **and** the firm's dividend payments, if any?
  5. If it did, how did the firm invest its excess cash?
  6. If not, what were the sources of cash the firm used to pay for the capital expenditures and/or dividends?
  7. Were the working capital (current asset and current liability) accounts other than cash and cash equivalents primarily sources of cash or users of cash?
  8. What other major items affected cash flows?

II.  What was the trend in:
  1. Net income?
  2. Cash flow from (continuing) operations?
  3. Capital expenditures?
  4. Dividends?
  5. Net borrowing (proceeds less payments of short- and long-term debt)?
  6. Working capital accounts?

III. Based on the evidence in the statement of cash flows alone, what is your assessment of the financial strength of this business? Why?

---

[1] Sometimes called net cash provided by operating activities, or cash flow from continuing operations.

[2] Alternatively referred to as income or loss from continuing operations.

[3] Also called investments in depreciable assets, or purchases of plant, property, and equipment.

## EXHIBIT 1
### Alpha Corporation, Consolidated Statements of Cash Flows ($ millions)

*Indirect Method*

| | Year Ended June 30, | | |
|---|---|---|---|
| | **1991** | **1990** | **1989** |
| **Operating Activities** | | | |
| Loss from continuing operations | $(377.9) | $(623.5) | $(320.6) |
| Depreciation | 168.4 | 220.1 | 263.4 |
| Amortization of capitalized software | 41.4 | 58.2 | 39.1 |
| Gain from sale of investments and other assets | (16.6) | (119.0) | — |
| Restructuring and other unusual items, net | 135.5 | 384.1 | 125.3 |
| Changes in other accounts affecting operations | | | |
|    Accounts receivable | 160.8 | 73.4 | (45.2) |
|    Inventory | 80.2 | 100.9 | (3.0) |
|    Other current assets | 17.0 | (1.2) | (13.0) |
|    Accounts payable and other current liabilities | (91.3) | (21.3) | 41.0 |
|    Other | 2.8 | 14.1 | (10.5) |
| Net cash provided by continuing operations | 120.3 | 85.8 | 76.5 |
| Net cash provided by (used in) discontinued operations | 4.9 | 3.5 | (29.7) |
| **Net cash provided by operating activities** | 125.2 | 89.3 | 46.8 |
| **Investing Activities** | | | |
| Investment in depreciable assets | (129.7) | (174.4) | (303.6) |
| Proceeds from disposal of depreciable and other assets | 157.0 | 242.0 | 94.1 |
| Proceeds from the sale of discontinued operations | 25.3 | 407.3 | — |
| Investment in capitalized software | (27.8) | (43.1) | (59.5) |
| Other | (6.0) | (13.0) | 14.2 |
| **Net cash provided by (used in) investing activities** | 18.8 | 418.8 | (254.8) |
| **Financing Activities** | | | |
| (Decrease) increase in short-term borrowings | (2.6) | (222.6) | 139.8 |
| Proceeds from long-term debt | 44.4 | 167.7 | 305.0 |
| Payments of long-term debt | (126.5) | (544.8) | (91.7) |
| Proceeds from sale of Class B common stock | 5.0 | 8.7 | 17.5 |
| Purchase of treasury stock | (.3) | (.6) | (18.8) |
| Dividends paid | — | (7.2) | (26.0) |
| **Net cash provided by (used in) financing activities** | (80.0) | (598.8) | 325.8 |
| Effect of changes in foreign exchange rates | .1 | 1.1 | (3.9) |
| **Increase (decrease) in cash equivalents** | 64.1 | (89.6) | 113.9 |
| **Cash and equivalents at beginning of year** | 169.1 | 258.7 | 144.8 |
| **Cash and equivalents at end of year** | $ 233.2 | $ 169.1 | $ 258.7 |

**EXHIBIT 2**
**Beta Corporation, Consolidated Statements of Cash Flows ($ thousands)**

Direct Method

| | Year Ended December 31, | | |
| --- | --- | --- | --- |
| | 1991 | 1990 | 1989 |
| **Cash Flows from Operating Activities:** | | | |
| Cash received from customers | $ 83,865 | $ 73,273 | $ 51,110 |
| Cash paid to suppliers and employees | (77,820) | (65,480) | (46,589) |
| Interest received | 643 | 355 | 132 |
| Interest paid | (536) | (1,046) | (908) |
| Income taxes paid | (2,233) | (102) | (75) |
| Net cash generated by operating activities | 3,919 | 7,000 | 3,670 |
| **Cash Flows from Investing Activities:** | | | |
| Capital expenditures | (6,031) | (4,600) | (3,650) |
| Marketable securities purchases | (8,000) | — | — |
| Net cash used in investing activities | (14,031) | (4,600) | (3,650) |
| **Cash Flow from Financing Activities:** | | | |
| Net payments under working capital line of credit | — | (2,000) | (860) |
| Net payments under equipment line of credit | (985) | (126) | (388) |
| Principal payments under capital lease obligations | (169) | (213) | (276) |
| Proceeds (payment) of subordinated debt | (5,000) | — | 4,400 |
| Proceeds from the issuance of common stock | 23,082 | 141 | 639 |
| Net cash provided by (used in) financing activities | 16,928 | (2,198) | 3,515 |
| Effect of exchange rate changes on cash | (4) | 14 | — |
| Net increase in cash and cash equivalents | 6,812 | 216 | 3,535 |
| Cash and cash equivalents at beginning of year | 5,375 | 5,159 | 1,624 |
| Cash and cash equivalents at end of year | $ 12,187 | $ 5,375 | $ 5,159 |
| **Reconciliation of Net Income to Net Cash** | | | |
| **Generated by Operating Activities:** | | | |
| Net income | $ 6,323 | $ 5,201 | $ 417 |
| **Adjustments to Reconcile Net Income to Net** | | | |
| **Cash Consumed by Operating Activities:** | | | |
| Bad debt provision | 99 | 47 | 98 |
| Depreciation and amortization | 4,028 | 2,701 | 2,231 |
| Amortization of original issue discount | 208 | 324 | 68 |
| Loss on disposition of assets | 17 | 9 | 58 |
| Compensation expense related to stock grants | 40 | 85 | — |
| **Changes in Assets and Liabilities:** | | | |
| (Increase) in accounts receivable | (10,837) | (613) | (1,550) |
| (Increase) decrease in inventory | (951) | (810) | 1,043 |
| (Increase) decrease in deposits and other assets | (665) | 366 | (762) |
| Increase (decrease) in accounts payable and accrued expenses | 5,657 | (310) | 2,067 |
| Total adjustments | (2,404) | 1,799 | 3,253 |
| Net cash generated by operating activities | $ 3,919 | $ 7,000 | $ 3,670 |

↓ = Indirect Method

**EXHIBIT 3**
**Gamma Corporation, Consolidated Statements of Cash Flows ($ thousands)**

Indirect Method

|  | June 29, 1991 | Year Ended June 30, 1990 | July 1, 1989 |
|---|---|---|---|
| **Cash Flows from Operating Activities:** | | | |
| Net income/(loss) | $ (617,427) | $ 74,393 | $1,072,610 |
| **Adjustments to Reconcile Net Income to** | | | |
| **Net Cash Provided by Operating Activities:** | | | |
| Depreciation and amortization | 828,560 | 796,201 | 686,738 |
| Other adjustments to income | 189,077 | 92,329 | 49,702 |
| (Increase)/decrease in accounts receivable | 105,977 | (241,357) | (373,248) |
| (Increase)/decrease in inventories | 18,616 | 99,743 | (62,942) |
| (Increase)/decrease in prepaid expenses | (47,239) | (90,602) | 18,965 |
| Increase/(decrease) in accounts payable | (17,694) | 107,001 | 30,645 |
| (Decrease) in taxes | (105,614) | (201,560) | (75,502) |
| Increase in deferred revenues and customer advances | 92,222 | 69,207 | 105,847 |
| Increase in restructuring reserve | 593,160 | 443,544 | — |
| Increase in other liabilities | 1,263 | 285,175 | 26,576 |
| Total adjustments | 1,658,328 | 1,359,681 | 406,781 |
| Net cash flows from operating activities | 1,040,901 | 1,434,074 | 1,479,391 |
| **Cash Flows from Investing Activities:** | | | |
| Purchase of plant, property, and equipment | (737,548) | (1,027,625) | (1,223,038) |
| (Increase) of other assets, net | (55,782) | (75,489) | (67,624) |
| Purchase of Kienzle business | (233,261) | — | — |
| Net cash flows from investing activities | (1,026,591) | (1,103,114) | (1,290,662) |
| Net cash flows from operating and investing activities | 14,310 | 330,960 | 188,729 |
| **Net Flows from Financing Activities:** | | | |
| Proceeds from issuance of debt | 14,249 | 17,661 | 40,425 |
| Payments to retire debt | (112,426) | (20,896) | (153,245) |
| Purchase of treasury shares | (240,719) | (270,231) | (814,958) |
| Issuance of treasury shares, including tax benefits | 239,653 | 296,225 | 230,733 |
| Net cash flows from financing activities | (99,243) | 22,759 | (697,045) |
| Net increase/(decrease) in cash and cash equivalents | (84,933) | 353,719 | (508,316) |
| Cash and cash equivalents at beginning of year | 2,008,983 | 1,655,264 | 2,163,580 |
| Cash and cash equivalents at end of year | $1,924,050 | $2,008,983 | $1,655,264 |

# Crystal Meadows of Tahoe, Inc.

**C**rystal Meadows of Tahoe (CMOT) was a holding company for two different alpine (downhill) ski resorts. The company had operated Crystal Meadows near Lake Tahoe, California, since 1962 and had purchased Lake Ridge in Utah in 1975. In addition, the company was involved in the development of a new ski resort in Nevada through a limited partnership in the Toiyabe Resort Company.

The ski business was both highly cyclical and highly seasonal. For the U.S. ski industry, on average 94% of revenues were received during the winter ski season. CMOT employed 100 people year round, but its employment swelled to 850 during the operating season. Because snowfall at given areas varied from year to year, the industry was cyclical as well. A string of several years of low snowfall at a given area could cause severe financial distress in order to cover fixed obligations.

Revenues at ski areas came primarily from the sale of lift tickets and related items such as ski rentals, ski lessons, and food and refreshments. **Exhibit 1** outlines the revenue sources for the average U.S. ski area. In addition, some ski areas were involved in the sale or rental of residential and commercial real estate around the ski area.

Costs for ski areas included labor for operating lifts, patrolling slopes, selling tickets, teaching lessons, and staffing cafeterias and shops. While some ski areas owned the land on which they operated, many leased land from the U.S. Forest Service or from other private owners. Ski areas typically invested

*This case is an update of Alpine Meadows of Tahoe, Inc. originally written by David J. Ellison under the supervision of Professor William J. Bruns, Jr. Some information taken from public documents has been reclassified, combined, or disguised for classroom use.*

Copyright © 1992 by the President and Fellows of Harvard College. Harvard Business School case 192-150.

significant sums in buildings, lifts, and snowmaking and snow grooming equipment. Other expenses included administration, marketing, and advertising, which typically were spread through the year.

CMOT owned both Crystal Meadows and Lake Ridge, two different types of ski areas. Crystal Meadows, with a capacity of 6,500 skiers per day, was a day and weekend ski area. Its clientele consisted primarily of skiers from Northern California, particularly Sacramento and the greater San Francisco Bay area. Crystal Meadows did not operate lodging at the ski area, although many of its skiers would stay somewhere in the Lake Tahoe area. Crystal Meadows competed with the other 18 ski areas in the greater Lake Tahoe area. On the other hand, Lake Ridge, with a capacity of 10,000 skiers per day, was primarily a destination resort, attracting people from all over the country. As a consequence, Lake Ridge competed with ski resorts all over the world, including locations in California, Idaho, Colorado, Wyoming, and Europe. As a holiday resort, Lake Ridge also competed with other vacation alternatives such as sun and beach resorts.

CMOT was a partner in the Toiyabe Resort Company, which was developing a year-round ski and recreational resort in the Lake Tahoe area. CMOT had invested $5.3 million in capital and capitalized interest costs in the venture by 1991. The project to that time had involved the designing, planning, and filing of applications for necessary permits. Construction of the resort was expected to start in 1992.

In addition to its ski operations, CMOT held some real estate that it would sell from time to time. This land was reported in a separate asset account in its financial statements.

Results from operations in fiscal year 1991, which ran from June 1, 1990 to May 31, 1991, were very positive for the company. Aftertax income was $.41 per share, more than twice that of 1990. Weather conditions at both ski areas were good, resulting in 839,000 skier days, the largest number in CMOT's history. Financial statements for fiscal years 1990 and 1991 are summarized in **Exhibits 2** and **3**.

During the year, the company had invested $2.7 million in new snowmaking equipment, as well as $2.6 million in other improvements. The 1992 capital expenditure plan was the most ambitious in company history at $8.2 million ($5.6 million at Lake Ridge and $2.6 million at Crystal Meadows). The planned expenditures included the replacement of two lifts at Lake Ridge and one lift at Crystal Meadows.

At the request of Julie Barnes, chief financial officer of CMOT, the accounting department had prepared a summary of some financial transactions affecting cash and cash balances during fiscal year 1991. A copy of the summary is shown in **Exhibit 4**.

## QUESTIONS

1. Prepare a statement of cash flows for CMOT for fiscal year 1991 using the indirect method. Organize the cash flows into cash flows from operating activities, cash flows from investing activities, and cash flows from financing activities. Does your statement explain the change in cash and cash equivalents between the beginning and end of 1991?

2. Prepare a schedule of cash flows from operations using the direct method. Is this schedule more or less informative about the company's operations than the one prepared by the indirect method in Question 1?

3. What does the analysis of cash flows reveal about CMOT that was not evident from analysis of the income statements and balance sheets?

**EXHIBIT 1**
**Average U.S. Ski Area Revenues (percent of total revenues)**

**Winter Season:**

| | |
|---|---:|
| Ski lift department | 55.0% |
| Ski school | 5.9 |
| Food service | 9.0 |
| Bar | 2.7 |
| Retail store | 4.0 |
| Rental shop | 3.7 |
| Accommodations | 3.9 |
| Other | 2.5 |
| Subtotal | 86.7% |

**Year-Round:**

| | |
|---|---:|
| Real estate | 5.3% |
| Utility | 0.6 |
| Miscellaneous | 1.5 |
| Subtotal | 7.4% |

**Summer Season:**

| | |
|---|---:|
| Lift department | 0.9% |
| Food service | 1.7 |
| Retail store | 0.4 |
| Sports department | 0.7 |
| Accommodations | 1.1 |
| Slide | 0.7 |
| Other | 0.3 |
| Subtotal | 5.8% |

Total  100.0%

---

Based on data included in *Economic Analysis of North American Ski Areas* (Boulder, Colorado, 1990).

**EXHIBIT 2**
**Crystal Meadows of Tahoe, Inc., Consolidated Statements of Operations,**
**Years Ended May 31 (thousands of dollars)**

| | 1991 | 1990 | Change from 1990 to 1991 |
|---|---|---|---|
| **Operating revenues:** | | | |
| Ticket sales | $19,274 | $16,319 | $2,955 |
| Ski school revenue | 2,623 | 2,281 | 342 |
| Other operating revenues | 3,246 | 2,636 | 610 |
| Total operating revenues | $25,143 | $21,236 | $3,907 |
| **Operating expenses:** | | | |
| Salaries and wages | 9,063 | 7,702 | 1,361 |
| Depreciation and amortization | 2,637 | 2,376 | 261 |
| Land rent | 1,447 | 1,412 | 35 |
| Other operating expenses | 9,702 | 8,360 | 1,342 |
| Total operating expenses | $22,849 | $19,850 | $2,999 |
| Income (loss) from operations | $ 2,294 | $ 1,386 | $ 908 |
| **Other income:** | | | |
| Interest income | $ 279 | $ 182 | $ 97 |
| Commercial property rent | 274 | 311 | (37) |
| Gain on sales of real estate | 329 | 0 | 329 |
| Miscellaneous income | 26 | 34 | (8) |
| Total other income | $ 908 | $ 527 | $ 381 |
| **Other expenses:** | | | |
| Interest expense | $ 1,073 | $ 956 | $ 117 |
| Miscellaneous expense | 132 | 101 | 31 |
| Total other expenses | $ 1,205 | $ 1,057 | $ 148 |
| Income (loss) before taxes | $ 1,997 | $ 856 | $1,141 |
| Income tax (provision) benefit | (579) | (185) | (394) |
| Net income (loss) | $ 1,418 | $ 671 | $ 747 |

**EXHIBIT 3**
**Crystal Meadows of Tahoe, Inc., Consolidated Balance Sheets, Years Ended May 31 (thousands of dollars)**

|  | 1991 | 1990 | Change from 1990 to 1991 |
|---|---|---|---|
| Assets: |  |  |  |
| Current assets: |  |  |  |
| Cash and equivalents | $ 4,097 | $ 3,272 | $ 825 |
| Accounts receivable | 140 | 199 | (59) |
| Prepaid expenses and other current assets | 337 | 343 | (6) |
| Total current assets | $ 4,574 | $ 3,814 | $ 760 |
| Real estate held for sale | 772 | 977 | (205) |
| Notes receivable | 967 | 927 | 40 |
| Plant & equipment, net | 17,826 | 15,317 | 2,509 |
| Investment in development stage resort | 5,299 | 4,883 | 416 |
| Other assets | 265 | 288 | (23) |
| Total Assets | $29,703 | $26,206 | $3,497 |
| Liabilities and Shareholders' Equity: |  |  |  |
| Current liabilities: |  |  |  |
| Long-term debt due within one year | $ 2,123 | $ 2,294 | $ (171) |
| Accounts payable | 864 | 619 | 245 |
| Accrued land rent | 1,544 | 1,525 | 19 |
| Accrued compensation | 614 | 462 | 152 |
| Deferred revenue | 607 | 363 | 244 |
| Income taxes payable | 100 | 0 | 100 |
| Other accrued liabilities | 465 | 286 | 179 |
| Total current liabilities | $ 6,317 | $ 5,549 | $ 768 |
| Long-term debt | 10,698 | 10,003 | 695 |
| Deferred income taxes | 1,041 | 562 | 479 |
| Other deferred credits | 570 | 354 | 216 |
| Total liabilities | $18,626 | $16,468 | $2,158 |
| Shareholders' equity: |  |  |  |
| Voting preferred stock, $.25 par value: |  |  |  |
| 1,750,000 shares authorized, 738,708 shares |  |  |  |
| issued and outstanding (839,069 in 1990) | $ 185 | $ 210 | $ (25) |
| Common stock, $.25 par value:  5,250,000 |  |  |  |
| shares authorized, 2,783,385 shares issued |  |  |  |
| and outstanding (2,657,024 in 1990) | 696 | 664 | 32 |
| Capital in excess of par value | 2,611 | 2,585 | 26 |
| Retained earnings | 7,585 | 6,279 | 1,306 |
| Total shareholders' equity | $11,077 | $ 9,738 | $1,339 |
| Total Liabilities and Shareholders' Equity | $29,703 | $26,206 | $3,497 |

## EXHIBIT 4
## Partial Summary of Cash and Other Financial Transactions During Fiscal Year 1991

1. Cash received in the course of operations during 1991 included:

   | | |
   |---|---:|
   | From customers and concessions | $25,446,000 |
   | Interest on investments | 279,000 |
   | Commercial property rental | 274,000 |
   | Other cash receipts | 26,000 |

2. Cash paid in the course of operations during 1991 included:

   | | |
   |---|---:|
   | Salaries and wages | $8,911,000 |
   | Land rentals | 1,428,000 |
   | Interest paid | 1,073,000 |
   | Other operating and miscellaneous expenses | 9,188,000 |

3. Cash dividends of $112,000 were paid in 1991.

4. CMOT made no tax payments in 1991 but expected to make an income tax payment of $100,000 early in fiscal year 1992.

5. From its inventory of real estate, CMOT sold land that had cost $221,000, resulting in a gain of $329,000. Of the total sales price, $110,000 was received in cash and the remainder in the form of a note receivable.

6. CMOT purchased plant and equipment with a total cost of $5,146,000 during 1991.

7. CMOT paid $416,000 in interest on funds borrowed to finance its investment in the Toiyabe resort, all of which was capitalized by adding the interest to prior CMOT investments in Toiyabe. Other investments in 1991 included:

   | | |
   |---|---:|
   | A loan (note receivable) to the Toiyabe Resort Company | $85,000 |
   | Capital expenditures relating to real estate held for sale | 16,000 |

   Notes receivable that were paid in full to CMOT during 1991 totaled $485,000, and $23,000 was received for miscellaneous other assets sold during the year.

8. Seasonal cash needs required CMOT to borrow $1,200,000 on a bank line of credit, all of which had been repaid by the end of the fiscal year.

9. CMOT borrowed an additional $3,344,000 in long-term debt during 1991. Some of the proceeds were used to repay $2,820,000 in long-term debt that had been outstanding at the beginning of the year.

10. During the year, a voting preferred stockholder exchanged 100,361 preferred shares for 100,361 shares of common stock. An additional 26,000 shares of common stock were issued for $33,000.

# Part Three
## Managing Financial Reporting

# Auditors and Their Opinions

**H**ow believable is the financial information that businesses—or any other organizations—make available to the public? There is a great deal in society that depends on this. If people are going to invest money in organizations, lend money to them, sell and buy things to and from them, even make contributions to them, they need to feel some confidence about what those organizations' resources are and how well they are being used. One job of auditors is to give people some confidence about financial information.

Making organizations' financial information believable is accomplished in different countries in different ways—with varying degrees of success. In the United States the primary mechanism for this was established in the aftermath of the stock market crash of 1929: Congress passed securities laws requiring almost all businesses whose stock is publicly traded to file with a governmental agency, on a regular basis, financial statements that have been examined by an independent auditor. These securities laws also gave that governmental agency (the Securities and Exchange Commission, or SEC) the authority to set accounting standards—that is, the way in which organizations' financial information is reported. For the most part, the SEC has outsourced this work of standard-setting to a nonprofit organization in the private sector, but it retains ultimate oversight over it.[1]

---

*Research Associate Jeremy Cott prepared this case under the supervision of Professor William J. Bruns, Jr.*

Copyright © 1997 by the President and Fellows of Harvard College. Harvard Business School case 197-113.

---

[1] Many organizations, both for-profit and not-for-profit, that are not legally required to have their financial statements audited do so nevertheless because potential investors, creditors, or vendors demand it.

There is a very serious social purpose behind all this—to reduce "information risk" and thus promote the efficient allocation of resources in society. No one knows whether a given business or organization is going to do well or badly in the future, but if people don't have reasonably believable information about an organization in the first place, they are not going to be able to allocate resources very well. At the very least, they will—if they want to invest in a business, for example—demand a "risk premium." Thus, setting up certain information rules and requirements ultimately reduces the risk premium that businesses have to pay and lowers their overall cost of capital.

Auditors express an "opinion" about whether an organization's financial statements present a fair picture of what is going on financially in that organization. The wording of their report is prescribed by a formal "statement of auditing standards" (published by the American Institute of Certified Public Accountants). An example is shown in **Exhibit 1**. The wording of the report may, on its surface, appear fairly bland and innocuous, but it is really a distillation of a great deal of thinking and history, with individual words chosen with great care—analogous to the wording of certain statutes or contracts. There is a lot riding on the auditor's report, including the assumption of legal responsibility.

## TITLE AND ADDRESS

The title of the report always includes the word "independent." This is meant to convey that the report is coming not from the company's managers but from accountants who are independent of them and who therefore wouldn't (presumably) be biased in what they say or do not say. (If, for example, an auditor owned some of the company's stock or held a seat on its Board of Directors, that person wouldn't be considered "independent."[2]) It has become customary, in fact, for the Board of Directors of a public corporation to assign the responsibility for hiring the auditors and responding to any concerns they may have to a special "audit committee," consisting entirely of outside directors. This is meant to provide even greater assurance of the auditors' independence, to provide a "buffer" between them and management. Moreover, the auditor's report is addressed not to the company's management but to its Board of Directors and stockholders.

The independent auditor's report contains three main sections: an *Introductory Paragraph*, which indicates the degree of responsibility that the auditor is taking; a *Scope Paragraph*, which indicates the scope of the auditor's work; and an *Opinion Paragraph*, which expresses the auditor's opinion about the validity of the financial statements in question.

---

[2]　These are the expectations in the United States. In some other countries, however, an auditor may sit on a company's Board of Directors or own some of the company's stock.

## INTRODUCTORY PARAGRAPH

This indicates who is responsible for what. The company is responsible for preparing the financial statements; the auditor is not. The auditor is carrying out more of an oversight function and is expressing an "opinion" about what people in the company have done. Furthermore, the auditor's report covers only the financial statements (and the related notes that are, as is often said, "an integral part of the financial statements"). But a company's Annual Report often contains much more than financial statements—for example, a letter from the Chief Executive, President, or Chairperson of the Board of Directors to stockholders; management's "discussion and analysis" of results; information about stock prices—and the audit has nothing to do with those other things.

## SCOPE PARAGRAPH

This indicates essentially what the auditor has done. A few words in the paragraph are really loaded:

- The audit is designed to obtain "reasonable" assurance, but not absolute assurance.
- The audit examines evidence on a "test basis," but not on a comprehensive basis. That is, it relies on a statistical sampling of the data; it doesn't examine every transaction and amount.
- The audit is designed to search for "material" misstatements, but not misstatements that are immaterial. What does "material" mean? Something that "matters," in a relative sense. For example, $10,000 may be material for a small business but completely immaterial for General Motors. The nature of an item is also a factor: a misstatement of $1,000,000 in a company's Cash balance is far more significant than a misstatement of $1,000,000 in the balance of Accumulated Depreciation. Auditing standards are ultimately quite practical in suggesting what is material: something is "material" if it is significant enough to influence the decision of a reasonable user of the financial statements (e.g., an investor or creditor or regulatory agency).

The implicit decision of society, reflected in the scope paragraph, is that there are costs as well as benefits to information and that an auditor can do only so much. What goes on in most public corporations is complicated. To require auditors to examine every financial transaction and amount—even if it were possible to do so—would cost too much, and investors wouldn't pay for it. The audit can provide only "reasonable assurance" of the validity of a company's financial statements. But that nevertheless represents a great deal: a company cannot give out whatever financial information it wants to in whatever form it wants.  There are standards against which their financial information will be judged.

## OPINION PARAGRAPH

The opinion paragraph typically consists of only one sentence.  It is the most important part of the report, however, and, for that reason, the entire report is sometimes referred to as "the auditor's opinion."

The sentence begins "In our opinion. . . ."  This means that the auditor is reasonably sure of his or her conclusions.  Earlier in the century, the typical auditor's report "certified" the company's financial statements as being "correct."  That kind of language was eventually dropped, however, because it gave the reader the incorrect impression that things could be measured exactly and without any ambiguity.  The auditor's opinion is an informed opinion, and it is extremely serious, but—like a doctor's opinion—it involves an exercise of judgment and doesn't provide any guarantees.

The key issue is whether the company's financial statements conform with "generally accepted accounting principles" (often referred to as "GAAP" in both the general business press and the accounting profession).  What *are* "generally accepted accounting principles"?  In fact, there isn't any official, definitive list.  In the United States, the SEC has the legal authority to specify acceptable accounting practices, and, for the most part, it has delegated that authority to a nonprofit organization in the private sector.[3]  What that organization says, however, is supplemented by the pronouncements and interpretations of various other professional organizations as well as by practices that become commonly accepted within certain industries.  Thus when an auditor decides whether or not a company's financial statements conform with "generally accepted accounting principles," that person not only has to consider a certain amount of ambiguity in the principles themselves but also has to exercise judgment about how general principles apply to very specific situations.  It is not a straightforward task.

The report shown in **Exhibit 1** is the standard auditor's report.  It represents an "unqualified" opinion (sometimes called a "clean" opinion).  This is what a company wants.  The report is saying essentially that the *quality* of the financial statements is fine (that is, they conform with GAAP), and there has been no problem with the *scope* of the audit (that is, nothing has prevented the auditors from gathering the evidence needed to support their opinion).

---

[3]  Since 1973, the organization that has been primarily responsible for issuing accounting standards for the private sector (both for-profit and not-for-profit organizations) is the Financial Accounting Standards Board (FASB), located in Norwalk, Connecticut.  To date, it has issued over 130 "Statements of Financial Accounting Standards."  Another organization, called the Government Accounting Standards Board (or GASB) issues accounting standards for the public sector (that is, governmental entities).

Sometimes the auditors will add some explanatory language to their report, even when they are expressing an unqualified opinion. This is a way of drawing attention to some special circumstance—for example, if part of the audit was carried out by other auditors, or if a legitimate change in accounting principles has occurred.

There are, however, three serious *exceptions* to an unqualified report:

- *Qualified opinion.*   This means that the financial statements contain some "material" departure from GAAP, or that there has been some "material" limitation placed on the scope of the auditors' work, but these problems do not overshadow the overall fairness of the statements. For example, a significant misstatement in the value of fixed assets might affect someone's willingness to lend money to the company if the assets were to be used as collateral, but the *overall* financial picture given of the company might still be fair. The wording of a qualified opinion would be similar to that of an unqualified opinion but would add the phrase "except for" and a brief explanation of what the problem is.
- *Adverse opinion.*   This is more serious. This means that the financial statements contain departures from GAAP that are so material or so pervasive that the financial statements as a whole are misleading.
- *Disclaimer of opinion.*   This means that the limitations placed on the scope of the auditors' work have been so material or so pervasive that the auditors simply do not have an adequate basis for expressing an opinion.

In practice, adverse opinions are rare because they would be of virtually no use to the client. Potential investors wouldn't invest in the company, and potential lenders wouldn't lend money to the company. If auditors feel that a client's financial statements contain such material departures from GAAP as to warrant an adverse opinion, this situation would be discussed with the company's audit committee or management, and management would probably agree to make the necessary changes because not doing so would carry intolerable implications. Auditing standards, moreover, prohibit auditors from sidestepping an adverse opinion by disclaiming an opinion.

## LEGAL IMPLICATIONS

What, however, happens in the real world? In the real world, auditors' opinions have come under increasing scrutiny and have provoked a good deal of litigation and scandal. Even harsh critics of the auditing profession in the United States acknowledge that, in the vast majority of cases, auditors' opinions are reliable.[4] In the 1980s and 1990s, however, there has been an enormous

---

[4] Mark Stevens, *The Big Six: The Selling Out of America's Top Accounting Firms* (Simon & Schuster, 1991), p. 254.

number of business failures, most significantly in the savings and loan industry, and many people—including some members of Congress—believe that auditors have not provided adequate warning to the public. People are astonished to see businesses file for bankruptcy not long after their auditors gave them a "clean" opinion. As a result, auditors in the United States have faced literally billions of dollars in damage claims.

Defenders of the profession regard many of the lawsuits as unjustified: when businesses fail, the auditors are sometimes seen as the only party left with "deep pockets," and investors and creditors may try to recoup their losses any way they can.

On the other hand, there clearly have been problems with the way in which auditors go about their work. A study by the federal government's General Accounting Office found that the audits of more than half of a sample number of bankrupt savings and loans failed "to meet professional standards." The National Commission on Fraudulent Financial Reporting, staffed by representatives of major accounting organizations, acknowledged that revenue and profit pressures in the auditing firms themselves detracted from the quality of their audits. The fact is that even though auditing firms have a responsibility to provide independent judgments about the believability of organizations' financial information—to be, in effect, a guardian of the public interest—they also have a private interest in making money. Naturally, they want to retain clients; they don't want to offend them. "As all accounting firms are well aware, clients determined to have their way on critical issues will often shop for the 'right' audit opinion, using the competition among the firms to find a 'cooperative' auditor. Those that fail to cooperate often lose the business."[5]

In response, expectations have been formally raised. Auditors used to be required to plan their search for material misstatements "within the limitations of the audit process."[6] Now they are required to be more proactive: auditors have to provide "reasonable assurance" of detecting material misstatement based on a documented assessment of specific risk factors for misstatement.[7] They first set up an audit plan, but if the risks of material misstatement appear to be greater than anticipated, they have to modify the plan. They may even have to modify it several times. A similar change has occurred regarding the possibility of bankruptcy. Auditors used to assume that their clients had the

---

[5] Ibid., p. 87.

[6] Statement of Auditing Standards 16 (effective in 1977).

[7] Statements of Auditing Standards 53 and 58 (effective in 1989) and 82 (effective in 1997). The second sentence of the "Scope Paragraph" in **Exhibit 1** ("[Generally accepted auditing standards] require that we plan and perform the audit to obtain reasonable assurance about whether the financial statements are free of material misstatement") is new to the standard auditor's report (as of 1989). The previous version of the standard auditor's report (in use since the late 1940s) contained no such assertion.

ability to continue as a "going concern."[8]  Now they are required to be more proactive on this issue as well.[9]

Finally, auditors used to assume that their clients were honest,[10] even though they were expected to carry out their work with an attitude of "professional skepticism."  Now they are expected to assume that their clients are neither honest nor dishonest.[11]

---

[8]  Statement of Auditing Standards 34 (effective in 1981).

[9]  Statement of Auditing Standards 59 (effective in 1989).

[10]  Stevens, op. cit., p. 60.

[11]  Statement of Auditing Standards 53 (effective in 1989).

**EXHIBIT 1**
**Standard Auditor's Report**

[*Title*]

**Report of Independent Auditors**

[*Addressed to:*]

**Board of Directors and Stockholders**
**of XYZ Corporation**

[*Introductory Paragraph*]

We have audited the accompanying balance sheets of XYZ Company as of June 30, 1997 and 1996, and the related statements of income, retained earnings, and cash flows for the fiscal years then ended. These financial statements are the responsibility of the Company's management. Our responsibility is to express an opinion on these financial statements based on our audits.

[*Scope Paragraph*]

We conducted our audits in accordance with generally accepted auditing standards. Those standards require that we plan and perform the audit to obtain reasonable assurance about whether the financial statements are free of material misstatement. An audit includes examining, on a test basis, evidence supporting the amounts and disclosures in the financial statements. An audit also includes assessing the accounting principles used and significant estimates made by management, as well as evaluating the overall financial statement presentation. We believe that our audits provide a reasonable basis for our opinion.

[*Opinion Paragraph*]

In our opinion, the financial statements referred to above present fairly, in all material respects, the consolidated financial position of XYZ Company as of June 30, 1997 and 1996, and the results of its operations and its cash flows for the years then ended in conformity with generally accepted accounting principles.

R. Smith & Co.
Certified Public Accountants

August 15, 1997

---

Source: Statement of Auditing Standards 58 (effective in 1989).

# Total Fitness, Inc. (A)

*As a major investor in Total Fitness, of course I was concerned with the financial well-being of the company. But for the past five years the company had grown at an average rate of at least 45% annually and had received clean audit reports. The foundation of the business seemed fine to me. . . . It turns out I was wrong.*

Jeff Sockal, investor and board member of Total Fitness, Inc.

*When I arrived in March 1991, I had not signed on for the kind of mess I have faced. I thought this was going to be some fun. I came out of retirement to return to New England and be closer to my husband's family. This was to be an exercise in turning an entrepreneurial firm into a full-fledged professionally managed company. The company had a robust market and sales were very strong. I thought it just needed to be cleaned up a bit. In the first few months I was at the company I even went out and sold $3.25 million in new equity. But by the end of the following fiscal year we had written off more than the aggregate total of all the historical income the company had ever earned.*

*In accounting there is no such thing as absolute truth. The same underlying reality can be accounted for using a range of assumptions. Throughout its entire history, Total Fitness had pushed the edge of the envelope. Instead of conservative accounting, the philosophy of this company was to choose the aggressive accounting alternative whenever there was a choice. Now with the help of new management we will change this. We hope to*

---

*Professor William J. Bruns, Jr. prepared this case with the assistance of Marc H. Zablatsky and Richard D. R. Stark, Research Associates.*

Copyright © 1994 by the President and Fellows of Harvard College. Harvard Business School case 194-019.

*present a realistic picture of our financial performance to the outside world. We need to regain the confidence of our suppliers, investors, the banks, and potential future investors. We are in business to provide a decent return for our investors, not to play creative accounting games.*

Gina LaRoche, new chief executive officer (CEO) of Total Fitness, Inc.

## COMPANY BACKGROUND

The roots of Total Fitness, Inc., dated back to 1983 when Fitness World was founded as a proprietorship. Fitness World, the first mail-order fitness reseller to focus on the needs of individuals wanting to work out at home, brought the company in close contact with the fitness community. Through this relationship, the company learned about the market and the needs of their customers. Seeing the potential to serve market niches where needs were not being met, the Fitness Products operation was founded, also as a sole proprietorship, to create and manufacture specific aerobic fitness products in 1984. In 1989 Fitness World and Fitness Products were incorporated and went public under the name Total Fitness, Inc.

Fitness World served as a "one-stop" shopping outlet for fitness professionals and amateurs, offering fitness products and related products and services. It also offered pre-sale technical support and product evaluation services. Fitness World targeted a well-defined market niche primarily through a "buyer's guide" catalog as well as specialty catalogs, direct mail solicitation, advertising, and telemarketing activities. The buyers guide catalog was distributed four times per year to approximately 450,000 fitness professionals, keen amateurs, and other potential users. Fitness World offered approximately 5,000 fitness products developed by companies ranging from small entrepreneurships to industry giants like Nordic Trak and Teva.

Fitness Products was a fitness developer which developed, manufactured, promoted, marketed, distributed, and supported fitness products. These included a family of products, the two most successful being heart rate and blood pressure monitors which were manufactured as convenient wrist units that could be worn during a workout. The company did not own these products but held exclusive, worldwide manufacturing, development, marketing, and distribution rights to them. Fitness Products and Fitness World were run as autonomous businesses.

## FIRST SIGNS OF TROUBLE

The first sign of trouble came in December 1990 (3rd quarter fiscal 1991), when there was an unusual sale of a small division of the company on the last day of the quarter that helped the company meet its earnings objective. This attracted the attention of the Board of Directors. Prior to this, no one had questioned the internal goings-on in the company because all that shareholders received were good reports with an impressive 40% to 50% compound annual growth rate, rising profits, and clean audits from a Big Six accounting firm (see **Exhibit 1**).

The Board of Directors had been concerned with the high rate of capitalization for product development costs, but it had been willing to accept management's explanation that this was all in the normal course of business. There also were rumors of loose internal control practices and insufficient reserves. But the company was hot and providing a decent return for investors, and problems tended to get swept under the rug. Despite their uneasiness, the Board approved every request for additional working capital. After all, Andrew Siebert, the founding entrepreneur, had lived up to every previous promise he had made.

By the fourth quarter of fiscal 1991 it was evident that, while sales growth had continued, profitability had declined significantly. There was also turmoil inside the company, due both to Andrew's marital problems that had distracted his attention from the business and to the firing of the corporate financial officer and a division head (two members of his senior management team) within a one-month period. The January 1991 Board of Directors meeting focused on the difficulties surrounding the company's first downturn in earnings. To satisfy the boards' concerns, Mr. Siebert asked Gina LaRoche, a retired industry expert, board member, and investor in the company, to come in and look the business over and offer constructive criticism.

## NEW MANAGEMENT AT TOTAL FITNESS, INC.

After LaRoche had spent a week on site, the nature of Siebert's request had changed. He now wanted Gina to become company president and chief operating officer (COO) and to move to Massachusetts. She accepted and became COO in March of 1991, and shortly thereafter the problems began to accelerate. By June LaRoche had been asked to take over as chief executive officer. As Gina LaRoche stated:

> When I started in March I thought everyone would see me as the good guy, the great savior on a white charger who would fix everything. But I did not know quite how loose the practices were. I was digging through this stuff and uncovering more and more questionable accounting practices and learning more and more each day. I began to wonder how in the world the auditors had bought off on this stuff. I had no idea of the extent of the problems. If I had known, I probably would not have taken on the job of turning the company around.

## THE ROAD BACK TO STABILITY

> The reason the company was in so much trouble was that Andrew had never understood that the company was no longer his once it went public in 1989.

*He continued to take the personal perks that he had in the past and to do whatever he damn well pleased. He did not understand his fiduciary responsibility to the shareholders, or the basic concepts of cash flow. When Gina came in we knew there were some internal control problems. The first request she made to the Board was that they form an audit committee. There needed to be more objectivity on the Board. In the past the company was simply controlled by Andrew. An additional outside board member was brought in to form the three-person audit committee.*

Jeff Sockal, investor and board member of Total Fitness, Inc.

Gina LaRoche started digging through the paper work for recent years. It took three or four months before the employees started to trust her, and then the true magnitude of the problem began to surface. By that time the company was already into fiscal 1992, and the books for the previous year had been closed.

What Gina LaRoche discovered was disturbing. In March of 1991 the company was running out of cash. When the bank account had been empty in the past, Andrew had simply raised more money. Andrew Siebert always seemed to be in the process of raising more money. He wanted to raise another $1 million, but this time the Board put its foot down and said no. At the company's current cash burn rate that would have lasted only 60 days. The Board demanded that he raise $3-4 million instead and get the company under control. Even before she became CEO, Gina LaRoche's mission was to get the company under control, literally and figuratively. Eventually $3.25 million in venture capital money was raised.

Gina LaRoche had been at Total Fitness only three months when the financing was completed. The fiscal 1991 audit had also already been completed. To address Gina's concerns the auditors had suggested a $60 thousand write-off. To be even more cautious, management decided that this reserve did not go deep enough and insisted on a further $150 thousand to protect the company against new areas of concern that were just being uncovered. No one knew the extent of the problems at this point, but the consensus was that the company had already dug pretty deep.

Management of Total Fitness had historically engaged in certain activities to encourage newer vendors to advertise their products in the company's catalog or to run cooperative advertising in fitness magazines such as *Shape*, *Fitness*, and *Self*. In lieu of paying cash for this advertising space, the company would sometimes accept products from these vendors and later resell those products for cash. The value of the resulting inventory depended upon the marketability of the advertisers' products. This practice was seen as a means of increasing advertising revenues, but the result was a rapid increase in slow-moving inventories beyond the company's ability to sell them. Within a month of her arrival, Gina LaRoche dramatically scaled back this practice, and at year end wrote down inventories in fiscal 1991 by $525 thousand. In fiscal 1992 management still felt that inventory was overvalued and a further charge of $714 thousand was taken against inventory.

Another problem that Gina quickly addressed was flexible pricing. Salespeople had been allowed to make deals with customers on the net selling price of the company's products. This practice had allowed the company to continue to achieve its aggressive sales growth objectives but had also dramatically affected company profitability. With the new conservatism Gina brought to the business, firm prices were set and guidelines for discounts were established and tracked.

Even before becoming CEO, Gina LaRoche set about creating a senior management team with the experience and expertise to redefine Total Fitness. It was not her explicit intention to go outside the company for the entire team, but it quickly became evident that existing management had some serious shortcomings, and that internal development of management caliber employees had not been successful.

As employees began to open up to Gina, and the realization set in that the dictatorial founder was no longer active in the company, it became clear that the magnitude of the problem was far greater than initially anticipated. Gina LaRoche was astonished by the practices that had been allowed to go unchecked by the auditors for the past few years. As she spoke of this situation her frustration was clear (see **Exhibit 2**, on the role of the independent auditor):

> *I believed that the auditors were culpable. If I could see stuff on the surface, I could not believe that the auditors did not catch some of the problems. I am referring to things like receivables from sales that were made on the last day of the fiscal year, never confirmed by the auditors, and eventually were 100% written-off . . . and receivables that were allowed to age way too long on our books with totally insufficient reserves.*
>
> *Another screwy thing the auditors never should have allowed to happen was the capitalization of development costs on products we did not even own. We had marketing rights and development obligations as part of the transaction with the third-party owners of these fitness products. But the auditors allowed the company to capitalize the development expenses and put them on our books as an asset. Firstly, how in the world can you have an asset on your books that you do not own? Secondly, we were allowed to amortize the costs over seven years, which is absolutely ludicrous in the fitness business when many products are obsolete within two years.*

During the first quarter of fiscal 1992, Gina LaRoche went to the head of the audit committee and expressed her belief that Total Fitness needed to switch auditors, or at least to switch audit partners. The audit committee believed that if the company switched auditors there would be a Securities and Exchange Commission investigation. The head of the audit committee therefore contacted the independent auditors and arranged for a new audit partner. The chairman of the audit committee took it as his personal responsibility to see to it that an adequate audit occurred.

With new management in place, a comprehensive review of Total Fitness's operations was undertaken to evaluate the ability of the company to manage effectively the profitable growth of the business with its existing organizational structure. As a result of this evaluation, the organizational structure was streamlined to eliminate redundancy, and a more traditional functional organization was instituted. In December of 1991, this reorganization resulted in the termination of 26 people (15% head count reduction) and employee severance costs of $429 thousand.

Another result of this comprehensive review was the realization that Total Fitness did not belong in the fitness development business. The Fitness Products division was bleeding cash at an alarming rate. Revenues of this division were declining, development costs were high, and the annual royalty payments were costing the company more than $1.75 million a year in cash. In March 1992, management decided to sell the Fitness Products division. This decision allowed the company to focus on the business activities at which it had been most successful and in which management believed the company had a stronger market position.

On May 28, 1992, the company sold Fitness Products' assets to Step International, Inc., for $6.7 million, of which $4.7 million was paid on the closing of the sale and the remaining $2 million was subject to certain contingencies. After including the cost of acquiring fitness products from their third-party owners and the cost of winding down Fitness Products, the transaction resulted in a loss on disposal of approximately $3.4 million. The company chose to account for the loss in fiscal 1992 instead of future time periods when the loss would actually be realized. This was consistent with management's new conservative accounting approach, since the decision to sell was made in fiscal 1992. The deal was structured in such a way that despite the losses incurred it was still a positive cash transaction (third-party owners received the majority of their compensation in equity).

With the "clean-up" behind them, management expected a difficult audit. But, since the company had initiated the write-downs and restructuring and was presenting a conservative set of financial statements to the auditors, a clean audit opinion, such as that given Total Fitness, Inc., by their auditors in 1991, was expected (see **Exhibit 3**).

## THE 1992 AUDIT

The 1992 audit took three months to complete, three times longer than audits in previous years. Everyone involved in the audit process was both physically and psychologically drained. With a new management team in place, a recent restructuring of the organization, and the sale of the financially draining Fitness Products division complete, Gina felt confident the company was well positioned to return to profitability. It was Gina's belief that the auditors would give the company a clean bill of health.

However, when the auditors finalized their opinion, they questioned the viability of Total Fitness as a "going concern."  Such a qualification had the potential to have very damaging effects on Total Fitness and its shareholders, and to significantly change relationships with suppliers, customers, lenders, and others.  The audited financial statements and auditors' opinion for 1992 are shown in **Exhibit 4**.

In the United States, a Form 10K must be filed by public companies within the 90-day period following the end of the fiscal year.  The Form 10K requires an audit opinion, and therefore Total Fitness was late in filing.

At roughly the same time as the audit opinion was finalized, the first quarter of fiscal 1993 closed with $1.4 million in cash, a positive cash flow, over $1 million in equity, and a small profit.  Immediately after filing the Form 10K a Form 10Q, which does not require an audit opinion, was filed for the first quarter ending June 30, 1992.

**EXHIBIT 1**
## The Big Six Auditing Firms in the United States

The Big Six are the premier accounting firms in the nation. Until 1989 and the megamergers that united Ernst & Whinney with Arthur Young and Deloitte Haskins & Sells with Touche Ross, the Big Eight dominated public accounting. The Big Six consist of Arthur Andersen, Coopers & Lybrand, Deloitte & Touche, Ernst & Young, KPMG Peat Marwick, and Price Waterhouse. Ranked by 1991 revenues and number of partners:

|                     | Revenues | Partners |
| ------------------- | -------- | -------- |
| Ernst & Young       | $2.26    | 2,131    |
| Arthur Andersen     | 1.99     | 1,322    |
| Deloitte & Touche   | 1.85     | 1,652    |
| KPMG Peat Marwick   | 1.77     | 1,881    |
| Coopers & Lybrand   | 1.28     | 1,252    |
| Price Waterhouse    | 1.10     | 845      |

The Big Six are no longer true "accounting firms." Consulting has grown to over 40% of their business. While the firms cling to the designation "CPAs" because of the access and image of professionalism it denotes, Mark Stevens, author of *The Big Six*, believes they are more correctly classified as holding companies, a mixture of semiautonomous service businesses functioning under a national brand.

However, overshadowed by the Big Six, the second tier of accounting firms are capable of supporting all but the largest multinationals. *Fortune 100* companies rarely stray from the "Good Housekeeping Seal of Approval" that a Big Six audit opinion denotes.

Source of Ranking Data: Bowman's Accounting Report.

## EXHIBIT 2
### The Role of the Independent Auditor

In *Statement of Financial Accounting Concepts No. 1*, the Financial Accounting Standards Board (FASB) clearly defines the role independent audits play in our free market economy:

> The effectiveness of individuals, enterprises, markets, and government in allocating scarce resources among competing uses is enhanced if those who make economic decisions have information that reflects the relative standing and performance of business enterprises to assist them in evaluating alternative courses of action and the expected returns, costs, and risks of each. . . . Independent auditors commonly examine or review financial statements and perhaps other information, and both those who provide and those who use information often view an independent auditor's opinion as enhancing the reliability or credibility of the information. (para. 16)

Below is an example of a typical engagement letter written by an auditor to a client. The engagement letter concisely states the fundamental responsibilities of both the auditor and the client in the audit process. While the engagement letter is not required by generally accepted auditing standards, it is customarily used to prevent misunderstandings about the auditor's responsibility for detecting errors, irregularities, and illegal acts, and to remind clients of the inherent limitations of an audit.

### Typical Engagement Letter

Audit Committee
X Corporation

This letter sets forth our understanding of the terms and objectives of our engagement, and the nature and scope of the services we will provide.

We will audit your financial statements as of and for the year ended December 31, 19XX, in accordance with generally accepted auditing standards. The objective of an audit is the expression of our opinion on whether the financial statements present fairly, in all material respects, the financial position, results of operations, and cash flows in conformity with generally accepted accounting principles.

As part of our audit, we will consider the Company's internal control structure, as required by generally accepted auditing standards, for the purpose of establishing a basis for determining the nature, timing, and extent of auditing procedures necessary for expressing our opinion on the financial statements. We will also read information included in the annual reports to shareholders and consider whether such information, including the manner of its presentation, is consistent with information appearing in the financial statements.

Our audit will include procedures designed to provide reasonable assurance of detecting errors and irregularities that are material to the financial statements. As you are aware, however, there are inherent limitations in the auditing process. For example, audits are based on the concept of selective testing of the data being examined and are, therefore, subject to the limitation that such matters, if they exist, may not be detected. Also, because of the

**EXHIBIT 2 (continued)**

characteristics of irregularities, including attempts at concealment through collusion and forgery, a properly designed and executed audit may not detect a material irregularity.

Similarly, in performing our audit we will be aware of the possibility that illegal acts may have occurred. However, it should be recognized that our audit provides no assurance that illegal acts, other than those having a direct and material effect on the determination of financial statements amounts, will be detected. We will inform you with respect to illegal acts or material errors and irregularities that come to our attention during the course of our audit.

You recognize that the financial statements and the establishment and maintenance of an internal control structure are the responsibility of management. Appropriate supervisory review procedures are necessary to provide reasonable assurance that adopted policies and prescribed procedures are adhered to and to identify errors and irregularities or illegal acts. As part of our aforementioned consideration of the Company's internal control structure, we will inform you of matters that come to our attention that represent significant deficiencies in the design or functioning of the internal control structure.

Generally accepted auditing standards require that we communicate certain additional matters to you or, alternatively, assure ourselves that management has appropriately made you aware of those matters. Such matters specifically include (1) the initial selection of and changes in significant accounting policies and their application; (2) the process used by management in formulating particularly sensitive accounting estimates and the basis for our conclusions regarding the reasonableness of those estimates; (3) audit adjustments that could, in our judgment, either individually or in the aggregate, have a significant effect on your financial reporting process; (4) any disagreements with management whether or not satisfactorily resolved, about matters that individually or in the aggregate could be significant to the financial statements or our report; (5) our views about matters that were the subject of management's consultations with other accountants about auditing and accounting matters; (6) major issues that were discussed with management in connection with the retention of our services, including, among other matters, any discussions regarding the application of accounting principles and auditing standards; and (7) serious difficulties that we encountered in dealing with management related to the performance of the audit.

At the conclusion of the engagement, we will be supplied with a representation letter, that among other things, will confirm management's responsibility for the preparation of the financial statements in conformity with generally accepted accounting principles, the availability of financial records and related data, the completeness and availability of all minutes of board of directors (and committee) meetings, and the absence of irregularities involving management or those employees who have significant roles in the control structure.

We shall be pleased to discuss this letter with you.

Source: *Montgomery's Auditing, 11th Edition.* Reprinted by permission of John Wiley & Sons, Inc.

**EXHIBIT 3**
**Report of Independent Auditors, 1991**

The Board of Directors and Shareholders
Total Fitness, Inc.

We have audited the accompanying consolidated balance sheets of Total Fitness, Inc., as of March 31, 1991 and 1990, and the related consolidated statements of income, stockholders' equity, and cash flows for each of the three years in the period ended March 31, 1991. These financial statements are the responsibility of the company's management. Our responsibility is to express an opinion on these financial statements based on our audit.

We conducted our audits in accordance with generally accepted auditing standards. Those standards require that we plan and perform the audit to obtain reasonable assurance about whether the financial statements are free of material misstatement. An audit includes examining, on a test basis, evidence supporting the amounts and disclosures in the financial statements. An audit also includes assessing the accounting principles used and significant estimates made by management, as well as evaluating the overall financial statement presentation. We believe that our audits provide a reasonable basis for our opinion.

In our opinion, the consolidated financial statements referred to above present fairly, in all material respects, the consolidated financial position of Total Fitness, Inc., as of March 31, 1991 and 1990, and the consolidated results of their operations and cash flows for each of the three years in the period ended March 31, 1991, in conformity with generally accepted accounting principles.

A Big Six Auditor

New York, New York
May 3, 1991

## EXHIBIT 4
### Financial Statements and Auditors' Opinion, 1992

Consolidated Statement of Operations—Total Fitness, Inc.

| | Years Ended March 31, | | |
| --- | --- | --- | --- |
| | 1992 | 1991 | 1990 |
| **Revenues:** | | | |
| Net product sales | $30,647,974 | $24,107,251 | $13,217,826 |
| Net marketing services income | 6,167,944 | 4,607,756 | 3,152,281 |
| | 36,815,918 | 28,715,007 | 16,370,107 |
| **Cost and expenses:** | | | |
| Cost of products sold | 23,574,260 | 17,185,498 | 9,414,572 |
| Cost of marketing services income | 4,135,029 | 4,473,075 | 2,107,618 |
| Selling, general, and administrative expenses | 9,672,072 | 7,564,625 | 4,176,133 |
| Restructuring charges | 429,000 | — | — |
| | 37,810,361 | 29,223,198 | 15,698,323 |
| | (994,443) | (508,191) | 671,784 |
| Interest expense, net | 276,084 | 169,778 | 63,469 |
| Other | (8,550) | 23,441 | — |
| (LOSS) INCOME FROM CONTINUING OPERATIONS BEFORE INCOME TAXES | (1,261,977) | (701,410) | 608,315 |
| Provision (benefit) for income taxes | (72,347) | (453,721) | 243,851 |
| (LOSS) INCOME FROM CONTINUING OPERATIONS | (1,189,630) | (247,689) | 364,464 |
| **Discontinued operation:** | | | |
| (Loss) income from discontinued operation (net of income taxes (benefit) of $(405,198), $653,721, and $173,149 in 1992, 1991, and 1990 respectively) | (3,306,553) | 356,870 | 258,793 |
| Provision for loss on disposal | (3,356,229) | — | — |
| NET (LOSS) INCOME | $ (7,852,412) | $ 109,181 | $ 623,257 |
| **Primary per share amounts:** | | | |
| From continuing operations | $(0.75) | $(0.10) | $0.18 |
| From discontinued operations | (3.26) | 0.15 | 0.12 |
| NET (LOSS) INCOME PER SHARE | $(4.01) | $ 0.05 | $0.30 |
| **Fully diluted per share amounts:** | | | |
| From continuing operations | — | — | $0.17 |
| From discontinued operations | — | — | 0.12 |
| NET INCOME PER SHARE | — | — | $0.29 |

## EXHIBIT 4 (continued)

Consolidated Balance Sheets—Total Fitness, Inc.

| | March 31, 1992 | March 31, 1991 |
|---|---|---|
| **ASSETS** | | |
| **Current Assets** | | |
| Cash and cash equivalents | $   579,386 | $   852,573 |
| Accounts receivable—trade, net of allowance for doubtful accounts of $471,353 in 1992 ($325,820 in 1991) | 3,180,316 | 3,387,900 |
| Accounts receivable—product, net of allowance for doubtful account of $139,070 in 1992 ($566,889 in 1991) | 638,598 | 330,730 |
| Inventory | 1,565,736 | 1,297,707 |
| Other current assets | 736,749 | 517,637 |
| Net current assets of discontinued operation | — | 874,639 |
| TOTAL CURRENT ASSETS | $ 6,700,785 | $ 7,261,186 |
| EQUIPMENT AND LEASEHOLD IMPROVEMENTS, net | 593,388 | 557,551 |
| NET NONCURRENT ASSETS RELATED TO DISPOSAL OF DISCONTINUED OPERATION | 2,000,000 | — |
| NET NONCURRENT ASSETS OF DISCONTINUED OPERATION | 58,041 | 1,758,340 |
| OTHER ASSETS | 96,634 | 485,201 |
| | $ 9,448,848 | $10,062,278 |
| **LIABILITIES AND STOCKHOLDERS' EQUITY (DEFICIT)** | | |
| **Current Liabilities** | | |
| Accounts payable—trade | $ 3,430,577 | $ 3,459,340 |
| Accrued payroll | 191,668 | 130,396 |
| Other accrued expenses | 704,903 | 286,936 |
| Accrued costs for disposal of discontinued operation | 366,021 | — |
| Customer advances | 151,308 | 168,358 |
| Line of credit | 2,400,000 | 2,500,000 |
| Current portion of long-term debt | — | 1,683 |
| Current portion of capitalized lease obligations | — | 15,263 |
| Net current liabilities of discontinued operation | 105,513 | — |
| TOTAL CURRENT LIABILITIES | $ 7,349,990 | $ 6,561,976 |
| LONG-TERM DEBT-RELATED PARTY | 300,000 | 300,000 |
| DEFERRED INCOME TAXES | — | 264,000 |
| LONG-TERM ACCRUED COST OF DISPOSAL OF DISCONTINUED OPERATION | 3,591,360 | — |
| COMMITMENTS AND CONTINGENCIES | | |
| STOCKHOLDERS' EQUITY (DEFICIT) | | |
| Preferred stock, $.01 par value, authorized 2,000,000 shares, 300,926 issued and outstanding | 3,009 | — |
| Common stock, voting, $.01 par value, authorized 10,000,000 shares; issued 2,081,172 shares (2,063,028 in 1991) | 20,811 | 20,630 |
| Additional paid-in capital | 5,235,624 | 2,114,561 |
| Cumulative translation adjustment | 6,125 | 6,770 |
| Retained (deficit) earnings | (6,974,414) | 877,998 |
| | $(1,708,845) | $ 3,019,959 |
| Less treasury stock at cost, 25,101 shares | (83,657) | (83,657) |
| TOTAL STOCKHOLDERS' EQUITY (DEFICIT) | $(1,792,502) | $ 2,936,302 |
| | $ 9,448,848 | $10,062,278 |

## EXHIBIT 4 (continued)

Consolidated Statements of Cash Flows—Total Fitness, Inc.

| | Years Ended March 31, | | |
| --- | --- | --- | --- |
| | 1992 | 1991 | 1990 |
| **Operating Activities** | | | |
| Net (loss) income from continuing operations | $(1,189,630) | $ (247,689) | $ 364,464 |
| Adjustments to reconcile net (loss) income to net cash provided by operating activities: | | | |
| Sale of advertising for product | (2,707,524) | (2,188,781) | (2,418,264) |
| Depreciation | 235,618 | 174,850 | 126,206 |
| Provision for losses on inventory | 667,333 | 75,000 | 36,435 |
| Provision for doubtful accounts receivable | 1,223,239 | 1,319,500 | 373,815 |
| Other | (8,550) | 23,441 | — |
| Deferred income tax provision | (264,000) | 106,000 | 113,000 |
| Change in assets and liabilities: | | | |
| Decrease (increase) in accounts receivable | 42,584 | (1,075,946) | (1,980,789) |
| Decrease in inventory | 406,055 | 1,334,518 | 953,738 |
| (Increase) decrease in other current assets | (219,112) | (286,523) | 344,010 |
| Decrease (increase) in other assets | 397,117 | (343,155) | (3,300) |
| (Decrease) increase in accounts payable | (28,763) | 1,334,527 | 1,247,749 |
| Increase (decrease) in accrued payroll | 61,272 | (41,737) | 135,114 |
| Increase (decrease) in other accrued expenses | 417,967 | (240,940) | 263,951 |
| (Decrease) increase in customer advances | (17,050) | 64,903 | 32,907 |
| Total adjustments | $ 206,186 | $ 255,657 | $ (775,428) |
| Net cash provided by (used for) continuing operating activities | $ (983,444) | $ 7,968 | $ (410,964) |
| Net cash used for discontinued operating activities | (2,024,950) | (841,596) | (405,571) |
| Net cash used for operating activities | $(3,008,394) | $ (833,628) | $ (816,535) |
| **Investing Activities** | | | |
| Capital expenditures for equipment and leasehold improvements | (271,455) | (514,819) | (243,524) |
| Other | — | (43,332) | — |
| Cash used for investing activities | $ (271,455) | $ (558,151) | $ (243,524) |
| **Financing Activities** | | | |
| Net proceeds from bank loans and line of credit | — | 2,200,000 | 991,250 |
| Principal debt payments | (101,683) | (674,774) | (240,489) |
| Principal payments under capital leases | (15,263) | (43,547) | (22,191) |
| Net proceeds from debt to related party | — | 300,000 | — |
| Proceeds from issuance of common stock and warrants | 59,252 | 318,500 | — |
| Proceeds from issuance of preferred stock | 3,065,001 | — | — |
| Cash provided by financing activities | $ 3,007,307 | $ 2,100,179 | $ 728,570 |
| Effect of exchange rate changes on cash | (645) | 6,770 | — |
| NET (DECREASE) INCREASE IN CASH AND CASH EQUIVALENTS | $ (273,187) | $ 715,170 | $ (331,489) |
| Cash and cash equivalents at beginning of year | 852,573 | 137,403 | 468,892 |
| CASH AND CASH EQUIVALENTS AT END OF YEAR | $ 579,386 | $ 852,573 | $ 137,403 |

## EXHIBIT 4 (continued)

Consolidated Statements of Cash Flows (Continued)—Total Fitness, Inc.

| | Years Ended March 31, | | |
| --- | --- | --- | --- |
| | 1992 | 1991 | 1990 |
| **Supplemental disclosures of cash flow information** | | | |
| Interest paid | $ 316,980 | $ 188,333 | $ 88,360 |
| Taxes paid | $    — | $ 285,829 | $ 143,825 |
| **Supplemental schedules of noncash investing and financing activities** | | | |
| Collection of accounts receivable—product | $ 1,341,417 | $ 1,738,180 | $ 1,461,438 |
| Net book value of Quik-Trim product line sold | $    — | $ 1,440,549 | $    — |
| Deferred gain on sale of Quik-Trim product line | $    — | $  (49,451) | $    — |
| Accrued cost for disposal of discontinued operation | $ 2,833,333 | $    — | $    — |

**EXHIBIT 4 (continued)**
**Report of Independent Auditors**

The Board of Directors and Stockholders
Total Fitness, Inc.

We have audited the accompanying consolidated balance sheets of Total Fitness, Inc., as of March 31, 1992 and 1991, and the related consolidated statements of operations, stockholders' equity (deficit), and cash flows for each of the three years in the period ended March 31, 1992. These financial statements are the responsibility of the company's management. Our responsibility is to express an opinion on these financial statements based on our audits.

We conducted our audits in accordance with generally accepted auditing standards. Those standards require that we plan and perform the audit to obtain reasonable assurance about whether the financial statements are free of material misstatement. An audit includes examining, on a test basis, evidence supporting the amounts and disclosures in the financial statements. An audit also includes assessing the accounting principles used and significant estimates made by management, as well as evaluating the overall financial statement presentation. We believe that our audits provide a reasonable basis for our opinion.

In our opinion, the consolidated financial statements referred to above present fairly, in all material respects, the consolidated financial position of Total Fitness, Inc., at March 31, 1992 and 1991, and the consolidated results of its operations and its cash flows for each of the three years in the period ended March 31, 1992, in conformity with generally accepted accounting principles.

The accompanying consolidated financial statements have been prepared assuming that Total Fitness, Inc., will continue as a going concern. The Company incurred a net loss for its fiscal year ended March 31, 1992, has had aggregate negative cash flow from continuing operations during its last three fiscal years, had a deficiency in its total working capital at March 31, 1992, and had borrowings of $2,400,000 under a line of credit expiring August 1, 1992, which line of credit has not been extended or refinanced. These conditions raised substantial doubt about the Company's ability to continue as a going concern. The consolidated financial statements do not include any adjustments to reflect the possible future effects on the recoverability and classification of assets or the amounts and classifications of liabilities that may result from the outcome of this uncertainty.

A Big Six Auditor

New York, New York
July 13, 1992

## Esperanto for Accountants

For nearly two decades, many American multinational corporations have urged the creation of financial Esperanto: a single set of accounting rules acceptable to investors and regulators in all of the world's major capital markets. But now that the London-based International Accounting Standards Committee (IASC) is close to rolling out universal accounting standards, some American companies are getting cold feet. That's because, looking down the road, many U.S. companies fear that standards set in London may one day replace standards currently used in the United States.

American companies are especially worried about the IASC's proposed rules in these four key areas:

**Accounting for mergers and acquisitions**  When U.S. companies acquire other companies for stock, they can often account for the acquired assets on a "pooling of interest" basis. In essence, this means the acquiring company can fold the new assets into its balance sheet without marking up (or down) the assets' values—important because it avoids loading the balance sheet with goodwill.

Under the proposed international rules, pooling would be effectively banned. This could make a huge difference to some companies' earnings. Take AT&T's $7.5 billion merger (for AT&T stock) with NCR. Using the pooling method, AT&T was able to combine NCR's assets into AT&T at book value. No goodwill was created. But the International Accounting Standards Committee's proposed rules would have forced AT&T to account for the transaction using the "purchase" method of business combinations. The purchase method could have put onto AT&T's books as much as $5.7 billion in goodwill, to be written off against earnings over several years.

---

*Roula Khalaf prepared this article.*

Reprinted by permission of FORBES Magazine © Forbes Inc., 1992.

Is that sound accounting?  A growing number of accountants think so.  "At some point, the Financial Accounting Standards Board will likely have to take up the issue," says Ernst & Young partner Norman Strauss.  International Accounting Standards Committee Chairman Arthur Wyatt defends his preference for purchase over pooling this way:  "If you go out and buy a television set for your business, you should record it at what it cost you.  But pooling brings old values into the balance sheet."

**Amortizing goodwill**  Current U.S. accounting rules allow companies to write off goodwill over as long as 40 years.  But the proposed international standards would cut that amortization period to a maximum of 20 years, with five years proposed for all but unusual situations.  If AT&T were forced to write off the NCR goodwill over five years, that would knock more than $1 billion a year off earnings.

Here, too, many accountants think shorter goodwill amortization periods are a good idea.  Says Dennis Beresford, former head of FASB:  "We might decide to limit goodwill amortization to 20 years, or certainly something less than 40."

There is some good news for U.S. companies here.  Currently, regulators in Britain, Germany, and Japan allow their companies to write off goodwill immediately against equity, with no charge to earnings.  Thus the IASC's goodwill proposals stand to hurt some of these companies more than U.S. companies.

**Inventory accounting**  U.S. companies typically choose between two inventory accounting methods:  LIFO (last in, first out) and FIFO (first in, first out).  More U.S. companies choose LIFO, which reduces inventory profits and tax bills.  But the proposed international rules would forbid LIFO and force companies to use FIFO.

"We were in support of the international effort up until the proposal to eliminate LIFO," says John Wulff, controller at Union Carbide.  Wulff says that if Union Carbide had been suddenly forced to switch from LIFO to FIFO in 1990, its reported $632 million pretax income would have jumped by $360 million.  That could have increased Carbide's tax bill by as much as $120 million.  Wulff's concern:  if the IASC bans LIFO, U.S. regulators may one day follow suit.

**Research and development**  In the United States, all R&D costs must be expensed against earnings in the year they are incurred.  But the proposed international rules would allow some development costs to be capitalized— recorded on the balance sheet as assets—if the company could prove there was a market for the products to which the development spending related, and costs could be recovered.  This would be a real boon to the bottom line of many U.S. drug and technology companies, although it might also give many foreign companies better access to U.S. capital markets.

Supported in theory by the Securities & Exchange Commission and regulators from other developed countries, new international rules may cause confusion. U.S. multinationals will continue to use U.S. standards when reporting to American shareholders, but could be forced to use international standards when reporting to Japanese and European shareholders. Meanwhile, foreign companies using U.S. financial markets will be allowed to use the international standards if approved by the SEC. Comparing the financial statements of IBM and Siemens will take more imagination than ever.

Longer term, the United States will be under pressure to conform to international standards, no matter how much that might hurt companies' bottom lines. "We're trying to reduce the uncertainties and the barriers that exist across the world's capital markets," says IASC chairman Wyatt. "If U.S. companies benefit, fine; if they suffer, that's too bad."

# WPP Group and Its Acquisitions

**M**artin Sorrell, chief executive officer (CEO) of London's WPP Group, supervised his firm's acquisition of New York's JWT Group, parent company of J. Walter Thompson, in 1987. Goodwill of $465 million was recognized on the deal and WPP took this amount out of its shareholders' equity account, leaving the company with a negative £64 million net worth at the end of that year. But in 1988, WPP said that the brand-name value of J. Walter Thompson and JWT's Hill and Knowlton public relations firm was £175 million. At the end of 1988, WPP reported shareholders' equity of positive £61 million. To outsiders, this change in value seemed impossible to explain, but the explanation could be found in a discrepancy between standard accounting procedures in the United States and the United Kingdom.

A year later, in mid-1989, Sorrell bought Ogilvy & Mather (O&M) for $862 million, bringing the controversy to the forefront again. The O&M brand name was also valued at £175 million. Now, even with the controversial accounting policy, WPP's balance sheet carried £600 million in long-term debt and negative stockholders' equity of £330 million. (See **Exhibit 1** for WPP 1987, 1988, and 1989 financial statements.)

## BACKGROUND

WPP Group PLC was an enormous communications empire with revenues of nearly £1 billion in 1989. WPP's six service sectors included strategic marketing, media advertising, public relations, market research, nonmedia advertising, and specialist communications.

*Susan S. Harmeling prepared this case under the supervision of Professor William J. Bruns, Jr.*

Copyright © 1991 by the President and Fellows of Harvard College. Harvard Business School case 192-038.

Martin Sorrell had built WPP from nothing.  From 1977, after earning his MBA from the Harvard Business School, until 1986, he was chief financial officer to the leading British advertising agency, Saatchi & Saatchi.  But Sorrell's responsibilities there went beyond financial matters.  He helped Maurice and Charles Saatchi build their small shop into an international firm touting the virtues of "global marketing," which to them meant selling a product the same way in every country.

Sorrell explained, "Maurice and Charles Saatchi used global marketing to differentiate themselves from others."[1]  Eventually, Sorrell came to believe that global marketing could work for a few choice brands like Coca-Cola and Marlboro, but in reality only a small portion of an advertising agency's revenues could realistically come from such products.

So in 1986, when Sorrell left Saatchi & Saatchi, he pursued a very different strategy.  He set out to acquire a number of small shops in specialty areas of marketing services.  He began by purchasing a British maker of grocery baskets and used it to acquire several small marketing firms.

At that time, in early 1986, Sorrell claimed that he was "three or four years away"[2] from making a big advertising agency purchase.  But at the end of 1986, a New York analyst mentioned JWT to Sorrell.  JWT, along with its affiliated public relations group Hill and Knowlton, had suffered two quarters of losses, the company's CEO and chairman had left, and major clients were putting their accounts up for review.

Meanwhile, Sorrell discovered that about 30% of JWT's business came from marketing services other than advertising in fast-growing sectors like public relations and market research.  In February 1987, Sorrell decided to acquire JWT, and with JWT's disappointing record on Wall Street, he had every reason to believe his bid would succeed.  WPP quietly accumulated just under 5% of JWT at an average price of $31 per share between March and June 1987.  On June 10, Sorrell surprised everyone with his $45 per share cash bid for JWT.  Five days later, he raised the bid to $50.50 per share as rumors of rival bidders surfaced.  After meeting with his advisers at First Boston Corp. on June 25, Sorrell delivered his clinching bid of $55.50 per share.  With the generous earnings multiples awarded to ad agencies in Britain, some $340 million of the $566 million purchase price came from a new stock offering and the remainder from long-term debt.

This acquisition marked the beginning of a heated debate over how to account for brand names and goodwill on the balance sheet and on income statements.  After the acquisitions were completed, the two brand names together were valued at £175 million, with JWT representing £150 million and Hill and

---

[1]  Marcia Berss, "The Bad Boy of Advertising," *Forbes,* July 8, 1991, p. 49.

[2]  Richard A. Melcher and Mark N. Vamos, "Hang On, Madison Avenue, Martin Sorrell Isn't Finished," *Business Week,* July 13, 1987, p. 81.

Knowlton £25 million. Such substantial valuation of brand names as intangible assets had many observers questioning WPP's accounting.

Two years later, Sorrell and WPP bought O&M for $862 million—26 times O&M's earnings. Sorrell rationalized the high prices he paid for both companies in the following three ways:

1. The pound was strong against the dollar, making U.S. properties relative bargains.
2. His stock was strong. When Sorrell bought JWT, WPP traded at about 35 times earnings, versus a multiple of about 15 for most U.S. ad companies.
3. U.K. accounting rules allowed goodwill to be written off as a charge to owners' equity when purchased, rather than capitalized to be expensed as a charge against earnings in future years (as practiced according to U.S. rules).[3]

With respect to Sorrell and WPP valuing the brand names and capitalizing them, in effect reversing part of the goodwill write-off, he said, "I see no difference between valuing a brand and valuing a piece of property. Advertising agencies' names can be brands in the same way as KitKat or Polo."[4] He was unmoved by the protests of accountants that such intangibles should not be taken into account on balance sheets. He observed, "I wanted our balance sheets to reflect a true and fair view of the value of the assets. It is unfortunate that accounting systems were designed for manufacturing companies and not for service companies."[5]

## THE GOODWILL CONTROVERSY

For the sake of debate, the issue of brands was "inextricably linked to the goodwill issue in the minds of most finance directors:"[6]

> *British firms used brand values primarily to boost their balance sheets; by recording brand values as intangible assets, they could magically increase their assets while drawing attention to their important brands. U.S. accounting rules didn't allow any such advantages.*
>
> *Brand valuations made sense for companies that were potential takeover targets, too. A company thinking that its stock was undervalued might make its brand values public in order to prompt an increase in the share price and thwart potential raiders. . . .*[7]

---

[3] Berss, *Forbes*, loc. cit.

[4] "The Art of Valuing Agency Brands," *Sunday Times, London*, July 2, 1989.

[5] Ibid.

[6] David Waller, "Gloves Will Soon Come Off in Goodwill Battle," *Financial Times*, August 3, 1989.

[7] Joanne Lipman, "British Value Brand Names—Literally," *The Wall Street Journal*, February 9, 1989, p. B4.

Many other companies, such as Grand Metropolitan and Ranks Hovis MacDougall, also put high brand values on their balance sheets.

Goodwill was treated very differently in the United States and the United Kingdom. In fact, the problem of goodwill was dealt with differently around the world. In the United States, the goodwill issue only arose when a purchaser was paying some amount in excess of the fair market value of identifiable assets of the target firm. This excess could arise, for example, because of a particularly strong brand name that was expected to be of some mutually agreed-upon value in the future. In the United States, goodwill was capitalized on the balance sheet and written off against the income statement over a maximum period of 40 years.

In the United Kingdom, goodwill was written off against shareholders' equity at the time of purchase. It was *not* charged as an expense item against income, so that companies in the United Kingdom did not have to burden their future earnings by charging goodwill against the income statement.

In certain firms, advertising agencies, for example, where tangible assets (desks, paper, office equipment) were quite small relative to intangible assets (the good reputation of the company, intellectual property, etc.), this discrepancy in accounting practices was significant indeed. For such firms in the United States, the write-off of these large intangible assets as an expense on the income statement had a greater impact on future earnings relative to firms in the United Kingdom, where the entire transaction was completed at the time of purchase.

## THE BRAND VALUATION PROCESS

In order to measure the value of a given brand name, it was necessary to develop a system that was both "objective and scientific." This was easier to do for consumer goods than for the "brand name" of a service firm such as an advertising agency. For consumer goods, the procedure, developed at the Henley Centre, an economic forecasting consultancy in London owned by WPP Group, worked as follows: First, the level of income arising from sales of a brand was split conceptually into two categories—those sales due to short-run marketing influences and those sales due to loyalty to the brand. The aim of this approach was to isolate short-run marketing influences by obtaining a mathematical formula based on statistical analysis to explain the sales of the brand in the recent past.

Once brand loyalty sales had been isolated, the profit element attributed to brand loyalty could be assessed. At any point in time, however, many factors could operate in determining the total level of sales of a brand. This range of factors likely to exercise a systematic and important influence on sales included spending power of consumers, demographics, price, competitors' price, advertising, competitors' advertising, promotion, and distribution. For each brand, a unique mathematical formula was generated, and the appraisers were allowed to choose which factors were important in a particular case. Once the formula was derived and tested, the level of brand loyalty sales could be calculated.

Although this technique was proven to work well for consumer goods, there were practical problems in obtaining information on these factors and especially in obtaining information on competitors, in the case of service firms. But even before consideration of those problems, there was a further point related to services that needed to be examined. This was the extent to which loyalty to the service depended upon the individual providing the service rather than the brand. (See **Exhibit 2** for a more detailed description of these problems.)

In addition, there was a major difference in auditing standards between the United States and the United Kingdom. In the United States, an auditor, working with the firm he or she was to represent, had to follow strict guidelines, the generally accepted accounting principles (GAAP). It was the responsibility of the auditor to follow these guidelines or risk prosecution for material misstatement or fraud (from *The New Auditor's Report* of the AICPA).

In the United Kingdom, the overriding requirement was to give a "true and fair view" of the value of the assets of any given company. The British philosophy was that rules alone could not necessarily result in a complete measure of value. Thus, all relevant information regarding value had to be weighed and taken into account in each specific case.

This approach was difficult to define and thus gave auditors in the United Kingdom more discretion in deciding what the "true and fair" value really was for each firm. In addition, while GAAP restricted U.S. auditors from certain "liberal" practices, the "true and fair" approach allowed U.K. auditors to measure value in closer accordance with the wishes of each firm's management team.

## EXHIBIT 1
**Excerpts from Annual Reports of the WPP Group PLC for the Years 1987, 1988, and 1989 (including the Consolidated Profit and Loss Accounts, End-of-Year Consolidated Balance Sheets, Selected Notes from the Annual Reports, and Auditors' Reports).**

### Consolidated Profit and Loss Account (for the year ended 31 December 1987)

|  | 1987 £000 | 1986 £000 | 1987 $000 | 1986 $000 |
|---|---|---|---|---|
| **Turnover** | £ 284,082 | £ 23,685 | $ 477,258 | $ 39,791 |
| Cost of sales | (65,160) | (17,761) | (109,469) | (29,839) |
| **Gross Profit** | £ 218,922 | £ 5,924 | $ 367,789 | $ 9,952 |
| Other operating expenses | (197,468) | (4,502) | (331,746) | (7,563) |
| **Operating Profit** | £ 21,454 | £ 1,422 | $ 36,043 | $ 2,389 |
| Interest receivable | 3,739 | 530 | 6,282 | 891 |
| Interest payable and similar charges | (11,076) | (195) | (18,608) | (328) |
| **Profit on Ordinary Activities before Taxation** | £ 14,117 | £ 1,757 | $ 23,717 | $ 2,952 |
| Tax on profit on ordinary activities | (6,810) | (613) | (11,441) | (1,030) |
| **Profit on Ordinary Activities after Taxation** | £ 7,307 | £ 1,144 | $ 12,276 | $ 1,922 |
| Minority interests | (222) | (75) | (373) | (126) |
| **Profit before Extraordinary Items** | £ 7,085 | £ 1,069 | $ 11,903 | $ 1,796 |
| Extraordinary items | — | 32 | — | 54 |
| **Profit for the Financial Year** | £ 7,085 | £ 1,101 | $ 11,903 | $ 1,850 |
| Dividends paid and proposed | (2,337) | (352) | (3,926) | (592) |
| **Retained Profit for the Year** | £ 4,748 | £ 749 | $ 7,977 | $ 1,258 |
| Earnings per share | 32.1p | 13.2p | $ 0.54 | $ 0.22 |

The main reporting currency of the group is the pound sterling and the accounts have been prepared on this basis. Solely for convenience, the accounts set out are also presented expressed in U.S. dollars using the approximate average rate for the year for the profit and loss account ($1.68 = £1), the rate in effect on 31 December 1987 for the balance sheets ($1.8785 = £1), and a combination of these for the statement of source and application of funds. This translation should not be construed as a representation that the pound sterling amounts actually represent or could be converted into U.S. dollars at the rates indicated.

**EXHIBIT 1 (continued)**
**Consolidated Balance Sheet (as at 31 December 1987)**

|  | 1987 £000 | 1986 £000 | 1987 $000 | 1986 $000 |
|---|---|---|---|---|
| **Fixed Assets** | | | | |
| Tangible assets | £  79,184 | £  4,801 | $ 148,747 | $  9,019 |
| Investments | 3,464 | — | 6,507 | — |
|  | £  82,648 | £  4,801 | $ 155,254 | $  9,019 |
| **Current Assets** | | | | |
| Stocks and work-in-progress | £  37,920 | £  1,810 | $  71,233 | $  3,400 |
| Debtors | 247,836 | 11,852 | 465,560 | 22,263 |
| Assets held for resale and investments | 115,273 | 1,040 | 216,540 | 1,954 |
| Cash at bank and in hand | 72,616 | 8,554 | 136,409 | 16,069 |
|  | £ 473,645 | £ 23,256 | $ 889,742 | $ 43,686 |
| **Creditors:** amounts falling due within one year | (454,733) | (21,510) | (854,216) | (40,407) |
| **Net Current Assets** | £  18,912 | £  1,746 | $  35,526 | $  3,279 |
| **Total Assets less Current Liabilities** | 101,560 | 6,547 | 190,780 | 12,298 |
| **Creditors:** amounts falling due after more than one year | (91,333) | (2,725) | (171,568) | (5,119) |
| **Provisions for Liabilities and Charges** | (74,719) | (300) | (140,360) | (563) |
| **Net Assets (Liabilities)** | £ (64,492) | £  3,522 | $(121,148) | $  6,616 |
| **Capital and Reserves** | | | | |
| Called-up share capital | £   3,670 | £  1,139 | $   6,894 | $  2,139 |
| Share premium | — | 8,396 | — | 15,772 |
| Merger reserve | (89,423) | (9,388) | (167,981) | (17,635) |
| Other reserves | 13,233 | 646 | 24,858 | 1,213 |
| Profit and loss account | 6,963 | 2,027 | 13,080 | 3,808 |
| **Shareholders' Funds** | £ (65,557) | £  2,820 | $(123,149) | $  5,297 |
| Minority interests | 1,065 | 702 | 2,001 | 1,319 |
| **Total Capital Employed** | £ (64,492) | £  3,522 | $(121,148) | $  6,616 |

Signed on behalf of the Board on 6 May 1988
R.E. Lerwill and M.S. Sorrell, Directors

The main reporting currency of the group is the pound sterling and the accounts have been prepared on this basis. Solely for convenience, the accounts set out are also presented expressed in U.S. dollars using the approximate average rate for the year for the profit and loss account ($1.68 = £1), the rate in effect on 31 December 1987 for the balance sheets ($1.8785 = £1), and a combination of these for the statement of source and application of funds. This translation should not be construed as a representation that the pound sterling amounts actually represent or could be converted into U.S. dollars at the rates indicated.

**EXHIBIT 1 (continued)**
**Notes to the Accounts (31 December 1987)**

**Note 11—Tangible Fixed Assets**
a)  Group
The movement in the year was as follows:

(£000)

| | Freehold | Long Leasehold | Short Leasehold | Plant and Machinery | Fixtures and Fittings | Motor Vehicles | Total |
|---|---|---|---|---|---|---|---|
| **Cost or valuation:** | | | | | | | |
| Beginning of year | 2,147 | 88 | 569 | 1,905 | 1,615 | 929 | **7,253** |
| New subsidiaries | 7,878 | 4,094 | 40,580 | 1,668 | 25,345 | 1,325 | **80,890** |
| Additions | 1,486 | 316 | 1,726 | 574 | 4,045 | 1,131 | **9,278** |
| Disposals | (429) | (112) | (883) | (322) | (1,949) | (635) | **(4,330)** |
| Exchange adjustments | 130 | (155) | (5,481) | (155) | (2,985) | (103) | **(8,749)** |
| Revaluation | 1,474 | — | — | — | — | — | **1,474** |
| End of year (see below) | 12,686 | 4,231 | 36,511 | 3,670 | 26,071 | 2,647 | **85,816** |
| **Depreciation:** | | | | | | | |
| Beginning of year | 35 | 4 | 93 | 1,044 | 891 | 385 | **2,452** |
| Charge | 190 | 389 | 1,744 | 728 | 3,287 | 487 | **6,825** |
| Disposals | (225) | (14) | (558) | (300) | (1,158) | (390) | **(2,645)** |
| End of year (see below) | — | 379 | 1,279 | 1,472 | 3,020 | 482 | **6,632** |
| **Net book value:** | | | | | | | |
| 31 December 1987 | 12,686 | 3,852 | 35,232 | 2,198 | 23,051 | 2,165 | **79,184** |
| 31 December 1986 | 2,112 | 84 | 476 | 861 | 724 | 544 | **4,801** |

Leased assets included above have a net book value of £322,000 (1986:  £142,000).

Basis of valuations:  Plant and machinery (including fixtures and fittings) are shown at cost.  Land and buildings include certain properties professionally revalued during 1987, by Messrs. James Andrew Badger (Surveyors & Valuers), on an open market, existing use basis.  The historic gross cost of such land and buildings is £1,859,000 (1986: £333,000).

**Auditor's Report**

To the members of WPP Group plc:

We have audited the accounts set out on pages 87 to 109 in accordance with approved Auditing Standards.

In our opinion, the accounts, which have been prepared under the historical cost convention, as modified by the revaluation of land and buildings, give a true and fair view of the state of affairs of the Company and of the Group at 31 December 1987 and of the Group profit and source and application of funds for the year then ended, and comply with the Companies Act 1985.

Arthur Andersen & Co.
London

6th May 1988

**EXHIBIT 1 (continued)**
**Consolidated Profit and Loss Account (for the year ended 31 December 1988)**

|  | 1988 (£000) | 1987 (£000) | 1988 ($000) | 1987 ($000) |
|---|---|---|---|---|
| **Turnover**[a] | £2,251,306 | £1,097,775 | $4,010,702 | $1,844,262 |
| **Revenue** | £ 547,129 | £ 284,082 | $ 974,710 | $ 477,258 |
| Cost of sales | (105,313) | (65,160) | (187,615) | (109,469) |
| **Gross Profit** | £ 441,816 | £ 218,922 | $ 787,095 | $ 367,789 |
| Other operating expenses (net) | (390,380) | (197,468) | (695,462) | (331,746) |
| **Operating Profit** | £ 51,436 | £ 21,454 | $ 91,633 | $ 36,043 |
| Interest receivable | 7,926 | 3,739 | 14,120 | 6,282 |
| Interest payable and similar charges | (19,044) | (11,076) | (33,926) | (18,608) |
| **Profit on Ordinary Activities before Taxation** | £ 40,318 | £ 14,117 | $ 71,827 | $ 23,717 |
| Tax on profit on ordinary activities | (18,930) | (6,810) | (33,724) | (11,441) |
| **Profit on Ordinary Activities after Taxation** | £ 21,388 | £ 7,307 | $ 38,103 | $ 12,276 |
| Minority interests | (266) | (222) | (474) | (373) |
| **Profit for the Financial Year** | £ 21,122 | £ 7,085 | $ 37,629 | $ 11,903 |
| Dividends paid and proposed | (7,033) | (2,337) | (12,529) | (3,926) |
| **Retained Profit for the Year** | £ 14,089 | £ 4,748 | $ 25,100 | $ 7,977 |
| Earnings per share | 55.0p | 32.1p | $ 0.98 | $ 0.54 |

The main reporting currency of the group is the pound sterling, and the accounts have been prepared on this basis. Solely for convenience, the accounts set out are also presented expressed in U.S. dollars using the approximate average rate for the year for the profit and loss account (1988: $1.7815 = £1; 1987: $1.6800 = £1), the rate in effect on 31 December for the balance sheets (1988: $1.8090 = £1; 1987: $1.8785 = £1), and a combination of these for the statement of source and application of funds. This translation should not be construed as a representation that the pound sterling amounts actually represent, or could be converted into, U.S. dollars at the rate indicated.

[a] Note on the difference between Turnover and Revenue:

"Turnover comprises the gross amounts billed to clients in respect of commission-based income together with the total of other fees earned. Revenue comprises commissions and fees earned in respect of turnover."

"Turnover and revenue are stated exclusive of VAT, sales taxes and trade discounts."

**EXHIBIT 1 (continued)**
**Consolidated Balance Sheet (as at 31 December 1988)**

|  | 1988 £000 | 1987 £000 | 1988 $000 | 1987 $000 |
|---|---|---|---|---|
| **Fixed Assets** |  |  |  |  |
| Intangible assets (Note 10) | £ 175,000 | £        — | $ 316,575 | $        — |
| Tangible assets (Note 11) | 86,378 | 79,184 | 156,258 | 148,747 |
| Investments | 4,678 | 3,464 | 8,463 | 6,507 |
|  | £ 266,056 | £   82,648 | $ 481,296 | $ 155,254 |
| **Current Assets** |  |  |  |  |
| Stocks and work-in-progress | £   34,340 | £   37,920 | $   62,121 | $   71,233 |
| Debtors | 266,405 | 247,836 | 481,927 | 465,560 |
| Investments and assets held for resale | 13,912 | 115,273 | 25,167 | 216,540 |
| Cash at bank and in hand | 92,591 | 72,616 | 167,497 | 136,409 |
|  | £ 407,248 | £ 473,645 | $ 736,712 | $ 889,742 |
| **Creditors:** amounts falling due within one year | (437,079) | (454,733) | (790,676) | (854,216) |
| **Net Current Assets (Liabilities)** | £ (29,831) | £   18,912 | $ (53,964) | $   35,526 |
| **Total Assets less Current Liabilities** | 236,225 | 101,560 | 427,332 | 190,780 |
| **Creditors:** amounts falling due after more than one year | (140,761) | (91,333) | (254,637) | (171,568) |
| **Provisions for Liabilities and Charges** | (34,603) | (74,719) | (62,597) | (140,360) |
| **Net Assets (Liabilities)** | £   60,861 | £ (64,492) | $ 110,098 | $ (121,148) |
| **Capital and Reserves** |  |  |  |  |
| Called-up share capital | £     3,973 | £     3,670 | $     7,187 | $     6,894 |
| Merger reserve | (150,603) | (89,423) | (272,441) | (167,981) |
| Other reserves | 185,259 | 13,233 | 335,134 | 24,858 |
| Profit and loss account | 21,052 | 6,963 | 38,083 | 13,080 |
| **Shareholders' Funds** | £   59,681 | £ (65,557) | $ 107,963 | $ (123,149) |
| Minority interests | 1,180 | 1,065 | 2,135 | 2,001 |
| **Total Capital Employed** | £   60,861 | £ (64,492) | $ 110,098 | $ (121,148) |

Signed on behalf of the Board on 9 May 1989
R.E. Lerwill and M.S. Sorrell, Directors

The main reporting currency of the group is the pound sterling and the accounts have been prepared on this basis. Solely for convenience, the accounts set out are also presented expressed in U.S. dollars using the approximate average rate for the year for the profit and loss account (1988: $1.7815 = £1; 1987: $1.6800 = £1), the rate in effect on 31 December for the balance sheets (1988: $1.8090 = £1; 1987: $1.8785 = £1), and a combination of these for the statement of source and application of funds. This translation should not be construed as a representation that the pound sterling amounts actually represent, or could be converted into, U.S. dollars at the rate indicated.

**EXHIBIT 1 (continued)**
**Notes to the Accounts (31 December 1988)**

**Note 10—Intangible Fixed Assets**

|                       | 1988<br>£000 | 1987<br>£000 |
|-----------------------|--------------|--------------|
| Corporate brand names | 175,000      | —            |

Corporate brand names represent the directors' valuation of the brand names J. Walter Thompson and Hill and Knowlton, which were acquired in 1987 as part of JWT Group, Inc. These assets have been valued under the Alternative Accounting Rules of the Companies Act 1985 in accordance with the group's accounting policy for intangible fixed assets. The directors in the course of their valuation have consulted their advisers Samuel Montagu & Co. Limited.

**Note 11—Tangible Fixed Assets**
a) Group
The movement in the year was as follows:

| (£000) | Land and Buildings | | | Plant and Machinery | Fixtures and Fittings | Motor Vehicles | Total |
|---|---|---|---|---|---|---|---|
| | Freehold | Long Leasehold | Short Leasehold | | | | |
| **Cost or valuation:** | | | | | | | |
| Beginning of year | 12,686 | 4,231 | 36,511 | 3,670 | 26,071 | 2,647 | **85,816** |
| New subsidiaries | 1,099 | 163 | 507 | 719 | 1,856 | 441 | **4,785** |
| Reclassification | — | (2,523) | 2,523 | — | — | — | **—** |
| Additions | 2,122 | 325 | 1,776 | 1,493 | 8,244 | 3,055 | **17,015** |
| Disposals | (5,732) | (26) | (2,022) | (1,274) | (2,188) | (990) | **(12,232)** |
| Exchange adjustments | 649 | 494 | 2,117 | 185 | 1,435 | 52 | **4,932** |
| Revaluation | 3,202 | — | 1,350 | — | — | — | **4,552** |
| End of year (see below) | 14,026 | 2,664 | 42,762 | 4,793 | 35,418 | 5,205 | **104,868** |
| **Depreciation:** | | | | | | | |
| Beginning of year | — | 379 | 1,279 | 1,472 | 3,020 | 482 | **6,632** |
| Charge | 275 | 154 | 3,896 | 599 | 5,572 | 1,123 | **11,619** |
| Disposals | (204) | (20) | (42) | (208) | (521) | (402) | **(1,397)** |
| Exchange adjustments | 40 | 31 | 677 | 110 | 760 | 18 | **1,636** |
| End of year (see below) | 111 | 544 | 5,810 | 1,973 | 8,831 | 1,221 | **18,490** |
| **Net book value:** | | | | | | | |
| 31 December 1988 | 13,915 | 2,120 | 36,952 | 2,820 | 26,587 | 3,984 | **86,378** |
| 31 December 1987 | 12,686 | 3,852 | 35,232 | 2,198 | 23,051 | 2,165 | **79,184** |

Leased assets (other than leasehold property) included above have a net book value of £1,373,000 (1987: £322,000).

Basis of valuation: Plant and machinery (including fixtures and fittings) are shown at cost. Land and buildings include certain properties professionally revalued during 1987 and 1988, by Messrs. James Andrew Badger (Surveyors & Valuers), on an open market, existing use basis. The historic net book value of such land and buildings is £6,511,000 (1987: £1,859,000).

**EXHIBIT 1 (continued)**
**Notes to the Accounts (31 December 1988)**

**Auditors' Report**

To the members of WPP Group plc:

We have audited the accounts set out on pages 63 to 84 in accordance with approved Auditing Standards.

In our opinion, the accounts, which have been prepared under the historical cost convention, as modified by the revaluation of land and buildings and corporate brand names, give a true and fair view of the state of affairs of the Company and of the Group at 31 December 1988 and of the Group profit and source and application of funds for the year then ended, and comply with the Companies Act 1985.

Arthur Andersen & Co.
London

9 May 1989

**EXHIBIT 1 (continued)**
**Consolidated Profit and Loss Account (for the year ended 31 December 1989)**

| | 1989 (£000) | 1988 (£000) | 1989 ($000) | 1988 ($000) |
|---|---|---|---|---|
| Turnover[a] *⌐Sales* | £4,406,898 | £2,251,306 | $7,190,735 | $4,010,702 |
| **Revenue** | £1,005,453 | £ 547,129 | $1,640,598 | $ 974,710 |
| **Gross Profit** | £ 843,032 | £ 441,816 | $1,375,575 | $ 787,095 |
| Other operating expenses (net) | (740,550) | (390,380) | (1,208,355) | (695,462) |
| **Operating Profit** | £ 102,482 | £ 51,436 | $ 167,220 | $ 91,633 |
| Interest receivable | 16,072 | 7,926 | 26,224 | 14,120 |
| Interest payable and similar charges | (43,515) | (19,044) | (71,003) | (33,926) |
| **Profit on Ordinary Activities before Taxation** | £ 75,039 | £ 40,318 | $ 122,441 | $ 71,827 |
| Tax on profit on ordinary activities | (34,532) | (18,930) | (56,346) | (33,724) |
| **Profit on Ordinary Activities after Taxation** | £ 40,507 | £ 21,388 | $ 66,095 | $ 38,103 |
| Minority interests | (2,306) | (266) | (3,763) | (474) |
| **Profit for the Financial Year** | £ 38,201 | £ 21,122 | $ 62,332 | $ 37,629 |
| Preference dividends | (8,413) | — | (13,727) | — |
| **Profit Attributable to Ordinary Shareholders** | £ 29,788 | £ 21,122 | $ 48,605 | $ 37,629 |
| Ordinary dividends ⟵ *US does not show on I.S.* | (9,913) | (7,033) | (16,175) | (12,529) |
| **Retained Profit for the Year** | £ 19,875 | £ 14,089 | $ 32,430 | $ 25,100 |
| **Earnings per Share** | | | | |
| Basic | 73.0p | 54.3p | $ 1.19 | $ 0.97 |
| Fully diluted | 71.2p | NA | $ 1.16 | NA |

The main reporting currency of the group is the pound sterling and the accounts have been prepared on this basis. Solely for convenience, the accounts set out are also presented expressed in U.S. dollars using the approximate average rate for the year for the profit and loss account (1989: $1.6317 = £1; 1988: $1.7815 = £1), the rate in effect on 31 December for the balance sheets (1989: $1.6125 = £1; 1988: $1.8090 = £1), and a combination of these for the statement of source and application of funds. This translation should not be construed as a representation that the pound sterling amounts actually represent, or could be converted into, U.S. dollars at the rate indicated.

[a] Note on the difference between Turnover and Revenue:

"Turnover comprises the gross amounts billed to clients in respect of commission-based income together with the total of other fees earned. Revenue comprises commissions and fees earned in respect of turnover."

"Turnover and revenue are stated exclusive of VAT, sales taxes and trade discounts."

**EXHIBIT 1 (continued)**
**Consolidated Balance Sheet (as at 31 December 1989)**

|  | 1989 £000 | 1988 £000 | 1989 $000 | 1988 $000 |
|---|---|---|---|---|
| **Fixed Assets** | | | | |
| Intangible assets (Note 9) — *Brand Valuation* | £   350,000 | £  175,000 | $   564,375 | $ 316,575 |
| Tangible assets | 156,583 | 86,378 | 252,400 | 156,258 |
| Investments | 19,774 | 4,678 | 31,886 | 8,463 |
|  | £   526,357 | £  266,056 | $   848,751 | $ 481,296 |
| **Current Assets** | | | | |
| Stocks and work-in-progress | £     91,004 | £    34,340 | $   146,744 | $   62,121 |
| Debtors | 648,778 | 266,405 | 1,046,155 | 481,927 |
| Investments and assets held for resale | 6,759 | 13,912 | 10,899 | 25,167 |
| Cash at bank and in hand | 233,617 | 92,591 | 376,707 | 167,497 |
|  | £   980,158 | £  407,248 | $ 1,580,505 | $ 736,712 |
| **Creditors:**  amounts falling due within one year | (1,149,858) | (437,079) | (1,854,146) | (790,676) |
| **Net Current Assets (Liabilities)** | £  (169,700) | £   (29,831) | $  (273,641) | $  (53,964) |
| **Total Assets less Current Liabilities** | 356,657 | 236,225 | (575,110) | 427,332 |
| **Creditors:**  amounts falling due after more than one year | (535,618) | (140,761) | (863,684) | (254,637) |
| **Provisions for Liabilities and Charges** | (151,170) | (34,603) | (243,762) | (62,597) |
| **Net (Liabilities) Assets** | £  (330,131) | £    60,861 | $  (532,336) | $ 110,098 |
| **Capital and Reserves** | | | | |
| Called-up share capital | £     25,505 | £      3,973 | $     41,127 | $     7,187 |
| Share premium | 192,721 | — | 310,763 | — |
| Goodwill reserve | (797,811) | (150,603) | (1,286,470) | (272,441) |
| Other reserves | 196,247 | 185,259 | 316,447 | 335,134 |
| Profit and loss account | 40,927 | 21,052 | 65,995 | 38,083 |
| **Shareholders' Funds** | £  (342,411) | £    59,681 | $  (552,138) | $ 107,963 |
| Minority interests | 12,280 | 1,180 | 19,802 | 2,135 |
| **Total Capital Employed** | £  (330,131) | £    60,861 | $  (532,336) | $ 110,098 |

Signed on behalf of the Board on 9 May 1989
R.E. Lerwill and M.S. Sorrell, Directors

The main reporting currency of the group is the pound sterling and the accounts have been prepared on this basis. Solely for convenience, the accounts set out are also presented expressed in U.S. dollars using the approximate average rate for the year for the profit and loss account (1989: $1.6317 = £1; 1988: $1.7815 = £1), the rate in effect on 31 December for the balance sheets (1989: $1.6125 = £1; 1988: $1.8090 = £1), and a combination of these for the statement of source and application of funds.  This translation should not be construed as a representation that the pound sterling amounts actually represent, or could be converted into, U.S. dollars at the rate indicated.

**EXHIBIT 1 (continued)**
**Notes to the Accounts (31 December 1989)**

### Note 9—Intangible Fixed Assets

| | £000 |
|---|---|
| Corporate brand names: | |
| Beginning of year | £175,000 |
| Additions at fair value to the group—Ogilvy & Mather | 175,000 |
| End of year | £350,000 |

Corporate brand names represent the directors' valuation of the brand names J. Walter Thompson and Hill and Knowlton which were valued in 1988 and Ogilvy & Mather acquired in 1989 as part of The Ogilvy Group, Inc. These assets have been valued in accordance with the group's accounting policy for intangible fixed assets and in the course of this valuation the directors have consulted their advisers, Samuel Montagu & Co. Limited.

**EXHIBIT 1 (continued)**
## Notes to the Accounts

### Note 10—Tangible Fixed Assets
a)  Group

The movement in the year was as follows:

| (£000) | Land and Buildings | | Fixtures, Fittings, | |
| | Freehold | Leasehold | and Equipment | Total |
|---|---|---|---|---|
| **Cost or valuation:** | | | | |
| Beginning of year | 14,026 | 45,426 | 45,416 | **104,868** |
| New subsidiaries | 3,969 | 24,060 | 30,181 | **58,210** |
| Additions | 139 | 7,108 | 19,112 | **26,359** |
| Disposals | (851) | (1,665) | (4,134) | **(6,650)** |
| Exchange adjustments | 419 | 4,974 | 5,334 | **10,727** |
| Revaluation | 2,445 | (350) | — | **2,095** |
| End of year (see below) | 20,147 | 79,553 | 95,909 | **195,609** |
| **Depreciation:** | | | | |
| Beginning of year | 111 | 6,354 | 12,025 | **18,490** |
| Charge | 146 | 4,780 | 14,903 | **19,829** |
| Disposals | (12) | (100) | (1,073) | **(1,185)** |
| Exchange adjustments | 34 | 411 | 1,447 | **1,892** |
| End of year (see below) | 279 | 11,445 | 27,302 | **39,026** |
| **Net book value:** | | | | |
| 31 December 1989 | 19,868 | 68,108 | 68,607 | **156,583** |
| 31 December 1988 | 13,915 | 39,072 | 33,391 | **86,378** |

Leasehold land and buildings comprises £3,485,000 (1988: £2,120,000) held on long leasehold and £64,623,000 (1988: £36,952,000) held on short leasehold.  Leased assets (other than leasehold property) included above have a net book value of £1,812,000 (1988:  £1,373,000).

Basis of valuation:  Fixtures, fittings, and equipment are shown at cost.  Land and buildings include certain properties professionally revalued during 1989, by Messrs. James Andrew Badger (Surveyors & Valuers), on an open market, existing use basis.  Other properties are included at historic cost.  The amount included in respect of revalued properties is £16,444,000 (1988: £12,314,000); the historic net book value of such land and buildings is £8,542,000 (1988:  £6,511,000).

### Auditors' Report

To the members of WPP Group plc:

We have audited the accounts set out on pages 41 to 63 in accordance with Auditing Standards.

In our opinion, the accounts give a true and fair view of the state of affairs of the Company and of the Group at 31 December 1989 and of the Group profit and source and application of funds for the year then ended, and comply with the Companies Act 1985.

Arthur Andersen & Co.
London
14 May 1990

## EXHIBIT 2

In thinking along the lines of corporate versus personalized loyalty it might be useful to introduce a simple analogy. If one thinks of a football team this is clearly a case of corporate loyalty. Individual players and managers may come and go, but the fans' loyalty is predominantly with that abstract corporate notion—the "team." On the other side of the coin, one can imagine a consultant's (e.g., a doctor's) relationship with a client—a relationship based primarily upon personal factors. Should the consultant in question leave his present firm it's quite conceivable that he will take his clients with him. The question now is where along this corporate-loyalty, personal-loyalty continuum lies the world of the advertising agency.

In approaching this question the following general factors need to be considered:

### A People Profession

Undoubtedly the advertising world is grounded upon a considerable degree of personal interaction. Within such an environment individual relationships and loyalties naturally flourish—even more so given the need for confidentiality and campaign consistency. The exact extent of the "personal factor" is difficult to quantify since it will vary from case to case and depend upon the influence of the person in question. There is no doubt, however, that in some cases a client's loyalty is primarily to their contact within an agency rather than with the agency itself. There have been some notable examples of this, through clients following key individuals when they leave the agency. A famous example in 1981 was a number of clients who followed Frank Lowe from Collet Dickenson Pearce to Lowe Howard-Spink. Recent examples include:

**Dec. 1988**—David Harrison leaves Leo Burnett Direct and formed RSCG Direct. He takes with him the Bankers Clearing Services Consortium account which he brought to the company when he joined.

**Dec. 1988**—David Pasley leaves FCB Pasley Woods and takes clients with him.

**1988**—Malcolm Gaskin leaves TBWA to form WMGO and takes the Wolverhampton and Dudley Breweries Account with him.

**Nov. 1987**—John Collington joins CTMC from Hilton Consumer and takes the Answercall account with him.

**June 1987**—Chris Davis seems set to leave AHH and industry sources suggest that if he leaves, a number of clients with whom he has worked will be prompted to review.

### A Capricious Profession

Given the advertising world's dependence upon creativity, there is an inherent danger of it becoming a hostage to fads and novelty. The continual quest for innovation makes it a volatile environment and can at times dictate against a lasting client-agency relationship. This tendency was demonstrated recently upon the transferral of H.R. Owen's account to Leagas Shafron, during which their marketing manager stated that "it wasn't that we were unhappy with Connell May and Stevenson, but it was felt that the time was right for a change." This type of philosophy can clearly impinge upon the loyalty of an agency's client-base.

## EXHIBIT 2 (continued)

### A Predatory Profession

The advertising world is, in a client sense, a highly acquisitive environment. *Advertising Age*, for example, found that 72% of its sample of company advertising directors had been approached within the previous three months by agencies trying to acquire their business. In such a competitive arena corporate (and individual) loyalty is put under a strain.

This volatility is further increased by the prevalence of new agencies; in the case of Britain an average of 20 a year (in 1981 there were 43 new agencies launched). The disruptive effect of these new players is increased by the fact that their very newness may, for the creative reasons alluded to earlier, be perceived as attractive in itself.

### Agency Size (Client Base)

To set against the above, the size of the agency is a very important fact. The larger the agency, the easier it is to replace important individuals with others of similar standing in the profession. Obviously in the case of JWT, its list of accounts is among the most comprehensive of all agencies on a world scale. Just as important though is the quality of the client base. Here, JWT is again impressive with names such as Kellogg, Rowntree Mackintosh, and Kraft on its books. The strength of these brands is in part attributable to JWT's own guidance, and it can be said that some of their brand strength has rubbed off on to JWT itself. This will be particularly true where the relationship is longstanding. In this sense JWT again looks good with an average length of service for its present clients standing at 13 years—with many accounts going back much further, e.g., Kraft 1926, Lever 1927, and Kellogg 1938. This evidence would suggest that to a large extent, JWT transcends the erratic nature of the advertising game. Moreover, this duration of client relationship would also imply that JWT's clients do not easily transfer their loyalty from the corporate body to individuals within it.

Most examples of accounts moving with individuals relate to the smaller agencies rather than to the major players in the game.

To illustrate this latter point, advertising agencies are categorized according to their age. This is most commonly expressed in the form of three separate "waves" of agencies. This corruption of Toffler's term represents a rather obtuse form of description, although it does provide a reasonably convenient way of approaching the subject.

Although exact definitions vary, the "first wave" is generally used to refer to those agencies, such as JWT, which existed prior to 1970. Those agencies which emerged in the next decade and a half tend to constitute the "second wave," and include such names as Lowe Howard-Spink and Saatchi and Saatchi. Finally, there is the "third wave," which goes back to the mid-1980s and is used to refer to new agencies such as Devito, Butterfield, Day, and Hockney.

Upon the basis of this schema we can make some general comments relating to the likely balance of corporate versus individual influences within the different categories of agency. In the case of the "first wave," for example, their client loyalty will have accrued over a long period of time and will be relatively independent of the qualities and influences of existing members of staff. This will be less true in the case of the "second wave," since it's likely that their founders will still be in control and will be personally responsible for much of the goodwill enjoyed by the agency. Finally, in the case of the "third wave" agencies, their brand value will tend to be heavily skewed towards their high-profile founders and other key personnel.

**EXHIBIT 2 (continued)**

Following on from the above approach it is clear that the names of the newer agencies tend to be synonymous with the name of their founders or other key personnel. In the event that one of these key personnel leaves the agency, then the agency's own name and state of continuity may be disrupted. In short, this type of agency is extremely susceptible to the mutilation of its brand image.

This will also tend to be the case with the second wave of agencies, although to a lesser extent since their longer existence will have imbued some level of brand value independent of those individuals of whom the agency is the namesake. Nevertheless, it would still be inconceivable to imagine that the likes of Saatchi and Saatchi could survive the departure of their founders with their reputation intact. Again, to a large extent these agencies are their key personnel.

In the case of the "first wave" agencies, such as JWT, the situation is entirely different. Put simply, the name JWT is not a derivative of any existing individuals within the agency. As such, its future brand value is not contingent upon its continued association with certain high-profile individuals. In discussing brands in general, Professor John Quelch of the Harvard Business School has stated that "brands of the highest stature are likely to be those coincidental with the companies' own name" (e.g., Heinz soup rather than "Head and Shoulders"). Adapting this to the case of advertising agencies, the opposite can seem to be the case; that is, the strongest and most secure brands are those where the product (i.e., the personnel) do not share the companies' name.

To conclude then, it appears from this analysis that JWT satisfies all those criteria which would suggest the existence of a strong client loyalty; a loyalty which is grounded upon corporate rather than individual allegiance.

In the case of the United States this strength would seem to be confirmed by the results of the *Advertising Age's* Agency Watch poll, which has consistently placed JWT in the number one position in terms of industry perceptions. This consistency, moreover, was not disrupted by the personnel problems experienced by JWT over the last few years: as *Advertising Age* (May 1988) itself expressed it, "JWT seems to be surviving the management turmoil of the past 18 months with its reputation intact."

In the British context this same strength is demonstrated by the high level of continuity of JWT's accounts. In 1986 and 1987, for example, around 96% of JWT's clients kept their business with the agency for the following year—an impressive level of retention given the possibility of "one off" campaigns (e.g., Government flotations) and the erratic nature of the industry.

As mentioned above, a practical problem with carrying out the brand valuation for an agency in the same way as for a consumer product arises from a lack of data. A more oblique way of approaching the question is required.

An extensive literature exists in economic theory relating to dominant firms and the likelihood of their decline. (See, for example, Geroski in Hay and Vickers (1987), *The Economics of Market Dominance*, for a recent critical survey.) In other words, given a firm which has a large market share, what is the likelihood of this declining substantially and by what processes will this decline come about? There is a presumption in theory that competitive forces will erode monopoly power and lead to the decline of even the most dominant firm. In practice, the theory is not supported all that well and powerful firms exercising dominance over markets can persist for a very long time.

Source:  *Valuing the JWT Brand*, a Henley Centre Report, January 1989, pp. 3-7.

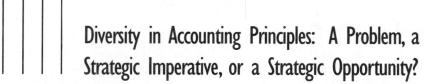

# Diversity in Accounting Principles:  A Problem, a Strategic Imperative, or a Strategic Opportunity?

In our study of accounting decision making, we have been reading and discussing situations in which managers have had choices about the way in which they would report on the results of operations and the financial condition of their organizations.  We have shown that managers must choose between using LIFO or FIFO in measuring and reporting on inventories, or between straight-line depreciation or accelerated depreciation in reporting on plant, property, and equipment.  For almost every classification of assets, liabilities, shareholders' equity, and revenue and expenses, alternative conventions, practices, and principles exist from which managers and their accountants can choose.  With such an array of methods and practices available, what is the meaning of "generally accepted accounting principles"?

## GENERALLY ACCEPTED ACCOUNTING PRINCIPLES

In general, when managers prepare reports for use by outsiders such as lenders, investors, regulatory authorities, or other interested groups, they must choose among accounting conventions, practices, and principles, which become bases for making the measurements necessary to prepare financial reports.  Once a choice is made, the concept of consistency demands that similar conventions and practices be used in subsequent periods unless there is a reason that an alternative method would be preferred.  We have seen how auditors refer to the use of "generally accepted" accounting principles in expressing their opinions on many financial statements prepared for the use of outsiders.

The use of the word "principles" is perhaps unfortunate, for it connotes something more basic than, in fact, most accounting principles are.  Accounting

Copyright © 1992 by the President and Fellows of Harvard College.  Harvard Business School case 193-045.

principles are not fundamental truths or even necessarily rules of conduct. They are methods used in observing, measuring, and reporting which are widely used or which have substantial, authoritative support. A generally accepted accounting principle is created whenever a method, practice, concept, or convention is widely used by those who prepare reports, or whenever an official pronouncement is made by a group such as the Financial Accounting Standards Board in the United States, the International Accounting Standards Committee, by a change to a Company's Act, or by a regulator with authority to influence reporting and securities trading.

The fact that wide use leads to general acceptance in accounting principles makes it critical to understand the accounting process and the way in which it operates. In preparing and distributing their reports, managers and their accountants participate in the development of accounting principles. Through the criteria its managers adopt in deciding which measurements should be made and reported, an organization supports and advances the development of principles that may be used even more widely in the future.

The idea of a set of generally accepted accounting principles is very important historically. When there were fewer constraints on the accounting practices that could be employed by managers in preparing reports, unscrupulous entrepreneurs often took advantage of investors, creditors, and other interested groups by rendering misleading reports about income and financial position. In an effort to avert such practices, professional accountants, regulators, independent authorities, and government agencies in most countries have sought to limit the kinds of practices that fall within the guidelines that generally accepted accounting principles provide.

Nevertheless, there is no definitive list of practices and principles that are "generally accepted." It is much easier to find lists or regulations of methods or practices that are not generally accepted. This means that in spite of all the efforts to reduce diversity in reporting practices, great diversity still remains, and anyone who seeks to use financial reports has to pay close attention to the methods used by the managers and accountants who prepared them.

Unfortunately, diversity in accounting principles presents an important problem to anyone who wants to compare the economic performance or financial position of an organization at two points in time, or with that of another organization, or to some normative standard or model. To merely look at the numbers that are reported without considering the methods that lie behind them creates the risk of faulty conclusions or errors in judgment. The next section demonstrates why this is so.

## DIVERSITY IN ACCOUNTING PRINCIPLES

The diversity in accounting principles is so great that it would be impossible to summarize in brief form all of the concepts, methods, and procedures that are at the present time acceptable in accounting practice. It is important at least to realize how many diverse practices are acceptable and the way in which the possibilities are multiplied if combinations of different principles and practices relating to assets, liabilities, shareholders' equity, revenues, and expenses are considered.  **Exhibit 1** lists some selected examples of diverse generally accepted accounting principles for presentation of financial information about important classifications.

It would be helpful if there were some normative standard against which diverse practices and their effect on financial reports might be compared.  If there were a normative standard, then accounting principles producing reports that were closest to the normative standard would be preferred.  By estimating the difference between a report in hand and one based on the normative standard, a financial report reader could make a judgment about the quality of information available in the financial report.  In the absence of a standard, each person who seeks to use accounting information needs to create his or her own reference point.  This is harder to do than it appears at first glance.  Consider the simple example that follows.

Assume that two identical companies start business at the same time, and that the events and transactions in which they engage during the first year of their operations are identical.  If managers of each company choose alternative accounting principles in preparing their reports, those reports may be quite different, even after only one year.  **Exhibit 2** shows the balance sheet  for each of the two companies to be the same when they begin operations.  **Exhibit 3** shows the events and transactions that affect both companies identically. **Exhibit 4** shows the accounting methods used by the managers of each company in reporting those identical events and transactions.  **Exhibit 5** shows the statement of income, balance sheets, and statement of cash flows that each company will prepare at the end of one year of operations.  And finally, **Exhibit 6** shows how the income of the two identical companies might be reconciled.

While this example is quite simple and is obviously hypothetical, differences like these arise in actual financial reporting.  Anyone who attempts to compare financial statements from two or more entities is faced with the task of identifying the accounting methods used.  Then, the impact that particular methods might have had on the reports must be estimated before any comparison of the two organizations can be made.  Even when examining the financial statements of a single company through time, attention must be given to possible changes in accounting principles and the impact these changes may have had before information contained in the financial reports can be used for many purposes.

## DIVERSITY:  STRATEGIC IMPERATIVE VS. STRATEGIC OPPORTUNITY

Financial reports are a showcase through which managers can fulfill their obligations to provide information to shareholders and other interested parties. The fact that periodic financial reporting is required shows how important the economic community and society think reporting by managers is in facilitating the free flow of capital and preventing one group from taking advantage of another because of the information available to it.  It is difficult to imagine how a modern free-enterprise economy could function without a financial reporting system that is somewhat effective.

The role that financial reporting plays in a modern economy requires that managers should be trying to report about the operations and financial condition of their organizations as accurately and informatively as possible.  Those who fear that managers might withhold information to use to their own advantage would argue that some minimum set of disclosure and reporting requirements is necessary to get managers to report effectively.  Whichever points of view you have about the environment in which financial reporting occurs, you must consider what managers should do if they discover that the accounting methods and principles they are using and reporting are not the right ones, and that a change is needed.

Why might managers or an organization be using accounting methods and principles that are incorrect or ineffective?  There are at least three obvious reasons.  First, it may be that the initial choice of an accounting method or principle was a poor one.  Since many initial choices of accounting principles or methods are made when a firm is small or when a problem is first encountered, the implications of those choices may not be obvious.  As the organization grows and develops, or as its activities stabilize, it may become obvious that the method or principle initially chosen does not provide as much or as good information as an alternative might.

A second reason why managers or an organization may need to change accounting methods or principles may be because conditions have changed.  The environment in which the organization is operating, or the relationships with various suppliers, investors, or financing sources, or a change in the product mix or strategy of the firm all may dictate that an alternative method or principle would be more informative than one previously employed.

A third reason why change may be necessary may be due to the actions of management itself.  In developing new strategies, in taking the organization in new directions, and in adopting new tactics to deal with the action of competitors, managers may want to signal that the old accounting methods supported the old strategy, but new accounting principles and methods are needed given the chosen change in strategic direction.

Regardless of which of these three reasons creates a need for change in the accounting method or principles used in reporting, management may view the need for change as imperative.  It is simply impossible to report effectively using the old method when it is obvious that a new method or principle would be more appropriate or effective.

Despite the demands for consistency that are created by the accountant's concept of consistency, an accounting change is permitted and even encouraged when it can be demonstrated that another method or principle would be preferable.  In other case studies, we have seen that auditors must note a change in accounting method, but they do not need to deny an unqualified auditor's opinion simply because managers have changed accounting methods or principles. In fact, in many circumstances the auditors append to their notice of change some phrase like "with which we concur" to signal that they are in agreement with and support the change that management has made in preparing its reports.

Unfortunately, the strategic imperative also creates the opportunity to use changes as a strategic opportunity. Selecting new accounting methods means that managers can present things differently. The results of operations or financial position can be presented in a light different than they would have been presented had the old methods or principles been retained. Because modern organizations and economic activities are so complex, what may to some managers be a strategic imperative to report things as clearly as possible may open the door to strategic opportunities to other managers who are less scrupulous or who desire to present things in a light particularly advantageous to themselves or their organization.

Diversity in accounting principles is unlikely to be eliminated by policy, law, or practice. Diversity exists because the arena in which financial communication, accounting measurement, and financial reporting takes place is a complex one. Those who use financial reports prepared in an atmosphere where accounting diversity is the norm must examine the accounting principles and methods used, consider what alternatives might have been available, and then decide how to use the information in reports. Those who prepare financial reports and are responsible for them must consider how to balance the strategic imperative to report as accurately and honestly as possible with the strategic opportunity to present information in such a way that some who see and use the information might be misled into drawing erroneous conclusions and taking undesirable actions.

**EXHIBIT 1**
## Selected Examples of Diversity in Generally Accepted Accounting Principles

### Cash
1. Include all cash on hand and in banks as one item.
2. Use separate captions for cash on hand, and/or cash in banks, and/or cash in banks that cannot be easily withdrawn, and/or separate currencies.

### Receivables
1. Show receivables at gross amount.
2. Show receivables at gross amount less allowances for unearned interest and doubtful accounts.
3. Show receivables classified by type (accounts, notes, etc.), and/or by time, and/or by source (customers, employees, government, etc.).
4. Exclude receivables unless earned and due, as in lease payments receivable.

### Marketable securities (temporary investments)
1. Show securities at cost.
2. Show securities at market value when below cost.
3. Show securities at cost plus interest earned but not yet paid.
4. Show securities at approximate market value.

### Inventories
1. Show inventories at gross cost and/or by classes (supplies, raw materials, work in process, finished goods ready for sale).
2. Show inventories at cost or market, whichever is lower.
3. Show inventories at market or selling price.
4. Determine "cost" or "price" by assuming average costs or standard costs.
5. Report flow of costs and value of goods remaining by assuming last-in first-out, or first-in first-out, or average costs in and out, or standard costs in and out, etc. (Also see **Cost of goods sold** below.)

### Land, plant, and equipment
1. Show land, plant, and equipment at original cost, and/or adjusted original cost, and/or cost or market value, whichever is lower.
2. Show plant and equipment at current value.
3. Show plant and equipment at cost less accumulated depreciation calculated by assuming straight-line allocation of cost to periods, or by an accelerated or decelerated rate of depreciation.
4. Charge all purchases of plant and equipment as expense in period purchased.
5. Show land at original cost less depletion caused by mining, harvesting, or extraction of gases or fluids.

## EXHIBIT 1 (continued)

### Investments

1. Show investments in other companies at cost.
2. Show investments in other companies at cost or market value, whichever is lower.
3. Show investments in other companies at cost plus any proportional share of earnings on investment not received.
4. Show investments at market value.

### Intangible assets

1. Exclude intangible assets, charging all costs related thereto as expense in the period of expenditure.
2. Show all intangible assets at cost.
3. Show intangible assets at cost but allocate costs over a few periods until only a nominal value remains.
4. Show intangible assets at cost but allocate cost to all periods of expected value.
5. Show intangible assets at cost but do not charge costs to periods unless value has clearly fallen.
6. Show intangible assets at estimated value at time of acquisition, adjusted for subsequent charges.

### Current liabilities

1. Show liabilities at face amount.
2. Show liabilities at amount at which obligations could be satisfied plus any costs of doing so.

### Long-term liabilities

1. Show long-term liabilities at face amount.
2. Show long-term liabilities at face amount adjusted for discounts or premiums given at acceptance and amortized over period of the liability.
3. Show liabilities, including commitments on leases, pensions, and other contractual agreements, at face amount or adjusted for effects of interest.

### Owners' equity

1. Show owners' equity as the amount of assets less the amount of liabilities.
2. Show owners' equity classified to show original source.
3. Show owners' equity classified by original source but modified by transactions between the entity and shareholders, and/or extraordinary reclassifications or adjustments.
4. Within owners' equity, segregate earnings retained by implied use of resources earned.

## EXHIBIT 1 (continued)

### Revenues
1. Recognize revenue in period when products or services are delivered.
2. Recognize revenue in period when product is ready for delivery (as in case of precious gems or metals).
3. Recognize revenue in period when payment is received from customer or client.

### Cost of goods sold
1. Recognize expense in the period and at purchase of product delivered.
2. Recognize expense in the period and at purchase cost of some assumed unit of product delivered.
3. Recognize expense in the period and at cost of replacement of the product delivered. (Also see **Inventories** above.)

### Expenses
1. Recognize, as expenses of the period, all or selected cash payments.
2. Recognize, as expenses of the period, all expenditures related to products or services sold in the period. All expenditures are assets or in satisfaction of obligations.
3. Recognize, as expenses in the period, all estimated declines in asset values and estimated increases in obligations not related to cost of goods sold.

### Net income
1. Show all increases or decreases in net value of owners' equity as net income, regardless of source.
2. Exclude from net income all adjustments relating to prior period reports, and/or extraordinary events.

**EXHIBIT 2**
**Balance Sheets, January 1, 1999**

| | Company A | | Company B | |
|---|---:|---:|---:|---:|
| **Assets** | | | | |
| Cash | | $ 500 | | $ 500 |
| Marketable securities | | 1,000 | | 1,000 |
| Inventories (100 units @ $10) | | 1,000 | | 1,000 |
| Building and equipment | | | | |
| (estimated life 10 years) | $2,000 | | $2,000 | |
| Less: Accumulated depreciation | — | | — | |
| | | 2,000 | | 2,000 |
| Total assets | | $4,500 | | $4,500 |
| **Equities** | | | | |
| Accounts payable | | $ 200 | | $ 200 |
| Bank loans | | 1,000 | | 1,000 |
| Total liabilities | | $1,200 | | $1,200 |
| Owners' equity: | | | | |
| Common Stock | | 3,300 | | 3,300 |
| Total equities | | $4,500 | | $4,500 |

**EXHIBIT 3**
**Events and Transactions of Companies A and Bª for the Year 1999**

| | | |
|---|---|---:|
| Sales of merchandise (200 units @ $40 each) | | $8,000 |
| Purchase of inventory on account | | |
| (a 3% discount is available if paid within 10 days): | | |

| | | |
|---|---|---:|
| March 31 | 50 units @ $10 | 500 |
| June 30 | 50 units @ $12 | 600 |
| September 30 | 50 units @ $15 | 750 |
| December 31 | 50 units @ $20 | 1,000 |

Paid accounts payable:

| | |
|---|---:|
| April 30 | 500 |
| July 31 | 600 |
| October 31 | 750 |

| | |
|---|---:|
| Paid salaries | $2,500 |
| Increased bank loan | $2,000 |
| Purchased new equipment (estimated life, 4 years) | $2,000 |
| Paid for research on new product not yet introduced | $  500 |
| Value of marketable securities, December 31, 1999 | $  950 |

---

ª  Assumed to be identical for each company

**EXHIBIT 4**
**Accounting Methods Used in Preparing Financial Reports by Companies A and B**

| Item | Company A | Company B |
|---|---|---|
| Cash | Report face amount on hand and in bank. | Report face amount on hand and in bank. |
| Marketable securities | Report at cost unless market is "materially" lower and sale contemplated. | Report at lower of market cost or market. |
| Inventory | Report at cost, assuming first-in, first-out. | Report at cost, assuming last-in, first-out. |
| Buildings and equipment | Report at cost less accumulated straight-line depreciation. | Report at cost less accumulated depreciation accelerated at two times straight-line rate. |
| Intangible assets | Hold as asset at cost until related revenues are realized. | Charge against revenues when cash expended. |
| Accounts payable | Report at amount due less discounts available. | Report at face amount. |
| Bank loan | Report at amount due. | Report at amount due. |
| Owners' equity | Assets – Liabilities | Assets – Liabilities |

**EXHIBIT 5**
**Financial Reports of Companies A and B**

| Statement of Income<br>For the Year 1999 | Company A | | Company B | |
|---|---|---|---|---|
| Sales revenues | | $8,000 | | $8,000 |
| Less cost of goods sold: | | | | |
| Beginning inventory | $1,000 | | $1,000 | |
| Add: Purchases | 2,850 | | 2,850 | |
| Available | $3,850 | | $3,850 | |
| Ending inventory | 1,750 | | 1,000 | |
| | | 2,100 | | 2,850 |
| Gross margin | | $5,900 | | $5,150 |
| Less expenses: | | | | |
| Salaries | $2,500 | | $2,500 | |
| Depreciation | 700 | | 1,400 | |
| Research on new product | — | | 500 | |
| | | 3,200 | | 4,400 |
| Operating income: | | $2,700 | | $ 750 |
| Add: Discount available | | 30 | | — |
| Less: Loss on securities held | | — | | 50 |
| Net Income | | $2,730 | | $ 700 |

| Balance Sheets,<br>December 31, 1999 | Company A | | Company B | |
|---|---|---|---|---|
| **Assets** | | | | |
| Cash | | $ 3,650 | | $3,650 |
| Marketable securities | | 1,000 | | 950 |
| Inventories | | 1,750 | | 1,000 |
| Building and equipment: | | | | |
| Cost | $4,000 | | $4,000 | |
| Accumulated depreciation | 700 | | 1,400 | |
| | | 3,300 | | 2,600 |
| Research on new product | | 500 | | — |
| Total assets | | $10,200 | | $8,200 |
| **Equities** | | | | |
| Accounts payable | | $ 1,170 | | $1,200 |
| Bank loans | | 3,000 | | 3,000 |
| Total liabilities | | $ 4,170 | | $4,200 |
| Owners' equity: | | | | |
| Common stock | | 3,300 | | 3,300 |
| Retained earnings | | 2,730 | | 700 |
| | | 6,030 | | 4,000 |
| Total equities | | $10,200 | | $8,200 |

**EXHIBIT 5 (continued)**

| Statement of Cash Flows For the Year 1999 | Company A | Company B |
|---|---|---|
| **Cash from Operations:** | | |
| Net income | $ 2,730 | $   700 |
| Add:  Depreciation | 700 | 1,400 |
| Decrease in marketable securities | — | 50 |
| Increase in inventories | (750) | — |
| Increase in accounts payable | 970 | 1,000 |
| Total cash from operations | $ 3,650 | $ 3,150 |
| **Cash from Inventories:** | | |
| Purchase of new equipment | $(2,000) | $(2,000) |
| Research on new product | (500) | — |
| Total cash from Inventory | $(2,500) | $(2,000) |
| **Cash from Financing:** | | |
| New bank loan | $ 2,000 | $ 2,000 |
| Total changes in cash | $ 3,150 | $ 3,150 |
| Cash, January 1, 1999 | 500 | 500 |
| Cash, December 31, 1999 | $ 3,650 | $ 3,650 |

**EXHIBIT 6**
**Reconciliation of Income for Companies A and B**

| | |
|---|---|
| Company B income | $   700 |
| Add $50 because Company A does not reduce value of marketable securities to market value of $950 | 50 |
| Add $750 because Company A uses FIFO instead of LIFO for inventory values and determining cost of goods sold | 750 |
| Add $700 because Company A uses straight-line depreciation instead of an accelerated method | 700 |
| Add $500 because Company A retains research costs as an asset | 500 |
| Add $30 because Company A reduced liabilities to discounted amount | 30 |
| Company A income | $2,730 |

# Kendall Square Research Corporation (A)

**K**endall Square Research Corporation (KSR) was founded in 1986 by Henry Burkhardt III and Steve Frank, another computer designer. KSR was the third computer company co-founded by Burkhardt, the first two having been Data General Corporation and Encore Computer Corporation. At KSR, Burkhardt chose a radical design for a supercomputer that would make the machines attractive for both government and university laboratories and for commercial users. The company delivered its first machine to the Oak Ridge National Laboratory in the fall of 1991, and Kendall Square Research reported that it reached break-even volume before the end of 1992.

From its beginning KSR funded its development and the design of its products through private placements of its equity and debt securities and an initial public stock offering in April 1992. A subsequent stock offering in April 1993 brought the total financing of the start-up to about $150 million, more than $80 million of which had come in two offerings of stock to the public. Shares in the first of the public offerings had more than doubled in price in less than 18 months. By October 1993, the market capitalization of the shares was about five times estimated 1993 sales and 45 times estimated 1993 earnings.[1]

From the time of its first sale, some critics questioned the criteria used by KSR to determine when revenue would be recognized. The company recognized revenue on product sales upon written customer acceptance of the

Copyright © 1994 by the President and Fellows of Harvard College. Harvard Business School case 194-068.

[1] Dorfman, John R. and William M. Bulkeley, "Heard on the Street: Supercomputer Maker Kendall Square's Effort to Crack Business Markets Has Some Skeptics," *The Wall Street Journal*, October 11, 1993, p. C2.

product. Acceptance often occurred before the configuration of a particular system was finalized or any payment had been received from a customer. Kendall Square Research fully disclosed its policy on revenue recognition in its financial reports to shareholders. (See **Exhibit 1** for excerpts from the 1992 Kendall Square Research Corporation Annual Report to Shareholders.)

## KENDALL SQUARE RESEARCH AND SUPERCOMPUTING[2]

Kendall Square Research recognized at its founding that a key to its success would be its ability to deliver more computing power at lower cost per computation than its competitors. Its approach was based on linking many low-cost minicomputers and dividing the computer task among them, rather than building larger mainframe computers or trying to improve programming and software to wring more performance from the computer architectures that were available. The concept of massively parallel processing had first surfaced in the 1980s, and several competitors felt that it had tremendous potential.

A large scale parallel computer was potentially faster and less expensive than traditional mainframes or available supercomputers. In addition to lower cost per computation or transaction, large scale parallel computers were theoretically scalable; bigger and more powerful machines could be assembled merely by adding processors and the memory and input and output devices to support them. However, as processors were added, programming became more difficult and cumbersome.

Kendall Square's founders believed that a highly successful parallel computer could succeed only if it could take advantage of the library of applications and languages that were already standard in the mainframe and supercomputer worlds. Their goal was to develop a standards-based multi-user system which could run multiple applications simultaneously, so that a sufficiently powerful system could serve an entire technical or business enterprise. Their ideal system would even be able to run scientific and business applications at the same time.

The technology which was needed to develop such a computer did not exist in 1986 when KSR was founded. For six years Kendall Square scientists and engineers invested in chip development technology that they hoped would turn their insight into a working computer. By 1992 they were sure they had succeeded. They had developed a large scale parallel computer which combined the power of massively parallel, distributed memory machines with the familiar shared-memory programming environment of conventional mainframes. The KSR1 family of computers was designed for high-performance computing requirements typical of scientific environments, for decision

---

[2] This section is based on information taken from the 1992 Annual Report of Kendall Square Research Corporation.

support and complex database query applications, and for on-line transaction-intensive environments such as automatic teller machines or airline reservation systems.

The KSR1 family of systems scaled from 16 to 1088 processors. A $975 thousand model with 16 processors could handle 1,200 transactions per second, a measure of commercial computer speed. Scalability allowed users to add computer resources in incremental and cost-effective steps without changes in software and without performance degradation. Therefore, a customer could add to an installation at a later date without the need to replace all software or to reprogram operating systems. While the scaling up of processors in massive parallel processing computer systems was not fully reliable, reports from users of KSR machines seemed to support the company's contention that they scale up more effectively than those of some other competitors.

In 1993 supercomputers with massive parallel processing were more commonly found in scientific applications than in commercial applications. One reason for this was the tendency for supercomputers to crash as users pushed their limits. In scientific applications users were often willing to sacrifice reliability for performance, but most commercial applications required computers to work reliably for months at a time. The business market for supercomputers had been estimated to be about $31 billion, far larger than the scientific and research market, which had been estimated to be about $4 billion.[3] In 1992, Kendall Square signed contracts with Neodata, a direct-mail company working with Electronic Data Systems (EDS), and AMR, the parent company of American Airlines, to work together to develop systems using KSR computers.

## REVENUE RECOGNITION AT KENDALL SQUARE RESEARCH CORP.

Critics of the revenue recognition practices used by KSR claimed that the company was far too liberal in what it called a sale of a machine or system. They cited cases in which laboratories had ordered or received equipment which was subsequently accepted but for which there was no prospective funding, or for which research grants had been requested but not yet granted. In such cases there was no assurance that the research grant would be received, and even if it was certain, there could be significant delays before the customer would pay KSR.

Other analysts thought that the liberal accounting practices used by KSR were not uncommon in the computer industry, but such practices were less visible in the financial statements of more mature companies such as IBM or Digital Equipment Corporation. These analysts pointed out that terms requiring payment in six or nine months, after a customer had received a grant from a government agency—often very slow payers—were not unusual. Such terms

---

[3] Dorfman and Bulkeley, loc. cit.

might be appropriate for the typical university or research laboratory that were the base of early KSR users.

> *Terms of Kendall's supercomputer deliveries were often extremely attractive to researchers. For example, Edward Lazowska, chairman of the department of computer science at the University of Washington, said that it has two KSR1 computers with a total of 60 processors. He said, "We paid $1 million for half of it, and the rest was a loan of equipment against future grants." Kendall . . . treated the entire shipment as a sale.*
>
> *William Goddard, a physicist at the California Institute of Technology, said he paid for 32 processors in September 1992 using a National Science Foundation grant. He liked it so much that last spring he wanted to double the size of the system and applied for more grant money. Kendall shipped him the computer immediately, but he and Kendall are still waiting for the grant award. "I'm committed to buying it," he said. "I am applying for two very large grants."[4]*

Other contracts included one for $1.5 million that could be cancelled if the second of two phases was not completed. Still others involved distributors that had the right to cancel the contract if a customer could not be found.

A second sales practice added to the concerns of critics of KSR's accounting policies. Some users purchased machines with fewer processors than were eventually thought to be needed. In these cases the processors purchased were booked as revenue and accounts receivable, but KSR had delivered additional processors to the customer for installation and use by the customer. The additional processors remained on KSR's balance sheet as inventory pending the customer's decision to keep the processors, apply for grants to buy them, or to otherwise make arrangements to pay for the loaned processors.

As a result of these practices, revenues recognized had exceeded cash collected from customers by significant amounts. Some critics thought this indicated that revenue was being recognized too early. Other observers thought this was normal for a new, growing company in the process of ramping up sales.

Of additional concern was the practice of KSR giving research grants to some users of its systems. Such grants had been reported to range between $5 thousand and $50 thousand or more. Mr. Burkhardt was reported to have agreed that grants ". . . sometimes do run into substantial amounts, but are legitimate expenses to foster software development, not disguised sales incentives. . . ."[5]

---

[4]  Bulkeley, William M., "Kendall Square . . . " *The Wall Street Journal*, December 2, 1993, p. A3.

[5]  Ibid.

## Kendall Square Research in 1993

In August 1993, *The Wall Street Journal* reported:

> **WALTHAM, Mass**   *Kendall Square Research Inc. is "quite comfortable" with analysts' estimates that it will earn 45 cents to 50 cents a share for the year, President Henry Burkhardt said.*
>
> *Mr. Burkhardt also said he is comfortable with estimates that revenue for the year will top $60 million, up from $20.7 million. And he said he is comfortable with third-quarter earnings estimates of 9 cents to 13 cents a share. For the year-earlier quarter, Kendall Square reported a net loss of 29 cents a share on revenue of $5.3 million.*[6]

## QUESTIONS

1.  Evaluate the revenue recognition policies used by Kendall Square Research.

    Do they conform to generally accepted accounting principles with respect to:
    a.  the timing of revenue recognition?
    b.  the amount of revenue recognized?
    c.  the matching of costs and expenses to revenue?
2.  The rapid growth in sales expected by Kendall Square Research managers will strain the company's ability to finance their expansion. How, if at all, should this fact affect the ways in which management chooses accounting principles and a reporting strategy?

---

[6] "Kendall Square Agrees With Profit Estimates for Quarter and Year," *The Wall Street Journal*, August 13, 1993, p. B5A.

**EXHIBIT 1**
**Excerpts from 1992 Annual Report of Kendall Square Research Corporation**

Management's Discussion and Analysis of
Financial Condition and Results of Operations

### Introduction

The Company was incorporated in February 1986 and sold its first computer system in September 1991. As of December 26, 1992, the Company had sold 22 systems, of which 11 were sold to customers in the United States and 11 to customers in Europe. Several of these customers have enlarged the size of their system configuration since initial installation. The Company's revenue for the fiscal year ended December 26, 1992, was $20.7 million. The Company has not been profitable on an annual basis since its inception and no assurance can be given that the Company will be able to operate on a profitable basis. As of December 26, 1992, the Company's accumulated deficit was approximately $69.7 million.

The Company's future operating results will depend on many factors, including the demand for the Company's products for both technical and commercial applications, the level of competition faced by the Company, and the ability of the Company to develop and market new products and control costs. The Company's sales and marketing strategy contemplates sales of its computer systems for both technical and commercial applications. To date, however, all of the computer systems have been sold for technical applications.

### Results of Operations

#### Years ended December 28, 1991 and December 26, 1992

The Company does not believe that the year-to-year comparison of various items of expense as a percentage of revenue is meaningful due to the significant growth in the Company's revenue from 1991 to 1992.

### Revenue

Revenue increased from $904,000 to $20,729,000. The Company shipped its first computer system in September 1991 and recorded its first revenue in the third quarter of 1991. The Company recorded revenue growth in each of the four quarters in 1992 as it increased the number of systems shipped. There can be no assurance that the Company will continue to achieve quarterly revenue growth in future periods. See "Quarterly Results." Sales to customers in Europe accounted for approximately 44% of revenue in 1992.

### Cost of Revenue

Cost of revenue increased from $332,000 to $9,189,000, or from 37% to 44% of revenue. These expenses include actual material, labor, and indirect costs associated with the manufacture of systems for which revenue has been recognized. The Company does not believe that the year-to-year comparison is meaningful due to the low level of revenues in fiscal 1991 as well as the allocation of certain start-up manufacturing costs in 1991 to other operating costs.

## EXHIBIT 1 (continued)

### Research and Development

Research and development expenses decreased by 11% from $15,786,000 to $14,113,000. Additionally, in 1992 the Company capitalized $3,506,000 of costs attributable to software license fees and software development. No such costs were capitalized in 1991. The Company increased research and development staffing levels from 79 to 115 persons from 1991 to 1992. In order to establish a competitive position and to develop new and enhanced products, the Company intends to continue to devote substantial resources to research and development. The Company expects that research and development expenses will fluctuate from quarter to quarter but will generally increase over time.

### Selling, General and Administrative

Selling, general and administrative expenses increased by 63% from $6,441,000 to $10,475,000. These expenses were comprised primarily of selling and marketing expenses, reflecting significant increases in sales, marketing, and support staffing levels from 49 to 66 persons from 1991 to 1992. These expenses are expected to continue to increase as the Company expands its selling and marketing efforts.

### Other Operating Costs and Expenses

Other operating costs in 1991 of $850,000 resulted from costs incurred in the establishment of the Company's manufacturing facilities and procedures and other initial manufacturing costs, including depreciation of test equipment. The manufacturing facilities and procedures became operational during the fourth quarter of 1991. There were no such costs incurred in 1992.

### Other Income (Expense), Net

The Company recorded other income of $326,000 in 1992, compared to other expense of $2,000 in 1991. Interest income increased by 104% from $380,000 to $775,000, which was partially offset by an 18% increase in interest expense from $382,000 to $449,000. The Company's average cash and investments balances were higher in 1992 than in 1991 as a result of the receipt of proceeds from convertible debt financings and the Company's initial public offering. All of the convertible debt was converted into shares of common stock upon the closing of the Company's initial public offering on April 3, 1992.

To date, inflation has not had a material impact on the Company's revenue or results of operations.

#### Years ended December 29, 1990 and December 28, 1991

### Revenue

Revenue for the year ended December 28, 1991, of $904,000 resulted from the Company's first shipment and customer acceptance of one KSR1-20 system. There were no shipments in the year ended December 29, 1990.

### EXHIBIT 1 (continued)

#### Cost of Revenue
Cost of revenue of $332,000 includes actual material, labor, and indirect costs associated with the manufacture of systems for which revenue was recognized.

#### Research and Development
Research and development expenses increased by 49% from $10,575,000 to $15,786,000. This increase resulted primarily from materials and other costs incurred in the design and development of product prototypes, as well as an increase in research and development staffing levels from 77 to 79 persons from 1990 to 1991.

#### Selling, General and Administrative
Selling, general and administrative expenses increased by 108% from $3,099,000 to $6,441,000. These expenses were comprised primarily of selling and marketing expenses, reflecting an increase in sales, marketing, and support staffing level from 24 to 49 persons from 1990 to 1991. These expenses were incurred as part of the Company's strategy to market its computer systems concurrently with its development efforts.

#### Other Operating Costs and Expenses
Other operating costs increased by 134% from $363,000 to $850,000. This increase resulted from costs incurred in the establishment of the Company's manufacturing facilities and procedures and other initial manufacturing costs, including depreciation of test equipment.

#### Other Income (Expense), Net
The Company recorded other expense of $2,000 in 1991 compared to other income of $687,000 in 1990. The Company had more proceeds from private equity and convertible subordinated debt financings in 1990 available for investment than in 1991 and earned higher average interest rates thereon. Additionally, interest expense was higher in 1991 as a result of higher capital lease obligations and the issuance in 1991 of $12,820,000 in convertible subordinated notes.

#### Quarterly Results
The following table presents unaudited quarterly financial information for the four fiscal quarters ended December 26, 1992. This information has been prepared by the Company on a basis consistent with the Company's audited consolidated financial statements and includes all adjustments (consisting only of normal recurring adjustments) which management considers necessary for a fair presentation of the results for such periods. The operating results for any quarter are not necessarily indicative of the results for any future period.

**EXHIBIT 1 (continued)**

| | 3 Months Ended | | | |
| | March 28, 1992 | June 27, 1992 | Sept. 26, 1992 | Dec. 26, 1992 |
| --- | --- | --- | --- | --- |
| | | (in thousands) | | |
| Revenue | $ 1,954 | $ 2,297 | $ 5,310 | $11,168 |
| Cost of revenue | 896 | 1,058 | 2,466 | 4,769 |
|    Gross profit | 1,058 | 1,239 | 2,844 | 6,399 |
| Cost and expenses: | | | | |
|    Research and development | 3,407 | 4,312 | 3,444 | 2,950 |
|    Selling, general and administrative | 1,890 | 2,160 | 2,859 | 3,566 |
| | 5,297 | 6,472 | 6,303 | 6,516 |
|    Loss from operations | (4,239) | (5,233) | (3,459) | (117) |
| Other income (expense): | | | | |
|    Interest income | 30 | 348 | 249 | 148 |
|    Interest expense | (323) | (61) | (40) | (25) |
| | (293) | 287 | 209 | 123 |
| Net income (loss) | $(4,532) | $(4,946) | $(3,250) | $ 6 |

Revenue in the first full year of shipments demonstrated successive quarterly growth, highlighted by fourth quarter revenue of $11,168,000 from the sale of systems to 13 new customers. The Company sold systems to eight new customers during the first three quarters of the year. Gross profit was approximately 54% of revenue throughout the first three quarters and improved to approximately 57% in the fourth quarter as revenues increased more rapidly than fixed costs. Research and development expenses increased in the second quarter primarily due to the shifting of development efforts to new products. The reduction in fourth quarter expenses was attributable to the capitalization of certain patents and trademarks and to increased capitalization of software development costs. Selling, general and administrative expenses reflect the increasing investment in the expansion of sales offices in Europe and the United States, staffing increases in sales, marketing and support staffing level, and marketing programs. Interest income increased in the second quarter as a result of the investment of the proceeds from the Company's initial public offering. Interest expense in the first quarter was primarily attributable to the outstanding convertible debt, which was converted into shares of common stock early in the second quarter. The balance of the year reflects the interest expense on capital leases.

**Selected Consolidated Financial Data**
The following data has been derived from financial statements audited by Price Waterhouse, independent accountants. The consolidated balance sheet at December 28, 1991, and December 26, 1992, and the related consolidated statements of operations, of stockholders' equity, and of cash flows for the three years ended December 26, 1992, and the notes thereto appear elsewhere in this Annual Report.

**EXHIBIT 1 (continued)**

| | | | Year Ended | | |
|---|---|---|---|---|---|
| | December 31, 1988 | December 30, 1989 | December 29, 1990 | December 28, 1991 | December 26, 1992 |
| | | | (in thousands except per share data) | | |
| **Statement of Operations Data:** | | | | | |
| Revenue | | | | $    904 | $ 20,729 |
| Cost of revenue | | | | 332 | 9,189 |
| Gross profit | | | | 572 | 11,540 |
| Costs and expenses: | | | | | |
| Research and development | $ 6,348 | $  8,253 | $ 10,575 | 15,786 | 14,113 |
| Selling, general and administrative | 902 | 2,494 | 3,099 | 6,441 | 10,475 |
| Other operating costs and expenses | | | 363 | 850 | |
| | 7,250 | 10,747 | 14,037 | 23,077 | 24,588 |
| Loss from operations | (7,250) | (10,747) | (14,037) | (22,505) | (13,048) |
| Other income (expense), net | 499 | 425 | 687 | (2) | 326 |
| Net loss | (6,751) | (10,322) | (13,350) | (22,507) | (12,722) |
| Pro forma net loss per share[a] | (2.31) | (2.92) | (2.77) | (3.90) | (1.22) |
| Weighted average shares outstanding[a] | 2,925 | 3,531 | 4,814 | 5,712 | 10,171 |

| | | | Year Ended | | |
|---|---|---|---|---|---|
| | December 31, 1988 | December 30, 1989 | December 29, 1990 | December 28, 1991 | December 26, 1992 |
| | | | (in thousands) | | |
| **Balance Sheet Data:** | | | | | |
| Working capital | $ 7,112 | $5,471 | $10,674 | $ 4,463 | $33,473 |
| Total assets | 10,298 | 9,226 | 15,959 | 13,129 | 48,733 |
| Long-term capital lease obligations | | 114 | 942 | 892 | 599 |
| Stockholders' equity[a] | 9,316 | 7,523 | 12,812 | 6,408 | 40,427 |

[a] Assumes the conversion of all outstanding shares of all series of convertible preferred stock and convertible subordinated notes outstanding prior to the closing of the Company's initial public offering on April 3, 1992, into common stock.  See Notes 1 and 4 of Notes to Consolidated Financial Statements.

**Price Range of Common Stock**
The Company's common stock is traded in the Over-the-Counter market on the National Association of Securities Dealers, Inc. Automated Quotation ("NASDAQ") National Market System under the symbol "KSRC."  The following table sets forth the range of high and low sale prices for the common stock for the periods indicated, as reported on the NASDAQ National Market System. Quotations represent prices between dealers and do not reflect retail mark-ups, markdowns, or commissions. There was no market for the Company's common stock prior to its initial public offering effective on March 27, 1992.

## EXHIBIT 1 (continued)

**Price Range of Common Stock**

|                | High   | Low   |
|----------------|--------|-------|
| First quarter  | $12    | $11   |
| Second quarter | 13¼    | 7½    |
| Third quarter  | 11½    | 7½    |
| Fourth quarter | 19½    | 5½    |

As of February 10, 1993, there were approximately 1,500 individual participants in security position listings for the Company's common stock.

**Report of Independent Accountants**

To the Board of Directors and Stockholders of
Kendall Square Research Corporation

In our opinion, the accompanying consolidated balance sheet and the related consolidated statements of operations, of stockholders' equity and of cash flow present fairly, in all material respects, the financial position of Kendall Square Research Corporation and its subsidiaries at December 26, 1992 and December 28, 1991, and the results of their operations and their cash flows for each of the three years in the period ended December 26, 1992, in conformity with generally accepted accounting principles. These financial statements are the responsibility of the Company's management; our responsibility is to express an opinion on these financial statements based on our audits. We conducted our audits of these statements in accordance with generally accepted auditing standards which require that we plan and perform the audit to obtain reasonable assurance about whether the financial statements are free of material misstatement. An audit includes examining, on a test basis, evidence supporting the amounts and disclosures in the financial statements, assessing the accounting principles used and significant estimates made by management, and evaluating the overall financial statement presentation. We believe that our audits provide a reasonable basis for the opinion expressed above.

Price Waterhouse
Boston, Massachusetts
February 8, 1993,
except as to Note 4, which is as of April 1, 1993

**EXHIBIT 1 (continued)**
## Consolidated Balance Sheet

| | December 28, 1991 | December 26, 1992 |
|---|---|---|
| | (in thousands, except share and per share data) | |

**Assets**
Current assets:

| | | |
|---|---|---|
| Cash and cash equivalents | $  4,035 | $  7,392 |
| Short-term investments | | 10,372 |
| Accounts receivable | 804 | 13,328 |
| Inventories | 4,316 | 8,939 |
| Prepaid expenses and other current assets | 1,137 | 1,149 |
| Total current assets | 10,292 | 41,180 |
| Fixed assets, net | 2,635 | 3,108 |
| Software development cost, net | | 3,451 |
| Other assets, net | 202 | 994 |
| | $ 13,129 | $ 48,733 |

**Liabilities and Stockholders' Equity**
Current liabilities:

| | | |
|---|---|---|
| Accounts payable | $  2,885 | $  3,001 |
| Accrued payroll costs | 1,019 | 1,575 |
| Other accrued expenses | 612 | 2,047 |
| Deferred revenue | 428 | 196 |
| Current portion of long-term capital lease obligations | 885 | 888 |
| Total current liabilities | 5,829 | 7,707 |
| Long-term capital lease obligations | 892 | 599 |

Stockholders' equity:

| | | |
|---|---|---|
| Convertible preferred stock | 50,098 | |
| Convertible subordinated notes, converted into common stock upon the closing of the initial public offering | 13,029 | |
| Common stock $.01 par value; 35,000,000 shares authorized; 375,578 and 11,356,517 shares issued at December 28, 1991 and December 16, 1992, respectively | 4 | 114 |
| Additional paid-in capital | 215 | 109,987 |
| Accumulated deficit | (56,938) | (69,660) |
| | 6,408 | 40,441 |
| Less 1,263 shares of common stock held in treasury, at cost | | (14) |
| Total stockholders' equity | 6,408 | 40,427 |
| Commitments (Note 7) | $ 13,129 | $ 48,733 |

The accompanying notes are an integral part of the financial statements.

**EXHIBIT 1 (continued)**
**Consolidated Statement of Operations**

| | December 29, 1990 | December 28, 1991 | December 26, 1992 |
|---|---|---|---|
| | | Year Ended | |
| | (in thousands, except per share data) | | |
| Revenue | | $    904 | $ 20,729 |
| Cost of revenue | | 332 | 9,189 |
| Gross profit | | 572 | 11,540 |
| Costs and expenses: | | | |
| Research and development | $ 10,575 | 15,786 | 14,113 |
| Selling, general and administrative | 3,099 | 6,441 | 10,475 |
| Other operating costs and expenses | 363 | 850 | — |
| | 14,037 | 23,077 | 24,588 |
| Loss from operations | (14,037) | (22,505) | (13,048) |
| Other income (expense): | | | |
| Interest income | 755 | 380 | 775 |
| Interest expense | (68) | (382) | (449) |
| | 687 | (2) | 326 |
| Net losses | $ (13,350) | $ (22,507) | $ (12,722) |
| Unaudited pro forma net loss per share assuming conversion of convertible preferred stock and convertible subordinated notes (Note 1) | $    (2.77) | $    (3.90) | $    (1.22) |
| Weighted average shares outstanding | 4,814 | 5,712 | 10,171 |

The accompanying notes are an integral part of the financial statements.

**EXHIBIT 1 (continued)**
**Consolidated Statement of Cash Flows Increase (Decrease) in Cash and Cash Equivalents**

| | December 29, 1990 | Year Ended December 28, 1991 | December 26, 1992 |
|---|---|---|---|
| | | (in thousands) | |
| **Cash flows from operating activities:** | | | |
| Cash received from customer | | $ 527 | $ 8,533 |
| Cash paid to suppliers and employees | $ (13,538) | (23,192) | (36,231) |
| Interest received | 636 | 530 | 681 |
| Interest paid | (68) | (173) | (177) |
| Net cash used for operating activities | (12,970) | (22,308) | (27,194) |
| **Cash flows from investing activities:** | | | |
| (Purchase) sale of short-term investments | (2,888) | 2,888 | (10,372) |
| Payment for capitalized software development costs | | | (3,506) |
| Purchase of fixed assets | (1,561) | (710) | (879) |
| Proceeds from sale of fixed assets | 242 | | |
| Net cash provided for (used for) investing activities | (4,207) | 2,178 | (14,757) |
| **Cash flows from financing activities:** | | | |
| Proceeds from sale and leaseback of equipment | 961 | | |
| Principal payments on capital lease obligations | (325) | (666) | (1,156) |
| Issuance of convertible subordinated notes | | 12,820 | 6,451 |
| Debt issuance costs | | | (288) |
| Issuance of convertible preferred stock | 18,817 | 3,059 | |
| Convertible preferred stock issuance costs | (195) | (47) | |
| Initial public offering of common stock | | | 44,000 |
| Initial public offering issuance costs | | | (3,964) |
| Proceeds from exercise of common stock options, warrants, and employee stock purchases | 17 | 64 | 279 |
| Repurchase of common stock | | | (14) |
| Net cash provided by financing activities | 19,275 | 15,230 | 45,308 |
| Net increase (decrease) in cash and cash equivalents | 2,098 | (4,900) | 3,357 |
| Cash and cash equivalents, beginning of period | 6,837 | 8,935 | 4,035 |
| Cash and cash equivalents, end of period | $ 8,935 | $ 4,035 | $ 7,392 |

The accompanying notes are in integral part of the financial statements.

**EXHIBIT 1 (continued)**
**Consolidated Statement of Cash Flows (continued)—Reconciliation**
**of Net Loss to Net Cash Used for Operating Activities (in thousands)**

|  | December 29, 1990 | Year Ended December 28, 1991 | December 26, 1992 |
|---|---|---|---|
| Net loss | $ (13,350) | $ (22,507) | $(12,722) |
| Adjustments to reconcile net loss to cash used for operating activities: |  |  |  |
| Depreciation and amortization | 1,526 | 1,786 | 2,115 |
| Gain on sale of fixed assets | (114) |  |  |
| Interest accrued on convertible subordinated notes |  | 209 | 277 |
| Change in assets and liabilities: |  |  |  |
| Increase in accounts receivable |  | (804) | (12,524) |
| Increase in inventories |  | (4,316) | (5,411) |
| Increase in prepaid expenses and other current assets | (860) | (81) | (12) |
| (Increase) decrease in other assets | (183) | 10 | (792) |
| Increase (decrease) in accounts payable | (161) | 2,190 | 116 |
| Increase in accrued payroll costs | 107 | 509 | 556 |
| Increase in other accrued expenses | 65 | 268 | 1,435 |
| Increase (decrease) in deferred revenue |  | 428 | (232) |
| Net cash used for operating activities | $ (12,970) | $ (22,308) | $(27,194) |

The accompanying notes are an integral part of the financial statements.

**EXHIBIT 1 (continued)**
## Notes to Consolidated Financial Statements

**Note 1:  Nature of Business and Summary of Significant Accounting Policies**
Kendall Square Research Corporation (the "Company") was incorporated on February 4, 1986. The Company develops, manufactures, markets, and supports a family of high performance, general purpose parallel computer systems for a broad range of mainstream applications, including numerically intensive computation, on-line transaction processing, and database management and inquiry.

**Principles of consolidation**  The consolidated financial statements include the accounts of the Company and its wholly-owned subsidiaries. All significant intercompany transactions are eliminated in consolidation.

**Fiscal year**  The Company's fiscal year ends on the last Saturday of December.

**Cash equivalents and short-term investments**  The Company considers all highly liquid debt instruments purchased with original maturities of three months or less to be cash equivalents. Short-term investments, which include treasury bills with original maturities of greater than three months, are recorded at cost which approximates market.

**Revenue recognition**  The Company recognizes revenue from product sales upon written customer acceptance. Warranty costs are accrued as product sales revenue is recognized.

**Inventories**  Inventories are stated at the lower of cost or market. Cost is determined by the first-in, first-out (FIFO) method.

**Fixed assets**  Fixed assets are recorded at cost and depreciated by use of the straight-line method over their estimated useful lives. Repair and maintenance costs are expensed as incurred.

**Software development costs**  Certain software development costs incurred subsequent to the establishment of technological feasibility are capitalized and amortized under straight-line and units-shipped methods over the lesser of the estimated economic life of the products or three years commencing when the products are available for general release. Amortization of software development costs is included in cost of revenue and in 1992 totaled $55,000.

**Note 2:  Inventories**
Inventories consist of the following (in thousands):

|  | December 28, 1991 | December 26, 1992 |
| --- | --- | --- |
| Raw materials and manufactured assemblies | $1,337 | $4,808 |
| Work in process | 1,906 | 1,272 |
| Finished goods | 1,073 | 2,859 |
|  | $4,316 | $8,939 |

Deposits on inventory purchases at December 28, 1991 and December 26, 1992 totaled $543,000 and $164, respectively, and are included in prepaid expenses and other current assets.

## EXHIBIT 1 (continued)

### Note 3:   Fixed Assets
Fixed assets consist of the following (in thousands):

|  | Useful Life in Years | December 28, 1991 | December 26, 1992 |
|---|---|---|---|
| Computer equipment and purchased software | 3 | $ 7,151 | $ 8,916 |
| Office furniture and equipment | 3-5 | 778 | 1,274 |
|  | Lease term | 345 | 617 |
| Leasehold improvements |  | 8,274 | 10,807 |
| Less accumulated depreciation and amortization |  | (5,639) | (7,699) |
|  |  | $ 2,635 | $ 3,108 |

The Company incurred capital lease obligations of $1,757,000, $844,000, and $866,000 in 1990, 1991, and 1992, respectively. Accumulated depreciation on equipment under capital leases totaled $1,229,000 and $2,219,000 at the end of 1991 and 1992, respectively.

In 1992, inventories totaling $788,000 were transferred to fixed assets.

The Company has a $2,600,000 lease line with a commercial lender for the leasing of fixed assets. At December 26, 1992, the Company has $1,734,000 available under the lease line.

### Note 4:   Stock Option and Purchase Plans
During 1991, the board of directors adopted the 1991 Stock Option Plan (the "Plan") under which it may issue both incentive and nonqualified stock options. The exercise price of incentive stock options will be no less than the fair market value of the common stock on the date of grant. The Plan allows for a maximum of 1,211,250 common shares to be granted under options over a ten-year period expiring in 2001. The options generally vest between three to five years. Options for the purchase of 210,625 common shares vest in seven years, however, the vesting may be accelerated based on the Company achieving certain revenue levels. All options to date have been issued at fair market value. At December 26, 1992, options for 181,492 shares were available for future grants. On February 8, 1993, the board of directors, subject to stockholder approval, authorized an increase of an additional 1,500,000 shares issuable under the Plan.

## EXHIBIT 1 (continued)

A summary of activity in the Plan is as follows:

| Incentive Stock Options | Incentive Stock Options | | Nonqualified Stock Options | |
| --- | --- | --- | --- | --- |
| | Number of Shares | Option Price | Number of Shares | Option Price |
| Balance at December 30, 1989 | 320,421 | $ .16–$ 1.60 | 48,750 | 1.60 |
| Granted | 50,656 | 1.60– 4.00 | | |
| Exercised | (22,646) | .16– 1.60 | | |
| Canceled | (32,031) | .80– 1.60 | | |
| Balance at December 29, 1990 | 316,400 | .80– 4.00 | 48,750 | 1.60 |
| Granted | 91,500 | 4.00– 9.00 | 23,125 | 4.00 |
| Exercised | (42,916) | .80– 4.00 | | |
| Canceled | (77,772) | .80– 4.00 | | |
| Balance at December 28, 1991 | 287,212 | .80– 9.00 | 71,875 | 1.60–4.00 |
| Granted | 432,099 | 9.00– 11.00 | | |
| Exercised | (26,986) | .80– 4.00 | (4,125) | 1.60 |
| Canceled | (22,946) | 1.60– 11.00 | — | |
| Balance at December 26, 1992 | 669,379 | .80– 11.00 | 67,750 | 1.60–4.00 |

At December 26, 1992, options for the purchase of 149,384 shares were exercisable.

On December 14, 1991, the Company's board of directors adopted the 1991 Employee Stock Purchase Plan (the "Purchase Plan") which provides for the issuance of up to 262,500 shares of common stock to participating employees of the Company through a series of four six-month offerings, beginning May 1, 1992. The Purchase Plan covers substantially all employees, subject to certain limitations. Each employee may elect to have up to 11% of base pay withheld and applied toward the purchase of shares in such offering. The price at which the shares of common stock may be purchased in an offering is 85% of the fair market value of the common stock on the date such offering commences or the date such offering terminates, whichever is lower. In 1992, 33,395 shares were purchased under the Purchase Plan.

The Company has reserved 1,412,892 shares of common stock for issuance upon the exercise of warrants (Note 4) and for use in the Plan and Purchase Plan.

## Note 6:   Income Taxes

Certain items of expense, primarily research and development, are recognized for income taxes in different periods than for financial reporting purposes. Certain research and development costs are capitalized for tax reporting purposes. Beginning in 1992, the Company is amortizing these costs over a period of 60 months. At December 26, 1992, unamortized research and development costs totaled $34,100,000.

At December 26, 1992, the Company has net operating loss carryforwards of approximately $64,100,000 and $26,500,000 for financial and tax reporting purposes, respectively. The net operating loss carryforwards expire through 2007. In addition, the Company has research and development tax credit carryforwards which expire through 2007 of approximately $2,900,000 available to offset future regular income tax liabilities. Under the Internal Revenue Code, certain substantial changes in the Company's ownership could result in an annual limitation on the amount of the carryforwards which could be utilized.

## EXHIBIT 1 (continued)

### Note 8:   Major Customers and Export Sales

Sales to one and three major customers accounted for $904,000 and $7,763,000, or 100% and 37% of revenue, for 1991 and 1992, respectively.  In 1992, revenue from European customers totaled $9,173,000.

### Note 10:   Line of Credit

The Company has a bank line of credit which provides for borrowings of up to $2,500,000.  Borrowings under the line of credit bear interest at the bank's base rate plus 2%.  In the event that the Company's quarterly net income exceeds $250,000, borrowings under the line of credit may increase to $5,000,000 and the interest will decrease to the bank's base rate plus ¾%.  All borrowings are secured by accounts receivable and inventories.  At December 26, 1992, there were no borrowings outstanding under the line of credit.

# Harnischfeger Corporation

In February 1985, Peter Roberts, the research director of Exeter Group, a small Boston-based investment advisory service specializing in turnaround stocks, was reviewing the 1984 annual report of Harnischfeger Corporation (**Exhibit 4**). His attention was drawn by the $1.28 per share net profit Harnischfeger reported for 1984. He knew that barely three years earlier the company had faced a severe financial crisis. Harnischfeger had defaulted on its debt and stopped dividend payments after reporting a hefty $7.64 per share net loss in fiscal 1982. The company's poor performance continued in 1983, leading to a net loss of $3.49 per share. Roberts was intrigued by Harnischfeger's rapid turnaround and wondered whether he should recommend the purchase of the company's stock (see **Exhibit 3** for selected data on Harnischfeger's stock).

## COMPANY BUSINESS AND PRODUCTS

Harnischfeger Corporation was a machinery company based in Milwaukee, Wisconsin. The company had originally been started as a partnership in 1884 and was incorporated in Wisconsin in 1910 under the name Pawling and Harnischfeger. Its name was changed to the present one in 1924. The company went public in 1929 and was listed on the New York Stock Exchange.

The company's two major segments were the P&H Heavy Equipment Group, consisting of the Construction Equipment and the Mining and Electrical Equipment divisions, and the Industrial Technologies Group, consisting of the Material Handling Equipment and the Harnischfeger Engineers divisions. The

---

*Professor Krishna Palepu prepared this case.*

Copyright © 1985 by the President and Fellows of Harvard College. Harvard Business School case 186-160.

sales mix of the company in 1983 consisted of Construction Equipment, 32%; Mining and Electrical Equipment, 33%; Material Handling Equipment, 29%; and Harnischfeger Engineers, 6%.

Harnischfeger was a leading producer of construction equipment. Its products, bearing the widely recognized brand name P&H, included hydraulic cranes and lattice boom cranes. These were used in bridge and highway construction and for cargo and other material handling applications. Harnischfeger had market shares of about 20% in hydraulic cranes and about 30% in lattice boom cranes. In the 1980s the construction equipment industry in general was experiencing declining margins.

Electric mining shovels and excavators constituted the principal products of the Mining and Electrical Equipment Division of Harnischfeger. The company had a dominant share of the mining machinery market. The company's products were used in coal, copper, and iron mining. A significant part of the division's sales were from the sale of spare parts. Because of its large market share and the lucrative spare parts sales, the division was traditionally very profitable. Most of the company's future mining product sales were expected to occur outside the United States, principally in developing countries.

The Material Handling Equipment Division of Harnischfeger was the fourth-largest supplier of automated material handling equipment with a 9% market share. The division's products included overhead cranes, portal cranes, hoists, monorails, and components and parts. The demand for this equipment was expected to grow in the coming years as an increasing number of manufacturing firms emphasized cost reduction programs. Harnischfeger believed that the material handling equipment business would be a major source of its future growth.

Harnischfeger Engineers was an engineering services division engaged in design, custom software development, and project management for factory and distribution automation projects. The division engineered and installed complete automated material handling systems for a wide variety of applications on a fee basis. The company expected such automated storage and retrieval systems to play an increasingly important role in the "factory of the future."

Harnischfeger had a number of subsidiaries, affiliated companies, and licensees in a number of countries. Export and foreign sales constituted more than 50% of the total revenues of the company.

## FINANCIAL DIFFICULTIES OF 1982

The machinery industry experienced a period of explosive growth during the 1970s. Harnischfeger expanded rapidly during this period, growing from $205 million in revenues in 1973 to $644 million in 1980. To fund this growth, the company relied increasingly on debt financing, and the firm's debt/equity ratio rose from 0.88 in 1973 to 1.26 in 1980. The worldwide recession in the early 1980s caused a significant drop in demand for the company's products starting in 1981 and culminated in a series of events that shook the financial stability of Harnischfeger.

Reduced sales and the high interest payments resulted in poor profit performance leading to a reported loss in 1982 of $77 million.  The management of Harnischfeger commented on its financial difficulties:

> *There is a persistent weakness in the basic industries, both in the United States and overseas, which have been large, traditional markets for P&H products.  Energy-related projects, which had been a major source of business of our Construction Equipment Division, have slowed significantly in the last year as a result of lower oil demand and subsequent price decline, not only in the U.S. but throughout the world.  Lack of demand for such basic minerals as iron ore, copper, and bauxite have decreased worldwide mining activity, causing reduced sales for mining equipment, although coal mining remains relatively strong worldwide. Difficult economic conditions have caused many of our normal customers to cut capital expenditures dramatically, especially in such depressed sectors as the steel industry, which has always been a major source of sales for all P&H products.*

The significant operating losses recorded in 1982 and the credit losses experienced by its finance subsidiary caused Harnischfeger to default on certain covenants of its loan agreements.  The most restrictive provisions of the company's loan agreements required it to maintain a minimum working capital of $175 million, consolidated net worth of $180 million, and a ratio of current assets to current liabilities of 1.75.  On October 31, 1982, the company's working capital (after reclassification of about $115 million long-term debt as a current liability) was $29.3 million, the consolidated net worth was $142.2 million, and the ratio of current assets to current liabilities was 1.12.  Harnischfeger Credit Corporation, an unconsolidated finance subsidiary, also defaulted on certain covenants of its loan agreements, largely due to significant credit losses relating to the financing of construction equipment sold to a large distributor.  As a result of these covenant violations, the company's long-term debt of $124.3 million became due on demand, the unused portion of the bank revolving credit line of $25.0 million became unavailable, and the unused short-term bank credit lines of $12.0 million were canceled.  In addition, the $25.1 million debt of Harnischfeger Credit Corporation also became immediately due.  The company was forced to stop paying dividends and began negotiations with its lenders to restructure its debt to permit operations to continue.  Price Waterhouse, the company's audit firm, qualified its audit opinion on Harnischfeger's 1982 annual report with respect to the outcome of the company's negotiations with its lenders.

## CORPORATE RECOVERY PLAN

Harnischfeger responded to the financial crisis facing the firm by developing a corporate recovery plan.  The plan consisted of four elements: (1) changes in the top management, (2) cost reductions to lower the break-even point, (3) reorientation of the company's business, and (4) debt restructuring and recapitalization. The actions taken in each of these four areas are described below.

To deal effectively with the financial crisis, Henry Harnischfeger, then chairman and chief executive officer of the company, created the position of chief operating officer. After an extensive search, the position was offered in August 1982 to William Goessel, who had considerable experience in the machinery industry. Another addition to the management team was Jeffrey Grade, who joined the company in 1983 as senior vice president of finance and administration and chief financial officer. Grade's appointment was necessitated by the early retirement of the previous vice president of finance in 1982. The engineering, manufacturing, and marketing functions were also restructured to streamline the company's operations (see **Exhibits 1** and **2** for additional information on Harnischfeger's current management).

To deal with the short-term liquidity squeeze, the company initiated a number of cost reduction measures. These included (1) reducing the workforce from 6,900 to 3,800; (2) eliminating management bonuses and reducing benefits and freezing wages of salaried and hourly employees; (3) liquidating excess inventories and stretching payments to creditors; and (4) permanent closure of the construction equipment plant at Escanaba, Michigan. These and other related measures improved the company's cash position and helped to reduce the rate of loss during fiscal 1983.

Concurrent with the above cost reduction measures, the new management made some strategic decisions to reorient Harnischfeger's business. First, the company entered into a long-term agreement with Kobe Steel, Ltd., of Japan. Under this agreement, Kobe agreed to supply Harnischfeger's requirements for construction cranes for sale in the United States as Harnischfeger phased out its own manufacture of cranes. This step was expected to significantly reduce the manufacturing costs of Harnischfeger's construction equipment, enabling it to compete effectively in the domestic market. Second, the company decided to emphasize the high technology part of its business by targeting for future growth the material-handling equipment and systems business. To facilitate this strategy, the Industrial Technologies Group was created. As part of the reorientation, the company stated that it would develop and acquire new products, technology, and equipment, and would expand its abilities to provide computer-integrated solutions to handling, storing, and retrieval in areas hitherto not pursued—industries such as distribution warehousing, food, pharmaceuticals, and aerospace.

While Harnischfeger was implementing its turnaround strategy, it was engaged at the same time in complex and difficult negotiations with its bankers. On January 6, 1984, the company entered into agreements with its lenders to restructure its debt obligations into three-year term loans secured by fixed as well as other assets, with a one-year extension option. This agreement required, among other things, specified minimum levels of cash and unpledged receivables, working capital, and net worth.

The company reported a net loss of $35 million in 1983, down from the $77 million loss the year before.  Based on the above developments during the year, in the 1983 annual report the management expressed confidence that the company would return to profitability soon.

> *We approach our second century with optimism, knowing that the negative events of the last three years are behind us, and with a firm belief that positive achievements will be recorded in 1984.  By the time the corporation celebrates its 100th birthday on December 1, we are confident it will be operating profitably and attaining new levels of market strength and leadership.*

During 1984 the company reported profits during each of the four quarters, ending the year with a pre-tax operating profit of $5.7 million, and a net income after tax and extraordinary credits of $15 million (see **Exhibit 4**).  It also raised substantial new capital through a public offering of debentures and common stock.  Net proceeds from the offering, which totaled $150 million, were used to pay off all of the company's restructured debt.  In the 1984 annual report the management commented on the company's performance as follows:

> *1984 was the Corporation's Centennial year and we marked the occasion by rededicating ourselves to excellence through market leadership, customer service, and improved operating performance and profitability.*

> \* \* \* \* \* \*

> *We look back with pride.  We move ahead with confidence and optimism.  Our major markets have never been more competitive; however, we will strive to take advantage of any and all opportunities for growth and to attain satisfactory profitability.  Collectively, we will do what has to be done to ensure that the future will be rewarding to all who have a part in our success.*

**EXHIBIT 1**
**Board of Directors, Harnischfeger Corporation, 1984**

| | | Director Since | Current Term | Shares Owned |
|---|---|---|---|---|
| Edward W. Duffy | Chairman of the Board and Chief Executive of United States Gypsum Company, manufacturer of building materials and products used in industrial processes, since 1983. Former Vice Chairman from 1981 to 1983; President and Chief Operating Officer from 1971 to 1981. Director American National Bank and Trust Company of Chicago, Walter E. Heller International Corporation, W. W. Grainger, Inc., and UNR Industries, Inc. Age 64. | 1981 | 1985 | 100 |
| Herbert V. Kohler, Jr. | Chairman, Chief Executive Officer, and Director of Kohler Company, manufacturer of plumbing and specialty products, engines and generators, since 1972; President since 1974. Age 44. | 1973 | 1985 | 700 |
| Taisuke Mori | Executive Vice Chairman and Director of Kobe Steel, Ltd., a Japanese manufacturer of steel and steel products, industrial machinery, construction equipment, aluminum, copper and alloy products, and welding equipment and consumables. Age 63. | 1981 | 1985 | None |
| William W. Goessel | President and Chief Operating Officer of the Corporation since 1982. Executive Vice President of Beloit Corporation from 1978, Director to 1982. Goulds Pumps, Inc. Age 56. | 1982 | 1986 | 15,000 |
| Henry Harnischfeger | Chairman of the Board and Chief Executive Officer of the Corporation since 1970; President from 1959 to 1982. Director, First Wisconsin Corporation and First Wisconsin National Bank of Milwaukee. Age 60. | 1945 | 1986 | 611,362 |
| Karl F. Nygren | Partner in Kirkland & Ellis, attorneys, since 1959. Age 56. | 1964 | 1986 | 2,000 |
| John P. Gallagher | Senior lecturer, Graduate School of Business, University of Chicago. Director, IC Industries, Inc., Stone Container Corporation, UNR Industries, Inc., American National Bank and Trust Company of Chicago, and Walter E. Heller International Corporation. Age 67. | 1979 | 1987 | 500 |
| Jeffrey T. Grade | Senior Vice President Finance and Administration and Chief Financial Officer of the Corporation since August 1, 1983. Vice President Corporate of IC Industries from 1981 to 1983; Assistant Vice President from 1976 to 1981. Age 40. | 1983 | 1987 | 3,750 |
| Donald Taylor | President, Chief Operating Officer, and Director of Rexnord, Inc., a major manufacturer of industrial components and machinery, since 1978. Director, Johnson Controls, Inc., Marine Corporation, and Marine Bank, N.A. Age 56. | 1979 | 1987 | 100 |
| Frank A. Lee | Director of Foster Wheeler Corporation since 1971; Chairman of the Board from 1981 to 1982; President and Chief Executive from 1978 to 1981. Director, Belco Pollution Control Corporation, International General Industries, Inc., and Banker's Life Insurance Co. Age 59. | 1983 | 1987 | None |

## EXHIBIT 2
## Executive  Compensation, Harnischfeger Corporation

The following table sets forth all cash compensation paid to each of the Corporation's five most highly compensated executive officers and to all executive officers as a group for services rendered to the Corporation and its subsidiaries during fiscal 1984.

Cash Compensation

| | | |
|---|---|---|
| Henry Harnischfeger | Chairman of the Board and Chief Executive Officer | $  364,004 |
| William W. Goessel | President and Chief Operating Officer | 280,000 |
| C. P. Cousland | Senior Vice President and group executive, P&H  Heavy Equipment | 210,000 |
| Jeffrey T. Grade | Senior Vice President Finance and Administration and Chief Financial Officer | 205,336 |
| Douglas E. Holt | President, Harnischfeger Engineers, Inc. | 152,839 |
| All persons who were executive officers during the fiscal year as a group (14 persons) | | 2,159,066 |

**1985 Executive Incentive Plan**
     In December 1984, the board of directors established an Executive Incentive Plan for fiscal 1985 which provides an incentive compensation opportunity of 40% of annual salary for 11 senior executive officers only if the Corporation reaches a specific net after-tax profit objective, and it provides an additional incentive compensation of up to 40% of annual salary for seven of those officers if the corporation exceeds the objective.  The Plan covered the chairman; president; senior vice presidents; president, Harnischfeger Engineers, Inc.; vice president, P&H World Services; vice president, material Handling Equipment; and secretary.  Awards made in respect to fiscal year 1984 are included in the compensation table above.

**EXHIBIT 3**
**Selected Stock Price and Market Data**

A.   **Stock Prices**

|  | Harnischfeger's Stock Price | | | S&P 400 Industrials Index | | |
|---|---|---|---|---|---|---|
|  | High | Low | Close | High | Low | Close |
| January 4, 1985 | 9 1/8 | 8 6/8 | 9 | 186.4 | 181.8 | 182.2 |
| January 11, 1985 | 10 6/8 | 8 7/8 | 10 5/8 | 188.2 | 182.2 | 182.8 |
| January 18, 1985 | 11 | 10 | 10 4/8 | 191.9 | 186.9 | 191.3 |
| January 25, 1985 | 11 2/8 | 10 1/8 | 11 | 199.7 | 191.3 | 198.6 |
| February 1, 1985 | 11 5/8 | 10 7/8 | 11 2/8 | 201.8 | 198.6 | 200.0 |

Harnischfeger's stock beta = 0.95 (Value Line estimate)

B.   **Market Data**

|  | February 1985 |
|---|---|
| Median P/E ratio of Dow Jones Industrials | 10.9 |
| Median P/E ratio of Value Line stocks | 11.3 |
| Median P/E ratio of machinery industry (construction and mining equipment) | 10.0 |
| Prime rate | 10.5% |
| 91-day Treasury bill rate | 8.4% |
| 30-year Treasury bond yield | 11.4% |
| Moody's Aaa corporate bond yield | 12.0% |

**EXHIBIT 4**
**1984 Annual Report—Edited**

### To Our Shareholders

The Corporation recorded gains in each quarter during fiscal 1984, returning to profitability despite the continued depressed demand and intense price competition in the world markets it serves.

For the year ended October 31, net income was $15,176,000 or $1.28 per common share, which included $11,005,000 or 93¢ per share from the cumulative effect of a change in depreciation accounting. In 1983, the Corporation reported a loss of $34,630,000 or $3.49 per share.

Sales for 1984 improved 24% over the preceding year, rising to $398.7 million from $321 million a year ago. New orders totaled $451 million, a $101 million increase over 1983. We entered fiscal 1985 with a backlog of $193 million, which compared to $141 million a year earlier.

### All Divisions Improved

All product divisions recorded sales and operating improvements during 1984.

Mining equipment was the strongest performer with sales up over 60%, including major orders from Turkey and the People's Republic of China. During the year we began the implementation of the training, engineering, and manufacturing license agreement concluded in November 1983 with the People's Republic of China, which offers the Corporation long-term potential in modernizing and mechanizing this vast and rapidly developing mining market.

Sales of material handling equipment and systems were up 10% for the year and the increasingly stronger bookings recorded during the latter part of the year are continuing into the first quarter of 1985.

Sales on construction equipment products showed some signs of selective improvement. In the fourth quarter, bookings more than doubled from the very depressed levels in the same period a year ago, although the current level is still far below what is needed to achieve acceptable operating results for this product line.

### Financial Stability Restored

In April, the financial stability of the Corporation was improved through a public offering of 2.15 million shares of common stock, $50 million of 15% notes due April 15, 1994, and $100 million of 12% subordinated debentures due April 15, 2004, with two million common stock purchase warrants.

Net proceeds from the offering totaled $149 million, to which we added an additional $23 million in cash, enabling us to pay off all of our long-term debt. As a result of the refinancing, the Corporation gained permanent long-term capital with minimal annual cash flow requirements to service it. We now have the financial resources and flexibility to pursue new opportunities to grow and diversify.

Furthermore, should we require additional funds, they will be available through a $52 million unsecured three-year revolving credit agreement concluded in June with ten U.S. and Canadian banks. An $80 million product financing capability was also arranged through a major U.S. bank to provide financing to customers purchasing P&H products.

## EXHIBIT 4 (continued)

### Outlook

Throughout 1985 we believe we will see gradual improvements in most of our U.S. and world markets.

For our mining excavator product line, coal and certain metals mining are expected to show a more favorable long-term outlook in selected foreign requirements and our capability to source equipment from the U.S., Japan, or Europe places us in a strong marketing position. In the U.S., we see only a moderate strengthening in machinery requirements for coal, while metals mining will remain weak.

Continuing shipments of the Turkish order throughout 1985 will help to stabilize our plant utilization levels and improve our operating results for this product line.

In our material handling and systems markets, particularly in the U.S., we are experiencing a moderately strong continuation of the improved bookings which we began to see in the third and fourth quarters of last year.

In construction lifting equipment markets, we expect modest overall economic improvement in the U.S., which should help to absorb the large numbers of idle lifting equipment that have been manufacturer, distributor, and customer inventories for the last three years. As this overhang on the market is reduced we will see gradual improvement in new sales. Harnischfeger traditionally exports half of its U.S.-produced lifting products. However, as with mining equipment, the continued strength of the U.S. dollar severely restricts our ability to sell U.S.-built products in world markets.

In addition to the strong dollar and economic instability in many foreign nations, overcapacity in worldwide heavy equipment manufacturing remains a serious problem in spite of some exits from the market as well as consolidations within the industry.

The Corporation continues to respond to severe price competition through systematic cost reduction programs and through expanded sourcing of P&H equipment from our European operation and, most importantly, through our 30-year association with our Japanese partner, Kobe Steel, Ltd. P&H engineering and technology have established world standards for quality and performance for construction cranes and mining equipment, which customers can expect from every P&H machine regardless of its source. More than a dozen new models of foreign-sourced P&H construction cranes will be made available for the first time in the U.S. during 1985, broadening our existing product lines and giving competitive pricing to our U.S. distributors and customers.

To improve our future operating results, we restructured our three operating divisions into two groups. All construction- and mining-related activities are in the new "P&H Heavy Equipment Group." All material handling equipment and systems activities are now merged into the "Industrial Technologies Group." More information on these Groups is reported in their respective sections.

We are pleased to announce that John P. Moran was elected Senior Vice President and Group Executive, Industrial Technologies Group, and John R. Teitgen was elected Secretary and General Counsel.

In September Robert F. Schnoes became a member of our Board of Directors. He is President and Chief Executive Officer of Burgess, Inc., and of Ultrasonic Power Corporation, and a member of the Board of Signode Industries, Inc.

## EXHIBIT 4 (continued)

### Beginning Our Second Century

1984 was the Corporation's Centennial year and we marked the occasion by rededicating ourselves to excellence through market leadership, customer service, and improved operating performance and profitability.

Our first century of achievement resulted from the dedicated effort, support and cooperation of our employees, distributors, suppliers, lenders, and shareholders, and we thank all of them.

We look back with pride.  We move ahead with confidence and optimism.  Our major markets have never been more competitive; however, we will strive to take advantage of any and all opportunities for growth and to attain satisfactory profitability. Collectively, we will do what has to be done to ensure that the future will be rewarding to all who have a part in our success.

**Henry Harnischfeger**
Chairman of the Board

**William W. Goessel**
President

January 31, 1985

### Management's Discussion & Analysis

### Results of Operation

#### 1984 Compared to 1983

Consolidated net sales of $399 million in fiscal 1984 increased $78 million or 24% over 1983.  Sales increases were 62% in the Mining and Electrical Equipment Segment and 10% in the Industrial Technologies Segment.  Sales in the Construction Equipment Segment were virtually unchanged, reflecting the continued low demand for construction equipment worldwide.

Effective at the beginning of fiscal 1984, net sales include the full sales price of construction and mining equipment purchased from Kobe Steel, Ltd., and sold by the Corporation, in order to reflect more effectively the nature of the Corporation's transactions with Kobe.  Such sales aggregated $28.0 million in 1984.

The $4.0 million increase in Other Income reflected a recovery of certain claims and higher license and technical service fees.

Cost of Sales was equal to 79.1% of net sales in 1984 and 81.4% in 1983; which together with the increase in net sales resulted in a $23.9 million increase in gross profit (net sales less cost of sales).  Contributing to this increase were improved sales of higher-margin replacement parts in the Mining Equipment and Industrial Technologies Segments and a reduction in excess manufacturing costs through greater utilization of domestic manufacturing capacity and economies in total manufacturing costs, including a reduction in pension expense.  Reductions of certain LIFO inventories increased gross profit by $2.4 million in 1984 and $15.6 million in 1983.

Product development selling and administrative expenses were reduced, due to the funding of R&D expenses in the Construction Equipment Segment pursuant to the

## EXHIBIT 4 (continued)

October 1983 Agreement with Kobe Steel, Ltd., to reductions in pension expenses and provision for credit losses, and to the absence of the corporate financial restructuring expenses incurred in 1983.

Net interest expense in 1984 increased $2.9 million due to higher interest rates on the outstanding funded debt and a reduction in interest income.

Equity in Earnings (Loss) of Unconsolidated Companies included 1984 income of $1.2 million of Harnischfeger Credit Corporation, an unconsolidated finance subsidiary, reflecting an income tax benefit of $1.4 million not previously recorded.

The preceding items, together with the cumulative effect of the change in depreciation method described in Financial Note 2, were included in net income of $15.2 million or $1.28 per common share, compared with net loss of $34.6 million or $3.49 per share in 1983.

The sales orders booked and unshipped backlogs of orders of the Corporation's three segments are summarized as follows (in million of dollars):

| Orders Booked | 1984 | 1983 |
|---|---|---|
| Industrial Technologies | $132 | $106 |
| Mining and Electrical Equipment | 210 | 135 |
| Construction Equipment | 109 | 109 |
| | $451 | $350 |

| Backlogs at October 31 | | |
|---|---|---|
| Industrial Technologies | $ 79 | $ 71 |
| Mining and Electrical Equipment | 91 | 50 |
| Construction Equipment | 23 | 20 |
| | $193 | $141 |

### 1983 Compared to 1982

Consolidated net sales of $321 million in fiscal 1983 were $126 million or 28% below 1982. This decline reflected, for the second consecutive year, the continued low demand in all markets served by the Corporation's products, with exports even more severely depressed due to the strength of the dollar. The largest decline was reported in the Construction Equipment Segment, down 34%; followed by the Mining and Electrical Equipment Segment, down 27%; and the Industrial Technologies Segment, down 23%.

Cost of Sales was equal to 81.4% of net sales in 1983 and 81.9% in 1982. The resulting gross profit was $60 million in 1983 and $81 million in 1982, a reduction equal to the rate of sales decrease.

The benefits of reduced manufacturing capacity and economies in total manufacturing costs were offset by reduced selling prices in the highly competitive markets. Reductions of certain LIFO inventories increased gross profits by $15.6 million in 1983 and $7.2 million in 1982.

Product development, selling, and administrative expenses were reduced as a result of expense reduction measures in response to the lower volume of business and undertaken in connection with the Corporation's corporate recovery program, and reduced provisions for credit losses, which in 1982 included $4.0 million in income support for Harnischfeger Credit Corporation.

**EXHIBIT 4 (continued)**

Net interest expense was reduced $9.1 million from 1982 to 1983, due primarily to increased interest income from short-term cash investments and an accrual of $4.7 million in interest income on refundable income taxes not previously recorded.

The Credit for Income Taxes included a federal income tax benefit of $5 million, based upon the recent examination of the Corporation's income tax returns and refund claims. No income tax benefits were available for the losses of the U.S. operations in 1983.

The losses from unconsolidated companies recorded in 1983 included $0.5 million in Harnischfeger Credit Corporation; $2.1 million in Cranetex, Inc., a Corporation-owned distributorship in Texas; and $0.8 million in ASEA Industrial Systems Inc., then a 49%-owned joint venture between the Corporation and ASEA AB and now 19%-owned with the investment accounted for on the cost method.

The preceding items were reflected in a net loss of $34.6 million or $3.49 per share.

**Liquidity and Financial Resources**

In April 1984, the Corporation issued in public offerings 2,150,000 shares of Common Stock, $50 million principal amount of 15% Senior Notes due in 1994, and 100,000 Units consisting of $100 million principal amount of 12% Subordinated Debentures due in 2004 and 2,000,000 Common Stock Purchase Warrants.

The net proceeds from the sales of the securities of $149 million were used to prepay substantially all of the outstanding debt of the Corporation and certain of its subsidiaries.

During the year ended October 31, 1984, the consolidated cash balances increased $32 million to a balance of $96 million, with the cash activity summarized as follows (in million of dollars):

| | |
|---|---:|
| Funds provided by operations | $10 |
| Funds returned to the Corporation upon restructuring of the Salaried Employees' Pension Plan | 39 |
| Debt repayment less the proceeds of sales of securities | (9) |
| Plant and equipment additions | (6) |
| All other changes—net | (2) |
| | $32 |

In the third quarter of fiscal 1984 the Corporation entered into a $52 million three-year revolving credit agreement with ten U.S. and Canadian banks. While the Corporation has adequate liquidity to meet its current working capital requirements, the revolver represents another step in the Corporation's program to strengthen its financial position and provide the required financial resources to respond to opportunities as they arise.

**EXHIBIT 4 (continued)**
**Consolidated Statement of Operations**

(Dollar amounts in thousands except per share figures)

| | Year Ended October 31 | | |
| --- | ---: | ---: | ---: |
| | 1984 | 1983 | 1982 |
| Revenues | | | |
| Net sales | $398,708 | $321,010 | $447,461 |
| Other income, including license and technical service fees | 7,067 | 3,111 | 5,209 |
| | 405,775 | 324,121 | 452,670 |
| Cost of sales | 315,216 | 261,384 | 366,297 |
| Operating Income | 90,559 | 62,737 | 86,373 |
| Less: | | | |
| Product development, selling and administrative expenses | 72,196 | 85,795 | 113,457 |
| Interest expense—net | 12,625 | 9,745 | 18,873 |
| Provision for plant closing | — | — | 23,700 |
| Income (Loss) before provision (credit) for income taxes, equity items and cumulative effect of accounting change | 5,738 | (32,803) | (69,657) |
| Provision (Credit) for income taxes | 2,425 | (1,400) | (1,600) |
| Income (Loss) before equity items and cumulative effect of accounting change | 3,313 | (31,403) | (68,057) |
| Equity items | | | |
| Equity in earnings (loss) of unconsolidated companies | 993 | (3,397) | (7,891) |
| Minority interest in (earnings) loss of consolidated subsidiaries | (135) | 170 | (583) |
| Income (Loss) before cumulative effect of accounting change | 4,171 | (34,630) | (76,531) |
| Cumulative effect of change in depreciation method | 11,005 | — | — |
| Net income (loss) | $ 15,176 | $ (34,630) | $ (76,531) |
| Earnings (Loss) per common and common equivalent share: | | | |
| Income (Loss) before cumulative effect of accounting change | $ .35 | $(3.49) | $(7.64) |
| Cumulative effect of change in depreciation method | .93 | — | — |
| Net income (loss) | $1.28 | $(3.49) | $(7.64) |
| Pro forma amounts assuming the changed depreciation method had been applied respectively: | | | |
| Net (Loss) | | $ (33,918) | $ (76,695) |
| (Loss) per common share | | $ (3.42) | $ (7.65) |

**EXHIBIT 4 (continued)**
## Consolidated Balance Sheet

(Dollar amounts in thousands except per share figures)

|  | October 31, 1984 | October 31, 1983 |
|---|---|---|
| **Assets** | | |
| Current Assets | | |
| Cash and temporary investments | $ 96,007 | $ 64,275 |
| Accounts receivable | 87,648 | 63,740 |
| Inventories | 144,312 | 153,594 |
| Refundable income taxes and related interest | 1,296 | 12,585 |
| Other current assets | 5,502 | 6,023 |
| Prepaid income taxes | 14,494 | 14,232 |
|  | 349,259 | 314,449 |
| Investments and Other Assets | | |
| Investments in and advances to: | | |
| Finance subsidiary, at equity in net assets | 8,849 | 6,704 |
| Other companies | 4,445 | 2,514 |
| Other assets | 13,959 | 6,411 |
|  | 27,253 | 15,629 |
| Operating Plants | | |
| Land and improvements | 9,419 | 10,370 |
| Buildings | 59,083 | 60,377 |
| Machinery and equipment | 120,949 | 122,154 |
|  | 189,451 | 192,901 |
| Accumulated depreciation | (93,259) | (107,577) |
|  | 96,192 | 85,324 |
|  | $472,704 | $ 415,402 |
| **Liabilities and Shareholders' Equity** | | |
| Current Liabilities | | |
| Short-term notes payable to banks by subsidiaries | $ 9,090 | $ 8,155 |
| Long-term debt and capitalized lease obligations payable within one year | 973 | 18,265 |
| Trade accounts payable | 37,716 | 21,228 |
| Employee compensation and benefits | 15,041 | 14,343 |
| Accrued plant closing costs | 2,460 | 6,348 |
| Advance payments and progress billings | 20,619 | 15,886 |
| Income taxes payable | 1,645 | 3,463 |
| Account payable to finance subsidiary | — | 3,436 |
| Other current liabilities and accruals | 29,673 | 32,333 |
|  | 117,217 | 123,457 |

**EXHIBIT 4 (continued)**
**Consolidated Balance Sheet (continued)**

(Dollar amounts in thousands except per share figures)

| | October 31, 1984 | 1983 |
|---|---|---|
| Long-Term Obligations | | |
| Long-term debt payable to: | | |
| Unaffiliated lenders | $128,550 | $139,092 |
| Finance subsidiary | — | 5,400 |
| Capitalized lease obligations | 7,870 | 8,120 |
| | 136,420 | 152,612 |
| Deferred Liabilities and Income Taxes | | |
| Accrued pension costs | 57,611 | 19,098 |
| Other deferred liabilities | 5,299 | 7,777 |
| Deferred income taxes | 6,385 | 134 |
| | 69,295 | 27,009 |
| Minority Interest | 2,400 | 2,405 |
| Shareholders' equity | | |
| Preferred stock $100 par value—authorized 250,000 shares: | | |
| Series A $7.00 cumulative convertible preferred shares: | | |
| authorized, issued and outstanding 117,500 shares in 1984 and 100,000 shares in 1983 | 11,750 | 10,000 |
| Common stock, $1 par value—authorized 25,000,000 shares: issued and outstanding 12,283,563 shares in 1984 and 10,133,563 shares in 1983 | 12,284 | 10,134 |
| Capital in excess of par value of shares | 114,333 | 88,332 |
| Retained earnings | 19,901 | 6,475 |
| Cumulative translation adjustments | (10,896) | (5,022) |
| | 147,372 | 109,919 |
| | $472,704 | $415,402 |

**EXHIBIT 4 (continued)**
**Consolidated Statement of Changes in Financial Position**

(Dollar amounts in thousands)

| | Year Ended October 31, | | |
| --- | --- | --- | --- |
| | 1984 | 1983 | 1982 |
| **Funds Were Provided by (Applied to):** | | | |
| Operations: | | | |
| Income (loss) before cumulative effect of accounting change | $ 4,171 | $ (34,630) | $(76,531) |
| Cumulative effect of change in depreciation method | 11,005 | — | — |
| Net income (loss) | 15,176 | (34,630) | (76,531) |
| Add (deduct)— | | | |
| Items included not affecting funds: | | | |
| Depreciation | 8,077 | 13,552 | 15,241 |
| Unremitted (earnings) loss of unconsolidated companies | (993) | 3,397 | 7,891 |
| Deferred pension contributions | (500) | 4,834 | — |
| Deferred income taxes | 6,583 | (3,178) | 1,406 |
| Reduction in accumulated depreciation resulting from change in depreciation method | (17,205) | — | — |
| Other—net | (2,168) | (67) | 2,034 |
| Decrease in operating working capital (see below) | 7,039 | 11,605 | 72,172 |
| Add (deduct) the effects on operating working capital of: | | | |
| Conversion of export and factored receivable sales to debt | — | 23,919 | — |
| Reclassification to deferred liabilities: | | | |
| Accrued pension costs | — | 14,264 | — |
| Other liabilities | — | 5,510 | — |
| Foreign currency translation adjustments | (6,009) | (1,919) | (5,943) |
| Funds provided by operations | 10,000 | 37,287 | 16,270 |
| **Financing, Investment and Other Activities:** | | | |
| Transactions in debt and capitalized lease obligations—Long-term debt and capitalized lease obligations: Proceeds from sale of 15% Senior Notes and 12% subordinated debentures, net of issue costs | 120,530 | — | — |
| Other increases | 1,474 | — | 25,698 |
| Repayments | (161,500) | (760) | (9,409) |
| Restructured debt | — | 158,058 | — |
| Debt replaced, including conversion of receivable sales of $23,919, and short-term bank notes payable of $9,028 | — | (158,058) | — |
| | (39,496) | (760) | 16,289 |
| Net increase (repayment) in short-term bank notes payable | 2,107 | (3,982) | (2,016) |
| Net increase (repayment) in debt and capitalized lease obligations | (37,389) | (4,742) | 14,273 |

**EXHIBIT 4 (continued)**
**Consolidated Statement of Changes in Financial Position (continued)**

(Dollar amounts in thousands)

| | Year Ended October 31, | | |
|---|---|---|---|
| | 1984 | 1983 | 1982 |
| Issuance of: | | | |
| Common stock | $ 21,310 | — | $    449 |
| Common stock purchase warrants | 6,663 | — | — |
| Salaried pension assets reversion | 39,307 | — | — |
| Plant and equipment additions | (5,546) | (1,871) | (10,819) |
| Advances to unconsolidated companies | (2,882) | — | — |
| Other—net | 269 | 1,531 | 848 |
| Funds provided by (applied to) financing, investment and other activities | 21,732 | (5,082) | 4,751 |
| Increase in cash and temporary investments | $ 31,732 | $ 32,205 | $ 21,021 |
| Cash Dividends | — | — | (2,369) |
| Increase in Cash and Temporary Investments | $ 31,732 | $ 32,205 | $ 18,652 |
| Decrease (increase) in operating working capital (excluding cash items, debt and capitalized lease obligations): | | | |
| Accounts receivable | $(23,908) | $ (5,327) | $ 42,293 |
| Inventories | 9,282 | 56,904 | 26,124 |
| Refundable income taxes and related interest | 11,289 | (2,584) | (6,268) |
| Other current assets | 259 | 10,008 | (439) |
| Trade accounts payable | 16,488 | (1,757) | (3,302) |
| Employee compensation and benefits | 698 | (15,564) | (3,702) |
| Accrued plant closing costs | (3,888) | (14,148) | 20,496 |
| Other current liabilities | (3,181) | (15,927) | (3,030) |
| Decrease in operating working capital | $   7,039 | $ 11,605 | $ 72,172 |

**EXHIBIT 4 (continued)**
**Consolidated Statement of Shareholders' Equity**

(Dollar amounts in thousands except per share figures)

| | Preferred Stock | Common Stock | Capital in Excess of Par Value of Shares | Retained Earnings | Cumulative Translation Adjustments | Total |
|---|---|---|---|---|---|---|
| Balance at October 31, 1981 | $10,000 | $10,085 | $ 87,932 | $120,005 | $   — | $228,022 |
| Cumulative translation adjustments through October 31, 1981 | | | | | (1,195) | (1,195) |
| Issuance of Common Stock: | | | | | | |
| 10,000 shares to Kobe Steel, Ltd. | | 10 | 91 | | | 101 |
| 38,161 shares under stock purchase and dividend reinvestment plans | | 39 | 309 | | | 348 |
| Net (loss) | | | | (76,531) | | (76,531) |
| Cash dividends paid on: | | | | | | |
| Preferred stock | | | | (350) | | (350) |
| Common stock $.20 per share | | | | (2,019) | | (2,019) |
| Translation adjustments, net of deferred income taxes of $128 | | | | | (2,928) | (2,928) |
| Balance at October 31, 1982 | 10,000 | 10,134 | 88,332 | 41,105 | (4,123) | 145,448 |
| Net (loss) | | | | (34,630) | | (34,630) |
| Translation adjustments, including deferred income taxes of $33 | | | | | (899) | (899) |
| Balance at October 31, 1983 | 10,000 | 10,134 | 88,332 | 6,475 | (5,022) | 109,919 |
| Issuance of: | | | | | | |
| 2,150,00 shares of common stock | | 2,150 | 19,160 | | | 21,310 |
| 2,000,000 common stock purchase warrants | | | 6,663 | | | 6,663 |
| 17,500 shares of Series A $7.00 cumulative convertible preferred stock in discharge of dividends payable on preferred stock | 1,750 | | | (1,750) | | — |
| Net income | | | | 15,176 | | 15,176 |
| Translation adjustments, net of deferred income taxes of $300 | | | | | (5,874) | (5,874) |
| Other | | | 178 | | | 178 |
| Balance at October 31, 1984 | $11,750 | $12,284 | $114,333 | $ 19,901 | $(10,896) | $147,372 |

**EXHIBIT 4 (continued)**
**Financial Notes**

### Note 1
### Summary of Significant Accounting Policies

**Consolidation**—The consolidated financial statements include the accounts of all majority-owned subsidiaries except a wholly-owned domestic finance subsidiary, a subsidiary organized in 1982 as a temporary successor to a distributor, both of which are accounted for under the equity method, and a wholly-owned Brazilian subsidiary, which is carried at estimated net realizable value due to economic uncertainty. All related significant intercompany balances and transactions have been eliminated in consolidation.

Financial statements of certain consolidated subsidiaries, principally foreign, are included, effective in fiscal year 1984, on the basis of their fiscal years ending September 30; previously, certain of such subsidiaries had fiscal years ending July (See Note 2). Such fiscal periods have been adopted by the subsidiaries in order to provide for a more timely consolidation with the Corporation.

**Inventories**—The Corporation values its inventories at the lower of cost or market. Cost is determined by the last-in, first-out (LIFO) method for inventories located principally in the United States, and by the first-in, first-out (FIFO) method for inventories of foreign subsidiaries.

**Operating Plants, Equipment, and Depreciation**—Properties are stated at cost. Maintenance and repairs are charged to expense as incurred and expenditures for betterments and renewals are capitalized. Effective in 1981, interest is capitalized for qualifying assets during their acquisition period. Capitalized interest is amortized on the same basis as the related asset. When properties are sold or otherwise disposed of, the cost and accumulated depreciation are removed from the accounts and any gain or loss is included in income.

Depreciation of plants and equipment is provided over the estimated useful lives of the related assets, or over the lease terms of capital leases, using, effective in fiscal year 1984, the straight-line method for financial reporting, and principally accelerated methods for tax reporting purposes. Previously, accelerated methods, where applicable, were also used for financial reporting purposes (See Note 2). For U.S. income tax purposes, depreciation lives are based principally on the Class Life Asset Depreciation Range for additions, other than buildings, in the years 1973 through 1980, and on the Accelerated Cost Recovery System for all additions after 1980.

Discontinued facilities held for sale are carried at the lower of cost less accumulated depreciation or estimated realizable value, which aggregated $4.9 million and $3.6 million at October 31, 1984 and 1983, respectively, and were included in Other Assets in the accompanying Balance Sheet.

**Pension Plans**—The Corporation has pension plans covering substantially all of its employees. Pension expenses of the principal defined benefit plans consist of current service costs of such plans and amortization of the prior service costs and actuarial gains and losses over periods ranging from 10 to 30 years. The Corporation's policy is to fund at a minimum the amount required under the Employee Retirement Income Security Act of 1974.

**EXHIBIT 4 (continued)**
**Financial Notes**

**Income Taxes**—The consolidated tax provision is computed based on income and expenses recorded in the Statement of Operations.  Prepaid or deferred taxes are recorded for the difference between such taxes and taxes computed for tax returns.  The Corporation and its domestic subsidiaries file a consolidated federal income tax return.  The operating results of Harnischfeger GmbH are included in the Corporation's U.S. income tax returns.

Additional taxes are provided on the earnings of foreign subsidiaries which are intended to be remitted to the Corporation.  Such taxes are not provided on subsidiaries' unremitted earnings which are intended to be permanently reinvested.

Investment tax credits are accounted for under the flow-through method as a reduction of the income tax provision, if applicable, in the year the related asset is placed in service.

**Reporting Format**—Certain previously reported items have been conformed to the current year's presentation.

**Note 2**
**Accounting Changes:**
Effective November 1, 1983, the Corporation includes in its net sales products purchased from Kobe Steel, Ltd. and sold by the Corporation, to reflect more effectively the nature of the Corporation's transactions with Kobe.  Previously only the gross margin on Kobe-originated equipment was included.  During fiscal year 1984 such sales aggregated $28.0 million.  Also, effective November 1, 1983, the financial statements of certain foreign subsidiaries are included on the basis of their fiscal years ended July 31.  This change had the effect of increasing net sales by $5.4 million for the year ended October 31, 1984.  The impact of these changes on net income was insignificant.

In 1984, the Corporation has computed depreciation expense on plants, machinery, and equipment using the straight-line method for financial reporting purposes.  Prior to 1984, the Corporation used principally accelerated methods for its U.S. operating plants.  The cumulative effect of this change, which was applied retroactively to all assets previously subjected to accelerated depreciation, increased net income for 1984 by $11.0 million or $.93 per common and common equivalent share.  The impact of the new method on income for the year 1984 before the cumulative effect was insignificant.

As a result of the review of its depreciation policy, the Corporation, effective November 1, 1983, has changed its estimated depreciation lives on certain U.S. plants, machinery and equipment, and residual values on certain machinery and equipment, which increased net income for 1984 by $3.2 million or $.27 per share.  No income tax effect was applied to this change.

The changes in accounting for depreciation were made to conform the Corporation's depreciation policy to those used by manufacturers in the Corporation's and similar industries and to provide a more equitable allocation of the cost of plants, machinery, and equipment over their useful lives.

**EXHIBIT 4 (continued)**
**Financial Notes**

**Note 3**
**Cash and Temporary Investments**
Cash and temporary investments consisted of the following (in thousands of dollars):

|  | October 31, | |
|  | 1984 | 1983 |
|---|---|---|
| Cash—in demand deposits | $ 2,155 | $11,910 |
| —in special accounts principally to support letters of credit | 4,516 | — |
| Temporary investments | 89,336 | 52,365 |
|  | $96,007 | $64,275 |

Temporary investments consisted of short-term U.S. and Canadian treasury bills, money market funds, time and certificates of deposit, commercial paper, and bank repurchase agreements and bankers' acceptances. Temporary investments are stated at cost plus accrued interest, which approximates market value.

**EXHIBIT 4 (continued)**
**Financial Notes**

### Note 4
**Long-Term Debt, Bank Credit Lines, and Interest Expense**
Outstanding long-term debt payable to unaffiliated lenders was as follows (in thousands of dollars):

|  | October 31, 1984 | October 31, 1983 |
|---|---|---|
| **Parent Company:** | | |
| 15% Senior Notes due April 15, 1994 | $ 47,700 | $    — |
| 12% Subordinated Debentures, with an effective interest rate of 16.3%; sinking fund redemption payments of $7,500 due annually on April 15 in 1994–2003, and final payment of $25,000 in 2004 | 100,000 | — |
| Term Obligations— | | |
| Insurance company debt: | | |
| 9% Notes | — | 20,000 |
| 9⅞ Notes | — | 38,750 |
| 8⅞ Notes | — | 40,500 |
| Bank debt, at 105% of prime | — | 25,000 |
| Paper purchase debt, at prime or LIBOR, plus 1¼% | — | 18,519 |
| 9.23% Mortgage Note due monthly to April 1998 | 4,327 | 4,481 |
|  | 152,027 | 147,250 |
| **Consolidated Subsidiaries** | | |
| Notes payable to banks in German marks | — | 9,889 |
| Contract payable in 1985–1989, in South African rands, with imputed interest rate of 12% | 1,024 | — |
| Other | — | 36 |
|  | 153,051 | 157,175 |
| Less: Amounts payable within one year | 644 | 17,799 |
| Unamortized discounts | 23,857 | 284 |
| Long-Term Debt—excluding amounts payable within one year | $128,550 | $139,092 |

**EXHIBIT 4 (continued)**
**Financial Notes**

**Note 5**
**Harnischfeger Credit Corporation and Cranetex, Inc.**
Condensed financial information of Harnischfeger Credit Corporation ("Credit"), an unconsolidated wholly-owned finance subsidiary, accounted for under the equity method, was as follows (in thousands of dollars):

| | October 31, | |
| Balance Sheet | 1984 | 1983 |
| --- | --- | --- |
| **Assets** | | |
| Cash and temporary investments | $ 404 | $19,824 |
| Finance receivables—net | 4,335 | 11,412 |
| Factored account note and current account receivable from parent company | — | 8,836 |
| Other assets | 4,181 | 661 |
| | $8,920 | $40,733 |
| | | |
| **Liabilities and Shareholder's Equity** | | |
| Debt payable | $ — | $32,600 |
| Advances from parent company | 950 | — |
| Other liabilities | 71 | 1,429 |
| | 1,021 | 34,029 |
| Shareholder's equity | 7,899 | 6,704 |
| | $8,920 | $40,733 |

| | Year Ended October 31, | | |
| Statement of Operations | 1984 | 1983 | 1982 |
| --- | --- | --- | --- |
| Revenues | $ 1,165 | $2,662 | $ 9,978 |
| Less: | | | |
| Operating expenses | 1,530 | 3,386 | 14,613 |
| Provision (credit) for income taxes | (1,560) | (222) | 180 |
| Net income (loss) | $ 1,195 | $ (502) | $(4,815) |

Credit's purchases of finance receivables from the Corporation aggregated $1.1 million in 1984, $46.7 million in 1983, and $50.4 million in 1982. In 1982, Credit received income support of $4.0 million from the Corporation.

In 1982, the Corporation organized Cranetex, Inc., to assume certain assets and liabilities transferred by a former distributor of construction equipment, in settlement of the Corporation's and Credit's claims against the distributor and to continue the business on an interim basis until the franchise can be transferred to a new distributor. The Corporation recorded provisions of $2.5 million in 1983 and $2.3 million in 1982, and Credit recorded a provision of $6.7 million in 1982 for credit losses incurred in the financing of equipment sold to the former distributor.

**EXHIBIT 4 (continued)**
**Financial Notes**

The condensed balance sheet of Cranetex, Inc., was as follows (in thousand of dollars):

|  | October 31, | |
|---|---|---|
|  | 1984 | 1983 |
| Assets | | |
| Cash | $ 143 | $ 49 |
| Accounts receivables | 566 | 428 |
| Inventory | 2,314 | 3,464 |
| Property and equipment | 1,547 | 1,674 |
|  | $4,570 | $ 5,615 |
| Liabilities & Deficit | | |
| Loans payable | $4,325 | $ 6,682 |
| Other liabilities | 338 | 620 |
|  | 4,663 | 7,302 |
| Shareholder's (deficit), net of accounts and advances payable to parent company | (93) | (1,687) |
|  | $4,570 | $ 5,615 |

The net losses at Cranetex, Inc., of $.2 million in 1984, $2.1 million in 1983, and $1.0 million in 1982 were included in Equity in Earnings (loss) of Unconsolidated Companies in the Corporation's Statement of Operations.

**EXHIBIT 4 (continued)**
**Financial Notes**

Note 6
**Transactions with Kobe Steel, Ltd., and ASEA Industrial Systems Inc.**

Kobe Steel, Ltd., of Japan ("Kobe"), has been a licensee for certain of the Corporation's products since 1955, and has owned certain Harnischfeger Japanese construction equipment patents and technology since 1981. As of October 31, 1984, Kobe held 1,030,000 shares or 8.4% of the Corporation's outstanding Common Stock. Kobe also owns 25% of the capital stock of Harnischfeger of Australia Pty. Ltd., a subsidiary of the Corporation. This ownership appears as the minority interest on the Corporation's balance sheet.

Under agreements expiring in December 1990, Kobe pays technical service fees on P&H mining equipment produced and sold under license from the Corporation, and trademark and marketing fees on sales of construction equipment outside of Japan. Net fee income received from Kobe was $4.3 million in 1984, $3.1 million in 1983, and $3.9 million in 1982; this income is included in Other Income in the accompanying Statement of Operations.

In October 1983, the Corporation entered into a ten-year agreement with Kobe under which Kobe agreed to supply the Corporation's requirements for construction cranes for sale in the United States as it phases out its own manufacture of cranes over the next several years, and to make the Corporation the exclusive distributor of Kobe-built cranes in the United States. The Agreement also involves a joint research and development program for construction equipment under which the Corporation agreed to spend at least $17 million over a three-year period and, provided it does so, Kobe agreed to pay this amount to the Corporation. Sales of cranes outside the United States continue under the contract terms described in the preceding paragraph.

The Corporation's sales to Kobe, principally components for mining and construction equipment, excluding the R&D expenses discussed in the preceding paragraph, approximated $5.2 million, $10.5 million, and $7.0 million during the three years ended October 31, 1984, 1983, and 1982, respectively. The purchases from Kobe of mining and construction equipment and components amounted to approximately $33.7 million, $15.5 million, and $29.9 million during the three years ended October 31, 1984, 1983, and 1982, respectively, most of which were resold to customers (See Note 2).

The Corporation owns 19% of ASEA Industrial Systems Inc. ("AIS"), an electrical equipment company controlled by ASEA AB of Sweden. The Corporation's purchases of electrical components from AIS aggregated $11.2 million in 1984 and $6.1 million in 1983 and its sales to AIS approximated $2.6 million in 1984 and $3.8 million in 1983.

The Corporation believes that its transactions with Kobe and AIS were competitive with alternative sources of supply for each party involved.

**EXHIBIT 4 (continued)**
## Financial Notes

### Note 7
### Inventories

Consolidated inventories consisted of the following (in thousand of dollars):

|  | October 31, 1984 | October 31, 1983 |
|---|---|---|
| At lower of cost or market (FIFO method): |  |  |
| Raw materials | $ 11,003 | $ 11,904 |
| Work in process and purchased parts | 88,279 | 72,956 |
| Finished goods | 79,111 | 105,923 |
|  | 178,393 | 190,783 |
| Allowance to reduce inventories to cost on the LIFO method | (34,081) | (37,189) |
|  | $144,312 | $153,594 |

Inventories valued on the LIFO method represented approximately 82% of total inventories at both October 31, 1984 and 1983.

     Inventory reductions in 1984, 1983, and 1982 resulted in a liquidation of LIFO inventory quantities carried at lower costs compared with the current cost of their acquisitions. The effect of these liquidations was to increase net income by 2.4 million or $.20 per common share in fiscal 1984, and to reduce the net loss by approximately $15.6 million or $1.54 per share in 1983 and by $6.7 million or $.66 per share in 1982; no income tax effect applied to the adjustment in 1984 and 1983.

### Note 8
### Accounts Receivable

Accounts receivable were net of allowances for doubtful accounts of $5.9 million and $6.4 million at October 31, 1984 and 1983, respectively.

### Note 9
### Research and Development Expense

Research and development expense incurred in the development of new products or significant improvements to existing products was $5.1 million in 1984 (net of amounts funded by Kobe Steel, Ltd.), $12.1 million in 1983, and $14.1 million in 1982.

**EXHIBIT 4 (continued)**
## Financial Notes

### Note 10
**Foreign Operations**
The net sales, net income (loss), and net assets of subsidiaries located in countries outside the United States and Canada and included in the consolidated financial statements were as follows (in thousands of dollars):

|  | Year Ended October 31, | | |
|  | 1984 | 1983 | 1982 |
|---|---|---|---|
| Net sales | $78,074 | $45,912 | $69,216 |
| Net income (loss) after minority interests | 828 | (1,191) | 3,080 |
| Corporation's equity in total net assets | 17,734 | 7,716 | 7,287 |

Foreign currency transaction losses included in Cost of Sales were $2.7 million in 1984, $1.2 million in 1983, and $1.3 million in 1982.

### Note 11
**Pension Plans and Other Postretirement Benefits**
Pension expense for all plans of the Corporation and its consolidated subsidiaries was $1.9 million in 1984, $6.5 million in 1983, and $12.2 million in 1982.

Accumulated plan benefits and plan net assets for the Corporation's U.S. defined benefit plans, at the beginning of the fiscal years 1984 and 1983, with the data for the Salaried Employees' Retirement Plan as in effect on August 1, 1984, were as follows (in thousands of dollars):

|  | 1984 | 1983 |
|---|---|---|
| Actuarial present value of accumulated plan benefits: | | |
| Vested | $52,639 | $108,123 |
| Nonvested | 2,363 | 5,227 |
|  | $55,002 | $113,350 |
| Net assets available for benefits: | | |
| Assets of the Pension Trusts | $45,331 | $112,075 |
| Accrued contributions not paid to the Trusts | 16,717 | 12,167 |
|  | $62,048 | $124,242 |

**EXHIBIT 4 (continued)**
**Financial Notes**

The Salaried Employees' Retirement Plan, which covers substantially all salaried employees in the U.S., was restructured during 1984 due to overfunding of the Plan. Effective August 1, 1984, the Corporation terminated the existing plan and established a new plan which is substantially identical to the prior plan except for an improvement in the minimum pension benefit. All participants in the prior plan became fully vested upon its termination. All vested benefits earned through August 1, 1984, were covered through the purchase of individual annuities at a cost aggregating $36.7 million. The remaining plan assets, which totaled $39.3 million, reverted to the Corporation in cash upon receipt of regulatory approval of the prior plan termination from the Pension Benefit Guaranty Corporation. For financial reporting purposes, the new plan is considered to be a continuation of the terminated plan. Accordingly, the $39.3 million actuarial gain which resulted from the restructuring is included in Accrued Pension Costs in the accompanying Balance Sheet and is being amortized to income over a ten-year period commencing in 1984. For tax reporting purposes, the asset reversion will be treated as a fiscal 1985 transaction. The initial unfunded actuarial liability of the new plan, computed as of November 1, 1983, of $10.3 million is also included in Accrued Pension Costs.

In 1982 and 1983, the Pension Trusts purchased certain securities with effective yields of 13% and 12%, respectively, and dedicated these assets to the plan benefits of a substantial portion of the retired employees and certain terminated employees with deferred vested rights. These rates, together with 9% for active employees in 1984, 8% in 1983, and 7¼% in 1982, were the assumed rates of return used in determining the annual pension expense and the actuarial present value of accumulated plan benefits for the U.S. plans.

The effect of the changes in the investment return assumption rates for all U.S. plans, together with the 1984 restructuring of the U.S. Salaried Employees' Plan, was to reduce pension expense by approximately $4.0 million in 1984 and $2.0 million in 1983, and the actuarial present value of accumulated plan benefits by approximately $60.0 million in 1984. Pension expense in 1983 was also reduced $2.1 million from the lower level of active employees. Other actuarial gains, including higher than anticipated investment results, more than offset the additional pension costs resulting from plan changes and interest charges on balance sheet accruals in 1984 and 1983.

The Corporation's foreign pension plans do not determine the actuarial value of accumulated benefits or net assets available for retirement benefits as calculated and disclosed above. For those plans, the total of the plans' pension funds and balance sheet accruals approximated the actuarially computed value of vested benefits at both October 31, 1984 and 1983.

The Corporation generally provides certain health care and life insurance benefits for U.S. retired employees. Substantially all of the Corporation's current U.S. employees may become eligible for such benefits upon retirement. Life insurance benefits are provided either through the pension plans or separate group insurance arrangements. The cost of retiree health care and life insurance benefits, other than the benefits provided by the pension plans, is expensed as incurred; such costs approximated $2.6 million in 1984 and $1.7 million in 1983.

**EXHIBIT 4 (continued)**
**Financial Notes**

**Note 12**
**Income Taxes**
Domestic and foreign income (loss) before income tax effects was as follows (in thousands of dollars):

|  | Year Ended October 31, | | |
|  | 1984 | 1983 | 1982 |
| --- | --- | --- | --- |
| Domestic | $1,578 | $(35,412) | $(77,600) |
| Foreign | | | |
| Harnischfeger GmbH | 432 | (2,159) | (475) |
| All other | 3,728 | 4,768 | 8,418 |
|  | 4,160 | 2,609 | 7,943 |
| Total income (loss) before income tax effects, equity items and cumulative effect of accounting change | $5,738 | $(32,803) | $(69,657) |

Provision (credit) for income taxes, on income (loss) before income tax effects, equity items, and cumulative effect of accounting change, consisted of (in thousands of dollars):

|  | 1984 | 1983 | 1982 |
| --- | --- | --- | --- |
| Currently payable (refundable): | | | |
| Federal | $ — | $(7,957) | $(9,736) |
| State | 136 | 297 | 70 |
| Foreign | 2,518 | 3,379 | 5,376 |
|  | 2,654 | (4,281) | (4,290) |
| Deferred (prepaid): | | | |
| Federal | — | 2,955 | 2,713 |
| State and foreign | (229) | (74) | (23) |
|  | (229) | 2,881 | 2,690 |
| Provision (credit) for income taxes | $2,425 | $(1,400) | $(1,600) |

Unremitted earnings of foreign subsidiaries which have been or are intended to be permanently reinvested were $19.1 million at October 31, 1984. Such earnings, if distributed, would incur income tax expense of substantially less than the U.S. income tax rate as a result of previously paid foreign income taxes, provided that such foreign taxes would become deductible as foreign tax credits. No income tax provision was made in respect of the tax-deferred income of a consolidated subsidiary that has elected to be taxed as a domestic international sales corporation. The Deficit Reduction Act of 1984 provides for such income to become nontaxable effective December 31, 1984.

**EXHIBIT 4 (continued)**
**Financial Notes**

At October 31, 1984, the Corporation had federal tax operating loss carryforwards of approximately $70.0 million, expiring in 1998 and 1999, for tax return purposes, and $88.0 million for book purposes. In addition, the Corporation had, for tax purposes, foreign tax credit carryforwards of $3.0 million (expiring in 1985 through 1989) and investment tax credit carryforwards of $1.0 million (expiring in 1997 through 1999). For book purposes, tax credit carryforwards are approximately $8.0 million. The carryforward will be available for the reduction of future income tax provisions, the extent and timing of which are not determinable.

Differences in income (loss) before income taxes for financial and tax purposes arise from timing differences between financial and tax reporting and relate to depreciation, consolidating eliminations for inter-company profits in inventories, and provisions, principally, for warranty, pension, compensated absences, product liability, and plant closing costs.

During 1983 an examination of the Corporation's 1977–1981 federal income tax returns and certain refund claims was completed by the Internal Revenue Service and, as a result, a current credit for federal income taxes of $8.0 million was recorded in 1983, $3.0 million of which was applied to the reduction of prepaid income taxes.

In 1984, tax credits fully offset any federal income tax otherwise applicable to the year's income, and in 1983 and 1982 the relationship of the tax benefit to the pre-tax loss differed substantially from the U.S. statutory tax rate due principally to losses from the domestic operations for which only a partial federal tax benefit was available in 1982. Consequently, an analysis of deferred income taxes and variance from the U.S. statutory rate is not presented.

**Report of Independent Accountants**

**Price Waterhouse**
**Milwaukee, Wisconsin**
**November 29, 1984**

**To the Directors and Shareholders of Harnischfeger Corporation**

In our opinion, the financial statements, which appear on pages 18 to 34 of this report, present fairly the consolidated financial position of Harnischfeger Corporation and its subsidiaries at October 31, 1984 and 1983, and the results of their operations and the changes in their financial position for each of the three years in the period ended October 31, 1984, in conformity with generally accepted accounting principles consistently applied during the period except for the change, with which we concur, in the method of accounting for depreciation expense as described in Note 2 of this report. Our examinations of these statements were made in accordance with generally accepted auditing standards and accordingly included such tests of the accounting records and such other auditing procedures as we considered necessary in the circumstances.

Price Waterhouse

# Part Four

## Cost Concepts and Analysis

Understanding Costs for Management Decisions

*Precision Worldwide, Inc.*

*Lille Tissages, S.A.*

*Prestige Telephone Company*

A Brief Introduction to Cost Accounting

*Hilton Manufacturing Company*

# Understanding Costs for Management Decisions

"Cost" is a word used in many different ways in management and management decision making. Cost is a measure of something that has been given up (or will be given up) in the process of doing things. The utility and versatility of the concepts of cost are what make the collection, analysis, and presentation of cost information so useful in solving management problems.

Many problems can be "solved" by first measuring and then using "cost" as a central part of the overall criteria or analysis. Sometimes managers want to predict or accomplish an objective in the least expensive manner. At other times they may want to compare cost to revenue to predict or achieve the highest profit or smallest loss. The least costly decision may not be the one ultimately selected because added benefits that can be gained by incurring greater costs may outweigh the greater cost itself.

Costs are often predicted and analyzed before decisions are made and implemented. These anticipated cost data are frequently used to control operations or to evaluate the effectiveness of decisions.

## TYPES OF COST

Three types of costs—*current costs, opportunity costs,* and *sunk costs*—are frequently used in management decision making. Each can be used in several ways in cost analysis.

Current costs are measured as activities take place. In measuring current costs, the accountant attempts to determine what has been (or must be) given up in order to either implement a decision or to carry out an activity. What is

Copyright © 1997 by the President and Fellows of Harvard College. Harvard Business School case 197-117.

given up can take many forms. Physical effort, raw material, or fees paid in the form of money to others may all be required to implement a decision or produce a product or service. Each of these may represent a current cost of that activity. Management accountants usually measure each component of current cost in terms of a monetary equivalent. This is done to make the process of measuring, accumulating, and storing information both more feasible and more convenient.

Opportunity costs can be thought of as the cost of the second best alternative. If cost is being incurred in producing product A, then it is not being incurred in producing product B. For example, if material is used in product A, it is not available for product B. In analyzing management options, it may be useful to think of the cost of product A as being what we gave up by not producing product B. Every management decision or option has an opportunity cost. Although opportunity costs are not always measured in financial terms and are rarely formally recorded in accounting records, they are important in management decision making and management accounting analyses.

The term "sunk" cost refers to expenditures of time, effort, material, and money that can never be recovered. In contrast to opportunity costs, which are rarely included in accounting records, sunk costs often are included. The nature of sunk costs must be clearly understood by managers. Sunk costs are irrelevant in analyzing future courses of action or in making decisions about which future courses of actions would be most advantageous given organizational goals.

The effectiveness with which information about costs can be developed and used depends upon an understanding of definitions and communication of types of "costs." Understanding what has been given up, or what will be given up, or what has been given up that can never be recovered (and, therefore, can be ignored in considering a current problem) is the beginning of effective cost analysis.

## COST VARIABILITY

The way in which costs change as activities change is important to determining the relevance of that cost in many decision problems. If the total amount of cost incurred because of a decision is not changed by that decision, that cost is *nonvariable, fixed,* or *nondifferential.* On the other hand, if the alternatives under consideration will result in changes in the amount of cost, that cost is *variable, differential,* or *incremental.*

Good cost analysis almost always begins with an attempt to determine whether—and how much—a cost will vary with alternatives that might be chosen. Sometimes, determining a variable cost is very simple. If each unit of product or service requires a specified amount of material, it is quite easy to both predict and measure the amount of cost that will be associated with the decision to produce a certain quantity of that product. By the same token, if a monthly fee such as rent must be paid in order to utilize a production facility and the facility can be used for any of several quantities of product or service, than the rent is a cost that relates to a period of time rather than the volume of production. The terms *nonvariable cost* or *variable cost* refer to how the total cost changes as the quantity of product or service produced changes.

Whether a cost is variable or nonvariable often depends upon the time horizon of a decision or course of action with which management is faced. If a factory or office is owned or has been rented under a contract, the occupancy costs and/or rent paid for may be nonvariable for the life of the building or contract. On the other hand, if the capacity of the building is insufficient to provide for the quantity of production under consideration and additional space will be required, then additional occupancy costs become variable costs (or *differential costs*) in the analysis. It is not possible to make categorical statements about whether a cost is nonvariable without considering the time period involved.

A final complication in any discussion of cost variability arises because many costs do not fall neatly into one or the other classification—variable or nonvariable. In addition, some costs are nonvariable within ranges of activity. If a decision will move activity beyond that range, however, then the level of cost will change significantly.

## ANALYZING COSTS IN SINGLE PERIOD DECISIONS

When a management problem or decision involves a relatively short time period, the cost analysis process can be fairly straightforward. Since nonvariable costs will not change in a short period of time (remember that the definition of a nonvariable cost is one that does not change), attention need be given only to those costs that will change (or the *variable* costs). Once a decision criterion of minimizing costs or maximizing the difference between revenues or benefits and costs has been chosen, most analyses will lead quickly to indicated courses of action. The only serious questions are likely to involve how certain are the measurements and predictions of costs and whether they are truly variable or nonvariable.

In analyzing single period decision problems, both managers and management accountants frequently use *contribution* analysis. The best decision will produce the most profit or make the highest "contribution" to covering nonvariable costs. Contribution analysis seeks to find the difference between the revenue or benefits and the variable costs that will result from a course of action.

For a unit of product or service, *contribution* is measured by the difference between the net selling price and the variable costs of producing a unit of the product or service. For a product line, it is measured by the revenue obtained by a given quantity of product or service delivered and sold to clients, less the total variable cost incurred in producing and delivering that quantity of product or service. Contribution is greater than profit because the nonvariable costs which are not changed as a result of the decision or action taken are excluded from the analysis. Contribution analysis is a simple yet powerful method of making short-term decisions.

In spite of its power, contribution analysis has many limitations. Conclusions reached by analyzing contribution are dependent on judgments that have been made about cost variability over the time period under consideration. In addition, when contribution analysis is used as an input to decision processes, we necessarily make the assumption that the predicted costs will be those actually incurred. Finally, in many situations the costs of various programs and activities interact, and it is difficult to separate these *joint costs*.

## COST ANALYSIS OVER MANY PERIODS

As soon as a management problem or a cost analysis problem extends beyond a short period of time, a number of additional complications can come into play. Uncertainties about the future increase as the horizon moves away from our current knowledge and experience. The concept of cost itself tends to change, for a current cost is different from one that will be incurred in the future.

Managers and accountants have developed techniques for analyzing multiperiod decision problems. These techniques are based upon or utilize the concept of *interest*. The concept of *compound interest* relates a financial cost at one point in time to the financial cost at another point in time using a *rate of return*, an *interest rate*, or a *cost of capital* appropriate to either the organization or the particular class of problem(s). While there are several techniques for doing this, two that are particularly popular are called the *net present value method* and the *internal rate of return method*.[1]

In the net present value method of analyzing multiperiod problems, all costs (and benefits) at future times are related to their present value equivalents by using an interest rate equal to either the cost of capital or the expected earnings rate within the organization. The net present value of a future cost can be considered to be the amount that the cost now represents when consideration is given to the return that could be obtained between the present time and the time at which the cost will be incurred. Some students find it useful to think of this amount as the amount that we could pay someone now to take care of the cost in the future—assuming that the person we would pay now could earn a given interest rate on our deposit.

*NPVe cost of Capital or*
*NPVe earnings rate.*

---

[1] Students who are not familiar with the use of compound interest in the analysis of multiperiod problems are referred to other references. Compound interest methods are appropriate whenever the planning or decision horizon extends beyond a single period.

The internal rate of return method for analyzing multiple period problems identifies the interest rate (or the cost of capital) that would make the various costs incurred and benefits received over the life of the project in question equal to each other in present value terms. In comparison to the net present value method, the internal rate of return method assumes that we know the costs to be incurred and the benefits to be received at the various points in time, and that we seek the interest rate that would allow us to treat them as equivalent. Both the net present value method and the internal rate of return method are based upon the same concepts and formulas, but technical differences in their application make them more or less useful in selected problems or to different managers.

Multiple period problems require that costs be measured in terms of cash or their cash equivalents. Both the present value and internal rate of return methods depend upon the identification of the cash flows that will result from alternative courses of action. If a cost does not consist of cash expenditure or if benefits are not obtained in the form of cash, it is necessary to seek their equivalence in cash before these analytical methods can be applied.

*Include Depreciation*

Among the most frequent problems encountered in multiple period analysis is the proper treatment of *depreciation*. The cash flow that relates to the cost of assets has usually been incurred in an earlier period. Therefore, when analyzing accounting costs in multiple period cost analysis, it is necessary to "correct" for the effects of depreciation accounting. Depreciation is an allocation of a previous cash flow to an accounting period. But depreciation cannot be ignored. Depreciation often affects other cash flows, such as the determination of taxes due.

Multiple period cost analysis is usually more complex than single period analysis. In almost every case where decisions or analyses cover several periods of time, the number of variables to be considered will be greater than they are in short-term decision making.

## COST AS A CRITERION FOR CHOICE

The concept of cost is a powerful one in economic decision making. If cost can be minimized for a given amount of output, or if more product or service can be obtained for the same amount of cost, economic efficiency will be enhanced. It is for this reason that managers in every organization seek an understanding of their costs and their cost of operations.

The process of cost analysis, however, must always proceed with some caution. The cost information utilized must be appropriate to the time period and the decision horizon of the problem at hand. The costs must be those that relate to actions that will be taken or have been taken. Careful analyses of costs that are irrelevant to the decision problem at hand are of little or no use.

Finally, cost analysis—taken by itself—will rarely lead to the discovery of new alternatives. For cost analysis to be effective as part of a total management system, there must be clear thinking about alternatives that could be taken or that might have been taken. This latter process should take place before, during, and after the cost analysis process. The effective manager or management accountant always brings imagination, ingenuity, and perseverance to every situation that requires information about costs.

# Precision Worldwide, Inc.

In late May 1997, Hans Thorborg, the general manager of the German plant of Precision Worldwide, Inc. (PWI), scheduled an afternoon meeting with his sales manager, accountant, and development engineer to discuss the introduction by the French firm Henri Poulenc (a competitor) of a plastic ring substitute for the steel retaining rings presently used in certain machines sold by Precision Worldwide. The plastic ring, new to the market, not only has a much longer life than the PWI steel ring but also apparently has a much lower manufacturing cost. Thorborg's problem stemmed from PWI's large quantity of steel rings on hand and the substantial inventory of special steel that had been purchased for their manufacture. After a thorough survey, he had found that the special steel could not be sold, even for scrap; the total book value of these inventories exceeded $390,000.

For nearly 90 years PWI had manufactured industrial machines and equipment for sale in numerous countries. The particular machines involved in Thorborg's dilemma were made only at the company's plant in Frankfurt, Germany, which employed more than one thousand people. The different models were priced between $18,900 and $28,900 and were sold by a separate sales organization. Repair and replacement parts, which accounted for a substantial part of the company's business, were sold separately. As with the steel rings, these parts could often be used on similar machines manufactured by competitors. The company's head office was in Toledo, Ohio, U.S.A. In general, plants outside the United States were allowed considerable leeway in administering their own affairs; the corporate headquarters, however, was easily

*Professor William J. Bruns, Jr. adapted this case from "Industrial Grinders N.V." (No. 175-246).*

Copyright © 1997 by the President and Fellows of Harvard College. Harvard Business School case 197-103.

accessible by telephone, email, or during executive visits to the individual plants.

In the early 1990s, competition had increased. Japanese manufacturers, with low-priced spare parts, had successfully entered the field. Other companies had appeared with lower-quality and lower-priced machines. There was little doubt that future competition would be more intense.

The steel ring manufactured by PWI had a normal life of about two months, depending upon the extent to which the machine was used. A worn-out ring could be replaced in a few seconds, and although different models of the machines required from two to six rings, the rings were usually replaced individually as they wore out.

The sales manager, Gerhard Henk, had learned of the new plastic ring shortly after its appearance and had immediately asked when PWI would be able to supply them, particularly for sale to customers in France, where Henri Poulenc was the strongest competition faced by PWI. Bodo Eisenbach, the development engineer, estimated that the plastic rings could be produced by mid-September. The necessary tools and equipment could be obtained for about $7,500. Eisenbach had initially raised the issue of the steel ring inventories that would not be used up by September. Henk believed that if the new ring could be produced at a substantially lower cost than the steel ones, the inventory problem was irrelevant; he suggested that the inventory be sold, or if that was impossible, thrown away. The size of the inventory, however, caused Thorborg to question this suggestion. He recalled that the size of the inventory resulted from having to order the highly specialized steel in large amounts so that a mill would be willing to handle the order.

Henk reported that Henri Poulenc was said to be selling the plastic ring at about the same price as the PWI steel ring; since the production cost of the plastic ring would be much less than the steel ring, he emphasized that PWI was ignoring a good profit margin if it did not introduce a plastic ring. As the meeting concluded, it was decided that the company should prepare to manufacture the new ring as soon as possible but that until the inventories of the old model and the steel were exhausted, the plastic ring would only be sold in those markets where it was offered by competitors. It was expected that the new rings would not be produced by any company other than Henri Poulenc for some time, and this meant that no more than 10% of Precision Worldwide's markets would be affected.

Shortly after this, Patrick Corrigan, from the parent company in Ohio, visited Frankfurt. During a review of company problems, the plastic ring question was discussed. Although the ring was only a small part of the finished machines, Corrigan was interested in the problem because the company wanted to establish policies for the production and pricing of all such parts that, in total, accounted for a substantial portion of PWI's revenues. Corrigan agreed that the company should proceed with plans for its production and try to find some other use for the steel; he then said, "If this does not seem possible, I would, of course, expect you to use this material and produce the steel rings."

A few days after Corrigan's visit, both Eisenbach and Henk came in to see Thorborg. Eisenbach came because he felt that since tests had indicated that the plastic ring had at least four times the wearing properties of the steel ring, it would completely destroy demand for the steel ring. He understood, however, that the price of the competitive ring was high, and he felt that the decision to sell the plastic ring only in markets where it was sold by competitors was a good one. He observed, "In this way we will probably be able to continue supplying the steel ring until stocks, at least of processed parts, are used up."

Henk still strongly opposed sales of any steel rings once the plastic ones became available. If steel rings were sold in some areas, he argued, while plastic rings were being sold elsewhere, customers who purchased steel rings would eventually find out. This would harm the sale of Precision Worldwide machines—the selling price of which was many times that of the rings. He produced figures to show that if the selling price of both rings remained at $1,350.00 per hundred, the additional profit from the plastic rings (manufactured at a cost of $279.65 per hundred versus the $1,107.90 per hundred for steel rings) would more than recover the value of the steel inventory, and do so within less than a year at present volume levels. Thorborg refused to change the decision of the previous meeting but agreed to have another discussion within a week.

Anticipating this third meeting and also having Corrigan's concern in mind, Thorborg obtained the data displayed in **Table A** from the cost accounting department on the cost of both plastic and steel rings.

Thorborg also learned that the inventory of special steel had cost $110,900 and represented enough material to produce approximately 34,500 rings. Assuming that sales continued at the current rate of 690 rings per week, without any further production, some 15,100 finished rings would be left on hand by mid-September. Thorborg then recalled that during the next two or three months the plant would not be operating at capacity; during slack periods, the company had a policy of employing excess labor (at about 70% of regular wages) on various make-work projects rather than laying workers off. He wondered if it would be a good idea to use some of this labor to convert the steel inventory into rings during this period.

## QUESTION

What action should Hans Thorborg take? Why?

## TABLE A

|  | 100 Plastic Rings | 100 Steel Rings |
|---|---|---|
| Material | $ 17.65 | $ 321.90 |
| Direct labor | 65.50 | 196.50 |
| Overhead[a] |  |  |
|   Departmental | 131.00 | 393.00 |
|   Administrative | 65.50 | 196.50 |
| Total (cost) | $279.65 | $1,107.90 |

[a] Overhead was allocated on the basis of direct labor cost. It was estimated that the variable overhead costs included here were largely fringe benefits related to direct labor and amounted to 80¢ per direct labor dollar or about 40% of the departmental amounts.

# Lille Tissages, S.A.

**E**arly in 1997, the marketing director and the finance director of Lille Tissages, S.A., met to prepare a joint pricing recommendation for Item 345. After the managing director had approved their recommendation, the company would announce the price in letters to its customers. In accordance with company and industry practice, announced prices were adhered to for the year unless radical changes in the market had occurred.

Lille Tissages was located in Lille, France. It was the largest company in its segment of the French textile industry; its 1996 sales had exceeded FF96 million. Company salesmen were on a straight salary basis, and each salesman sold the full line. Most of Lille Tissages' competitors were small. Usually, they waited for Lille Tissages to announce prices before mailing out their own price lists.

Item 345, an expensive yet competitive fabric, was the sole product of a department whose facilities could not be utilized on other items in the product line. In January 1995, Lille Tissages had raised its price from FF15 to FF20 a meter. This had been done to bring the profit per meter on Item 345 up to that of other products in the line. Although the company was in a strong position financially, it would require considerable capital in the next few years to finance a recently approved long-term modernization and expansion program. The 1995 pricing decision had been one of several changes advocated by the directors in an attempt to strengthen the company's working capital position so as to ensure that adequate funds would be available for this program.

Competitors of Lille Tissages had held their prices on products similar to Item 345 at FF15 during 1995 and 1996. The industry and Lille Tissages volume for Item 345 for the years 1991–96, as estimated by the sales director, are shown

Copyright © 1997 by the President and Fellows of Harvard College. Harvard Business School case 198-005.

in **Exhibit 1**. As shown by this exhibit, Lille Tissages had lost a significant portion of its former market position. In the sales director's opinion, a reasonable forecast of industry volume for 1997 was 700,000 meters. He was certain that the company could sell 25% of the 1997 industry total if it adopted the FF15 price. He feared a further volume decline if it did not meet the competitive price. As many consumers were convinced of the superiority of the Lille Tissages product, the sales director reasoned that sales of Item 345 would probably not fall below 75,000 meters, even at a FF20 price.

During the pricing discussions, the finance director and the marketing director had considered two other aspects of the problem. The finance director was concerned about the possibility that competitors would reduce their prices below FF15 if Lille Tissages announced a FF15 price for Item 345. The marketing director was confident that competitors would not go below FF15 because they all had higher costs and several of them were in tight financial straits. He believed that action taken on Item 345 would not have had any substantial repercussions on other items in the line.

The finance director prepared estimated costs of Item 345 at various volumes of production (see **Exhibit 2**). These estimated costs reflected projected labor and material costs. They were based on past experience except for the estimates of 75,000 and 100,000 meters. The company had produced more than 100,000 meters in each of the last ten years, and earlier experience was not applicable because of equipment changes and increases in labor productivity.

## QUESTIONS

1.  Should Lille Tissages lower the price to FF15? (Assume no intermediate prices are being considered.)
2.  If the department that produces Item 345 was a profit center and if you were the manager of that department, would it be to *your* financial advantage to lower the price?
3.  Is there any possibility that the competition might raise their prices if Lille Tissages maintains its price of FF20? If so, how do you take this factor into your analysis?
4.  At FF15, will Lille Tissages earn a profit on Item 345? How do you decide?

**EXHIBIT 1**
**Item 345, Prices and Production, 1991–1996**

| Year | Volume of Production (meters) | | Price (French francs) | |
| | Industry Total | Lille Tissages | Charged by Most Competitors | Lille Tissages |
| --- | --- | --- | --- | --- |
| 1991 | 610,000 | 213,000 | 20.00 | 20.00 |
| 1992 | 575,000 | 200,000 | 20.00 | 20.00 |
| 1993 | 430,000 | 150,000 | 15.00 | 15.00 |
| 1994 | 475,000 | 165,000 | 15.00 | 15.00 |
| 1995 | 500,000 | 150,000 | 15.00 | 20.00 |
| 1996 (est.) | 625,000 | 125,000 | 15.00 | 20.00 |

**EXHIBIT 2**
**Estimated Cost per Meter of Item 345 at Various Volumes of Production (in French francs)**

| | 75,000 | 100,000 | 125,000 | 150,000 | 175,000 | 200,000 |
| --- | --- | --- | --- | --- | --- | --- |
| Direct labor[a] | 4.00 | 3.90 | 3.80 | 3.70 | 3.80 | 4.00 |
| Material | 2.00 | 2.00 | 2.00 | 2.00 | 2.00 | 2.00 |
| Material spoilage | .20 | .20 | .19 | .19 | .19 | .20 |
| Department expense: | | | | | | |
|   Direct[b] | .60 | .56 | .50 | .50 | .50 | .50 |
|   Indirect[c] | 4.00 | 3.00 | 2.40 | 2.00 | 1.71 | 1.50 |
| General overhead[d] | 1.20 | 1.17 | 1.14 | 1.11 | 1.14 | 1.20 |
| Factory cost | 12.00 | 10.83 | 10.03 | 9.50 | 9.34 | 9.40 |
| Selling & administrative expense[e] | 7.80 | 7.04 | 6.52 | 6.18 | 6.07 | 6.11 |
|     Total Cost | 19.80 | 17.87 | 16.55 | 15.68 | 15.41 | 15.51 |

[a] Any workers made redundant as a result of a decrease in the volume of sales of Item 345 could be economically absorbed in other departments.

[b] Indirect labor, supplies, repairs, powers, etc.

[c] Depreciation, supervision, etc.

[d] Thirty percent of direct labor, consisting principally of general plant administrative costs (plant supervision, plant services, etc.) and occupancy costs.

[e] Sixty-five percent of factory cost.

# Prestige Telephone Company

In April 1997, Daniel Rowe, president of Prestige Telephone Company, was preparing for a meeting with Susan Bradley, manager of Prestige Data Services, a company subsidiary. Partial deregulation and an agreement with the state Public Service Commission had permitted Prestige Telephone to establish a computer data service subsidiary to perform data processing for the telephone company and to sell computer service to other companies and organizations. Mr. Rowe had told the commission in 1994 that a profitable computer services subsidiary would reduce pressure for telephone rate increases. However, by the end of 1996 the subsidiary had yet to experience a profitable month. Ms. Bradley felt only more time was needed, but Rowe felt action was necessary to reduce the drain on company resources.

Prestige Data Services had grown out of the needs of Prestige Telephone for computer services to plan, control, and account for its own operations in the metropolitan region it served. The realization by Prestige that other businesses in the metropolitan region needed similar services and that centralized service could be provided over telephone circuits suggested that Prestige could sell computer time not needed by telephone operations. In addition, the state Public Service Commission had encouraged all public utilities under its jurisdiction to seek new sources of revenue and profits as a step toward deregulation and to reduce the need for rate increases which higher costs would otherwise bring.

Because it operated as a public utility, the rates charged by Prestige Telephone Company for telephone service could not be changed without the approval of the Public Service Commission. In presenting the proposal for the new subsidiary, Mr. Rowe had argued for a separate but wholly owned entity

Copyright © 1997 by the President and Fellows of Harvard College. Harvard Business School case 197-097.

whose prices for service would not be regulated. In this way, Prestige could compete with other computer service organizations in a dynamic field; in addition, revenues for use of telephone services might also be increased. The commission accepted this proposal subject only to the restriction that the average monthly charge for service by the subsidiary to the parent not exceed $82,000, the estimated cost of equivalent services used by Prestige Telephone Company in 1994. All accounts of Prestige Data Services were separated from those of Prestige Telephone, and each paid the other for services received from the other.

From the start of operations of Prestige Data Services in 1995 there had been problems. Equipment deliveries were delayed. Personnel had commanded higher salaries than expected. And most important, customers were harder to find than earlier estimates had led the company to expect. By the end of 1996, when income of Prestige Telephone was low enough to necessitate a report to shareholders revealing the lowest return on investment in seven years, Rowe felt it was time to reassess Prestige Data Services. Susan Bradley had asked for more time, as she felt the subsidiary would be profitable by March. But when the quarterly reports came (**Exhibits 1** and **2**), Rowe called Bradley to arrange their meeting.

Rowe received two reports on operations of Prestige Data Services. The summary of computer utilization (**Exhibit 1**) summarized the use of available hours of computer time. Service was offered to commercial customers 24 hours a day on weekdays and eight hours on Saturdays. Routine maintenance of the computers was provided by an outside contractor who took the computer off-line for eight hours each week for testing and upkeep. The reports for the quarter revealed a persistent problem; available hours, which did not provide revenue, remained high.

Revenue and cost data were summarized in the quarterly report on results of operations (**Exhibit 2**). Intracompany work was billed at $400 per hour, a rate based on usage estimates for 1997 and the Public Service Commission's restrictions that cost to Prestige Telephone should not exceed an average of $82,000 per month. Commercial sales were billed at $800 per hour.

While most expenses summarized in the report were self-explanatory, Rowe reminded himself of the characteristics of a few. Space costs were all paid to Prestige Telephone. Prestige Data Services rented the ground floor of a central exchange building owned by the company for $8,000 per month. In addition, a charge for custodial service based on the estimated annual cost per square foot was paid by Data Services, as telephone personnel provided these services.

Computer equipment had been acquired by lease and by purchases; leases had four years to run and were noncancelable. Owned equipment was all salable but probably could not bring more than its book value in the used equipment market.

Wages and salaries were separated in the report to show the expense of four different kinds of activities. Operating salaries included those of the six persons necessary to run the center around the clock as well as amounts paid hourly help who were required when the computer was in operation. Salaries of the programming staff who provided service to clients and maintained the operating system were reported as system development and maintenance. Sales personnel, who called upon and serviced present and prospective commercial clients, were also salaried.

Because of its relationship with Prestige Telephone, Prestige Data Services was able to avoid many costs an independent company would have. For example, all payroll, billing, collections, and accounting were done by telephone company personnel. For those corporate services, Prestige Data Services paid Prestige Telephone an amount based on wages and salaries each month.

Although Rowe was discouraged by results to date, he was reluctant to suggest to Bradley that Prestige Data Services be closed down or sold. The idea behind the subsidiary just seemed too good to give up easily. Besides, he was not sure that the accounting report really revealed the contribution that Data Services was making to Prestige Telephone. In other cases, he felt that the procedures used in accounting for separate activities in the company tended to obscure the costs and benefits they provided.

After examining the reports briefly, Rowe resolved to study them in preparation for asking Bradley to estimate the possible effects on profits of increasing the price to customers other than Prestige Telephone, reducing prices, increasing sales efforts and promotion, and of going to two-shift rather than 24-hour operations.

# QUESTIONS

1.  Appraise the results of operations of Prestige Data Services. Is the subsidiary really a problem to Prestige Telephone Company? Consider carefully the differences between reported costs and costs relevant for decisions that Daniel Rowe is considering.
2.  Assuming the company demand for service will average 205 hours per month, what level of commercial sales of computer use would be necessary to break even each month?
3.  Estimate the effect on income of each of the options Rowe has suggested if Bradley estimates as follows:
    a.  Increasing the price to commercial customers to $1,000 per hour would reduce demand by 30%.
    b.  Reducing the price to commercial customers to $600 per hour would increase demand by 30%.
    c.  Increased promotion would increase sales by up to 30%. Bradley is unsure how much promotion this would take. (How much could be spent and still leave Prestige Data Services with no reported loss each month if commercial hours were increased 30%?)
    d.  Reducing operations to 16 hours on weekdays and eight hours on Saturdays would result in a loss of 20% of commercial revenue hours.
4.  Can you suggest changes in the accounting and reporting system now used for operations of Prestige Data Services which would result in more useful information for Rowe and Bradley?

**EXHIBIT 1**
**Prestige Data Services Summary of Computer Utilization, First Quarter 1997**

| Revenue Hours | January | February | March |
|---|---|---|---|
| Intercompany | 206 | 181 | 223 |
| Commercial | 123 | 135 | 138 ✓ |
| Total revenue hours | 329 | 316 | 361 |
| | | | |
| Service hours | 32 | 32 | 40 |
| Available hours | 175 | 188 | 167 |
| Total hours | 536 | 536 | 568 |

**EXHIBIT 2**
**Prestige Data Services Summary Results of Operations, First Quarter 1997**

|  | January | February | March |
|---|---|---|---|
| Revenues |  |  |  |
| Intercompany sales | $ 82,400 | $ 72,400 | $ 89,200 |
| Commercial sales |  |  |  |
| Computer use | 98,400 | 108,000 | 110,400 |
| Other | 9,241 | 9,184 | 12,685 |
| Total revenue | $190,041 | $189,584 | $212,285 |
| Expenses |  |  |  |
| Space costs: |  |  |  |
| Rent | $ 8,000 | $ 8,000 | $ 8,000 FC |
| Custodial services | 1,240 | 1,240 | 1,240 FC |
|  | 9,240 | 9,240 | 9,240 |
| Equipment costs |  |  |  |
| Computer leases | 95,000 | 95,000 | 95,000 FC |
| Maintenance | 5,400 | 5,400 | 5,400 FC |
| Depreciation: |  |  |  |
| Computer equipment | 25,500 | 25,500 | 25,500 FC |
| Office equipment and fixtures | 680 | 680 | 680 FC |
| Power | 1,633 | 1,592 | 1,803 — Mixed |
|  | 128,213 | 128,172 | 128,383 |
| Wages and salaries |  |  |  |
| Operations | 29,496 | 29,184 | 30,264 — Mixed |
| Systems development and maintenance | 12,000 | 12,000 | 12,000 FC |
| Administration | 9,000 | 9,000 | 9,000 FC |
| Sales | 11,200 | 11,200 | 11,200 FC |
|  | 61,696 | 61,384 | 62,464 |
| Materials | 9,031 | 8,731 | 10,317 VC |
| Sales promotions | 7,909 | 7,039 | 8,083 FC — use Avg Value |
| Corporate services | 15,424 | 15,359 | 15,236 — Not Relevant |
| Total expenses | $231,513 | $229,925 | $233,723 |
| Net income (loss) | $ (41,472) | $ (40,341) | $ (21,438) |

# A Brief Introduction to Cost Accounting

Organizations and managers are almost always interested in and concerned about costs. Control of past, present, and future costs is part of every manager's job. In companies that try to earn profits, control of costs directly affects the amount of profit earned. Knowledge of the cost of products or services is indispensable for decisions about pricing or product and service mix. In nonprofit organizations, control of costs influences the level of services that can be provided and the future survival of the organization.

Cost accounting systems can be important sources of information for managers. For this reason, effective managers understand the strengths and limitations of cost accounting systems and actively participate in the evaluation and evolution of cost measurement and management systems. Unlike accounting systems that support the preparation of periodic financial reports, cost accounting systems and reports are not subject to rules or standards such as generally accepted accounting principles. Managers are permitted to exercise as much creativity and ingenuity as they wish in the quest for information on costs. As a result, there is much variety in cost accounting systems used in different companies and sometimes even in different parts of the same organization.

This brief introduction to cost accounting will review the principal uses of cost data, provide some vocabulary for cost accounting, and present several of the questions managers have to answer in designing or using a cost accounting system. Its purpose is to provide the beginner with some vocabulary and ideas to use in learning about and exploring how cost management systems are designed and used by managers. While many of the references are to products

Copyright © 1991 by the President and Fellows of Harvard College. Harvard Business School case 192-068.

and manufacturing environments, the vocabulary and concepts are equally applicable to services.

# SOME USES OF INFORMATION ABOUT COSTS

Information about costs is used for two purposes in most organizations. Cost accounting systems provide information for evaluating the performance of an organizational unit or its manager. They also provide a means for estimating the costs of units of product or service that the organization may manufacture or provide to others.

## Performance Measurement

Reports on the costs incurred by part of an organization—a department or a division, for example—are one means by which efficiency and effectiveness can be evaluated. By comparing *actual costs* to those that were expected—to *standard costs* or *budgeted costs*—the degree to which costs have been controlled can be judged. Deviations from expectations—*variances*—can be identified, evaluated, and discussed by managers. If needed, corrective actions can be taken or expectations can be modified to incorporate previously unexpected efficiencies.

Performance measurement reporting is usually periodic and systematic. Costs are assigned to parts of an organization that are identified as *cost centers*. When managers are held accountable for the costs incurred in a cost center, they are sometimes called *responsibility centers*. Performance reports provide information on the achievement of established objectives, efficiency of operations, and opportunities for cost control or cost reduction. Performance reports are used for both information and performance measurement and evaluation.

## Product Costs and the Cost of Services

**Inventory cost**   In manufacturing companies, product costs must be measured to determine the cost of items transferred from work-in-process to finished goods inventory. To satisfy the demands created by the *cost concept* used in financial reporting, a cost accounting system must measure all of the costs of the manufacturing process and assign some part of those costs to each unit of product. The costs of obtaining, maintaining, and managing the manufacturing facility need to be added to the costs of material and productive labor that each unit requires. The former costs are called *indirect costs*, and the latter are called *direct costs*. Generally accepted accounting principles require that inventory cost includes a "fair share" of total manufacturing costs, including indirect costs. In practice, there is considerable variation in how indirect costs are assigned to products.

$CM = SP - VC$

$GM = SP - TC$

**Profitability analysis**   Information on costs is indispensable for analyzing the profitability of a product or product line.  Product cost information allows managers to evaluate *contribution margin*—the difference between price and variable costs—and *gross margin*—the difference between price and total product costs.  Information about sales, marketing, and distribution costs allows managers to evaluate the profitability of a product or product line.  Without good information about costs, managers have no way to associate net income with actions or products about which they make decisions and over which they exercise control.

**Product mix**   In companies that offer more than one product or service, information about costs is a key to managing the mix of products or services offered to customers or clients.  With cost and profitability information, a manager can direct sales and marketing effort to the most profitable products.  Unprofitable products can be eliminated, repriced, or bundled with more profitable products.  The importance of product line decisions to future profitability requires confidence that product costs have been accurately determined.

**Pricing**   Although prices are determined by market forces of supply and demand, product differentiation and marketing offer many managers some degree of latitude in setting prices.  Product costs and trends in product costs often provide signals to managers that prices should be changed.  In particular, a change in the cost of a critical material or component may signal the need to reconsider the prices asked for products.

**Cost of service**   Many products require the seller to provide additional services to customers.  In such cases, information about the cost of services is as important to managers as product costs.  The same is true for managers of companies or organizations that provide only services.  Unless the cost of service is measured, there is no way to know if providing the service is profitable or not and whether changes in pricing or marketing strategy are needed.

## COST BEHAVIOR—RELATION OF COSTS TO VOLUME

Basic knowledge about cost behavior is a prerequisite for understanding, using, or designing cost accounting or cost management systems.  The level of cost can be a function of either or both the *volume* of activity or *time* when the cost is incurred.  Because prices of material, labor, and other resources change as time passes, and because time allows changes in manufacturing methods or service delivery, comparing costs at two points in time can be informative about efficiency.  However, understanding the effect of changes in volume on costs is essential to measuring, analyzing, and using information about costs for both performance measurement and product costing.

    If a company changes the amount of product or service it provides to customers or clients, its total costs will usually change as well.  If more product is manufactured and sold, then we should expect the higher volume to cause costs to increase. However, in many instances, the increase in costs will not be proportional to the increase in product volume. To understand why, the concepts of *variable costs* and *fixed costs* must be understood.

**Variable costs**　A cost which changes in strict proportionality with volume is called a variable cost. That is, if volume increases by 50%, a variable cost will increase in total by 50% as well. Materials used to create a product are a common example of a variable cost item. The total cost of materials to manufacture 20 units is double the cost to manufacture 10 units.

**Nonvariable costs**　A cost that does not vary at all with volume is called a nonvariable, or fixed, cost. Over time the level of a fixed cost may change, but the change is independent of the volume of activity. Building rent is usually a nonvariable cost. The rent paid is independent of the number of units of product or service produced in the building or the number of customers served. Nonvariable costs can often be changed by management decisions, but they do not change simply because the volume of activity changes.

**Semivariable costs**　Many costs include a combination of variable costs and nonvariable costs. The total amount of these costs varies in the same direction as volume, but less than proportionately with changes in volume. Sometimes semivariable costs can be separated into a fixed portion and a variable portion by isolating elements of the cost. The total cost of driving an automobile is semivariable with respect to the number of miles driven, but the cost of gasoline, oil, tires, and maintenance may be variable, whereas insurance and registration fees are probably fixed.

**Chunky costs**　Often costs are assumed to be variable when they actually are incurred in chunks. Such costs, also known as *step-function costs*, are fixed for a range of volume of production but change in a chunk when volume drops below or exceeds the limits of the *relevant range* of volume. The costs of stockroom employees are often chunky. As volume of inventory or products increases, one stockroom employee may be able to handle material and finished goods until the volume level increases to the point where another employee must be added. The new staffing level will then be sufficient even as volume rises further until another "step" is reached. Chunky costs and costs that are not easily related to volume measures usually require special analysis and management.

## ACCOUNTING FOR COSTS

### Classifying Costs

The word *cost* is used many different ways in accounting and by managers. For clarity, other words are often attached to the word *cost* to enhance its meaning.

In cost accounting, costs are usually classified into two categories: direct costs and indirect costs.

**Direct costs**   Direct costs can be specifically traced to or are caused by a product, project, organizational unit, or activity.  Materials specifically used in the manufacture of a product are an example of a direct cost.  Labor specifically employed to provide a service would be another example.  Many direct costs are variable costs, but nonvariable costs can also be direct costs if they can be traced directly to a project, organizational unit, or activity.

**Indirect costs**   When a cost cannot be traced directly to a single product, project, organizational unit, or activity, it is classified as an indirect cost.  The rental cost of a factory building making more than one product is an indirect cost with respect to each product.  There is no feasible way to associate specifically an indirect cost with an individual unit or batch of products.

Indirect costs are included in *overhead cost*, or *burden*.  To account for the full cost of manufacturing products, some portion of the overhead cost must be associated with each unit of product.  The methods by which overhead costs are associated with products or services comprise the essence of most cost accounting systems.

## Accounting for Direct Costs

A simplified cost flow chart for a manufacturing company is shown in **Exhibit 1**.  Resources are acquired for cash or on credit and are classified as materials, payroll, or overhead.  Payroll, which is classified as indirect cost, becomes part of overhead.  In the production process, material, labor, and overhead cost become the cost of work-in-process inventory. When completed, work in process becomes finished goods and, later, cost of goods sold.

It is easy to understand the accounting for direct costs such as material and productive labor.  As material is converted to product by the effort of production labor, the costs of material used and labor can be associated with products.  As products are completed and transferred to finished goods and cost of goods sold, these direct costs are transferred with them.  All the cost accountant has to do is keep track of how much material and labor cost is used in producing each unit of product.  (Actually, this is a little more complicated than it may sound here, but this brief description captures the essence of the accounting process for these direct costs.)

## Accounting for Indirect Costs

Accounting for indirect costs is more complicated than accounting for direct costs.  Costs must be collected and associated with activities before they can be assigned to products.  The relationship between expenditures or costs and products or services is often far from obvious.  Assignment to activities is often based on arbitrary decisions about the possible relationships between the reason for an expenditure and an activity. For example, rent for a building that houses both manufacturing and sales activities might be assigned to each activity in the same ratio as the floor space occupied by each. Then, the manufacturing rent cost may be assigned to products manufactured using a measure of volume or some other measure of effort or activity.

Almost all cost accounting systems use a two-stage procedure for assigning indirect costs to products or other *cost objects*. First, costs are assigned to cost centers, or *cost pools*. Second, costs are assigned from each pool to products using *cost drivers*. The concept of a cost driver is based on the idea that products drive the consumption of resources.

The first question that the cost accounting system designer has to answer concerns how many cost centers to use. Using more cost centers than necessary adds complexity and cost to the cost accounting process itself. But using too few cost pools can create a risk that assigned costs will have little relationship to the activities and products that caused the cost to be incurred and resources to be consumed. In a manufacturing plant, the number of cost pools needed may be as small as one if machines, labor, and products are homogenous, or the number needed may be much larger if there is greater diversity in activities or products. In some manufacturing plants, each department, or even each machine, may be treated as a separate cost center.

The second set of questions the cost accounting system designer has to answer concerns how to assign costs to each cost center or cost pool. Expenditures for indirect costs may be assigned based on direct labor cost, floor space, head counts, or direct costs. More complex systems will attempt to implement as much direct charging to each cost pool as possible by using actual measures of the resources used by each cost center.

The third set of questions the cost accounting system designer has to answer concerns how to assign the costs collected for each cost center to the products that are manufactured by or pass through that center. Often the costs are assigned in proportion to the use of a resource that is easily measured. Each unit product may be assigned the same proportion of indirect cost as it consumes labor time, labor cost, machine time, or material cost, for example.

Given the number and complexity of choices facing the cost accounting system designer and the fact that there are no constraining "generally accepted principles of cost accounting," it should be obvious that there is great diversity in the cost accounting systems used by different organizations. A new manager or employee has no choice but to learn about the systems the company uses before using the cost information the system has produced. Every manager has to be continually alert to be sure the cost information available is the right information for the decision or task at hand.

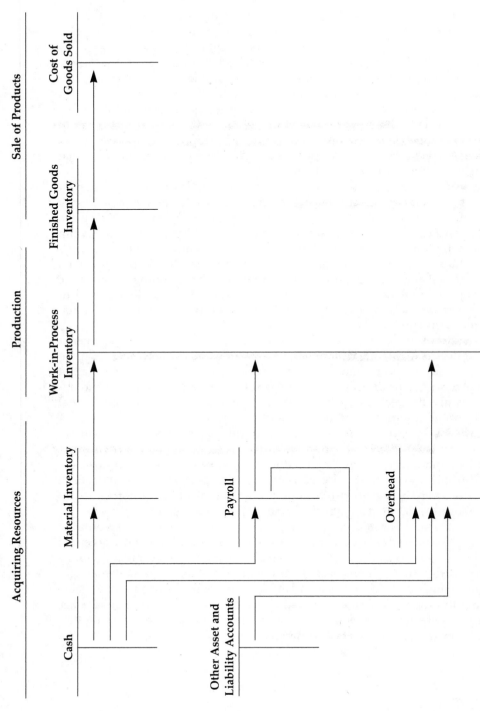

**EXHIBIT 1**
**Cost Flow Chart for a Manufacturing Company**

# Hilton Manufacturing Company

In February 1991, George Weston was appointed general manager by Paul Hilton, president of Hilton Manufacturing Company. Weston, age 56, had wide executive experience in manufacturing products similar to those of the Hilton Company. The appointment of Weston resulted from management problems arising from the death of Richard Hilton, founder and, until his death in early 1990, president of the company. Paul Hilton had only four years' experience with the company, and in early 1991 was 34 years old. His father had hoped to train Paul over a 10-year period, but the father's untimely death had cut short this seasoning period. The younger Hilton became president after his father's death and had exercised full control until he hired Mr. Weston.

Paul Hilton knew that he had made several poor decisions during 1990 and that the morale of the organization had suffered, apparently through lack of confidence in him. When he received the 1990 income statement (**Exhibit 1**), the loss of almost $200,000 during a good year for the industry convinced him that he needed help. He attracted Weston from a competitor by offering a stock option incentive in addition to salary, knowing that Weston wanted to acquire financial security for his retirement. The two men came to a clear understanding that Weston, as general manager, had full authority to execute any changes he desired. In addition, Weston would explain the reasons for his decisions to Mr. Hilton and thereby train him for successful leadership upon Weston's retirement.

Hilton Manufacturing Company made only three industrial products, 101, 102, and 103, in its single plant. These were sold by the company sales force for use in the processes of other manufacturers. All of the sales force, on a salary basis, sold the three products but in varying proportions. Hilton sold through-

Copyright © 1991 by the President and Fellows of Harvard College. Harvard Business School case 192-063.

out New England, where it was one of eight companies with similar products. Several of its competitors were larger and manufactured a larger variety of products. The dominant company was Catalyst Company, which operated a plant in Hilton's market area. Customarily, Catalyst announced prices, and the other producers followed suit.

Price cutting was rare; the only variance from quoted selling prices took the form of cash discounts. In the past, attempts at price cutting had followed a consistent pattern; all competitors met the price reduction, and the industry as a whole sold about the same quantity but at the lower prices. This continued until Catalyst, with its strong financial position, again stabilized the situation following a general recognition of the failure of price cutting. Furthermore, because sales were to industrial buyers and the products of different manufacturers were similar, Hilton was convinced it could not unilaterally raise prices without suffering volume declines.

During 1990, Hilton's share of industry sales was 12 percent for type 101, 8 percent for 102, and 10 percent for 103. The industrywide quoted selling prices were $9.41, $9.91, and $10.56, respectively.

Weston, upon taking office in February 1991, decided against immediate major changes. Rather, he chose to analyze 1990 operations and to wait for results of the first half of 1991. He instructed the accounting department to provide detailed expenses and earnings statements by products for 1990 (see **Exhibit 2**). In addition, he requested an explanation of the nature of the costs including their expected future behavior (see **Exhibit 3**).

To familiarize Paul Hilton with his methods, Weston sent copies of these reports to Hilton, and they discussed them. Hilton stated that he thought product 103 should be dropped immediately as it would be impossible to lower expenses on product 103 as much as 83 cents per hundredweight (cwt.). In addition, he stressed the need for economies on product 102.

Weston relied on the authority arrangement Hilton had agreed to earlier and continued production of the three products. For control purposes, he had the accounting department prepare monthly statements using as standard costs the actual costs per cwt. from the 1990 profit and loss statement (**Exhibit 2**). These monthly statements were his basis for making minor marketing and production changes during the spring of 1991. Late in July 1991, Weston received from the accounting department the six months' statement of cumulative standard costs including variances of actual costs from standard (see **Exhibit 4**). They showed that the first half of 1991 was a successful period.

During the latter half of 1991, the sales of the entire industry weakened. Even though Hilton retained its share of the market, its profit for the last six months would be small. For January 1992, Catalyst announced a price reduction on product 101 from $9.41 to $8.64 per cwt. This created an immediate pricing problem for its competitors. Weston forecast that if Hilton Manufacturing Company held to the $9.41 price during the first six months of 1992, its unit sales would be 750,000 cwt. He felt that if Hilton dropped its price to $8.64 per cwt., the six months' volume would be 1,000,000 cwt. Weston knew that competing managements anticipated a further decline in activity. He thought a general decline in prices was quite probable.

The accounting department reported that the standard costs in use would probably apply during the first half of 1992, with two exceptions: materials and supplies would be about 5 percent above standard; and light and heat would increase about 7 percent.

Weston and Hilton discussed the product 101 pricing problem. Hilton observed that especially with the anticipated increase in materials and supplies costs, a sales price of $8.64 would be below cost. He therefore wanted to hold the price at $9.41, since he felt the company could not be profitable while selling a key product below cost.

## QUESTIONS

1. If the company had dropped product 103 as of January 1, 1991, what effect would that action have had on the $158,000 profit for the first six months of 1991?
2. In January 1992, should the company reduce the price of product 101 from $9.41 to $8.64?
3. What is Hilton's most profitable product?
4. What appears to have caused the return to profitable operations in the first six months of 1991?

**EXHIBIT 1**
**Hilton Manufacturing Company, Income**
**Statement for Year Ending December 31, 1990**

| | | |
|---|---:|---:|
| Gross sales | | $40,690,234 |
| Cash discount | | 622,482 |
| Net sales | | 40,067,752 |
| Cost of sales | | 25,002,386 |
| Gross margin | | 15,065,366 |
| Less:  Selling expense | $7,058,834 | |
|     General administration | 2,504,597 | |
|     Depreciation | 5,216,410 | 14,779,841 |
| Operating income | | 285,525 |
| Other income | | 78,113 |
| Income before interest | | 363,638 |
|    Less:  interest expense | | 555,719 |
| Income (loss) | | $    (192,081) |

**EXHIBIT 2**
**Hilton Manufacturing Company, Analysis of Profit and Loss by Product, Year Ended December 31, 1990**

| | Product 101 | | Product 102 | | Product 103 | | Total |
|---|---|---|---|---|---|---|---|
| | Thousands | $ per Cwt. | Thousands | $ per Cwt. | Thousands | $ per Cwt. | Thousands |
| Rent | 721 | 0.3383 | 603 | 0.5856 | 718 | 0.7273 | 2,042 |
| Property taxes | 240 | 0.1125 | 192 | 0.1862 | 153 | 0.1555 | 585 |
| Property insurance | 201 | 0.0941 | 153 | 0.1486 | 202 | 0.2047 | 556 |
| Compensation insurance | 317 | 0.1486 | 167 | 0.1620 | 172 | 0.1747 | 656 |
| Direct labor | 4,964 | 2.3282 | 2,341 | 2.2740 | 2,640 | 2.6746 | 9,945 |
| Indirect labor | 1,693 | 0.7941 | 814 | 0.7903 | 883 | 0.8947 | 3,390 |
| Power | 86 | 0.0403 | 96 | 0.0929 | 116 | 0.1171 | 298 |
| Light and heat | 57 | 0.0269 | 49 | 0.0472 | 39 | 0.0392 | 145 |
| Building service | 38 | 0.0180 | 30 | 0.0288 | 28 | 0.0288 | 96 |
| Materials | 2,935 | 1.3766 | 1,809 | 1.7572 | 1,862 | 1.8862 | 6,606 |
| Supplies | 201 | 0.0941 | 183 | 0.1774 | 135 | 0.1363 | 519 |
| Repairs | 68 | 0.0319 | 57 | 0.0557 | 39 | 0.0396 | 164 |
| Total | 11,522 | 5.4036 | 6,493 | 6.3059 | 6,986 | 7.0787 | 25,002 |
| Selling expense | 3,496 | 1.6397 | 1,758 | 1.7069 | 1,805 | 1.8286 | 7,059 |
| General administration | 1,324 | 0.6209 | 499 | 0.4850 | 681 | 0.6904 | 2,505 |
| Depreciation | 2,169 | 1.0172 | 1,643 | 1.5955 | 1,404 | 1.4223 | 5,216 |
| Interest | 201 | 0.0941 | 153 | 0.1490 | 202 | 0.2043 | 556 |
| Total cost | 18,711 | 8.7755 | 10,546 | 10.2423 | 11,078 | 11.2243 | 40,338 |
| Less other income | 39 | 0.0184 | 20 | 0.0192 | 19 | 0.0192 | 78 |
| | 18,672 | 8.7571 | 10,526 | 10.2231 | 11,059 | 11.2051 | 40,260 |
| Sales (net) | 19,847 | 9.3084 | 9,977 | 9.6900 | 10,243 | 10.3784 | 40,068 |
| Profit (loss) | 1,175 | 0.5513 | (549) | (0.5331) | (816) | (0.8267) | (192) |
| Unit sales (cwt.) | 2,132,191 | | 1,029,654 | | 986,974 | | |
| Quoted selling price | $9.41 | | $9.91 | | $10.56 | | |
| Cash discounts taken, percent of selling price | 1.08% | | 2.22% | | 1.72% | | |

Note:  Figures may not add exactly because of rounding.

## EXHIBIT 3
## Accounting Department's Commentary on Costs

*Direct labor:*   Variable.  Nonunion shop at going community rates.  No abnormal demands foreseen.  It may be assumed that direct labor dollars is an adequate measure of capacity utilization.

*Compensation insurance:*   Variable.  Five percent of direct and indirect labor is an adequate estimate.

*Materials:*   Variable.  **Exhibit 2** figures are accurate.  Includes waste allowances.

*Power:*   Variable.  Rates are fixed.

*Supplies:*   Variable.  **Exhibit 2** figures are accurate.

*Repairs:*   Variable.  Varies as volume changes within normal operating range.  Lower and upper limits are fixed.

*General administrative, selling expense, indirect labor, interest:*   Almost nonvariable.  Can be changed by management decision.

*Cash discount:*   Almost nonvariable.  Average cash discounts taken are consistent from year to year.  Percentages in **Exhibit 2** are accurate.

*Light and heat:*   Almost nonvariable.  Heat varies only with fuel cost changes.  Light is a fixed item regardless of level of production.

*Property taxes:*   Almost nonvariable.  Under the lease terms, Hilton Manufacturing Company pays the taxes; assessed valuation has been constant, the rate has risen slowly.  Any change in the near future will be small and independent of production volume.

*Rent:*   Nonvariable.  Lease has 12 years to run.

*Building service:*   Nonvariable.  At normal business level, variances are small.

*Property insurance:*   Nonvariable.  Three-year policy with fixed premium.

*Depreciation:*   Nonvariable. Fixed dollar total.

**EXHIBIT 4**
**Hilton Manufacturing Company, Profit and Loss by Product, at Standard, Showing Variations from January 1 to June 30, 1991**

| Item | Product 101 Standard per Cwt. | Product 101 Total at Standard | Product 102 Standard per Cwt. | Product 102 Total at Standard | Product 103 Standard per Cwt. | Product 103 Total at Standard | Total Standard (thousands) | Total Actual (thousands) | Variances |
|---|---|---|---|---|---|---|---|---|---|
| Rent | 0.3383 | 337 | 0.5856 | 417 | 0.7273 | 365 | 1,119 | 1,021 | + 98 |
| Property taxes | 0.1125 | 112 | 0.1862 | 133 | 0.1555 | 78 | 323 | 307 | + 16 |
| Property insurance | 0.0941 | 94 | 0.1486 | 106 | 0.2047 | 103 | 302 | 278 | + 24 |
| Compensation insurance | 0.1486 | 148 | 0.1620 | 115 | 0.1747 | 88 vc | 351 | 348 | + 3 |
| Direct labor | 2.3282 | 2,321 | 2.2740 | 1,619 | 2.6746 | 1,341 vc | 5,281 | 5,308 | – 27 |
| Indirect labor | 0.7941 | 792 | 0.7903 | 563 | 0.8947 | 448 | 1,803 | 1,721 | + 82 |
| Power | 0.0403 | 40 | 0.0929 | 66 | 0.1171 | 59 vc | 165 | 170 | – 5 |
| Light and heat | 0.0269 | 27 | 0.0472 | 34 | 0.0392 | 20 | 80 | 83 | – 3 |
| Building service | 0.0180 | 18 | 0.0288 | 21 | 0.0288 | 14 | 53 | 50 | + 3 |
| Materials | 1.3766 | 1,372 | 1.7572 | 1,251 | 1.8862 | 946 vc | 3,569 | 3,544 | + 25 |
| Supplies | 0.0941 | 94 | 0.1774 | 126 | 0.1363 | 68 vc | 288 | 288 | — |
| Repairs | 0.0319 | 32 | 0.0557 | 40 | 0.0396 | 20 vc | 91 | 88 | + 3 |
| Total production cost | 5.4036 | 5,387 | 6.3059 | 4,490 | 7.0787 | 3,548 | 13,425 | 13,206 | +219 |
| Selling expense | 1.6397 | 1,635 | 1.7069 | 1,215 | 1.8286 | 917 | 3,767 | 3,706 | + 62 |
| General administration | 0.6209 | 619 | 0.4850 | 345 | 0.6904 | 346 | 1,310 | 1,378 | – 68 |
| Depreciation | 1.0172 | 1,014 | 1.5955 | 1,136 | 1.4223 | 713 | 2,863 | 2,686 | +177 |
| Interest | 0.0941 | 94 | 0.1490 | 106 | 0.2043 | 102 | 302 | 290 | + 12 |
| Total cost | 8.7755 | 8,748 | 10.2423 | 7,294 | 11.2243 | 5,626 | 21,668 | 21,266 | +402 |
| Less other income | 0.0184 | 18 | 0.0192 | 14 | 0.0192 | 10 | 42 | 42 | — |
| | 8.7571 | 8,730 | 10.2231 | 7,280 | 11.2051 | 5,617 | 21,626 | 21,224 | +402 |
| Actual sales (net) | 9.3084 | 9,279 | 9.6900 | 6,900 | 10.3784 | 5,202 | 21,382 | 21,382 | — |
| Profit or loss | 0.5513 | 550 | (0.5331) | (380) | (0.8267) | (414) | (244) | 158 | +402 |
| Unit Sales (cwt.) | | 996,859 | | 712,102 | | 501,276 | | | |

Note: Figures may not add exactly because of rounding.

# Part Five

## Product Costing and an Introduction to Cost Management

Accounting for Indirect Costs

*Seligram, Inc.: Electronic Testing Operations*

Activity Accounting: Another Way to Measure Costs

*Destin Brass Products Co.*

*Siemens Electric Motor Works (A) Process-Oriented Costing*

*Kanthal (A)*

Standard Costs and Variance Analysis

*Waltham Motors Division*

*Mile High Cycles*

*Polysar Limited*

# Accounting for Indirect Costs

**W**hen resources are used in the process of creating a product or service, but a causal linkage between the use of resources and the product or service cannot be established, *indirect costs* are incurred. Indirect costs are not assigned directly to a cost object.

The goal in accounting for indirect costs is to select cost centers and bases of allocation that will relate resource consumption to products or services accurately. Achieving this goal is usually impossible. A more practical objective is to try to measure costs well enough that the information produced is good enough to improve the quality of decisions about pricing, product design, and product mix and to reduce the possibility of mistakes or errors.

In most cost accounting systems, indirect costs are budgeted in advance, and predetermined overhead allocation rates are calculated. Then, as production takes place, indirect costs are applied to (or absorbed into) cost objects. Determining a predetermined overhead rate involves selecting the *cost centers* (or *cost pools*) into which costs will be placed, estimating the total cost to be incurred in each cost center, and choosing cost drivers to allocate resource costs to cost objects.

Predetermined overhead rates normally are used, rather than actual overhead rates, for three reasons:

1. Predetermined overhead rates permit indirect costs to be applied to cost objects at the same time direct costs are applied, rather than waiting for the end of the accounting period;
2. Predetermined overhead rates provide anticipated product or service cost information that can be used in pricing or product-line decisions; and

Copyright © 1992 by the President and Fellows of Harvard College. Harvard Business School case 193-070.

3.  Predetermined overhead rates reduce the amount of effort required to maintain the system because the overhead rates do not have to be recalculated each period.

## THE ALLOCATION PROCESS

Even though overhead rates are almost always predetermined, it is easier to think about the process of allocating indirect costs to cost objects as if allocations were done during or after the production process has taken place. After production has taken place, there is no uncertainty about what resources were consumed and what was produced.

The production process, whether for products or services, consumes resources. To obtain or replenish those resources, cash must be expended. For example, supervisors of direct labor must be paid, along with landlords, insurance agents, and building service suppliers. The first step in allocating indirect costs is to assign these expenditures to cost centers. Some cost centers may not be directly involved in the process of production, but they provide services to production cost centers. The costs of these *service centers* need to be allocated to production cost centers so that they can be allocated to products. For example, the costs of a payroll department in a manufacturing plant might be allocated among the production cost centers served by the payroll department. Any costs of service centers not allocated to production cost centers are treated as period costs, which may cause the measured full cost of cost objects produced to be understated.

Many different allocation bases are used to allocate different costs to cost centers. Some commonly used bases include payroll, number of employees in the cost center, space occupied or used by the cost center, value of materials processed in the cost center, the number of transactions within the cost center or with other cost centers, and the overall level of activity with the cost center.

Once all indirect costs are assigned to production cost centers, cost drivers need to be identified to assign the costs to products or services. Ideally, the cost drivers selected should allocate a fair share of the indirect cost to each unit. If all units of products or services are homogeneous, then a cost driver related to volume is usually appropriate. However, when a variety of products or services is produced, cost drivers such as labor hours, machine hours, number of setups, or transactions are often used. **Exhibit 1** is a schematic diagram for a cost accounting system for a manufacturing plant with a rented building, depreciation for building fixtures and three productive machines, and supervision.

Since overhead allocation rates are predetermined, the amount of indirect costs actually applied to products or services will almost never be equal to the expenditures on resources consumed. The difference between the actual indirect costs and those assigned to products or services arises because of a failure to predict indirect cost expenditures and activity levels perfectly, and is usually called an *overhead variance*.  If small, overhead variances are usually charged as period costs.  If large, further cost analysis may be justified, and the entire process of allocating indirect costs may be repeated to allow managers to figure out what is really going on as they create products or services.

**EXHIBIT 1**
**A Schematic Diagram for Accounting for Indirect Costs**

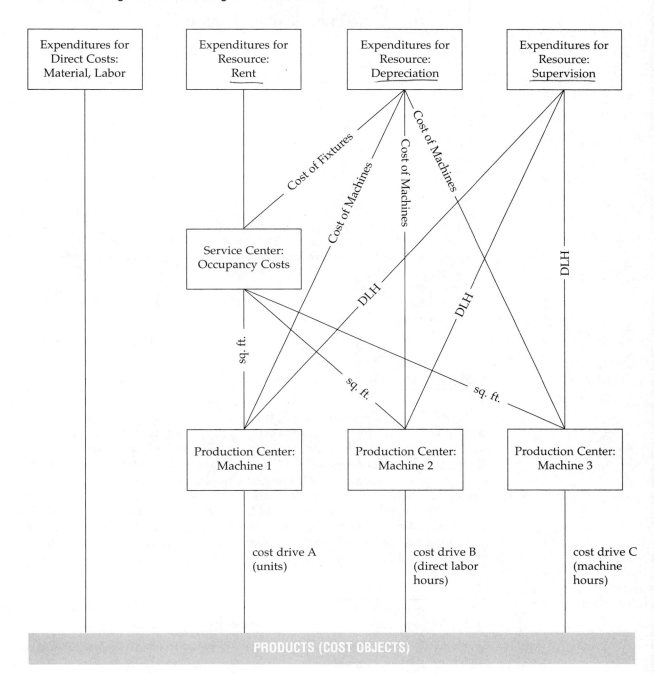

# Seligram, Inc.: Electronic Testing Operations

*We put in a piece of automated equipment a year ago that only fits the requirements of one customer. This equipment reduced the direct labor required to test his components and, because of our labor-based burden allocation system, substantially reduced his costs. But putting a $40,000 machine into the general burden pool raised the costs to our other customers. It just doesn't make sense shooting yourself in the foot at the same time you are lowering the company's cost of operations.*

Paul Carte, Manager

## INTRODUCTION

Electronic Testing Operations (ETO), a division of Seligram, Inc., provided centralized testing for electronic components such as integrated circuits. ETO was created as a result of a decision in 1979 to consolidate electronic testing from 11 different divisions of Seligram. ETO commenced services to these divisions in 1983. It was estimated that centralization would save Seligram in excess of $20 million in testing equipment investment over the next five years.

ETO operated as a cost center and transferred products to other divisions at full cost (direct costs plus allocated burden). Although ETO was a captive division, other divisions within Seligram were allowed to use outside testing services if ETO could not meet their cost or service requirements. ETO was

---

*This case was prepared by Professor Peter B. B. Turney, Portland State University, and Christopher Ittner, Doctoral Student, under the supervision of Professor Robin Cooper.*

Copyright © 1991 by the President and Fellows of Harvard College. Harvard Business School case 189-084.

permitted to devote up to 10% of its testing capacity to outside customers but chose to work mainly with other Seligram divisions due to limited marketing resources.

ETO employed approximately 60 hourly personnel and 40 administrative and technical staff members. Budgeted expenses were $7.9 million in 1988 (see **Exhibit 1**).

## Testing Procedures

ETO expected to test between 35 and 40 million components in 1988. These components included integrated circuits (ICs), diodes, transistors, capacitors, resistors, transformers, relays, and crystals. Component testing was required for two reasons. First, if defective components were not caught early in the manufacturing cycle, the cost of repair could exceed the manufacturing cost of the product itself. Studies indicated that a defective resistor caught before use in the manufacturing process cost two cents. If the resistor was not caught until the end product was in the field, however, the cost of repair could run into the thousands of dollars. Second, a large proportion of Seligram's work was defense related. Military specifications frequently required extensive testing of components utilized in aerospace and naval products. By 1988, ETO had the ability to test 6,500 different components. Typically, however, the division tested about 500 different components each month and between 3,000 and 3,500 per year. Components were received from customers in lots; in 1988, ETO would receive approximately 12,000 lots of components.

ETO performed both electrical and mechanical testing. Electrical testing involved measuring the electrical characteristics of the components and comparing these measurements with the components' specifications. For example, the specifications for an amplifier may have called for a 1-volt input to be amplified into a 10-volt output. ETO would deliver a 1-volt input to the component. By measuring the amplifier's output, ETO gauged its conformance with specifications.

Mechanical testing included solderability, component burn-in, thermal shock, lead straightening, and leak detection. Solderability involved the inspection of components to see if they held solder. Burn-in was the extended powering of components at high temperature. Thermal shock involved the cycling of components between high and low temperatures. Lead straightening was the detection and correction of bent leads on components such as axial components. Leak detection examined hermetically sealed ICs for leaks.

Components varied significantly in the number and type of electrical and mechanical testing procedures they required. This variation resulted in about 200 different standard process flows for the division. Process flows were determined by the different combinations of tests and specifications requested by the customer. Based on these combinations, ETO planners determined the routing of components between testing equipment and the type of tests to be performed at each station.  ICs, for example, could follow six different flows through the facility.  While some ICs only required electrical testing at room temperature (solderability and leak detection, for instance), others also required thermal shock and burn-in testing.

Each type of component required separate software development, and custom tools and fixtures were often required.  Software, tools, and fixtures were developed by the engineering group, which was made up of specialists in software development, equipment maintenance, calibration and repair, tooling and fixturing, and testing equipment operation.  Software engineers developed programs for specific applications.  The programs were then retained in a software library for future use.  ETO had 6,500 different software programs on file, of which 1,300 were programs developed in the past year.  ETO also had an inventory of 1,500 tools and fixtures, of which 300 had been developed in the past year.  The large number of tools and fixtures allowed the testing of components with a wide variety of leads, pin combinations, and mating configurations.

The testing facility was divided into two rooms.  The main testing room contained the equipment used for electrical testing.  The mechanical room contained the equipment used for mechanical testing, plus incoming receiving and the stockroom.  A total of 20 people worked in the two rooms on each of two main shifts, and 10 people worked on the night shift.

## Cost Accounting System

The cost accounting system measured two components of cost: direct labor and burden.  Burden was grouped into a single cost pool that included burden costs associated with each of the testing rooms as well as the engineering burden costs related to software and tooling development and the administrative costs of the division.  Total burden costs were divided by the sum of testing and engineering labor dollars to arrive at a burden rate per direct labor dollar.  The division costed each lot of components.  Burden was calculated for each lot by multiplying the actual direct labor dollars associated with the lot by the 145% of burden rate.  The resulting burden was then added to the actual direct labor costs to determine the lot's total cost.  In 1988, the facility-wide burden rate was 145% of each direct labor dollar, of which more than 40% was attributable to equipment depreciation (see **Exhibit 2**).

## Signs of Obsolescence

Several trends pointed to the obsolescence of the labor-based burden allocation process.  Since the founding of the division in 1983, direct labor hours per lot tested had been steadily declining (see **Exhibit 3**).  This trend was aggravated by an increased dependence on vendor certification.  Vendor certification was a key component of just-in-time (JIT) delivery.  With vendor certification, Seligram's suppliers did the primary testing of components.  ETO then utilized statistical sampling to verify that the supplier's production process was still in control. Thus, whereas JIT led to an increased number of smaller lots being received by ETO, vendor certification reduced the number of tests performed. Early indications were that JIT deliveries would account for 30% of Seligram's shipments within the next five years.

In addition to declining direct labor content and fewer test lots, the obsolescence of the labor-based allocation system was intensified by a shift from simple inspection services to broader-based test technology. On complex parts requiring screening, environmental conditioning, and testing, the division was consistently cheaper than outside services. Where only elementary testing was required, however, low-technology outside laboratories were often cheaper, especially on large lots. The advantage that the division brought customers over the outside labs was that the latter provided essentially no engineering support, whereas ETO with its resident engineering resources was able to support such service on a rapid and cost-effective basis. The shift to more technically sophisticated services prompted a shift in the labor mix from direct to indirect personnel. The division expected to see a crossover between engineering head count and hourly head count early in the 1990s.

Finally, the introduction of high-technology components created the need for more automatic testing, longer test cycles, and more data per part. Digital components, for example, were currently tested for up to 100 conditions (combinations of electrical input and output states). The new generation of digital components, on the other hand, would be much more complex and require verification of up to 10,000 conditions. These components would require very expensive highly automated equipment. This increase in automation would, in turn, lead to a smaller base of direct labor to absorb the depreciation costs of this new equipment.

There were fears that the resulting increase in burden rates would drive some customers away. ETO had already noticed an increase in the number and frequency of complaints from customers regarding the rates they were charged for testing.

The division's accounting manager proposed a new cost accounting system to alleviate the problem. Under this new system, burden would be directly traced to two cost pools. The first pool would contain burden related to the administrative and technical functions (division management, engineering, planning, and administrative personnel). This pool would be charged on a rate per direct labor dollar. The second pool would include all other burden costs and would be charged based on machine hours. **Exhibit 4** provides the proposed burden rates.

Shortly after the accounting manager submitted his proposal, a consultant hired by Seligram's corporate management prepared an assessment of ETO's cost system. He recommended the implementation of a three-burden-pool system utilizing separate burden centers for each test room and a common technical and administrative pool. Burden would be directly traced to each of the three burden pools. Like the accounting manager's system, burden costs in the test rooms would then be allocated on a machine-hour basis.  Technical and administrative costs would continue to be charged on a rate per direct labor dollar.

To examine the impact of the two alternative systems, ETO management asked that a study be conducted on a representative sample of parts.  **Exhibit 5** provides a breakout of actual direct labor and machine-hour requirements per lot for the five components selected for the study.

### Technological Future

In 1988, the division faced major changes in the technology of testing that required important equipment acquisition decisions.  The existing testing equipment was getting old and would not be able to keep pace with developments in component technology.  Existing components, for example, had between 16 and 40 input/output terminations (e.g., pins or other mating configurations), and ETO's equipment could handle up to 120 terminations.  Although the 120-termination limit had only been reached a couple of times in the past few years, a new generation of components with up to 256 terminations was already being developed.  Similarly, the upper limit of frequency on existing components was 20 MHz (million cycles per second), whereas the frequency on the next generation of components was expected to be 50 MHz.

The equipment required to test the next generation of components would be expensive.  Each machine cost approximately $2 million.  Testing on this equipment would be more automated than existing equipment, with longer test cycles and the generation of more test data per part.  It was also likely that lot sizes would be larger.  The new equipment would not replace the existing equipment but would merely add capabilities ETO did not currently possess.  Additionally, the new equipment would only be needed to service the requirements of one or two customers in the foreseeable future.  **Exhibit 6** provides a summary of the new equipment's economics and operating characteristics.

The impact of this new equipment would be an acceleration in the decline in direct labor hours per lot of components.  At the same time, burden would increase with the additional depreciation and engineering costs associated with the new equipment.  This would result in a large increase in the burden rate per direct labor dollar.  As Paul Carte, manager of ETO, saw it, the acquisition of the new equipment could have a disastrous effect on the division's pricing structure if the labor-based allocation system remained in use:

> *We plan on investing $2 million on a large electronic testing machine to test the chips of one or two customers.  This machine will be very fast and will require little direct labor.  Its acquisition will have a significant effect on our per direct labor dollar burden rate, which will result in an increase in charges to our other customers.  It is clear that a number of customers will walk away if we try to pass this increase on.  I am afraid that we will lose 25% of our customer base if we don't change our cost system.*

**EXHIBIT 1**
**Seligram Inc.:  Electronic Testing Operations**

### 1988 Budgeted Expenses

| | | |
|---|---:|---:|
| Direct Labor | | $3,260,015 |
| Overhead | | |
| Indirect Labor | $ 859,242 | |
| Salary Expense | 394,211 | |
| Supplies & Expenses | 538,029 | |
| Services[a] | 245,226 | |
| Personnel Allocations[b] | 229,140 | |
| Service Allocations[c] | 2,448,134 | |
| Total Overhead | | 4,713,982 |
| Total Budgeted Expenses | | $7,973,997 |

[a] Includes tool repair, computer expenses, maintenance stores, and service cost transfers from other divisions.
[b] Includes indirect and salaried employee fringe benefits, personnel department, security, stores/warehousing, and holidays/vacations.
[c] Includes building occupancy, telephones, depreciation, information systems, and data control.

**EXHIBIT 2**
**Seligram, Inc.:  Electronic Testing Operations**

### Calculation of Burden Rate
Based on 1988 Plan

$$\text{Burden Rate} = \frac{\text{Total Burden Dollars[a]}}{\text{Direct Labor Dollars}}$$

$$= \frac{\$4,713,982}{\$3,260,015}$$

$$= 144.6\%$$

$$\text{Effective Rate} = 145\%$$

[a] Cost Breakdown:

| | | Fixed | | |
|---|---:|---:|---:|---:|
| | Variable | Depreciation | Other | Total |
| Total Burden | $1,426,317 | $1,288,000 | $1,999,665 | $4,713,982 |

**EXHIBIT 3**
**Seligram, Inc.: Electronic Testing Operations**

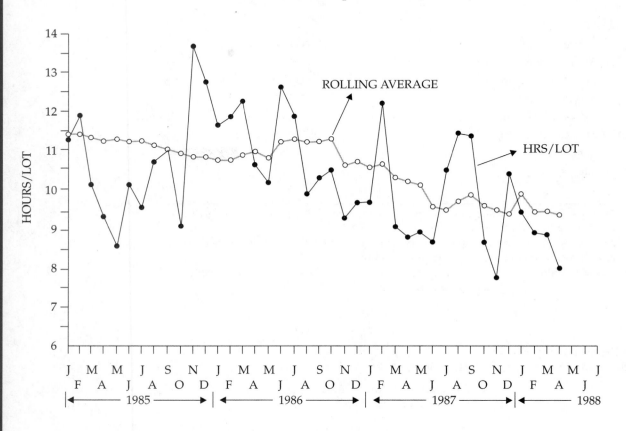

Direct Labor Hours per Lot Chart

**EXHIBIT 4**
**Seligram, Inc.: Electronic Testing Operations**

**Proposed Burden Rates**
Based on 1988 Plan

| Machine-Hour Rate | Machine Hours | Burden Dollars[a] | |
|---|---|---|---|
| Main Test Room | 33,201 – ABC | $2,103,116 – ABC | 2103116/33201 = $63/hr |
| Mechanical Test Room | 17,103 ABC | 1,926,263 – ABC | = 113$/hr |
| Total | 50,304 | $4,029,379 | |

$$\text{Machine-Hour Rate} \quad \frac{\text{Test Room Burden Dollars}}{\text{Machine Hours}} = \frac{\$4,029,379}{50,304} = \$80.10$$

Effective Machine-Hour Rate  =  $80.00 / machine hr.

Direct Labor Hour Rate

Total Engineering & Administrative Burden Dollars  =  $684,603

Total Direct Labor Dollars  =  $3,260,015[b]

$$\text{Burden Rate} = \frac{\text{Engineering \& Administrative Burden Dollar}}{\text{Direct Labor Dollar}} = \frac{\$684,603}{\$3,260,015} = 21\% / DLhr$$

Effective Burden Rate per Direct Labor Dollar  =  20%

---

[a] Cost Breakdown

| | | Fixed | | |
|---|---|---|---|---|
| | Variable | Depreciation | Other | Total |
| Main Test Room | $ 887,379 | $ 88,779 | $1,126,958 | $2,103,116 |
| Mechanical Test Room | 443,833 | 808,103 | 674,327 | 1,926,263 |
| Test Room Burden | $1,331,212 | $ 896,882 | $1,801,285 | $4,029,379 |
| Engineering & Admin. | 95,105 | 391,118 | 198,380 | 684,603 |
| Total Burden | $1,426,317 | $1,288,000 | $1,999,665 | $4,713,982 |

[b] Includes all direct labor costs, including direct labor costs incurred in both test rooms as well as in engineering.

**EXHIBIT 5**
**Seligram, Inc.: Electronic Testing Operations**

### Direct Labor and Machine-Hour Requirements
### Actuals For One Lot

| Product | Direct Labor ($) | Machine Hours Main Room | Mech. Room | Total |
|---|---|---|---|---|
| ICA | $  917 | 8.5 | 10.0 | 18.5 |
| ICB | 2,051  per Lot | 14.0 | 26.0 | 40.0 |
| Capacitor | 1,094 | 3.0 | 4.5 | 7.5 |
| Amplifier | 525 | 4.0 | 1.0 | 5.0 |
| Diode | 519 | 7.0 | 5.0 | 12.0 |

**EXHIBIT 6**
**Seligram, Inc.: Electronic Testing Operations**

### New Testing Equipment Economics and Operating Characteristics

| | |
|---|---|
| Cost: | $2 million |
| Useful Life: | 8 years |
| Depreciation Method: | Double declining balance (First year depreciation costs of $500,000) |
| Location: | Main test room |
| Utilization: | 10% first year, rising to 60% by third year and in all subsequent years, based on 4,000 hours per year availability (2 shifts × 2,000-hour year) |
| Direct Labor Requirements: | Approximately five minutes per hour of operation; average labor rate of $30 per hour |
| Engineering Requirements: | $75,000 in installation and programming costs in first year |
| Estimated Overhead (nonengineering depreciation): | $250,000 ($100,000 variable, $150,000 fixed) |

# Activity Accounting: Another Way to Measure Costs

Traditional cost accounting systems operate on the assumption that producing products and services is what causes costs to occur. For this reason, direct material, direct labor, and other direct costs are assigned to products, and all other costs are grouped as indirect and then allocated among the products that are produced, usually based on some measure of product volume. There is an implicit assumption that the indirect costs that must be allocated are necessary, or they would not have been incurred. Because the costs are necessary, each unit of product or service must bear its fair share of these costs.

These traditional assumptions work fairly well in situations where managers have successfully attained efficiency in organizational tasks related to a single product, homogeneous products, or services, or if indirect costs are small relative to direct materials and direct labor. In these situations, the assumption that costs should be allocated based on the volume of direct material, direct labor hours, direct labor dollars, units of product, or some other volume measure creates few significant problems. Because of the homogeneity of products or services, each unit of product or service gets what might be called its fair share of indirect costs. But in actuality, few manufacturing plants or organizations are as simple or homogeneous as the assumption demands. As product mix and product diversity increase, allocating indirect costs by volume alone may introduce distortions that allow high-volume products to subsidize low-volume products because the high-volume products carry more than their fair share of the actual indirect costs that are incurred.

In the last decade, increased attention has been given to another kind of cost accounting system. These *activity-based cost (ABC) systems* are built on the

Copyright © 1992 by the President and Fellows of Harvard College. Harvard Business School case 193-044.

assumption that activities cause costs, and that products or services and customers are the reasons that activities must be performed.  Therefore, for example, if a customer's special order requires us to order material, receive it, take it to the production line, prepare a check to pay the supplier, and prepare new product specifications for that special order, each of these activities and the cost of performing them should be measured and assigned to the units produced. The cost of the special order can be compared with the revenue generated to assess the profitability of the customer's order. *An ABC system attempts to trace the cost of each activity as closely as possible to the reason why organizational resources were consumed in support of the necessary activities.*

This approach, which is also called transaction-based costing, or activity accounting, focuses on what an organization does, the way time is spent, and the outputs of those processes.  To do this requires at least four steps:

1.    Identify activities;
2.    Trace the costs of resources to the activities performed;
3.    Identify activity measures (outputs) by which the costs of a process vary most directly; and
4.    Trace activity costs to cost objects such as products, processes, and customers based on the usage of activities.

By this method, the cost of support departments, which might otherwise be accumulated as indirect costs and assigned based on volume in a traditional cost accounting system, are assigned to activities performed, such as setting up machines, receiving and handling material, and shipping finished products. Then, the expenses of each activity are assigned to products or customers based on their demand for the activities, such as the number of setups, the number of inbound material shipments, or the number of separate shipments to the customer.

ABC systems are similar to more traditional cost systems in that they capture costs, assign them to cost centers (activity centers), and then assign those costs to products based on the demand that the product or customer places on the activity itself.  Some activities, such as machine setup, will occur each time a production run is initiated.  Other activities, such as product engineering, may have nothing to do with how many units or batches of the products are produced.

ABC systems differ from more traditional volume-based systems because they focus on what causes a cost to occur rather than on simply allocating what has been spent.  In many respects, you can think of ABC systems as abandoning the traditional ideas that a cost can be variable or fixed. Resources are consumed because something (activities) made a demand on them.  The ABC system seeks to understand what that something (activities) is and to associate the costs of the resources consumed with whatever made the demand.  The system creates the mechanism for tracing resource consumption to whatever caused spending to acquire the resource.

Proponents of introducing and using ABC systems usually concede that such systems are more complex and more costly than the traditional cost systems that they replace. However, they also feel that the following three benefits of using ABC systems outweigh the costs of designing, installing, and using such systems.

First, ABC systems produce more accurate product costs, particularly in circumstances where indirect costs are important in the total cost structure of the organization and where there is great diversity in products or services, the processes of producing them, or customers. With more accurate costs, the risk of poor decisions is reduced, and the revelation of competitive opportunity is likely to be more complete.

Second, focusing on the consumption of resources rather than merely allocating costs to products or services raises questions about why resources are being consumed in the way that they are. For example, if the cost of processing orders is high because each order has a special characteristic, the savings possible by producing a standard line can easily be uncovered with an ABC system. In addition, focusing on resources used can direct attention to reducing the cost (increasing the efficiency) of activities and business processes.

Third, the need for special cost analyses when confronted with usual situations is frequently reduced with more accurate cost information and management's improved understanding of what causes costs to be incurred.

Two HBS case studies, "Destin Brass Products Co." and "Siemens Electric Motor Works (A) Process-Oriented Costing" introduce basic techniques used in ABC systems. One should be aware, however, that each ABC system will differ from another because every system must be closely tied to the technology and economic characteristics of the organization it supports. Although only a relatively small proportion of companies are using ABC systems to date, it is expected that many more will be experimenting with them over the next decade. Organizations that have developed and used such systems express enthusiasm for them, and managers agree that ABC developments have been one of the most exciting events in the development of cost accounting during this century.

# Destin Brass Products Co.

*Every month it becomes clearer to me that our competitors either know some-
thing that we do not know, or they are crazy. I realize that pumps are a major
product in a big market for all of us, but with the price cutting that is going
on, it is likely that no one will be able to sell pumps profitably if they keep
forcing us to match their lower prices. I guess we should be grateful that
competitors seem to be overlooking the opportunities for profit in flow controllers. Even with the 12½% price increase we made there, our sales representatives report no new competition.*

Roland Guidry, president of Destin Brass Products Co., was discussing
product profitability in the latest month with Peggy Alford, his controller, and
John Scott, his manufacturing manager. The meeting among the three was taking place in an atmosphere tinged with apprehension because competitors
had been reducing prices on pumps, Destin Brass Products' major product
line. With no unique design advantage, managers at Destin had seen no alternative except to match the reduced prices while trying to maintain volumes.
Moreover, the company's profits in the latest month had slipped again to be
lower than those in the prior month.

The purpose of the meeting was to try to understand the competitive
trends and to develop new strategies for dealing with them if new strategies
were appropriate. The three managers, along with Steve Abbott, sales and marketing manager, who could not attend because he was away, were very concerned because they held significant shares of ownership in Destin Brass
Products. Locally, they were a success story; the company had grown to be a
significant business in Destin, Florida, better known for its white sand beaches
and as "the Luckiest Fishing Village in the World."

---

Copyright © 1989 by the President and Fellows of Harvard College. Harvard Business
School case 190-089.

## THE COMPANY

Destin Brass Products Co. was established by Abbott, Guidry, and Scott, who purchased a moribund commercial machine shop in 1984. Steve Abbott had sensed an opportunity in a conversation with the president of a large manufacturer of water purification equipment who was dissatisfied with the quality of brass valves available. John Scott was a local legend because of the high-quality brass boat fittings he had always manufactured for the fishing fleet along the Florida Gulf Coast. Roland Guidry had recently retired from the United States Air Force, where he had a long record of administrative successes. The three then selected Peggy Alford, an accountant with manufacturing experience, to join them.

John Scott was quick to analyze the nature of problems other manufacturers were having with water purification valves. The tolerances needed were small, and to maintain them required great labor skill or expensive machine controls, or both. Within weeks of forming the company, Scott and his shop crew were manufacturing valves that met or exceeded the needed specifications. Abbott negotiated a contract with the purification equipment manufacturer, and revenues soon were earned.

The company had grown quickly because the demand for water purification equipment increased, and Destin Brass Products became the sole supplier of valves to its customer. However, Abbott and Guidry both had greater ambitions. Knowing that the same manufacturing skills used in machining valves could also be used in manufacturing brass pumps and flow controllers, they created an engineering department and designed new products for those markets. Pumps were known to be an even larger market than valves, and flow controllers were often used in the same fluid distribution systems as valves and pumps. Moreover, by specializing in brass, the company could exploit Scott's special knowledge about working with the material.

Destin did no foundry work. Instead, components were purchased from brass foundries and then were precisely machined and assembled in the company's new modern manufacturing facility. The same equipment and labor were used for all three product lines, and runs were scheduled to match customer shipping requirements. The foundries had agreed to just-in-time deliveries, and products were packed and shipped as completed. Guidry described the factory to his friends as "a very modern job shop in specialized products made from brass."

## THE PRODUCTS

Valves (24% of company revenues) were created from four brass components. Scott had designed machines that held each component in jigs while it was machined automatically. Each machinist could operate two machines and assemble the valves as machining was taking place. The expense of precise machining made the cost of Destin's valves too high to compete in the nonspecialized valve market, so all monthly production of valves took place in a single production run, which was immediately shipped to its single customer upon completion. Although Scott felt several competitors could match Destin's quality in valves, none had tried to gain market share by cutting price, and gross margins had been maintained at a standard 35%.

Pumps (55% of revenues) were created by a manufacturing process that was practically the same as that for valves. Five components required machining and assembly. The pumps were then shipped to each of seven industrial product distributors on a monthly basis. To supply the distributors, whose orders were fairly stable as long as Destin would meet competitive prices, the company scheduled five production runs each month.

Pump prices to distributors had been under considerable pressure. The pump market was large, and specifications were less precise than those for valves. Recently, it seemed as if each month brought new reports of reduced prices for pumps. Steve Abbott felt Destin had no choice but to match the lower prices or give up its place as a supplier of pumps. As a result, gross margins on pump sales in the latest month had fallen to 22%, well below the company's planned gross margin of 35%. Guidry and Alford could not see how the competitors could be making profits at current prices unless pumps were being subsidized by other products.

Flow controllers (21% of revenues) were used to control the rate and direction of flow of liquids. As with pumps, the manufacturing operations required for flow controllers were similar to those for valves. More components were needed for each finished unit, and more labor was required. In recent months, Destin had manufactured 4,000 flow controllers in 10 production runs, and the finished flow controllers had been distributed in 22 shipments to distributors and other customers.

Steve Abbott was trying to understand the market for flow controllers better because it seemed to him that Destin had almost no competition in the flow controller market. He had recently raised flow controller prices by 12½% with no apparent effect on demand.

## THE MEETING

After the latest month's results had been summarized and reported, Roland Guidry called Peggy Alford and John Scott into his office to discuss what changes they could or should make in their course of actions. The meeting opened with his statement above concerning competition in pumps versus flow controllers. Guidry had a copy of the product profitability analysis (**Exhibit 1**) on his desk.

**John Scott (Manufacturing manager):** It really is amazing to me as well that our competitors keep reducing prices on pumps. Even though our manufacturing process is better than theirs, I truly do not believe we are less efficient or cost effective. Furthermore, I can't see what their motives can be. There are many manufacturers of pumps. Even if we or even several competitors were to drop out of the market, there would still be so many competitors that no monopoly or oligopoly pricing could be maintained. Maybe the competitors just don't realize what their costs are. Could that be, Peggy?

**Peggy Alford (Controller):**   That does not seem likely to me! Cost accounting is a well-developed art, and most competent managers and cost accountants have some understanding of how product costs can be measured. In manufacturing businesses like ours, material and labor costs are pretty easily related to products produced, whether in the product design stage or after the fact. So, if anything, our competitors must be making some different assumptions about overhead costs or allocating them to products in some other way. Or, as you said Roland, maybe they have stupidly forgotten that in the long run, prices have to be high enough to provide product margins that cover corporate costs and produce return to owners.

**Roland Guidry (President):**   Peggy, I know you have explained to me several times already the choices we could make in allocating overhead to products. In fact, last month you almost sold me on what you called a "modern costing approach," which I rejected because of the work and cost of the changeover. I also was worried about the discontinuity it might cause in our historical data. But I feel that I might need another lesson to help me understand what is happening to us. Could you try once more to explain what we do?

**Peggy Alford:**   I would be happy to try again. We have a very traditional cost accounting system that meets all of our needs for preparing financial reports and tax returns. It is built on measurements of direct and indirect costs and on assumptions about our production and sales activity (**Exhibit 2**). Each unit of product is charged for material cost and labor cost; material cost is based on the prices we pay for components, and labor cost is based on the standard times for production-run labor times the labor pay rate of $16 per hour. Overhead cost is assigned to products in a two-stage process. First, the overhead costs are assigned to production—in our situation, we have only one producing department so we know all overhead costs are assigned correctly at the first stage. Then, we allocate the total overhead cost assigned to production on the basis of production-run labor cost. Every $1.00 of run labor cost causes $4.39 of overhead to be allocated to the product to which the labor was applied. You can see how this works in our standard unit costs sheet, which I brought with me (**Exhibit 3**). This is a fairly inexpensive way to allocate overhead cost because we have to accumulate direct labor cost to prepare factory payroll, and we just use the same measurement in product costing.

**Roland Guidry:**   All this looks familiar to me. But remind me again what the choices we discussed earlier were.

**Peggy Alford:**   Well, one choice advocated by some would be to forego the overhead cost allocation altogether.  Overhead costs could be charged each month as period expenses.  Product profitability would then be measured at the contribution margin level, or price less all variable costs, which in our situation are direct material costs.  We would still have to make some adjustments at the end of any period we held inventory to satisfy reporting and tax return requirements, but the effort to do that would be fairly trivial.  The bigger danger would be that we would forget that all overhead costs have to be covered somehow, and we might allow our prices to slip.

**John Scott:**   Yeah, the salesman's mentality in Steve Abbott would make that kind of direct cost accounting dangerous.  He would be looking for marginal customers willing to pay marginal prices based on marginal costs.  From the outset, we have succeeded in part because we insisted on trying to maintain a 35% gross margin on costs *including* allocated overhead.

**Roland Guidry:**   John, the competitors are real and so are their prices.  If we want to stay in pumps, we probably have to meet them head-on.  Peggy, please go on.

**Peggy Alford:**   The last time we discussed this, Roland, I showed you these revised standard unit costs (**Exhibit 4**).  These are based on a more modern view of the proper way to allocate costs.  I put these together in an attempt to better allocate overhead based on activities.  First, I identified material-related overhead, the cost of receiving and handling material, and allocated that to each product line based on the cost of material.  The justification for this change is that material handling does not have any relationship to the labor cost of machining.  Second, I took setup labor cost out of the total overhead and allocated it to each product line.  This is a small amount, but the cost of setups also had no relationship whatever to the total labor cost of a production run.  Finally, I substituted machine hours for labor dollars as a basis for allocating the remaining factory overhead.  John [Scott] has really done wonders with our machines, but our expenses for machines are probably more than double the cost of labor.  Therefore, it seems to me that machine hours better reflect use of an expensive resource and should be used to allocate overhead costs.

The results of this proposal made sense to me and may contain a clue about why competitors are chasing lower prices in the pump market.  The revised standard cost for pumps is more than $4.00 below our present standard and would show a gross margin percentage of 27% compared to our current 22%.  Maybe our competitors just have more modern cost accounting!

**Roland Guidry:**   And you said this modern approach would not cost much more to maintain once we adopted it?

**Peggy Alford:**   No, it wouldn't.  All I really did was to divide the overhead costs into two pools, each of which is allocated on a different measure of activity.

**Roland Guidry:** And we could use the same numbers for financial reports and tax returns?

**Peggy Alford:** Absolutely.

(John Scott had been examining the revised unit costs and suddenly spoke up.)

**John Scott:** Peggy! This new method makes valves look more costly and flow controllers even more profitable than we know they are.

**Peggy Alford:** . . . or, thought they were! The profit for each product line will change if we change the way we allocate overhead costs to products.

**John Scott:** I realize that. But it seems to me that product costs should have more to do with the costs caused by producing and selling the product. That's usually true for material and maybe direct labor, but it is not true for most of these overhead costs. For example, we probably spend one-half of our engineering effort on flow controllers, but whether you use direct labor dollars or machine hours to allocate engineering costs to products, flow controllers don't get much of the engineering costs.

I've been thinking about this a lot since last week when I attended an "Excellence in Manufacturing" conference in Tallahassee. One presentation was about "Cost Accounting for the New Manufacturing Environment." I couldn't follow all of the arguments of the speaker, but the key seemed to be that activity, rather than production volume, causes costs. In our operations, it is receiving and handling material, packing and shipping, and engineering orders that cause us to incur costs, not the length of any production run.

If I understood what this speaker was advocating, it was that whenever possible overhead costs that cannot be traced directly to product lines should be allocated on the basis of transactions—since transactions cause costs to be incurred. A product that required three times as many transactions to be incurred than another product would be allocated three times as much of the overhead cost related to those transactions than the other product would be allocated. Or said another way, a product that causes 3% of the total transactions for receiving components would be allocated 3% of the total cost of receiving components. At a basic level, this seems to make sense to me.

**Peggy Alford:** Recently I've been reading a lot in my professional magazines about this activity-based costing (ABC) . . . .

**Roland Guidry:** But, to cost products that way has got to be more expensive. It's more complex; also, who keeps count of transactions?

**Peggy Alford:** It can't be too hard. All overhead allocation is somewhat arbitrary. We could experiment with estimates to see how the product costs might be affected. The product costs for material, direct labor, and setup labor will be the same as for my revised unit costs, and to allocate other overhead costs, we just need to estimate how many transactions occur in total and are caused by each product.

**John Scott:**   I'd like to ask Peggy to put together an analysis for us.  The managers at the conference from companies that have used these transaction-based costing systems really seemed excited about what they said they learned.

**Roland Guidry:**   OK.  Peggy, you and John get together this afternoon to put together the activity estimates you need.  Get back to me as quickly as you can.  Maybe we can figure out why the competitors think they should sell pumps regardless of price.

## LATER

After lunch, Peggy Alford and John Scott met in Peggy's office.  They discussed transactions and effort related to each type of overhead cost.  The result was the overhead cost activity analysis shown in **Exhibit 5**.

## QUESTIONS

1.   Use the Monthly Overhead Cost Activity Analysis in **Exhibit 5** and other data on manufacturing costs to estimate product costs for valves, pumps, and flow controllers.
2.   Compare the estimated costs you calculate to existing standard unit costs (**Exhibit 3**) and the revised unit costs (**Exhibit 4**).  What causes the different product costing methods to produce such different results?
3.   What are the strategic implications of your analysis?  What actions would you recommend to the managers at Destin Brass Products Co.?
4.   Assume that interest in a new basis for cost accounting at Destin Brass Products remains high.  In the following month, quantities produced and sold, activities, and costs were all at standard.  How much higher or lower would the *net income* reported under the activity-transaction-based system be than the *net income* that will be reported under the present, more traditional system?  Why?

**EXHIBIT 1**
**Product Profitability Analysis**

|  | Valves | Pumps | Flow Controllers |
|---|---|---|---|
| Standard unit costs | $37.56 | $63.12 | $56.50 |
| Target selling price | $57.78 | $97.10 | $86.96 |
| Planned gross margin (%) | 35% | 35% | 35% |
| **Last Month** | | | |
| Actual selling price | $57.78 | $81.26 | $97.07 |
| Actual gross margin | 35% | 22% | 42% |

**EXHIBIT 2**
**Monthly Product and Cost Summary**

| Product Lines | Valves | Pumps | Flow Controllers | |
|---|---|---|---|---|
| Monthly production | 7,500 units (1 run) | 12,500 units (5 runs) | 4,000 units (10 runs) | |
| Monthly shipments | 7,500 units (1 shipment) | 12,500 units (7 shipments) | 4,000 units (22 shipments) | |
| **Manufacturing Costs** | | | | **Monthly Total** |
| Material | 4 components | 5 components | 10 components | |
| | 2 @ $2 = $ 4 | 3 @ $2 = $ 6 | 4 @ $1 = $ 4 | |
| | 2 @ $6 =  12 | 2 @ $7 =  14 | 5 @ $2 =  10 | |
| | | | 1 @ $8 =   8 | |
| Total material | $16 | $20 | $22 | $458,000 |
| Labor ($16 per hour including employee benefits) | | | | |
| Setup labor | 8 hours per production run | 8 hours per production run | 12 hours per production run | 168 hours |
| Run labor  D.L. | .25 hours per unit | .50 hours per unit | .40 hours per unit | 9,725 hours |
| Machine usage | .50 hours per unit | .50 hours per unit | .20 hours per unit | 10,800 hours |

**Manufacturing Overhead**

| | |
|---|---|
| Receiving | $ 20,000 |
| Materials handling | 200,000 |
| Engineering | 100,000 |
| Packing and shipping | 60,000 |
| Maintenance | 30,000 |
| Total | $410,000 |

| | |
|---|---|
| Machine depreciation (units-of-production method) $25 per hour of use | $270,000 |

**EXHIBIT 3**
**Standard Unit Costs**

|  | Valves | Pumps | Flow Controllers |
|---|---|---|---|
| Material | $16.00 | $20.00 | $22.00 |
| Direct labor | 4.00 | 8.00 | 6.40 |
| Overhead @ 439% of direct labor $ | 17.56 | 35.12 | 28.10 |
| Standard unit cost | $37.56 | $63.12 | $56.50 |

**Overhead**

| | |
|---|---|
| Machine depreciation | $270,000 |
| Setup labor | 2,688 |
| Receiving | 20,000 |
| Materials handling | 200,000 |
| Engineering | 100,000 |
| Packing and shipping | 60,000 |
| Maintenance | 30,000 |
| | $682,688 |

Total run labor = 9,725 hours × $16 = $155,600

Overhead rate $\dfrac{682,688}{155,600} = 439\%$

**EXHIBIT 4**
**Revised Unit Costs** — *Not Using ABC*

| | | Valves | Pumps | Flow Controllers |
|---|---|---|---|---|
| Material | Direct C, | $16.00 ✓ | $20.00 | $22.00 |
| Material overhead (48%) | Burden | 7.68 | 9.60 | 10.56 |
| Setup labor | Burden | .02 | .05 | .48 |
| Direct labor | Direct C. | 4.00 ✓ | 8.00 | 6.40 |
| Other overhead (machine hour basis) | | 21.30 | 21.30 | 8.52 |
| Revised standard cost | | $49.00 | $58.95 | $47.96 |

**Material Related Overhead**

| | | |
|---|---|---|
| Receiving | Burden | $ 20,000 |
| Materials handling | | 200,000 |
| Total | | $220,000 |

**Overhead Absorption Rate**

$$\frac{\$220,000}{\$458,000} = 48\% \text{ (materials cost basis)}$$

**Other Overhead**

| | | |
|---|---|---|
| Machine depreciation | Burden | $270,000 |
| Engineering | | 100,000 |
| Packing and shipping | | 60,000 |
| Maintenance | | 30,000 |
| Total | | $460,000 |

**Overhead Absorption Rate**

$$\frac{\$460,000}{10,800 \text{ hours}} = \$42.59 \text{ per machine hour}$$

**EXHIBIT 5**
**Monthly Overhead Cost Activity Analysis**   ABC Drivers

| | Valves | Pumps | Flow Controllers |
|---|---|---|---|
| **Receiving and Materials Handling:** | | | |
| Receive each component once per run | 4 transactions (3%) | 25 transactions (19%) | 100 transactions (78%) |
| Handle each component once per run | 4 transactions (3%) | 25 transactions (19%) | 100 transactions (78%) |
| **Packing and Shipping:** | | | |
| One packing order per shipment | 1 transaction (3%) | 7 transactions (23%) | 22 transactions (73%) |
| **Engineering:** | | | |
| Estimated engineering work-order percentage (subjective) | 20% | 30% | 50% |
| **Maintenance:** | | | |
| Machine-hour basis | 3,750 hours (35%) | 6,250 hours (58%) | 800 hours (7%) |

# Siemens Electric Motor Works (A)
# Process-Oriented Costing

*Ten years ago, our electric motor business was in real trouble. Low labor rates allowed the Eastern Bloc countries to sell standard motors at prices we were unable to match. We had become the high-cost producer in the industry. Consequently, we decided to change our strategy and become a specialty motor producer. Once we adopted our new strategy, we discovered that while our existing cost system was adequate for costing standard motors, it was giving us inaccurate information when we used it to cost specialty motors.*

—Mr. Karl-Heinz Lottes, Director of Business Operations, EMW

## SIEMENS CORPORATION

Headquartered in Munich, Germany, Siemens AG, a producer of electrical and electronic products, was one of the world's largest corporations. Revenues totaled 51 billion deutschemarks (DM) in 1987, with roughly one-half this amount representing sales outside the Federal Republic of Germany. The Siemens organization was split into seven major groups and five corporate divisions. The largest group, Energy and Automation, accounted for 24% of total revenues. Low-wattage alternating current (A/C) motors were produced at the Electric Motor Works (EMW), which was part of the Manufacturing Industries Division of the Energy and Automation Group. High-wattage motors were produced at another facility.

*Professor Robin Cooper and Professor Karen Hopper Wruck prepared this case.*

Copyright © 1988 by the President and Fellows of Harvard College. Harvard Business School case 189-089.

## THE ELECTRIC MOTOR WORKS

Located in the small town of Bad Neustadt, the original Siemens EMW plant was built in 1937 to manufacture refrigerator motors for "Volkskuhlschraenke" (people's refrigerators). Less than a year later, Mr. Siemens decided to halt the production of refrigerator motors and began to produce electric motors for other applications. At the end of World War II, the Bad Neustadt plant was the only Siemens factory in West Germany capable of producing electric motors. All the other Siemens production facilities had been completely destroyed or seized by Eastern Bloc countries. After an aggressive rebuilding program, Bad Neustadt emerged as the firm's primary producer of electric motors.

Throughout the 1970s, EMW produced about 200 different types of standard motors, at a total annual volume of approximately 230,000 motors. Standard motors accounted for 80% of sales volume—the remaining 20% was customized motors. The production process was characterized by relatively long runs of a single type of motor. Because identical motors were used by a wide range of customers, standard motors were inventoried and shipped as orders were received. Production of standard A/C motors was extremely competitive. The key to success was to reduce costs so that the firm could price aggressively while making a profit. Despite a major expansion and automation program begun in 1974, by the early 1980s it had become obvious that the lower labor rates of the Eastern Bloc competitors gave them an insurmountable cost advantage.

## CHANGE IN STRATEGY

An extensive study of EMW's production capabilities and the market for electric motors indicated that EMW was in a position to become a profitable producer of low-volume, customized A/C motors. To help implement this strategy, the Bad Neustadt plant was enlarged and dedicated to the manufacture of A/C motors with power ratings ranging from 0.06 to 18.5 kilowatts. These motors supported a number of applications, including automation engineering, machine tools, plastic processing, and paper and printing machines.

Adopting this new strategy required the ability to manufacture efficiently many more types of motors in smaller production runs. Between 1985 and 1988, EMW spent DM50 million a year on its production facilities. By replacing almost every machine on the shop floor, EMW created a production environment that supported its new strategy.

As a result of the capital expenditures program, by 1987 the production process was highly automated, with numerically controlled machines, flexible machining centers, and robotically fed production processes used throughout the factory. High-volume common components were manufactured using the appropriate automated equipment, whereas low-volume components might be made by hand. Where possible, flexible manufacturing was used to mass-produce small-volume specialty components. While a normal annual production volume for common components might be 100,000 units, a single component could have up to 10,000 custom variations that might have to be produced one at a time.

To design a custom motor, modifications were made to a standard motor design. The process involved determining where standard components could not be used. These standard components were replaced by custom components that provided the functionality required by the customer.

In 1987, 65,625 orders were accepted. Of these orders, 90% were for custom motors. A total of 630,000 motors were produced. Including all customized variations, Siemens EMW produced about 10,000 unique products.

## CHANGE IN THE CALCULATION OF PRODUCT COSTS

Beginning in 1926, EMW had used a cost system to calculate product costs. This system assigned material and labor costs directly to the products and divided overhead costs into three categories: material-related, production-related, and support-related overhead. Material-related overhead contained costs associated with material acquisition and was allocated based on deutschemarks of direct materials consumed by a product. Production-related overhead was directly traced into cost pools and allocated to products using either direct labor hours or machine hours, but not both. For more manually intensive machine classes, direct labor hours was used. For machines whose operation required few direct labor hours, machine hours was used. In 1987, EMW used 600 cost pools, one per machine class. Support-related overhead was allocated to products based on the sum of direct material and direct labor costs, material-related overhead, and production-related overhead. The breakdown of each cost category as a percentage of total costs was as follows:

| | Percentage of Total Costs | Burden Rate |
|---|---|---|
| Direct material | 29% | |
| Direct labor | 10 | |
| Materials-related overhead | 2 | 6% of material cost |
| Production-related overhead | 33 | |
| Support-related overhead | 26 | 35% of pre-support manufacturing cost |

Two years after the change in strategy, problems with the traditional cost system became apparent. Management's concern with the traditional cost system was in its inability to capture the relationship between the increased support costs and the change in product mix. Under the traditional system, support costs were allocated to each motor based on its consumption of direct materials, direct labor, and either direct labor hours or machine hours.

Management felt that the support costs were more closely related to the number of orders received or the number of customized components required.

As shown in **Exhibit 1**, 74% of the orders accepted for production by EMW after the change in strategy was for less than five motors. This simultaneous increase in the number of orders and reduction in the number of motors per order increased the load on the production support departments. An analysis of the way work was generated by orders in the order-receiving, product-costing, bidding, shipping, and billing departments indicated that the same resources were required to process an order of one custom motor as were required to process an order of 100 standard motors.

The increase in the number of products with special options similarly caused the technical examination of incoming orders, scheduling and production control, and inventory handling to increase and the product-costing and bidding, product development, purchasing, and receiving departments to expand. An analysis of the way work was generated by special components in these departments indicated that it was not the number of special components produced but the number of different types of special components in each motor design that determined the work load. For example, processing an order of 50 custom motors with a design requiring 10 special components per unit generated the same amount of work as processing an order of one custom motor also requiring 10 special components. For each order, 10 special components had to be processed, making a total of 20 special components processed. In 1987, EMW filled 65,625 orders. These orders required over 30,000 different types of special components, each of which was issued its own stock number. Production orders and requisitions were prepared 325,000 times to call special components from inventory or initiate special component production. Each production order and requisition listed the type of special component by stock number and the quantities of each stock number required. Management thought that it was the number of these production orders and requisitions that drove the costs related to special components. In total, over one million special components were produced.

An extensive study was undertaken to identify the support costs that management believed were driven by processing orders and processing special components. Part of each of the following departments' costs was allocated to two new overhead cost pools:

### Costs Related to Order Processing
Order Receiving
Product Costing and Bidding
Shipping
Billing

### Costs Related to Special Components
Technical Examination of Incoming Orders
Scheduling and Production Control

Inventory Handling
Product Costing and Bidding
Product Development
Purchasing
Receiving

Once these costs were identified, they were removed from the support-related cost pool and assigned to two new cost pools. **Exhibit 2** illustrates the formation of the two process-oriented cost pools for 1987. The first column presents total costs grouped by traditional costing system definitions. To move to process-oriented costing (PROKASTA[1]), DM6.3 million was removed from the engineering costs and DM27 million from administrative costs; these DM33.3 million of costs were then assigned to the new cost pools—DM13.8 million to order processing costs and DM19.5 million to special components costs.

With process-oriented costing, the cost of the base motor from which the customized product was derived and the cost of each custom component were calculated using the traditional cost system but with the new smaller support-related cost pool (see **Exhibit 3**). This was called the pre-PROKASTA unit cost. The PROKASTA cost elements were then added.

## EFFECT OF THE PROCESS-ORIENTED COST SYSTEM

In 1987, EMW received close to DM1 billion in orders, but accepted only DM450 million. Production volume ran at 115% of rated capacity. The product cost information generated by the PROKASTA system played an integral role in helping EMW managers determine which orders were profitable and should be accepted.

Mr. Karl-Heinz Lottes, Director of Business Operations, EMW, commented on the role of the new cost system in helping to establish the new strategy:

> *Without PROKASTA, our new strategy would have failed. With the information generated by the process-oriented cost system, we can identify those orders we want to accept. While some orders we lose to competitors, most we turn down because they are not profitable. Anyone who wants to understand the importance of PROKASTA to EMW simply has to look at the costs of some typical orders under the traditional system and PROKASTA.*

---

[1] PROKASTA is an abbreviation for **PRO**zessorientierte **KA**lkulation fuer **STA**ffelkosten, which translated means Process-Oriented Calculation for Cost Schedule.

**EXHIBIT 1**
**Distribution of Orders Accepted for Production in 1987**

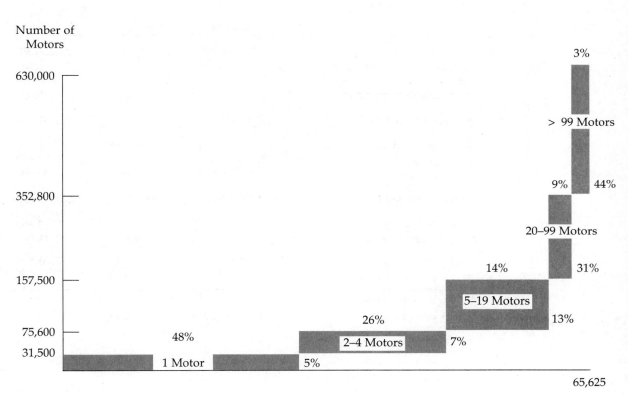

Number of Orders

**EXHIBIT 2**
**1987 Reconciliation of Traditional Cost System to**
**Process-Oriented Costing System (000 in deutschemarks)**

|  | Traditional | Transferred | Process Oriented |
|---|---|---|---|
| Material | DM105,000 |  | DM105,000 |
| Material-Related Overhead | 6,000 |  | 6,000 |
| Labor | 36,000 |  | 36,000 |
| Production-Related Overhead | 120,000 |  | 120,000 |
| **Manufacturing Cost[a]** | **267,000 (74%)** |  | **267,000 (74%)** |
| Engineering Costs | 12,000 | 6,300 | 5,700 |
| Tooling Costs | 22,500 | 0 | 22,500 |
| Administrative Costs | 60,000 | 27,000 | 33,000 |
| **Support-Related Cost[a]** | **94,500 (26%)[b]** | **33,300 (9%)** | **61,200 (17%)** |
| Order-Processing Cost |  | 13,800 | 13,800 |
| Special Components Cost |  | 19,500 | 19,500 |
| Total Cost | DM361,500 | 0 | DM361,500 |

[a]  Percent of total cost

[b]  This corresponds to the 26% labeled support-related overhead on page 5-32.

**EXHIBIT 3**
**Pre-PROKASTA Unit Costs for Five Motor Orders**

|  | A | B | C | D | E |
|---|---|---|---|---|---|
| Cost of Base Motor[a] (Pre-PROKASTA) | DM304.0 | DM304.0 | DM304.0 | DM304.0 | DM304.0 |
| Cost of All Special Components[b] (Pre-PROKASTA) | DM39.6 | DM79.2 | DM118.8 | DM198.0 | DM396.0 |
| # of Different Types of Special Components per Motor | 1 | 2 | 3 | 5 | 10 |
| # of Motors Ordered | 1 | 1 | 1 | 1 | 1 |

**Notes:**
The cost of the base motor and the cost of each special component were calculated using the traditional cost system but with the new smaller support-related cost pool. This was called the pre-PROKASTA unit cost. The PROKASTA cost elements were then added.

[a]Cost of Base Motor

| Material | DM90 |
|---|---|
| Material-Related Overhead | 5 |
| Direct Labor | 35 |
| Production-Related Overhead | 117 |
|  | DM247 |
| Support-Related Overhead[1] | 57 |
|  | DM304 |

[b]Cost of Special Components[2]

| Material | DM12.0 |
|---|---|
| Material-Related Overhead | 0.7 |
| Direct Labor | 4.5 |
| Production-Related Overhead | 15.0 |
|  | DM32.2 |
| Support-Related Overhead[1] | 7.4 |
|  | DM39.6 |

[1] Excluding order processing cost and special components cost.

[2] For illustrative purposes, all different types of special components are assumed to cost 39.6 a piece.

# Kanthal (A)

**C**arl-Erik Ridderstråle, president of Kanthal, was describing his motivation for developing a system to measure customer profitability.

> Before, when we got an order from a big, important customer, we didn't ask questions. We were glad to get the business. But a small company, competing around the world, has to concentrate its sales and marketing resources. We needed an account management system if we were to achieve our strategy for higher growth and profitability. An account management system as part of the Kanthal 90 Strategy will enable us to get sales managers to accept responsibility for promoting high-margin products to high-profit customers.

## HISTORY

Kanthal, the largest of six divisions in the Kanthal-Hoganas group of Sweden, was headquartered in Hallstahammar, a town of 17,000 persons about 150 km. northwest of Stockholm. The company's history can be traced back to an ironworks founded in the 17th century to exploit the water power available from the stream running through the town. Kanthal specialized in the production and sales of electrical resistance heating elements. "We work for a warmer world" was its motto.

---

*Professor Robert S. Kaplan prepared this case.*

Copyright © 1989 by the President and Fellows of Harvard College. Harvard Business School case 190-002.

Kanthal had about 10,000 customers and 15,000 items that it produced. Sales during 1985 through 1987 had been level at about SEK 850 million.[1] Export sales, outside of Sweden, accounted for 95% of the total. Summary statistics for the past two years appear in **Exhibit 1**.

Kanthal consisted of three divisions:

*Kanthal Heating Technology supplied manufacturers of electrical appliances and heating systems with wire that generated heat through electrical resistance. Products included heating wire and ribbon, foil elements, machinery, and precision wire. Kanthal's 25% market share made it a world leader in supplying heating alloys. Sales growth was sluggish in Europe and the United States but rapid growth was occurring in the Far East and Latin America.*

*Kanthal Furnace Products produced a wide range of heating elements for electric industrial furnaces. Its 40% market share gave it a dominant position in the large markets of the United States, Japan, West Germany, and the United Kingdom. A new product, Kanthal Super, was generating substantial growth because of its substantially improved performance over conventional materials, including longer service life, lower service costs, and higher operating temperatures.*

*Kanthal Bimetals was one of the few companies in the world with fully integrated manufacturing of thermo-bimetals for temperature control devices used in the manufacture of thermostats, circuit breakers, and household appliances.*

Kanthal's manufacturing facilities were located in Hallstahammar, Brazil, the United Kingdom, West Germany, the United States, and Italy.

## KANTHAL 90

Ridderstråle, upon becoming president in 1985, saw the need for a strategic plan for Kanthal.

*The company had been successful in the past. We needed to use this base of experience to influence the future. We had to have a consolidated view to ensure that we did not sub-optimize in narrow markets or with a narrow functional view. Resources were to be allocated so that we could increase profits while maintaining a return on employed capital in excess of 20%.*

The Kanthal 90 plan specified overall profit objectives by division, by product line, and by market. Currently, however, salespersons were compensated mostly on gross sales volume. Higher commissions were being paid for

---

[1]  In 1988, the Swedish kronor (SEK) was worth about US$0.16.

selling higher-margin products, such as Super, and higher bonuses were being awarded for achieving sales targets in the high-margin products. But Ridderstråle wanted to achieve the additional growth planned under Kanthal 90 without adding sales and administrative resources to handle the increased volume anticipated.

> *We needed to know where in the organization the resources could be taken from and redeployed into more profitable uses. We did not want to eliminate resources in a steady-state environment. We wanted to reallocate people to generate future growth.*
>
> *With our historically good profitability, and lacking any current or imminent crisis, we could not realistically consider laying off people at the Hallstahammar plant. But we wanted to be able to redeploy people so that they could earn more profit for us; to move people from corporate staff to divisions, from the parent company to operating subsidiaries, and from staff functions into sales, R&D, and production. Ideally, if we could transform an accounting clerk at Hallstahammar into a salesman of Kanthal-Super in Japan, we could generate a substantial profit increase.*

**Exhibit 2** shows the distribution of Kanthal's incurred costs. The existing cost system treated most sales, marketing, and administrative costs as a percentage of sales revenue. Therefore, customers whose selling price exceeded the standard full cost of manufacturing plus the percentage mark-up for general, selling, and administrative expenses appeared to be profitable, while a customer order whose selling price was below standard manufacturing cost plus the percentage mark-up appeared unprofitable. Ridderstråle knew, however, that individual customers made quite different demands on Kanthal's administrative and sales staff.

> *Low-profit customers place high demands on technical and commercial service. They buy low-margin products in small orders. Frequently they order non-standard products that have to be specially produced for them. And we have to supply special selling discounts in order to get the business.*
>
> *High-profit customers buy high-margin, standard products in large orders. They make no demands for technical or commercial service, and accurately forecast for us their annual demands.*

He felt that a new system was needed to determine how much profit was earned each time a customer placed a particular order. The system should attempt to measure the costs that individual customer orders placed on the production, sales, and administrative resources of the company. The goal was to find both "hidden profit" orders, those whose demands on the company were quite low, and the "hidden loss" orders, those customer orders that under the existing system looked profitable but which in fact demanded a disproportionate share of the company's resources to fulfill.

Ridderstråle pointed out the weaknesses with the present method of profitability measurement:

*We distribute resources equally across all products and customers. We do not measure an individual customer's profitability or the real costs of individual orders. In this environment, our sales and marketing efforts emphasize volume more than profits. In the future, we want Kanthal to handle significantly increased sales volume without any corresponding increase in support resources, and to gain the share in our most profitable products.*

Our current method of calculating product costs may show two customers to be equally profitable on a gross margin basis. But there could be hidden profits and hidden costs associated with these customers that we are not seeing (see **Exhibit 3**). If we could get more accurate information about our own manufacturing cost structure, as well as the costs of supplying individual customers and orders, we could direct our resources to customers with hidden profits and reduce our efforts to customers with the hidden losses. We might end up with the same market share, so that our competitors would not even see this shift in our strategy, but our profitability would be much higher. To execute such a strategy, however, we need better information about the profitability of each order, each product, and each customer.

The biggest barrier we have to overcome is the notion that production overhead, selling, and administrative costs are "fixed." The definition of strategy is to recognize that all costs are variable. Our salespeople must learn how to deploy resources to their most profitable use.

## THE NEW ACCOUNT MANAGEMENT SYSTEM

Per O. Ehrling, financial manager of Kanthal, worked with SAM, a Swedish management advisory group, to develop a system to analyze production, sales, and administrative costs at the Hallstahammar facility. Over a period of several months, finance managers and the consultants conducted extensive interviews with all department heads and key personnel. The interviews were designed to elicit information about the nature of the activities being performed by support department personnel and the events that triggered the demands for these organizational activities. Ehrling described the philosophy of the new approach:

*In our previous system, indirect costs were either manufacturing costs that were allocated to products based on direct labor, or they were selling and administrative costs that were treated as period expenses and were unanalyzed. This treatment may have been correct 100 years ago when we had one bookkeeper for every ten blacksmiths, but today we have eight bookkeepers for every three blacksmiths. This means that most of our costs today are indirect and our previous system didn't know how to allocate them.*

*We wanted to move away from our traditional financial accounting categories. We found that most of our organizational costs could be classified either as order-related or volume costs.  Actually, we did investigate three additional cost drivers—product range, technical support, and new products. But the total costs assigned to these three categories ended up being less than 5% of total costs so we eliminated them.*

Using the interview information, the project team determined how much of the expenses of each support department related to the volume of sales and production and how much related to handling individual production and sales orders (see **Exhibit 4**). The *manufacturing volume* costs, in addition to material, direct labor, and variable overhead, also included the costs of production orders to replenish inventory stocks. Only 20% of Kanthal's products were stocked in inventory, but these products represented 80% of sales orders, so the cost of continually replenishing these products was assumed to be related to the volume of production. *Manufacturing order* costs, therefore, included only the cost of setup and other activities that were triggered when a customer ordered a product not normally stocked. Manufacturing order costs were calculated separately for each major product group. The *sales order* costs represented the selling and administrative costs that could be traced to processing an individual customer's order.  The selling and administrative costs that remained after subtracting *sales order* costs were treated as *sales volume* costs and were allocated proportionately to the *manufacturing volume* costs.

For example, the Sales Department activities relating to preparing a bid for an order, negotiating with the customer about the order, and following up with the customer after the order was delivered were classified as "order-related." All remaining activities, such as public relations and sales management, that could not be traced to individual orders were classified as "volume-related."

Follow-up interviews were conducted to corroborate the split of effort in each department between volume- and order-related activities. Sample calculations are shown in **Exhibit 5**.

Bo Martin Tell, controller of the Furnace Products Division, recalled the amount of tedious work required to collect all the numbers.

*It took almost a year to develop a system to collect the data in the proper form. Even in production, we had problems identifying the costs that related to stocked and non-stocked orders.*

## INITIAL OUTPUT FROM THE ACCOUNT MANAGEMENT SYSTEM

**Exhibit 6** shows a profitability report for a sample of individual orders from Swedish customers. Profit margins on these individual orders ranged from −179% to +65%.  Previously, almost all of these orders would have appeared profitable.  Similar reports were prepared to show total profitability by customer, by product group, or by all the orders received from customers in a country.  For example, **Exhibit 7** shows the sales volume and profitability of a sample of Swedish customers for a given product group—Finished Wire N.

Leif Rick, general manager of Heating Technology, remembered the initial reactions to the account management reports:

*The study was a real eye-opener. We saw how the traditional cost accounting system had been unable to truly report costs and profits by market, product, and customer.*

*At first, the new approach seemed strange. We had to explain it three or four times before people started to understand and accept it. People did not want to believe that order costs could be so high; that order costs had to be treated as an explicit cost of selling. Most surprising was finding that customers thought to be very profitable were actually break-even or even loss customers. Salespeople initially thought the approach was part of a master plan to get rid of small customers. But people who have been working with the system now are convinced of its value and are beginning to take sensible actions based on the information.*

**Exhibit 8** shows the profits from Swedish customers, ranked by customer profitability. The results surprised even Ridderstråle. Only 40% of Kanthal's Swedish customers were profitable, and these generated 250% of realized profits. In fact, the most profitable 5% of the customers generated 150% of the country's profits. The least profitable 10% of customers lost 120% of the profits (see cumulative profitability chart in **Exhibit 9**).

Even more surprising, two of the most unprofitable customers turned out to be among the top three in total sales volume. These two customers had gone to just-in-time (JIT) delivery for its suppliers. They had pushed inventory back onto Kanthal, which had not recognized the new demands being placed on its production and order-handling processes by the JIT approach. Moreover, further investigation revealed that one of these customers was using Kanthal as a back-up supplier, to handle small special orders of a low-priced item when its main supplier could not deliver. Because of the size and prestige of the two customers, Kanthal people had always welcomed and encouraged their orders. Ridderstråle now realized how expensive it had become to satisfy them.

The immediate problem was to devise a strategy for the large number of nonprofitable customers, particularly the very high-volume ones. Corporate management had started a series of meetings with the general and sales managers of the operating divisions in Sweden to discuss how to handle these customers.

Also, while the account management system had been developed for the Swedish operating divisions, some overseas divisions remained skeptical about the value of the exercise. The account management system was seen as yet another intrusion of the headquarters staff into their operations. Ridderstråle knew he faced an uphill battle gaining acceptance for the account management system around the world.

**EXHIBIT 1**
**Summary of Operations**

|                              | 1986  | 1987  |
|------------------------------|-------|-------|
| Invoiced sales (MSEK)        | 839   | 849   |
| Profit after financial items | 87    | 107   |
| Return on capital            | 20%   | 21%   |
| Number of employees          | 1,606 | 1,591 |

**EXHIBIT 2**
**Cost Structure**

| Cost Component                | Percentage |
|-------------------------------|------------|
| Materials                     | 23         |
| Production salaries and wages | 19         |
| Variable processing costs     | 5          |
| Fixed processing costs        | 16         |
| Subcontracted services        | 3          |
| Selling and administrative    | 34         |
| Total costs                   | 100        |

**EXHIBIT 3**
**Hidden Profit and Hidden Cost Customers**

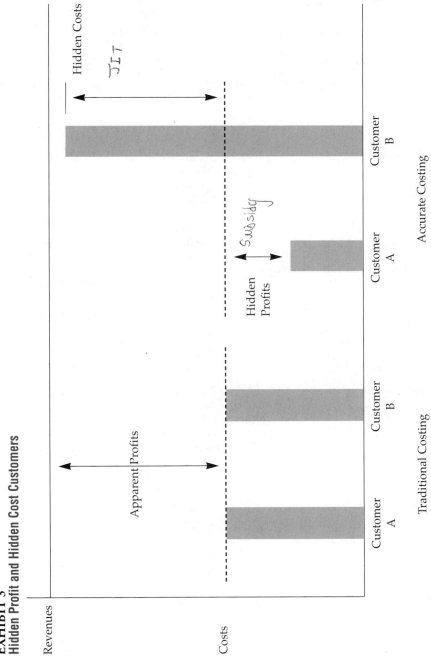

**EXHIBIT 4**
**Order and Volume Costs**

| Type of Personnel | Order-Related Work | Volume-Related Work |
|---|---|---|
| **Production** | | |
| Stock Replenishment | None | All Activities |
| Production Planning | Order Planning<br>Order Follow-up | Inventory Management |
| Operators | Setup<br>Start-up Expense | Direct Hours |
| Foremen | Order Planning<br>Order Support | Machine Problems |
| Stock | Order Input<br>Order Output | Order Handling |
| Transportation | Order Planning<br>Order Handling | |
| **Selling and Administrative** | | |
| Management | Offer Discussion<br>Offer Negotiation | General Management |
| Sales | Offer Work<br>Order Negotiation<br>Delivery Follow-up | Sales—Unrelated to Orders<br>General Public Relations<br>Sales Management |
| Secretarial | Offer Typing | |
| Administration | Order Booking<br>Order Adjustment<br>Invoice Typing<br>Customer Ledger<br>Supervision | Accounting |

**EXHIBIT 5**
**Sample Calculation of Order and Volume Costs: By Product Group**

**Step 1.   Calculate Selling & Administrative (S&A) Order Costs**

| | | |
|---|---:|---:|
| Total Selling & Administrative Order Costs | | SEK 2,000,000 |
| Total Number of Orders | 2,000 | |
| Stocked Products | 1,500 | |
| Non-Stocked Products | 500 | |
| S&A Order Costs per Order | | SEK     1,000 |

*— why not for both types? because they say they know by indv. order pg 5-42.*

**Step 2.   Calculate Manufacturing Order Cost for Non-Stocked Products**

| | |
|---|---:|
| Total Manufacturing Order Costs (for non-stocked products) | SEK 1,000,000 |
| Number of Orders for Non-Stocked Products | 500 |
| Manufacturing Order Costs per Non-Stocked Order | SEK     2,000 |

**Step 3.   Calculate Allocation Factor for S&A Volume Costs**

| | | |
|---|---:|---:|
| Compute Total Manufacturing and S&A Costs: | | SEK 7,000,000 |
| Subtract Order Costs: | | |
| Non-Stocked Products | 1,000,000 | |
| Selling & Administrative Order Costs | 2,000,000 | 3,000,000 |
| Total Volume Costs | | SEK 4,000,000 |
| Manufacturing Volume Costs of Goods Sold (CGS) | 3,200,000 | |
| Selling & Administrative Volume-Related Costs | 800,000 | |
| S&A Volume Allocation Factor: S&A Volume Costs / Mfg. Volume CGS (800/3,200) | | 25% |

**Step 4.   Calculate Operating Profit on Individual Orders for Non-Stocked Product**   *Per Order*

| | |
|---|---:|
| Sales Value | SEK   10,000 |
| Less:  Volume Costs: Manufacturing Cost of Goods Sold (@ 40% of Sales Value) | 4,000 |
| Volume Costs: Selling & Administrative (@ 25% of Mfg. CGS)  *— New* | 1,000 |
| Margin on Volume-Related Costs | 5,000 |
| Less:  Mfg. Order Cost for Non-Stocked Product | 2,000 |
| Selling & Administrative Order Cost | 1,000 |
| Operating Profit for Order | SEK     2,000 |

*why a blended #?. Stocked + Non-Stocked*

**EXHIBIT 6**
**Customer Order Analysis** — by Customer

Standard order cost: SEK572
Manufacturing order cost for non-stocked products:   Foil Elements:  SEK1508
Finished Wire:  SEK2340

| Country Customer | Order Lines | Invoiced Value (SEK) | Volume Cost (SEK) | Order Cost (SEK) | Non-Stocked (SEK) | Operating Profit (SEK) | Profit Margin |
|---|---|---|---|---|---|---|---|
| **Sweden** | | | | *Standard Cost* | | | |
| S001 | 1 | 1,210 | 543 | 572 | 0 | 95 | 8% |
| S002 | 3 | 46,184 | 10,080 | 1,716 | 4,524 | 29,864 | 65 |
| S003 | 8 | 51,102 | 50,567 | 4,576 | 12,064 | (16,105) | −32 |
| S004 | 9 | 98,880 | 60,785 | 5,148 | 13,572 | 19,375 | 20 |
| S005 | 1 | 3,150 | 1,557 | 572 | 2,340 | (1,319) | −42 |
| S006 | 5 | 24,104 | 14,889 | 2,860 | 4,680 | 1,675 | 7 |
| S007 | 2 | 4,860 | 2,657 | 1,144 | 4,680 | (3,621) | −75 |
| S008 | 1 | 2,705 | 1,194 | 572 | 0 | 939 | 35 |
| S009 | 1 | 518 | 233 | 572 | 0 | (287) | −55 |
| S010 | 8 | 67,958 | 51,953 | 4,576 | 12,064 | (635) | −1 |
| S011 | 2 | 4,105 | 1,471 | 1,144 | 0 | 1,490 | 36 |
| S012 | 8 | 87,865 | 57,581 | 4,576 | 12,064 | 13,644 | 16 |
| S013 | 1 | 1,274 | 641 | 572 | 2,340 | (2,279) | −179 |
| S014 | 2 | 1,813 | 784 | 1,144 | 0 | (115) | −6 |
| S015 | 2 | 37,060 | 15,974 | 1,144 | 3,016 | 16,926 | 46 |
| S016 | 2 | 6,500 | 6,432 | 1,144 | 3,016 | (4,092) | −63 |

Note:  All financial data reported in Swedish kroner (SEK).

*- A product* *New Cost Pools*

**EXHIBIT 7**
**Finished Wire N Customer List**

| Customer # | Invoiced Sales (SEK) | Volume Costs (SEK) | Order Cost (SEK) | Non-Stocked Cost (SEK) | Operating Profit (SEK) | Profit Margin |
|---|---|---|---|---|---|---|
| 33507 | 3,969 | 1,440 | 750 | 0 | 1,779 | 45% |
| 33508 | 4,165 | 1,692 | 750 | 2,150 | (427) | –10 |
| 33509 | 601 | 139 | 750 | 2,150 | (2,438) | –406 |
| 33510 | 13,655 | 6,014 | 750 | 2,150 | 4,741 | 35 |
| 33511 | 2,088 | 350 | 750 | 2,150 | (1,162) | –56 |
| 33512 | 1,742 | 637 | 750 | 0 | 355 | 20 |
| 33513 | 4,177 | 932 | 750 | 2,150 | 345 | 8 |
| 33514 | 7,361 | 3,134 | 750 | 0 | 3,477 | 47 |
| 33515 | 1,045 | 318 | 750 | 0 | (23) | –2 |
| 33516 | 429,205 | 198,277 | 9,000 | 0 | 221,928 | 52 |
| 33517 | 31,696 | 13,128 | 3,750 | 0 | 14,818 | 47 |
| 33518 | 159,612 | 58,036 | 2,250 | 6,450 | 92,876 | 58 |
| 33519 | 48,648 | 17,872 | 9,750 | 12,900 | 8,126 | 17 |
| 33520 | 5,012 | 1,119 | 750 | 2,150 | 993 | 20 |
| 33521 | 4,933 | 2,170 | 1,500 | 4,300 | (3,037) | –62 |
| 33522 | 17,277 | 7,278 | 1,500 | 0 | 8,499 | 49 |
| 33523 | 134 | 120 | 1,500 | 4,300 | (5,786) | –4,318 |
| 33524 | 1,825 | 523 | 1,500 | 0 | (198) | –11 |
| 33525 | 13,874 | 4,914 | 3,750 | 6,450 | (1,240) | –9 |
| 33526 | 3,762 | 1,452 | 750 | 0 | 1,560 | 41 |
| 33527 | 64,875 | 18,559 | 3,750 | 8,600 | 33,966 | 52 |
| 33528 | 13,052 | 5,542 | 3,000 | 6,450 | (1,940) | –15 |
| 33529 | 39,175 | 12,683 | 3,750 | 8,600 | 14,142 | 36 |
| 33530 | 383 | 87 | 750 | 0 | (454) | –119 |
| 33531 | 6,962 | 1,865 | 750 | 2,150 | 2,197 | 32 |
| 33532 | 1,072 | 314 | 1,500 | 0 | (742) | –69 |
| 33533 | 14,050 | 6,333 | 1,500 | 2,150 | 4,067 | 29 |
| 33534 | 820 | 244 | 750 | 0 | (174) | –21 |
| 33535 | 809 | 181 | 750 | 2,150 | (2,272) | –281 |
| 33536 | 1,366 | 316 | 750 | 2,150 | (1,850) | –135 |
| 33537 | 155,793 | 65,718 | 21,750 | 49,450 | 18,875 | 12 |
| 33538 | 7,593 | 2,772 | 2,250 | 2,150 | 421 | 6 |
| Total | 1,060,731 | 434,159 | 84,000 | 131,150 | 411,422 | 39% |

Note:    All financial data reported in Swedish kroner (SEK).

**EXHIBIT 8**
**Customer Profitability: Ranked from Most to Least Profitable Customers**

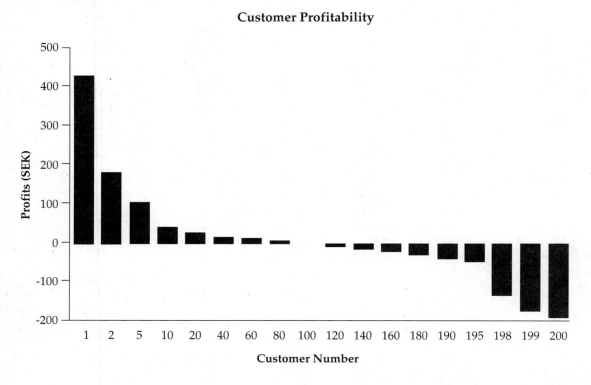

**EXHIBIT 9**
**Cumulative Profitability by Customers**

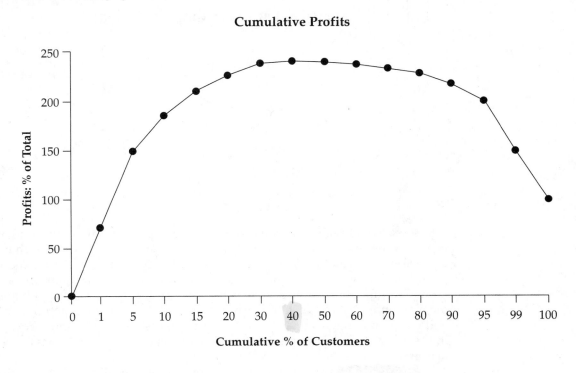

# Standard Costs and Variance Analysis

**A** *budget* is a quantitative expression of a plan of action. It serves as a goal that the organization strives to achieve. It is also used as a benchmark against which actual performance can be evaluated. Budgets span a specific period of time such as a month, a quarter, or a year. Organizations prepare a number of different budgets such as the sales budget, the production budget, the marketing costs budget, the cash budget, and the capital budget. This note will focus on budgets for product costs—direct costs (material and labor) and indirect costs (overhead)—and their role in managing the overall costs of products and services.

*Standard costs* are developed based on the budgeted direct and indirect costs. A standard cost is a measure of how much one unit of product or service should cost to produce or deliver. A standard cost for a product is made up of the costs of the components required to produce the product. For example, the standard cost of a leather jacket includes the cost of the materials (the leather, zipper, snaps, etc.), the cost of the labor (the time required to cut the pattern, stitch it, etc., at the production employee's wage rate), plus an allocation of the indirect or overhead costs related to it (the sewing machine depreciation, power, lights, etc.).

Once a standard cost is established, it provides a basis for decisions, for analyzing and controlling costs, and for measuring inventory accounts and cost of goods sold. Standard costs may be established using careful analysis of the product or service and the materials and process used to create it. Standard costs established in this way can be thought of as ideal costs. Other ways of

---

*Lecturer Donella M. Rapier prepared this note.*

Copyright © 1996 by the President and Fellows of Harvard College. Harvard Business School case 196-121.

determining standard costs, however, are also common. For example, last year's actual cost to produce a product or service can be used as the standard cost for this year.

Standard costs serve as benchmarks against which actual costs are compared. Differences between actual costs and standard costs are called *variances*. Actual costs may differ from standard costs because of price differences, quantity differences, errors or mistakes, or less than ideal conditions. Determining the reasons for variances may suggest corrective action or highlight that products are actually costing more or less than anticipated.

Although the remainder of this note emphasizes standard costs and variances in a manufacturing setting, many of the same concepts can be applied to the delivery of services. The focus on manufacturing allows a clearer discussion of material, labor, and overhead variances, which are often harder to conceptualize in service organizations.

## DIRECT COSTS

Direct costs are costs, such as material and labor costs, that can be directly attributed to one unit of product. The standard cost for the direct costs of a product involves two components: a price component and a quantity component. The standard cost for a unit of production is the standard quantity to be used multiplied by the standard price per the unit of measure.

Example: Assume that our leather jacket contains on average four yards of leather with a cost of $8.00 per yard, one zipper with a cost of $1.00, and two snaps with a cost of $0.25 each. Based on a time study recently done by management, one jacket requires an average of 5 hours of an employee's time to produce. Production workers are paid an average wage of $10 per hour including benefits. The standard cost for the direct costs (indirect costs will be discussed in the next section) would be as follows:

|  | Quantity | × | Price | = | Standard Cost |
|---|---|---|---|---|---|
| Materials: |  |  |  |  |  |
| Leather | 4 yards |  | $ 8.00 |  | $32.00 |
| Zipper | 1 |  | 1.00 |  | 1.00 |
| Snaps | 2 |  | .25 |  | .50 |
| Total material cost |  |  |  |  | $33.50 |
| Labor cost | 5 hours |  | 10.00 |  | 50.00 |
| Total direct cost |  |  |  |  | $83.50 |

Throughout the year, our leather jacket company will acquire leather, zippers, and snaps and will hire and pay production workers. The actual amounts paid for these items, however, may not equal the amounts budgeted that formed the basis of the standard costs. For instance, the company may find leather at a lower price from a new discount supplier. A new machine purchased by the company may minimize the amount of material required for each jacket by reducing scrap material. Due to a significant order, the company might work its employees overtime, which must be paid at time-and-a-half (150% of wage rate). The new machine might improve productivity so that it takes less than five hours to put a jacket together. These differences will give rise to variances between the actual and the budgeted standard costs.

An analysis of the year's results shows that the actual costs on average for the year for one jacket are as follows (no variances are assumed for zippers and snaps for simplicity):

|  | Quantity | × | Price | = | Actual Cost |
|---|---|---|---|---|---|
| Materials: |  |  |  |  |  |
| Leather | 3.5 yards |  | $ 7.50 |  | $26.25 |
| Zipper | 1 |  | 1.00 |  | 1.00 |
| Snaps | 2 |  | .25 |  | .50 |
| Total material cost |  |  |  |  | $27.75 |
| Labor cost | 4.8 hours |  | 12.00 |  | 57.60 |
| Total direct cost |  |  |  |  | $85.35 |

It is easy to see that jackets cost $1.85 more than budgeted. But without further analysis, a manager might miss potential opportunities for improving the business. For instance, a manager might miss the significance of the new supplier and the need to nurture this relationship. Or, without understanding the impact that the overtime pay has had, a manager might overlook the possibility of hiring additional workers instead of running overtime shifts. A manager might also misunderstand which department was responsible for savings, such as purchasing, and which was responsible for cost overruns, like production. Also, he or she would potentially miss the magnitude of the impact of the new machine and the possible opportunity to invest in additional machines.

In order to understand a variance, it must be broken into its component parts. An analysis of the materials variance is as follows:

| Materials | Quantity | × | Price | = | Total |  |
|---|---|---|---|---|---|---|
| Leather: |  |  |  |  |  |  |
| Budgeted | 4.0 yards |  | $8.00 |  | $32.00 |  |
| Actual | 3.5 yards |  | 7.50 |  | 26.25 |  |
|    Materials variance |  |  |  |  | $ 5.75 | favorable |
| Price variance | ($8.00 − $7.50) × 3.5 yards |  |  | = | $ 1.75 | favorable |
| Quantity variance | (4.0 − 3.5) × $8.00 |  |  | = | 4.00 | favorable |
|    Materials variance |  |  |  |  | $ 5.75 | favorable |

An analysis of the labor variance is as follows:

| Labor | Quantity | × | Price | = | Total |
|-------|----------|---|-------|---|-------|
| Labor: | | | | | |
| Budgeted | 5.0 hours | | $10.00 | | $50.00 |
| Actual | 4.8 hours | | 12.00 | | 57.60 |
| Labor variance | | | | | $ 7.60 unfavorable |
| | | | | | |
| Price variance | ($10.00 − $12.00) × 4.8 hours | | | = | $ 9.60 unfavorable |
| Quantity variance | (5.0 − 4.8) × $10.00 | | | = | 2.00 favorable |
| Labor variance | | | | | $ 7.60 unfavorable |

The total variance is summed up as follows:

| | |
|---|---|
| Standard cost | $83.50 |
| Actual cost | 85.35 |
| Total variance | $ 1.85 unfavorable |
| | |
| Materials variance | $ 5.75 favorable |
| Labor variance | 7.60 unfavorable |
| Total variance | $ 1.85 unfavorable |

Formulas for analyzing variances can be expressed as follows:

| | | |
|---|---|---|
| Price variance | = | (SP − AP) × AQ |
| Quantity variance | = | (SQ − AQ) × SP |
| Total variance | = | (SP × SQ) − (AP × AQ) |

= Price Variance + Quantity Variance

Where:
SP = Standard price
AP = Actual price
SQ = Standard quantity
AQ = Actual quantity

Rather than worrying about whether to put standard or actual first in the formulas or about trying to keep track and understand whether a negative result is favorable or unfavorable, just think about whether the variance is good or bad. If the actual price is lower than the standard, it is a good or favorable variance; if the actual quantity is more than the standard, it is a bad or unfavorable variance, etc.

Note that by convention, price variance is computed using *actual* quantities, whereas quantity variance is computed using *standard* prices. This enables the purchasing agents to be assessed for price variations on quantities actually purchased. Production managers are assessed for quantity differences at standard prices, ignoring price fluctuations. While there are other ways of carving up the variances, this approach is the most typical.

A materials price variance is often called a *purchase price variance,* and a materials quantity variance is often called a *materials usage variance.* A labor price variance is often called a *labor rate variance,* and a labor quantity variance is often called a *labor efficiency variance.*

## INDIRECT COSTS

Direct costs vary in relation to the volume of units produced. Indirect or overhead costs, however, have elements that vary directly with volume (variable overhead) and other elements that do not (fixed overhead). The volume of production will fluctuate depending on many factors, such as demand for the company's products, labor shortages, etc. The effects of these variations in volume create additional complexities in analyzing performance relative to an overhead budget.

**Overhead budgets**   One approach to overhead budgeting ignores the volume considerations. This approach is called *fixed overhead budgeting.* Under a fixed budget approach, management determines the amount of overhead that should be incurred at the normal or most likely production level. This expense total becomes the budget against which cost performance is measured regardless of the level of production output actually achieved. An example would be as follows:

Allowed Overhead (in thousands)

| | |
|---|---|
| Rent | $   500 |
| Depreciation | 500 |
| Supervision | 1,000 |
| Supplies | 800 |
| Power | 800 |
| | $3,600 |

Performance at the end of the year would be measured against the $3,600,000 total. This approach, however, by disregarding the true nature of the costs, may lead a manager to make some inaccurate conclusions about performance. For instance, assume that this budget is based on a "normal" production level of 160,000 leather jackets. Also assume that the power costs, representing in part the cutting and sewing machines, vary with the level of production. If 200,000 jackets are produced during the year, the power costs would exceed $800,000, say these costs total $1,000,000. Comparing this to the fixed budget, a manager might conclude that the warehouse supervisor did a poor job of managing the power costs, when in fact the overspending relates solely to the extra 40,000 jackets produced.

The more conceptually sound approach to determining overhead standards is called *flexible budgeting.* A flexible overhead budget specifies allowable cost at each possible output level. Once a period is completed and the actual production volume is known, the budget standard is determined by reference to the flexible budget for the actual level of output. This is a direct parallel to the way a budget for direct material and direct labor is determined.

An example of a simplified flexible budget might look something like the following:

### Flexible Budget

|  |  |  |  | "Normal" ↓ |  |  |
|---|---|---|---|---|---|---|
| Capacity Utilization: | 40%[a] | 60% | 70% | 80% | 100% | |
| Labor Cost (piece rate): | $4,000 | $6,000 | $7,000 | $8,000 | $10,000 | |
| Allowed Overhead |  |  |  |  |  | Cost Behavior |
| Rent | $ 500 | $ 500 | $ 500 | $ 500 | $ 500 | Pure nonvariable or "fixed" |
| Depreciation | 500 | 500 | 500 | 500 | 500 | Pure nonvariable or "fixed" |
| Supervision | 500 | 1,000 | 1,000 | 1,000 | 1,500 | "Step" cost[b] |
| Supplies | 400 | 600 | 700 | 800 | 1,000 | Pure variable at 10% of labor |
| Power | 600 | 700 | 750 | 800 | 900 | Semivariable: $400 + 5% of labor |
| Total | $2,500 | $3,300 | $3,450 | $3,600 | $4,400 | |

[a] It is assumed that volume would never fall below 40% of capacity.

[b] A "step" cost is one which does not vary directly with production but does increase in lump-sum jumps when volume rises substantially. An example would be adding a second supervisor when volume rose to the level where a second shift was needed.

A flexible budget allows us to more intelligently analyze variable overhead spending.

**Overhead absorption**   Now that our flexible overhead budget is established, we need a way to allocate the overhead to our products. The cost of a product should include all costs incurred in bringing the product to its completed form. Therefore, in addition to the direct labor and material costs, the standard cost of a product includes indirect costs as well. But labor and material are easily measured and assigned to the products. It is much more difficult to determine how much rent, supplies, or depreciation is consumed by a particular product.

Accountants resolve this dilemma by using an allocation method. This is termed *overhead absorption,* as the costs are *absorbed* into inventory. Overhead costs are first collected in *cost pools.* One pool might include all rent, another all costs related to inspection, another might be supervisory expenses. The cost pools are then allocated down to the products using a *cost driver.* For simplicity, in the remainder of this note, we will assume that all overhead is aggregated into a single pool. Assume that all of our overhead expenses for our leather jacket company are set forth in the table above and are accumulated in one cost pool for allocation to products.

In single-product firms, the overhead pool might be allocated on a per-unit basis, i.e., using units as the cost driver. The total budgeted overhead ($3.6 million using the example above) would be divided by the planned production volume (assume 200,000 jackets for this illustration). Then for every jacket produced, $18.00 ($3.6 million divided by 200,000) would be applied as overhead. The standard cost for a jacket under this method would thus be as follows:

| Standard Cost: | |
| --- | --- |
| Materials | $ 33.50 |
| Labor | 50.00 |
| Overhead | 18.00 |
| Total standard cost | $101.50 |

In multiproduct firms, however, it is necessary to use an allocation method or cost driver other than number of units produced in order to more fairly apportion the overhead. For instance, if our company made leather gloves in addition to jackets, and the gloves could be manufactured in one-quarter of the time it takes to produce a jacket, it would be unfair to burden each pair of gloves with the same dollar amount of overhead as a jacket. Some other measure of capacity utilization must be used, such as labor hours, labor dollars, or machine hours. The choice of a volume measure in a particular business should be based on which variable best measures the level of capacity utilization for that business. For example, a machine depreciation cost pool might be allocated using number of machine hours per product as the driver. A supervision cost pool might be allocated using direct labor hours as the cost driver.

Since our jacket production process is fairly labor-intensive, we will use direct labor dollars as our allocation method. Using direct labor dollars, the standard overhead cost for a jacket would be $0.45 for every direct labor dollar ($3.6 million total budgeted overhead divided by $8 million budgeted labor cost). So for one jacket, $22.50 would be applied ($50.00 labor dollars per jacket multiplied by the $0.45 per labor dollar overhead rate). The total standard cost would be as follows:

| Standard Cost: | |
| --- | --- |
| Materials | $ 33.50 |
| Labor | 50.00 |
| Overhead | 22.50 |
| Total standard cost | $106.00 |

This is the amount that would be accumulated as inventory throughout the year for every jacket produced. However, differences in planned versus actual volume will give rise to a *volume variance*.

Above we demonstrated how variable overhead would fluctuate with volume and, therefore, could not be intelligently compared to a fixed or static budget. On the other hand, fixed overhead does not vary with volume. As indicated in our flexible budget above, rent and depreciation are the same amounts under all levels of production. But, let's think about the mechanics for a moment. If, throughout the year, $22.50 is allocated or absorbed into inventory for every jacket produced, what if the number of jackets is different than we planned? Certainly, if we produced the exact number planned, 160,000, the overhead absorbed would equal the actual overhead (assuming no spending variances).

| | | |
|---|---|---|
| Labor per jacket | $ | 50.00 |
| Overhead rate | × | .45 |
| Overhead/jacket | $ | 22.50 |
| Number of jackets | × | 160,000 |
| Total overhead applied | | $3,600,000 |

This would be equal to the total overhead planned. If, on the other hand, only 140,000 jackets were produced, the amount absorbed would be as follows:

| | | |
|---|---|---|
| Labor per jacket | $ | 50.00 |
| Overhead rate | × | .45 |
| Overhead/jacket | $ | 22.50 |
| Number of jackets | x | 140,000 |
| Total overhead applied | | $3,150,000 |

Let's assume that all of the $3.6 million overhead is fixed. At the end of the year, our accounts would show that $3.15 million of overhead was absorbed into inventory but our actual costs were $3.6 million. This gives us a variance of $450 thousand. What does this variance tell us? Does this tell us much about how we managed our overhead? Not really. The costs were fixed at $3.6 million and that's what was spent. It does indicate that at a lower level of production, our per-unit cost is higher as our fixed costs are spread over fewer units, but this is, to some extent, merely a function of the planned production chosen at the beginning of the year that we used to derive our overhead rate.

This variance, called a *volume variance*, is essentially just the mathematical difference that arises because overhead is applied as if it were a variable expense (a budgeted rate times a cost driver such as direct labor dollars), but it is actually fixed. The absorption rate is set to just absorb into inventory the planned overhead when the company operates at its normal volume. It is necessary to isolate the volume variance from the spending variance, which is much more managerially significant, because otherwise we would make inappropriate conclusions about our performance against the budget.

## ANALYZING THE TOTAL OVERHEAD VARIANCE

Now that we have isolated the separate pieces of the overhead variance, the spending variance and the volume variance, let's work through an example. Assume the following:

| | |
|---|---|
| Planned production | 160,000 |
|    80% capacity | |
|    $8 million direct labor dollars | |
| Actual production | 140,000 |
|    70% capacity | |
|    $7 million direct labor dollars | |
| | |
| (in thousands) | |
| Absorbed overhead | $3,150  ($7,000 labor dollars at $0.45) |
| Actual overhead | 3,610 |
| Unfavorable variance | $  460 |

**Spending variance**  To analyze the spending variance, compare the actual overhead to the flexible budget at 70% capacity:

| | Flexible Budget Allowance at Actual Volume of $7,000 Direct Labor Dollars | Actual Expense at Actual Volume | Spending Variance |
|---|---|---|---|
| Rent | $  500 | $  500 | — |
| Depreciation | 500 | 600 | $100U |
| Supervision | 1,000 | 1,050 | 50U |
| Supplies | 700 | 690 | 10F |
| Power | 750 | 770 | 20U |
| Total | $3,450 | $3,610 | $160U |

The difference between actual overhead incurred and the flexible budget at this level of output is the *overhead spending variance*. It measures cost control performance.

**Volume variance**  To analyze the volume variance, compare the allowed overhead at 70% capacity to the absorbed overhead (in thousands):

| | |
|---|---|
| Allowed overhead (70% capacity) | $3,450 |
| Absorbed overhead | 3,150 |
| Unfavorable volume variance | $  300 |

The difference between the allowed overhead and the absorbed overhead at this level of output is the *production volume variance*. It results from the difference between planned and actual production volume. It is made up of under- or overabsorbed *fixed manufacturing overhead*. It does not include any variable overhead because items that vary directly with production are treated identically in both the absorption rate and in the flexible budget.

**Total variance** You will note that the sum of the spending variance and the volume variance is equal to the total variance. To express the variance analyses mathematically:

(Actual OH − Allowed OH) + (Allowed OH − Absorbed OH) =

(Actual OH − Absorbed OH)

| Spending Variance | + | Volume Variance | = | Total Variance |

Plugging in our amounts from above (in thousands):

| ($3,610 − $3,450) | + | ($3,450 − $3,150) | = | ($3,610 − $3,150) |
| $160 | + | $300 | = | $460 |

Another way to look at the total variance is as follows:

| Total variance | = | Actual OH − Absorbed OH |
| Spending variance | = | Actual OH − Allowed OH *e Flex. budget* |
| Volume variance | = | Allowed OH − Absorbed OH |

To proof:

| Spending variance | + | Volume variance | = | Total variance |

## CONCLUSION

The important questions that follow the calculation of variances concern *why* actual costs are different from standard costs. Variances provide clues for managers to investigate further. Sometimes the answers are obvious, but often they are not. For example, favorable materials price variances may be caused by lower quality but cheaper material being used. This may lead to more labor time being spent by workers of high skill (and higher wages) leading to an unfavorable labor usage (quantity) variance. Skilled managers analyzing variances often try to weave clues together into a "story" to explain why the variances arose in order to make appropriate decisions to improve performance in the future.

# Waltham Motors Division

W hen Sharon Michaels arrived at her office at Waltham Motors Division on June 4, 1991, she was pleased to find the monthly performance report for May on her desk. Her job as division controller was to analyze results of operations each month and to prepare a narrative report on operations that was to be forwarded to the corporate headquarters of Marco Corporation. Waltham Motors was a wholly owned subsidiary of Marco. The atmosphere at the division had been one of apprehensiveness throughout the month of May, and today would provide a chance to find out how well division management had compensated for the recent loss of a major customer contract.

## THE CURRENT SITUATION

Waltham Motors manufactured electric motors of a single design that were sold to household appliance manufacturers. Originally a family-owned business, the division had been acquired in late 1990 by the Marco Corporation. Few changes had been made in either the company's operating procedures or systems because Marco's management had chosen to delay changing procedures and systems until it was able to observe how well those already in use at Waltham functioned. In April, Sharon Michaels, who had earned a master's degree in business administration in 1989, was transferred from the corporate headquarters controller's office to Waltham Motors. She was joined in late May by David Marshall, also from Marco, who was to be the new division manager.

*Professor William J. Bruns, Jr. prepared this case. The case was updated by Susan S. Harmeling.*

Copyright © 1984 by the President and Fellows of Harvard College. Harvard Business School case 184-169.

Because of the lost contract, Michaels had asked the plant accountant to as-semble the May figures as quickly as possible, but she was amazed that they were ready so soon. At headquarters, monthly results had rarely been available until several days after the end of each month. Even though the plant accoun-tant had promised Sharon that he would be able to prepare the report in a sin-gle day with some overtime work, she was surprised that he had been able to do so.

The division had prepared a budget for 1991 based on estimated sales and production costs. Because sales were not subject to seasonal fluctuations, the monthly budget was merely one-twelfth of the annual budget. No adjustments had been made to the May budget when the contract was lost in April.

## THE PERFORMANCE REPORT

A glance at the performance report confirmed Michaels' worst fears. Instead of a budgeted profit of $91,200, the report showed the division had lost $7,200 in May. Even allowing for the lost volume, she had expected a better showing than indicated by the performance report. The plant accountant had attached the following memo to the report:

June 3, 11:00 P.M.

Sharon:

As promised, here is the performance report for May. (I told you smaller is better; we'll show headquarters how efficient our plant accounting depart-ment is!) I am sure you'll find the bottom line as disappointing as I did, but plant performance really looks good, and the crews there may deserve our compliments. Note how they are at or under budget on every single cost ex-cept for supervision. I suspect that the unfavorable variance in supervision was caused directly by the work involved in controlling other costs.

Because I worked late, I am taking a day off tomorrow. The other data you requested are as follows:

1. There were no beginning and ending inventories in work in progress or finished goods.
2. Per-unit standard costs used in budgeting this year were:
   Direct material        $ 6
   Direct labor           16
3. We are still using two hours per unit as standard labor time.
4. Actual material prices have been 5% less than expected.
5. Actual direct labor costs have been $8.20 per hour due to the increase in medical benefits granted last January.

A copy of the performance report is shown as **Exhibit 1**.

## QUESTIONS

1.   Using budget data, how many motors would have to be sold for Waltham Motors Division to break even?
2.   Using budget data, what was the total expected cost per unit if all manufacturing and shipping overhead (both variable and fixed) was allocated to planned <u>production</u>?  What was the actual per unit cost of <u>production</u> and shipping?
3.   Comment on the performance report and the plant accountant's analysis of results.  How, if at all, would you suggest the performance report be changed before sending it on to the division manager and Marco Corporation headquarters?
4.   Prepare your own analysis of the Waltham Division's operations in May. Explain in as much detail as possible why income differed from what you would have expected.

**EXHIBIT 1**
**Performance Report, May 1991**

| | Budget | Actual | Variance | |
|---|---|---|---|---|
| Units | 18,000 | 14,000 | 4,000 | |
| Sales | $864,000 | $686,000 | $178,000 | U |
| *Variable manufacturing costs:* | | | | |
|    Direct material | $108,000 | $ 85,400 | $ 22,600 | F |
|    Direct labor | 288,000 | 246,000 | 42,000 | F |
|    Indirect labor | 57,600 | 44,400 | 13,200 | F |
|    Idle time | 14,400 | 14,200 | 200 | F |
|    Cleanup time | 10,800 | 10,000 | 800 | F |
|    Miscellaneous supplies | 5,200 | 4,000 | 1,200 | F |
|    Total variable manufacturing cost | $484,000 | $404,000 | $ 80,000 | F |
| *Variable shipping costs* | 28,800 | 28,000 | 800 | F |
|    Total variable costs | $512,800 | $432,000 | $ 80,800 | F |
| Contribution margin | $351,200 | $254,000 | $ 97,200 | U |
| *Nonvariable manufacturing costs:* = FIXED | | | | |
|    Supervision | $ 57,600 | $ 58,800 | $ 1,200 | U |
|    Rent | 20,000 | 20,000 | — | |
|    Depreciation | 60,000 | 60,000 | — | |
|    Other | 10,400 | 10,400 | — | |
|    Total nonvariable manufacturing costs | $148,000 | $149,200 | $ 1,200 | U |
| *Selling and administrative costs* (Period Exp.) → | 112,000 | 112,000 | — | |
|    Total nonvariable and programmed costs | $260,000 | $261,200 | $ 1,200 | U |
| Operating income (loss) | 91,200 | (7,200) | (98,400) | U |

# Mile High Cycles

In 1989, Bob Moyer was reviewing production costs for Mile High Cycles. Located in Denver, Colorado, the company sold high-quality, hand-crafted mountain bikes to bicycle retailers throughout the country. Sales for the company were $13 million that year.

Bob Moyer had been an avid cyclist in college, racing for the Stanford University cycling team while completing his degree in mechanical engineering. After working for a few years as a design engineer for a company in Denver, Bob decided to start his own business. As a hobby, he had designed and built several prototypes of a mountain bike, which had been enthusiastically received by his mountain-biking friends. Approaching several friends and relatives for start-up money, Mile High Cycles was founded in 1987.

A mountain bike was a bicycle with 15 to 21 speeds, designed and built to take the punishment of riding on dirt trails and roads. The bikes were first made by avid cyclists who customized their 10-speed road bikes in order to ride on mountain trails and dirt roads. Some with framebuilding experience began to experiment with making their own frames in order to better handle the additional demands of off-road riding. By 1982, several small companies selling bicycles specifically designed for riding under these conditions had emerged.

During the rest of the 1980s, mountain bikes took off in popularity, not only for use off-road but also for use in the city, where their sturdy construction could withstand the pounding from potholes and curbs. In addition, many casual cyclists preferred the mountain bike's more upright riding position to the

---

*David J. Ellison prepared this case under the supervision of William J. Bruns, Jr.*

Copyright © 1990 by the President and Fellows of Harvard College. Harvard Business School case 191-056.

hunched position of the 10-speed road bike. Sales of all bicycles in the United States had declined from 12.6 million units in 1987 to 9.9 million units in 1988. However, over the same time period, sales of mountain bikes increased from 1.5 million units to 2.1 million units.

Bob Moyer had planned to produce 10,000 bikes in 1989, all of one model. Operations at Mile High Cycles consisted of three departments: frames, wheel assembly, and final assembly. In frames, steel tubing was cut to length for the components of the frame. Then the pieces were carefully welded together to form the completed frameset. This part of the process was quite time-consuming, requiring frequent inspection and measurement to ensure that the frameset was aligned perfectly. After welding, the frame was painted in one of ten different color schemes and prepared for final assembly.

In wheel assembly, front and rear wheels were assembled from their key components: hubs, spokes, and rims. All of the components were purchased from an outside supplier. Mile High Cycles used a high-quality automatic lacing and truing machine to build its wheels. This machine would lace the spokes between the hub and rim and then automatically tighten the spokes to the appropriate tension. The machine was quite precise but would occasionally damage spokes during the insertion process. In such a case, the operator would replace any damaged parts and restart the machine. Each wheel would also be inspected and trued by hand in order to ensure that the wheels were in perfect alignment.

In final assembly, the frame and wheels were combined with other purchased parts to create the final package that would then be shipped to bicycle dealers. In this area, the front fork and many other key components were attached to the frame, and the inner tubes and tires were mounted on the wheels. In order to minimize damage while shipping, some of the bicycles' components were left packaged for the bicycle dealer to assemble before selling the bike to the final customer. All of the components were purchased from outside suppliers and then were combined to form kits for the bicycles. Mile High Cycles carried an inventory of spare parts to replace any parts damaged during assembly or shipping, although such replacement was infrequent.

In reviewing his costs, Bob noted that he had produced 10,800 bicycles in 1989, 800 more than planned. Bob thought that operations during the year had done well to meet the additional demand, but he wondered if Mile High Cycles was doing a good job in managing its costs. **Exhibit 1** shows the planned material, labor, and overhead costs for 1989. **Exhibit 2** shows the actual material, labor, and overhead costs for that year.

## QUESTIONS

1.  Determine the direct cost and overhead variances. What might be causing each of the variances to occur?
2.  Should Bob Moyer be concerned about Mile High Cycles' performance? Where should he be prepared to direct his attention? What additional information should he try to obtain?
3.  Are there any purposes for which a total, per-unit variance would be more useful than a series of functional variances? If so, for what?

**EXHIBIT 1**
**1989 Production Budget**

Budget based on 10,000 bicycles production

**Frame assembly:**

| | | |
|---|---|---|
| Steel tubing | $  3,300,000 | (110,000 lbs. @ $30.00/lb.) |
| Paint | 25,000 | (1,250 gals. @ $20.00/gal.) |
| Labor | 1,500,000 | (100,000 hrs. @ $15.00/hr.) |
| Total frame assembly | $  4,825,000 | |

**Wheel assembly:**

| | | |
|---|---|---|
| Parts | $  1,200,000 | (10,000 kits @ $120.00/kit) |
| Labor | 65,000 | (5,000 hrs. @ $13.00/hr.) |
| Total wheel assembly | $  1,265,000 | |

**Final assembly:**

| | | |
|---|---|---|
| Parts | $  3,500,000 | (10,000 kits @ $350.00/kit) |
| Labor | 105,000 | (7,500 hrs. @ $14.00/hr.) |
| Total final assembly | $  3,605,000 | |

**Overhead costs:**

| | | |
|---|---|---|
| Rent | $     250,000 | |
| Office staff | 100,000 | |
| Depreciation | 100,000 | |
| Other costs | 750,000 | (estimated to be 2/3 variable) |
| Total overhead | $  1,200,000 | |
| Total annual costs | $10,895,000 | |

**EXHIBIT 2**
**1989 Production Costs**

Actual production: 10,800 bicycles

**Frame assembly:**

| | | |
|---|---:|---|
| Steel tubing | $ 3,572,100 | (113,400 lbs. @ $31.50/lb.) |
| Paint | 28,187 | (1,375 gals. @ $20.50/gal.) |
| Labor | 1,528,050 | (100,200 hrs. @ $15.25/hr.) |
| Total frame assembly | $ 5,128,337 | |

**Wheel assembly:**

| | | |
|---|---:|---|
| Parts | $ 1,317,600 | (10,800 kits @ $122.00/kit) |
| Rework parts | 25,000 | (spokes and rims) |
| Labor | 74,250 | (5,500 hrs. @ $13.50/hr.) |
| Total wheel assembly | $ 1,416,850 | |

**Final assembly:**

| | | |
|---|---:|---|
| Parts | $ 3,963,600 | (10,800 kits @ $367.00/kit) |
| Rework parts | 45,000 | (miscellaneous parts) |
| Labor | 116,000 | (8,000 hrs. @ $14.50/hr.) |
| Total final assembly | $ 4,124,600 | |

**Overhead costs:**

| | |
|---|---:|
| Rent | $    250,000 |
| Office staff | 100,000 |
| Depreciation | 100,000 |
| Other costs | 850,000 |
| Total overhead | $ 1,300,000 |
| Total annual costs | $ 11,969,787 |

# Polysar Limited

As soon as Pierre Choquette received the September report of operations for NASA Rubber (**Exhibits 1** and **2**), he called Alf Devereux, Controller, and Ron Britton, Sales Manager, into his office to discuss the year-to-date results. Next week, he would make his presentation to the Board of Directors, and the results for his division for the first nine months of the year were not as good as expected. Pierre knew that the NASA management team had performed well. Sales volume was up and feedstock costs were down, resulting in a gross margin that was better than budget. Why did the bottom line look so bad?

As the three men worked through the numbers, their discussion kept coming back to the fixed costs of the butyl rubber plant. Fixed costs were high. The plant had yet to reach capacity. The European Division had taken less output than projected.

Still, Choquette felt that these factors were outside his control. His division had performed well—it just didn't show in the profit results.

Choquette knew that Henderson, his counterpart in Europe, did not face these problems. The European rubber profits would be compared to those of NASA. How would the Board react to the numbers he had to work with? He would need to educate them in his presentation, especially concerning the volume variance. He knew that many of the Board members would not understand what that number represented or that it was due in part to the actions of Henderson's group.

Pierre Choquette, Alf Devereux, and Ron Britton decided to meet the next day to work on a strategy for the Board presentation.

---

*Professor Robert Simons prepared this case. The financial data have been developed to illustrate the issues involved and are not representative of the true financial results of the company.*

Copyright © 1987 by the President and Fellows of Harvard College. Harvard Business School case 187-098.

# POLYSAR LIMITED

In 1986, Polysar Limited was Canada's largest chemical company with $1.8 billion in annual sales. Based in Sarnia, Ontario, Polysar was the world's largest producer of synthetic rubber and latex and a major producer of basic petrochemicals and fuel products.

Polysar was established in 1942 to meet wartime needs for a synthetic substitute for natural rubber. The supply of natural rubber to the Allied forces had been interrupted by the declaration of war against the United States by Japan in December 1941. During 1942 and 1943, ten synthetic rubber plants were built by the governments of the United States and Canada, including the Polysar plant in Sarnia.

After the war, the supply of natural rubber was again secure and the nine U.S. plants were sold to private industry or closed. Polysar remained in operation as a Crown Corporation, wholly owned by the government of Canada. In 1972, by an Act of Parliament, the Canada Development Corporation (CDC) was created as a government-owned, venture capital company to encourage Canadian business development; at that time, the equity shares of Polysar were transferred to the Canada Development Corporation. In 1986, Polysar remained wholly owned by the CDC; however, in a government sponsored move to privatization, the majority of the shares of the CDC were sold to the Canadian public in the period 1982 to 1985.

Through acquisition and internal growth, Polysar had grown considerably from its original single plant. Polysar now employed 6,650 people, including 3,100 in Canada, 1,050 in the U.S., and 2,500 in Europe and elsewhere. The company operated 20 manufacturing plants in Canada, the United States, Belgium, France, The Netherlands, and West Germany.

# STRUCTURE

The operations of the company were structured into three groups: basic petrochemicals, rubber, and diversified products (**Exhibit 3**).

### Basic Petrochemicals

Firman Bentley, 51, was Group Vice President of Basic Petrochemicals. This business unit produced primary petrochemicals such as ethylene as well as intermediate products such as propylene, butadiene, and styrene monomers. Group sales in 1985 were approximately $800 million, of which $500 million was sold to outside customers and the remainder was sold as intermediate feedstock to Polysar's downstream operations.

## Rubber

The Rubber Group was headed by Charles Ambridge, 61, Group Vice President. Polysar held 9% of the world synthetic rubber market (excluding communist bloc countries). As the largest group in the company, the Rubber Group produced 46% of Polysar sales. Major competitors included Goodyear, Bayer, Exxon, and Dupont.

Rubber products, such as butyl and halobutyl, were sold primarily to manufacturers of automobile tires (six of the world's largest tire companies[1] accounted for 70% of the world butyl and halobutyl demand); other uses included belting, footwear, adhesives, hose, seals, plastics modification, and chewing gum.

The Rubber Group was split into two operating divisions that were managed as profit centers: NASA (North and South America) and EROW (Europe and rest of world). In addition to the two operating profit centers, the Rubber Group included a Global Marketing Department and a Research Division. The costs of these departments were not charged to the two operating profit centers, but instead were charged against group profits.

## Diversified Products

John Beaton, 48, was Vice President of Diversified Products, a group that consisted of the Latex, Plastics, and Specialty Products Divisions. This group was composed of high-technology product categories that were expected to double sales within five years. In 1985, the group provided 27% of Polysar's sales revenue.

Bentley, Ambridge, and Beaton reported to Robert Dudley, 60, President and Chief Executive Officer.

# RUBBER GROUP

A key component of Polysar's strategy was to be a leader in high-margin, specialty rubbers. The leading products in this category were the butyl and halobutyl rubbers. Attributes of butyl rubber include low permeability to gas and moisture, resistance to steam and weathering, high energy absorption, and chemical resistance. Butyl rubber was traditionally used in inner tubes and general purpose applications. Halobutyl rubber, a modified derivative, possesses the same attributes as regular butyl with additional properties that allow bonding to other materials. Thus, halobutyls were used extensively as liners and sidewalls in tubeless tires.

---

[1] Michelin, Goodyear, Bridgestone, Firestone, Pirelli, and Dunlop.

Butyl and halobutyl rubber were manufactured from feedstocks such as crude oil, naphtha, butane, propane, and ethane (**Exhibit 4**). Polysar manufactured butyl rubbers at two locations: NASA Division's Sarnia plant and EROW Division's Antwerp plant.

### NASA Butyl Plant

The original Sarnia plant, built in 1942, manufactured regular butyl until 1972. At that time, market studies predicted rapid growth in the demand for high-quality radial tires manufactured with halobutyl. Demand for regular butyl was predicted to remain steady since poor road conditions in many countries of the world necessitated the use of tires with inner tubes. In 1972, the Sarnia plant was converted to allow production of halobutyls as well as regular butyl.

By the 1980s, demand for halobutyl had increased to the point that Polysar forecast capacity constraints. During 1983 and 1984, the company built a second plant at Sarnia, known as Sarnia 2, to produce regular butyl. The original plant, Sarnia 1, was then dedicated solely to the production of halobutyl.

Sarnia 2, with a capital cost of $550 million, began full operations late in 1984. Its annual nameplate (i.e., design) production capacity for regular butyl was 95,000 tonnes. During 1985, the plant produced 65,000 tonnes.

### EROW Butyl Plant

The EROW Division's butyl plant was located in Antwerp, Belgium. Built in 1964 as a regular butyl unit, the plant was modified in 1979–80 to allow it to produce halobutyl as well as regular butyl.

The annual nameplate production capacity of the Antwerp plant was 90,000 tonnes. In 1985, as in previous years, the plant operated near or at its nameplate capacity. The Antwerp plant was operated to meet fully the halobutyl demand of EROW customers; the remainder of capacity was used to produce regular butyl.

In 1981, the plant's output was 75% regular butyl and 25% halobutyl; by 1985, halobutyl represented 50% of the plant's production. Since regular butyl demand outpaced the plant's remaining capacity, EROW took its regular butyl shortfall from the Sarnia 2 plant; in 1985, 21,000 tonnes of regular butyl were shipped from NASA to EROW.

## PRODUCT SCHEDULING

Although NASA served customers in North and South America and EROW serviced customers in Europe and the rest of the world, regular butyl could be shipped from either the Sarnia 2 or Antwerp plant. NASA shipped approximately one-third of its regular butyl output to EROW. Also, customers located in distant locations could receive shipments from either plant due to certain cost or logistical advantages. For example, Antwerp sometimes shipped to Brazil and Sarnia sometimes shipped to the Far East.

A Global Marketing Department worked with Regional Directors of Marketing and Regional Product Managers to coordinate product flows. Three sets of factors influenced these analyses. First, certain customers demanded products from a specific plant due to slight product differences resulting from the type of feedstock used and the plant configuration. Second, costs varied between Sarnia and Antwerp due to differences in variable costs (primarily feedstock and energy), shipping, and currency rates. Finally, inventory levels, production interruptions, and planned shutdowns were considered.

In September and October of each year, the NASA and EROW divisions prepared production estimates for the upcoming year. These estimates were based on estimated sales volumes and plant loadings (i.e., capacity utilization). Since the Antwerp plant operated at capacity, the planning exercise was largely for the benefit of the managers of the Sarnia 2 plant who needed to know how much regular butyl Antwerp would need from the Sarnia 2 plant.

## Product Costing and Transfer Prices

Butyl rubbers were costed using standard rates for variable and fixed costs.

Variable costs included feedstocks, chemicals, and energy. Standard variable cost per tonne of butyl was calculated by multiplying a standard utilization factor (i.e., the standard quantity of inputs used) by a standard price established for each unit of input. Since feedstock prices varied with worldwide market conditions and represented the largest component of costs, it was impossible to establish standard input prices that remained valid for extended periods. Therefore, the company reset feedstock standard costs each month to a price that reflected market prices. Chemical and energy standard costs were established annually.

A purchase price variance (were input prices above or below standard prices?) and an efficiency variance (did production require more or less inputs than standard?) were calculated for variable costs each accounting period.

Fixed costs comprised three categories of cost. Direct costs included direct labor, maintenance, chemicals required to keep the plant bubbling, and fixed utilities. Allocated cash costs included plant management, purchasing department costs, engineering, planning, and accounting. Allocated noncash costs represented primarily depreciation.

Fixed costs were allocated to production based on a plant's "demonstrated capacity" using the following formula:

$$\frac{\text{Standard Fixed}}{\text{Cost Per Tonne}} = \frac{\text{Estimated Annual Total Fixed Costs}}{\text{Annual Demonstrated Plant Capacity}}$$

To apply the formula, production estimates were established each fall for the upcoming year. Then, the amount of total fixed costs applicable to this level of production was estimated. The amount of total fixed cost to be allocated to each tonne of output was calculated by dividing total fixed cost by the plant's demonstrated capacity. **Exhibit 5** reproduces a section of the Controller's Guide that defines demonstrated capacity.

Each accounting period, two variances were calculated for fixed costs. The first was a spending variance calculated as the simple difference between actual total fixed costs and estimated total fixed costs. The second variance was a volume variance calculated using the formula:

$$\begin{matrix} \text{Volume} \\ \text{Variance} \end{matrix} = \begin{pmatrix} \text{Standard Fixed} \\ \text{Cost Per Tonne} \end{pmatrix} \times \left( \begin{bmatrix} \text{Actual Tonnes} \\ \text{Produced} \end{bmatrix} - \begin{bmatrix} \text{Demonstrated} \\ \text{Capacity} \end{bmatrix} \right)$$

Product transfers between divisions for performance accounting purposes were made at standard full cost, representing, for each tonne, the sum of standard variable cost and standard fixed cost.

## Compensation

Employees at Polysar had in the past been paid by fixed salary with little use of bonuses except at the executive level of the company. In 1984, a bonus system was instituted throughout the company to link pay with performance and to strengthen the profit center orientation.

## Non-Management Employees

The bonus system varied by employee group but was developed with the intention of paying salaries that were approximately five percent less than those paid by a reference group of 25 major Canadian manufacturing companies. To augment salaries, annual bonuses were awarded, in amounts up to 12% of salary, based on corporate and divisional performance. Hourly workers could receive annual bonuses in similar proportions based on performance.

All bonuses were based on achieving or exceeding budgeted profit targets. For salaried workers, for example, meeting the 1985 corporate profit objective would result in a 5% bonus; an additional $25 million in profits would provide an additional 4% bonus. Meeting and exceeding division profit targets could provide an additional 3% bonus.

Using periodic accounting information, divisional vice presidents met in quarterly communication meetings with salaried and wage employees to discuss divisional and corporate performance levels.

## Management

For managers, the percent of remuneration received through annual bonuses was greater than 12% and increased with responsibility levels.

The bonuses of top division management in 1985 were calculated by a formula that awarded 50% of bonus potential to meeting and exceeding divisional profit targets and 50% to meeting or exceeding corporate profit targets.

## INTERVIEWS WITH RUBBER GROUP VICE PRESIDENTS[2]

### Pierre Choquette

Pierre Choquette, 43, was Vice President[3] of the NASA Rubber Division. A professional engineer, Choquette had begun his career with Polysar in plant management. Over the years, he had assumed responsibilities for product management in the U.S., managed a small subsidiary, managed a European plant, and directed European sales.

> *This business is managed on price and margin. Quality, service, and technology are also important, but it is difficult to differentiate ourselves from other competitors on these dimensions.*
>
> *When the price of oil took off, this affected our feedstock prices drastically, and Polysar's worldwide business suffered. Now that prices are back down, we are trying to regroup our efforts and bring the business back to long-term health. Polysar will break even in 1985 and show a normal profit again in 1986. Of course, the Rubber Division will, as in the past, be the major producer of profit for the company.*
>
> *As you know, this is a continuous process industry. The plant is computerized so that we need the same number of people and incur most of the same overhead costs whether the plant is running fast or slow.*
>
> *The regular butyl plant, Sarnia 2, is running at less than capacity. Although the plant should be able to produce 95,000 tonnes, its demonstrated capacity is 85,000. Last year, we produced 65,000. This leaves us sitting with a lot of unabsorbed fixed costs, especially when you consider depreciation charges.*
>
> *Still, NASA Rubber has been growing nicely. I think that this is in part due to our strong commitment to run the divisions as profit centers. We have*

---

2 Pierre Choquette was interviewed at Harvard Business School in 1985; Doug Henderson was interviewed at Harvard in 1986. Both men were attending the thirteen-week Advanced Management Program that was developed to strengthen the management skills of individuals with potential to become chief executive officers of their companies. In addition to Choquette and Henderson, Polysar had sent Firman Bentley to the program in 1984.

3 Due to its relatively large size, the Rubber Group was the only group with regional vice presidents. Regional responsibilities of the Basic Petrochemicals Group and the Diversified Products Group were managed by lower-ranking general managers.

*been pushing hard to build both volume and efficiency and I am pleased that our programs and incentives are paying off.*

*Our transfers to EROW are still a problem. Since the transfers are at standard cost and are not recorded as revenue, these transfers do nothing for our profit. Also, if they cut back on orders, our profit is hurt through the volume variance. Few of our senior managers truly understand the volume variance and why profit results are so different in the two regions. The accounting is not a problem, but having to continuously explain it to very senior-level managers is. It always comes down to the huge asset that we carry whether the plant is at capacity or not.*

*We run our businesses on return on net assets, which looks ridiculous for NASA. I worry that if I am not around to explain it, people will form the wrong conclusion about the health of the business. Also, you sometimes wonder if people ascribe results to factors that are outside your control.*

## Doug Henderson

Doug Henderson, 46, Vice President of the EROW Rubber Division, was also a professional engineer. His career included management responsibilities in plant operations, market research, venture analysis and corporate planning, running a small regional business in Canada, and Director of European Sales.

*The Antwerp plant produces about 45,000 tonnes of halobutyl and 45,000 tonnes of regular butyl each year. In addition, we import approximately 15,000 to 20,000 tonnes of regular butyl from Sarnia each year (**Exhibit 6**).*

*We inform Sarnia each fall of our estimated regular butyl needs. These estimates are based on our predictions of butyl and halobutyl sales and how hard we can load our plant. The overall sales estimates are usually within ten percent, say plus or minus 8,000 tonnes, unless an unexpected crisis occurs.*

*The EROW business has been extremely successful since I arrived here in 1982. We have increased our share in the high growth halobutyl market; the plant is running well; and we have kept the operation simple and compact.*

*Looking at our Statement of Net Contribution (**Exhibit 7**), our margins are better than NASA's. For one thing, there is a great surplus of feedstock in Europe and we benefit from lower prices. Also, market dynamics are substantially different.*

*We pay a lot of attention to plant capacity. For example, we budgeted to produce 250 tonnes per day this year and we have got it up to 275. We are also working hard to reduce our "off-spec" material as a way of pushing up our yield. If we can produce more, it's free—other than variable cost, it goes right to the bottom line.*

*Given these factors, Pierre loves it when I tell him jokingly that our success at EROW is attributable to superb management.*

**EXHIBIT 1**
**Operations Report**

NASA RUBBER DIVISION
Regular Butyl Rubber
Statistics and Analyses

September 1986

|  | 9 Months Ended September 30, 1986 | | |
|---|---|---|---|
| Volume—Tonnes | Actual (000's) | Budget (000's) | Deviation (000's) |
| Sales | 35.8 | 33.0 | 2.8 |
| Production | 47.5 | 55.0 | −7.5 |
| Transfers | | | |
|    to EROW | 12.2 | 19.5 | −7.3 |
|    from EROW | 2.1 | 1.0 | 1.1 |
| Productions Costs | ($000's) | ($000's) | ($000's) |
| Fixed Cost—Direct | −21,466 | −21,900 | 434 |
|    —Allocated Cash | − 7,036 | − 7,125 | 89 |
|    —Allocated Noncash | −15,625 | −15,600 | − 25 |
| Fixed Cost to Production | −44,127 | −44,625 | 498 |
| Transfers to/from FG Inventory | 1,120 | 2,450 | −1,330 |
| Transfers to EROW | 8,540 | 13,650 | −5,110 |
| Transfers from EROW | − 1,302 | − 620 | − 682 |
| Fixed Cost of Sales | −35,769 | −29,145 | −6,624 |

Note: As indicated on p. 5-71 of the case, financial data have been disguised and do not represent the true financial results of the company.

**EXHIBIT 2**
**Operations Report**

NASA RUBBER DIVISION
Regular Butyl Rubber
Statement of Net Contribution

September 1986

| | 9 Months Ended September 30, 1986 | | |
|---|---|---|---|
| | Actual ($000's) | Budget ($000's) | Deviation ($000's) |
| Sales Revenue—Third Party | 65,872 | 61,050 | 4,822 |
| —Diversified Products Group | 160 | 210 | - 50 |
| —Total | 66,032 | 61,260 | 4,772 |
| Delivery Cost | - 2,793 | - 2,600 | - 193 |
| Net Sales Revenue | 63,239 | 58,660 | 4,579 |
| *Variable Costs* | | | |
| Standard | -22,589 | -21,450 | -1,139 |
| Cost Adjustments | 54 | — | 54 |
| Efficiency Variance | 241 | — | 241 |
| Total | -22,294 | -21,450 | - 844 |
| Gross Margin—$ | 40,945 | 37,210 | 3,735 |
| *Fixed Costs* | | | |
| Standard | -25,060 | -23,100 | -1,960 |
| Cost Adjustments | 168 | 80 | 88 |
| Spending Variance | 498 | — | 498 |
| Volume Variance | - 11,375 | - 6,125 | -5,250 |
| Total | -35,769 | -29,145 | -6,624 |
| Gross Profit—$ | 5,176 | 8,065 | -2,889 |
| —% of NSR | 8.2% | 13.7% | - 5.5% |
| *Period Costs* | | | |
| Administration, Selling, Distribution | - 4,163 | - 4,000 | - 163 |
| Technical Service | - 222 | - 210 | - 12 |
| Other Income/Expense | 208 | 50 | 158 |
| Total | - 4,177 | - 4,160 | - 17 |
| Business Contribution | 999 | 3,905 | -2,906 |
| Interest on Working Capital | - 1,875 | - 1,900 | 25 |
| Net Contribution | - 876 | 2,005 | -2,881 |

Note: As indicated on p. 5-71 of the case, financial data have been disguised and do not represent the true financial results of the company.

**EXHIBIT 3**
**Polysar Limited Organization Chart**

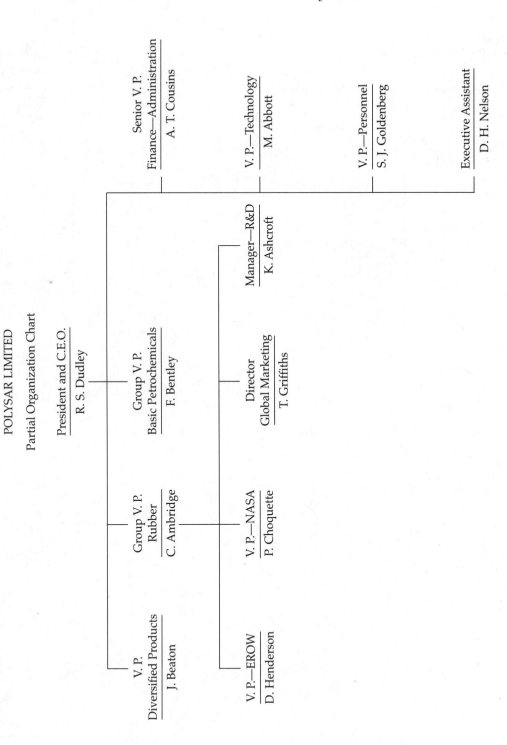

POLYSAR LIMITED
Partial Organization Chart

President and C.E.O.
R. S. Dudley

Senior V. P.
Finance—Administration
A. T. Cousins

V. P.—Technology
M. Abbott

V. P.—Personnel
S. J. Goldenberg

Executive Assistant
D. H. Nelson

Group V. P.
Basic Petrochemicals
F. Bentley

Manager—R&D
K. Ashcroft

Director
Global Marketing
T. Griffiths

Group V. P.
Rubber
C. Ambridge

V. P.—NASA
P. Choquette

V. P.
Diversified Products
J. Beaton

V. P.—EROW
D. Henderson

**EXHIBIT 4**
**Rubber Production Process**

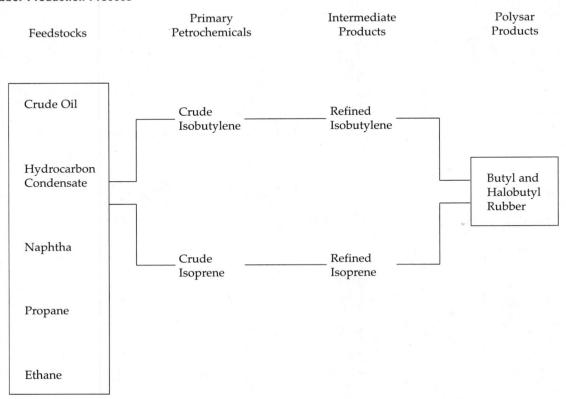

**EXHIBIT 5**
**Controller's Guide**

| POLYSAR LIMITED—CONTROLLER'S GUIDE | NUMBER | 03:02 | |
|---|---|---|---|
| | PAGE 1 OF 14 PAGES | | |

| SUBJECT | NEW | REPLACES |
|---|---|---|
| ACCOUNTING FOR INVENTORIES | x | |
| | ISSUE DATE | Jan. 1/81 |

| ISSUED BY | Director Accounting | AUTHORIZED BY | Corporate Controller |
|---|---|---|---|

*PURPOSE*

To set out criteria and guidelines for the application of the Company's accounting policy for inventories:

> "Inventories are valued at the lower of FIFO (first-in, first-out) cost and net realizable value except for raw materials and supplies which are valued at the lower of FIFO cost and replacement cost."

*SPECIFIC EXCLUSION*

This release does not apply to SWAP transactions.

*DEFINITIONS*

*By-products*—one or more products of relatively small per-unit market value that emerge from the production process of a product or products of greater value.

*Cost system*—a system to facilitate the classification, recording, analysis, and interpretation of data pertaining to the production and distribution of products and services.

*Demonstrated capacity* is the actual annualized production of a plant which was required to run full out within the last fiscal year for a sufficiently long period to assess production capability after adjusting for abnormally low or high unscheduled shutdowns, scheduled shutdowns, and unusual or annualized items which impacted either favourably or unfavourably on the period's production. The resulting adjusted historical base should be further modified for changes planned to be implemented within the current fiscal year.

    a) Where a plant has not been required to run full out within the last fiscal year, production data may be used for a past period after adjusting for changes (debottlenecking/inefficiencies) since that time affecting production.

    b) Where a plant has never been required to run full out, demonstrated capacity could be reasonably considered as "nameplate" capacity after adjusting for

        i) known invalid assumptions in arriving at "nameplate"
        ii) changes to original design affecting "nameplate"
        iii) a reasonable negative allowance for error.

**EXHIBIT 6**
**Schedule of Regular Butyl Shipments from NASA to EROW**

|      | Actual Tonnes | Budget Tonnes |
|------|--------------:|--------------:|
| 1985 | 21,710        | 23,500        |
| 1984 | 12,831        | 13,700        |
| 1983 | 1,432         | 4,000         |
| 1982 | 792           | 600           |
| 1981 | 1,069         | 700           |

**EXHIBIT 7**
**Statement of Net Contribution**

EROW RUBBER DIVISION
Regular Butyl Rubber
Condensed Statement of Net Contribution

September 1986

|  | 9 Months Ended September 30, 1986 |
| --- | --- |
| Sales Volume—Tonnes | 47,850 |
|  | ($000's) |
| Sales Revenue | 94,504 |
| Delivery Cost | – 4,584 |
| Net Sales Revenue | 89,920 |
| *Variable Cost* |  |
| Standard | –28,662 |
| Purchase Price Variance | 203 |
| Inventory Revaluation | – 46 |
| Efficiency Variance | 32 |
| Total | –28,473 |
| Gross Margin—$ | 61,447 |
| *Fixed Cost to Production* |  |
| Depreciation | – 4,900 |
| Other | –16,390 |
|  | –21,290 |
| Transfers to/from Finished Goods Inventory | – 775 |
| Transfers to/from NASA | – 7,238 |
|  | –29,303 |
| Gross Profit—$ | 32,144 |
| Period Costs | – 7,560 |
| Business Contribution | 24,584 |
| Interest on W/C | – 1,923 |
| Net Contribution | 22,661 |

Notes:

[1] Fixed costs are allocated between regular butyl production (above) and halobutyl production (reported separately).

[2] As indicated on p. 5-71 of the case, financial data have been disguised and do not represent the true financial results of the company.

# Part Six

## Analysis for Capital Investment Decisions

# Basic Capital Investment Analysis

**D**ecisions about new investments in machines, a plant, or other assets are among the most important decisions that managers make for their organizations. In many cases, a decision to invest means that the organization will have to live with the effects of the investment for many years to come. Consequently, when new investments are considered it is of great importance that managers have all possible relevant information and that the information be analyzed with care in a meaningful manner.

Capital investment analysis always should begin with a careful search for alternatives. This is not always as easy as it first appears, because some alternatives may be more difficult to identify than others. Often investment alternatives have a sponsor who stands to gain if his or her alternative is selected, and other alternatives will be ignored or not mentioned by the sponsor. Or an investment perpetuates a traditional way of doing business when a more modern approach would prove more successful in the long run. All reasonable alternatives to any proposed investment need to be considered, and any that cannot be eliminated before formal investment analysis begins need to be studied and analyzed.

## ESTIMATING CASH FLOWS

Once alternatives have been identified, the cash flows which will occur if each is accepted need to be determined. Usually the cash flows that result from making the proposed investment are compared to the alternative of doing nothing.

Copyright © 1997 by the President and Fellows of Harvard College. Harvard Business School case 198-004.

For example, if the proposal is to acquire a new machine to replace one already owned, the cash flows that will take place if the new machine is acquired can be compared to the cash flows if no action is taken to determine the *differential cash flows* that are associated with the new machine. Only the differential *future* cash flows are of interest and concern. If there are several alternatives, a separate study of each will allow comparison to determine which is best.

## TWO TECHNIQUES FOR EVALUATING CAPITAL INVESTMENT PROPOSALS

Two techniques are often used to help decide whether a capital investment should be made or not made. The *net present value* (NPV) method uses an interest rate, cost of capital, or a desired rate of return to determine whether or not the present value of all future cash flows from the proposal is positive or negative. If it is positive, a decision to make the investment is supported. The *internal rate of return* (IRR) method seeks the interest rate that will equate the present value of all cash outflows to the present value of all cash inflows. If this internal rate of return (or *yield*) exceeds the *hurdle rate* (cost of capital or desired rate of return), a positive decision to make the investment is supported.

Each of these techniques is based on the same algebraic formula. The difference lies in the unknown variable that is the focus of the solution. In NPV, the focus is on the net present value of all cash flows at a desired interest rate. In IRR, the focus is on the interest rate that will equate the present value of all cash outflows with the present value of all cash inflows. The formula looks like this:

$$\text{Net Present Value} = \text{Cash Flow}^{(CF)}{}_{0} + \frac{CF_1}{(1 + i)^1} + \frac{CF_2}{(1 + i)^2} + \frac{CF_n}{(1 + i)^n}$$

where $i$ is the desired rate of return.

If the net present value is set to 0 and the equation is solved for $i$, $i$ is the *internal rate of return*.

It is rare that anyone actually has to work with the formula above because it is built into all financial or business calculators, computer spreadsheet software, and many personal computers, and compound interest tables are widely available.

Each of these techniques requires the analyst to identify:

1. The amount of all cash outflows that the investment requires and their timing.
2. The amount of all net cash inflows that will result from the investment and their timing.
3. The criterion for acceptability of new investments of the type under consideration.

## A SIMPLE EXAMPLE

Suppose that a proposed investment were $27,500 and the anticipated net cash flows were $9,000 each year (received at the end of each year) for five years.

If the desired rate of return is 15%, the NPV is $2,669.

If the desired rate of return is 20%, the NPV is $(584).

If the NPV is set to 0, the IRR is found to be 19%.

If the managers will make any investment that returns more than 15%, or if they find an IRR of 19% acceptable, they may make this investment. If they demand a return of 20%, the proposed investment is unacceptable.

## SOME THINGS TO KEEP IN MIND

Cash flows, not earnings, are the focus of investment analysis. This means that the effects of income taxes and the deductibility of depreciation must always be considered if they affect cash flows. If the analysis begins with an estimate of the positive cash flows that will be obtained by making the investment, and these will be taxed, only the cash flow after taxes should be used in the analysis. However, if depreciation is deductible for tax purposes, that may shield some of the new positive cash flows from taxes.

If there is existing equipment that can be sold, the total net new investment required should reflect the sales price that the old equipment will bring. A trade-in of the old equipment has a similar effect, reducing the new investment required. Likewise, if there is a gain or loss on the sale of the old equipment that will add to or reduce income taxes, that must be taken into account in the amount of investment or future cash flows.

New investments may change the amount of working capital that is required, and working capital requirements should always be considered when analyzing investments. Even though additional working capital required because of a new investment will be recovered at the end of the new investment's life, the use of compound interest methods will make the present value of the recovered working capital a fraction of the investment in working capital required when the new investment is made.

A final consideration in investment analysis concerns pricing trends that may affect the amount of new investment required. It may be possible that the cost of the new investment will fall if the investment is delayed one year or more. When a price reduction seems likely, the benefits of investing now should be compared with the benefits of waiting to invest in the future. Sometimes the price reduction will be great enough to offset the cost of waiting to gain the benefits of the investment.

Effective capital investment analysis requires clear identification of strategies and competitive initiatives, ingenuity and imagination to uncover alternatives, and careful attention to factors that will affect current and future cash flows. Often early analyses will lead to new questions that can be answered only through study or research. But the objective should be held clearly in mind—managers want to make the best decisions possible based on the best information available, carefully analyzed. The future success of their organization depends on making the best investments at the most favorable times.

# Riverbend Telephone Company

T he Riverbend Telephone Company is independently owned and operates in the area between the west bank of the Short River and the state line. The company provides local telephone service to customers in several adjacent communities, and its lines connect with those of other companies to provide long-distance telephone service. Operating as a public utility, the Riverbend Telephone Company is subject to regulation by the State Public Service Commission, which periodically reviews service and must approve all changes in rates.

In recent years, the population of the area served by the company had grown rapidly as a result of a new bridge which facilitated daily commuting over the Short River to a nearby city. As a result of this growth, company personnel and equipment had been hard pressed to meet all demands for installation of new telephone lines and maintenance. For a time, the company had used an outside contractor to handle overload work, but several poor experiences had caused abandonment of that practice. By late 1997, it was obvious that the company needed at least one new maintenance truck and crew.

The need to obtain a new truck arose at a critical period for the company. Earlier, Riverbend had made heavy commitments to purchase telephone equipment needed to improve service. Recent payments for new equipment had strained the net working capital position of the firm. Stockholders were unable to provide additional resources and hoped to avoid selling additional shares which would dilute their ownership. Interest rates were quoted at 8% on short-term notes, and above 9% for long-term rates. Since the company had been earning only about 10% on net assets, the firm hoped to avoid unnecessary borrowing.

Copyright © 1997 by the President and Fellows of Harvard College. Harvard Business School case 197-104.

In November 1997, Warren Freeman, general manager of Riverbend, requested bids for the new trucks from four truck dealers. The lowest bid received was from the Reliable Motors Company, which quoted a cash price of $24,300, including all taxes and delivery charges. As an alternative, Reliable would lease the truck to Riverbend Telephone for five years at an annual rate of $7,200.

The truck which Riverbend Telephone Company needed was similar to several others which it already owned. At Mr. Freeman's request, the accounting department used records to estimate the cost of operating the new truck. Those estimates are shown in **Exhibit 1**. The truck was expected to last for five years, at which time it could probably be sold for about $1,800. If the truck were purchased, it would be depreciated by the straight-line method because that was the only method allowed by the State Public Service Commission.

If the truck were leased, Riverbend Telephone would have to pay the annual lease charge on or before the first day of each year. In addition, they would be responsible for all costs of operation and maintenance of the truck, except for tires which Reliable Motors would supply. The proposed agreement also made Riverbend responsible for all risks to the truck and property damage, collision, personal injury, fire, and theft. Finally, Riverbend would reimburse Reliable for all costs of vehicle registration and taxes.

Mr. Freeman was unsure how he should view the alternatives presented by Reliable Motors. Leasing the truck would reduce the immediate demands on Riverbend Telephone's financial resources. Still, the prospect of paying $36,000 over five years when the truck could be purchased new for $24,300 raised questions about how well he would be serving company stockholders if he leased rather than purchased the truck. On the other hand, the operating expenses and lease payments would be allowable expense deductions in calculating income for tax purposes. Since the company had been paying and expected to continue paying income taxes of 40%, an increase in expenses of $7,200 per year would not really cost that much.

The effect of his choice on Riverbend's rate of return earned on net assets was also important to Mr. Freeman. In 1997, the State Public Service Commission had allowed another telephone company to raise its rates to provide revenues to increase its rate of return to just above 11% on net assets. In an attempt to raise Riverbend's return without requesting higher rates, Mr. Freeman had not approved any new investments that would provide a rate of return on investment below 12% unless they were absolutely necessary. Since the truck had to be acquired and the choice was only whether it should be leased or purchased, Mr. Freeman was unsure whether his 12% return minimum made any difference in this case.

Mr. Freeman also wanted to consider how the State Public Service Commission might view leased assets in evaluating rates of return earned by utilities. Purchased assets were always included in total investment net of accumulated depreciation, and all operating expenses, including depreciation, were allowable deductions in determining annual income. While he was not able to ascertain exactly what the Commission might want, he reasoned that Riverbend could probably include all operating expenses and the lease payments among annual expenses in reports to the Commission, but he was unsure whether investment should be increased by the "fair value" of the leased asset before calculating return on net assets.

## QUESTIONS

1.  Should the company buy or lease the new truck? (Assume that Riverbend Telephone uses the straight-line method of depreciation for tax purposes as well as for reports to shareholders and the State Public Service Commission.)
2.  If Riverbend Telephone purchased the truck and chose to depreciate it for income tax purposes only using the double-declining balance method, would this affect your decision to buy or lease? Assume that the annual depreciation would be as follows:

| Year | Depreciation |
| --- | --- |
| 1998 | $9,720 |
| 1999 | 5,832 |
| 2000 | 3,500 |
| 2001 | 2,100 |
| 2002 | 1,348 |

3.  If the truck is leased, how should Mr. Freeman report investment and annual income for the Riverbend Telephone Company to the State Public Service Commission?

**EXHIBIT 1**
**Estimated Operating Expense of Maintenance Truck**

| Type of Expenses | Year of Operation | | | | |
|---|---|---|---|---|---|
| | 1 | 2 | 3 | 4 | 5 |
| Gasoline | $ 3,600 | $ 3,600 | $ 3,600 | $ 3,600 | $ 3,600 |
| Repairs and maintenance | 800 | 928 | 1,048 | 1,160 | 1,264 |
| Tires | — | 760 | 760 | 760 | 760 |
| Insurance | 2,400 | 2,400 | 2,400 | 2,400 | 2,400 |
| Registration and taxes | 848 | 720 | 600 | 488 | 384 |
| Depreciation (straight-line method) | 4,500 | 4,500 | 4,500 | 4,500 | 4,500 |
| Total expenses | $12,148 | $12,908 | $12,908 | $12,908 | $12,908 |

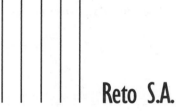

# Reto S.A.

In December 1997, R. E. Torgler was trying to decide whether to add a new line of injection molded plastic products to those already manufactured and distributed by Reto S.A. In order to do so, the firm would have to buy new injection molding equipment; none of the existing equipment could be adapted to perform the necessary operations and Torgler was anxious to retain control of manufacturing. Actually, new injection molding equipment of the type needed had been considered before, but a decision to purchase the equipment had been postponed because the product concept was judged to need additional development. But now the products seemed ready.

Sales of the new product were forecast at SFr. 2,000,000[1] per year, from which a sales commission of 15 percent would be paid to Reto's sales agents. Direct manufacturing costs were budgeted at SFr. 600,000 for materials and SFr. 900,000 for labor, leaving an annual cash flow before taxes of SFr. 200,000. The new equipment would cost SFr. 600,000, delivered and installed, and was expected to have an economic life of 10 years before it would become worthless.

Reto was able to borrow money at 8 percent, although it did not plan to negotiate a loan specifically for the purchase of this equipment.

Copyright © 1997 by the President and Fellows of Harvard College. Harvard Business School case 197-102.

[1] Actual sales were made in several different currencies, but for simplicity here all money measurements are stated in their Swiss franc equivalents. The approximate exchange rate at the time of writing the case was SFr. 1.45 = U.S. $1.00.

## QUESTIONS

1. Ignoring the effect of taxes, what is the internal rate of return (IRR) on the proposed investment? Assume the new equipment would be installed by January 1, 1998, and begin producing on that date.

2. The cost of the equipment can be deducted from annual cash flows before they are subjected to taxation. Assuming that the equipment will last 10 years, that an equal amount of the cost of SFr. 600,000 will be deducted each year, and that the tax rate is expected to be 45 percent, what is the IRR on an after-tax basis?

3. Torgler has stated that Reto should be willing to purchase this machine as long as it yielded a return of 12 percent after taxation. Should he make the investment?

4. To stimulate industrial development, the tax rules allow up to one-third of the cost of any such investment to be deducted from cash flows in the first year after the investment, and up to one-fifth of the remainder of the un-amortized investment amount can be deducted in the second year. Thereafter, annual deductions are computed on a straight-line basis such that no more than the original cost of the equipment is depreciated over its economic life. How, if at all, does this affect the attractiveness of the investment?

5. Reto has learned that investment in working capital (receivables and inventories, less payables) amounts to approximately 15 percent of sales. Will the additional SFr. 300,000 investment for the new line decrease the rate of return on investment to less than the 12 percent criterion Torgler has been using?

6. In late December 1997, Reto purchased the equipment, and the operating results turned out as forecast. A year later, Torgler learned that the manufacturer of the equipment had introduced new models which were more automated. The new equipment sold for SFr. 1,000,000 and would permit labor savings of SFr. 200,000 per year, thus doubling the net operating cash flow on the product. As a result of the technological advance, Torgler expected the one-year-old machine could be sold for only SFr. 200,000 despite the fact that its book value was SFr. 400,000. If Reto buys the new machine and depreciates it using allowed tax depreciation over 10 years, would the investment meet the 12 percent after-tax criterion?

7. If the one-year-old machine had no salvage value at all, would replacing it with the new machine still be desirable?

8. Torgler was loathe to throw away a nearly new machine and thought he might be better off to keep it one more year and then replace it. Would he be better off? How would you go about addressing this issue?

9. During 1998, the rate of inflation remained low, and it was expected that it would average about 4 percent for the year. Torgler wondered how Reto's analysis should reflect this rate of inflation, which he expected might continue for several years. Should an assumed inflation rate change his decision?

# The Super Project

In March 1967, Crosby Sanberg, manager of financial analysis at General Foods Corporation, told a casewriter, "What I learned about incremental analysis at the Business School doesn't always work." He was convinced that under some circumstances sunk costs were relevant to capital project evaluations. He was also concerned that financial and accounting systems did not provide an accurate estimate of incremental costs and revenues, and that this was one of the most difficult problems in measuring the value of capital investment proposals. Sanberg used the Super project[1] as an example.

Super was a new instant dessert, based on a flavored, water-soluble, agglomerated[2] powder. Although four flavors would be offered, it was estimated that chocolate would account for 80% of total sales.

General Foods was organized along product lines in the United States, with foreign operations under a separate division. Major U.S. product divisions included Post, Kool-Aid, Maxwell House, Jell-O, and Birds Eye. Financial data for General Foods are given in **Exhibits 1**, **2**, and **3**.

The $200,000 capital investment project request for Super involved $80,000 for building modifications and $120,000 for machinery and equipment.

*Lecturer Harold E. Wyman prepared this case. This case was made possible by the cooperation of General Foods Corporation.*

Copyright © 1967 by the President and Fellows of Harvard College. Harvard Business School case 112-034.

---

[1]  The name and nature of this new product have been disguised to avoid the disclosure of confidential information.

[2]  Agglomeration is a process by which the processed powder is passed through a steam bath and then dried. This fluffs up the powder particles and increases solubility.

Modifications would be made to an existing building, where Jell-O was manufactured. Since available capacity of a Jell-O agglomerator would be used in
the manufacture of Super, no cost for the key machine was included in the
project. The $120,000 machinery and equipment item represented packaging
machinery.

## THE MARKET

A Nielsen survey indicated that powdered desserts constituted a significant
and growing segment of the total dessert market, as shown in **Table A**. On the
basis of test market experience, General Foods expected Super to capture a 10%
share of the total dessert market. Eighty percent of this expected Super volume
would come from growth in total market share or growth in the powders segment, and 20% would come from erosion of Jell-O sales.

**TABLE A**
**Dessert Market, August–September 1966 Compared with August–September 1965**

|  | | Change from Aug.–Sept. 1965 | |
| --- | --- | --- | --- |
|  | Aug.–Sept. 1966 | Share Points | Volume (%) |
| Jell-O | 19.0% | 3.6 | 40.0 |
| Tasty | 4.0 | 4.0 | (new) |
| Total powders | 25.3 | 7.6 | 62.0 |
| Pie fillings and cake mixes | 32.0 | –3.9 | (no change) |
| Ice cream | 42.7 | –3.4 | 5.0 |
| Total market | 100.0% |  | 13.0 |

## PRODUCTION FACILITIES

Test market volume was packaged on an existing line, inadequate to handle
long-run requirements. Filling and packaging equipment to be purchased had
a capacity of 1.9 million units on a two-shift, five-day workweek basis. This
represented considerable excess capacity, since 1968 requirements were expected to reach 1.1 million units, and the national potential was regarded as 1.6
million units. However, the extra capacity resulted from purchasing standard
equipment, and a more economical alternative did not exist.

## CAPITAL BUDGETING PROCEDURE

The General Foods Accounting and Financial Manual identified four categories of capital investment project proposals: (1) safety and convenience,

(2) quality, (3) increase profit, and (4) other.  Proposal procedures and criteria for accepting projects varied according to category (see **Exhibit 4**).  In discussing these criteria, Sanberg noted that the payback and return guidelines were not used as cut-off measures and added:

> *Payback and return on investment are rarely the only measure of acceptability. Criteria vary significantly by type of project.  A relatively high return might be required for a new product in a new business category.  On the other hand, a much lower return might be acceptable for a new product entry which represents a continuing effort to maintain leadership in an existing business by, for example, filling out the product line.*

Super fell into the third category, as a profit-increasing project.  Estimates of payback and return on funds employed were required for each such project requiring $50,000 or more of new capital funds and expense before taxes.  The payback period was the length of time required for the project to repay the investment from the date the project became operational.  In calculating the repayment period, only incremental income and expenses related to the project were used.

Return on funds employed (ROFE) was calculated by dividing 10-year average profit before taxes by the 10-year average funds employed.  Funds employed included incremental net fixed assets plus or minus related working capital.  Start-up costs and any profits or losses incurred before the project became operational were included in the first profit and loss period in the financial evaluation calculation.

## CAPITAL BUDGETING ATMOSPHERE

A General Foods accounting executive commented on the atmosphere within which capital projects were reviewed:

> *Our problem is not one of capital rationing.  Our problem is to find enough good solid projects to employ capital at an attractive return on investment. Of course, the rate of capital inputs must be balanced against a steady growth in earnings per share. The short-term impact of capital investments is usually an increase in the capital base without an immediate realization of profit potential.  This is particularly true in the case of new products.*
>
> *The food industry should show a continuous growth.  A cyclical industry can afford to let its profits vary.  We want to expand faster than the gross national product.  The key to our capital budgeting is to integrate the plans of our eight divisions into a balanced company plan which meets our overall growth objectives. Most new products show a loss in the first two or three years, but our divisions are big enough to introduce new products without showing a loss.*

## DOCUMENTATION FOR THE SUPER PROJECT

**Exhibits 5** and **6** document the financial evaluation of the Super project. **Exhibit 5** is the summary appropriation request prepared to justify the project to management and to secure management's authorization to expend funds on a capital project. **Exhibit 6** presents the backup detail. Cost of the market test was included as "Other" expense in the first period because a new product had to pay for its test market expense, even though this might be a sunk cost at the time capital funds were requested. The "Adjustments" item represented erosion of the Jell-O market and was calculated by multiplying the volume of erosion times a variable profit contribution. In the preparation of this financial evaluation form, costs of acquiring packaging machinery were included but no cost was attributed to Jell-O agglomerator capacity to be used for the Super project because the General Foods Accounting and Financial Manual specified that capital project requests be prepared on an incremental basis:

> *The incremental concept requires that project requests, profit projections, and funds-employed statements include only items of income and expense and investment in assets which will be realized, incurred, or made directly as a result of, or are attributed to, the new project.*

## EXCHANGE OF MEMOS ON THE SUPER PROJECT

After receiving the paperwork on the Super project, Sanberg studied the situation and wrote a memorandum arguing that the incremental approach advocated by the manual should not be applied to the Super project. His superior agreed with the memorandum and forwarded it to the corporate controller with the cover note contained in **Appendix A**. The controller's reply is given in **Appendix B**.

**EXHIBIT 1**
**Consolidated Balance Sheet of General Foods Corporation,**
**Fiscal Year Ended April 1, 1967 ($ millions)**

**Assets**

| | |
|---|---:|
| Cash | $ 20 |
| Marketable securities | 89 |
| Receivables | 180 |
| Inventories | 261 |
| Prepaid expenses | 14 |
| Current assets | 564 |
| Land, buildings, equipment (at cost, less depreciation) | 332 |
| Long-term receivables and sundry assets | 7 |
| Goodwill | 26 |
| Total | $929 |

**Liabilities and Stockholders' Equity**

| | |
|---|---:|
| Notes payable | $ 22 |
| Accounts payable | 86 |
| Accrued liabilities | 73 |
| Accrued income taxes | 57 |
| Current liabilities | 238 |
| Long-term notes | 39 |
| 3³⁄₈% debentures | 22 |
| Other noncurrent liabilities | 10 |
| Deferred investment tax credit | 9 |
| Stockholders' equity | |
| Common stock issued | 164 |
| Retained earnings | 449 |
| Common stock held in treasury, at cost | (2) |
| Stockholders' equity | 691 |
| Total | $929 |
| Common stock—shares outstanding at year-end (millions) | 25.127 |

**EXHIBIT 2**
**Common Stock Prices of General Foods Corporation, 1958–1967**

| Year | Low | High |
|------|------|------|
| 1958 | $24 | $39 |
| 1959 | 37 1/8 | 53 7/8 |
| 1960 | 49 1/8 | 75 1/2 |
| 1961 | 68 5/8 | 107 |
| 1962 | 57 | 96 |
| 1963 | 77 5/8 | 90 1/2 |
| 1964 | 78 1/4 | 93 1/4 |
| 1965 | 77 1/2 | 89 7/8 |
| 1966 | 62 | 83 |
| 1967 | 65 1/4 | 81 |

**EXHIBIT 3**
**Summary of Statistical Data of General Foods Corporation,**
**Fiscal Years 1958–1967 ($ millions, except assets per employee and figures on a share basis)**

| | 1958 | 1959 | 1960 | 1961 | 1962 | 1963 | 1964 | 1965 | 1966 | 1967 |
|---|---|---|---|---|---|---|---|---|---|---|
| **Income Statement** | | | | | | | | | | |
| Sales to customers (net) | $1,009 | $1,053 | $1,087 | $1,160 | $1,189 | $1,216 | $1,338 | $1,478 | $1,555 | $1,652 |
| Cost of sales | 724 | 734 | 725 | 764 | 769 | 769 | 838 | 937 | 965 | 1,012 |
| Marketing, administrative, and general expenses | 181 | 205 | 236 | 261 | 267 | 274 | 322 | 362 | 406 | 449 |
| Earnings before income taxes | 105 | 115 | 130 | 138 | 156 | 170 | 179 | 177 | 185 | 193 |
| Taxes on income | 57 | 61 | 69 | 71 | 84 | 91 | 95 | 91 | 91 | 94 |
| Net earnings | $ 48 | $ 54 | $ 61 | $ 67 | $ 72 | $ 79 | $ 84 | $ 86 | $ 94 | $ 99 |
| Dividends on common shares | 24 | 28 | 32 | 35 | 40 | 45 | 50 | 50 | 53 | 55 |
| Retain earnings—current year | 24 | 26 | 29 | 32 | 32 | 34 | 34 | 36 | 41 | 44 |
| Net earnings per common share[a] | $ 1.99 | $ 2.21 | $ 2.48 | $ 2.69 | $ 2.90 | $ 3.14 | $ 3.33 | $ 3.44 | $3.73 | $ 3.93 |
| Dividends per common share[a] | 1.00 | 1.15 | 1.30 | 1.40 | 1.60 | 1.80 | 2.00 | 2.00 | 2.10 | 2.20 |
| **Assets, Liabilities, and Stockholders' Equity** | | | | | | | | | | |
| Inventories | 169 | 149 | 154 | 189 | 183 | 205 | 256 | 214 | 261 | 261 |
| Other current assets | 144 | 180 | 200 | 171 | 204 | 206 | 180 | 230 | 266 | 303 |
| Current liabilities | 107 | 107 | 126 | 123 | 142 | 162 | 202 | 173 | 219 | 238 |
| Working capital | 206 | 222 | 230 | 237 | 245 | 249 | 234 | 271 | 308 | 326 |
| Land, buildings, equipment, gross | 203 | 221 | 247 | 289 | 328 | 375 | 436 | 477 | 517 | 569 |
| Land, buildings, equipment, net | 125 | 132 | 148 | 173 | 193 | 233 | 264 | 283 | 308 | 332 |
| Long-term debt | 49 | 44 | 40 | 37 | 35 | 34 | 23 | 37 | 54 | 61 |
| Stockholders' equity | 287 | 315 | 347 | 384 | 419 | 454 | 490 | 527 | 569 | 611 |
| Stockholders' equity per common share[a] | 11.78 | 12.87 | 14.07 | 15.46 | 16.80 | 18.17 | 19.53 | 20.99 | 22.64 | 24.32 |
| **Capital Program** | | | | | | | | | | |
| Capital additions | 28 | 24 | 35 | 40 | 42 | 57 | 70 | 54 | 65 | 59 |
| Depreciation | 11 | 14 | 15 | 18 | 21 | 24 | 26 | 29 | 32 | 34 |
| **Employment Data** | | | | | | | | | | |
| Wages, salaries, and benefits | $ 128 | $ 138 | $ 147 | $ 162 | $ 171 | $ 180 | $ 195 | $ 204 | $ 218 | $ 237 |
| Number of employees (in thousands) | 21 | 22 | 22 | 25 | 28 | 28 | 30 | 30 | 30 | 32 |
| Assets per employee ($ thousands) | $ 21 | $ 22 | $ 23 | $ 22 | $ 22 | $ 23 | $ 24 | $ 25 | $ 29 | $ 29 |

[a] Per share figures calculated on shares outstanding at year end and adjusted for 2-for-1 stock split in August 1960.

**EXHIBIT 4**
**Criteria for Evaluating Projects by General Foods Corporation**

The basic criteria to be applied in evaluating projects within each of the classifications are set forth in the following schedule:

**Purpose of Project**
**a.    Safety and Convenience:**
1.    Projects required for reasons of safety, sanitation, health, public convenience, or other overriding reason with no reasonable alternatives.  Examples:  sprinkler systems, elevators, fire escapes, smoke control, waste disposal, treatment of water pollution, etc.
2.    Additional nonproductive space requirements for which there are no financial criteria.  Examples:  office space, laboratories, service areas (kitchens, restrooms, etc.).

**b.    Quality:**
Projects designed primarily to improve quality.

**c.    Increase Profit:**
1.    Projects that are justified primarily by reduced costs.
2.    Projects that are designed primarily to increase production capacity for an existing product.
3.    Projects designed to provide facilities to manufacture and distribute a new product or product line.

**d.    Other:**
This category includes projects which by definition are excluded from the three preceding categories. Examples:  standby facilities intended to ensure uninterrupted production, additional equipment not expected to improve profits or product quality and not required for reasons of safety and convenience, equipment to satisfy marketing requirements, etc.

**Payback and ROFE Criteria**
Payback—return on funds projections not required but the request must clearly demonstrate the *immediate* need for the project and the lack or inadequacy of alternative solutions.

Requests for nonproductive facilities, such as warehouses, laboratories, and offices, should indicate the advantages of owning rather than leasing, unless no possibility to lease exists. In those cases where the company owns a group of integrated facilities and wherein the introduction of rented or leased properties might complicate the long-range planning or development of the area, owning rather than leasing is recommended.  If the project is designed to improve customer service (such as market-centered warehouses) this factor is to be noted on the project request.

If Payback and ROFE cannot be computed, it must be clearly demonstrated that the improvement is identifiable and desirable.

Projects with a payback period *up to 10 years* and a 10-year return on funds as *low as 20%* PBT are considered worthy of consideration, provided (1) the end product involved is believed to be a reasonably permanent part of our line or (2) the facilities involved are so flexible that they may be usable for successor products.

**EXHIBIT 4 (continued)**

Projects for a proven product where the risk of mortality is small, such as coffee, Jell-O Gelatin, and cereals, should assure a payback in *no more than 10 years* and 10-year PBT return on funds of *no less* than 20%.

Because of the greater risk involved, such projects should show a high potential return on funds (not less than a 10-year PBT return of 40%). Payback period, however, might be as much as *10 years* because of losses incurred during the market development period.[a]

While standards of return may be difficult to set, some calculations of financial benefits should be made where possible.

---

Source:  The General Foods Accounting and Financial Manual

[a] These criteria apply to the United States and Canada only. Profit-increasing capital projects in other areas in categories c1 and c2 should offer at least a 10-year PBT return of 24% to compensate for the greater risk involved. Likewise, foreign operation projects in the c3 category should offer a 10-year PBT return of at least 48%.

## EXHIBIT 5
## Capital Project Request Form of General Foods Corporation

NY1292-A 12-63
PTD. In U.S.A.
"Super" Facilities                    66-42
*Project Title & Number*

Jell-O Division      —      St. Louis
*Division & Location*

### Project Description
To provide facilities for
production of Super,
chocolate dessert. This
project included finishing
a packing room in
addition to filling and
packaging equipment.

December 23, 1966
*Date*

Expansion-New Product
*Purpose*

New Request  [X]       Supplement ☐   [X] A  ☐ R

| Summary of Investment | |
| --- | --- |
| New Capital Funds Required | $200M |
| Expense Before Taxes | — |
| Less: Trade-in or Salvage, If Any | — |
| Total This Request | $200M |
| Previously Appropriated | — |
| Total Project Cost | $200M |

| Financial Justification | |
| --- | --- |
| ROFE (PBT Basis) - 10 Yr. Average | 62.9 |
| Payback Period    April, F'68    Feb, F'75<br>From    To | 6.83 Yrs. |
| Not Required | ☐ |
| * Based on Total Project Cost and Working Fund of | $510M |

| Estimated Expenditure Rate | |
| --- | --- |
| Quarter Ending Mar.  F19  67 | $160M |
| Quarter Ending June  F19  68 | 40M |
| Quarter Ending       F19 | |
| Quarter Ending       F19 | |
| Remainder | |

| Other Information | |
| --- | --- |
| Major ☐    Specific Ordinary ☐    Blanket ☐ | |
| Included in Annual program   Yes ☐    No ☐ | |
| Percent of Engineering Completed | 80% |
| Estimated Start-Up Cost | $15M |
| Estimated Start-Up Date | April |

**Level of Approval Required**

☐ Board      ☐ Chairman      ☐ Exec. V.P.      ☐ Gen. Mgr.

| For Division Use—Signatures | |
| --- | --- |
| Name & Title | Date |
| | |
| | |
| | |
| | |
| | |

| Signatures | | Date |
| --- | --- | --- |
| Director Corp. Eng. | | |
| Director B&A | | |
| General Manager | | |
| Exec. Vice President | | |
| President | | |
| Chairman | | |

**EXHIBIT 5 (continued)**
## Instructions for Capital Project Request Form NY 1292-A

The purpose of this form is to secure management's authorization to commit or expend funds on a capital project. Refer to Accounting and Financial Manual Statement No. 19 for information regarding projects to which this form applies.

**New Request—Supplement**   Check the appropriate box.

**Purpose**   Identify the primary purpose of the project in accordance with the classifications established in Accounting and Financial Statement No. 19, i.e., Sanitation, Health and Public Convenience, Nonproductive Space, Safety, Quality, Reduce Cost, Expansion—Existing Products, Expansion—New Products, Other (specify). Also indicate in the appropriate box whether the equipment represents an addition or a replacement.

**Project Description**   Comments should be in sufficient detail to enable Corporate Management to appraise the benefits of the project. Where necessary, supplemental data should be attached to provide complete background for project evaluation.

### Summary of Investment

**New Capital Funds Required**   Show gross cost of assets to be acquired.

**Expense Before Taxes**   Show incremental expense resulting from project.

**Trade-in or Salvage**   Show the amount expected to be realized on trade-in or sale of a replaced asset.

**Previously Appropriated**   When requesting a supplement to an approved project, show the amount previously appropriated even though authorization was given in a prior year.

### Financial Justification

**ROFE**   Show the return on funds employed (PBT basis) as calculated on Financial Evaluation Form NY 1292-C or 1292-F. The appropriate Financial Evaluation Form is to be attached to this form.

**Not Required**   Where financial benefits are not applicable or required or are not expected, check the box provided. The nonfinancial benefits should be explained in the comments.

In the space provided, show the sum of the Total Project Cost plus Total Working Funds (line 20, Form NY 1292-C or line 5, Form NY 1292-F) in either of the first three periods, whichever is higher.

**Estimated Expenditure Rate**   Expenditures are to be reported in accordance with accounting treatment of the asset and related expense portion of the project. Insert estimated quarterly expenditures beginning with the quarter in which the first expenditure will be made. The balance of authorized funds unspent after the fourth quarter should be reported in total.

**EXHIBIT 5 (continued)**
**Instructions for Capital Project Request Form NY 1292-A (continued)**

**Other Information**    Check whether the project is major, specific ordinary, or blanket, and whether or not the project was included in the annual program. Show estimated percentage of engineering completed; this is intended to give management an indication of the degree of reliability of the funds requested. Indicate the estimated start-up costs as shown on line 32 of Financial Evaluation Form NY 1292-C. Insert anticipated start-up date for the project; if start-up is to be staggered, explain in the comments.

**Level of Approval Required**    Check the appropriate box.

---

Source:  General Foods

**EXHIBIT 6**
**Financial Evaluation Form of General Foods Corporation ($ in thousands)**

NY 1292-C  10-64
PTD. In U.S.A.

Division: Jell-O  Location: St. Louis  Project Title: The Super Project  Project No.: 67–89  Supplement No. _____  Date _____

| Project Request Detail | 1st Per. | 2nd Per. | 3rd Per. | 4th Per. | 5th Per. |
|---|---|---|---|---|---|
| 1. Land | $ | | | | |
| 2. Buildings | 80 | | | | |
| 3. Machinery & Equipment | 120 | | | | |
| 4. Engineering | | | | | |
| 5. Other (Explain) | | | | | |
| 6. Expense Portion (Before Tax) | | | | | |
| 7. Subtotal | $200 | | | | |
| 8. Less: Salvage Value (Old Asset) | | | | | |
| 9. Total Project Cost* | $200 | | | | |
| 10. Less: Taxes on Exp. Portion | | | | | |
| 11. Net Project Cost | $200 | | | | |

*Same as Project Request

**Return on New Funds Employed—10-Yr. Avg.**

| | PAT (C ÷ A) | PBT (B ÷ A) |
|---|---|---|
| A—New Funds Employed (Line 21) | $380 | $380 |
| B—Profit Before Taxes (Line 35) | | $239 |
| C—Net Profit (Line 37) | $115 | |
| D—Calculated Return | 30.2% | 62.0% |

**Payback Years From Operational Date**

| | |
|---|---|
| Part Year Calculation for First Period | —Yrs. |
| Number of Full Years to Payback | 6.00 Yrs. |
| Part Year Calculation for Last Period | 0.83 Yrs. |
| Total Years to Payback | 6.83 Yrs. |

| Funds Employed | 1st Per. F 68 | 2nd Per. F 69 | 3rd Per. F 70 | 4th Per. F 71 | 5th Per. F 72 | 6th Per. F 73 | 7th Per. F 74 | 8th Per. F 75 | 9th Per. F 76 | 10th Per. F 77 | 11th Per. — | 10-Yr. Avg. |
|---|---|---|---|---|---|---|---|---|---|---|---|---|
| 12. Net Project Cost (Line 11) | $200 | 200 | 200 | 200 | 200 | 200 | 200 | 200 | 200 | 200 | | |
| 13. Deduct Depreciation (Cum.) | 19 | 37 | 54 | 70 | 85 | 98 | 110 | 121 | 131 | 140 | | |
| 14. Capital Funds Employed | $181 | 163 | 146 | 130 | 115 | 102 | 90 | 79 | 69 | 60 | | 113 |
| 15. Cash | 124 | 134 | 142 | 151 | 160 | 160 | 169 | 169 | 178 | 178 | | 157 |
| 16. Receivables | 207 | 222 | 237 | 251 | 266 | 266 | 281 | 281 | 296 | 296 | | 260 |
| 17. Inventories | | | | | | | | | | | | |
| 18. Prepaid & Deferred Exp. | | | | | | | | | | | | |
| 19. Less Current Liabilities | (2) | (82) | (108) | (138) | (185) | (184) | (195) | (195) | (207) | (207) | | (150) |
| 20. Total Working Funds (15 Thru 19) | 329 | 274 | 271 | 264 | 241 | 242 | 255 | 255 | 267 | 267 | | 267 |
| 21. Total New Funds Employed (14 + 20) | $510 | 437 | 417 | 394 | 356 | 344 | 345 | 334 | 336 | 327 | | 380 |

(continued)

**EXHIBIT 6 (continued)**
**Financial Evaluation Form of General Foods Corporation ($ in thousands) (continued)**

| Profit and Loss | 1st Per. F 68 | 2nd Per. F 69 | 3rd Per. F 70 | 4th Per. F 71 | 5th Per. F 72 | 6th Per. F 73 | 7th Per. F 74 | 8th Per. F 75 | 9th Per. F 76 | 10th Per. F 77 | 11th Per. — | 10-Yr. Avg. |
|---|---|---|---|---|---|---|---|---|---|---|---|---|
| 22. Unit Volume (in thousands) | 1100 | 1200 | 1300 | 1400 | 1500 | 1500 | 1600 | 1600 | 1700 | 1700 | | 1460 |
| 23. Gross Sales | $2200 | 2400 | 2600 | 2800 | 3000 | 3000 | 3200 | 3200 | 3400 | 3400 | | 2920 |
| 24. Deductions | 88 | 96 | 104 | 112 | 120 | 120 | 128 | 128 | 136 | 136 | | 117 |
| 25. Net Sales | 2112 | 2304 | 2496 | 2688 | 2880 | 2880 | 3072 | 3072 | 3264 | 3264 | | 2803 |
| 26. Cost of Goods Sold | 1100 | 1200 | 1300 | 1400 | 1500 | 1500 | 1600 | 1600 | 1700 | 1700 | | 1460 |
| 27. Gross Profit | 1012 | 1104 | 1196 | 1288 | 1380 | 1380 | 1472 | 1472 | 1564 | 1564 | | 1343 |
| Gross Profit % Net Sales | | | | | | | | | | | | |
| 28. Advertising Expense | 1100 | 1050 | 1000 | 900 | 700 | 700 | 730 | 730 | 750 | 750 | | 841 |
| 29. Selling Expense | | | | | | | | | | | | |
| 30. Gen. and Admin. Cost | | | | | | | | | | | | |
| 31. Research Expense | | | | | | | | | | | | |
| 32. Start-Up Costs | 15 | | | | | | | | | | | 2 |
| 33. Other (Explain) Test Mkt. | 360 | | | | | | | | | | | 36 |
| 34. Adjustments (Explain) Erosion | 180 | 200 | 210 | 220 | 230 | 230 | 240 | 240 | 250 | 250 | | 225 |
| 35. Profit Before Taxes | $(643) | (146) | (14) | 168 | 450 | 450 | 502 | 502 | 564 | 564 | | 239 |
| 36. Taxes | (334) | (76) | (7) | 87 | 234 | 234 | 261 | 261 | 293 | 293 | | 125 |
| 36A. Add: Investment Credit | (1) | (1) | (1) | (1) | (1) | (1) | (1) | (1) | — | — | | (1) |
| 37. Net Profit | (308) | (69) | (6) | 82 | 217 | 217 | 242 | 242 | 271 | 271 | | 115 |
| 38. Cumulative Net Profit | $(308) | (377) | (383) | (301) | (84) | 133 | 375 | 617 | 888 | 1159 | | |
| 39. New Funds to Repay (21 Less 38) | $818 | 814 | 800 | 695 | 440 | 211 | (30) | (283) | (552) | (832) | | |

See Accounting & Financial Manual Policy No. 19 for Instructions.

**EXHIBIT 6 (continued)**
## Instructions for Preparation of Form NY 1292-C Financial Evaluation

This form is to be submitted to Corporate Budget and Analysis with each profit-increasing capital project request requiring $50,000 or more of capital funds and expense before taxes.

Note that the 10-year term has been divided into 11 periods. The first period is to end on March 31 following the operational date of the project, and the P&L projection may thereby encompass any number of months from 1 to 12, e.g., if the project becomes operational on November 1, 1964, the first period for P&L purposes would be 5 months (November 1, 1964 through March 31, 1965). The next nine periods would be fiscal years (F '66, F '67, etc.) and the 11th period would be 7 months (April 1, 1974 through October 30, 1974). This has been done primarily to facilitate reporting of projected and actual P&L data by providing for fiscal years. See categorized instructions below for more specific details.

**Project Request Detail**   *Lines 1 through 11* show the breakdown of the Net Project Cost to be used in the financial evaluation. *Line 8* is to show the amount expected to be realized on trade-in or sale of a replaced asset. *Line 9* should be the same as the "Total Project Cost" shown on Form NY 1292-A, Capital Project Request. Space has been provided for capital expenditures related to this project which are projected to take place subsequent to the first period. Indicate in such space the additional cost only; do not accumulate them.

## Funds Employed

**Capital Funds Employed**   *Line 12* will show the net project cost appearing on Line 11 as a constant for the first 10 periods except in any period in which additional expenditures are incurred; in that event show the accumulated amount of Line 11 in such period and in all future periods.

Deduct cumulative depreciation on *Line 13*. Depreciation is to be computed on an incremental basis, i.e., the net increase in depreciation over present depreciation on assets being replaced. In the first period depreciation will be computed at one-half of the first year's annual rate; no depreciation is to be taken in the 11th period. Depreciation rates are to be the same as those used for accounting purposes. *Exception:* When the depreciation rate used for accounting purposes differs materially from the rate for tax purposes, the higher rate should be used. A variation will be considered material when the first full year's depreciation on a book basis varies 20% or more from the first full year's depreciation on a tax basis.

The 10-year average of Capital Funds Employed shall be computed by adding Line 14 in each of the first 10 periods and then dividing the total by 10.

**Total Working Funds**   Refer to Financial Policy No. 21 as a guide in computing new working fund requirements. Items which are not on a formula basis and which are normally computed on a five-quarter average shall be handled proportionately in the first period. For example, since the period involved may be less than 12 months, the average would be computed on the number of quarters involved. Generally, the balances should be approximately the same as they would be if the first period were a full year.

**EXHIBIT 6 (continued)**

Cash, based on a formula which theorizes a two weeks' supply (2/52nds), should follow the same theory. If the first period is for three months, two-thirteenths (2/13th) should be used; if it is for five months, two-twenty-firsts (2/21sts) should be used, and so forth.

Current liabilities are to include one-half of the tax expense as the tax liability. The 10-year averages of Working Funds shall be computed by adding each line across or the first 10 periods and then dividing each total by 10.

## Profit and Loss Projection

**P&L Categories (Lines 22 through 37)**   Reflect only the incremental amounts which will result from the proposed project; exclude all allocated charges. Include the P&L results expected in the individual periods comprising the first 10 years of the life of the project. Refer to the second paragraph of these instructions regarding the fractional years' calculations during the first and eleventh periods.

Any loss or gain on the sale of a replaced asset (see Line 8) shall be included on Line 33.

As indicated in the caption Capital Funds Employed, no depreciation is to be taken in the eleventh period.

The 10-year averages of the P&L items shall be computed by adding each line across for the 11 periods (10 full years from the operational date) and dividing the total by 10.

**Adjustments (Line 34)**   Show the adjustment necessary, on a before-tax basis, to indicate any adverse or favorable incremental effect the proposed project will have on any other products currently being produced by the corporation.

**Investment Credit**   To be included on Line 36-A. The Investment Credit will be spread over 8 years, or fractions thereof, as an addition to PAT.

**Return on New Funds Employed**   Ten-year average returns are to be calculated for PAT (projects requiring Board approval only) and PBT. The PAT return is calculated by dividing average PAT (Line 37) by average new funds employed (Line 21); the PBT return is derived by dividing average PBT (Line 35) by average new funds employed (Line 21).

## Payback Years from Operational Date

**Part Year Calculation for First Period**   Divide number of months in the first period by 12. If five months are involved, the calculation is 5/12 = 0.4 years.

**Number of Full Years to Payback**   Determined by the last period, excluding the first period, in which an amount is shown on Line 39.

**Part Year Calculation for Last Period**   Divide amount still to be repaid at the end of the last full period (Line 39) by net profit plus the *annual* depreciation in the following year when payback is completed.

**Total Years to Payback**   Sum of full and part years.

## APPENDIX A
## Memos to Controller

To:　　　J. C. Kresslin, Corporate Controller

From:　　J. E. Hooting, Director, Corporate Budgets and Analysis

March 2, 1967

**Super Project**

At the time we reviewed the Super project, I indicated to you that the return on investment looked significantly different if an allocation of the agglomerator and building, originally justified as a Jell-O project, were included in the Super investment. The pro rata allocation of these facilities, based on the share of capacity used, triples the initial gross investment in Super facilities from $200,000 to about $672,000.

I am forwarding a memorandum from Crosby Sanberg summarizing the results of three analyses evaluating the project on an:

I.　　Incremental basis
II.　　Facilities-used basis
III.　　Fully allocated facilities and costs basis

Crosby has calculated a 10-year average ROFE using these techniques. Please read Crosby's memo before continuing with my note.

*　*　*　*　*

Crosby concludes that the fully allocated basis, or some variation of it, is necessary to understand the long-range potential of the project.

I agree. We launch a new project because of its potential to increase our sales and earning power for many years into the future. We must be mindful of short-term consequences, as indicated by an incremental analysis, but we must also have a long-range frame of reference if we are to really understand what we are committing ourselves to. This long-range frame of reference is best approximated by looking at fully allocated investment and "accounted" profits, which recognize fully allocated costs because, in fact, over the long run all costs are variable unless some major change occurs in the structure of the business.

Our current GF preoccupation with only the incremental costs and investment causes some real anomalies that confuse our decision making. Super is a good example. On an incremental basis the project looks particularly attractive because, by using a share of the excess capacity built on the coattails of the lucrative Jell-O project, the incremental investment in Super is low. If the excess Jell-O capacity did not exist, would the project be any less attractive? In the short term, perhaps yes because it would entail higher initial risk, but in the long term it is not a better project just because it fits a facility that is temporarily unused.

Looking at this point from a different angle, if the project exceeded our investment hurdle rate on a short-term basis but fell below it on a long-term basis (and Super comes close to doing this), should we reject the project? I say yes because over the long run, as "fixed" costs become variable and as we have to commit new capital to support the business, the continuing ROFE will go under water.

In sum, we have to look at new project proposals from both the long-term and the short-term point of view. We plan to refine our techniques of using a fully allocated basis as a long-term point of reference and will hammer out a policy recommendation for your consideration. We would appreciate any comments you may have.

**APPENDIX A (continued)**

To:     J. E. Hooting, Director, Corporate Budgets and Analysis

From:     C. Sanberg, Manager, Financial Analysis

February 17, 1967

**Super Project: A Case Example of Investment Evaluation Techniques**
This will review the merits of alternative techniques of evaluating capital investment decisions using the Super project as an example. The purpose of the review is to provide an illustration of the problems and limitations inherent in using incremental ROFE and payback and thereby provide a rationale for adopting new techniques.

**Alternative Techniques**
The alternative techniques to be reviewed are differentiated by the level of revenue and investment charged to the Super project in figuring a payback and ROFE, starting with incremental revenues and investment. Data related to the alternative techniques outlined below are summarized [at the end of this memo].

## Alternative I. Incremental Basis

**Method**     The Super project as originally evaluated considered only incremental revenue and investment, which could be directly identified with the decision to produce Super. Incremental fixed capital ($200M) basically included packaging equipment.

**Result**     On this basis the project paid back in 7 years with a ROFE of 63%.

**Discussion**     Although it is General Foods' current policy to evaluate capital projects on an incremental basis, this technique does not apply to the Super project. The reason is that Super extensively utilizes existing facilities, which are readily adaptable to known future alternative uses.

Super should be charged with the "opportunity loss" of agglomerating capacity and building space. Because of Super the opportunity is lost to use a portion of agglomerating capacity for Jell-O and other products that could potentially be agglomerated. In addition, the opportunity is lost to use the building space for existing or new product volume expansion. To the extent there is an opportunity loss of existing facilities, new facilities must be built to accommodate future expansion. In other words, because the business is expanding Super utilizes facilities that are adaptable to predictable alternative uses.

## Alternative II. Facilities-Used Basis

**Method**     Recognizing that Super will use half of an existing agglomerator and two-thirds of an existing building, which were justified earlier in the Jell-O project, we added Super's pro rata share of these facilities ($453M) to the incremental capital. Overhead costs directly related to these existing facilities were also subtracted from incremental revenue on a shared basis.

**Result**     ROFE 34%

## APPENDIX A (continued)

**Discussion**    Although the existing facilities utilized by Super are not incremental to this project, they are relevant to the evaluation of the project because potentially they can be put to alternative uses. Despite a high return on an incremental basis, if the ROFE on a project was unattractive after consideration of the shared use of existing facilities, the project would be questionable. Under these circumstances, we might look for a more profitable product for the facilities.

In summary, the facilities-used basis is a useful way of putting various projects on a common ground for purposes of *relative* evaluation. One product using existing capacity should not necessarily be judged to be more attractive than another practically identical product which necessitates an investment in additional facilities.

### Alternative III.  Fully Allocated Basis

**Method**    Further recognizing that individual decisions to expand inevitably add to a higher overhead base, we increased the costs and investment base developed in Alternative II by a provision for overhead expenses and overhead capital. These increases were made in year five of the 10-year evaluation period, on the theory that at this point a number of decisions would result in more fixed costs and facilities. Overhead expenses included manufacturing costs, plus selling and general and administrative costs on a per-unit basis equivalent to Jell-O. Overhead capital included a share of the distribution system assets ($40M).

**Result**    ROFE 25%

**Discussion**    Charging Super with an overhead burden recognizes that overhead costs in the long run increase in proportion to the level of business activity, even though decisions to spend more overhead dollars are made separately from decisions to increase volume and provide the incremental facilities to support the higher volume level. To illustrate, the Division-F1968 Financial Plan budgets about a 75% increase in headquarters' overhead spending in F1968 over F1964. A contributing factor was the decision to increase the sales force by 50% to meet the demands of a growing and increasingly complex business. To further illustrate, about half the capital projects in the F1968 three-year Financial Plan are in the "non-payback" category. This group of projects comprised largely "overhead facilities" (warehouses, utilities, etc.), which are not directly related to the manufacture of products but are necessary components of the total business activity as a result of the cumulative effect of many decisions taken in the past.

The Super project is a significant decision which will most likely add to more overhead dollars as illustrated above. Super volume doubles the powdered dessert business category; it increases the Division businesses by 10%. Furthermore, Super requires a new production technology: agglomeration and packaging on a high-speed line.

## APPENDIX A (continued)

### Conclusions

1. The incremental basis for evaluating a project is an inadequate measure of a project's worth when existing facilities with a known future use will be utilized extensively.
2. A fully allocated basis of reviewing major new product proposals recognizes that overhead increases in proportion to the size and complexity of the business and provides the best long-range projection of the financial consequences.

### Alternative Evaluations of Super Project ($ in thousands)

|  | I.<br>Incremental<br>Basis | II.<br>Facilities-Used<br>Basis | III.<br>Fully<br>Allocated |
|---|---|---|---|
| **Investment** |  |  |  |
| Working capital | $267 | $267 | $267 |
| Fixed capital |  |  |  |
| Gross | 200 | 653 | 672 |
| Net | 113 | 358 | 367 |
| **Total net investment** | **380** | **625** | **634** |
| **Profit before taxes**[a] | **239** | **211** | **157** |
| **ROFE** | **63%** | **34%** | **25%** |

**Jell-O project**

| | |
|---|---|
| Building | $200 × 2/3 = $133 |
| Agglomerator | 640 × 1/2 = 320 |
| | $453 |

Note: Figures based on 10-year averages.

[a] Assumes 20% of Super volume will replace existing Jell-O business.

### APPENDIX B
### Controller's Reply

To:        Mr. J. E. Hooting, Director, Corporate Budgets and Analysis

From:    Mr. J. C. Kresslin, Corporate Controller

Subject:   Super Project

March 7, 1967

On March 2 you sent me a note describing Crosby Sanberg's and your thoughts about evaluating the Super project. In this memo you suggest that the project should be appraised on the basis of fully allocated facilities and production costs.

In order to continue the dialogue, I am raising a couple of questions below.

It seems to me that in a situation such as you describe for Super, the real question is a *management decision* as to whether to go ahead with the Super project or not go ahead. Or to put it another way, are we better off in the aggregate if we use half the agglomerator and two-thirds of an existing building for Super, or are we not, on the basis of our current knowledge?

It might be assumed that, for example, half of the agglomerator is being used and half is not and that a minimum economical size agglomerator was necessary for Jell-O and, consequently, should be justified by the Jell-O project itself. If we find a way to utilize it sooner by producing Super on it, aren't we better off in the aggregate, and the different ROFE figure for the Super project by itself becomes somewhat irrelevant? A similar point of view might be applied to the portion of the building. Or if we charge the Super project with half an agglomerator and two-thirds of an existing building, should we then go back and relieve the Jell-O projects of these costs in evaluating the management's original proposal?

To put it another way, since we are faced with making decisions at a certain time on the basis of what we then know, I see very little value in looking at the Super project all by itself. Better we should look at the total situation before and after to see how we fare.

As to allocated production costs, the point is not so clear. Undoubtedly, over the long haul, the selling prices will need to be determined on the basis of a satisfactory margin over fully allocated costs. Perhaps this should be an additional requirement in the course of evaluating capital projects, since we seem to have been surprised at the low margins for "Tasty" after allocating all costs to the product.

I look forward to discussing this subject with you and with Crosby at some length.

# Part Seven
## Measurements for Management Control

# Control in an Age of Empowerment

**A** fundamental problem facing managers in the 1990s is how to exercise adequate control in organizations that demand flexibility, innovation, and creativity. Competitive businesses with demanding and informed customers must rely on employee initiative to seek out opportunities and respond to customers' needs. But pursuing some opportunities can expose businesses to excessive risk or invite behaviors that can damage a company's integrity.

Consider the spate of management control failures that have made headlines in the past several years: Kidder, Peabody & Company lost $350 million when a trader allegedly booked fictitious profits; Sears, Roebuck and Company took a $60 million charge against earnings after admitting that it recommended unnecessary repairs to customers in its automobile service business; Standard Chartered Bank was banned from trading on the Hong Kong stock market after being implicated in an improper share support scheme. The list goes on. In each case, employees broke through existing control mechanisms and jeopardized the franchise of the business. The cost to the companies—in damaged reputations, fines, business losses, missed opportunities, and diversion of management attention to deal with the crises—was enormous.

How do senior managers protect their companies from control failures when empowered employees are encouraged to redefine how they go about doing their jobs? How do managers ensure that subordinates with an entrepreneurial flair do not put the well-being of the business at risk? One solution is to go back to the fundamentals of control developed in the 1950s and 1960s for machinelike bureaucracies. In that era, managers exercised control by telling people how to do their jobs and monitoring them with constant surveillance to guard against surprises. Although this approach sounds anachronistic

---

*Robert Simons authored this article. Reprinted by permission from* Harvard Business Review, *March-April 1995, 80-88. Reprint 95211.*

Copyright © 1995 by the President and Fellows of Harvard College.

for modern businesses, it is still effective when standardization is critical for efficiency and yield, such as on an assembly line; when the risk of theft of valuable assets is high, such as in a casino; or when quality and safety are essential to product performance, such as at a nuclear power plant.

However, in most organizations operating in dynamic and highly competitive markets, managers cannot spend all their time and effort making sure that everyone is doing what is expected. Nor is it realistic to think that managers can achieve control by simply hiring good people, aligning incentives, and hoping for the best. Instead, today's managers must encourage employees to initiate process improvements and new ways of responding to customers' needs—but in a controlled way.

Fortunately, the tools to reconcile the conflict between creativity and control are at hand. Most managers tend to define control narrowly—as measuring progress against plans to guarantee the predictable achievement of goals. Such diagnostic control systems are, however, only one ingredient of control. Three other levers are equally important in today's business environment: beliefs systems, boundary systems, and interactive control systems.

Each of the four control levers has a distinct purpose for managers attempting to harness the creativity of employees. Diagnostic control systems allow managers to ensure that important goals are being achieved efficiently and effectively. Beliefs systems empower individuals and encourage them to search for new opportunities. They communicate core values and inspire all participants to commit to the organization's purpose. Boundary systems establish the rules of the game and identify actions and pitfalls that employees must avoid. Interactive control systems enable top-level managers to focus on strategic uncertainties, to learn about threats and opportunities as competitive conditions change, and to respond proactively.

## DIAGNOSTIC CONTROL SYSTEMS

Diagnostic control systems work like the dials on the control panel of an airplane cockpit, enabling the pilot to scan for signs of abnormal functioning and to keep critical performance variables within preset limits. Most businesses have come to rely on diagnostic control systems to help managers track the progress of individuals, departments, or production facilities toward strategically important goals. Managers use these systems to monitor goals and profitability and to measure progress toward targets such as revenue growth and market share. Periodically, managers measure the outputs and compare them with preset standards of performance. Feedback allows management to adjust and fine-tune inputs and processes so that future outputs will more closely match goals.

But diagnostic control systems are not adequate to ensure effective control. In fact, they create pressures that can lead to control failures—even crises. Whether managers realize it or not, there are built-in dangers when empowered employees are held accountable for performance goals—especially for difficult ones—and then left to their own devices to achieve them. For example, Nordstrom, the upscale fashion retailer known for extraordinary customer service, recently found itself embroiled in a series of lawsuits and investigative reports related to its sales-per-hour performance-measurement system. Used to track the performance of its entrepreneurial salespeople, the system was designed to support the service orientation for which Nordstrom is famous. But without counterbalancing controls, the system created the potential for both exemplary customer service and abuse. Some employees claimed that first-line supervisors were pressuring them to underreport hours on the job in an attempt to boost sales per hour. Settling those claims cost Nordstrom more than $15 million.

I recently conducted a study of ten newly appointed chief executive officers to understand better how they used measurement and control systems to implement their agendas. Within the first months of taking charge, many of the new CEOs established demanding performance goals for division managers and increased the rewards and punishments associated with success and failure in achieving those goals. In response to the pressures, several division managers manipulated financial data by creating false accounting entries to enhance their reported performance. The managers were fired, but not before they had inflicted damage on their organizations. In one memorable case, a retail company had been making inventory and markdown decisions based on the falsified data, a practice that resulted in significant losses. These are not isolated incidents. The Big Six accounting firms have observed a substantial increase in errors and fraud over the past five years as organizations downsize and reduce the resources devoted to internal controls. With the elimination of many middle management jobs, basic internal controls, such as segregation of duties and independent oversight, have often been sacrificed.

One of the main purposes of diagnostic measurement systems is to eliminate the manager's burden of constant monitoring. Once goals are established and people have performance targets on which their rewards will be based, many managers believe they can move on to other issues, knowing that employees will be working diligently to meet the agreed-upon goals. Yet the potential for control failures as the performance bar is raised and employees' rewards are put at risk underscores the need for managers to think about the three other essential levers of control.

## BELIEFS SYSTEMS

Companies have used beliefs systems for years in an effort to articulate the values and direction that senior managers want their employees to embrace. Typically, beliefs systems are concise, value-laden, and inspirational. They draw employees' attention to key tenets of the business: how the organization creates value ("Best Customer Service in the World"); the level of performance the organization strives for ("Pursuit of Excellence"); and how individuals are expected to manage both internal and external relationships ("Respect for the Individual").

Senior managers intentionally design beliefs systems to be broad enough to appeal to many different groups within an organization: salespeople, managers, production workers, and clerical personnel. Because they are broad, beliefs statements are often ridiculed for lacking substance. But this criticism overlooks the principal purpose of the statements: to inspire and promote commitment to an organization's core values. Still, the statements achieve their ends only if employees believe, by watching the actions of senior managers, that the company's stated beliefs represent deeply rooted values. If employees suspect that managers are going through the motions of the latest fad, cynicism will set in.

Indeed, some managers adopt missions and credos not out of any real commitment but because they seem fashionable. However, managers who use their missions as living documents—as part of a system to guide patterns of acceptable behavior—have discovered a powerful lever of control. At Johnson & Johnson, for example, senior managers meet regularly with subordinates throughout the company to review and reaffirm the beliefs recorded in J&J's long-standing credo, which articulates clearly and passionately the company's responsibilities to customers, employees, local communities, and stockholders. Managers throughout the organization recognize the value that senior managers place on the exercise and respond accordingly. When problems arise, such as when J&J faced the Tylenol crisis, the strong beliefs system embedded in its credo provided guidance regarding the types of solutions to search for.

In the past, a company's mission was usually understood without reference to core values or formal beliefs; employees knew that they worked for a bank or a telephone company or a company that made shock absorbers. However, businesses have become much more complex in recent years, making it more difficult for individuals to comprehend organizational purpose and direction. Moreover, in many businesses, downsizing and realignment have shattered strongly held assumptions about the values and foundations of businesses and their top-level managers. Employees no longer know whom to trust. At the same time, their expectations for meaningful careers have risen as education levels have increased. Without a formal beliefs system, employees in large, decentralized organizations often do not have a clear and consistent understanding of the core values of the business and their place within the business. In the absence of clearly articulated core values, they are often forced to make assumptions about what constitutes acceptable behavior in the many different, unpredictable circumstances they encounter.

Beliefs systems can also inspire employees to create new opportunities: they can motivate individuals to search for new ways of creating value. We all have a deep-seated need to contribute—to devote time and energy to worthwhile endeavors. But companies often make it difficult for employees to understand the larger purpose of their efforts or to see how they can add value in

**Harness Employees' Creativity with the Four Levers of Control**

| Potential | Organizational Blocks | Managerial Solution | Control Lever |
|---|---|---|---|
| To contribute | Uncertainty about purpose | Communicate core values and mission | Beliefs systems |
| To do right | Pressure or temptation | Specify and enforce rules of the game | Boundary systems |
| To achieve | Lack of focus or of resources | Build and support clear targets | Diagnostic control systems |
| To create | Lack of opportunity or fear of risk | Open organizational dialogue to encourage learning | Interactive control systems |

a way that can make a difference. Individuals want to understand the organization's purpose and how they can contribute, but senior managers must unleash this potential. Effective managers seek to inspire people throughout their organizations by actively communicating core values and missions. As top-level managers rely increasingly on empowered employees to generate new ideas and competitive advantage, participants from all parts of an organization need to understand as clearly as possible their company's purposes and mission.

Beliefs systems can augment diagnostic control systems to give today's managers greater amounts of control. But they are only part of the answer. Think of them as the yang of Chinese philosophy—the sun, the warmth, and the light. Opposing them are dark, cold boundaries—the yin—which represent the next lever of control.

## BOUNDARY SYSTEMS

Boundary systems are based on a simple, yet profound, management principle that can be called the "power of negative thinking."[1] Ask yourself the question, If I want my employees to be creative and entrepreneurial, am I better off telling them what to do or telling them what *not* to do? The answer is the latter. Telling people what to do by establishing standard operating procedures and rule books discourages the initiative and creativity unleashed by empowered, entrepreneurial employees. Telling them what *not* to do allows innovation, but within clearly defined limits.

---

[1] Professor Charles Christenson coined this term in a 1972 Harvard Business School working paper.

Unlike diagnostic control systems (which monitor critical performance outcomes) or beliefs systems (which communicate core values), boundary systems are stated in negative terms or as minimum standards. The boundaries in modern organizations, embedded in standards of ethical behavior and codes of conduct, are invariably written in terms of activities that are off-limits. They are an organization's brakes. Every business needs them, and, like racing cars, the fastest and most performance-oriented companies need the best brakes.

Human beings are inventive, and, when presented with new opportunities or challenging situations, they often search for ways to create value or overcome obstacles. But empowerment—fueled by inspiration and performance rewards—should never be interpreted as giving subordinates a blank check to do whatever they please. People generally want to do the right thing—to act ethically in accordance with established moral codes. But pressures to achieve superior results sometimes collide with stricter codes of behavior. Because of temptation or pressure in the workplace, individuals sometimes choose to bend the rules. As the recent problems at Kidder, Peabody and Salomon Brothers show, entrepreneurial individuals sometimes blur or misinterpret the line between acceptable and unacceptable behavior. At Salomon Brothers, a creative trader attempting to increase investment returns violated U.S. Treasury bidding rules and short-circuited existing controls; the aftermath of the scandal destroyed careers and impaired Salomon's franchise. Similar problems at Kidder, Peabody involving fictitious securities trades resulted in massive losses and ultimately led to the sale of the business. Clearly, the consequences of a misstep can be severe.

Boundary systems are especially critical in those businesses in which a reputation built on trust is a key competitive asset. A well-respected bank with a global franchise states as a part of its business principles that its three main assets are people, capital, and reputation. Of all these, it notes, the last is the most difficult to regain if impaired. To guard against damage to its reputation, the bank's code of conduct forbids individuals both from developing client relationships in "undesirable" industries, such as gambling casinos, and from acting as intermediaries in unfriendly takeovers, which senior managers believe could undermine the perceived trustworthiness of the company.

Large consulting firms like McKinsey & Company and the Boston Consulting Group routinely work with clients to analyze highly proprietary strategic data. To ensure that their reputations for integrity are never compromised, the firms enforce strict boundaries that forbid consultants to reveal information—even the names of clients—to anyone not employed by the firm, including spouses. They also clearly state in their codes of professional conduct that individuals must not misrepresent themselves when attempting to gather competitive information on behalf of clients.

Unfortunately, the benefits of establishing business conduct boundaries are not always apparent to senior managers. Too often, they learn the hard way. Many codes of conduct are instituted only after a public scandal or an internal investigation of questionable behavior. Over the years, General Electric has instituted codes of business conduct that prohibit activities relating to improper payments, price fixing, and improper cost allocation on government contracts. Each of those codes was instituted after a major crisis impaired the integrity of the business. For instance, when GE was forced to suspend its $4.5 billion business as supplier to the U.S. government in 1985, CEO Jack Welch responded by strengthening internal controls and issuing a clear policy statement that forbade the behaviors that had landed GE in trouble: improper cost allocations on government contracts. Similarly, senior managers at Wall Street investment firms did not pay much attention to business conduct boundary systems until the disclosure of improper behavior by a small number of employees at Salomon Brothers nearly destroyed the business. Again, senior managers at investment firms across the country scrambled to install compliance systems to avoid a similar crisis in their own firms.

Effective managers anticipate the inevitable temptations and pressures that exist within their organizations. They spell out the rules of the game based on the risks inherent in their strategy and enforce them clearly and unambiguously. Some behaviors are never tolerated: the firing of the manager who inflated his or her expense report by $50 is a familiar story in many organizations. On the surface, the punishment may seem too harsh for the crime, but the purpose of such punishment is to signal clearly to all managers and employees that the consequences of stepping over ethical boundaries are severe and

**Renew Strategy with the Four Levels of Control**

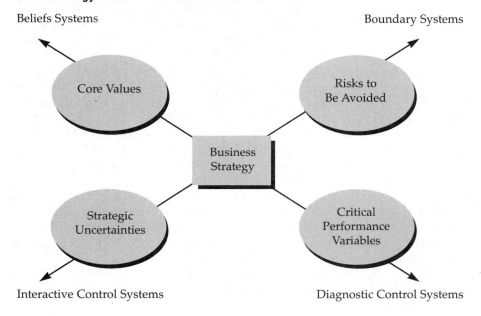

nonnegotiable. As performance-oriented organizations grow and become more decentralized, the risks of failure increase. Managers must rely more and more on formal systems in order to ensure that the boundaries are communicated and understood.

Not all boundaries concern standards of ethical conduct. Strategic boundaries focus on ensuring that people steer clear of opportunities that could diminish the business's competitive position. A large computer company, for example, uses its strategic planning process to segregate its product and market opportunities into what managers call *green space* and *red space*. Green space is the acceptable domain for new initiatives. Red space represents products and markets in which senior managers have decided they do not want to pursue new opportunities, although the organization could compete in those products and markets given its competencies. A British relief organization uses a similar system to monitor strategic boundaries; it maintains a *gray list* of companies whose contributions it will neither solicit nor accept. Managers at Automatic Data Processing (ADP) use a strategic boundary list that delineates the types of business opportunities that managers must avoid. The guidelines provide ADP managers with clarity and focus. This technique has contributed to 133 consecutive quarters of double-digit growth in earnings per share—a record unmatched by any other company traded on the New York Stock Exchange.

Working together, boundary systems and beliefs systems are the yin and yang that together create a dynamic tension. The warm, positive, inspirational beliefs are a foil to the dark, cold constraints. The result is a dynamic tension between commitment and punishment. Together, these systems transform limitless opportunity into a focused domain that employees and managers are encouraged to exploit actively. In combination, they establish direction, motivate and inspire, and protect against potentially damaging opportunistic behavior.

## INTERACTIVE CONTROL SYSTEMS

When organizations are small, key managers and employees can sit around the same table and informally explore the impact of emerging threats and opportunities. But as organizations grow larger and senior managers have less and less personal contact with people throughout the organization, new formal systems must be created to share emerging information and to harness the creativity that often leads to new products, line extensions, processes, and even markets. Unfortunately, diagnostic control systems, which highlight shortfalls against plans, won't suffice. Instead, senior managers need sensing systems more like the ones used by the National Weather Service. Ground stations all over the country monitor temperature, barometric pressure, relative humidity, cloud cover, wind direction and velocity, and precipitation. Balloons and satellites provide additional data. These data are monitored continuously from a central location in an effort to identify patterns of change.

Managers need similar scanning mechanisms.  Like weather-tracking systems, interactive control systems are the formal information systems that managers use to involve themselves regularly and personally in the decisions of subordinates.  These systems are generally simple to understand. Through them, senior managers participate in the decisions of subordinates and focus organizational attention and learning on key strategic issues.

Making a control system interactive invariably demands attention from participants throughout the business.  At Pepsico, for example, the weekly release of new Nielsen market-share numbers creates a flurry of activity as 60 or 70 people throughout the organization begin working on the data in anticipation of the inevitable scrutiny and queries of senior management.  Senior managers schedule weekly meetings to discuss the new Nielsen information, to challenge subordinates to explain the meaning of changed circumstances, and to review action plans that subordinates have developed to react to problems and opportunities.

Interactive control systems have four characteristics that set them apart from diagnostic control systems.  First, they focus on constantly changing information that top-level managers have identified as potentially strategic. Second, the information is significant enough to demand frequent and regular attention from operating managers at all levels of the organization.  Third, the data generated by the interactive system are best interpreted and discussed in face-to-face meetings of superiors, subordinates, and peers.  Fourth, the interactive control system is a catalyst for an ongoing debate about underlying data, assumptions, and action plans.

Interactive control systems track the strategic uncertainties that keep senior managers awake at night—the shocks to the business that could undermine their assumptions about the future and the way they have chosen to compete.  Depending on the business, these uncertainties might relate to changes in technology, customers' tastes, government regulation, and industry competition.  Because interactive control systems are designed to gather information that might challenge visions of the future, they are, by definition, hot buttons for senior managers.

A senior manager's decision to use a specific control system interactively—in other words, to invest time and attention in face-to-face meetings to review new information—sends a clear signal to the organization about what's important.  Through the dialogue and debate that surround the interactive process, new strategies often emerge.  Consider the case of a well-known hospital supply company.  The company is a low-cost producer, supplying disposable hospital products for intravenous drug delivery such as plasma containers, tubing, and syringes.  Even though efficiency, quality, and cost control are important competencies, these concerns do not keep managers awake at night. (They are well understood and can be managed effectively with diagnostic control systems.) Instead, senior managers worry that technological breakthroughs will undermine their ability to deliver products valued by the market. Accordingly, they use a project management system interactively to focus organizational attention on a dozen or so emerging technological issues. Senior managers meet monthly for several days to debate the impact of technologies—introduced by competitors or in related industries, or developed in-house—on their business. These meetings become intense as the managers challenge one another to assess the impact of new information and develop responses. From this dialogue, new strategies emerge.

Senior managers at *USA Today*, Gannett Company's daily newspaper, use a similar process to review information contained in a simple package of reports delivered each Friday. Three weekly reports give senior managers a picture of how they have done in the previous week and what conditions lie ahead for the upcoming few weeks. The data in the Friday packet range from year-to-date figures to daily and account-specific information. These data provide insight into changing industry conditions and the advertising strategies of key customers. They allow managers to look at the big picture and provide enough detail to identify specific vulnerabilities, opportunities, and the source of any problems that require proactive responses.

Each week, senior managers at *USA Today* schedule intensive face-to-face meetings with key subordinates to analyze and interpret the report data. Among the regular topics of discussion and debate are advertising volume against plan, committed future volume by issue, and new business by type of client. In addition to looking for unexpected shortfalls, managers also look for unexpected successes. From these meetings, significant innovations have been proposed to deal with unanticipated downturns and to capitalize on unanticipated opportunities. Innovations have included launching a new market-survey service for automotive clients, introducing fractional-page color advertising, selling exclusive inserts dedicated to specific customers and products, and using circulation salespeople to sell ad space in regional locations.

Of course, managers in other businesses choose different kinds of control systems to use interactively depending on the strategic uncertainties associated with their business strategies. For example, Johnson & Johnson uses its profit-planning system interactively to focus attention on the development and protection of innovative products in its various markets. Managers periodically reestimate the predicted effects of competitive tactics and new product rollouts on their profit plans for the current and the following year. The recurring questions posed by managers are: What has changed since our last forecast? Why? What are we going to do about it? The results are new ideas and action plans.

## BALANCING EMPOWERMENT AND CONTROL

Effective managers empower their organizations because they believe in the innate potential of people to innovate and add value. For instance, the reason Nordstrom salespeople provide exceptional customer service is that they are selected and trained to act entrepreneurially. In turn, they have the freedom and motivation to tailor their service to each customer's needs. To unleash this type of potential, senior managers must give up control over many kinds of decisions and allow employees at lower levels of the organization to act independently. Good managers work constantly to help employees rise to their potential. In small organizations, managers do this informally. While eating or traveling together, they communicate core values and missions, the rules of the game, and current targets—and they learn about significant changes. As companies become larger, more decentralized, and geographically dispersed, senior managers are no longer in constant contact with all the employees who will identify and respond to emerging problems and opportunities. Nonetheless, the guiding principles of communication and control are every bit as important.

A large international construction company respected for its quality and customer service provides a clear illustration of how the control levers support one another. The company has more than 25 offices in the United States and abroad; as a result, project managers and employees make multimillion-dollar decisions far from the company's top-level managers. The senior managers who set the company's overall direction and strategy ensure that they have adequate control of their far-flung operations by using all four levers of control.

To communicate core values, they rely on a beliefs system. The company's widely circulated credo refers to the importance of responsibility, of collective pride in engineering quality, of financial success, and of integrity. It concludes with an overall objective handed down by the founder: "To be the best."

These inspirational beliefs are offset by clear boundaries. Managers are forbidden, for example, to work in certain countries where facilitating payments and bribes are required to do business, because these sorts of actions jeopardize the company's belief in integrity. The company also maintains a *turkey list* to communicate to managers the types of projects that the company has learned are not profitable and should be avoided. (For example, senior managers have learned from bitter experience to steer clear of sewage-disposal-plant construction.) The list is adjusted from time to time as managers learn where their competencies lie and where they don't.

Managers gain still more control by using a variety of diagnostic controls—among them profit plans, budgets, and goals and objectives. These control systems do not require very much attention from senior management other than the time spent setting annual goals and monitoring exceptions to see that events unfold according to plan. One control system, however, is used interactively. The project management system focuses attention on the strategic uncertainties that managers want everyone to monitor: the company's reputation in the trade, the shifting perceptions of customers, and the ideal skill mix required in various project teams. The new data are used as a catalyst to force regular face-to-face discussions in which managers share information and attempt to develop better ways to customize their services and adjust their strategies in a changing market.

Collectively, these four levers of control set in motion powerful forces that reinforce one another. As organizations become more complex, managers will inevitably deal with increasing opportunity and competitive forces and decreasing time and attention. By using the control levers effectively, managers can be confident that the benefits of innovation and creativity are not achieved at the expense of control.

# Indianapolis: Implementing Competition in City Services

In November 1991, Stephen Goldsmith was elected mayor of Indianapolis, Indiana. Indianapolis, with a population of 800,000, was the 12th largest city in the United States. As a Republican candidate, Goldsmith campaigned on the basis of neighborhood revitalization and making city government more effective by providing better services more efficiently, being more responsive to its people, and avoiding increases in property taxes. He was opposed by the existing bureaucracy, which wanted to maintain job stability and security, and the unionized city workers, who enjoyed monopolies over the provision of nearly all city services and were concerned about his threatened privatization of these services.

Goldsmith called for profound changes in the way the city was run. Skeptics argued that the city was in excellent shape. It had produced operating surpluses for several years, and its bonds were rated AAA—the highest possible by Moody's Investors Service, Inc. "Why fix what ain't broke?" they asked. Moreover, Goldsmith was following a popular Republican who had been mayor since 1976. The voters, however, seemed to agree with the 44-year-old Goldsmith that the services provided the public for the taxes they paid were not returning a good value. Rising taxes and deteriorating public services were driving both companies and the citizenry to the suburbs.

## COMPETITION AND COMPETITIVENESS

Newly elected Mayor Goldsmith realized that drastic action was needed to stop this "flight of wealth." He also knew that he would have to move quickly while

*Professor William J. Bruns, Jr. and Professor Roger Atherton of Northeastern University prepared this case.*

Copyright © 1996 by the President and Fellows of Harvard College. Harvard Business School case 196-099.

he still had the momentum and enthusiasm of his supporters and before coalitions could form to block his ideas. Although he had campaigned advocating "privatization," a policy of transferring city services to private contractors, he realized soon after taking office that public monopolies were likely to be only slightly less efficient than private monopolies. He was frequently quoted as saying that "if we had only one McDonald's in town, even with the best restaurant managers in charge, over time the price of the hamburger would go up while the quality deteriorated."

Goldsmith worked hard to put in place "the most comprehensive competition and competitiveness effort of any major city or maybe any governmental entity in the United States." In his presentations, he made it very clear that "we do not have a privatization effort in Indianapolis." Instead, he coined the term "marketization." His approach combined many existing ideas in an unusual combination. The application of competition to the public sector attracted so much local, national, and even international attention that it could help vault him into the governorship and perhaps even higher.

## THE FIRST STEPS

Mayor Goldsmith created the Service, Efficiency, and Lower Taxes for Indianapolis Commission (SELTIC) in February 1992. SELTIC was comprised of nine entrepreneurs who volunteered their time to recommend ways to decrease costs, eliminate waste, and improve government services and make them more efficient. Each member led a group of private sector volunteers and some of the most enterprising employees in each city department. The commission and its 100 volunteers inventoried city assets to determine whether they should be sold and looked at city services, identifying about 150 that they recommended be opened to competition.

Goldsmith, soon after taking office, set up a separate Office of Enterprise Development and placed Skip Stitt, a 30-year-old lawyer, in charge, reporting directly to the mayor. It was Stitt's job to challenge all of the basic assumptions about city government—to ask why do we do things the way we do, why do we capture numbers this way, how could we do this service better, why are we in this business at all? In the mayor's opinion, it was Stitt's ability to confront a director directly that led to great debates and improvements in city government. Over time, the directors learned to challenge the assumptions that had built up over the years and stood in the way of making their departments more efficient. The mayor commented that:

> It was Stitt's job to torment everybody else in government until we reached
> the right equilibrium between the private side and the public side.

Stitt quickly recognized that if the city was going to use competition as a core strategy, the managers would have to know their real costs. At that time the city had no financial or accounting tools in place that would tell them their real costs. Stitt also realized they would need additional management tools if they were going to be successful in creating a more efficient and responsive government.

## STRATEGIC TOOLS

Four new practices, which became known as the "Strategic Tools Initiative," were developed. Stitt explained the first three of these as follows:

1.  **Activity-based costing (ABC)**    The city needed to know how much every service and activity cost. This tool was originally developed in a manufacturing environment, so that manufacturers who were making finished goods could determine what it cost to provide, to prepare, and to deliver each of the components. That way they could decide whether they should manufacture in-house or should buy them through out-sourcing (what we would call privatization in government) from another vendor. ABC was an important tool for managing costs. It also facilitated continuous improvement. To the extent you could identify the cost of services, you could carefully and predictively compare yourself to other government providers, and even within the city we could compare the costs of snow removal services in one part of the city with the costs in another quadrant. ABC was particularly helpful as our in-house work force started thinking about competition. It allowed them to borrow the best ideas from other areas in the city and to implement the best management practices in their own activities.

2.  **Performance measures**    Cost was not the only issue. Quality assurance required the city to develop performance standards for assessing how well city services were provided. Competitive contracting also required very clear standards from the city about how the contracts would be evaluated. It was important to know expected outcomes to measure performance against other public sector and private sector entities. Performance measures were critically important so that we knew what it was we were doing, how well we were doing it, and how much we needed to do in terms of monitoring those services. These have also been helpful in our increasing emphasis on pay-for-performance.

3.  **Popular budgets**    By combining activity-based costing with performance measures, the city created a "popular budget" that explained to citizens what they were purchasing with every dollar of their budget. The focus was on such output measures as the miles of streets plowed or repaired, the number of park lawns mowed, or the number of police officers on the streets rather than on such input measures as the number of plows purchased, labor hours used, or budgeted dollars.

One other strategic tool was developed: customer surveys. There was no point to being efficient delivering a service that was not wanted. City managers believed that regular customer surveys, coupled with the popular budget, enabled them to make informed decisions about trade-offs between services.

## THE RESULTS

By 1996 more than 60 city services had been moved into the competitive marketplace. The estimated cost savings from the public-private competition were substantial: $6.5 million in 1992, $12 million in 1993, and $27.6 million in 1994. Total predicted savings to the city are estimated to exceed $150 million. In addition, nearly $1 million of unused or underutilized city assets had been sold or not replaced. Some details are shown in **Exhibits 1** and **2**.

The new mayor eliminated about 450 of 4,700 full-time employees in the first 16 months, including 160 managerial-level employees within the first three months. He reduced city employment from 4,675 on December 31, 1991 to 3,641 on December 31, 1995. Excluding public safety, public employment in the city decreased 40% to the lowest level in 20 years. Some of the savings were used to enhance public safety and to pay for the largest infrastructure rebuilding program in city history. The 1996 budget of $439 million included operating expenses that were $26 million less than were incurred in 1992. The property tax rate had remained constant for eight consecutive years.

## PUTTING ANALYSIS INTO ACTION: LOOKING FOR SMOOTH STREETS

A small cadre of young managers, selected by Steve Goldsmith, led the change in the delivery of city services. One of the most effective was Mitch Roob, a 30-year-old CPA who had earned an MBA at Notre Dame, and whom Goldsmith appointed director of the former Department of Transportation. It was Roob's job to bring competitiveness to the department that maintained the city's streets and alleys.

In 1995, Roob described how the effort began:

*When the mayor ran four years ago he talked at length about the need to compete services and about privatization. He was endorsed by the regular Republican organization and opposed by AFCSME (the city employees' labor union). When he won, there was great concern on the part of organized labor that Steve Goldsmith's goal in life was to go after organized labor. There was great glee on the part of the Republican organization folks that they had secured their jobs for another four years. During the campaign, neither side had listened very well.*

*When Steve came into office and we decided to compete services, we looked at potholes. One of the reasons we chose potholes was that it had high public visibility. At about the same time we opened microfilming city records to competition. Does the public care about microfilm? No, they don't.  Quite frankly, we wanted to make an early political statement.  We did that with potholes.  Other than snow removal and backed-up toilets, there are very few things that the public cares about more than potholes.  They hate potholes.  So by competing street repair we could get the public's and the media's attention.*

*With the help of KPMG Peat Marwick, we figured that it cost $425 per ton of asphalt to fix potholes.  Having an outside firm estimate the costs through activity-based costing really helped because it made those costs credible.  We did not know whether this was a good price or a bad price, so we had to find out.  We told the people in street maintenance that they now had an opportunity to compete.*

*The union was very concerned about this.  They thought they would lose this opportunity to compete and be out of their jobs, that this was just a polite way to fire all of them.  So the union leadership came to us and said, "You've got too many managers.  You've got 32 managers and 94 workers. You cannot expect us to be competitive if you keep that much overhead, so you've got to do something about it." That made sense to us.  Just incidentally, about half of the managers were Republican-precinct committeemen. But we began eliminating managerial positions.*

*That action sent a pretty strong message to folks in the union.  If management was willing to fire those who had supported them in the election, if we do not get the price right, what will they do to us? We intentionally wanted them to feel that way.  This was a very charged environment.  It was as stressful a time in my life as I have had.*

*Business theorists suggest that fear is a poor long-term motivator, and there seems to be a significant amount of anecdotal evidence that this is the case.  However, fear is an extraordinary good motivator in the short term. We used fear to reorient our employees, and then after they began performing the way we wanted them to, we started to be really nice to them.*

*After we had scared the union guys, we worked with them to change their behavior, and we showed them what they could gain by working with us.  We showed the union that they were in too many lines of business, and it was to everyone's benefit to get out of some of them.  We had to focus on the infrastructure management business.*

*We needed to show the union workers the advantages of preserving paved roads by sealing cracks earlier in their life at a cost of about $700 per mile in order to postpone patching or repaving them at a cost of $100 thousand per mile or replacing them at a cost of $1 million per mile because the cracks had not been sealed.  To explain this, we had to put these concepts in terms of preventative maintenance on houses and cars, which they understood.  Then, we told them that in the future we were going to buy the services to do the preventative maintenance.  After we explained that we could go to either a private company or to them, they quickly saw that they should be more into the crack sealing business, and that they should invest in the*

*technology to do better work faster. They came to believe that they could ef-
fectively compete.*

*We explained to them that if they could not do their work effectively and
efficiently, we would get someone who would. We got them to behave the
way we wanted them to behave, by treating them the same way we would
have treated any other contractor.*

*When we did that, the union and management came back to us and said
they could fill potholes more cost effectively than they did before. "We don't
really need two trucks in every pothole crew. We don't really need to have
eight people in a pothole crew. We could have only six people in a pothole
crew. We could raise the crack sealing goal from two lane miles per day to
three lane miles per day." Let's face it, necessity was the mother of invention.
They felt the need to become competitive. When they did that, the $425
dropped to $307 for laying a ton of asphalt.*

*Once I had a group of lower-level union officials come to me and ask me
to remove an equipment operator from their crew because he was not very
good. They did not want to be burdened with him because he did not work
fast enough, and they thought they were going to lose bids because he slowed
them down.*

*Another thing that affected what happened was that my predecessor
was a pretty typical government manager with a military background, and
he had managed as if he were still in the army. At first, crews were surprised
to find me out on jobs working with them. Or they would be out working
and I would be bringing them drinks. They soon felt that somebody cared
about them more than the previous administration did. And I dealt fairly
often with the guys right on the front line. I knew most of them by face, if
not by name.*

*This was a style that worked well for me, but it probably also had the ef-
fect of undercutting the relationship that managers had with their workers.
The managers were used to living in a command and control structure. They
would often hear about my suggestions no sooner, and sometimes later, than
their employees did. I destroyed their existing management paradigm, and I
did not give them a new one.*

*Another thing that helped us was that we concentrated our work in the
central city where most of our employees lived, instead of focusing on the
suburbs, as our predecessors had done. Our employees saw our commitment
to their own neighborhoods. They saw their streets being resurfaced, and
they were being paid to fix the streets where they lived.*

*Our relationship with the union started out as bad as it could be. These
guys had supported Steve Goldsmith's opponent, and they were convinced
that we were going to destroy them. They started off believing the worst of
us. Actually, that was a really good place to start, because anything we did
to show that we were not bad was seen as positive. Our relationship improved because it had started so low. The kinds of messages that we sent*

*signaled that we were all in this thing together, and if they did not work with us, none of us would have jobs. We tried to encourage a we vs. them spirit in the sense of the public sector vs. private sector.*

*We had a sense of leadership that flowed from Steve Goldsmith through the rest of us. He had the vision and the willingness to inspire the rest of us to do things like being on the job at 2:30 a.m. on Christmas morning, giving hot chocolate to the drivers who were plowing streets in the middle of a snow storm. Those guys worked harder for us because they knew we cared about them.*

Bob Larsen, a manager with the former Department of Transportation in 1995, described the changes from his perspective:

*We've gone from 32 supervisors in February 1992 to six right now. When a bid comes up we have a meeting between the management and the union, and we decide whether or not to bid. If it is something that we do, we get a bid team together. We inspect the job and try to figure out a way to do it.*

*We used to go out with five or six people patching or filling potholes. We do it with three people now. The teams are watching their mix of man-power and equipment because the costs are derived through activity-based costing. We have large trucks like tandem duals which you need only for snow. You do not need that large a truck out there to fill potholes. So they go out with a single axle, or a crew cab, or a one-ton dump truck.*

*Our performance measures in 1992 had crack sealing at two lane miles per day. We knew we could not win a bid at two lane miles per day, so we bid the contract at three lane miles per day. We won that bid. By adjusting our manpower and equipment to lower costs (see **Exhibits 3** and **4** for dia-grams and changes in manpower and equipment), we actually averaged four lane miles per day and successfully completed the job at $20,000 under our bid. The Department of Transportation shared some of those savings with all of us in the form of an unexpected cash bonus. That really made an impres-sion on our workers.*

*During the 1992 bid, I chewed our crews out if it took too long to get to the job site. In 1993 we had already cut back half of our supervision, and the crew leaders of the line employees took over.*

*In 1993 we put a class together on how to prepare bids. We held the class for roughly 70 people, union and management, about half our work force. We started out with showing them what a company would have to do. For example, our license plate costs $5, while theirs would cost $258. They have to put so much money as a bid bond. Their average worker works 1,520 hours a year in private construction because of the weather; while we are still working, those guys are sitting at home. A lot of them don't have full medi-cal and dental coverage. We have an outstanding plan. We let them in on the idea that if our guys get out there and do a good job, the work tilts toward the city worker.*

*After the bid team training, another manager came in and gave a one-hour introduction to ABC that snowed the hell out of everybody. Now I sit down with two or three guys and we just talk about the assumptions and methodology. I take my laptop and get right in the back of a crew cab and say, "We have six guys on this job, what do we need six guys for?" They say, "It is a narrow road so we need a flagger," but I say, "Why can't the truck driver get out and wave his arms so that we can do the job with just five?" Then, they see that the cost per ton goes down. They have been picking up these ideas.*

*We were successful on some of our bids, but we learned some lessons. We didn't have any historical data on concrete sealing, so when we bid the concrete we bid it just like an asphalt street. But concrete takes three times as much material, so it is going to take you longer to do it. So we lost some money on concrete work in 1993. But we made money on the asphalt contracts. The one bid on concrete on which we made money was one on which we had doubled our estimated labor time from 10 hours to 20, and then we added another hour just to be on the safe side. Our actual time was 19½ hours to do 4.95 lane miles of concrete.*

*We had one contract in which a pothole team put in a bid assuming they were going to use a DuraPatcher. That is a machine that mixes the tak and stone in a hopper, which is cheaper. Instead of $22 per ton, you are putting out the material at $14 per ton. They had so many potholes that they went and grabbed a big tandem axle dual that cost $55 an hour when they had put the bid in at $17.50 a unit. But with the bigger truck they were able to go out and do ten tons in seven hours instead of seven tons. They figured this out on their own; no one told them to do it.*

*By 1994 we had been able to train half the work force on how to calculate a bid, and to explain to them that everything we do is watched by internal audit, which wants to see all of the paperwork that goes with all of the contract work. Also all of the work is inspected. This schedule (**Exhibit 5**) shows the steps we used in preparing a bid.*

*All of our bids are based on costs that we keep up-to-date. (See **Exhibit 6**.)*

*There are still problems with ABC. If garbage goes in, garbage comes out. If there are errors in the ABC cost estimates, they foul up all of the ABC information that we use in bidding.*

*Once we win a bid, I prepare spreadsheets from the source documents that I get from the crew chiefs. I keep a running record on every bid, on a day-by-day basis. (See **Exhibits 7** through **10** for some of the daily reports used to monitor costs.) That was how I discovered that concrete was costing us too much. Sometimes if I think we are getting in trouble on costs, I go out to see the crews and to talk to them.*

*These reports show me and my boss where we stand. (See **Exhibits 11** and **12**.) She may ask whether she should be worried about being $1,000* *down, and I can tell her yes or no, because I keep track of what is actually going on.*

Ray Wallace, Stephen Goldsmith's special assistant, summarized his views on why the competitiveness effort had been so successful:

*Our success really all comes down to competition.  What our people needed was a tool to measure their efficiency so that they could compare their work to that of others.  Anytime you can install competition into a process, it is going to bring out the best people have to offer.  Once people knew that they had to win bids or lose their jobs, and that eventually they might share in savings, they began to look for ways to do their work better and at a lower cost.*

**EXHIBIT 1**
## Highlights of the Indianapolis Competition Effort

**What is the Indianapolis privatization effort?**

Actually, Indianapolis does not have a privatization effort. It has a comprehensive effort to let private sector companies compete against government workers for contracts to provide services and manage assets. Regardless of whether the private sector or city government wins, the result is reduced costs and more responsive services for the taxpayers. Indianapolis is moving the provision of municipal services into the marketplace, and breaking up government monopolies.

**Why is this necessary?**

The environment in which cities operate is changing. Wealth and jobs are rapidly leaving our urban areas, chased out by crime, taxes, and other factors. In order for Indianapolis to remain successful in the next century, it must reduce the cost of providing government services so that it can keep taxes as low as possible.

**What have these savings meant for the city?**

Indianapolis has been able to balance the budget, cut the non-public safety work force by 40%, reduce the budget by $26 million, and use the approximately $150 million it has identified in savings to put more officers on the street and to undertake the largest infrastructure improvement program in the city's history—all without raising taxes. Indianapolis has enjoyed four consecutive years of record-setting job creation and now has one of the lowest unemployment rates in the country.

**What are some of the successes of competition?**

Private management of the Indianapolis International Airport will save $100 million over 10 years, helping to make Indianapolis one of the pre-eminent passenger and cargo hubs in the country.

Private management of the city's advanced wastewater treatment plants is saving taxpayers $65 million over five years. The work force at the plants has dropped from 328 to 176, while the quality of the treated water leaving the plants has risen significantly.

Competitively bidding trash collection is saving taxpayers more than $15 million over three years. Collapsing the city's 25 trash collection districts into 11 districts and competing out contracts for them reduced the cost of providing trash collection from approximately $85 per household annually to about $68. City workers reengineered their work plans to win the maximum territory in the competition.

City workers reduced their budget, cut their work force, and increased their productivity to win a bid to maintain and service city vehicles. The agreement saves taxpayers $8 million.

In total, more than 60 services have been moved into the marketplace, with total savings to taxpayers of $150 million. Competition has improved services and made them more responsive in many areas throughout government.

**EXHIBIT 2**
**Report Card from the Indianapolis Effort to Competitively Bid the Delivery of City Services**

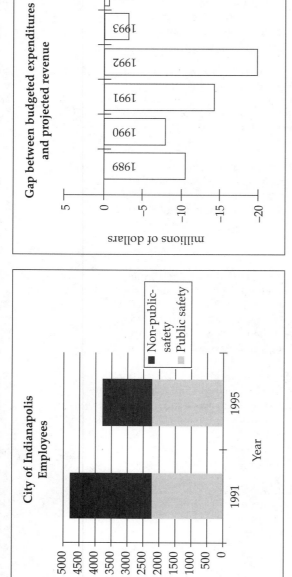

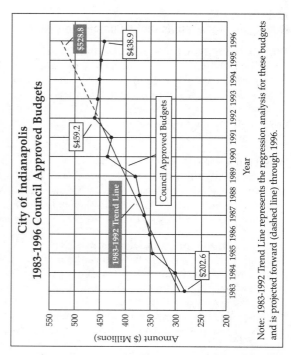

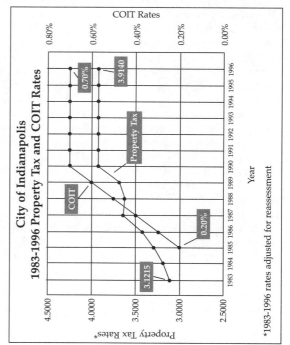

**EXHIBIT 3**
**The Old Way to Seal Cracks**

| DOT PLANNING | | | | | | | |
|---|---|---|---|---|---|---|---|
| CRACK REPAIR 1993 | | LOCATION: | | | | | |
| | THE OLD WAY | | | | | | |
| JOB REQUIREMENTS | INSPECTION | ASPHALT | CONCRETE | MOVE IN/OUT | USE | UNIT COST | COST |
| TRUCK DRIVER | | 5 | 0 | | 5 | $30.00 | 150 |
| LABORER | | 5 | 0 | | 5 | $20.00 | 100 |
| CREW LEADER | | 1 | 0 | | 1 | $34.00 | 34 |
| EQUIP OP | | | | | 0 | $33.87 | 0 |
| OVERHEAD | 0 | 11 | 0 | 0 | 11 | $23.00 | 253 |
| STAKE BED | | 0 | 0 | | 0 | $15.00 | 0 |
| CREW CAB | | 1 | 0 | | 1 | $20.00 | 20 |
| DOUBLE BOILER | | 1 | 0 | | 1 | $35.00 | 35 |
| 1 TON DUMP | | | | | 0 | $15.00 | 0 |
| 3/4 TON PU | | 0 | 0 | | 0 | $15.00 | 0 |
| TRAILER | | | | | 0 | $18.00 | 0 |
| ROUTER | | | | | 0 | $40.00 | 0 |
| COMPRESSOR | | 1 | 0 | | 1 | $3.34 | 3.34 |
| MINI PICKUP | | | 0 | | 0 | $15.00 | 0 |
| ARROW BOARD | | | 0 | | 0 | $2.00 | 0 |
| SINGLE AXEL DUMP | 2 | | | | 2 | $16.55 | 33.1 |
| CRUM RUBBER | 200 | 0 | | | 200 | $0.30 | 60 |
| TOTAL COST | | | | | | | 688.44 |

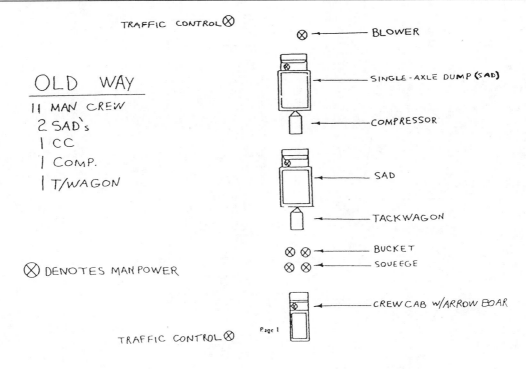

TRAFFIC CONTROL ⊗

⊗ ←—— BLOWER

OLD WAY

11 MAN CREW
2 SAD's
1 CC
1 COMP.
1 T/WAGON

⊗ DENOTES MAN POWER

←———— SINGLE-AXLE DUMP (SAD)

←———— COMPRESSOR

←———— SAD

←———— TACKWAGON

⊗ ⊗ ←—— BUCKET
⊗ ⊗ ←—— SQUEEGE

←———— CREW CAB w/ARROW BOAR

TRAFFIC CONTROL ⊗    Page 1

**EXHIBIT 4**
**The New Way to Seal Cracks**

| DOT PLANNING | | | | | | | |
|---|---|---|---|---|---|---|---|
| CRACK REPAIR 1993 | | LOCATION: | | | | | |
| | THE BETTER WAY | | | | | | |
| JOB REQUIREMENTS | INSPECTION | ASPHALT | CONCRETE | MOVE IN/OUT | USE | UNIT COST | COST |
| TRUCK DRIVER | | 3 | 0 | | 3 | $30.00 | 90 |
| LABORER | | 2 | 0 | | 2 | $20.00 | 40 |
| CREW LEADER | | 1 | 0 | | 1 | $34.00 | 34 |
| EQUIP OP | | | | | 0 | $33.87 | 0 |
| OVERHEAD | 0 | 6 | 0 | 0 | 6 | $23.00 | 138 |
| STAKE BED | | 1 | 0 | | 1 | $15.00 | 15 |
| CREW CAB | | 1 | 0 | | 1 | $20.00 | 20 |
| DOUBLE BOILER | | 1 | 0 | | 1 | $35.00 | 35 |
| 1 TON DUMP | | | | | 0 | $15.00 | 0 |
| 3/4 TON PU | | 0 | 0 | | 0 | $15.00 | 0 |
| TRAFFIC CONTROL | | 2 | | | 2 | $15.00 | 30 |
| ROUTER | | | | | 0 | $40.00 | 0 |
| COMPRESSOR | | 1 | 0 | | 1 | $3.34 | 3.34 |
| MINI PICKUP | | | 0 | | 0 | $15.00 | 0 |
| ARROW BOARD | | | 0 | | 0 | $2.00 | 0 |
| SINGLE AXEL DUMP | | | | | 0 | $16.55 | 0 |
| CRUM RUBBER | | 200 | 0 | | 200 | $0.30 | 60 |
| TOTAL COST | | | | | | | 465.34 |

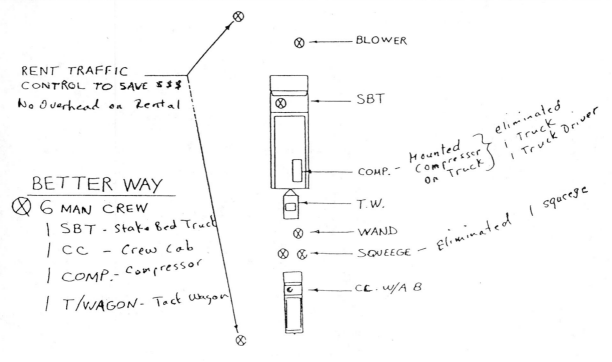

RENT TRAFFIC CONTROL TO SAVE $$$
No Overhead on Rental

BLOWER

SBT

COMP. - Mounted Compressor on Truck } eliminated 1 Truck Driver

T.W.

WAND

SQUEEGE - Eliminated 1 squeege

CC. W/A B

BETTER WAY
⊗ 6 MAN CREW
1 SBT - Stake Bed Truck
1 CC - Crew Cab
1 COMP. - Compressor
1 T/WAGON - Tact Wagon

**EXHIBIT 5**

## BID PREPARATION

BID NOTIFICATION
   MAIL NOTICE TO BIDDERS POST CARD RECEIVE TUESDAY OF 1ST WEEK
   NEWSPAPER APPEARS MONDAY 1ST WEEK AND 2ND WEEK

PICK UP BID ROOM 1522 CITY COUNTY BUILDING
   MAKE ADDITIONAL COPIES OF BID PACKAGE
   SAFEGUARD ORIGINAL BID PROPOSAL

ASSEMBLE THE BID TEAM
   MANAGEMENT REPRESENTATIVE
   UNION REPRESENTATIVE
   PEOPLE WHO WILL DO THE WORK

BID TEAM MEETING
   REVIEW BID PACKAGE
   DO WE BID?
   IDENTIFY PROBLEMS
   ASSIGN JOBS

FIELD INSPECTION
   IS IT FEASIBLE?
   HOW DO WE DO IT?

PUT THE BID TOGETHER

SUBMIT THE BID BY THURSDAY OF THE 3RD WEEK

BID OPENS 10:00 AM

BE AT DCAM BOARD TO ANSWER ANY QUESTIONS

PRE-CON & TONICE TO PROCEED MEET CONSULTANT/INSPECTOR

CONTRACT SCHEDULE

TRACK COST

FINAL ACCEPTANCE

SUBMIT PO TO GET PAID

SET UP COMPLETE FILE FOR HISTORICAL DATA, INTERNAL AUDIT, & FINAL ANALYSIS

**EXHIBIT 6**

## OUTPUT COST SUMMARY

|                            | 1993       | 1994       |          |
|----------------------------|------------|------------|----------|
| BASE REPAIR                | $    29.11 | $    16.09 | sq. yds. |
| BRIDGE CLEANING            | $   304.89 | $   298.16 | ea.      |
| CLEAN RIGHT-OF-WAY         | $    71.59 | $     4.87 | hrs.     |
| CONSTRUCT NEW SURFACE      | $    25.00 | $    44.67 | sq. yds. |
| CURBS REMOVE/REPLACE       | $    18.00 | $    23.49 | lin. ft. |
| DOUBLE BOILER SEALING      | $1,815.00  | $1,519.57  | ln. mi.  |
| HAND MOWING/BRUSH CUT      | $    77.00 | $    46.24 | hrs.     |
| HAULING TRASH/RUBBLE       | $    41.00 | $    41.18 | cu. yds. |
| HUMP REMOVAL               | $   261.00 | $   234.40 | ea.      |
| INLET CLEANING             | $    38.00 | $    37.25 | ea.      |
| OTHER WORK                 | $    30.00 | $    48.32 | hrs.     |
| PATCHING                   | $   311.00 | $   211.19 | tons     |
| SIDEWALKS REMOVE/REPLACE   | $   108.00 | $   128.17 | sq. yds. |
| SNOW CONTROL               | $   150.79 | $    86.53 | hrs.     |
| STRIP PATCHING             | $   166.00 | $    97.12 | tons     |
| TRACTOR MOWING             | $    48.00 | $    55.54 | hrs.     |
| UNPAVED ALLEY REPAIR       | $     1.93 | $     2.46 | lin. ft. |
| UNPAVED BERM REPAIR        | $     3.19 | $     1.44 | lin. ft. |

**EXHIBIT 7**
**FAX on Planned Work**

| | |
|---|---|
| *To:* | MICHAEL FINGER, P.E.<br>PROJECT ENGINEER<br>UNITED SURVEYING, INC. |
| *From:* | DAVID WALDROP<br>CREW LEADER |
| *Date:* | *5-23-95* |
| *Number of Pages:* | 1 |
| *Phone:* | 253-4996 |
| *Fax:* | 253-5385 |

# FAX

*Remarks:* WE PLAN ON PATCHING ON WASHINGTON STREET STARTING AT __*3800*__ THROUGH ____*?*____. WE PLAN TO START AT ____*9:30*____ HOURS.

THANK YOU.

*David Waldrop*

*DISTRICT 1 - OPERATIONS DIVISION*
*DEPARTMENT OF PUBLIC WORKS*
*2001 DR. MARTIN LUTHER KING JR. STREET*
*INDIANAPOLIS, INDIANA 46202*

**EXHIBIT 8**

Milestone Contractors, L.P.
2810 Columbia Avenue
Plant 14

**Milestone**

SOLD        CITY OF INDPLS / D.P.W.
TO:          P.O.# UD 49029                                              NO.  02585

| TIME | DATE | PLANT # | CUSTOMER # | TICKET # | TYPE MATERIAL | TRUCK # |
|------|------|---------|------------|----------|---------------|---------|
| 10:02 | 05/23/95 | 14 | 22440 | 02585 | #12 SURF | SA |

| PRODUCT #—NAME/LOAD #—ACCUMULATED TOTALS(TONS) | | |
|---|---|---|
| 03-#8  BIND | 02-#12 SURF<br>003-0013.20 | 99-OTHERS |

| TRUCK WEIGHT IN TONS | | |
|---|---|---|
| GROSS | TARE | NET |
| 17.37 | 11.94 | 5.43 |

DRIVER _____*Harold*_____ RECVD. BY _____

ALL WEIGHTS ARE IN POUNDS UNLESS OTHERWISE SPECIFIED

| NO. | TARE | 1 | 2 | 3 | 4 | 5 | 6 | 7 | TARE | ASPHALT | BATCH TOTAL |
|-----|------|---|---|---|---|---|---|---|------|---------|-------------|
|  |  |  |  |  |  |  |  |  |  |  |  |

5.0 *W. Wash* 95.050

43 *Country Club Rd.* 2100

| INSPECTOR'S SIGNATURE | *David Wallup* | | LOAD TOTAL | 10860 |
|---|---|---|---|---|

**EXHIBIT 9**
**Daily Work Sheet**

DATE: 5-23-95    WALDROP    DAILY WORK REPORT    TUESDAY-FRIDAY    MARTIN LUTHER KING

| ACTY | LOCATION | LABOR | 1 | 2 | 3 | 4 | 5 | 6 | TOTAL |
|---|---|---|---|---|---|---|---|---|---|
| 1  3 0 3 7 | MLK  Walkup - 4SSPH ST EQU.  Bus Trip | DW  HB  JC  VB  RYAN | 4.0  4.0  4.0 | 6.0  5.0  5.0 | 1.0  1.0  1.0 | 10.0 | 10.0 | | |
| 2  3 0 0 7 | W. Wash.  3800 - 3100 E. Bowes | TOTAL | | | | | | | |
| 3  3 0 0 7 | County Club rd 5100  Dispala | VEHICLE  1403  2039 | 4.5  4.0 | 5.0  5.0 | 1.0  1.0 | 4 | 5 | 6 | |
| 4  7 5 0 0 | Leave | | | | | | | | |
| 5  9 9  9 9 | Allan to 15 | MATERIAL  5150  5210 | 1 | 5.0  16 | 43 | 4 | 5 | 6 | |
| 6 | | NOTES: | | | | | | | |

CREW LEADER  David Wallac    MGR/SUPV  _____    DATE ENTERED/INITIAL 5/30 B+

**EXHIBIT 10**

DPW OPERATIONS
STREET MAINTENANCE/MARTIN LUTHER KING
(c) De Lew, Cather & Company

DAILY WORK REPORT DATA

Page:   1
Date:   06/02/95
TIME:   4:02 pm

| DATE | MGMT UNIT | REF# | ACTIVITY | SUB-ACTIVITY | SYSTEM/ROAD CLASS |
|---|---|---|---|---|---|
| 05/23/95 | 01 | 757 | 3875 PATCHING | | |

WORK REQUEST NO'S:

***EQUIPMENT***

| CLASS/ SPEC. | DESCRIPTION | HOURS ON JOB | CLASS/ SPECF. | DESCRIPTION | HOURS ON JOB |
|---|---|---|---|---|---|
| 1623 | CREWCAB PU | 0.5 | 2039 | PATCHMAKER TRK | 5.0 |

***MATERIAL***

| CLASS/ SPECF. | DESCRIPTION | QTY USED | UNIT OF MEASURE | CLASS/ SPECF. | DESCRIPTION | QTY USED | UNIT OF MEASURE |
|---|---|---|---|---|---|---|---|
| 5150 | HOT MIX | 5.0 | TON | 5210 | TACK COAT | 10.0 | GALLON |

***ACCOMPLISHMENT***

| LOCATION | QTY |
|---|---|
| 95-001 | 5.0 |

NOTES:
WORK UNIT: TONS

| REG CLASS/ B HRS SPECF.R | NAME | OVERTIME CODE | HRS | REG CLASS/ B HRS SPECF.R | NAME | OVERTIME CODE | HRS |
|---|---|---|---|---|---|---|---|
| 5.0 DW | DAVID WALDROP | | | 5.0 HB | JEFF CATT | 5.0 JC | |

**EXHIBIT 11**
**Daily Report**

**Sheet 1**

| CITY OF INDIANAPOLIS | | | | | | |
|---|---|---|---|---|---|---|
| DEPARTMENT OF PUBLIC WORKS | | | 3400-3800W | | | |
| OPERATIONS | WASHINGTON CHUCK HOLES WEST | | | | | |
| 23-MAY-95 | | | | | | |
| REQUIREMENT | REG TIME | | | REG COST | | TOTAL COST |
| CREW LEADER | 5 | | $ | 20.00 | $ | 100.00 |
| TRUCK DRIVER | 10 | | $ | 17.00 | $ | 170.00 |
| LABORER | | | $ | 14.00 | $ | — |
| OVERHEAD | 15 | | $ | 14.85 | $ | 222.75 |
| PATCHMAN | 5 | | $ | 26.91 | $ | 134.55 |
| CREW CAB | 5 | | $ | 8.21 | $ | 41.05 |
| 1 TON DUMP | | | $ | 11.54 | $ | |
| HOT BOX | | | $ | 9.32 | $ | |
| HOT MIX | 5 | | $ | 19.90 | $ | 99.50 |
| SPECIAL MIX | | | $ | 23.07 | $ | — |
| TACK | 10 | | $ | .99 | $ | 9.90 |
| DURAPATCH | | | $ | 17.05 | $ | — |
| | | | | | | |
| | | | | | | |
| | | | | | | |
| COST PER TON | $155.55 | | | MANPOWER | $ | 270.00 |
| | | | | EQUIPMENT | $ | 175.60 |
| | | | | MATERIAL | $ | 109.40 |
| | | | | OVERHEAD | $ | 222.75 |
| | | | | | $ | 777.75 |

**EXHIBIT 12**

**Sheet 1**

| WASHINGTON STREET | COST PER TON | $160.00 | | | | | RFL |
|---|---|---|---|---|---|---|---|
| EMERGENCY RESPONSE | COST MOBILIZATION | $180.00 | | | | | |
| WASH-95-001 POTHOLE | | | | | DATE AS OF | 20-JUN-95 | |
| LOCATION | DATE/TIME NOTIFIED | DATE/TIME REPAIRED | TONNAGE | OUR COST | AMOUNT TO BILL | PROFIT (LOSS) | COST PER TON |
| 2300-2900W | PATCHING | 4/21/95 | 1 | $ 150.18 | $ 160.00 | $ 9.82 | $150.18 |
| 3800-4200W | PATCHING | 4/26/95 | 4.07 | $ 360.21 | $ 651.20 | $ 290.99 | $ 88.50 |
| 4200-5000W | PATCHING | 4/28/95 | 5.83 | $ 767.87 | $ 932.80 | $ 164.93 | $131.71 |
| 5000-4200W | PATCHING | 5/12/95 | 2.41 | $ 582.65 | $ 385.60 | $ (197.05) | $241.76 |
| 7000-8000E | PATCHING | 5/10/95 | 0.5 | $ 166.76 | $ 80.00 | $ (86.76) | $333.52 |
| 7000-8000E | PATCHING | 5/11/95 | 3.53 | $ 870.58 | $ 635.40 | $ (235.18) | $246.62 |
| 500-7930E | PATCHING | 5/23/95 | 3 | $ 681.19 | $ 480.00 | $ (201.19) | $227.06 |
| 3400-3800W | PATCHING | 5/23/95 | 5 | $ 777.75 | $ 800.00 | $ 22.25 | $155.55 |
| 3400-39002 | PATCHING | 6/6/95 | 3.03 | $ 611.15 | $ 484.80 | $ (126.35) | $201.70 |
| 2900-1800W | PATCHING | 6/7/95 | 4.02 | $ 993.66 | $ 643.20 | $ (350.46) | $247.18 |
| 1800-3400W | PATCHING | 6/8/95 | 1.41 | $ 596.88 | $ 225.60 | $ (371.28) | $423.32 |
| | | | | | | $ — | #DIV/0! |
| | | | | | | $ — | #DIV/0! |
| | | | | | | $ — | #DIV/0! |
| | | | | | | $ — | #DIV/0! |
| | | | | | | $ — | #DIV/0! |
| | | | 33.8 | $6,558.87 | $5,478.60 | $(1,080.27) | $194.05 |

# Nordstrom: Dissension in the Ranks? (A)

T he first time Nordstrom sales clerk Lori Lucas came to one of the many "mandatory" Saturday morning department meetings and saw the sign—"Do Not Punch the Clock"—she assumed the managers were telling the truth when they said the clock was temporarily out of order. But as weeks went by, she discovered that on subsequent Saturdays the clock was always "broken" or the time cards were not accessible. When she and several colleagues hand-wrote the hours on their time cards, they discovered that their manager whited-out the hours and accused them of not being "team players." Commenting on the variety of tasks that implicitly had to be performed after hours, Ms. Lucas said, "You couldn't complain, because then your manager would schedule you for the bad hours, your sales per hour would fall, and next thing you know, you're out the door."[1]

Patty Bemis, who joined Nordstrom as a sales clerk in 1981 and quit eight years later, told a similar story:

> Nordstrom recruiters came to me. I was working at The Broadway as Estee Lauder's counter manager and they said they had heard I had wonderful sales figures. We'd all heard Nordstrom was the place to work. They told me how I would double my wages. They painted a great picture and I fell right into it. . .

---

[1] Susan Faludi, "At Nordstrom Stores, Service Comes First—But at a Big Price," *The Wall Street Journal*, February 20, 1990, p. A1.

---

*Hilary Weston prepared this case from public sources under the supervision of Professor Robert Simons.*

Copyright © 1990 by the President and Fellows of Harvard College. Harvard Business School case 191-002.

*The managers were these little tin gods, always grilling you about your sales. . . . You felt like your job was constantly in jeopardy. They'd write you up for anything, being sick, the way you dressed. . . . The girls around me were dropping like flies. Everyone was always in tears. . . .*

*Working off the clock was just standard. In the end, really serving the customer, being an All-Star, meant nothing; if you had low sales per hour, you were forced out. . . .*

*I just couldn't take it anymore—the constant demands, the grueling hours. I just said one day, life's too short.*[2]

Despite employee grievances such as those of Lori Lucas and Patty Bemis, top management at the fashion specialty retailer acknowledged no serious problems with its management systems. Jim Nordstrom, co-chairman of the company with his brother John and cousin Bruce, explained management's position in a statement to the press:

*We haven't seen any complaints from the union. . . . If employees are working without pay, breaks, or days off, then it's isolated or by choice.*

*A lot of them say, "I want to work every day." I have as many people thank us for letting them work all these hours as complain. I think people don't put in enough hours during the busy time. We need to work harder.*

*A lot of what comes out makes it sound like we're slave drivers. If we were that kind of company, they wouldn't smile, they wouldn't work that hard. Our people smile because they want to.*[3]

## BACKGROUND OF THE CURRENT SITUATION

John W. Nordstrom founded Nordstrom in 1901 as a shoe store. Nearly a century later, by the end of 1989, the company had grown to become the nation's leading specialty retailer of apparel, shoes, and accessories. The company operated 59 department stores in six states and was implementing a national expansion plan that called for store openings in several additional states in the early 1990s. By the end of 1989, sales were approaching $3 billion and Nordstrom enjoyed one of the highest profit margins in its industry.

Nordstrom, which issued shares to the public in 1971, had always been run by members of the Nordstrom family, who still owned roughly half of the company. The third generation of Nordstrom family managers, who had been at the helm since 1970, upheld the management philosophy of the company's founder: offer the customer the best in service, selection, quality, and value.

Superior customer service was Nordstrom's strongest competitive advantage and consequently a major source of its financial success. The retailer had

---

[2]  Ibid.

[3]  Ibid.

enjoyed nearly twenty years of uninterrupted (primarily double-digit) earnings growth before reporting a decline for the 1989 fiscal year. **Exhibit 1** provides a history of Nordstrom's financial performance. With sales per square foot of $380 in 1988,[4] Nordstrom was among the most productive in the industry, generating roughly double the 1988 industry average for specialty retailers of $194 per square foot.[5]

Throughout the 1980s, Nordstrom's salespeople were the envy of the industry in terms of their quality and productivity. The caliber of the company's sales clerks seemed to withstand the pressures of rapid growth as the company's work force expanded geographically and grew from 5,000 employees in 1980 to 30,000 in 1989. The clerks' "heroics" (as they called their exceptional customer service efforts) helped to build the store's alluring image, its extremely strong customer loyalty, and its lofty sales per square foot.

At Nordstrom's, it was common practice for sales clerks, or "Nordies" as they called themselves, to:

- drive to another Nordstrom store to retrieve a desired item in an out-of-stock size or color;
- drive to a customer's home to deliver purchases;
- call a valued customer to alert her or him of newly arriving merchandise;
- help a customer assemble a complete outfit by retrieving items from several different departments; and
- write thank-you notes to customers for their purchases.

Sales clerks were also known for performing such heroics as changing a customer's flat tire in the store parking lot, paying a customer's parking ticket if his or her shopping time outlasted the parking meter, lending a few dollars to a customer short on cash in order to consummate a purchase, and taking a customer to lunch.

By performing these extraordinary services—which were often performed outside of a sales clerk's scheduled time on the selling floor—sales clerks earned their customers' praise, gratitude, and loyalty. (**Exhibit 2** reproduces a typical customer letter.) In addition to customer loyalty, industrious clerks could earn over $80,000 a year. The average Nordstrom sales clerk earned $20,000 to $24,000 per year, compared to the national average for all retail sales clerks of $12,000 per year.[6]

During the 1980s, more and more rivals such as R. H. Macy, Bloomingdales, and Neiman Marcus began to emulate Nordstrom's service-oriented strategy. According to one industry expert:

---

[4] Richard W. Stevenson, "Watch Out Macy's, Here Comes Nordstrom," *New York Times*, August 27, 1989, p. 34.

[5] National Retail Merchants Association, *Financial & Operating Results of Department & Specialty Stores*, 1989 ed.

[6] Faludi, op. cit.

*All retailers in America have awakened to the Nordstrom threat and are struggling to catch up.  Nordstrom is the future of retailing. . . . [It] is the most Darwinian of retail companies today.*[7]

At the end of the decade, Nordstrom's much heralded reputation was formally acknowledged with the 1989 National Retail Merchants Association's Gold Medal—considered by many to be the most prestigious award in the industry.[8]

## POLICIES, PRACTICES, AND MEASUREMENT SYSTEMS

In the mid-1960s, to support its high-service strategy and motivate its salespeople, Nordstrom introduced an innovative commission system—revolutionary among specialty retail and department stores.  Top management combined this incentive compensation system—which was driven by sales per hour (SPH)—with other distinctive policies to guide, motivate, and measure the performance of its sales staff.  Although its established set of management systems and policies had proven very effective for over 20 years, problems began to emerge at the end of the 1980s.

### Sales-Per-Hour Incentives

The following account[9] describes the mechanics of Nordstrom's commission-selling system as well as the explicit and implicit ways in which it affected employees:

> *Interviews with a dozen current and former Nordstrom employees in California illustrate the contradictory pressures that workers can experience in a system that tries to give equal emphasis to service, profitability, and middle-managerial autonomy.*
>
> *Most of those interviewed said no manager ever formally told them to go off the clock, an order that would flatly violate state and federal fair labor standards laws.  Rather, they said, it becomes clear to most Nordstrom salespeople soon after they are hired that the store's commission-selling program effectively penalizes any salesperson who insists on getting paid for every hour worked.*
>
> *The reason is that Nordstrom carefully evaluates salespeople on their sales-per-hour ratio.  Each employee is given a target SPH ratio—a quota—based on his or her base hourly wage and store department.  The actual SPH for the past two weeks—sales minus merchandise returned by customers, divided by hours worked—appears on each paycheck stub.*

[7]  Stevenson, op. cit.

[8]  Jean Bergmann, "Nordstrom Gets the Gold," *STORES*, January 1990, p. 44.

[9]  Bob Baker, "The Other Nordstrom," *Los Angeles Times*, February 4, 1990, p. D1.

*If the actual SPH is higher than the target SPH, the employee is paid a 6.75% to 10% commission on net sales, depending on the department. If the SPH is below the target, the employee is paid the base hourly wage (roughly $9.00, with variations by department).[10] Failure to meet the target SPH often results in decreased hours or, in some cases, termination. Meeting or surpassing the target SPH means more working hours—including better hours when the shopping is heavier—and a better chance of promotion to a department manager job.*

*Stories of some Nordstrom workers making $40,000 to $60,000 or more a year thanks to hefty commissions are widespread. But critics of the system say rank-and-file salespeople are often torn in this environment.*

*To chalk up the most impressive SPH ratio, salespeople must be on the floor selling. But to carry out the Nordstrom credo of being a "team player" or a "Nordie," they also must be available to run themselves ragged meeting each customer's needs, which can take considerable time. Time also must be spent in routine merchandise stocking, store display activities, or attending numerous sales staff meetings. These hours, if formally recorded, lower the SPH.*

*Initially your feeling is, "I've got to punch in for every minute I'm there," said Joel Kirk, who worked as a salesman and a men's clothing manager for several years in Northern California before leaving Nordstrom last summer to return to college. "Then you find you're at the bottom on SPH, or near it. Then someone nudges you. It's there but it's not said. It's an underlying factor that everyone eventually realizes.*

*"There is pressure on (department) managers to get people with the biggest SPH into the most hours. You're not told that if you don't (go off the clock) you'll get your hours cut. It becomes an inferred thing. The more you sell per hour, the more hours you get," said Kirk, who spoke on the condition that his real name not be used.*

*As a result, critics of the system say, people making blue-collar wages and governed by hourly wage laws find themselves having to make time-management decisions usually reserved for white-collar "professionals" who are paid much higher weekly salaries and, in exchange, are expected to work some uncompensated hours.*

*Nordstrom says to salespeople, "This is your own business, treat it like your own business, but it's not said outright that you're going to have to do all these extra things," said Kirk, who emphasized that he has no hard feelings against the company. "They don't sit you down and say the calling of past customers for new business is important, the thank-you cards are*

---

[10]  Newly hired sales clerks began at an hourly rate of approximately $4.50, and in each of the four quarters of their first year they received wage increases to bring them up to the maximum base rate for their department, which was roughly $9.00 per hour, depending on the department.

*important, taking things to the customer's house is important, running things out to a local tailor when Nordstrom's tailor is backed up is important."*

*To honor those who thrive, Nordstrom awards its top sellers annual membership in the company's Pace Setters Club, entitling them to 33% discounts on merchandise. The posting of SPH figures creates peer pressure that is regarded by retail analysts as a strong motivator.*

*However . . . dissident salespeople complain about intense competition between individual salespeople. Often cited is the court case in King County, Washington, where a jury last fall awarded $180,000 to a former Nordstrom saleswoman who claimed that she was wrongfully dismissed because co-workers wrote anonymous letters claiming that she stole from them by falsely crediting herself with their commissions.*

## Examples of Compensation Determination

The following two examples, one for a sales clerk generating $8,000 in weekly sales and one for a clerk generating $5,000 in weekly sales, illustrate the incentives built in to Nordstrom's SPH compensation system:[11]

**Assumptions:**

| | |
|---|---|
| • Guaranteed base wage: | $9.45 per hour |
| • Hours scheduled per week: | 40 |
| • Sales per hour (SPH) target: | $140 |
| • Sales per week target: | 40 hrs. × $140 SPH = $5,600 |
| • Commission rate: | 6.75% (if sales *exceed* target) |
| • Overtime pay (O/T) for hours in excess of 40 hours/week: | 0.5 × average regular-time hourly earnings |

**Example 1:**

A sales clerk who works 50 hours per week and generates weekly sales of $8,000.

a)  If hours reported = 40, then
    SPH = $8,000/40 = $200, and
    Weekly earnings = .0675 × $8,000 = $540

b)  If hours reported = 50, then
    SPH = $8,000/50 = $160, and
    Weekly earnings = (.0675 × $8,000) + (premium for 10 hours O/T)
                           = $540 + (10 hours × .5 × $9.45) = $587.25

---

[11] These hypothetical examples are based on descriptions of Nordstrom's compensation system provided by multiple public sources, including the Washington State Department of Labor and Industries.

As this example illustrates, a sales clerk would earn more for this week's work by reporting overtime hours; however, this option would result in a lower SPH. A low SPH could reduce a clerk's ranking among peers and could work against him or her when the supervisor assigns shifts.[12] As a result, a sales clerk may choose to sacrifice pay in the short term for better shifts and more hours in the future. The higher SPH also may improve a clerk's chances for promotion.

**Example 2:**

A sales clerk who works 50 hours per week and generates weekly sales of $5,500.

a)   If hours reported = 40, then
     SPH = $5,500/40 = $137.50 (which is less than target), and
     Weekly earnings = 40 hours × $9.45 = $378 (no commissions earned)

b)   If hours reported = 50, then
     SPH = $5,500/50 = $110 (which is less than target), and
     Weekly earnings = 50 hours × $9.45 + (premium for 10 hours O/T)
                     = $472.50 + (10 hours × .5 × $9.45) = $519.75

As in the first example, the sales clerk stands to gain financially by reporting all hours worked. If the clerk does so, however, the SPH drops substantially below his or her target level. According to employees' descriptions of the system, a substandard SPH can result in fewer scheduled hours, worse shifts, and—if such performance persists for several pay periods—termination, not to mention stressful peer pressure. Again, employees may opt to work off the clock rather than report all hours.

The lack of a clear distinction between "selling time" and "non-sell" work time exacerbated the pressures on employees. For example, an hour of extra work defined as "non-sell" (e.g., annual stock-taking) by Nordstrom entitled an employee to the guaranteed base wage with no effect on his or her SPH. If the same hour was considered selling time, his or her SPH would be affected negatively. Moreover, the clerk was considered to be fully compensated for all selling hours through commissions (assuming targets were exceeded) and was therefore not entitled to any extra pay for reporting the extra hour worked. **Exhibit 3** reproduces an internal memo distributed by top management in an effort to clarify its system of differentiating between selling and non-selling time on the job.

## Additional Elements of the Management System

Although SPH monitoring was the heart of Nordstrom's distinctive management strategy, the SPH system was complemented by other organizational

---

[12]   Faludi, op. cit.

factors.  For example, the composition of the sales force was well-suited to the competitive work environment.  Nordstrom sales clerks tended to be young, often college-educated people looking for a career in retailing.  They were willing to work hard in exchange for the retailer's relatively high salaries and opportunities for rapid advancement.[13]  The company's policy of promoting only from within also enhanced the overall level of Nordstrom experience within middle management, and helped to motivate ambitious and hard-working employees.

The availability of desirable merchandise in appropriate colors and sizes was critical to Nordstrom's success.  Department managers worked closely with buyers and often had direct buying authority.  Since the sales-per-hour commission system rewarded turnover, Nordie's were committed to working with their department managers to anticipate customer buying patterns and ensuring adequate stock.

Throughout the chain's rapid growth, top management endorsed a decentralized system of operations; department, store, and regional managers were relatively free to make their own decisions.[14]  Moreover, they were eligible for bonuses tied to the achievement of their budget goals.  Thus, decision-making responsibility and rewards were delegated directly to the front-line salespeople who were closest to the customer.  At the same time, however, such decentralization limited top management's control over the application of sales force management systems.  Such systems were originally centralized when the organization was much smaller.  Without meaningful control over their use, however, these systems—which supported sales force scheduling, compensation, and promotions—could be vulnerable to abuse.

Another aspect of the Nordstrom's work environment that had both positive and negative ramifications was the role of group recognition and peer pressure.  At monthly store meetings, managers read aloud customers' letters of praise.  Sales staffs responded with applause and cheers.  The salespeople who elicited such written praise were honored as "Customer Service All-Stars" and their pictures were usually displayed by the customer-service desk.  The All-Stars also received added discounts on clothing and had their efforts documented in their personnel files.[15]  The pressure to become an All-Star, however, could result in undesired behavior, such as "sharking"—the term Nordstrom employees used to describe stealing credit for sales made by other staff.

Competition was also promoted on the sales floor via various types of sales contests.  For example, a free dinner might be awarded to the employee who generated the most multiple-item sales to individual customers.  Such public fanfare helped to keep Nordstrom's sales clerks motivated and its incentive system alive on a day-to-day and hour-to-hour basis.  Peer pressure

---

[13]  Stevenson, op. cit.

[14]  Nordstrom's 1987 Annual Report.

[15]  Stevenson, op. cit.

was also strong among management ranks where an elaborate and very public goal-setting process transpired. Every year the company's managers gathered in large meetings where they individually proclaimed their store or departmental goals for the next 12 months. Then, immediately following each announcement, the boss of the particular manager stood up to unveil his or her previously hidden goal for that manager. Again, cheering and howling was a common accompaniment.

One last ingredient that helped to support Nordstrom's sales force management strategy was the use of automation: salespeople were able to track their performance on computer printouts available in back offices. The printouts listed individual sales by employee identification number so that clerks could compare their performance to both their own targets and their peers' performance. The ease of access to such information helped employees at all levels to determine precisely their achievement relative to their peers.

Nordstrom management believed their system worked. The company claimed that employees earned one of the highest base pay rates in the industry—as much as $10 an hour—and especially industrious employees could make as much as $80,000 a year. Moreover, Nordstrom's corporate policy of promoting only from within and its policy of decentralization combined to give managers unusual freedom to make decisions that would enhance customer service.[16]

## FROM A LOCAL UNION DISPUTE TO CLASS ACTION SUITS[17]

In the second half of 1989, the same company policies and compensation systems to which much of Nordstrom's success was attributed became the target of a barrage of employee complaints, union allegations, lawsuits, and regulatory orders that tainted the company's reputation and blemished its financial performance. By the spring of 1990, the escalating accusations and events remained under dispute and it was not yet clear whether Nordstrom's change of fortune was temporary or long term.

In the summer of 1989, a discontent minority of Nordstrom's sales clerks chose to risk their reputation as "the most helpful and cheerful in the industry" and voice their grievances against the company. Angered by management's actions during contract negotiations, the United Food and Commercial Workers (UFCW) Local 1001 began a publicity campaign against Nordstrom, challenging the legality of the company's labor practices. Local 1001 was based in the state of Washington and represented roughly 1,500 of Nordstrom's nearly 30,000 employees. Local 367 represented another 200 sales clerks in the state.

---

[16] Ibid.

[17] This section provides a chronological summary of the events that transpired between June 1989 and April 1990 as reported in the press.

The Washington employees were the only unionized members of the Nordstrom workforce; no other Nordstrom employees were unionized.

Representatives of Local 1001 complained that the company coerced employees to work "off the clock" without being paid. They maintained that Nordstrom neither recorded nor compensated employees for all the time they spent performing certain duties that were not directly related to selling—such as delivering packages to customers' homes, attending department meetings, writing thank-you notes to customers, doing inventory work, and general bookkeeping. Moreover, the union claimed that Nordstrom's use of sales per hour as a performance measure—for determining which employees were eligible for commissions (versus hourly wages), which were assigned the most and best shifts, and which were at risk of being fired—implicitly encouraged employees to work off the clock.

In an effort to quantify their claim, Local 1001's union officials distributed back-pay forms to the unionized sales clerks on which they could calculate and submit their individual claims. By late November 1989, the union reported to the press that they had collected $1 million in back-pay claims from several hundred sales clerks.

In November 1989, Local 1001 filed a formal complaint with the Employment Standards Section of the Washington State Department of Labor and Industries. (**Exhibit 4** reproduces the Department of Labor summary of the complaint.) At the same time, members of the union also voiced their complaints through pamphlets, pickets, and the press, demanding that management reimburse employees the millions of dollars of back pay which they were owed.

Nordstrom management denied the allegations and dismissed them as a union ploy "to drum up support for their cause" at the bargaining table. (Contract negotiations had been at a stalemate since July 1989.) A company spokesperson said that the complaints were unsubstantiated and maintained that the company policy had "always been to pay employees for the time that they've worked."[18]

At the same time, the company was also forced to respond to a variety of charges filed against them by the National Labor Relations Board (NLRB).[19] The NLRB claimed that Nordstrom's bargaining tactics with the UFCW

---

[18] Robert Spector, "Union Says Nordstrom Owes Workers Millions," *Footwear News*, November 6, 1989, p. 8.

[19] The National Labor Relations Board (NLRB) is an independent federal agency responsible for enforcing the National Labor Relations Act—a body of federal law that governs relations between labor unions and employers engaged in interstate commerce. In addition to conducting unionization elections, the NLRB investigates, prosecutes, and remedies employers' and unions' labor practices that are in violation of the NLR Act. The agency operates out of 52 offices throughout the U.S. and employs nearly 3,000 people. Its leadership (a general counsel and five-member board) are appointed by the president.

violated federal labor laws and that management had failed to provide the union with requested wage-related data and time card records.

The union complaints triggered a three-month investigation by the Washington State Department of Labor and Industries. On February 15, 1990, the department released their findings, which concurred with several of Local 1001's allegations. The administrative ruling stated that Nordstrom systematically violated state wage and hour laws in their failure both to record all hours worked and to pay sales clerks for performing certain services. The state regulatory agency ordered the company to bolster its record-keeping operations, to pay two years' of back pay to all Washington employees affected by the charge, and to pay employees in the future for time spent on such tasks as deliveries, meetings, and writing thank-you notes. The regulators did not specify the number of employees affected or the dollars involved in the back-pay reimbursements. **Exhibit 5** reproduces the department's conclusions and its order.

Local 1001 President Joe Peterson estimated that Nordstrom could be liable for as much as $30 to $40 million in back-pay claims from its Washington employees alone, and for several hundred million dollars if the union followed through with a nationwide class action suit on behalf of all Nordstrom employees.[20] By mid-February, the union said it had doubled its November "back-pay" collection and held individual claims totaling over $2 million from roughly 400 sales clerks in Washington, California, and Oregon. According to media reports, the sales clerks who submitted claims worked an average of 8 to 10 hours per week off the clock. Peterson asserted, "Nordstrom is doing a disservice to its reputation, employees, and stockholders by continuing to deny that they have a culture. . . that requires employees to work without pay."[21]

In response, company co-chairman Bruce Nordstrom affirmed management's intentions to "fully comply with the law" and to review their record-keeping procedures and pay practices for any weaknesses.[22] Management announced that it was refining its time-keeping procedures to correct for any shortcoming. But, at the same time, Bruce Nordstrom denied that there was a "pattern" of abuse and maintained that complying with the law would "not alter our culture nor affect our continued commitment to customer service."[23]

As part of their efforts to illustrate their good intentions, Nordstrom management vowed to compensate employees for any past errors in its record-keeping and pay practices. To do so, they set up a procedure by which all employees nationwide could submit claims for back pay. The procedure offered employees the opportunity to collect a lump sum payment based on their

---

[20]  George Tibbits, *Financial News* (API newswire), February 26, 1990, time: 13:59 PST.

[21]  Blackburn Katia, *Financial News* (API newswire), February 16, 1990, time: 17:21 PST.

[22]  Bob Baker, "Agency Orders Nordstrom to Pay Back Wages," *Los Angeles Times*, February 17, 1990, p. D1.

[23]  Francine Schwadel, "Nordstrom to Post Its First Decline in Annual Profit," *The Wall Street Journal*, February 20, 1990, p. A16.

choice of either length of service or their own detailed individual claims. In the former case, the payment was for $300, $700, or $1,000, depending on an employee's length of service. Initially, this back-pay offer was mailed only to current employees outside of Washington because management had to consult the State Labor and Industries Department and the local union before extending the offer to Washington employees.[24] Management was also designing a process by which former employees entitled to back pay could collect from the company. To fund the back-pay claims program, Nordstrom voluntarily established a $15 million reserve—which had a substantial effect on fourth quarter earnings.[25]

In addition to setting up the back-pay fund, management took steps to improve the existing system and restore its integrity. They first sent a memo to employees detailing company pay policies and reassuring sales clerks that they would be paid for all store meetings, inventory work, and deliveries. They also initiated several procedural changes, including the adoption of sign-out sheets. Under the new system, sales clerks who planned to do extra work at home or on the way home (i.e., deliveries) could punch out on the time clock at the end of their shift but also indicate on the sign-out sheet that they were doing work after hours. The next day they would submit a time sheet showing the amount of extra time worked.

Local 1001 President Peterson argued that this arrangement was placing the burden on employees to keep records, when it was Nordstrom's responsibility.[26] Peterson also criticized another Nordstrom policy: the classification of tasks performed off the sales floor into "selling" and "non-selling" activities. By continuing to classify certain behind-the-scenes tasks as "selling" duties, time spent writing "thank-you" letters and similar activities would remain in the denominator of sales-per-hour performance measures. Consequently, Peterson contended, employees would continue to feel pressure not to report all their hours spent on these tasks.

On February 27, 1990, Nordstrom became the target of another unhappy constituency. Immediately after fourth quarter earnings were released, three individual Nordstrom stockholders filed a suit against the company (for unspecified damages) in Seattle's King County Superior Court. They claimed to have suffered financial losses due to Nordstrom management's failure to disclose adequately their labor problems and the early claims for unpaid work. The suit requested that it be made a class action suit on behalf of Nordstrom's

---

[24] Francine Schwadel, "Nordstrom Creates $15 Million Reserve for Back Wages," *The Wall Street Journal*, February 27, 1990, p. A3.

[25] Although the $15 million provision was not made public until late February 1990, it was recorded as an expense against Nordstrom's 1989 fourth-quarter earnings (quarter ending January 31, 1990).

[26] Stuart Silverstein, "Nordstrom to Change Its Timekeeping Procedures," *Los Angeles Times*, February 24, 1990, p. D2.

more than 75,000 stockholders.[27]  (See **Exhibit 6** for a history of Nordstrom's stock price.)

Within a two-day period, Nordstrom became the target of a second class action suit.  On February 28, 1990, UFCW Locals 1001 and 367, together with five individually named plaintiffs employed by Nordstrom, filed suit on behalf of approximately 50,000 current and former Nordstrom employees (union and nonunion) nationwide.  The lawsuit accused the company of numerous violations of state and federal wage and hour laws and requested that the King County Superior Court order Nordstrom to improve its record-keeping and award damages equal to twice the amount of unpaid wages (plus additional damages determined at trial and attorneys' fees).  **Exhibit 7** reproduces the union's alleged "facts."  Union officials had decided to launch the suit because they considered Nordstrom's response to the Washington State order, both the policy changes and the $15 million provision for back pay, inadequate.[28]

Reaction to the suit among employees was mixed.  Many remained loyal to Nordstrom and came to its defense.  Several employee-organized rallies took place outside stores in Seattle and California, featuring signs and chants such as "We Love Nordstrom," "My Job is #1," and "I Love Being a Nordie."  The demonstrators resented the local unions' assertion that the union spoke for all Nordstrom employees.

Nevertheless, the national publicity elicited by the suit brought into question the image and systems that Nordstrom's competitors had sought to emulate. According to one retail consultant, the company long considered the epitome of retailing excellence and superior service had actually enjoyed an unfair advantage by not paying fully for employees' work.  If the apparent means of Nordstrom's success proved true, he believed, other retailers would probably become less eager to replicate the Nordstrom retailing model.

In the spring of 1990, Nordstrom management was defending itself on multiple fronts.

First, on March 16, 1990, Nordstrom's lawyers petitioned the court to void the Washington State Department of Labor and Industries' ruling (dated February 15) on the grounds that the department's investigation and release of findings had violated Nordstrom's constitutional rights to due process and equal protection.  (The Labor and Industries Department subsequently filed a counter-claim in defense of its actions.)  If Nordstrom and the agency could not resolve their differences directly, the agency would have to take Nordstrom to court to enforce its ruling.

Also, the NLRB maintained their charges that Nordstrom had illegally circumvented the union in communicating with its employees.  If the agency could not persuade Nordstrom to settle out of court, it planned to bring its allegations before an administrative judge.

---

[27]  *Financial News* (newswire), February 27, 1990, time: 20:27 PST.

[28]  *Financial News* (API newswire), February 28, 1990, time: 21:30 PST.

In addition to dealing with state and federal regulatory agencies, Nordstrom remained embroiled in the dispute surrounding both the shareholders' and the union's class action suits against it. In May 1990, *60 Minutes,* the popular CBS news magazine show, televised a twenty-minute segment on Nordstrom's incentive systems and related problems.

According to the assistant director of the Washington State Department of Labor and Industries:[29]

> *We're looking at what is likely to be the highest wage claim in the history of the state. These are employment practice patterns the company engaged in, not isolated incidents.*

## THE JURY WAS OUT

In Nordstrom's 1989 Annual Report, released in March 1990, the company's executive committee summarized its position:

> *We are disappointed that there is now litigation regarding the payment of retroactive wages and related issues. Our policy has always been to pay our employees for the work that they perform, and this policy has not changed over the years. Employee initiative and enthusiasm has always been important in servicing the needs of customers, and we appreciate the efforts of our employees. They are the foundation of the Company's success. Some mistakes have been made in compensating our employees, and we are in the process of correcting them. We believe, however, that our sales employees are the highest paid in our industry. And we also believe that they will continue to provide the customer service that they have become known for because they enjoy selling for the Company and because they are rewarded for their efforts through commissions on their sales.*

As of April 1990, there were no indications of emerging consensus among Nordstrom's 50,000 current and former employees as to the seriousness of the problem. While over a thousand employees had mailed in to Local 1001 back-pay claims (averaging $5,000 each),[30] hundreds of other fiercely loyal "Nordies" came to management's defense. Some loyalists expressed their sentiments by signing a petition to decertify the union and some participated in "pro-Nordstrom" rallies.

Confusion around the merits of Nordstrom's management systems and culture was evident in the contradictory claims of outspoken current and former employees. Some of these were negative:

---

[29]  Faludi, op. cit.

[30]  Telephone interview with Joe Peterson, president of UFCW Local 1001, May 16, 1990.

*We have the sworn testimony of a supervisor. He said it was routine in this department that people would come in and do the markdowns in preparation for a sale on their own time, on their day off, off the clock. If they didn't get it done in time, he'd punish them by not scheduling them to work on the first day of the sale. This is no petty violation, and it goes far beyond customer service. It goes right down to the core of the business.[31]*

\* \* \* \* \*

*It was like a snake pit. They'd throw you into the arena, and the strong would survive.[32]*

\* \* \* \* \*

*The system fosters a lot of pettiness and jealousy. . . . It's fear that provides great customer service.[33]*

Other comments, however, were positive:

*I've never been asked to work overtime or make deliveries or do anything I didn't feel in my heart I wanted to do for many reasons. And my paycheck reflects that service I give. Everything I do, I'm compensated for in many, many ways.[34]*

As the crisis escalated, national newspapers began printing letters to their editors which expressed opinions on the Nordstrom grievances. One letter challenged directly a basic assumption of the union grievance action:

*When I worked at Nordstrom's Anchorage and Spokane stores, I was paid to the minute for all the time I was in the store as an hourly employee. When I was in management, I received a salary and bonus structure that rivaled that of many other professionals. The awards and sales incentives were fair and generous.*

*The people dismayed with the long hours required do not grasp a fundamental of retail: The shopkeeper must be available to the customer at the customer's whim, not to suit the employees' or owners' desires.[35]*

When confronted by reporter Morley Safer during a *60 Minutes* interview on the problem, Bruce and Jim Nordstrom summarized Nordstrom management's beliefs:

---

[31] *60 Minutes* (CBS news documentary on national television), May 6, 1990.

[32] Ibid.

[33] Baker, op. cit.

[34] *60 Minutes*, op. cit.

[35] Letter to the Editor, *The Wall Street Journal*, March 14, 1990, p. A19.

*The system is to have self-empowered people who have an entrepreneurial spirit, who feel that they're in this to better themselves and to feel good about themselves and to make more money and to be successful.  That's the system.*

*[We have] expectations on our people.  And when people apply for a job anyplace, they want to work hard and they want to do a good job.  That's their intention.  And our intention is to allow them the freedom to work as hard as they want to work.*[36]

---

[36]  *60 Minutes,* op. cit.

**EXHIBIT 1**
**Nordstrom, Inc. and Subsidiaries Ten-Year Statistical Summary**

| | 1990 | 1989 | 1988 | 1987 | 1986 | 1985 | 1984 | 1983 | 1982 | 1981 |
|---|---|---|---|---|---|---|---|---|---|---|
| **Operations** | | | | | | | | | | |
| Net sales | 2,671,114 | 2,327,946 | 1,920,231 | 1,629,918 | 1,301,857 | 958,678 | 768,677 | 598,666 | 512,188 | 400,614 |
| Total costs and expenses | 2,491,705 | 2,129,514 | 1,757,498 | 1,489,679 | 1,214,478 | 886,167 | 694,838 | 550,353 | 468,513 | 364,059 |
| Earnings before income taxes | 179,409 | 198,432 | 162,733 | 140,239 | 87,379 | 72,511 | 73,839 | 48,313 | 43,675 | 36,555 |
| Net earnings | 114,909 | 123,332 | 92,733 | 72,939 | 50,079 | 40,711 | 40,239 | 27,013 | 24,775 | 19,655 |
| Fully diluted earnings per share | 1.41 | 1.51 | 1.13 | .91 | .65 | .54 | .54 | .38 | .35 | .29 |
| **Stores and Facilities** | | | | | | | | | | |
| Company-operated stores | 59 | 58 | 56 | 53 | 52 | 44 | 39 | 36 | 34 | 31 |
| Total square footage | 6,898,000 | 6,374,000 | 5,527,000 | 5,098,000 | 4,727,000 | 3,924,000 | 3,213,000 | 2,977,000 | 2,640,000 | 2,166,000 |

**EXHIBIT 2**
**Sample Customer Letter**

*10-23-89*

*Dear Mr. Nordstrom,*

*I shopped in your store October 7th. As always it was a fun experience. One of your employees, Anne Smith, was particularly nice. Your store did not have my size in a jacket I loved. Ms. Smith found out that I was from Oregon & wanted the jacket for a party on the 14th. She drove to South Center and picked it up (after work) and I came in later that evening and purchased it. She deserves recognition!*

*I supervise several employees and recognize outstanding employees when I see them. Ms. Smith went out of her way to see that the*

# nordstrom

800 Tacoma Mall
Tacoma, WA 98409-7273
(206) 475-3630

October 31, 1989

Ms. Cheryl Johnson
1321 Lawnridge Ave.
Springfield, OR 97477

Dear Ms. Johnson:

Thank you for your thoughtful letter about the good service you received from Anne Smith in our Individualist department. I'm glad Anne followed through for you and located the jacket you wanted.  Customer service is our number one priority at Nordstrom Tacoma Mall and salespeople like Anne help set a positive example for the rest of the store to emulate.  It will be my pleasure to share your kind note with Anne and her department manager.  I really appreciate your feedback.

Sincerely,

signed by Peter E. Nordstrom

Peter E. Nordstrom
Store Manager

PEN:cam

cc:   Tracy Magnuson, Individualist Manager, Tacoma

---

Source: Washington State Department of Labor and Industries, ESAC Division, Nordstrom Investigation.

**EXHIBIT 3**
**Nordstrom Compensation Memo**

TO:      ALL STORE AND DEPARTMENT MANAGERS
FROM:   THE NORDSTROM FAMILY
SUBJ:    EMPLOYEE COMPENSATION FOR TIME WORKED
DATE:    AUGUST 1, 1989

The following information is offered as a review of some long-standing Company business practices. First of all, the Nordstrom policy of employee compensation is based on the premise that "all employees will be paid for time worked." Although it would be impossible to outline all examples of work activities, we'll attempt to review some common Company practices that warrant employee compensation.

"Hand carries"—merchandise that is picked up by an employee at one store and delivered to another. If done during regular work hours, employee remains on time clock. If effort is made going to and from work, the employee may be entitled to be paid for time over and above their normal commute time. ("Hand carries" that facilitate a personal sale are considered an extension of the selling process and regular "selling-time" would be paid. If the employee has been requested to pick up and deliver merchandise other than for a personal customer, their time would be compensated as "non-sell.")

"Home deliveries"—merchandise that is delivered to a customer's home, office, hotel, hospital room, etc. The same criteria as "hand carries" would apply.

Although there are many functions related to each employee's job, listed below are a number of activities that are part of the selling/customer service process. These efforts are to be performed at the workplace. Also, when work is performed outside the workplace (i.e., at home), then, depending on the circumstances, an employee may be entitled to compensation.

- Time spent locating merchandise from other stores via the telephone.
- Stock assignments, floor moves, and work parties, i.e., picking up "dead wood," "singles parties," "running hash," or any other merchandise-handling activity.
- Sales promotion activities and customer correspondence, i.e., thank-you notes, addressing sale notices, etc.
- MNS book documentation efforts.
- Customer Service Board, Human Resource Committee, and Safety Committee tasks and activities.
- "Personal Touch" department seminars and activities.
- Employee meetings that are mandatory. In addition, if the meeting is voluntary, then our people should never suffer criticism for not attending.

Again, this partial list does not pretend to encompass all possible job-related functions. However, the intent is to reiterate and possibly clarify some compensatory work activities at Nordstrom.

Source: Washington State Department of Labor and Industries, ESAC Division, Nordstrom Investigation.

**EXHIBIT 4**
**Summary of UFCW Local 1001 Complaint from the**
**Department of Labor and Industries, State of Washington**

February 15, 1990


Mr. Wayne Hansen
Lane Powell Moss & Miller
1420 Fifth Avenue, Suite 4100
Seattle, Washington 98101-2338

Dear Mr. Hansen:

On November 21, 1989, The Employment Standards Section of the Department of
Labor and Industries received a complaint from Local 1001 of the United Food and
Commercial Workers Union representing the employees of Nordstrom Inc.  The basis
of the complaint was:

1.    Nordstrom employees are required or encouraged to attend store, depart-
      ment, and group meetings, outside normal work hours, without compensa-
      tion, where the purpose of the meeting is to discuss work objectives and
      other work-related topics.

2.    Nordstrom employees are required or encouraged to locate merchandise at
      other stores, either by phone or in person, outside of normal work hours,
      without compensation.  This would include deliveries of merchandise to
      customers' homes, called "hand carries."

3.    Employees are required or encouraged to perform stock work outside of
      normal work hours, without compensation.  This includes floor moves, sale
      set-ups, inventory preparation, mark downs and ticketing, and other
      merchandise-handling activities.

4.    Employees are required or encouraged to write customer correspondence
      including thank-you notes, as well as addressing advertising circulars, sales
      notices, and maintaining personal trade books, all outside of normal work
      hours, without compensation.

5.    Employees are required or encouraged to work on "Make Nordstrom
      Special" projects outside of normal work hours, without compensation.
      This also includes Customer Service Book preparation and maintenance, as
      well as attendance at Customer Service Board meetings.

6.    Employees' overtime rates are not adjusted upward when commission pay-
      ments increase their gross earnings during weeks when overtime is worked.

**EXHIBIT 4 (continued)**

On December 5, 1989, the Department requested certain records from Nordstrom Inc. A copy of one of those letters is attached. The investigation was assigned to the Seattle Service Location, and was coordinated by the Regional Supervisor, Cindy Hanson.

On December 11, 1989, the Department met with officials from Nordstrom Inc. and the company's attorneys. The majority of the records requested were provided at that time, with the remaining records being delivered on December 19, 1989.

Following is an overview of each allegation contained in the complaint, Nordstrom's position taken regarding the allegation, and the findings made by the Department. This overview is based on the complaint and documents submitted on behalf of the employees (See Exhibit 1), records provided by Nordstrom (See Exhibit 2), information obtained from the meeting with Nordstrom officials on December 5, 1989, and various telephone conversations with Nordstrom and employee representatives.

Source: Washington State Department of Labor and Industries, ESAC Division, Nordstrom Investigation.

**EXHIBIT 5**
**Department of Labor and Industries Conclusion and Order**

## II.  CONCLUSIONS

Based on the above findings of fact, the Department makes the following conclusions:

1.   There is no indication that any of the voluntary meetings referenced in allegation 1 would meet the Department's position on unpaid training time (See Exhibit 3).  An example given by Nordstrom at our meeting and the records received indicate that all meetings held are directly related to the employees' jobs.  Therefore, the company is in violation of RCW 49.46.020 and RCW 49.46.130, where applicable, for not properly compensating its employees for all time spent in meetings.  In addition, Nordstrom has not kept records of this time worked, in violation of RCW 49.46.070 and WAC 296-128-010.

2.   Records reviewed indicate employees have made deliveries of merchandise to other stores, in person, outside of normal work hours.  Certain hours worked by employees locating and delivering merchandise would be considered hours worked under Chapter 49.46 RCW.  Therefore, the company is in violation of RCW 49.46.020 for failing to properly compensate employees for all time worked.

In addition, Nordstrom has failed to record these hours of work performed by employees as specified in RCW 49.46.070 and WAC 296-128-010(6).

3.   Nordstrom has failed to record the actual hours of work performed by cosmetic line managers as specified in RCW 49.46.070 and WAC 296-128-010(6). Employees are required to perform inventory duties on their own time and the payment received for these hours worked by cosmetic line managers is not accurate or in accordance with the state overtime provisions as specified in RCW 49.46.130 and WAC 296-128-550.

4.   Nordstrom permits the writing of thank-you notes by employees on their own time, without proper compensation, in violation of RCW 49.46.020. Nordstrom has failed to record actual hours of this work performed by employees as specified in RCW 49.46.070 and WAC 296-128-010.

5.   Work performed by employees in preparing Customer Service Books and "Make Nordstrom Special" projects/books is considered time worked.  In reviewing the documentation, the Department found nothing to substantiate the allegations that employees are encouraged or required to work on "Make Nordstrom Special" projects outside of normal work hours without compensation.

6.   Nordstrom has not paid overtime to employees in violation of the state overtime provisions, as specified in RCW 49.46.130.

**EXHIBIT 5 (continued)**

### III.   ORDER

Based on the above findings of fact and conclusions of law, the Department of Labor and Industries hereby orders Nordstrom Inc. to immediately from this date forward:

1. Compensate employees for attending various store meetings, when the meeting is held in the interest of the employer or is directly related to the employees' job, pursuant to RCW 49.46.020 and RCW 49.46.130; and to

2. Comply with record-keeping provisions pursuant to RCW 49.46.070 and WAC 296-128-010; and to

3. Compensate employees for all hours of work, pursuant to RCW 49.46.020; and to

4. Compensate employees for overtime hours worked pursuant to RCW 49.46.130; and to

5. Retroactively compensate all current and former employees who were not compensated for all hours worked, or who were not properly compensated for overtime hours worked, pursuant to RCW 49.46.020 and RCW 49.46.130.

BY:

Signed by Michael Pellegrini

Michael Pellegrini
Supervisor of Employment Standards

2-15-90

Date

cc:   Joe Peterson, UFCW Local 1001
      Mark McDermott, Assistant Director, ESAC Division

---

Source: Washington State Department of Labor and Industries, ESAC Division, Nordstrom Investigation.

**EXHIBIT 6**
**Nordstrom Stock Price History**

|      |           | Monthly Close ($/share) |
|------|-----------|-------------------------|
| 1989 | January   | 32-4/8                  |
|      | February  | 31-2/8                  |
|      | March     | 33-2/8                  |
|      | April     | 33-6/8                  |
|      | May       | 34-4/8                  |
|      | June      | 31-2/8                  |
|      | July      | 35-6/8                  |
|      | August    | 41-6/8                  |
|      | September | 39-4/8                  |
|      | October   | 36-6/8                  |
|      | November  | 37-4/8                  |
|      | December  | 37-2/8                  |
| 1990 | January   | 33-4/8                  |
|      | February  | 27-6/8                  |
|      | March     | 31-4/8                  |

**EXHIBIT 7**
**UFCW Local 1001 Complaint for Declaratory and Injunctive**
**Relief, Damages, and Statutory Penalties (Class Action)**

III.  Facts.

11.  Nordstrom and Local 1001 have been parties to a series of collective bargaining agreements, the most recent of which expired on July 31, 1989.  Nordstrom and Local 367 have been parties to a series of collective bargaining agreements, the most recent of which expired on July 31, 1989.  The Unions do not bring the claims herein under these agreements.

12.  Nordstrom has individual employment contracts with its employees, which contracts are formed from company-wide employment policies and practices.  Under these employment contracts, employees are compensated as follows:  Most sales employees are paid an hourly wage for time spent in selling activities ("selling time") and non-selling activities ("non-sell time").  In addition, employees may receive additional wages for selling time in the form of commissions based on sales of goods and services above each employee's sales quota.  Each employee's sales quota is determined by dividing the hourly guaranteed wage rate by the commission rate applicable to the merchandise or services sold.  For example, the sales quota for an employee who is guaranteed $9.75 per hour and has a commission rate of 6.75 percent is $9.75 per hour divided by 0.0675, or $144.44 of sales per hour.  Some sales employees are paid an hourly wage plus a commission on sales of goods and services.  Non-sales employees and some sales employees are paid an hourly wage.

**EXHIBIT 7 (continued)**

13.  Nordstrom has company-wide policies applicable to all employees, including employees represented by the Unions and unrepresented employees, the terms of which are included in individual employment contracts between Nordstrom and its employees. These policies require payment for all work Nordstrom has permitted to be performed for its benefit, including, but not limited to, the location and acquisition of merchandise from other stores; the delivery of merchandise to a customer's home, office, or other location; the performance of various stock assignments; the performance of sales promotion activities, including writing and addressing thank-you notes and addressing sale notices to customers; various customer service promotions, including "Make Nordstrom Special" projects, the preparation and maintenance of customer service books, and attendance at customer service board and other company meetings; and various other work activity all for the benefit of Nordstrom.

14.  Nordstrom has consistently and routinely failed to pay wages to employees represented by the Unions, individual plaintiffs, and employees similarly situated, for activities for which compensation is required by individual employment contract or by law, including the activities identified in the preceding paragraph.

15.  Officers, directors, and responsible managers of Nordstrom knew that employees were performing the work described in paragraph 13 above without being paid as required by individual employment contract or by law and yet continued to promote or permit these activities to continue.

**EXHIBIT 7 (continued)**

16.   In failing to pay wages to employees as alleged in paragraphs 13 through 15 above, Nordstrom has acted willfully and with the intent of depriving employees of such wages.

17.   Nordstrom has failed to keep accurate records of the time worked by employees performing the activities alleged in paragraph 13 above.

18.   Nordstrom has discouraged employees from submitting claims for compensation for work performed "off the clock" and has subjected employees who submit such claims to reprisal and threat of reprisal.

19.   Nordstrom has compelled, coerced, or required employees to purchase clothing from Nordstrom to wear while working at stores operated by Nordstrom.

20.   Nordstrom has withheld from wages earned by employees the amount of commissions that were paid on merchandise that is subsequently returned, where such merchandise was not sold by the employee against whom the commission was charged.

21.   By its conduct alleged in paragraphs 13 through 20 above, Nordstrom has irreparably harmed employees represented by the Unions, the individual plaintiffs, and other employees similarly situated for which they have no adequate remedy at law.

---

Source:  Washington State Department of Labor and Industries, ESAC Division, Nordstrom Investigation.

# Codman & Shurtleff, Inc.: Planning and Control System

"This revision combines our results from January to April with the preliminary estimates supplied by each department for the remainder of the year. Of course, there are still a lot of unknown factors to weigh in, but this will give you some idea of our preliminary updated forecast."

As the Board members reviewed the document provided to them by Gus Fleites, vice president of Information and Control at Codman & Shurtleff, Roy Black, president, addressed the six men sitting at the conference table, "This revised forecast leaves us with a big stretch. We are almost two million dollars short of our profit objective for the year. As we discussed last week, we are estimating sales to be $1.1 million above the original forecast. This is due in part to the early introduction of the new Chest Drainage Unit. However, three major factors that we didn't foresee last September will affect our profit plan estimates for the remainder of the year.

"First, there's the currency issue: our hedging has partially protected us, but the continued rapid deterioration of the dollar has pushed our costs up on European specialty instruments. Although this has improved Codman's competitive market position in Europe, those profits accrue to the European company and are not reflected in this forecast. Second, we have an unfavorable mix variance; and finally, we will have to absorb inventory variances due to higher than anticipated start-up costs of our recently combined manufacturing operations.

"When do we have to take the figures to Corporate?" asked Chuck Dunn, vice president of Business Development.

"Wednesday of next week," replied Black, "so we have to settle this by Monday. That gives us only tomorrow and the weekend to wrap up the June

---

*Professor Robert Simons prepared this case.*

Copyright © 1987 by the President and Fellows of Harvard College. Harvard Business School case 187-081.

budget revision. I know that each of you has worked on these estimates, but I think that the next look will be critical to achieving our profit objective."

"Bob, do you have anything you can give us?"

Bob Dick, vice president of Marketing, shook his head, "I've been working with my people looking at price and mix. At the moment, we can't realistically get more price. Most of the mix variance for the balance of the year will be due to increased sales of products that we are handling under the new distribution agreement. The mix for the remainder of the year may change, but with 2,700 active products in the catalogue, I don't want to move too far from our original projections. My expenses are cut right to the bone. Further cuts will mean letting staff go."

Black nodded his head in agreement. "Chuck, you and I should meet to review our research and development priorities. I know that Herb Stolzer will want to spend time reviewing the status of our programs. I think we should be sure that we have cut back to reflect our spending to date. I wouldn't be surprised if we could find another $400,000 without jeopardizing our long-term programs."

"Well, it seems our work is cut out for us. The rest of you keep working on this. Excluding R&D, we need at least another $500,000 before we start drawing down our contingency fund. Let's meet here tomorrow at two o'clock and see where we stand."

# CODMAN & SHURTLEFF, INC.

Codman & Shurtleff, Inc., a subsidiary of Johnson & Johnson, was established in 1838 in Boston by Thomas Codman to design and fashion surgical instruments. The company developed surgical instrument kits for use in Army field hospitals during the Civil War and issued its first catalogue in 1860. After the turn of the century, Codman & Shurtleff specialized in working with orthopedic surgeons and with pioneers in the field of neurosurgery.

In 1986, Codman & Shurtleff supplied hospitals and surgeons worldwide with over 2,700 products for surgery, including instruments, equipment, implants, surgical disposables, fiber-optic light sources and cables, surgical head lamps, surgical microscopes, coagulators, and electronic pain control simulators and electrodes. These products involved advanced technologies from the fields of metallurgy, electronics, and optics.

Codman & Shurtleff operated three manufacturing locations in Randolph, New Bedford, and Southbridge, Massachusetts, and a distribution facility in Avon, Massachusetts. The company employed 800 people in the United States.

In 1964, Codman & Shurtleff was acquired by Johnson & Johnson, Inc., as an addition to its professional products business. Johnson & Johnson operated manufacturing subsidiaries in 46 countries, sold its products in most countries of the world, and employed 75,000 people worldwide. 1985 sales were $6.4 billion with before tax profits of $900 million (**Exhibit 1**).

Roy Black had been president of Codman & Shurtleff since 1983. In his 25 years with Johnson & Johnson, Black had spent 18 years with Codman, primarily in the Marketing Department. He had also worked at Ethicon and Surgikos. He described his job:

> *This is a tough business to manage because it is so complex. We rely heavily on the neurosurgeons for ideas in product generation and for the testing and ultimate acceptance of our products. We have to stay in close contact with the leading neurosurgeons around the world. For example, last week I returned from a tour of the Pacific Rim. During the trip, I visited eight Johnson & Johnson/Codman affiliates and 25 neurosurgeons.*
>
> *At the same time, we are forced to push technological innovation to reduce costs. This is a matter of survival. In the past, we concentrated on producing superior quality goods, and the market was willing to pay whatever it took to get the best. But the environment has changed; the shift has been massive. We are trying to adapt to a situation where doctors and hospitals are under severe pressure to be more efficient and cost-effective.*
>
> *We compete in 12 major product groups. Since our markets are so competitive, the business is very price sensitive. The only way we can take price is to offer unique products with cost-in-use benefits to the professional user.*
>
> *Since the introduction of DRG costing[1] by hospitals in 1983, industry volume has been off approximately 20%. We have condensed 14 locations to 4 and have reduced staff levels by over 20%. There have also been some cuts in R&D, although our goal is to maintain research spending at near double the historical Codman level.*

Chuck Dunn, vice president of Business Development, had moved three years earlier from Johnson & Johnson Products to join Codman as vice president for Information and Control. During his 24 years with Johnson & Johnson, he had worked with four different marketing divisions as well as the Corporate office. He recalled the process of establishing a new mission statement at Codman:

> *When I arrived here, Codman was in the process of defining a more clearly focused mission. Our mission was product-oriented, but Johnson & Johnson was oriented by medical specialty. On a matrix, this resulted in missed product opportunities as well as turf problems with other Johnson & Johnson companies.*

---

[1] On October 1, 1983, Medicare reimbursement to hospitals changed from a cost-plus system to a fixed-rate system as called for in the 1983 Social Security refinancing legislation. The new system was called "prospective payment" because rates were set in advance of treatment according to which of 467 "diagnostic-related groups" (or DRGs) a patient was deemed to fall into. This change in reimbursement philosophy caused major cost-control problems for the nation's 5,800 acute-care hospitals, which received an average of 36% of their revenues from Medicare and Medicaid.

*It took several years of hard work to arrive at a new worldwide mission statement oriented to medical specialty, but this process was very useful in obtaining group consensus. Our worldwide mission is now defined in terms of a primary focus in the neuro-spinal surgery business. This turns out to be a large market and allows better positioning of our products.*

*In addition to clarifying our planning, we use the mission statement as a screening device. We look carefully at any new R&D project to see if it fits our mission. The same is true for acquisitions.*

## REPORTING RELATIONSHIPS AT JOHNSON & JOHNSON

In 1985, Johnson & Johnson comprised 155 autonomous subsidiaries operating in three health care markets: consumer products, pharmaceutical products, and professional products.

Johnson & Johnson was managed on a decentralized basis as described in the following excerpt from the 1985 Annual Report:

*The Company is organized on the principles of decentralized management and conducts its business through operating subsidiaries which are themselves, for the most part, integral, autonomous operations. Direct responsibility for each company lies with its operating management, headed by the president, general manager, or managing director who reports directly or through a Company group chairman to a member of the Executive Committee. In line with this policy of decentralization, each internal subsidiary is, with some exceptions, managed by citizens of the country where it is located.*

Roy Black at Codman & Shurtleff reported directly to Herbert Stolzer at Johnson & Johnson headquarters in New Brunswick, New Jersey. Mr. Stolzer, 59, was a member of the Executive Committee of Johnson & Johnson, with responsibility for 16 operating companies in addition to Codman & Shurtleff (**Exhibit 2**). Stolzer had worked for Johnson & Johnson for 35 years with engineering, manufacturing, and senior management experience in Johnson & Johnson Products and at the Corporate office.

The senior policy and decision-making group at Johnson & Johnson was the Executive Committee, comprising the chairman, president, chief financial officer, vice president of administration, and eight Executive Committee members with responsibilities for company sectors. The 155 business units of the Company were organized in sectors based primarily on products (e.g., consumer, pharmaceutical, professional) and secondarily on geographic markets.

## FIVE- AND TEN-YEAR PLANS AT JOHNSON & JOHNSON

Each operating company within Johnson & Johnson was responsible for preparing its own plans and strategies. David Clare, president of Johnson &

Johnson, believed that this was one of the key elements in their success. "Our success is due to three basic tenets: a basic belief in decentralized management, a sense of responsibility to our key constituents, and a desire to manage for the long term. We have no corporate strategic planning function nor one strategic plan. Our strategic plan is the sum of the strategic plans to each of our 155 business units."

Each operating company prepared annually a five- and ten-year plan. Financial estimates in these plans were limited to only four numbers: estimated unit sales volume, estimated sales revenue, estimated net income, and estimated return on investment. Accompanying these financial estimates was a narrative description of how these targets would be achieved.

To ensure that managers were committed to the plan that they developed, Johnson & Johnson required that the planning horizon focus on two years only and remain fixed over a five-year period. Thus, in 1983, a budget and second-year forecast was developed for 1984 and 1985 and a strategic plan was developed for the years 1990 and 1995. In each of the years 1984 through 1987, the five- and ten-year plan was redrawn in respect of only years 1990 and 1995. Only in year 1988 would the strategic planning horizon shift five years forward to cover years 1995 and 2000. These two years will then remain the focus of subsequent five- and ten-year plans for the succeeding four years, and so on.

At Codman & Shurtleff, work on the annual five- and ten-year plan commenced each January and took approximately six months to complete. Based on the mission statement, a business plan was developed for each significant segment of the business. For each competitor, the marketing plan included an estimated *pro forma* income statement (volume, sales, profit) as well as a one-page narrative description of their strategy.

Based on the tentative marketing plan, draft plans were prepared by the other departments, including research and development, production, finance, and personnel. The tentative plan was assembled in a binder with sections describing mission, strategies, opportunities and threats, environment, and financial forecasts. This plan was debated, adjusted, and approved over the course of several meetings in May by the Codman Board of Directors (see **Exhibit 3**), comprising the president and seven key subordinates.

In June, Herb Stolzer travelled to Boston to preside over the annual review of the five- and ten-year plan. Codman executives considered this a key meeting that could last up to three days. During the meeting Stolzer reviewed the plan, aired his concerns, and challenged the Codman Board on assumptions, strategies, and forecasts. A recurring question during the session was, "If your new projection for 1990 is below what you predicted last year, how do you intend to make up the shortfall?"

After this meeting, Roy Black summarized the plan that had been approved by Stolzer in a two-page memorandum that he sent directly to Jim Burke, chairman and chief executive officer of Johnson & Johnson.

Based on the two-page "Burke letters," the five- and ten-year plans for all operating companies were presented by Executive Committee members and debated and approved at the September meeting of the Executive Committee in New Brunswick. Company presidents, including Roy Black, were often invited to prepare formal presentations. The discussion in these meetings was described by those in attendance as "very frank," "extremely challenging," and "grilling."

## FINANCIAL PLANNING AT JOHNSON & JOHNSON

Financial planning at Johnson & Johnson comprised annual budgets (i.e., profit plans) for the upcoming operating year and a second-year forecast. Budgets were detailed financial documents prepared down to the expense center level for each operating company. The second-year forecast was in a similar format but contained less detail than the budget for the upcoming year.

Revenues and expenses were budgeted by month. Selected balance sheet items, e.g., accounts receivable and inventory, were also budgeted to reflect year-end targets.

Profit plan targets were developed on a bottom-up basis by each operating company by reference to two documents: (1) the approved five- and ten-year plan and (2) the second-year forecast prepared the previous year.

Chuck Dunn described the budgeting process at Codman & Shurtleff:

*We wrote the initial draft of our 1987 profit plan in the Summer of 1986 based on the revision of our five- and ten-year plan. By August, the profit plan is starting to crystallize; we have brought in the support areas such as accounting, quality assurance, R&D, and engineering to ensure that they "buy in" to the new 1987 profit and marketing plans.*

*The first year of the strategic plan is used as a basis for the departments to prepare their own one-year plans for both capital and expense items. The production budget is based on standard costs and nonstandard costs such as development programs and plant consolidations. As for the R&D budget, the project list is always too long, so we are forced to rank the projects. For each project, we look at returns, costs, time expended, sales projections, expected profit, and gross profit percentages as well as support to be supplied to the plants.*

*The individual budgets are then consolidated by the Information and Control Department. We look very carefully at how this budget compares with our previous forecasts. For example, the first consolidation of the 1986 profit plan revealed a $2.4 million profit shortfall against the second-year forecast that was developed in 1984 and updated in June 1985. To reconcile this, it was necessary to put on special budget presentations by each department to remove all slack and ensure that our earlier target could be met if possible. The commitment to this process is very strong.*

*We are paying more and more attention to our second-year forecast since it forces us to re-examine strategic plans. The second-year forecast is*

*also used as a benchmark for next year's profit plan and, as such, it is used
as hindsight to evaluate the forecasting ability and performance of managers.*

The procedure for approving the annual profit plan and second-year
forecast followed closely the procedures described above for the review of the
five- and ten-year plans.  During the early fall, Herbert Stolzer reviewed the
proposed budget with Roy Black and the Codman & Shurtleff Board of
Directors.  Changes in profit commitments from previous forecasts and the
overall profitability and tactics of the Company were discussed in detail.

After all anticipated revenues and expenses were budgeted, a separate
contingency expense line item was added to the budget; the amount of the contingency changed from year to year and was negotiated between Stolzer and
Black based on the perceived uncertainty in achieving budget targets.  In 1986,
the Codman & Shurtleff contingency was set at $1.1 million.

Stolzer presented the budget for approval at the November meeting of the
Johnson & Johnson Executive Committee.

## BUDGET REVISIONS AND REVIEWS

During the year, budget performance was monitored closely.  Each week, sales
revenue performance figures were sent to Herb Stolzer.  In addition, Roy Black
sent a monthly management report to Stolzer that included income statement
highlights and a summary of key balance sheet figures and ratios.  All information was provided with reference to (1) position last month, (2) position this
month, and (3) budgeted position.  All variances that Black considered significant were explained in a narrative summary.

The accuracy of budget projections was also monitored during the year
and formally revised on three occasions.  The first of these occasions occurred
at the March meeting of the Executive Committee.  Going around the table,
each Executive Committee member was asked to update the Committee on his
most recent estimates of sales and profits for each operating company for the
current year.  Herb Stolzer relied on Roy Black to provide this information for
Stolzer's review prior to the March meeting.

The "June Revision" referred to the revised budget for the current year
that was presented to the Executive Committee in June.  The preparation of
this revised budget required managers at Codman & Shurtleff and all other
Johnson & Johnson companies to re-budget in May for the remainder of the fiscal year.  This revision involved rechecking all budget estimates, starting with
the lowest level expense center, as well as revising the second-year forecast
when necessary.

The third review of budget projections was the "November update,"
which was presented to the Executive Committee at the November meeting
concurrently with the consideration of the budget and second-year forecast for
the upcoming budget year.  The November update focused on results for the

ten months just completed and revised projections for the remaining two months. At Codman & Shurtleff, preparation of the November update involved performance estimates from all departments but was not conducted to the same level of detail as the June revision.

## CORPORATE VIEW OF THE PLANNING AND CONTROL PROCESS

David Clare, president of Johnson & Johnson:

> *The sales and profit forecasts are always optimistic in the five- and ten-year plans, but this is O.K. We want people to stretch their imagination and think expansively. In these plans we don't anticipate failure; they are a device to open up thinking. There is no penalty for inaccuracies.*
>
> *The profit plan and second-year forecast are used to run the business and evaluate managers on planning, forecasts, and achievements.*
>
> *We ask our managers to always include in their plans an account of how and why their estimates have changed over time. That is why we use the five- and ten-year planning concept rather than a moving planning horizon. This allows us to revise our thinking over time and allows for retrospective learning.*
>
> *If a manager insists on a course of action and we (the Executive Committee) have misgivings, nine times out of ten we will let him go ahead. If we say, 'No,' and the answer should have been, 'Yes,' we say, 'Don't blame us, it was your job to sell us on the idea and you didn't do that.'*
>
> *Johnson & Johnson is extremely decentralized, but that does not mean that managers are free from challenge as to what they are doing. In the final analysis, managing conflict is what management is all about. Healthy conflict is about what is right, not who is right.*
>
> *Our Company philosophy is to manage for the long term. We do not use short-term bonus plans. Salary and bonus reviews are entirely subjective and qualitative and are intended to reward effort and give special recognition to those who have performed uniquely. The Executive Committee reviews salary recommendations for all managers above a certain salary level, but Company presidents, such as Roy Black, have full discretion as to how they remunerate their employees.*

Herbert Stolzer, Executive Committee member:

> *The planning and control systems used in Johnson & Johnson provide real benefits. These systems allow us to find problems and run the business. This is true not only for us at Corporate, but also at the operating companies where they are a tremendous tool. Once a year, managers are forced to review their businesses in depth for costs, trends, manufacturing efficiency, marketing plans, and their competitive situation. Programs and action plans result.*

*You have to force busy people to do this.  Otherwise, they will be caught up in day-to-day activities—account visits, riding with salesmen, standing on the manufacturing floor.*

*Our long-term plans are not meant to be a financial forecast; rather, they are meant to be an objective way of setting aspirations.  We never make those numbers—who can forecast sales five or ten years out with unforeseen markets, products, and competitors?  Even the accuracy of our two-year fore-cast is bad.  The inaccuracy is an indication of how fast our markets are changing.  Our businesses are so diverse, with so many competitors, that it is difficult to forecast out two years.*

*I visit at least twice a year with each operating company board.  We usually spend the better part of a week going over results, planning issues, strategic plans, and short- and long-term problems.  The Executive Com-mittee, to the best of my knowledge, never issues quantitative performance targets before the bottom-up process begins.*

*At the Executive Committee meetings, a lot of argument takes place around strategic planning issues.  How fast can we get a business up to higher returns?  Are the returns in some businesses too high?  Are we mov-ing too fast?  However, the outcome is never to go back to the operating com-pany and say we need 8% rather than 6%.  The challenge has already taken place between the Executive Committee member and the Company Board.  If the EC member is satisfied with the answers provided by the Board, that's the end of it.*

*It happens very rarely that the consolidated budget is unacceptable.  Occasionally, we might say, 'We really could use some more money.'  However, in the second review, this may not turn up any extra.  If so, that's O.K.*

*Our systems are not used to punish.  They are used to try and find and correct problems.  Bonuses are not tied to achieving budget targets.  They are subjectively determined, although we use whatever objective indicators are available—for example, sales and new product introductions for a marketing vice president.*

*The key to our whole system is the operating Company presidents.  We are so decentralized that they define their own destiny.  A successful Company president needs to be able to stand up to pressure from above.  He or she needs to have the courage to say, 'I have spent hours and hours on that forecast and for the long-term health of the Company, we have to spend that budget.'*

Clark Johnson, corporate controller:

*At the Executive Committee review meetings, we always review the past five years before starting on the forecast.  We look at volume growth rates—sales growth adjusted for inflation—and discuss problems.  Then, we compare growth rate against GNP growth.  We keep currency translation out of it.*

*We evaluate foreign subsidiaries in their own currency and compare growth against country-specific GNP. We are looking for market share by country. On almost any topic, we start with forecast versus past track record.*

*The Committee never dictates or changes proposals—only challenges ideas. If it becomes clear to the individual presenting that the forecast is not good enough, only that person decides whether a revision is necessary. These discussions can be very frank and sometimes acrimonious. The result of the review may be agreement to present a revision at the next meeting, specific action items to be addressed, or personal feedback to David Clare.*

*This process cascades down the organization. Executive Committee members review and challenge the proposals of Company presidents. Company presidents review and challenge the proposals of their vice presidents.*

### Thursday, May 8, 1986—8:00 P.M.

Following the Codman & Shurtleff Board meeting to discuss the June budget revision on the afternoon of Thursday, May 8 (described at the beginning of the case), Roy Black, Chuck Dunn, Bob Dick, and Gus Fleites worked into the evening going over the list of active R&D projects. Their review focused on R&D projects that had been included in the original 1986 budget. They searched for projects that could be eliminated due to changed market conditions or deferred to 1987 because of unplanned slowdowns. After discussing the progress and priority of each major project, Roy Black asked Chuck Dunn to have his staff work the next morning to go over the 40 active projects in detail and look for any savings that could be reflected in the June revision of the budget.

### Friday, May 9, 1986—7:45 A.M.

In addition to Chuck Dunn, four people were seated around the table in the small conference room. Bob Sullivan and Gino Lombardo were program managers who reported to Bill Bailey, vice president of Research. John Smith was manager, Technical Development, of the research facility in Southbridge that specialized in microscopes, fiber-optics, and light scopes. Gordon Thompson was the research accountant representing the Finance Department.

After coffee was delivered, Chuck closed the door and turned to the others:

*Here's the situation. We are approximately two million short of the June revision pre-tax profit target. As you know, our sales volume this year has been good—better than budget, in fact—but a few recent unpredictable events, including unfavorable product mix and that large variance in the cost of specialty European products, are hurting our profit projection.*

*This morning, I want the four of you to look at our original spending projections to see where we stand.  For example, we know that R&D underspent $200,000 in the first quarter.  Therefore, I think we should take it as a starting point that R&D has $200,000 to give up from its 1986 budget.  I know that you can argue that this is just a timing difference, but you know as well as I do that, given the record of the R&D department, this money will probably not be spent this year.*

*It's time to get the hopes and dreams out of the R&D list.  If we roll up our sleeves, we can probably find $400,000 without sacrificing either our 1986 objectives or our long-term growth.*

*We worked late last night looking at the project list and I think it can be done.  I have to meet again today at 2:00 with the Board and I want to be able to tell them that we can do it.  That leaves it up to you to sift through these projects and find that money.  We're looking for projects that have stalled and can be put on hold, and some belt-tightening on ongoing work.*

After Chuck Dunn had left the group to its work, Gordon led the group through the list of projects.  For each project, the group discussed spending to date, problems with the project, and spending needed for the remainder of the year.  For each project, Gordon asked if anything could be cut and occasionally asked for points of clarification.  On a separate sheet of paper, he kept track of the cuts to which the R&D managers had agreed.  He turned to Project 23:

*How about 23?  You were planning on a pilot run of 100 prototypes this year. Should that still be included in the schedule?*

*Yes, the project is on track and looks promising.  I suppose we could cut the run to 50 without sacrificing our objective.  Would anyone have a problem with that?*

*It's a bad idea.  That item has a very high material component and we have a devil of a time getting it at a reasonable price, even for a run of 100. If we cut the volume any more, the unit material cost will double.*

*O.K., we'll stick with 100.  How about the sales samples?  Is there anything there?*

*If we reduced the number of samples by a third, we could save $20,000. I suppose I could live with that, but I don't know how that will impact the marketing plan.  Let me call Bob Dick and see what he thinks.*

Gordon kept a running total of the expense reductions as the morning progressed.  Dunn stopped in approximately once an hour to ask how the work was coming.

### Friday, May 9—2:00 P.M.

Roy Black opened the meeting, "Gus, do you have the revised budget with the changes we've made?  What does it look like?"

As Gus Fleites distributed copies of the budget document to the Codman & Shurtleff Board, Chuck Dunn interjected, "Roy, at the moment, we have found $300,000 in R&D. That reflects adjusting our priority list for the rest of the year and cutting the fat out of ongoing projects. As for the last $100,000, we are still working on recasting the numbers to reflect what I call our 'project experience factor.' In other words, I think we can find that $100,000 by recognizing that our projects always take longer than originally planned. My people say that we've cut right to the bone on ongoing programs. The next round of cuts will have to be programs themselves, and we know we don't want to do that."

"We've discussed this before," responded Black, "and I think we all agree on the answer. In the past, we have authorized more projects than we can handle and have drawn the work out over too long a time. The way to go is fewer projects, sooner. It's the only thing that makes sense. Our mission is more focused now and should result in fewer projects. It's unfortunate that Bill Bailey is unavailable this week, but we are going to have to go ahead and make those decisions."

As Fleites briefed the Board on the revised budget, Roy Black turned to Bob Dick to discuss inventory carrying costs. "Bob, don't you think that our inventory level is too high on some of our low turnover products? Wouldn't we be better to cut our inventory position and take a higher back-order level? With 2,700 products, does it make sense to carry such a large inventory?"

Bob Dick nodded his head in agreement, "You're right, of course, our stocking charges are substantial and we could recover part of our shortfall if we could cut those expenses. But our first concern has to be our level of service to customers."

"Agreed. But perhaps there is room here to provide fast turnaround on a core of critical products and risk back orders on the high-specialty items. The 80/20 rule applies to most of our business. For example, say we offered top service for all our disposables and implants and flagged set-up products for new hospital construction in our catalogue as '90-day delivery' or 'made to order.' We could then concentrate on the fastest possible turnaround for products where that is important and a slower delivery for products that are usually ordered well in advance in any case."

"I think that may be a good tactic. It won't help us for the June revision, but I'll have our market research people look at it and report back next month."

"Good," responded Black, "that just leaves our commercial expenses. We need some donations from each of you. What I am suggesting is that each of you go back to your departments and think in terms of giving up two percent of your commercial expenses. If everyone gives up two percent, this will give us $500,000. In my opinion, we have to bring the shortfall down to $900,000 before we can draw down part of our contingency fund. We're a long way from the end of the year and it's too early to start drawing down a major portion of the contingency."

Black turned to Bob Marlatt, vice president of Human Resources. "Bob, where do we stand on headcount projections?"

"The early retirement program is set to clear our Corporate Compensation Department next month. That should yield 14 headcount reductions. Otherwise, no changes have been made in our projections through the end of the year. I think that we could all benefit from thinking about opportunities to reduce staff and pay overtime on an as-needed basis to compensate."

Black summed up the discussion:

*Well, I think we all know what is needed. Chuck, keep working on that last $100,000. All of you should think in terms of giving up two percent on commercial expenses and reducing non-critical headcount. That means that you will have to rank your activities and see what you can lose at the bottom end. Bob, I think that we should go back and look at our marketing plan again to see if we can make any changes to boost revenues.*

*We need to take a revised budget to Stolzer that is short by no more than $250,000. If necessary, I think we can live with drawing down the contingency to make up the difference.*

*So, your work is cut out for you. See you back here on Monday. Have a nice weekend! (laughter all around)*

After the meeting, Roy Black reflected on what had transpired, and his role as an operating manager in Johnson & Johnson.

*These meetings are very important. We should always be thinking about such issues, but it is tough when you are constantly fighting fires. The Johnson & Johnson system forces us to stop and really look at where we have been and where we are going.*

*We know where the problems are. We face them every day. But these meetings force us to think about how we should respond and to look at both the upside and downside of changes in the business. They really get our creative juices flowing.*

*Some of our managers complain. They say that we are planning and budgeting all the time and that every little change means that they have to go back and re-budget the year and the second-year forecasts. There is also some concern that the financial focus may make us less innovative. But we try to manage this business for the long term. We avoid at all costs actions that will hurt us long term. I believe that Herb Stolzer is in complete agreement on that issue.*

*It is important to understand what decentralized management is all about. It is unequivocal accountability for what you do. And the Johnson & Johnson system provides that very well.*

**EXHIBIT 1**
**Johnson & Johnson and Subsidiaries, Consolidated Statement of Earnings and Retained Earnings**

| Dollars in Millions Except Per Share Figures (Note 1) | 1985 | 1984 | 1983 |
|---|---|---|---|
| **Revenues** | | | |
| Sales to customers | $6,421.3 | $6,124.5 | $5,972.9 |
| Other revenues | | | |
|     Interest income | 107.3 | 84.5 | 82.9 |
|     Royalties and miscellaneous | 48.1 | 38.0 | 49.4 |
| **Total revenues** | $6,576.7 | $6,247.0 | $6,105.2 |
| **Costs and expenses** | | | |
| Cost of products sold | $2,594.2 | $2,469.4 | $2,471.8 |
| Selling, distribution and administrative expenses | 2,516.0 | 2,488.4 | 2,352.9 |
| Research expense | 471.1 | 421.2 | 405.1 |
| Interest expense | 74.8 | 86.1 | 88.3 |
| Interest expense capitalized | (28.9) | (35.0) | (36.9) |
| Other expenses including nonrecurring charges (Note 2) | 50.3 | 61.8 | 99.9 |
| Total costs and expenses | $5,677.5 | $5,491.9 | $5,381.1 |
| Earnings before provision for taxes on income | $ 899.2 | $ 755.1 | $ 724.1 |
| Provision for taxes on income (Note 8) | 285.5 | 240.6 | 235.1 |
| **Net earnings** | $ 613.7 | $ 514.5 | $ 489.0 |
| Retained earnings at beginning of period | $3,119.1 | $2,824.5 | $2,540.1 |
| Cash dividends paid (per share: 1985, $2.175; 1984, $1.175; 1983, $1.075) | (233.2) | (219.9) | (204.6) |
| Retained earnings at end of period | $3,499.6 | $3,119.1 | $2,824.5 |
| **Net earnings per share** | $ 3.36 | 2.75 | 2.57 |

**EXHIBIT 1 (continued)**
**Johnson & Johnson and Subsidiaries, Consolidated Statement of Earnings and Retained Earnings**

Segments of Business

| (Dollars in Millions) | 1985 | 1984 | 1983 | Percent Increase (Decrease) 1985 vs. 1984 | Percent Increase (Decrease) 1984 vs. 1983 |
|---|---|---|---|---|---|
| **Sales to customers (2)** | | | | | |
| Consumer—Domestic | $1,656.0 | $1,588.3 | $1,502.5 | 4.3% | 5.7% |
| International | 1,118.5 | 1,161.4 | 1,185.3 | (3.7) | (2.0) |
| Total | $2,774.5 | $2,749.7 | $2,687.8 | .9 | 2.3 |
| Professional—Domestic | $1,553.9 | $1,429.3 | $1,465.5 | 8.7 | (2.5) |
| International | 653.1 | 626.1 | 620.3 | 4.3 | .9 |
| Total | $2,207.0 | $2,055.4 | $2,085.8 | 7.4 | (1.5) |
| Pharmaceutical—Domestic | $ 780.0 | $ 718.3 | $ 642.5 | 8.6 | 11.8 |
| International | 659.8 | 601.1 | 556.8 | 9.8 | 8.0 |
| Total | $1,439.8 | $1,319.4 | $1,199.3 | 9.1 | 10.0 |
| Worldwide total | $6,421.3 | $6,124.5 | $5,972.9 | 4.8% | 2.5% |
| **Operating profit** | | | | | |
| Consumer | $ 408.7 | $ 323.4 | $ 422.7 | 26.4% | (23.5)% |
| Professional | 149.2 | 118.7 | 120.0 | 25.7 | (1.1) |
| Pharmaceutical | 461.1 | 440.4 | 358.4 | 4.7 | 22.9 |
| Segments total | $1,019.0 | $ 882.5 | $ 901.1 | 15.5 | (2.1) |
| Expense not allocated to segments (3) | (119.8) | (127.4) | (177.0) | | |
| **Earnings before taxes on income** | $ 899.2 | $ 755.1 | $ 724.1 | 19.1% | 4.3% |
| **Identifiable assets at year end** | | | | | |
| Consumer | $1,616.2 | $1,560.1 | $1,535.9 | 3.6% | 1.6% |
| Professional | 1,876.1 | 1,717.6 | 1,673.5 | 9.2 | 2.6 |
| Pharmaceutical | 1,343.8 | 1,024.3 | 996.2 | 31.2 | 2.8 |
| Segments total | $4,836.1 | $4,302.0 | $4,205.6 | 12.4 | 2.3 |
| General corporate | 259.0 | 239.4 | 255.9 | | |
| Worldwide total | $5,095.1 | $4,541.4 | $4,461.5 | 12.2% | 1.8% |

**EXHIBIT 2**
**Johnson & Johnson Organization Chart**

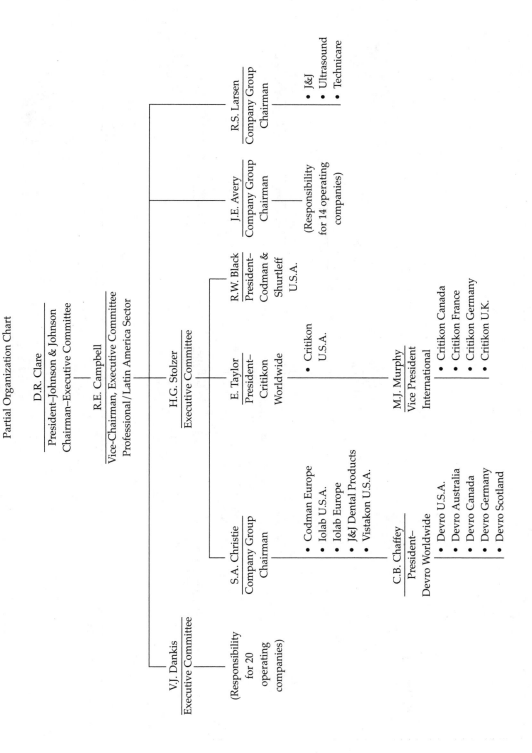

JOHNSON & JOHNSON
Partial Organization Chart

**EXHIBIT 3**
**Board of Directors**

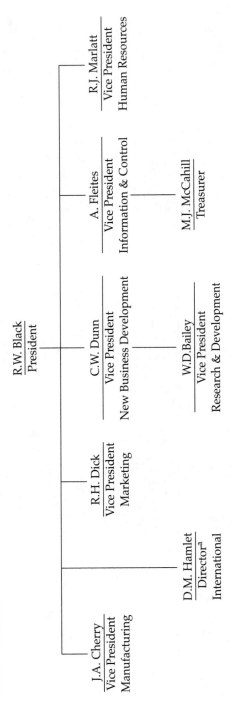

[a] Not a board member

# Responsibility Centers and Performance Measurement

**M**anagement control depends on measurement. Effective measurement of operations and performance requires assignment and acceptance of responsibility for performance. Performance measurements should meet three criteria: (1) they should be timely, informing when action can be taken; (2) they should be seen as fair; and (3) they should be congruent with the goals of the organization. Goal congruence assures that an improved measure of performance means the organization is nearer to achieving one or more of its objectives.

Measurements are used by managers for two reasons. First, measurements inform management about performance in the past, and they help managers answer questions about how they and the organization are performing. Second, they affect future behaviors by informing and motivating managers in the present and future.

Financial control of responsibility centers is achieved by measuring the dimensions of finance performance that managers can affect or control. Most responsibility centers can be classified by their focus on costs or expenses, margin or profit, or return on investment. Ideally, the financial measure should include any revenue or cost that managers can affect, even though they may not have complete control over revenues, expenses, or investments.

## COST CENTERS AND EXPENSE CENTERS

When only the resources consumed in a responsibility center can be measured, it can be classified as a *cost center* or an *expense center*. Performance is measured

Copyright © 1993 by the President and Fellows of Harvard College. Harvard Business School case 193-101.

by a financial measure of the resources used. Control is achieved by comparing performance to a reference point, which may be a standard, budget, or prior period expenditure. Service centers, such as an accounting department, are often managed as expense centers because it is easy to measure the cost of providing the service but hard to measure the benefit or value of the output of the center.

A report for an expense center is shown in **Exhibit 1**. Actual expenses are compared to a budgeted amount. Control depends on the effective establishment of a reference point to which the actual expenses can be compared. Even then, however, no measure of the effectiveness or efficiency of the expense center can be made because the report does not show how well the accounting department performed, how good its services were, or how much more efficiently the department could have performed the service it provided.

## FINANCIAL PERFORMANCE CENTERS

When both the inputs and the outputs of a responsibility center can be measured, a *financial performance center* or *profit center* can be created. As with cost centers, control is achieved by comparing actual margin or profit to an expected or budgeted margin or profit. Detail in the financial measurements provides information on problems and the need for management attention and action.

**Exhibit 2** shows several possible performance reports for a financial performance center. The appropriate bottom-line measure depends on the extent to which costs or expenses are controllable or can be influenced by a manager. The broader a manager's responsibility, the more costs and expense are likely to be relevant. If a financial performance center supplies or is supplied by another in the same organization, a mechanism for determining *transfer prices* must be established as well. Some organizations go beyond income or profit as it is usually measured in accounting for financial performance centers by adding a charge to conventional expenses for the assets or resources that managers use to generate revenue and income. This *residual income* approach is thought to avoid some problems that can be encountered when an investment center is measured by return on investment.

### Investment Centers

A manager of an *investment center* is held responsible for not only the inputs and outputs of that center but also for the amount of investment used to produce the outputs. A proper measurement of margin or profit needs to be selected, and the investment supporting the center needs to be measured. Investments can be measured by using their original cost, book value, current value, or replacement value. Control is best achieved by comparing expected return on investment to that achieved.

Two problems sometimes arise when investment centers are created. First, managers may be motivated to sell or dispose of assets that would have future utility to the organization, if doing so would give the appearance of improved financial performance. Second, managers may be reluctant to make new investments that would provide a return above the organization's cost of capital but below the current rate of return. Each of these two potential problems is illustrated in **Exhibit 3**.

## Matching Performance Measures with Strategy

Because measurements motivate and affect the behavior of managers, care must be taken to be sure that the performance measures support the organization's strategy. An organization committed to superior service may find treating responsibility centers that interface with clients or customers as expense centers undermines its strategy. An organization committed to being a technological leader may find that charging a profit center manager for research and development costs leads to less effective research and development. The most effective organizations use a carefully selected mix of financial performance measures and continually evaluate their effectiveness.

**EXHIBIT 1**
**Example of a Performance Measurement Report for an Expense Center**

|          | Budget   | Actual   | Variance |
|----------|----------|----------|----------|
| Salaries | $3,070   | $3,070   | 0        |
| Overtime | 0        | 206      | (206)    |
| Total    | $3,070   | $3,276   | (206)    |

**EXHIBIT 2**
**Profit Concepts for Financial Performance Centers**

Summary of Activities in the Retail Division, July ($ 000s)

| | |
|---|---|
| Revenue | $1,000 |
| Direct division expenses | |
|     Variable | 700 |
|     Nonvariable controllable | 100 |
|     Nonvariable noncontrollable | 50 |
| Indirect division expenses: | |
|     Allocated corporate overhead | 60 |
| Required earnings rate | 10% |

Income Statements

| Retail Division, July ($ 000s) | Division Contribution Margin | Division Controllable Income | Division Direct Income | Division Net Income | Division Residual Income |
|---|---|---|---|---|---|
| Revenue | $1,000 | $1,000 | $1,000 | $1,000 | $1,000 |
| Less: Direct division variable expenses | 700 | 700 | 700 | 700 | 700 |
| Division contribution margin | $ 300 | | | | |
| Nonvariable controllable expense | | 100 | 100 | 100 | 100 |
| Division controllable income | | $ 200 | | | |
| Nonvariable noncontrollable expenses | | | 50 | 50 | 50 |
| Division direct income | | | $ 150 | | |
| Indirect division expenses | | | | 60 | 60 |
| Division net income | | | | $ 90 | |
| Capital charge (10%) on investment of $1,100 | 110 | 110 | 110 | | 110 |
| Residual income | $ 190 | $ 90 | $ 40 | | $ ( 20) |

**EXHIBIT 3**
**Examples of Performance Measures for Investment Centers**

Measuring Investment for the Retail Division ($ 000s)

|  | Cost | Accumulated Depreciation | Replacement Value |
|---|---|---|---|
| Fixed assets: |  |  |  |
| Land and buildings | $ 500 | $ 200 | $ 900 |
| Store fixtures | 100 | 25 | 150 |
| Total | $ 600 | $ 225 | $1,050 |
| Current assets: |  |  |  |
| Cash | $ 50 |  | $ 50 |
| Receivables (net) | 200 |  | 200 |
| Inventories | 250 |  | 275 |
|  | $1,100 |  | $1,575 |

*Investments*
| Gross historical | $1,100 |
| Historical cost net of accumulated depreciation | 875 |
| Replacement value | 1,575 |

*Return on investment*

$$\frac{Income}{Investment} = Return\ on\ investment$$

$$\frac{Division\ net\ income}{Gross\ historical\ cost} = \frac{\$90}{\$1,100} = 8.2\%$$

*Residual income* reports income as absolute dollar amount after a *capital charge*, or return, expected of all divisions. In most cases it encourages investments that are profitable (return more than capital charge rate) but below current rate of return.

Example:
A wholesale division currently earns $300,000 on an investment of $1,500,000 and has a rate of return of 20%. An investment of $500,000 can be made that will raise income $75,000.

|  | Return on investment | Residual income (capital charge = 10%) |
|---|---|---|
| Without investment | 20% | $150 |
| After new investment | 18.75% | $175 |

# Western Chemical Corporation: Divisional Performance Measurement

*The fact is that we really have not yet figured out the best way to measure and report on the performance of some of our foreign operations. Because of different ownership arrangements and the use of local financing, when we use conventional accounting principles and standards, we often get financial reports that seem to contradict what we believe to be the true results of operations. This creates problems within the company because people who are not familiar with particular operations see the reports and draw erroneous conclusions about how this one or that one is performing relative to others.*

*Now that you are beginning to get questions from shareholders and analysts about how some of these investments are performing, I realized that Cynthia and I had better brief you on what some of the problems are that we have with division performance measurement.*

Stan Rogers, president of Western Chemical Corporation (WCC), was meeting with Samantha Chu, recently appointed director of Investor Relations, and Cynthia Sheldon, who had recently been appointed vice president and controller. Chu had that morning received an inquiry from a well-known chemical industry analyst who had some fairly specific questions about some of the company's investments in Europe and the Far East. When she questioned Sheldon, Cynthia suggested that they meet with Rogers to examine some of the issues that Rogers and Sheldon had been discussing, so that Chu could answer the analyst's requests more accurately.

The information on the financial performance of WCC's foreign operations was prepared by the same accountants who maintained the company's

---

*Professor William J. Bruns, Jr. and Professor Roger Atherton of Northeastern University prepared this case.*

Copyright © 1995 by the President and Fellows of Harvard College. Harvard Business School case 196-079.

accounts and who prepared its quarterly and annual reports. A single database for all accounting had been established some years earlier in the belief that it could serve all accounting needs of both managers and those external to the company. A common chart of accounts and accounting policies was used throughout the company and in all of its subsidiaries.

A variety of new alliances and ownership arrangements had been used in recent international ventures to speed entry to new international markets and to minimize investment and risk. Because of these, Rogers became convinced that some of the reports the accountants were preparing about some of the ventures could be quite misleading. It was for that reason that he and Sheldon were already discussing alternative ways to measure divisional performance, and that Sheldon thought Chu should be brought into their discussion before trying to answer the analyst's queries.

## THE COMPANY AND INTERNATIONAL VENTURES

In 1995, WCC was a 75-year-old, *Fortune 300* chemical company. Its largest business marketed chemicals and chemical programs for water and waste treatment. Additional products and chemical services targeted manufacturing processes where the quality of a customer's product could be enhanced. The company was proud of its industry reputation for quality of its solutions to customer problems and exceptional service to customers. WCC had 4,900 employees and operated more than 35 plants in 19 countries. Financial information by geographic area is shown in **Exhibit 1**.

WCC manufactured in many different countries using a variety of ownership arrangements. Some plants were wholly-owned manufacturing sites; others were operated as joint ventures with local affiliates. Three of these plants were useful illustrations as background for discussing the problems the company faced in measuring the performance of its international ventures. All had been constructed and had come on-stream in the 1991–1993 period.

A chemical plant on the outskirts of Prague in the Czech Republic was operated as a joint venture with a local partner. Total investment in the plant was between $35 and $40 million, including working capital. WCC retained a controlling interest in the joint venture and operated the plant. The company had invested about $5 million in the venture, and the balance of the investment had come from the venture partner and local borrowing.

A similar plant in Poland was 100% owned, and the total capital investment of $40 to $45 million including working capital had been funded by WCC. The venture itself had no external debt.

A third plant in Malaysia was also 100% owned. The plant was built to add capacity in the Pacific region, but the plant was considered part of the company's production capacity serving the global market. WCC had invested approximately $35 million in this Malaysian plant.

## MEASURING THE PERFORMANCE OF THREE INTERNATIONAL VENTURES

Cynthia Sheldon had prepared some exhibits using representative numbers, and she began by explaining the income statement for the venture in the Czech Republic to Samantha Chu.

*The first case is Prague. It is pretty much a classic situation. What I have put together here is a basic income statement for the facility for the first three quarters of 1995 (**Exhibit 2**). What this helps to show is how the difference between the ownership structures in Prague and Poland lead to apparent differences in reported income.*

*This is a nine-month year-to-date income statement for the joint venture. Earnings before interest and taxes of $869,000 is what we would normally report internally for a wholly-owned subsidiary, and that is what would be consolidated. As you proceed down the income statement, there is a charge for interest because we have the ability to leverage these joint ventures fairly highly, anywhere from 60% to 80%. This is interest on external debt—cash going out. We account for it this way because the venture has its own Board of Directors, even though we have management control and retain much of the ability to influence operations, which is not always the case. The fees of $867,000 are coming to WCC under a technical agreement that we have with the joint venture, as a percentage of revenues. In this case, we have put a minority interest line to get down to a net income for WCC. That is the actual income that we would report to the outside world.*

*We are reporting externally a loss of $646,000 on this business, when in truth, relative to our other businesses which are reported before interest charges and before fees, it is contributing to our corporate income. This report makes it appear that we are operating at a loss of just under $1.2 million, $532,000 of which is the share of our joint venture partner, and our share is the $646,000.*

Stan Rogers described the investment:

*In this business WCC has invested, in addition to its technical knowledge and technology, $5 million of its money. In addition, we do not guaranty the debt, which is off balance sheet so far as WCC is concerned. One other way that we can look at these businesses is to look at cash flows to WCC, and cash return on investment to WCC. When we do that, because of the $867,000 in fees which are paid to WCC, there is some return. Although the return is small, it is reasonable at this stage of development of a new business. This business, because of the fees, has been in a loss position, but because of the fees it has shown a positive cash return on investment to WCC.*

Sheldon continued:

*Our actual return consists of the fees paid to WCC, or $867,000, and our share of the reported operating losses, for a net income of $221,000. That is* *the return on our approximately $5 million investment. If the subsidiary were wholly owned with a total investment of approximately $40 million, we would be looking at the $869,000 income before interest and taxes, to which we might decide to apply a tax, on the investment of $40 million. That is how we measure the performance of wholly-owned divisions.*

*One of the reasons that this report appears as it does was that, a few years ago, then-current management decided to work from a single database and to have one group prepare both the external financial reports and the management reports for internal use. It was a fine decision, except for the fact that the external reporters did not have the interest or ability to report what was actually going on in the affiliates.*

*Now, let's look at the report for our subsidiary in Poland (**Exhibit 3**). This plant is 100% owned, so we do not report any interest or fees. The total capital investment was funded by the company and totaled about $40 or $45 million including working capital. There is no external debt or minority interest and no fees. The other charges include the amortization of interest that was capitalized during the construction of the plant. The cost of sales includes some profit from materials that are purchased from other plants, but the prices paid are reasonable if you compare them with competitors' prices. This is another interesting problem that we struggle with, since we are probably reporting $2 or $3 million in profits elsewhere because of these plant purchases. But consider how this would look if we were deducting interest on $30 million of debt, and fees of 8% of revenues as we do in the case of the Prague affiliate. We would then be showing a loss from the business of about $3 million. The accountants do not consider this, and their report makes it appear that the business was doing just fine.*

Samantha Chu spoke up:

*Your explanation implies that there must be some other measures of performance that tell you how these plants are performing. What are those?*

Sheldon:

*We use budgets and the original business plans. We look at the performance against those expectations.*

Rogers:

*Also, although we do not monitor cash flows to the degree that we ought to, we have in our head the cash contribution compared to the amounts that we have invested. In the Czech Republic we can look ahead and see that in the future we will have a 35% to 45% cash on cash return. Poland is draining cash out of us at a remarkable rate, and we have not yet figured out a way to stop it. There are still a lot of unresolved business problems. Compared to the original business plan we have not been able to generate the revenues that were forecasted and the costs have been higher. We do not present cash flow reports to our managers, so these analyses all have to be done in our heads. The information we would need to bring this about formally is all available, but we just have not asked anyone to do it.*

*What we have are three new plants built at about the same time, each having very complex and different financial reporting issues that lead you to have completely different views of the business. Cynthia, show Samantha the report on the plant in Malaysia and what happens when we introduce an economic value added (EVA) approach.*

Sheldon:

*The third plant was built to supply a high margin part of our business. That part of our business is truly a global business in that we can actually ship our product from any of several plants to anywhere in the world. When the decision to build a plant in Malaysia was made we were running out of capacity. We made a strategic decision that we wanted to be located in Malaysia, but this was to be part of our production facilities to serve the global market. We do not usually build a separate plant to supply only the high margin products. The volumes sold and shipped tend to be small, and adding the technostructure of technical service and laboratories to a plant makes the economics somewhat unfavorable unless there are several other units in the same plant producing higher volume products to help carry the costs of these necessary add-ons.*

*Looking at the column labeled "Region of Manufacture," you can see the sales and profitability of the manufacturing facility in Malaysia (**Exhibit 4**). It sells $12 million worth of product, and you can see that with the costs being what they are, the plant is losing a lot of money. The capital charge that we show is an attempt to get a measure of the economic value added by the plant. As was the case with Poland, this report does not include any interest on the total investment of almost $35 million, or any fees.*

*The EVA approach uses a 12% capital charge based on the assets employed including working capital and including accounts payable and fixed capital. Depreciation is included in cost of sales. I think the way we use EVA is very simple, exactly the way it is employed by other folks, but some get much more sophisticated about allocations, capitalized research and development, and the like. We do not do that.*

*In addition, we have recently started to look not just at "region of manufacture" but also at "region of sale," primarily to get an understanding of whether or not a market is attractive. The second column labeled "Region of Sale" is all product being sold in Southeast Asia, even if it is manufactured outside the area, so it includes the cost of manufacturing the product, shipping it, and delivering it to customers in the region. On that basis the earnings before interest and taxes are about $4 million. If we wanted to get down to economic value added we would need to deduct taxes* *and a capital charge; the economic value added would still be negative but not so much so that we could not develop some reasonable strategies to fix it compared to the region of manufacture measure, which is pretty daunting.*

Stan Rogers interjected:

*There is an incremental layer of complexity here in that this plant is starting to produce for the rest of the world because we are running out of capacity and are using this plant as the swing plant. Those shipments will show up in the region of manufacture numbers, but they will not show up in the region of sale numbers. We have not yet sorted this out, but my suspicion is that you cannot look at it this way and get an intriguing view—a solid view—of the business. We probably have to look at the whole system and analyze the incremental revenues and costs of the whole business.*

*The reason why I see this as another iteration or complexity of the same problem is that in Prague and Poland we had the different corporate structures that led to different accounting treatments of interest and fees, which gave us completely warped views on what was going on in the business. This presents the same challenge but adds the dimensions of region of manufacture and region of sale accounting and the need for total system analysis.*

Samantha Chu broke the silence of the pause which followed:

*Have you found a solution to the problem yet?*

Rogers answered:

*We understand it. We have not institutionalized a management reporting system that would lead someone who is intelligent but does not understand the background to understand what is really going on. We do not have a management reporting system in place that shows the relative performance of the three plants in a clear manner. On this basis the system does not work.*

## SOME POSSIBLE SOLUTIONS TO THE PERFORMANCE MEASUREMENT PROBLEM

Cynthia Sheldon began a discussion of some possible solutions to the division performance measurement problem:

*We are scratching away at a solution, perhaps using the concept of economic value added. We probably will also separate the people who are preparing the managerial reports from those who are concerned with external reporting, even though both groups will be working from the same databases. Until now, when we report to external public relations and to the Chairman about the performance of the business, we have used external reporting standards and bases. I have concluded that to get away from that we have to have a separate group engaged with the businesses.*

Stan Rogers chimed in:

> *From a business standpoint we understand this. When we want to do a pre-sentation we will do a one-time analysis, pulling the numbers together that we think best reflect the situation. But we do not have a disciplined, repetitious reporting system that produces an analysis of how these businesses are doing in any other way than the way the external reporting system does it. That is an issue of priorities. We just do not have the time or resources to fix the system now. It is not that we do not understand the problem, or that we could not do it. I think we understand the problem, and we understand the intellectual underpinnings of a solution.*
>
> *I know that does not help you in responding to the analyst's questions today, so you will just have to respond very carefully.*

Cynthia Sheldon continued:

> *We are really just beginning to use EVA as a tool to get people to understand the issues. There is nothing wrong with using cash flow, return on net assets, and other familiar financial measures. There are always problems with any single financial measure, but right now in order to get people to focus it is easier to have one number, and EVA is the most effective single number. We know that in order to make the business viable in our Southeast Asia region we have to go down a path of expanding the business. When you expand, EVA goes down, so if you focus on only that measure you risk saying that I do not want to do that. That is not the right answer. We are already seeing that kind of problem. But at least EVA gets people to focus on the cost of the capital associated with the income that they earn, and it gets more of a sense of cash flow, but we do not rely solely on it.*

Stan Rogers summed up his feelings on the division performance measurement problems, echoing some of the conclusions of Sheldon:

> *You know, I would say the same thing. There is not a planning department here that thinks about EVA and all that kind of stuff. We probably could use better numbers, but driving the business off any single number probably would not work.*

## QUESTIONS

1.  What is causing the problems in measuring division performance at Western Chemical Corporation?
2.  Are there alternative methods for measuring division performance that would avoid the problems that WCC management is having with the methods that they have been using?
3.  Evaluate the approach to using economic value added (EVA) that WCC management is discussing and using experimentally. What are the strengths and weaknesses of this approach?
4.  How should the performance of divisions of WCC be measured?
5.  What should Samantha Chu tell the analyst if he asks specifically about the investments in the Czech Republic, Poland, and Malaysia?

**EXHIBIT 1**
**Financial Information by Geographic Area**

Western Chemical Corporation (WCC) is engaged in the worldwide manufacture and sale of highly specialized service chemical programs.  This includes production and service related to the sale and application of chemicals and technology used in water treatment, pollution control, energy conservation, and other industrial processes as well as a super-absorbent product for the disposable diaper market.

Within WCC, sales between geographic areas are made at prevailing market prices to customers minus an amount intended to compensate the sister WCC company for providing quality customer service.

Identifiable assets are those directly associated with operations of the geographic area.  Corporate assets consist mainly of cash and cash equivalents; marketable securities; investments in unconsolidated partnerships, affiliates, and leveraged leases; and capital assets used for corporate purposes.

Geographic Area Data (in millions)

|  | 1994 | 1993 | 1992 |
|---|---|---|---|
| **Sales** | | | |
| North America | $   886.9 | $   915.1 | $   883.7 |
| Europe | 288.9 | 315.6 | 346.5 |
| Latin America | 72.2 | 66.4 | 60.7 |
| Pacific | 127.7 | 116.7 | 108.2 |
| Sales between areas | (30.1) | (24.4) | (24.6) |
|  | $1,345.6 | $1,389.4 | $1,374.5 |
| **Operating Earnings** | | | |
| North America | $   181.6 | $   216.9 | $   211.3 |
| Europe | (10.2) | 41.8 | 48.9 |
| Latin America | 9.3 | 11.4 | 10.0 |
| Pacific | 14.3 | 14.4 | 14.4 |
| Expenses not allocated to areas | (20.3) | (21.6) | (24.3) |
|  | $   174.7 | $   262.9 | $   260.3 |
| **Identifiable Assets** | | | |
| North America | $   485.2 | $   566.6 | $   562.2 |
| Europe | 245.2 | 227.4 | 225.5 |
| Latin America | 66.9 | 45.4 | 42.7 |
| Pacific | 147.9 | 126.3 | 124.7 |
| Corporate | 337.0 | 246.7 | 395.5 |
|  | $1,282.2 | $1,212.4 | $1,350.6 |

Amounts for North America sales in the tabulation above include exports to the following areas:

| (in millions) | 1994 | 1993 | 1992 |
|---|---|---|---|
| Latin America | $21.9 | $19.2 | $16.0 |
| All other | 7.3 | 13.0 | 12.0 |

The decrease in operating earnings in 1994 was mainly attributable to the pretax provision of $68 million for consolidation expenses.  Of that amount, approximately $34 million was included in European operations.

**EXHIBIT 2**
**Income from Czech Republic Joint Venture ($ in thousands)**

|  | 9/95 Year-to-Date |
|---|---|
| Revenues | $11,510 |
| Cost of sales | (9,541) |
| Selling, technical expenses, and administrative expenses | (891) |
| Other income/Other charges | (209) |
| Income before interest and taxes | $ 869 |
| Interest | (1,120) |
| Fees | (867) |
| Foreign exchange | (60) |
| Income (loss) | $ (1,178) |
| Minority interest | 532 |
| Taxes | — |
| Net income (loss) | $ (646) |

*Real Cash Here.* (handwritten, pointing to Fees)

**EXHIBIT 3**
**Income from Poland Plant ($ in thousands)**

|  | 9/95 Year-to-Date |
|---|---|
| Revenues | $ 32,536 |
| Cost of sales | (28,458) |
| Selling, technical expenses, and administrative expenses | (2,529) |
| Other income/Other charges | (121) |
| Income before interest and taxes | $ 1,428 |
| Interest | — |
| Fees | — |
| Foreign exchange | 34 |
| Income | $ 1,462 |
| Minority interest | — |
| Taxes | — |
| Net income (loss) | $ 1,462 |

**EXHIBIT 4**
**Income from Malaysia and Southeast Asia ($ in thousands)**

|  | Region of Manufacture | Region of Sale |
|---|---|---|
|  | 9/95 Year-to-Date | 9/95 Year-to-Date |
| Revenues | $ 12,020 | $ 36,052 |
| Cost of sales | (12,392) | (26,648) |
| Selling, technical expenses, and administrative expenses | (3,775) | (4,845) |
| Other income/Other charges | (685) | (285) |
| Income before interest and taxes | $ (4,832) | $ 4,274 |
| Taxes (40%) | — | (1,710) |
| Net income | $ (4,832) | $ 2,564 |
| Capital charges | (3,600)[a] | (6,686)[b] |
| Economic value added | $ (8,432) | $ (4,122) |

[a] $30,000 @ 12% = $3,600

[b] $110,000 @ 12% × [(36,052 − 12,020) / 102,800] + 30,000 @ 12% = $6,686

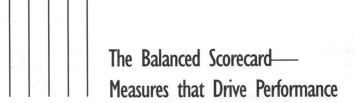

# The Balanced Scorecard—
# Measures that Drive Performance

**W**hat you measure is what you get. Senior executives understand that their organization's measurement system strongly affects the behavior of managers and employees. Executives also understand that traditional financial accounting measures like return-on-investment and earnings-per-share can give misleading signals for continuous improvement and innovation—activities today's competitive environment demands. The traditional financial perfor-mance measures worked well for the industrial era, but they are out of step with the skills and competencies companies are trying to master today.

As managers and academic researchers have tried to remedy the inade-quacies of current performance measurement systems, some have focused on making financial measures more relevant. Others have said, "Forget the financial measures. Improve operational measures like cycle time and defect rates; the financial results will follow." But managers should not have to choose between financial and operational measures. In observing and working with many companies, we have found that senior executives do not rely on one set of measures to the exclusion of the other. They realize that no single measure can provide a clear performance target or focus attention on the critical areas of the business. Managers want a balanced presentation of both financial and operational measures.

During a year-long research project with 12 companies at the leading edge of performance measurement, we devised a "balanced scorecard"—a set of measures that gives top managers a fast but comprehensive view of the business. The balanced scorecard includes financial measures that tell the results

*Robert S. Kaplan and David P. Norton authored this article. Reprinted by permission from* Harvard Business Review, *January-February, 1992, 71–79. Reprint 92105.*

Copyright © 1991 by the President and Fellows of Harvard College.

of actions already taken.  And it complements the financial measures with operational measures on customer satisfaction, internal processes, and the organization's innovation and improvement activities—operational measures that are the drivers of future financial performance.

Think of the balanced scorecard as the dials and indicators in an airplane cockpit.  For the complex task of navigating and flying an airplane, pilots need detailed information about many aspects of the flight.  They need information on fuel, air speed, altitude, bearing, destination, and other indicators that summarize the current and predicted environment.  Reliance on one instrument can be fatal.  Similarly, the complexity of managing an organization today requires that managers be able to view performance in several areas simultaneously.

The balanced scorecard allows managers to look at the business from four important perspectives. (See the exhibit on the following page, "The Balanced Scorecard Links Performance Measures.")  It provides answers to four basic questions:

- How do customers see us? (customer perspective)
- What must we excel at? (internal business perspective)
- Can we continue to improve and create value? (innovation and learning perspective)
- How do we look to shareholders? (financial perspective)

While giving senior managers information from four different perspectives, the balanced scorecard minimizes information overload by limiting the number of measures used.  Companies rarely suffer from having too few measures.  More commonly, they keep adding new measures whenever an employee or a consultant makes a worthwhile suggestion.  One manager described the proliferation of new measures at his company as its "kill another tree program."  The balanced scorecard forces managers to focus on the handful of measures that are most critical.

Several companies have already adopted the balanced scorecard.  Their early experiences using the scorecard have demonstrated that it meets several managerial needs.  First, the scorecard brings together, in a single management report, many of the seemingly disparate elements of a company's competitive agenda: becoming customer oriented, shortening response time, improving quality, emphasizing teamwork, reducing new product launch times, and managing for the long term.

Second, the scorecard guards against suboptimization.  By forcing senior managers to consider all the important operational measures together, the balanced scorecard lets them see whether improvement in one area may have been achieved at the expense of another.  Even the best objective can be achieved badly.  Companies can reduce time to market, for example, in two very different ways: by improving the management of new product introductions or by releasing only products that are incrementally different from existing products.  Spending on setups can be cut either by reducing setup times or by increasing

**The Balanced Scorecard Links Performance Measures**

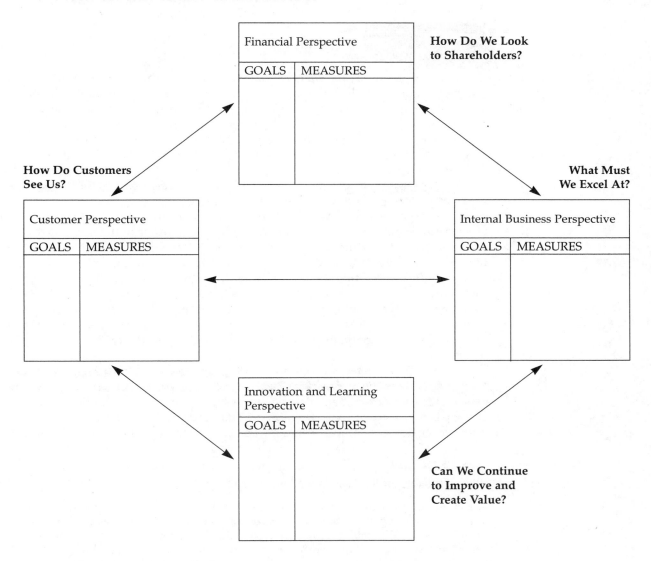

batch sizes. Similarly, production output and first-pass yields can rise, but the increases may be due to a shift in the product mix to more standard, easy-to-produce but lower-margin products.

We will illustrate how companies can create their own balanced scorecard with the experiences of one semiconductor company—let's call it Electronic Circuits Inc. (ECI). ECI saw the scorecard as a way to clarify, simplify, and then operationalize the vision at the top of the organization. The ECI scorecard was designed to focus the attention of its top executives on a short list of critical indicators of current and future performance.

## CUSTOMER PERSPECTIVE: HOW DO CUSTOMERS SEE US?

Many companies today have a corporate mission that focuses on the customer. "To be number one in delivering value to customers" is a typical mission statement. How a company is performing from its customers' perspective has become, therefore, a priority for top management. The balanced scorecard demands that managers translate their general mission statement on customer service into specific measures that reflect the factors that really matter to customers.

Customers' concerns tend to fall into four categories: time, quality, performance and service, and cost. Lead time measures the time required for the company to meet its customers' needs. For existing products, lead time can be measured from the time the company receives an order to the time it actually delivers the product or service to the customer. For new products, lead time represents the time to market, or how long it takes to bring a new product from the product definition stage to the start of shipments. Quality measures the defect level of incoming products as perceived and measured by the customer. Quality could also measure on-time delivery, the accuracy of the company's delivery forecasts. The combination of performance and service measures how the company's products or services contribute to creating value for its customers.

To put the balanced scorecard to work, companies should articulate goals for time, quality, and performance and service and then translate these goals into specific measures. Senior managers at ECI, for example, established general goals for customer performance: get standard products to market sooner, improve customers' time to market, become customers' supplier of choice

---

### Other Measures for the Customer's Perspective

A computer manufacturer wanted to be the competitive leader in customer satisfaction, so it measured competitive rankings. The company got the rankings through an outside organization hired to talk directly with customers. The company also wanted to do a better job of solving customers' problems by creating more partnerships with other suppliers. It measured the percentage of revenue from third-party relationships.

The customers of a producer of very expensive medical equipment demanded high reliability. The company developed two customer-based metrics for its operations: equipment up-time percentage and mean-time response to a service call.

A semiconductor company asked each major customer to rank the company against comparable suppliers on efforts to improve quality, delivery time, and price performance. When the manufacturer discovered that it ranked in the middle, managers made improvements that moved the company to the top of customers' rankings.

---

through partnerships with them, and develop innovative products tailored to customer needs. The managers translated these general goals into four specific goals and identified an appropriate measure for each. (See the exhibit on the following page, "ECI's Balanced Scorecard.")

To track the specific goal of providing a continuous stream of attractive solutions, ECI measured the percent of sales from new products and the percent of sales from proprietary products. That information was available internally. But certain other measures forced the company to get data from outside. To assess whether the company was achieving its goal of providing reliable, responsive supply, ECI turned to its customers. When it found that each customer defined "reliable, responsive supply" differently, ECI created a database of the factors as defined by each of its major customers. The shift to external measures of performance with customers led ECI to redefine "on time" so it matched customers' expectations. Some customers defined "on time" as any shipment that arrived within five days of scheduled delivery; others used a nine-day window. ECI itself had been using a seven-day window, which meant that the company was not satisfying some of its customers and over-achieving with others. ECI also asked its top ten customers to rank the company as a supplier overall.

Depending on customers' evaluations to define some of a company's performance measures forces that company to view its performance through customers' eyes. Some companies hire third parties to perform anonymous customer surveys, resulting in a customer-driven report card. The J.D. Powers quality survey, for example, has become the standard of performance for the automobile industry, while the Department of Transportation's measurement of on-time arrivals and lost baggage provides external standards for airlines. Benchmarking procedures are yet another technique companies use to compare their performance against competitors' best practice. Many companies have introduced "best of breed" comparison programs: the company looks to one industry to find, say, the best distribution system, to another industry for the lowest cost payroll process, and then forms a composite of those best practices to set objectives for its own performance.

In addition to measures of time, quality, and performance and service, companies must remain sensitive to the cost of their products. But customers see price as only one component of the cost they incur when dealing with their suppliers. Other supplier-driven costs range from ordering, scheduling delivery, and paying for the materials; to receiving, inspecting, handling, and storing the materials; to the scrap, rework, and obsolescence caused by the materials; and schedule disruptions (expediting and value of lost output) from incorrect deliveries. An excellent supplier may charge a higher unit price for products than other vendors but nonetheless be a lower cost supplier because it can deliver defect-free products in exactly the right quantities at exactly the right time directly to the production process and can minimize, through electronic data interchange, the administrative hassles of ordering, invoicing, and paying for materials.

**ECI's Balanced Business Scorecard**

## Customer Perspective

| GOALS | MEASURES |
|---|---|
| New products | Percent of sales from new products |
| | Percent of sales from proprietary products |
| Responsive supply | On-time delivery (defined by customer) |
| Preferred supplier | Share of key accounts' purchases |
| | Ranking by key accounts |
| Customer partnership | Number of cooperative engineering efforts |

## Internal Business Perspective

| GOALS | MEASURES |
|---|---|
| Technology capability | Manufacturing geometry vs. competition |
| Manufacturing excellence | Cycle time Unit cost Yield |
| Design productivity | Silicon efficiency Engineering efficiency |
| New product introduction | Actual introduction schedule vs. plan |

## Innovation and Learning Perspective

| GOALS | MEASURES |
|---|---|
| Technology leadership | Time to develop next generation |
| Manufacturing learning | Process time to maturity |
| Product focus | Percent of products that equal 80% sales |
| Time to market | New product introduction vs. competition |

## Financial Perspective

| GOALS | MEASURES |
|---|---|
| Survive | Cash flow |
| Succeed | Quarterly sales growth and operating income by division |
| Prosper | Increased market share and ROE |

## INTERNAL BUSINESS PERSPECTIVE: WHAT MUST WE EXCEL AT?

Customer-based measures are important, but they must be translated into measures of what the company must do internally to meet its customers' expectations. After all, excellent customer performance derives from processes, decisions, and actions occurring throughout an organization. Managers need to focus on those critical internal operations that enable them to satisfy customer needs. The second part of the balanced scorecard gives managers that internal perspective.

The internal measures for the balanced scorecard should stem from the business processes that have the greatest impact on customer satisfaction—factors that affect cycle time, quality, employee skills, and productivity, for example. Companies should also attempt to identify and measure their company's core competencies, the critical technologies needed to ensure continued market leadership. Companies should decide what processes and competencies they must excel at and specify measures for each.

Managers at ECI determined that submicron technology capability was critical to its market position. They also decided that they had to focus on manufacturing excellence, design productivity, and new product introduction. The company developed operational measures for each of these four internal business goals.

To achieve goals on cycle time, quality, productivity, and cost, managers must devise measures that are influenced by employees' actions. Since much of the action takes place at the department and workstation levels, managers need to decompose overall cycle time, quality, product, and cost measures to local levels. That way, the measures link top management's judgment about key internal processes and competencies to the actions taken by individuals

---

### Other Measures for the Internal Business Perspective

One company recognized that the success of its TQM program depended on all its employees internalizing and acting on the program's messages. The company performed a monthly survey of 600 randomly selected employees to determine if they were aware of TQM, had changed their behavior because of it, believed the outcome was favorable, or had become missionaries to others.

Hewlett-Packard uses a metric called breakeven time (BET) to measure the effectiveness of its product development cycle. BET measures the time required for all the accumulated expenses in the product and process development cycle (including equipment acquisition) to be recovered by the product's contribution margin (the selling price less manufacturing, delivery, and selling expenses).

A major office products manufacturer, wanting to respond rapidly to changes in the marketplace, set out to reduce cycle time by 50%. Lower levels of the organization aimed to radically cut the times required to process customer orders, order and receive materials from suppliers, move materials and products between plants, produce and assemble products, and deliver products to customers.

---

that affect overall corporate objectives.  This linkage ensures that employees at lower levels in the organization have clear targets for actions, decisions, and improvement activities that will contribute to the company's overall mission.

Information systems play an invaluable role in helping managers disaggregate the summary measures.  When an unexpected signal appears on the balanced scorecard, executives can query their information system to find the source of the trouble. If the aggregate measure for on-time delivery is poor, for example, executives with a good information system can quickly look behind the aggregate measure until they can identify late deliveries, day by day, by a particular plant to an individual customer.

If the information system is unresponsive, however, it can be the Achilles' heel of performance measurement.  Managers at ECI are currently limited by the absence of such an operational information system.  Their greatest concern is that the scorecard information is not timely; reports are generally a week behind the company's routine management meetings, and the measures have yet to be linked to measures for managers and employees at lower levels of the organization.  The company is in the process of developing a more responsive information system to eliminate this constraint.

## INNOVATION AND LEARNING PERSPECTIVE:
## CAN WE CONTINUE TO IMPROVE AND CREATE VALUE?

The customer-based and internal business process measures on the balanced scorecard identify the parameters that the company considers most important for competitive success.  But the targets for success keep changing.  Intense global competition requires that companies make continual improvements to their *existing* products and processes and have the ability to introduce entirely new products with expanded capabilities.

A company's ability to innovate, improve, and learn ties directly to the company's value.  That is, only through the ability to launch new products, create more value for customers, and improve operating efficiencies continually can a company penetrate new markets and increase revenues and margins—in short, grow and thereby increase shareholder value.

ECI's innovation measures focus on the company's ability to develop and introduce standard products rapidly, products that the company expects will form the bulk of its future sales.  Its manufacturing improvement measure focuses on new products; the goal is to achieve stability in the manufacturing of new products rather than to improve manufacturing of existing products.  Like many other companies, ECI uses the percent of sales from new products as one of its innovation and improvement measures.  If sales from new products are trending downward, managers can explore whether problems have arisen in new product design or new product introduction.

In addition to measures on product and process innovation, some companies overlay specific improvement goals for their existing processes. For example, Analog Devices, a Massachusetts-based manufacturer of specialized semiconductors, expects managers to improve their customer and internal business process performance continuously. The company estimates specific rates of improvement for on-time delivery, cycle time, defect rate, and yield.

Other companies, like Milliken & Co., require that managers make improvements within a specific time period. Milliken did not want its "associates" (Milliken's word for employees) to rest on their laurels after winning the Baldridge Award. Chairman and CEO Roger Milliken asked each plant to implement a "ten-four" improvement program: measures of process defects, missed deliveries, and scrap were to be reduced by a factor of ten over the next four years. These targets emphasize the role for continuous improvement in customer satisfaction and internal business processes.

## FINANCIAL PERSPECTIVE: HOW DO WE LOOK TO SHAREHOLDERS?

Financial performance measures indicate whether the company's strategy, implementation, and execution are contributing to bottom-line improvement. Typical financial goals have to do with profitability, growth, and shareholder value. ECI stated its financial goals simply: to survive, to succeed, and to prosper. Survival was measured by cash flow, success by quarterly sales growth and operating income by division, and prosperity by increased market share by segment and return on equity.

But given today's business environment, should senior managers even look at the business from a financial perspective? Should they pay attention to short-term financial measures like quarterly sales and operating income? Many have criticized financial measures because of their well-documented inadequacies, their backward-looking focus, and their inability to reflect contemporary value-creating actions. Shareholder value analysis (SVA), which forecasts future cash flows and discounts them back to a rough estimate of current value, is an attempt to make financial analysis more forward looking. But SVA still is based on cash flow rather than on the activities and processes that drive cash flow.

Some critics go much further in their indictment of financial measures. They argue that the terms of competition have changed and that traditional financial measures do not improve customer satisfaction, quality, cycle time, and employee motivation. In their view, financial performance is the result of operational actions, and financial success should be the logical consequence of doing the fundamentals well. In other words, companies should stop navigating by financial measures. By making fundamental improvements in their operations, the financial numbers will take care of themselves, the argument goes.

Assertions that financial measures are unnecessary are incorrect for at least two reasons. A well-designed financial control system can actually enhance rather than inhibit an organization's total quality management program. (See the insert, "How One Company Used a Daily Financial Report to Improve

Quality.") More important, however, the alleged linkage between improved operating performance and financial success is actually quite tenuous and uncertain. Let us demonstrate rather than argue this point.

### How One Company Used a Daily Financial Report to Improve Quality*

In the 1980s, a chemicals company became committed to a total quality management program and began to make extensive measurements of employee participation, statistical process control and key quality indicators. Using computerized controls and remote data entry systems, the plant monitored more than 30,000 observations of its production processes every four hours. The department managers and operating personnel who now had access to massive amounts of real-time operational data found their monthly financial reports to be irrelevant.

But one enterprising department manager saw things differently. He created a daily income statement. Each day, he estimated the value of the output from the production process using estimated market prices and subtracted the expenses of raw materials, energy, and capital consumed in the production process. To approximate the cost of producing out-of-conformance product, he cut the revenues from off-spec output by 50% to 100%.

The daily financial report gave operators powerful feedback and motivation and guided their quality and productivity efforts. The department head understood that it is not always possible to improve quality, reduce energy consumption, and increase throughput simultaneously; tradeoffs are usually necessary. He wanted the daily financial statement to guide those tradeoffs. The difference between the input consumed and output produced indicated the success or failure of the employees' efforts on the previous day. The operators were empowered to make decisions that might improve quality, increase productivity, and reduce consumption of energy and materials.

That feedback and empowerment had visible results. When, for example, a hydrogen compressor failed, a supervisor on the midnight shift ordered an emergency repair crew into action. Previously, such a failure of a noncritical component would have been reported in the shift log, where the department manager arriving for work the following morning would have to discover it. The midnight shift supervisor knew the cost of losing the hydrogen gas and made the decision that the cost of expediting the repairs would be repaid several times over by the output produced by having the compressor back on line before morning.

The department proceeded to set quality and output records. Over time, the department manager became concerned that employees would lose interest in continually improving operations. He tightened the parameters for in-spec production and reset the prices to reflect a 25% premium for output containing only negligible fractions of impurities. The operators continued to improve the production process.

The success of the daily financial report hinged on the manager's ability to establish a financial penalty for what had previously been an intangible variable: the quality of output. With this innovation, it was easy to see where process improvements and capital investments could generate the highest returns.

---

* Source: "Texas Eastman Company," by Robert S. Kaplan, Harvard Business School case 9-190-039.

Over the three-year period between 1987 and 1990, a NYSE electronics company made an order-of-magnitude improvement in quality and on-time delivery performance. Outgoing defect rate dropped from 500 parts per million to 50, on-time delivery improved from 70% to 96%, and yield jumped from 26% to 51%. Did these breakthrough improvements in quality, productivity, and customer service provide substantial benefits to the company? Unfortunately not. During the same three-year period, the company's financial results showed little improvement, and its stock price plummeted to one-third of its July 1987 value. The considerable improvements in manufacturing capabilities had not been translated into increased profitability. Slow releases of new products and a failure to expand marketing to new and perhaps more demanding customers prevented the company from realizing the benefits of its manufacturing achievements. The operational achievements were real, but the company had failed to capitalize on them.

The disparity between improved operational performance and disappointing financial measures creates frustration for senior executives. This frustration is often vented at nameless Wall Street analysts who allegedly cannot see past quarterly blips in financial performance to the underlying long-term values these executives sincerely believe they are creating in their organizations. But the hard truth is that if improved performance fails to be reflected in the bottom line, executives should reexamine the basic assumptions of their strategy and mission. Not all long-term strategies are profitable strategies.

Measures of customer satisfaction, internal business performance, and innovation and improvement are derived from the company's particular view of the world and its perspective on key success factors. But that view is not necessarily correct. Even an excellent set of balanced scorecard measures does not guarantee a winning strategy. The balanced scorecard can only translate a company's strategy into specific measurable objectives. A failure to convert improved operational performance, as measured in the scorecard, into improved financial performance should send executives back to their drawing boards to rethink the company's strategy or its implementation plans.

As one example, disappointing financial measures sometimes occur because companies don't follow up their operational improvements with another round of actions. Quality and cycle-time improvements can create excess capacity. Managers should be prepared to either put the excess capacity to work or else get rid of it. The excess capacity must be either used by boosting revenues or eliminated by reducing expenses if operational improvements are to be brought down to the bottom line.

As companies improve their quality and response time, they eliminate the need to build, inspect, and rework out-of-conformance products or to reschedule and expedite delayed orders. Eliminating these tasks means that some of the people who perform them are no longer needed. Companies are understandably reluctant to lay off employees, especially since the employees may have been the source of the ideas that produced the higher quality and reduced cycle time.  Layoffs are a poor reward for past improvement and can damage the morale of remaining workers, curtailing further improvement.  But companies will not realize all the financial benefits of their improvements until their employees and facilities are working to capacity—or the companies confront the pain of downsizing to eliminate the expenses of the newly created excess capacity.

If executives fully understood the consequences of their quality and cycle-time improvement programs, they might be more aggressive about using the newly created capacity.  To capitalize on this self-created new capacity, however, companies must expand sales to existing customers, market existing products to entirely new customers (who are now accessible because of the improved quality and delivery performance), and increase the flow of new products to the market.  These actions can generate added revenues with only modest increases in operating expenses. If marketing and sales and R&D do not generate the increased volume, the operating improvements will stand as excess capacity, redundancy, and untapped capabilities.  Periodic financial statements remind executives that improved quality, response time, productivity, or new products benefit the company only when they are translated into improved sales and market share, reduced operating expenses, or higher asset turnover.

Ideally, companies should specify how improvements in quality, cycle time, quoted lead times, delivery, and new product introduction will lead to higher market share, operating margins, and asset turnover or to reduced operating expenses.  The challenge is to learn how to make such explicit linkage between operations and finance.  Exploring the complex dynamics will likely require simulation and cost modeling.

## MEASURES THAT MOVE COMPANIES FORWARD

As companies have applied the balanced scorecard, we have begun to recognize that the scorecard represents a fundamental change in the underlying assumptions about performance measurement.  As the controllers and finance vice presidents involved in the research project took the concept back to their organizations, the project participants found that they could not implement the balanced scorecard without the involvement of the senior managers who have the most complete picture of the company's vision and priorities.  This was revealing because most existing performance measurement systems have been designed and overseen by financial experts.  Rarely do controllers need to have senior managers so heavily involved.

Probably because traditional measurement systems have sprung from the finance function, the systems have a control bias.  That is, traditional performance measurement systems specify the particular actions they want employees to take and then measure to see whether the employees have in fact taken those actions. In that way, the systems try to control behavior. Such measurement systems fit with the engineering mentality of the Industrial Age.

The balanced scorecard, on the other hand, is well suited to the kind of organization many companies are trying to become. The scorecard puts strategy and vision, not control, at the center. It establishes goals but assumes that people will adopt whatever behaviors and take whatever actions are necessary to arrive at those goals. The measures are designed to pull people toward the overall vision. Senior managers may know what the end result should be, but they cannot tell employees exactly how to achieve that result, if only because the conditions in which employees operate are constantly changing.

This new approach to performance measurement is consistent with the initiatives under way in many companies: cross-functional integration, customer-supplier partnerships, global scale, continuous improvement, and team rather than individual accountability. By combining the financial, customer, internal process and innovation, and organizational learning perspectives, the balanced scorecard helps managers understand, at least implicitly, many interrelationships. This understanding can help managers transcend traditional notions about functional barriers and ultimately lead to improved decision making and problem solving. The balanced scorecard keeps companies looking—and moving—forward instead of backward.

# Chadwick, Inc.:
# The Balanced Scorecard (Abridged)

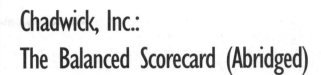

*The "Balanced Scorecard"[1] article seemed to address the concerns of several division managers who felt that the company was over-emphasizing short-term financial results. But the process of getting agreement on what measures should be used proved a lot more difficult than I anticipated.*

Bill Baron, Comptroller of Chadwick, Inc.

## COMPANY BACKGROUND

Chadwick, Inc., was a diversified producer of personal consumer products and pharmaceuticals. The Norwalk Division of Chadwick developed, manufactured, and sold ethical drugs for human and animal use. It was one of five or six sizable companies competing in these markets and, while it did not dominate the industry, the company was considered well-managed and was respected for the high quality of its products. Norwalk did not compete by supplying a full range of products. It specialized in several niches and attempted to leverage its product line by continually searching for new applications for existing compounds.

Norwalk sold its products through several key distributors who supplied local markets, such as retail stores, hospitals and health service organizations,

---

*Professor Robert S. Kaplan prepared this case.*

Copyright © 1996 by the President and Fellows of Harvard College. Harvard Business School case 196-124.

---

[1] Robert S. Kaplan and David P. Norton, "The Balanced Scorecard: Measures that Drive Performance," *Harvard Business Review* (January-February 1992).

and veterinary practices. Norwalk depended on its excellent relations with the distributors who served to promote Norwalk's products to end users and also received feedback from the end users about new products desired by their customers.

Chadwick knew that its long-term success depended on how much money distributors could make by promoting and selling Norwalk's products. If the profit from selling Norwalk products was high, then these products were promoted heavily by the distributors and Norwalk received extensive communication back about future customer needs. Norwalk had historically provided many highly profitable products to the marketplace, but recent inroads by generic manufacturers had been eroding distributors' sales and profit margins. Norwalk had been successful in the past because of its track record of generating a steady stream of attractive, popular products. During the second half of the 1980s, however, the approval process for new products had lengthened and fewer big winners had emerged from Norwalk's R&D laboratories.

## RESEARCH AND DEVELOPMENT

The development of ethical drugs was a lengthy, costly, and unpredictable process. Development cycles now averaged about 12 years. The process started by screening a large number of compounds for potential benefits and use. For every drug that finally emerged as approved for use, up to 30,000 compounds had to be tested at the beginning of a new product development cycle. The development and testing processes had many stages. The development cycle started with the discovery of compounds that possessed the desirable properties and ended many years later with extensive and tedious testing and documentation to demonstrate that the new drug could meet government regulations for promised benefits, reliability in production, and absence of deleterious side effects.

Approved and patented drugs could generate enormous revenues for Norwalk and its distributors. Norwalk's profitability during the 1980s was sustained by one key drug that had been discovered in the late 1960s. No blockbuster drug had emerged during the 1980s, however, and the existing pipeline of compounds going through development, evaluation, and test was not as healthy as Norwalk management desired. Management was placing pressure on scientists in the R&D lab to increase the yield of promising new products and to reduce the time and costs of the product development cycle. Scientists were currently exploring new bio-engineering techniques to create compounds that had the specific active properties desired rather than depending on an almost random search through thousands of possible compounds. The new techniques started with a detailed specification of the chemical properties that a new drug should have and then attempted to synthesize candidate compounds that could be tested for these properties. The bio-engineering procedures were costly, requiring extensive investment in new equipment and computer-based analysis.

A less expensive approach to increase the financial yield from R&D investments was to identify new applications for existing compounds that had already been approved for use.  While some validation still had to be submitted for government approval to demonstrate the effectiveness of the drug in the new applications, the cost of extending an existing product to a new application was much less expensive than developing and creating an entirely new compound.  Several valuable suggestions for possible new applications from existing products had come from Norwalk salespeople in the field.  The salespeople were now being trained not only to sell existing products for approved applications, but also to listen to end users who frequently had novel and interesting ideas about how Norwalk's products could be used for new applications.

## MANUFACTURING

Norwalk's manufacturing processes were considered among the best in the industry. Management took pride in the ability of the manufacturing operation to quickly and efficiently ramp up to produce drugs once they had cleared governmental regulatory processes.  Norwalk's manufacturing capabilities also had to produce the small batches of new products that were required during testing and evaluation stages.

## PERFORMANCE MEASUREMENT

Chadwick allowed its several divisions to operate in a decentralized fashion. Division managers had almost complete discretion in managing all the critical processes: R&D, Production, Marketing and Sales, and administrative functions such as finance, human resources, and legal.  Chadwick set challenging financial targets for divisions to meet. The targets were usually expressed as Return on Capital Employed (ROCE).  As a diversified company, Chadwick wanted to be able to deploy the returns from the most profitable divisions to those divisions that held out the highest promise for profitable growth. Monthly financial summaries were submitted by each division to corporate headquarters.  The Chadwick Executive Committee, consisting of the chief executive officer, the chief operating officer, two executive vice presidents, and the chief financial officer met monthly with each division manager to review ROCE performance and backup financial information for the preceding month.

## THE BALANCED SCORECARD PROJECT

Bill Baron, the comptroller of Chadwick, had been searching for improved methods for evaluating the performance of the various divisions. Division managers complained about the continual pressure to meet short-term financial objectives in businesses that required extensive investments in risky projects to yield long-term returns. The idea of a balanced scorecard appealed to him as a constructive way to balance short-run financial objectives with the long-term performance of the company.

Baron brought the article and concept to Dan Daniels, the president and chief operating officer of Chadwick. Daniels shared Baron's enthusiasm for the concept, feeling that a balanced scorecard would allow Chadwick divisional managers more flexibility in how they measured and presented their results of operations to corporate management. He also liked the idea of holding managers accountable for improving the long-term performance of their division.

After several days of reflection, Daniels issued a memorandum to all Chadwick division managers. The memo had a simple and direct message: Read the Balanced Scorecard article, develop a scorecard for your division, and be prepared to come to corporate headquarters in 90 days to present and defend the divisional scorecard to Chadwick's Executive Committee.

John Greenfield, the division manager at Norwalk, received Daniels' memorandum with some concern and apprehension. In principle, Greenfield liked the idea of developing a scorecard that would be more responsive to his operations, but he was distrustful of how much freedom he had to develop and use such a scorecard. Greenfield recalled:

> *This seemed like just another way for corporate to claim that they have decentralized decision-making and authority while still retaining ultimate control at headquarters.*

Greenfield knew that he would have to develop a plan of action to meet corporate's request but, lacking a clear sense of how committed Chadwick was to the concept, he was not prepared to take much time from his or his subordinates' existing responsibilities for the project.

The next day, at the weekly meeting of the Divisional Operating Committee, Greenfield distributed the Daniels memo and appointed a three-person committee, headed by the divisional controller, Wil Wagner, to facilitate the process for creating the Norwalk balanced scorecard.

Wagner approached Greenfield later that day:

> *I read the Balanced Scorecard article. Based on my understanding of the concept, we must start with a clearly defined business vision. I'm not sure I have a clear understanding of the vision and business strategy for Norwalk. How can I start to build the scorecard without this understanding?*

Greenfield admitted: "That's a valid point. Let me see what I can do to get you started."

Greenfield picked up a pad of paper and started to write. Several minutes later he had produced a short business strategy statement for Norwalk (see **Exhibit 1**). Wagner and his group took Greenfield's strategy statement and started to formulate scorecard measures for the division.

**EXHIBIT 1**
**Norwalk Pharmaceutical Division—Business Strategy**

1.  Manage Norwalk portfolio of investments
    *   minimize cost of executing our existing business base
    *   maximize return/yield on all development spending
    *   invest in discovery of new compounds

2.  Satisfy customer needs

3.  Drive responsibility to the lowest level
    *   minimize centralized staff overhead

4.  People development
    *   industry training
    *   unique mix of technical and commercial skills

# Review Cases

Consulting Partners & Co.

Kings Mountain Distillery, Inc.

# Consulting Partners & Co.

*The chairman's office just called with a special request. The Management Committee will be meeting this afternoon to discuss issues surrounding the National Training Center. The preliminary report on the Center's operations during 1993 has just arrived on his desk, and he is quite upset that the costs seem to be about one-third higher than he expected. Before he chairs the meeting this afternoon, he would like you to take a look at the costs and prepare an analysis of the performance of the Center last year. In addition, he has some idea that perhaps training costs should be treated as an asset in the firm's balance sheet. This would encourage partners to seek training themselves and to be more willing to release staff members for training. If training costs were capitalized (recorded to asset accounts), they would not be deducted from income immediately and they would not reduce the current year's distribution of income to partners. Finally, now that the National Training Center is up and running, he thinks we ought to pay some attention to establishing a management control system and performance measures that will allow us to determine the extent to which the Center is accomplishing its mission each year.*

Robert Sampson, director of human resources at Consulting Partners & Co. (CPC), was speaking with Patricia Ryan, who had recently joined CPC as a specialist in personnel and human relations. Three-and-one-half years earlier, Ryan had earned a Master of Business Administration degree and accepted a position on the human relations staff of a Big Six accounting firm. In November 1993, a headhunter called and she was convinced to resign her position and join CPC.

Copyright © 1993 by the President and Fellows of Harvard College. Harvard Business School case 194-057.

Sampson continued:

*The chairman specifically asked that this assignment go to you. So whether you have time to take it on this morning or not, it's yours. His office has already faxed a copy of the summary report on operations for 1993 at the National Training Center (**Exhibit 1**). From my file, I found a copy of the proposal for the Center on which the July 1992 decision to establish a training center was based (**Exhibit 2**). The chairman's office also promised to fax his more specific questions as soon as they can get them typed up.*

## THE FIRM

Consulting Partners & Co. was established late in 1991 by the merger of four separate consulting firms, each of which had been competing on a national basis. The concept of the merger was that a larger firm would be able to offer stronger and more diversified services on a nationwide basis in the United States and compete internationally with larger firms in the industry. The combined firms had nearly 1,400 partners and employed almost 10,000 personnel in 51 offices in the United States, London, Paris, Frankfurt, and Mexico City.

Much consolidation and reorganization was necessary as a result of the merger. In the cities where the newly merged firms each had offices, consolidation was inevitable. Real estate leases had to be negotiated or renegotiated to achieve economies of operation. Fortunately, the newly merged firm had sufficient operating capital so that the restructuring could take place quickly, and the consolidation was mostly completed by mid-1993.

Even before the merger had taken place, the new firm had decided that required training for all professional staff would be one of the new firm's hallmarks. Initially, it was determined that all partners would be required to engage in a training activity for at least one week each year on average, and all other staff consultants would be required to spend two weeks each year in training. While such a requirement was not unprecedented in the professional services industry, CPC's standard would be a costly one: not only would the firm have to bear the cost of training, but during training consultants would not be available to serve on assignments and earn fees. Nevertheless, the partners in the new venture were convinced that professional training would provide a competitive edge until other professional service firms matched them.

Initially, the training requirement could be met in two ways. Consultants could choose to participate in professional development seminars run by universities or other training agents. Alternatively, individual offices of CPC could organize their own training sessions. The problem with the second alternative was that it was hard to achieve economies of scale within a single office without effectively shutting down that office during the time training was taking place.

Against that background, the Management Committee proposed to develop or purchase a training facility that would provide regular training for partners and staff of CPC on a cost-effective and firm-specific basis. Training would be based on CPC consulting principles and would be consistent with the culture that the new firm hoped to create and maintain. In early 1992, CPC learned that the entire campus of Sandown College in suburban Chicago was for sale, and a decision was made to purchase the property, renovate buildings, and establish the National Training Center.

## THE NATIONAL TRAINING CENTER

In July 1992, CPC purchased Sandown College. Included in the $4 million purchase price was an administrative building that housed several classrooms, several residence halls, and other incidental buildings. Half of the purchase price was allocated to the land and half was allocated to the buildings. All buildings on the property were in substantial disrepair, as Sandown had struggled financially for several years before closing. In 1992, CPC had all buildings except the administrative and classroom building and one residence hall destroyed and immediately began renovating the two buildings which would become the National Training Center.

Each of the two buildings to be renovated was allocated half of the purchase cost of $2 million for the buildings, or $1 million each. The cost of renovations was great. A total of $7.5 million was spent renovating the residence hall, while renovations to the office and classroom building required an expenditure of just over $8 million. In both cases, the costs of renovation exceeded estimates because of unknown structural problems and the need for unexpected asbestos removal.

The proposal to create the National Training Center envisioned a permanent full-time staff devoted to training programs for partners and staff consultants, and a separate staff responsible for management and operation of the residence hall and its associated cafeteria. The capacity of the National Training Center would be 120 participants for the 48 weeks it would operate each year. Programs for partners would have space for 30 partners each week, while those for staff consultants could accommodate 90, usually in two sections of 45 each. While CPC would employ a professional training staff, they would also use external trainers from both professional firms and professors from universities with national reputations. Though the cost of external trainers was expected to be high, it would distinguish CPC's training effort from those of other professional service firms that did all of their own training in-house.

With renovations complete and the staff hiring nearly complete by the end of 1992, the National Training Center opened during the first week of January in 1993. Many on the professional staff had been reluctant initially to support the idea of a national training center. However, evaluations from participants in company-sponsored training programs held at the Center during 1993 were extremely positive. The renovations had resulted in comfortable accommodations, and the classrooms were state-of-the-art with equipment for case discussions, multimedia presentations, and computer-based learning. As the year progressed word went out through the firm that the National Training Center was a great place to go to study with, and to get to know, other members of the professional staff of CPC.

The proposal on which the decision to establish the National Training Center had been based estimated an expenditure of $16.5 million for the purchase of Sandown College and building renovations. On a per-week basis, the forecasted cost of operating the National Training Center was estimated to be $784 dollars a week per participant, including the transportation cost of getting staff members from their home base to the National Training Center and back again. The decision to have the Center cover transportation cost was designed to minimize the reluctance of local offices to send people to the National Center instead of conducting their own training locally.

Robert Sampson had explained to Patricia Ryan that the costs of training had been a topic for lively discussion among the partners before the decision was made to establish the National Training Center. In addition to the out-of-pocket costs of training sessions, training incurs other kinds of costs. While they are participating in training sessions, staff consultants, partners, and principals are not working on client projects and are unable to bill clients for their time. In round numbers, the cost to the firm of this use of time is about $3,500 per week for a staff consultant and about $7,400 per week for a partner or principal, based on estimates for 1993. In addition, staff consultants continue to earn their salaries while they are in training sessions.

Robert Sampson and Patricia Ryan had just had time to note that the cost per participant per week at the National Training Center shown on the report on operations for 1993 was $1,047—about 33% higher than that forecasted in the proposal. Sampson had just commented that it was no wonder the chairman wanted to figure out what was happening at the Center when the facsimile machine beeped its message that the chairman's questions had arrived. Ryan knew that it was time to get to work. This would be the first work that she had done directly for the chairman. She wanted to be as thorough and complete as she could be in the four hours that were available before she was to deliver her outline, notes, analysis, and conclusions to the chairman to study before the Management Committee met.

## THE CHAIRMAN'S MEMO AND QUESTIONS

To:        Patricia Ryan (and Robert Sampson)
           Office of Human Resources

From:    David Li, Chairman

Date:     January 18, 1994

Subject:  Questions about the National Training Center

The first year of operations at the National Training Center is now history, and the Management Committee will be discussing the performance of the Center at our meeting this afternoon. I would very much appreciate your analysis and recommendations about three issues which concern me. First, I need some help in thinking about the proper accounting for the costs we are incurring because of the important role of training in the firm's strategy; it seems to me that we are creating something of great value to the firm and its future, and I think our balance sheet should reflect that value in some way. Second, the summary report on operations (copy faxed to Sampson this morning) concerns me a great deal; it looks to me that the costs of the Center are running about one-third higher for each participant than we forecast at the time the Center was proposed in 1992. Third, my concerns about the costs lead me to conclude that we should explicitly discuss establishing management control systems for the Center so that we can assess its effectiveness on an ongoing basis.

### Questions on Accounting for Training Costs:

1.  On January 1, 1993, the Statement of Financial Position for CPC showed the National Training Center at its cost to the firm, or $19.5 million. The investment that we had made by purchasing Sandown College and renovating our two buildings there was fully disclosed to our partners, all of whom took great pride in our decision to create the Center. Now, with a year's operations behind us, it seems to me that we have created some valuable human capital and that our balance sheet should reflect the added value of the firm because of the training programs we have conducted at the Center. **I realize that if we were a firm subject to generally accepted accounting principles this would be difficult or impossible because our auditors would probably object, but CPC is a partnership and is privately owned by the partners only.** For this reason, application of the accounting principles of accrual, matching, and realization all seem to me to support the idea that some or all of the training costs that we incurred in 1993 should be capitalized this year so that these potential expenses can be matched with the additional revenues we hope our trained professional staff will generate. Do you agree? Why, or why not?
2.  Regardless of your answer to Question 1, which of the training costs incurred in 1993 are the best candidates for capitalization? If you suggest that some, but not all, of the training costs incurred in 1993 are good candidates for capitalization, what are the criteria that permit you to separate those that might be capitalized from those that should not be capitalized? Are there other costs incurred by CPC that are related to its training activities that should be capitalized?
3.  If we adopt a policy of capitalizing some of the training costs that we incur at the Center, then we will have to adopt a policy for when those costs should be recognized as expenses. According to the presentation that

Robert Sampson made to our partners at last year's Partners' Meeting, the average employment of a newly hired professional as a staff consultant will be just over three years; 30% will leave the firm before three years, and only 30% still will be with the firm at the end of the fourth year. Only about one in ten staff members is likely to become a partner or principal. At any one time, the average partner or principal will be a member of the firm for seven years from the current date. I am not sure how these data fit together with the idea that every staff consultant should spend two weeks in training each year and each partner or principal should average one week in training each year. If some training costs are capitalized, over what time period should they be matched with revenues? Please outline a possible accounting policy that I can present to and discuss with the Management Committee.

4.   If we do adopt a policy of capitalizing some training costs, the operating income that we will report to partners will be higher for 1993 than if we do not capitalize some training costs. How, if at all, should this affect the cash payout to partners and principals for 1993? How will the capitalization of training costs affect the cash flows for the firm?

## Questions on the Operations of the National Training Center:

5.   Please analyze as completely as you can for me why the 1993 actual cost per participant of $1,047 per week exceeded the proposal estimate of $784 per week. I expect that there are going to be questions about this from the Management Committee, so the more clearly you can present and reconcile what we expected to what actually happened will help me very much. Do you have any possible hypotheses about why the differences occurred or what might have caused them?

6.   I am not really very happy about the ways in which we are tracking the cost of training at the Center. Can you outline a system or ways we might do this better in the future?

## Questions about the Future Management Controls for the Training Activity:

7.   At the present time we have no established management control system in place at the National Training Center or for the training activity in our firm. Please outline your ideas for a management control system. What should be our objectives, how should we try to achieve them, and what should we be measuring to know that we are achieving them? Please be as detailed as possible in the time available to you.

8.   One problem that we have had at the National Training Center is filling the available training weeks for partners and principals. Whenever I ask about this I am told that these people are reluctant to attend training at the Center because it means that those hours and days cannot be billed to

clients, and billable time is part of the formula we use to distribute profits to partners and principals at the end of each operating year. Do you have any suggestions about changes to the firm's management control systems or incentive systems to encourage partners and principals to use the Center to its capacity?

Thank you for your help with this on such short notice. It is great to have you on our staff.

**EXHIBIT 1**
**Consulting Partners & Co., The National Training Center Report on Operations—1993 ($ thousands except for cost per participant week)**

Annual Costs:
   Training:

| | | |
|---|---:|---:|
| Training staff | $560 | |
| Office staff | 310 | |
| Equipment and supplies | 190 | |
| Fees—external trainers | 900 | |
| Depreciation | 400 | |
| Other expenses | 152 | $2,512 |
| Travel expenses | | 1,298 |

Residences:

| | | |
|---|---:|---:|
| Managers and staff | $251 | |
| Depreciation | 425 | |
| Cafeteria staff | 142 | |
| Maintenance and supplies | 50 | |
| Food and beverages | 298 | |
| | | 1,166 |
| TOTAL ANNUAL COSTS | | $4,976 |

Training in 1993:

| | | |
|---|---:|---|
| Partner training | 672 | weeks |
| Staff training | 4,080 | weeks |
| | 4,752 | participant weeks |
| Cost per participant per week | $1,047 | |

**EXHIBIT 2**
**Consulting Partners & Co., The National Training Center Proposal—**
**July 1992 ($ thousands, except for cost per participant week)**

|  | Purchase of Sandown College: | | |
|---|---|---|---|
|  | Land | $2,000 |  |
|  | Buildings | 2,000 |  |
|  |  |  | $ 4,000 |
|  | Renovations: |  |  |
| (actual = 7.5 mil.) | Residence halls | $6,500 |  |
| (actual = 8.0 mil.) | Offices and classrooms | 6,000 |  |
|  |  |  | 12,500 |
|  | **Annual Costs—Training:** |  |  |
|  | Training staff | $ 550 |  |
|  | Office staff | 350 |  |
|  | Equipment and supplies | 200 |  |
|  | Fees—external trainers | 900 |  |
|  | Other expenses | 150 |  |
|  |  |  | $ 2,150 |
|  | Travel expenses |  | 1,620 |
|  | **Annual Costs—Residences:** |  |  |
|  | Residence managers and staff | $ 242 |  |
|  | Cafeteria staff | 140 |  |
|  | Maintenance supplies | 50 |  |
|  | Food and beverages | 315 |  |
|  |  |  | 747 |
|  | TOTAL ANNUAL COSTS |  | $ 4,517 |

Capacity is 120 participants for 48 weeks[a] = 5,760 participant
weeks. Cost per participant per week = $784.

---

[a] Thirty partners per week for 48 weeks; 90 staff per week for 48 weeks.

# Kings Mountain Distillery, Inc.

In early August 1996, Ralph Harmon, president and chief operating officer (COO) of Kings Mountain Distillery, Inc. (KMD) of Bessemer City, North Carolina, sat in his office pondering the previous day's meeting of the board of directors and wondering if he should submit the 1996 financial statements (**Exhibits 1** and **2**) to the GastoniaBanc of Gastonia, North Carolina. KMD had requested a new loan of $4 million from the bank in July, and the bank was waiting for the new financial statements before making a decision on the new KMD loan.

At the board meeting the day before, there had been considerable discussion about the 1996 reported loss of almost $1.2 million and the manner in which it had been determined. A great deal of controversy had arisen about the accounting treatment of various expenses and costs and the manner in which they were reported in the 1996 financial statements. Harmon felt that the issues raised had to be resolved quickly because the company had reached a point where additional working capital was needed immediately to maintain KMD's solvency.

## COMPANY HISTORY

Robert Lee Hager, known as "Lee," began distilling whiskey in 1921 on the lower slopes of Kings Mountain, which is between Gastonia and Bessemer City. The previous year, the 18th Amendment to the Constitution of the United States had banned the export, import, manufacture, sale, and transportation of alcoholic beverages in the United States and its territories. In a small, heavily

---

Copyright © 1996 by the President and Fellows of Harvard College. Harvard Business School case 197-042.

wooded valley surrounded by high knolls, Hager began to distill bourbon whiskey using the pure water from a local stream. Although the business was very risky due to its illegality, demand grew steadily. Remarkably, the distilling operation was never shut down by local authorities.

When the 21st Amendment to the U.S. Constitution repealed prohibition in the United States, Hager moved his distilling equipment to Bessemer City and into a barn beside his home. There he began to produce a high-quality, distinctive bourbon whiskey which he marketed as "Hager's Own." Sales grew from $100 thousand in 1935 to nearly $5 million in 1941. During that time, the distillery was moved into more extensive and suitable facilities in downtown Bessemer City. Lee Hager emphasized quality, and the distillery was one of the first in the state to have its own chemical testing laboratory. The quality of the ingredients and product was constantly monitored from 1939. In addition, only the finest fire-charred white oak barrels, made locally by the Harmon family, were used in the aging process.

Production of "Hager's Own" was restricted during World War II, when more than half of the plant capacity was converted to the production of commercial alcohol for military purposes in the defense effort.

In 1985, Ralph Harmon, son-in-law of Lee Hager, took over as COO of the company. During the next 10 years, sales revenues nearly doubled. Harmon felt that the company had grown because of the stress it placed on marketing a distinctive, high-quality product and because of its concentration on only one brand of fine bourbon whiskey—Hager's Own. The company's advertising stressed the quality of its ingredients, processes, and its use of the Harmon family-produced "specially prepared and cured fire-charred white oak barrels." Promotions had been very effective in establishing a brand image of Hager's Own in the consumer's mind that connoted a family-produced product from rural North Carolina where people still worked hard to make a living and still cared about quality.

In 1995, the company produced less than 1% of the whiskey distilled in the United States and thus was one of the smaller distillers in the industry. Since the mid-1980s, the company's production had been stable; the financial statements for 1995 (**Exhibits 1** and **2**) were typical of the results of the preceding several years. After a surge in demand in the 1980s, no special effort had been made to gain a larger share of the market, but at a board meeting in December 1995, a decision had been made to expand production to try to capture a larger proportionate share of the increase in whiskey consumption that industry research had forecast.

This market research forecast that consumption of straight bourbon whiskey would increase as the baby boom generation matured and Generation X became more regular liquor consumers. Based on this report and other industry data, Harmon expected a doubling of straight whiskey consumption from 1995 to 2003. In view of this assumption, and because bourbon whiskey had to be aged at least four years, the board had decided to increase the production of whiskey in 1996 by 50% of the 1995 volume (see **Exhibit 2**) in order to meet the anticipated increase in consumer demand for straight bourbon whiskey in general, and for Hager's Own in particular.

## THE MANUFACTURING PROCESS

Hager's Own was a straight bourbon whiskey and thus, by law, had to be made from a mixture of grains containing at least 51% corn and be aged in new (not reused) charred white oak barrels. The process began when the ground corn was mixed with pure water in a large vat. To this mixture was added a certain amount of ground barley malt and rye. It was then heated slowly until the starches were converted to sugars, thus completing the "mashing" process. This mash was then pumped into a cypress fermenting vat where yeast and certain other ingredients were added. This mixture was allowed to ferment for several days until the yeast had converted the sugars into alcohol, at which time the fermenting process was complete and the mash was pumped into a distillation tower (or still) where the alcohol was separated from the "slurry," or spent mash, through a series of distillation tanks and condensers. The distilled liquor was then mixed with pure water to obtain the desired proof (percent alcohol by volume where one degree of proof equals .5% alcohol).

At this point, the whiskey was a clear liquid with a sharp, biting taste and had to be mellowed before consumption. For this process, it was pumped into 50-gallon barrels and moved to an aging warehouse. The cost accumulated in the product prior to its entry into barrels, including all direct and indirect materials and labor consumed in the production process, was approximately $1.50 per gallon (see **Exhibit 2**). The volume of production had been the same for each of the years 1991 to 1995, and all costs during this period had been substantially the same as the 1995 costs shown in **Exhibit 2**.

## MATURING OR AGING PROCESS

In order to mellow the whiskey, improve its taste, and give it a rich amber color, the new bourbon whiskey had to be matured or aged for a period of time of not less than four years under controlled temperature and humidity conditions. The new whiskey reacted with the charred oak and assimilated some of the flavor and color of the fire-charred oak during the period of aging.

Since the quality of the aging barrel was an important factor in determining the ultimate taste and character of the final product, KMD had its barrels manufactured under a unique patented process at a cost of $89 per barrel. The barrels could not be reused for aging future batches of bourbon whiskey, but the barrels could be sold to used barrel dealers for about $1.50 each at the end of the aging period.

The filled barrels were next placed in open "ricks" in an aging warehouse rented by KMD or in part of the factory building that was available for warehouse space. The increased production in 1996 necessitated the leasing of an additional warehouse at an annual cost of $280,000. The temperature and humidity of the warehouse space had to be controlled, since the quality of the whiskey could be impaired by aging too rapidly or too slowly, a process determined in part by temperature and humidity conditions.

Every six months the barrels had to be rotated from a high rick to a lower rick or vice versa or between warehouses (because of uneven temperatures at different locations in the warehouses) and sampled for quality and character up to that point in the aging process. A small amount of liquid was removed from representative barrels at this time and sent to the sampling laboratory for quality inspection (some of which was performed by skilled tasters). If the quality of the whiskey was not up to standard, certain measures were taken to adjust the aging process to bring the whiskey up to standard. At this time, each barrel was also checked for leaks or seepage, and the required repairs were made.

At the end of the four-year aging period, the barrels were removed from the ricks and dumped into regauging tanks where the charred oak residue was filtered out and volume was measured. On average, the volume of liquid in a barrel declined by 30% during the aging process because of evaporation and leakage. Thus, a barrel originally filled with 50 gallons of raw bourbon would produce about 35 gallons of aged bourbon. The regauging operation was supervised by a government liquor tax agent, since it was at this point that the excise taxes of $29.50 per gallon were levied on the whiskey removed from the warehouse. Once the bourbon had been removed from the aging warehouse, it was bottled and shipped to wholesalers with the greatest speed possible because of the large amount of cash tied up in taxes on the finished product. During both 1995 and 1996, the company sold 30,000 regauged barrels of whiskey, equivalent to about 43,000 barrels of original production.

## EXCERPTS FROM THE BOARD OF DIRECTORS' MEETING—AUGUST 5, 1996

**Ralph Harmon (President and COO)**   "I'm quite concerned over the prospect of obtaining the $4 million loan we need in light of our 1996 loss of $1.2 million. We have shown annual profits every year since 1980, and our net sales of $59 million this year are the same as last year, and yet we incurred a net loss for the year. I think I understand the reason for this, but I am afraid that the loan officers at GastoniaBanc will hesitate in granting KMD a new loan on the basis of our most recent performance. It looks like we are becoming less efficient in our production operation."

**Mac Hager (Production Manager)**   "That is not true Ralph. You know as well as I do that we increased production by 50% this year, and with this increased production our costs were bound to increase. We cannot produce something for nothing."

**Claudette Morgan (Controller)**   "Yes, but that should not necessarily reduce our income.  Granted that our production costs must rise when production increases, but our inventory account takes care of the increased costs of deferring these product costs until a future period when the product is actually sold.  As you can see by looking at our 1995 income statement, our cost of goods sold did not increase in 1996, since the volume of sales was the same in 1996 as in 1995.  The largest share of the increase in production costs has been deferred until future periods, as you can see by looking at the increase in our inventory account of almost $1.5 million.  I believe that the real reason for our loss this year was the large increase in other costs, composed chiefly of warehousing costs.  The 'Occupancy costs' category in our income statement is really the summation of a group of expense accounts, including building depreciation, rent, heat, light, power, building maintenance, labor and supplies, real estate taxes, and insurance.  In addition, warehouse labor cost also rose substantially in 1996.  Administrative and general expenses went up, due primarily to higher interest expense on the additional money needed to finance our increase in inventory.  Selling, distribution, and advertising expenses increased because we incurred costs to restructure relationships with all our distributors.  Also, our smaller distributors ordered more frequently than they did previously."

**Ralph Harmon**   "Well, what's our explanation for the large increase in warehousing costs, Mac?"

**Mac Hager**   "As I said before, Ralph, we increased production, and this also means an increase in warehousing costs, since the increased production has to be aged for several years.  You just can't age 50% more whiskey for the same amount of money."

**Ralph Harmon**   "But I thought Claudette said that increased production costs were taken care of in the inventory account.  Isn't that so, Claudette?"

**Claudette Morgan**   "Well, yes and no, Ralph.  The inventory account can only be charged with those costs associated with the direct production of whiskey, and our warehousing costs are handling or carrying costs, certainly not production costs."

**Mac Hager**   "Now just a minute, Claudette, I think that some of those costs are just as valid production costs as are direct labor and materials going into the distillation of the new bourbon.  The manufacturing process doesn't stop with the newly produced bourbon; why, it isn't even marketable in that form.  Aging is an absolutely essential part of the manufacturing process, and I think the cost of barrels and part of the warehouse labor should be treated as direct costs of the product."

**Ralph Harmon**   "Great, Mac!  I agree with you that warehousing and aging costs are an absolutely essential ingredient of our final product.  We certainly couldn't market the bourbon before it had been aged. I think that all the costs associated with aging the product should be charged to the inventory account. I think that most of the "other costs" should be considered a cost of the product. Don't you agree, Claudette?"

**Claudette Morgan**    "Sure, Ralph! Let's capitalize depreciation, interest expenses, your salary, the shareholders' dividends, our advertising costs, your secretary's salary—why, let's capitalize all our costs! That way we can show a huge inventory balance and small expenses! I'm sure GastoniaBanc and the income tax authorities would be happy to cooperate with us on it! Why, we'll revolutionize the accounting profession!"

**Ralph Harmon**    "I think you're being facetious, Claudette. Be reasonable about this. I'm afraid I really don't see why we couldn't charge some of those costs you mentioned to the inventory account, since it seems to me that they are all necessary ingredients in producing our final product. What distinction do you draw between these so-called "direct" costs you mentioned and the aging costs?"

**Claudette Morgan**    "By direct costs, I mean those costs that are necessary to convert raw materials into the whiskey that goes into the aging barrels. This is our cost of approximately $1.50 per gallon and includes the cost of raw materials going into the product, such as grain, yeast, and malt; the direct labor necessary to convert these materials into whiskey; and the cost of any other overhead items that are needed to permit the workers to convert grain into whiskey. I don't see how aging costs can be included under the generally accepted accounting definition of the inventory cost of the product."

**Ralph Harmon**    "I think we'd better defer further discussion of this entire subject until our meeting next month. In the meantime, I am going to try to get this thing squared away in my own mind. I have never really thought that financial statements had much meaning, but now I am not at all sure that they aren't truly misleading documents!

"Let's move on to selling, distribution, and advertising expenses. I can't understand why these costs have increased as much as they have in 1996 since sales to each of our distributors are exactly the same as in 1995. The only change I was expecting here was the increase in advertising costs of $149,000, from $385,000 to $534,000, because of higher advertising rates."

**Sally Shields (Sales and Distribution Manager)**    "We have 40 distributors. Based on the market research forecasts, I began to restructure relationships with our distributors. I had consultants prepare files on distributor characteristics, visited our distributors for discussions, drew up new legal contracts, and designed a system to evaluate distributor performance over time. I also had to give them promotional allowances and new point-of-sales material including our very popular antique neon signs. I gather from the information Claudette sent me that we spent $6,000 per distributor. In 1995 these costs were $500 per distributor.

"Of our 40 distributors, 10 are large distributors while 30 are small specialty distributors. In 1995 and 1996 we sold the equivalent of 1,200 barrels of regauged whiskey to each of our large distributors and 600 barrels to each of our small distributors. During 1995, both our large and our small distributors placed five orders each. In 1996, each of our large distributors continued to place five orders but each of our small distributors placed 10 orders rather than five. Each time an order is placed, we incur costs to confirm and input the order into the order-entry system, set aside the correct number of gallons, organize shipment and delivery, verify that the order is correctly packed, ensure that the delivery is made, send invoices, and follow up for payments. Claudette's department calculated costs of $400 for performing the activities pertaining to each order.

"In addition to the above costs, we continue to incur selling and distribution costs of $57 per barrel sold (for sales commissions and freight)."

**Ralph Harmon**    "I see what you are trying to get at but I am still confused. For all these years now the selling and distribution costs per barrel have been essentially unchanged. I would like all of us to think through the implications of these higher selling and distribution costs.

"Well, let's turn briefly to the question of our developing needs for a more formal set of management controls as we grow and prepare to turn the business over to the next generation. Because we have always been essentially a family business, we really have never had much in the way of formal controls or a formal planning and control system. Now, Mac and I are thinking about retiring or at least cutting back on the time we spend in Bessemer City, and most of the family members who might have been suitable replacements have moved to Charlotte, Atlanta, and beyond and seem to have little interest in returning here.

"Several things are very different than when Lee invited me to come into the Distillery. We are much larger, and if we have evaluated the future potential of the business correctly, we will grow even larger in the next decade. As we grow, I expect that we will have to add additional facilities, just as we had to do this year as we needed more aging space. We are out of land here in the center of Bessemer City, so these new locations are likely to be physically removed from our traditional locations. Finally, the businesses of liquor production and distribution are changing to favor larger distribution organizations than we have developed, and I think that in the long run we may find that we should grow into distributors and take on other distillers' products to let us grow into a larger and more efficient distributing organization.

"Because these problems are relatively new to me, I really need some help in thinking about how we might go about assessing our management control environment, developing a management control strategy, and implementing some new management control systems that will help us and our successors to control KMD successfully.

"We have to adjourn now, but I would really appreciate your spending some time thinking about this problem and getting your ideas back to me before our next board of directors' meeting."

## QUESTIONS

**Part I (60%)**

1.  In your opinion, what costs should be included in Kings Mountain Distillery's inventory?
2.  Assuming KMD decided to charge only barrel costs (but not other warehousing and aging costs) to inventory, how would the 1996 income statement and balance sheet change? What account balances would change? Would the balances increase or decrease? By what amounts? (Assume that there would be no change to "Inventory in process.")
3.  An alternative to charging the barrel costs directly to inventory would be to treat the barrels as if they were machines, capitalizing their cost and depreciating them over their useful lives. Would you recommend that KMD consider using this accounting method? Why or why not?
4.  What methods of accounting would you recommend that KMD use in preparing the annual financial statements to be submitted to Gastonia-Banc? If these methods of accounting had been used in preparing the financial statements in the years between 1992 and 1995, approximately what would have been the reported income of KMD in 1995?

**Part II (20%)**

5.  What could be the explanation for the increase in selling, advertising, and distribution expenses between 1995 and 1996? What actions, if any, would you recommend Kings Mountain Distillery take with respect to selling, advertising, and distribution costs?
6.  Would Kings Mountain Distillery, Inc., benefit from the introduction of transaction-based or activity-based costing (ABC) in its manufacturing operations? If you feel that it would, explain why and also how you would go about deciding the number of cost pools and activity measures (cost drivers) to use for such a system. If you feel they would not benefit from introducing ABC, explain why not, and speculate about changes in the company or conditions that might cause you to reconsider at a later date.

**Part III (20%)**

7.  Laboratory labor and supplies expense are direct and variable costs with respect to number of barrels in the aging vats. The standard number of tests done in the chemical laboratory in 1996 was one test for every eight barrels in the aging process. The standard cost for each test in 1996 was $8.

In 1996, the laboratory did 23,200 tests at $10 per test. Evaluate the laboratory's performance in 1996, calculating, interpreting, and commenting on any variances you think would be useful.

8.  What are some of the management control problems and future management control problems that KMD is facing or may face as it grows and changes and as the experienced management team is replaced by managers who have not grown up in the business? What controls may need reconsideration now, and how would you think about developing new controls and control systems for use in the future? Assume that you have been asked by a member of the board of directors to prepare a draft of a memorandum to Ralph Harmon as suggested by his remarks at the end of the board of directors' meeting on August 5, 1996. Be as specific as you can be in your analysis and suggestions.

## EXHIBIT 1
### Kings Mountain Distillery, Inc., Balance Sheet as of June 30, 1995 and 1996 ($ thousands)

|  | 1995 | | 1996 | |
|---|---|---|---|---|
| **Current Assets** | | | | |
| Cash | | $ 3,560 | | $   942 |
| Accounts receivable—(net of allowance for doubtful accounts) | | 3,996 | | 5,127 |
| Inventories: | | | | |
| Bulk whiskey in barrels at average production cost | | | | |
| (no excise tax included) | | 12,625 | | 14,093 |
| Bottled and cased whiskey, 175,000 gallons in each year at an | | | | |
| average cost of $31.50 per gallon (including excise tax) | | 5,513 | | 5,513 |
| Inventory in process | | 283 | | 283 |
| Raw materials and supplies | | 1,120 | | 661 |
| Prepaid expenses | | 1,233 | | 1,088 |
| Total current assets | | $28,330 | | $27,707 |
| **Fixed Assets** | | | | |
| Cash surrender value of insurance | | 90 | | 98 |
| Land | | 84 | | 84 |
| Building[a] | $5,348 | | $5,908 | |
| Less: Accumulated depreciation | 2,240 | 3,108 | 2,495 | 3,413 |
| Equipment | 322 | | 402 | |
| Less: Accumulated depreciation | 140 | 182 | 202 | 200 |
| Total fixed assets | | 3,464 | | 3,795 |
| Total assets | | $31,794 | | $31,502 |
| **Current Liabilities** | | | | |
| Notes payable: | | | | |
| Short-term to banks | | $ 3,080 | | $ 4,200 |
| Current maturities of long-term debt | | 644 | | 1,352 |
| Accounts payable | | 2,408 | | 1,173 |
| Accrued liabilities | | 557 | | 322 |
| Federal excise taxes payable | | 1,148 | | — |
| Total current liabilities | | $ 7,837 | | $ 7,047 |
| **Noncurrent Liabilities** | | | | |
| Notes payable (7½%) secured by deed of trust on warehouse | | | | |
| property (less current maturities of $644,000 for 1995 and | | | | |
| $1,352,000 for 1996) | | 9,800 | | 11,480 |
| **Stockholders' Equity** | | | | |
| Common stock held principally by members of the Hager and | | | | |
| Harmon families | | 5,040 | | 5,040 |
| Earnings retained in the business | | 9,117 | | 7,935 |
| Total liabilities and capital | | $31,794 | | $31,502 |

[a]  In June 1996, payment was made for work that had been performed during the year in adding to and improving the warehousing space in the building owned by Kings Mountain Distillery.

**EXHIBIT 2**
**Kings Mountain Distillery, Inc., Statement of Income for the Years Ended June 30, 1995 and 1996 ($ thousands)**

| | | 1995 | | 1996 |
|---|---|---|---|---|
| Net sales | | | | |
| Sale of whiskey to wholesalers | | $58,800 | | $58,800 |
| Cost of goods sold: | | | | |
| Federal excise taxes—on barrels sold | | 44,247 | | 44,247 |
| Cost of product charged to sales: | | | | |
| Bulk whiskey inventory July 1, of each year—172,000 barrels | $12,625 | | $12,625 | |
| Plus: Cost of whiskey produced to inventory (43,000 barrels in 1995 and 63,000 barrels in 1996 at an average cost of $73.40/50-gallon barrel in both years) | 3,156 | | 4,624 | |
| | 15,781 | | 17,249 | |
| Less: Bulk whiskey inventory June 30 of respective year (172,000 and 192,000 barrels, at average production cost) | 12,625 | 3,156 | 14,093 | 3,156 |
| Cased goods and in process July 1, of respective year | 5,796 | | 5,796 | |
| Cased goods and in process June 30, of respective year | 5,796 | — | 5,796 | — |
| | | $47,403 | | $47,403 |
| Other costs charged to Cost of Goods Sold: | | | | |
| Cost of barrels used during year at $89.00 per barrel | 3,827 | | 5,607 | |
| Occupancy costs: Factory building | 371 | | 416 | |
| Rented buildings | 380 | | 791 | |
| Warehouse labor and warehouse supervisor | 263 | | 468 | |
| Labor and supplies expense of chemical laboratory | 190 | | 232 | |
| Depreciation: Factory equipment | 34 | | 34 | |
| Warehouse equipment | 17 | | 27 | |
| Cost of government supervision and bonding facilities | 8 | | 20 | |
| Cost of bottling liquor (labor, glass, and miscellaneous supplies) | 641 | 5,731 | 641 | 8,236 |
| Total cost of goods sold | | $53,134 | | $55,639 |
| Gross profit from operations | | $ 5,666 | | $ 3,161 |
| Less: Selling, distribution, and advertising expenses | 2,195 | | 2,624 | |
| Administrative and general expense including income taxes | 1,400 | 3,595 | 1,719 | 4,343 |
| Net profit (loss) | | $ 2,071 | | $ (1,182) |

# Index

## Plateau

*From the Cascade Range in northwestern Canada, south to the Sierra Nevada*

Cayuse
Coeur d'Alene
Flathead
Kalispel
Klamath
Kutenai
Lillooet
Modoc
Nez Perce
Nicola
Okanagan
Palouse
Sanpoil
Shuswap
Spokane
Thompson
Umatilla
Walla Walla
Wanapam
Yakima

## Great Basin

*Desert region, including Nevada and parts of Utah, California, Idaho, Wyoming, and Oregon*

Bannock
Goshute
Kawaiisu
Paiute
Shoshone
Ute
Washo

## Southwest

*An area that includes Arizona, New Mexico, southern Utah, parts of Texas and northern Mexico*

Apache:
    Chiricahua
    Cibecue
    Jicarilla
    Lipan
    Mescalero
    Mimbreño
    San Carlos
    Tonto
    White Mountain
Coahuiltec
Cocopa

Havasupai
Jumeño
Karenkawa
Maricopa
Mayo
Mojave
Navajo
Pima
Pueblo:
    Hopi
    Keres
    Tano
    Tewa
    Northern Tiwa
    Southern Tiwa
    Towa
    Zuni
Quechan
Seri
Tarahumara
Tehueco
Tepecano
Tepehuan
Tohono O'odham
    (Papago)
Walapai
Yaqui
Yavapai

## Plains

*Canada to southern Texas; Mississippi River, west to the Rocky Mountains*

Arapaho
Ankara
Assiniboine
Blackfoot:
    Blood
    Gros Ventre
    Piegan
    Sarcee
    Sikiska (Northern
    Blackfoot)
Cheyenne
Comanche
Crow
Hidatsa
Iowa
Kansa
Kiowa
Kiowa-Apache
Lakota (Sioux):
    Santee
    Teton
    Yankton
    Yanktonai
Mandan

Missouri
Omaha
Osage
Oto
Pawnee
Ponca
Quapaw
Tonkawa
Wichita

## Northeast Woodlands

*Nova Scotia and Maine, west to Minnesota, south to Kentucky*

Abnaki
Algonquin
Anishinabe
    (Chippewa/
    Ojibwa)
Beothuk
Delaware (Lenape):
    Munsee
    Unalachtigo
    Unami
Erie
Fox (Mesquakie)
Huron
Illinois
Iroquois:
    Cayuga
    Mohawk
    Onondaga
    Oneida
    Seneca
    Tuscarora
Kickapoo
Mahican
Maliseet
Massachuset
Menominee
Miami
Micmac
Mohegan
Nanticoke
Narraganset
Neutral
Ottawa
Pequot
Potawatomi
Powhatan
Sauk
Shawnee
Susquehanna
Wampanoag
Winnebago

## Southeast

*Carolinas to southern Florida, west to Texas*

Ais
Alabama
Apalachee
Atakapa
Caddo
Calusa
Catawba
Cherokee
Chickasaw
Chitimacha
Choctaw
Coushatta
Creek
Hitchiti
Lumbee
Natchez
Seminole
Timucua
Tunica
Yamasee
Yazoo
Yuchi

## Arctic

*Arctic Circle area*

Aivilik Inuit
Aleut
Baffinland Inuit
Bering Strait Inuit
Caribou Inuit
Copper Inuit
East Greenland Inuit
Iglulik Inuit
Labrador Inuit
Mackenzie Inuit
Netsilik Inuit
North Alaskan Inuit
Pacific Yuit
Polar Inuit
Southwest Alaskan
Inuit
West Greenland Inuit

The Lakota Sun Dance is only one of many similar rituals performed by peoples of the Great Plains, the vast grassland region of central North America, and only one of hundreds of religious ceremonies that Native peoples conduct throughout North America. For 75 years at the end of the 19th century and the beginning of the 20th, it was illegal for Native Americans in the United States and Canada to observe their religious ceremonies. The survival of the Sun Dance ceremony and of many other ceremonies shows the determination of Native Americans to preserve and practice their religions, even in the face of opposition.

## THE HISTORY OF NATIVE AMERICAN RELIGIONS

Long before European explorers reached North American shores, the land was home to hundreds of groups of Native Americans. These native peoples lived in villages that dotted the North American continent, sustaining themselves by hunting, fishing, and farming. It has been estimated that in the 1600s, before contact with European cultures, well over 1 million Native Americans were living in North America north of what is now the Mexican border, the area covered in this book.

## LANGUAGE AND COMMUNICATION

Each tribe was distinct and different from the others. For one thing, each spoke its own language. Although some neighboring tribes might have languages similar enough that people could understand each other, that was not always the case. Native Americans spoke languages that were in places as different from one another as, for example, English and Hungarian. Scholars estimate that at one time there may have been 2,200 different Native American languages, and they have identified seven different language families among the Indians of the Plains alone. In that area, where tribes with very different languages often met, they developed a sign language, a kind of international code that enabled them to communicate. In addition to speaking different languages, each tribe had its own culture and customs and its own way of building homes and making clothing and everyday objects such as tools, weapons, and utensils. Each tribe also had its own set of beliefs and religious practices closely associated with its particular culture.

## NATIVE AMERICAN RELIGIONS

There is no single "Native American religion." Similarities can be found among native religions, just as similarities can be found between Christianity and Islam or between Daoism and Buddhism, but the religious customs of different tribes can be and are quite varied.

Native American religions differ from "organized" religions in several ways. They are not "systematic." In other words, they have no church buildings and no church hierarchy or organizational structure. Although some tribal tales recall the deeds of famous tribe members, most Native American religions do not rely on central historical figures such as Moses, Jesus, or Buddha, and they are more strongly tied to nature and its rhythms than to individual historic events.

## AN ORAL TRADITION

Traditional Native American culture has always been oral, with information passed down by word of mouth. There is no written set of beliefs, no "rules" that "followers" must adhere to. There is no holy book, such as the Bible or Quran. In many ways Native American spirituality is similar to other religions with folk roots, such as Shinto or Daoism. The fact that there is no written creed does not suggest that there were no standards of behavior or ethics, however. Strict rules for living a decent and ethical life governed all Native American cultures. Tribe members were taught by example, and those guiding principles were not memorized in formal lessons but were internalized from childhood and became a part of daily life.

## COMPLEX BELIEFS

When European settlers first came into contact with Native peoples, the differences they saw led them to conclude that the Indians

An Alaskan bald eagle in flight. Flying higher than any other bird, the eagle embodies a strong spiritual presence, one that communicates between Earth and the most powerful forces of the universe. Eagle feathers are used ritually by many tribes to invoke the bird's spirit power.

had no religion, or at least no "real" religion. The Native Americans they met had no written language so there were no books from which the newcomers might learn about Native religions. In addition, few non-Indians bothered to learn Native American languages, and the Native Americans often deliberately excluded the outsiders from their holiest rituals. Not until the early years of the 20th century did people finally begin to examine Native American belief systems. They found that far from being a simplistic form of "nature worship," Native American beliefs were often rich, deep, and complex.

In recent years, as knowledge of Native American customs has become more widespread, so has respect for their religious traditions. Many Native Americans have returned to their roots, seeking spiritual renewal in traditional rituals and practices. Ceremonies for purification and healing, for celebrating the cycles of nature, and for renewing the land attract participants and observers from many backgrounds, those people who find the ceremonies and celebrations spiritually meaningful.

## BASIC CONCEPTS

Although the ways of expressing spiritual belief vary widely from region to region and tribe to tribe, certain basic concepts or ideas do occur in most Native American religions.

- Great Spirit: A Great Power, sometimes called Great Spirit or Great Mystery (Wakan Tanka, Manitou, Orenda, among other names) underlies all creation. This power is not a personal god, such as the Judeo-Christian God, and it cannot be imagined in human form. Rather it is a universal force to which all of nature is attuned. All of nature, including human nature, is the creation of this Great Power.
- Spirits in the universe: All things in the universe are alive and contain spirit within them. Spirit forces actively affect human lives in ways that can be both good and bad. The Earth, which nourishes and sustains life, and to which people return after death, is particularly endowed with spirit and is to be respected and revered. All forms of life interact and depend on all others.
- Walk in the sacred way: The individual is called on to "walk in the sacred way"—that is, to live in balance and harmony with the universe and the spirit world. People find their own sacred way by seeking clues to the sacred in dreams and visions.
- Oral tradition and ceremonies: Values, beliefs, morals, ethics, and sacred traditions are passed on through an oral tradition and through ceremonies. Cultural bonding takes place through rituals developed by each group over centuries. These often include dancing, singing, drumming, and feasting, as well as purification rites, fasting, and physical ordeals.

- **Medicine men and women:** Certain people (sometimes called shamans, medicine men or women, or singers) have special ties to the higher powers. Their special calling enables them to mediate between the spirit world and the Earthly world for healing, spiritual renewal, and the good of the community.
- **Humor:** Humor is a part of the sacred way because people need to be reminded of their foolishness.

## ORIGINS OF NATIVE AMERICAN RELIGIONS

Native American religions go back to distant prehistory. Scholars who study ancient cultures believe that the ancestors of the Native Americans may have migrated to the North American continent from Asia more than 12,000 years ago, traveling across a land bridge that once linked Siberia to Alaska across what is now the Bering Strait. These peoples moved in bands, or tribes,

Ancient Native American cave paintings in Arizona. In their myths, many tribes tell of a time when there was no difference between animals and humans who spoke the same language. The prehistoric Native American civilization centered around the present-day Four Corners area of the southwest United States that emerged around 1200 B.C.E.

gradually spreading south and east across North America. These first Americans probably brought their religious beliefs with them, gradually adapting them to the environment they settled.

## SHAMANISM

In Native American religions students of prehistory find a continuous thread of shamanism, humankind's "oldest religion," in which mediation between the visible and spirit worlds is brought about by shamans. Shamans, or holy people, are healers and interpreters of the will of the spirit world, and shamanism is one of the earliest traceable forms of religion. Another feature of shamanism was animism, the belief that all things contain spirit, or life. This was a distinctive feature of Native American religion.

## LINKS WITH ASIA

Scholars point to religious similarities between the Siberian tribes of Asia and the Inuit tribes of Canada and Alaska. The parallels they find suggest that these religions have common origins. Native American religions also share ideas—particularly about the importance of balance and harmony with the universe—with Asian religions such as Daoism and Confucianism, which developed in ancient China out of the same religious roots, and with Shinto, the native religion of Japan, which had the same Asian influences.

## NATIVE AMERICANS TODAY

Approximately 4 million people living in the United States and Canada identify themselves as Native Americans. What makes someone a Native American is a matter of both heritage and law. Some tribal groups, such as the Cherokee, admit to full tribal membership anyone who can

## CREATION STORIES

The traditions of Native peoples themselves often hold that their tribes originated in their ancestral lands and spread outward from there. The Navajo, for example, point to a place in the mountains of southeastern Colorado where the First People emerged from the underworld and began to create life on this Earth. Similarly, the Umatilla of eastern Washington State hold that their people were created in that place and have been there since the beginning of time. The creation stories of most Native Americans support their beliefs that they have always been in North America, connected to and part of the land.

At Wind River Reservation in Wyoming, a father helps his young son dress in traditional costume for a powwow, a gathering of Native American tribes, to talk, dance, sing, and socialize. It offers an opportunity for tribes to celebrate their culture and can vary in length from one to several days.

trace any Cherokee ancestry; other tribes admit only those who are at least one-quarter or one-eighth Native American by blood; still other tribes have other rules governing tribal membership.

The Native peoples who live on tribal lands, such as the Hopi and the Navajo in the southwestern United States and the Inuit peoples in Alaska and Canada, are most likely to have preserved the religious practices of their forebears and continued their religious traditions. Most people who declare themselves to be Native American, however, whether they live on reservations or in cities, do follow at least some Native American cultural and religious practices and attempt to pass on their culture and sacred history to the next generation.

## ONE SACRED WAY

Native Americans do not segment their lives into the secular and the religious. Their culture and their religion are one, so closely united that many Native American languages have no word for *religion*. All work is considered prayer. A woman making a basket may pray to the spirit of the grass as she cuts it. Later the designs she weaves into the basket may have symbolic meaning. The art of basketry itself is a kind of spiritual gift for which to be grateful. The successfully completed basket, too, a work of both beauty and usefulness, is an occasion for thanks. Thus even a common utensil has a sacred dimension. Hunters and farmers invoke the spirits of game and fertility so that their efforts and the outcome of their labors will be blessed. Ideally people live with a constant awareness of the spirit world around them and act in ways that honor this awareness.

## A SACRED POWER

Although they do not separate their religion from their everyday existence, Native Americans have traditionally believed in a higher power that created and informs all of life, and they have followed traditions and rituals meant to connect humans with that power, the basic tenet of all religions. Whether their traditions came with them from another continent or sprang from American soil, the religions of Native peoples represent an ancient tradition of deep spirituality.

# CHAPTER 2

# THE SPIRIT WORLD AND THE SACRED WAY

The Algonquins speak of Manitou, the Iroquois of Orenda, and the Lakota of Wakan Tanka, words usually translated as "Great Spirit" or "Great Mystery." These words all refer to the indefinable power that underlies all creation. However else their traditions may vary, almost all Native American peoples believe in a great sacred force from which all things come and which keeps the universe in motion.

## THE GREAT SPIRIT

When Native peoples first came in contact with European religions they recognized parallels between the white man's God and their Great Spirit, and some groups incorporated the notion of a personal god into their beliefs. However traditionally the Great Spirit is not a supreme being, such as the Judeo-Christian God or

Speaking Rock, the left-hand column, and Spider Rock, the right-hand column, in Canyon de Chelly National Monument in Arizona are sacred sites for the Navajo people. Spider Rock is the traditional home of Spider Woman, a legendary holy person who taught the Navajo the art of weaving. Canyon de Chelly is unique among national park service units as it is composed entirely of Navajo tribal trust land.

Islam's Allah, who speaks to humankind. It is more like the Dao of Daoism, an immense and universal power that is above and in all things. The words *Wakan Tanka,* for example, literally mean "most sacred," and when people speak of Wakan Tanka they are more likely to be speaking of the sacred power of the universe rather than of a personal god formed by imagination.

The Great Spirit cannot be seen or touched, but it is present in the cycles and visible signs of nature. People can find evidence of it in the continuing change of seasons; in day and night; growth and death; and in the movement of the Sun, Moon, and stars.

People traditionally learned about the Great Spirit, or Great Mystery, through oral tradition, the tales of magical beings and important events and ancestors passed down from one genera-

Ancient rock paintings of humanlike figures with earrings and headdresses. The figures are believed to represent spirits that can be found in all things that have life, from the sky, Sun, and wind to the smallest of creatures.

tion to the next. They also experience this mysterious power directly through dreams and visions. Children learn from an early age to pay attention to their dreams and to examine them for meaning. They learn to be aware of the spirit world, which is all around them, a kind of parallel universe that is always close at hand. Later in life they may actively seek a vision for spiritual guidance through periods of fasting and self-denial.

## THE CREATOR

Although all things come from the Great Spirit, the Great Spirit is not the creator of the world. In Native American belief that function is performed by a supernatural being with special creative powers, a being whom scholars call a culture hero. This being may have human form, such as First Man and First Woman of the Navajo, World-Maker of the Yakima, or Earth Starter of the Ojibwa, or a dual human-animal form, such as Raven of the Northwest or Coyote of the western plains. In addition to creating the world and placing humans on it, he or she gives the first human beings the ceremonies and cultural institutions that they will use on Earth.

## THE WORLD OF SPIRITS

A central concept of Native American religions is the idea that everything in the world that can be seen or touched is alive with spirit or breath. All of the environment has a life. The water that comes out

### Wakan Power

*The most wonderful things which a man can do are different from the works of nature. When the seasons changed, we regarded it as a gift from the Sun, which is the strongest of all the mysterious wakan powers . . . We cannot see the thunder, and we say it is wakan, but we see the lightning and we know that the thunder and the lightning are a sign of rain, which does good to the earth. Anything which has a similar power is wakan, but above all is the Sun, which has the most power of all...*

—Anonymous, Teton Sioux

(In Peggy V. Beck, *Sacred: Ways of Knowledge, Sources of Life*.)

### Teton Sioux Prayer

*Wakan Tanka
when I pray to him
heard me
whatever is good
he grants me*

—sung by Lone Man

(In Alan R. Velie, *American Indian Literature, an Anthology*.)

Everything in the world is inhabited by spirits, which can be grouped into several different kinds:

The sky beings, such as star gods, the Sun, and the Moon.

Spirits of the atmosphere, such as the four winds, whirlwinds, rain, and Thunderbird, a huge bird—perhaps like an eagle—whose flapping wings create thunder and whose flashing eyes create lightning.

The rulers of animals and plants, such as Buffalo Spirit or Corn Spirit; also those connected with natural places such as mountains, waterfalls, and the sea.

The powers of the underworld, such as Mother or Grandmother Earth, snakes and cougars, and the ruler of the dead.

of the earth is alive, as are the rocks and the hills. Each comes from the Earth, which is itself alive and revered as the mother—or, as some say, grandmother—of all. The spirit of the air can be felt in a breath of wind and the sound of the breeze as it moves through the leaves. The spirit of the rain can be felt in moisture on the earth. The spirits of rocks, trees, grass, wind, and rain cannot be seen, but they are a constant reality, influencing all aspects of human life.

The spirits of the dead may live as ghosts on Earth or may be reborn as animals. Ghosts are potentially dangerous, however, and are to be avoided for the harm they can do.

## SKY SPIRITS

Many people shared the belief that the Milky Way, the broad band of faint light that can be seen in the night sky, was a "path of souls" to which people went after death. The Luiseño of California explain that the First People went to the sky when their work on Earth was done, taking their families with them and becoming star people. The Navajo think of stars as "friendly beings" because they lighten the night sky and also because the stars help them tell time and mark the seasons.

According to Pawnee creation stories, their tribe is descended from the Morning Star. The Pawnee settled on the banks of the Loup, Platte, and Republican Rivers in Nebraska. In their tales Morning Star overcame the others and directed them to stand in their appointed places. Morning Star wed Evening Star, and their daughter traveled to Earth, where she married the child of the Sun and the Moon. From this union came the Pawnee people.

In the Southwest the Sun has special significance. The Zuni welcome the Sun each day as "father," sprinkling a little cornmeal and offering a prayer to this great power that awakens the Earth's fertility. And in California the Chumash hold the Sun to be the greatest supernatural being, the one who carries the torch that lights the world. He is both loved and feared, because although he brings light and heat, he also brings death.

## ANIMAL SPIRITS

In their mythic histories many tribes recall a time when there was no distinction between animals and humans. All spoke the same language and each received special powers from the creator who made them. Humans, indeed, are often portrayed as the weakest and least able of all the beings in creation. Animals such as bears and badgers, deer and mice, are seen as having distinct spirits and as being "people" of another order.

Many spirit beings, such as Raven of the Tlingit and Buffalo Calf Woman who brought the Lakota their seven sacred rites, have the ability to change from animal to human and back again. Animal spirits may convey the traits attributed to that animal,

An American bison, which came to be called the buffalo by European settlers, grazing on the plains. Among the Plains tribes the buffalo was considered a special messenger from the Great Spirit. Throughout Native American culture animals had distinct spirits, and hunters traditionally prayed to the animals they killed in thanks for giving their lives to the tribe.

such as speed or courage. Birds, especially the eagle, are respected for their freedom in flight. The oral traditions of many tribes portray birds as special beings with the power to carry messages to the sky and back to Earth. For this reason the feathers of the eagle are a mark of special power and esteem.

Native hunters traditionally prayed to the spirit of the game they killed for food, thanking the deer, the buffalo, or the salmon for giving up its life so that people might eat and remain alive. People understood that only with the help of the spirit world could they succeed in life. Someone who neglected to respect the life of the deer he had taken might find that the other deer spirits rose up against him and hindered future hunts. In Cherokee tradition certain illnesses, such as rheumatism, came to the hunter who ignored his duty to honor the animals he hunted.

## PLANT SPIRITS

Plants also have spirit, which can be seen in the way they respond to their environment. Plants that are not cared for or treated with respect do not survive. If they are overharvested they will not return. They draw their spirit from the earth, as do other living things. Native Americans saw plants as friendly to humans. To Native peoples there were few if any plants that could not be used as food, as medicine, in making shelter or useful objects, or in rituals. Many different tribes viewed certain food plants, particularly maize (Indian corn), beans, and squash or pumpkin, as gifts of divine origin, provided for their use by the Great Spirit. These traditional foods, grown and eaten by the many agricultural tribes that lived on a largely vegetarian diet, provided balanced nutrition that kept people healthy and strong.

Native people lived particularly close to the land and had a deep understanding of its value. Everything was not sacred, but almost anything, particularly if it was used to help sustain life, might be sacred, and its spirit had to be respected. People had to act in ways that would keep the world in balance and harmony. Overusing a plant or killing too much game could result in total loss. However recognizing the spiritual dimension of all things kept Native hunters and gatherers constantly aware of their responsibility to save and preserve them even as they used them to preserve their own lives.

## SACRED TOBACCO

Native Americans considered tobacco a sacred plant and used it in rituals as a way of communicating with the spirit world. They grew and cured a special, strong tobacco. Its scented smoke, rising to the skies, carried human prayers to the spirits. Among the Crow just planting and growing tobacco brought good fortune, and they performed rituals for its planting and harvest. Tobacco was widely grown, and tribes that did not grow it traded for it with other tribes. Present-day rituals still make use of tobacco.

As part of a ceremony holy men and tribal leaders smoked tobacco in a pipe or rolled into a cigar, or they sprinkled it on an open fire. They also placed dried tobacco leaves on water or on the ground as an offering. Many tribes had tales concerning its sacredness, in which it was described as a special gift from the spirit world.

## THE SPIRIT IN PLACES

Places were particularly endowed with spiritual significance. Mountain spirits, water spirits, lake spirits, rock spirits—all interacted to make a particular area sacred. Within their tribal boundaries groups had areas—high mountains, bluffs, dense woods, springs, lakes, and waterfalls—that had special spiritual power, much as a great cathedral or a temple might have for a Christian or a Buddhist. People went to these places to seek communion with the Great Spirit, to conduct ceremonies and rituals, and to be healed. In the Navajo tradition, for example, there are four kinds of sacred land:

- Lands mentioned in sacred stories.
- Lands where supernatural events occurred.
- Lands where healing plants, minerals, or waters can be found.
- Lands where people can communicate with spirits.

Land might become sacred when people experienced visions there or, in some cultures, when tribe members were buried on it. Creation stories and other parts of the oral tradition were often tied to specific places, giving the tribe's ancestral grounds special spiritual meaning.

## INTERACTION WITH THE SPIRIT WORLD

In Native American belief people interact continually with spirits, both seen and unseen, as they interact with the natural world. The spirit world speaks to those who are attuned to it. The spirits require respect and attention. If no one speaks to them they may

## MEDICINE WHEELS

The ancestors of the Plains Indians left behind hundreds of stone circles, often laid out like the spokes of a wheel around a central cairn, or pile of rocks, and with other cairns placed at intervals around them. Archaeologists now believe that these medicine wheels, as they are called, helped Native Americans follow the progress of the year by charting the movement of the Sun and stars. Medicine wheels are associated with spirit forces, and the land on which they lie is sacred. Sacrifices and sacred items were often left within them.

A medicine wheel in Sedona, Arizona.